THIRD EDITION

PSYCHOLOGY   A Concise Introduction

Terry F. Pettijohn is Professor of Psychology at Ohio State University, where he has taught introductory psychology for nearly two decades. He has been recognized for his teaching efforts, including twice being a recipient of the University Award for Distinguished Teaching. He received his Ph.D. in experimental psychology from Bowling Green State University in 1974. His current research interests include the study of animal social behavior and computer-assisted learning. When he is not teaching or revising this book, Dr. Pettijohn enjoys traveling with his family, participating in church activities, taking photographs, and building his music collection. He is a member of the American Psychological Society, the Psychonomic Society, the Animal Behavior Society, the Society for Computers in Psychology, and the American Psychological Association, where he is affiliated with the Division of the Teaching of Psychology.

THIRD EDITION

PSYCHOLOGY

A Concise Introduction

Terry F. Pettijohn

Ohio State University

DPG

The Dushkin Publishing Group, Inc.

Credits & Acknowledgments

Cover: *Head of a Woman* by Jacques Villon. Museum of Art, Rhode Island School of Design, Mary B. Jackson Fund. Photography by Cathy Carver. Cover design by Harry Rinehart; 5 United Nations; 6 Pamela Carley Petersen; 8 The Bettmann Archive, Inc.; Brown Brothers; 9 UPI/Bettmann; 10 The Bettman Archive, Inc.; Harvard University Archives; 11 Culver Pictures, Inc.; 12 UPI/Bettmann; The Bettmann Archive, Inc.; 36 AP/Wide World; 37 © Mark Antman—The Image Works; 38 Professor José M. R. Delgado; 52 Jason Laure, 1978—Woodfin Camp & Associates; 53 "Infant Visual Preference" adapted from "The Origin of Form Perception" by Robert L. Fantz, copyright © 1961 by Scientific American, Inc., all rights reserved; 55 Mr. & Mrs. Daniel Petit; Mr. & Mrs. Richard Yarian; 56 Pamela Carley Petersen; 57 Elizabeth Crews—Stock • Boston; 58 University of Wisconsin, Primate Lab; 59 Leonard Freed, © Magnum Photo; 60 Yves de Braine—Black Star; 61 Zimbel—Monkmeyer; 63 Bob Fitch—Black Star; 68 United Nations photo by L. Barns; 69 courtesy SNET: 70-71 United Nations photos by John Isaac; 77 Topham—The Image Works; 87 Figure 4.14 from *Gesetze des Sehens* by Wolfgang Metzger, 1953, Frankfurt am Main, Germany: Verlag Waldemar Kramer, p. 313; 87 David H. Wells—The Image Works; 88 New School for Social Research; UPI/Bettmann; The Granger Collection; 89 State of Minnesota; Department of Economic Development; 90 Greater Boston Convention & Tourist Bureau; 91 United Nations photo by Shelley Rotner; 96 Roswell Angier—Stock • Boston; 97 Pamela Carley Petersen; 100 "Pain Mechanisms: A New Theory" by Melzack and Wall, Nov. 1985, *The Journal of Science*, 150 (3699), p. 975; 100 © W. Hill, Jr.—The Image Works; 101 Don Hogan Charles—NYT Pictures; 105 NYT Pictures; 106 Florida News Bureau; 109 "Sequence of Sleep Stages" from *Some Must Watch While Some Must Sleep* by William C. Dement, copyright 1976 by William C. Dement, used by permission of the Stanford Alumni Association and William C. Dement; 109 Stanford Sleep Disorder Center; 111 Figure 5.5 from "Ontogenetic Development of the Human Sleep-Dream Cycle" by H. P. Roffwarg, J. N. Muzio, and W. C. Dement in *Science*, Vol. 152, pp. 604-619, copyright 1966 by The American Association for the Advancement of Science; 112 courtesy Detroit Institute of Arts; 115 United Nations photo by Jane Schreibman; 116 © Dean Abramson, Stock • Boston; 117 EPA Documerica; 120 Dr. H. W. Leeman and R. W. Frei, 1955, Triangle, *Sandoz Journal of Medical Science*, Vol. II, pp. 119-123; 122 Ray Ellis—Photo Researchers; 123 © David Powers—Stock • Boston; 129 courtesy Dr. B. F. Skinner; 131 The Bettman Archive, Inc.; 132 Pamela Carley Petersen; 133 Elaine Ward; 137 George N. Peet—The Picture Cube; 138 Teachers College Library, Columbia University; 139 San Diego Convention and Visitors Bureau; 140 Will Rapport; 141 Wm. S. Sahakian, Ph.D.; 142 Wm. S. Sahakian, Ph.D.; "Schedules of Reinforcement" from "Teaching Machines" by B. F. Skinner, copyright © 1961 by Scientific American, Inc., all rights reserved; 143 Las Vegas News Bureau; 145 John Watles—Miami Herald; 146 David Powers—Stock • Boston; 147 United Nations photo by John Isaac; 148 George W. Gardner—The Image Works; 149 © Three Lions; 151 Thomas McAvoy, *Life* magazine © 1955 Time Inc.; 156 The Bettmann Archive, Inc.; 164 UPI/Bettmann Newsphotos; 165 courtesy Elizabeth F. Loftus; 177 Ed Keating—NYT Pictures; 179 Figure 8.2 from *The Speech Chain* by Peter B. Denes and Elliot N. Pinson, copyright © 1963 by Bell Telephone Laboratories, Inc., used by permission of Doubleday, a division of Bantam Doubleday Dell Publishing Group, Inc.; Figure 8.3 from *Aspects of the Theory of Syntax* by N. Chomsky, 1965, MIT Press; 180 Figure 8.4 from "The Acquisition of Language" by B. A. Moscowitz, copyright © 1978 by Scientific American, Inc., all rights reserved; 181 Lee Lockwood—Black Star; 182 B. T. and R. A. Gardner, Department of Psychology, University of Nevada; 185 "Problem Solving," by M. Scheerer, April 1963, *Scientific American*, 208 (4), Atlanta, GA; 188 & 190 "Nine-Dot Problem and Solution from "Problem Solving" by Martin Scheerer, copyright © 1963 by Scientific American, Inc., all rights reserved; 194 The Bettmann Archive, Inc.; 197 Mr. and Mrs. Langenderfer; 198 Figure 8.20 from "Familial Studies of Intelligence: A Review by T. J. Bouchard and M. McGue, *Science*, Vol. 212, May 29, 1981, pp. 1055-1959, copyright 1981 by the American Association for the Advancement of Science; 200 United Nations photo by John Isaac; 201 © Alan Carey—The Image Works; 202 United Nations photo by Jane Hanckel; 203 © 1989 Nita Winter—The Image Works; 209 courtesy Peter M. Milner, McGill University; 211 Ron Garrison © Zoological Society of San

continued on page 469

Psychology: A Concise Introduction, 3rd Edition

Printed in the United States of America

Library of Congress Catalog Card Number: 91-77531

International Standard Book Number (ISBN) 1-56134-063-4

First Printing

The Dushkin Publishing Group, Inc., Sluice Dock, Guilford, Connecticut 06437

Preface

"Vigorous writing is concise," counseled William Strunk, Jr., in *The Elements of Style*. "This requires," he went on, "not that the writer make all his sentences short, or that he avoid all detail and treat his subjects only in outline, but that *every* word tell."

I have strived to maintain the conciseness of the previous editions and to expand judiciously some topics, such as personality and health. In an attempt to provide an even clearer visual organization than before, I have added more topic headings. In addition, I have included a significant number of new references and have updated many others.

I have reorganized some topics within chapters as well as moved some topics within the textbook. For example, the material on animal communication was moved to chapter 9, "Motivation." And research on primate language is now discussed in chapter 8, "Language and Intelligence."

Most topics throughout the book have been updated since the last edition. The latest research findings have been included, as well as the current theories in the field. Thanks to an article by C. James Goodwin in the *American Journal of Psychology* (Spring 1991, vol. 104), an illustration showing a dog undergoing a classical conditioning experiment, erroneously attributed to Pavlov in previous editions of this textbook (as in most other textbooks), has been corrected in this edition. Further research has also led to the deletion from this edition of a series of drawings of cats, traditionally, but mistakenly, attributed to a schizophrenic patient. Many areas have been expanded in this edition. We now have expanded coverage of neurotransmitters in chapter 2, "Psychobiology," adulthood issues in chapter 3, "Development," love in chapter 10, "Emotion," and personality measurement in chapter 11, "Personality." A number of current topics in psychology have been added to the third edition, including daydreaming (chapter 5), the MMPI-2 (chapter 11), health enhancement behavior (chapter 12), and conflict and peace (chapter 15). In addition, a number of chapter opening stories and application highlights are new to this edition.

I believe that psychology is a delicate blend of rigorous science and humanistic perspective. I have tried to balance an intellectual approach to the subject matter with personal anecdotes and examples that I hope will give students an understanding and appreciation of the science of psychology.

As before, I have included a number of features in the textbook to help make it an effective learning tool.

CHAPTER OUTLINE   At the beginning of each chapter I provide a brief outline consisting of the major headings in the chapter as a preview for students and to let them know what to expect in the chapter. The Chapter Outline is related to the Chapter Objectives and the Chapter Review for a complete learning program.

CHAPTER OBJECTIVES   The Chapter Objectives provide a guidepost for students to begin their learning of the chapter material. The objectives are always found on the first page of the chapter so students can easily find them and refer to them as they study. The major topics in each chapter are included in the objectives. Each objective is directly keyed to an item in the Chapter Review at the end of the chapter.

INTRODUCTORY PARAGRAPH   Each chapter begins with a short paragraph set in italics that provides a glimpse of what the chapter covers. This should be especially useful when students first skim the chapter.

OPENING STORY   Each chapter begins with a story of an important research study in psychology. The stories are nontechnical, and read easily. They often raise issues that are discussed in the chapter, and present interesting and useful information that is integrated with the chapter material. One of the goals of the opening story is to motivate the student to understand the topics covered in the chapter. Opening stories describe the work of psychologists such as Eleanor Gibson, Elizabeth Loftus, Jean Piaget, Stanley Schachter, Martin Seligman, and B. F. Skinner.

INTRODUCTORY DEFINITIONAL SECTIONS   Following the opening story, each chapter contains a WHAT IS? section. Here the general chapter topics are introduced and the main concepts are defined. After reading "What is Therapy?" in chapter 14, "Therapy," for example, students know that there are two major forms of therapy for psychological disorders, and have learned the names of the major types of each form of therapy. Of course, they then have to read the rest of the chapter to discover the details of the therapies mentioned.

APPLICATIONS   Each chapter has one or two Applications, which demonstrate how psychological theory can be applied to everyday situations. Applications include topics such as hormones and premenstrual syndrome, eating disorders, improvement of love relationships, biofeedback, stages of parenthood, television and aggression, jury selection, memory improvement, computers and programmed learning, education and learning disabilities, and stress and performance. In this edition, each Application is fully integrated into the appropriate section in a chapter. This does not break up the flow of reading and facilitates the understanding of the material.

BIOGRAPHICAL HIGHLIGHTS   All chapters (with the exception of chapter 13) have one or two Biographical Highlights that present in-depth information on a psychologist who was instrumental in shaping psychology as we know it today. These biographies make psychology more personal for students, and provide them with knowledge of the important figures in the field, including historically important psychologists like Sigmund Freud, William James, John Watson, and Abraham Maslow, and contemporary psychologists such as Elizabeth Loftus, Stanley Milgram, Anne Anastasi, and Robert Sternberg. New to this edition is a Biographical Highlight of early black American psychologists.

CHAPTER REVIEW

At the end of each chapter is a review, consisting of a brief summary of the main points in the chapter. Each summary paragraph is keyed to a Chapter Objective found at the beginning of the chapter. For example, in chapter 2, "Psychobiology," Objective 2 asks students to identify the parts of a neuron, and in the Chapter Review, number 2 describes the neuron as having a cell body, dendrites, and an axon. I regard this as a key feature of the text, helping students learn the material by providing immediate specific feedback. One suggestion for effective studying is for students to write out answers to the Chapter Objectives and then check their answers in the Chapter Review.

FIGURES

A purposeful program of illustration was included in making this book. Many of the figures extend the text material by presenting details of research studies or illustrating theories. This edition has many charts that help summarize key points. The photographs help make the concepts clear to students by presenting examples. Figures are expressly referred to when they contain research data that is important in understanding a concept, and otherwise appear on the same page as the text material. The captions provide information that extends or supports the text and can be used by students as a quick review. New to this edition is a four-page insert of full-color illustrations covering the topics of fetal development, visual perception, and the study of the brain.

CROSS-REFERENCES

An important feature is the extensive system of cross-references used throughout the text to emphasize the importance of the interrelatedness of principles in psychology.

GLOSSARY

Important terms and concepts are underlined in the text and defined in the glossary at the end of the text. Other important concepts are in italics. In addition, the glossary items for each chapter are included in the corresponding chapter of the student study guide that accompanies the text, so that students may have ready access to the definitions when they study.

SUPPLEMENTS

I have written all the supplements in conjunction with the textbook. For students, there is the *Study Guide to Accompany Psychology: A Concise Introduction, 3rd Edition,* which includes both learning and self-testing activities designed to reinforce and extend the material in the textbook. For instructors, a teaching resource manual, *Teaching and Testing From Psychology: A Concise Introduction, 3rd Edition,* is available, and contains a variety of aids for teaching, including discussion suggestions, classroom activities, audiovisual information, and an array of practical tips to improve teaching. The testbank included in the teaching resource manual, *Testing From Psychology: A Concise Introduction, 3rd Edition,* contains a wide array of test items for measuring student accomplishments in learning concepts and principles of psychology. A microcomputer test program, *EZ TEST® to Accompany Psychology: A Concise Introduction, 3rd Edition,* is designed to help teachers prepare tests for students. Transparency masters are available to help students visualize the important concepts while in the classroom. Also available is a computer-assisted study program. All these supplements have been carefully coordinated for maximum effectiveness.

FLEXIBILITY

Because this book is concise, instructors of psychology will be able to expand on important topics and assign entire chapters to students. The use of frequent cross-references to other chapters where topics are also discussed makes it easy for students to find related material. Instructors will also be able to use outside readings or short books for discussions of specific topics. One choice might be *Annual Editions: Psychology*, an anthology of current readings in psychology issued in a new edition each spring. Many of the readings parallel discussions in the text and provide students additional insight into psychology. *Taking Sides: Clashing Views on Controversial Psychological Issues* is another option for those who wish to use a more structured tool to involve students in issues of concern in psychology today. Because of the low price of *Psychology: A Concise Introduction, 3rd Edition*, students are able to purchase a supplemental reader along with the textbook for less expense than the typical text alone costs.

ACCURACY, CURRENCY, AND RESEARCH

Psychology is an evolving science, and it is important to make sure that students have accurate and current information about the research findings in the field. I have checked and rechecked all of the sources in *Psychology: A Concise Introduction, 3rd Edition*. Many of the references in the book are from the recent decade, but the classic theories and historical research are also included for a full picture of psychology. The findings and theories that are discussed in the book have all been derived from important research studies and are documented according to standard practice. Students can easily find a particular citation in the References section.

APPLICATION

Memorizing numerous theories and definitions is of little use to students unless they can use the theories and definitions to better understand people and their behavior. I have tried to help students appreciate the importance of the information gained from psychological research by showing them how it is applied to everyday situations. In addition to the Applications in each chapter, I have included sections on practical applications in many other places in the book. For example, in chapter 6, "Learning," special in-text sections explain applications of operant and classical conditioning. Time and stress management techniques are discussed in chapter 12, "Adjustment and Health." Procedures for applying for a position in business are discussed in chapter 16, "Applied Psychology." Compliance techniques are discussed in chapter 15, "Social Psychology," and relaxation techniques are described in chapter 14, "Therapy." Each chapter presents the basic theoretical background of the important topics in psychology and also shows how these principles are applied to everyday life.

RELEVANCE AND CHALLENGE

Students do better when they can relate topics they are studying to their personal lives. I have attempted to help students feel that the information presented is personal and relevant to each of them. Thus I have provided a variety of situations in which students are challenged to think about the issues. The Applications in each chapter raise issues in which students evaluate their own beliefs and feelings. In this edition I have attempted to introduce cultural and ethnic viewpoints where relevant.

ORGANIZATION

The organization of *Psychology: A Concise Introduction, 3rd Edition* is traditional. Part 1, "Foundations," presents the basic foundations for studying psychology, including history and methods, and the topics of biology and human development. In Part 2, "Perceptual Processes," the areas of sensation, perception, and consciousness are reviewed. In part 3, "Learning and Cognitive Processes," students learn about learning, memory, language, thinking, and intelligence. In

Part 4, "Motivation and Emotion," students are presented with the theories and research findings concerned with motivation and emotion. In Part 5, "Personality and Adjustment," personality assessment and theories are presented, along with material on stress, adjustment, and health. Part 6, "Psychological Disorders and Therapy," covers the areas of abnormal psychology and therapy. And Part 7, "Social Processes," examines social psychology and applied psychology.

Writing a textbook takes much more of just about everything than I ever imagined. Five years ago the first edition was published. Now, I have completed the third edition, which I believe is much improved over the first two editions, and combines all of the elements of a successful teaching program for the instructor. I am very proud of the finished product, and hope that you find it extremely useful, relevant, challenging, exciting, and informative. I love teaching psychology and have attempted to convey my enthusiasm for the subject here.

ACKNOWLEDGMENTS

Although only one name appears on the cover, many individuals have contributed in countless ways to the text. A number of psychologists and instructors reviewed the book at various stages in the writing process. I am particularly fortunate to have colleagues who spent hours reading parts of chapters or the entire book.

I wish to thank the following whose ideas and suggestions were immeasurably valuable in guiding my writing and revising efforts for the third edition: Kerm Almos, Capital University; Edward C. Caldwell, West Virginia University; Mary Ann Dickman, Marion Technical College; Carl R. Gaetano, Cuyahoga Community College; Stephen Hamilton, Mt. San Antonio College; Marge Hazelett, Ohio State University; James L. Lloyd, Western Wisconsin Technical Institute; Sara Staats, Ohio State University; and Peter Suedfeld, University of British Columbia. The specific feedback from Ed Caldwell was singularly beneficial throughout the revision process. I also want to acknowledge the special contribution of Evelyn Blanch, Wilberforce University, for her suggestions on black psychology issues and minority concerns.

Others who have been extremely helpful with previous editions of the book include: Edward Arees, Northeastern University; John Broida, University of Southern Maine; Robert Bruel, Kean College of New Jersey; Ernest Chavez, Colorado State University; Dan Christie, Ohio State University; Michael Compton, University of Hawaii; Christopher Cozby, California State University-Fullerton; Gary Dunbar, Central Michigan University; Thomas Eckle, Modesto Junior College; Robert Gordon, Wittenberg University; Shelia Greenlee, Ohio State University; W. Richard Krall, South Central Community College; James Lamiell, Georgetown University; Gerhard Lang, Montclair State College; Richard McCrady, New Mexico State University; Marilyn Milligan, Santa Rosa Junior College; Alicia O'Neill, Monterey Peninsula College; Chris Paterson, University of Miami; Robert Plutchik, Albert Einstein College of Medicine; Mary Helen Spear, Prince George's Community College; Larry Vandervert, Spokane Falls Community College; Gary Verett, Richland College; and David Wolfe, Ocean County College.

Students, of course, are particularly important in the final evaluation of a textbook, and during the writing and revising of this book, many students helped review, critique, and proofread sections. Over 300 students provided in-depth critiques of each chapter of the second edition. Those who contributed significantly to the project include Linda Banks, Kathy Barkley, Mickey Bloom, Ray Coleman, Chris Cover, Pat Ellefson, Linda Feltner, Meg Hiss, Julie Hoffman, Joan Jernigan, Kim Kurts, Sandi Larcomb, Jennifer Levitsky, John Matthews, Susan Matthews, Glenn McCleese, Kari McDonough, Debbie Monroe, Craig Philips, Ed Shirley, Susie Sobas, Juli Swartz, Tina Thompson, Mary Trimmer, Lynn Vance, Gretch Walker, Roger Wren, and Sue Yanok.

The Dushkin Publishing Group has been outstanding in its support and guidance. Especially important in ensuring an excellent product are publisher Rick Connelly, and managing editor John Holland. I also very much appreciate the efforts of Pam Petersen in obtaining the figures and illustrations for this book. I am grateful, too, to Darylle Steiner and the entire sales service staff for their continuing efforts in providing me with valuable information from the many users of the text. In the first edition I acknowledged the sterling efforts of Michael Werthman in preparing my manuscript. In the second edition I gave special credit to Marcuss Oslander for her valuable criticism and excellent editing skills. In this edition, I wish to acknowledge the truly outstanding editorial work of Bob Mill. He caught every weak spot and his suggestions helped tremendously to improve the readability of the book.

I would like to thank my family, whose patience, help, feedback, and understanding have all been extremely valuable through the project. My wife, Bernie, and children Terry, Karen, and Tommy have been supportive throughout the revision process and have made sacrifices so that I could work on the book. Bernie again typed and proofread much of the revised manuscript. My son Terry even field-tested it when he used the book in his psychology course. Once again I can finally tell my friends and colleagues that I am doing something other than "revising my book."

Terry F. Pettijohn

Contents in Brief

Contents

PART II   PERCEPTUAL PROCESSES   74

4

Sensation and Perception   76

5

Sleep and Consciousness   104

PART III   LEARNING AND COGNITIVE PROCESSES   126

6

Learning   128

7

Human memory 154

8

Language and Intelligence 176

PART IV MOTIVATION AND EMOTION 206

9

Motivation 208

10

Emotion 232

PART VII   SOCIAL PROCESSES   344

15

Social Psychology   346

16

Applied Psychology   376

Applications and Biographical Highlights

To the Student

AN INVITATION TO PSYCHOLOGY

Psychology is an exciting field that will contribute much to your life. This book serves as an integral part of your course in psychology. It will help you in numerous ways during the course and afterwards. A little effort on your part in noting the format and goals of the textbook, and the suggested study procedures, will pay off in an increased understanding of psychology (and in a better course grade).

As you read this textbook, you will learn about many facts, theories, and applications of psychological information that will give you a working knowledge of what psychology is all about. Many of these concepts are interrelated, and you will learn to identify the principles of psychology every day of your life.

You will also gain a better understanding of your own behavior and the behavior of those around you. You will better understand motivation, personality, social interactions, and biological forces on behavior. This will help you make better decisions concerning what *you* want to do and why other people behave as they do. Ultimately, this should result in increased happiness and successful adjustment for you.

I think psychology is the most exciting discipline, in part because it is an ongoing activity. We don't have all of the answers, and current research continuously provides us with new information, as evidenced by the large number of references from the 1980s and 1990s. I really hope you enjoy the book, and that it helps you better understand psychologists, psychological research, and of course, yourself.

HOW TO STUDY FROM *PSYCHOLOGY: A CONCISE INTRODUCTION, 3rd EDITION*

Learning is a complex adventure that involves a variety of approaches. You will learn much in the classroom as well as from reading and studying the book. There are some procedures that help enhance your learning from your book.

In chapter 7, "Human Memory," we discuss the SQ5R study technique. This procedure requires that you survey a chapter, ask questions, read carefully, record the main ideas, recite to ensure understanding, review the material, and then reflect on what you have learned. This is an excellent study procedure, and is explained in more detail in *Study Guide to Accompany Psychology: A Concise Introduction, 3rd Edition*.

Psychology: A Concise Introduction, 3rd Edition has been designed so you can effectively learn from it. It has a number of important characteristics that help guide you through the learning process. For every chapter you study, there are several steps you should take to enhance your learning:

1. SURVEY the chapter. Examine the brief outline at the beginning of the chapter, read the introductory paragraph, quickly read the introductory story, and then skim the rest of the chapter, noting the major headings and points of interest. This skimming is designed not to provide details, but rather to give you an overall picture or preview of what you will be covering.

2. QUESTION what you will be learning. A unique feature of the book is the incorporation of the Chapter Objectives at the beginning of the chapter. Use these to develop questions about important material in the chapter. You will notice that each objective corresponds to a major section of the textbook, usually identified with a heading. In addition, the book has been constructed so that each Chapter Objective is discussed in the Chapter Review at the end of the chapter. Take the objectives and turn them into questions as you read the chapter.

3. READ the chapter carefully, paragraph by paragraph, trying to identify the main ideas and important details in each section. Note that there are usually 3 to 5 main sections, with several detailed sections under each main section. You might want to read only one section before you stop and review what you have learned. But carefully read each section, as well as the special Applications that provide insight into how psychology is applied to everyday life. Take time to think about how you feel about the issues raised in the chapter. The important point in reading is that you learn and understand the information being presented.

4. RECORD the main ideas in each section. This encourages you to read the book actively to discover the important ideas contained in it. You can underline key words, write important points in the margin, or write a summary in your notebook. Keep your writing brief and focus on the really important ideas that you will need to remember for your test.

5. RECITE what you have learned by returning to the Chapter Objectives and writing a very brief response to each objective, then check your responses with the corresponding items in the Chapter Review. You might orally give your responses, but only if you really write them can you be absolutely sure you actually have learned the material. If you have problems, you can at this time go back to the section in the book and study the material again until you do learn. Also, using *Study Guide to Accompany Psychology: A Concise Introduction, 3rd Edition* at this time will help ensure that you master the main ideas and important details. You should also look at the underlined terms in each chapter and see if you can briefly write definitions, which can be checked for accuracy with the glossary.

6. REVIEW what you have learned by quickly going back over the outline, Chapter Objectives, and Chapter Review. Check to make sure that everything makes sense to you, and that you have no questions. Reviewing is a step that you should do periodically to make sure you don't forget anything. Again, the study

guide will help you review the important information, and should be used on a regular basis.

7. REFLECT on the main ideas that you have learned. This step allows you to think critically about the important issues raised in the chapter. It is important to take some time to organize the information you have recently learned. Here you can develop examples and applications of the major principles, and evaluate the various theories and viewpoints. This helps you remember and use the information more effectively.

Study Guide to Accompany Psychology: A Concise Introduction, 3rd Edition is an integral part of your study program, and should be incorporated into the process as much as possible. After you read the textbook and record the main ideas is the ideal time to recite, review, and reflect with the study guide. This will allow you to identify the major concepts presented in the chapter, study the relevant theories of psychology, and evaluate your knowledge of the material through practice tests.

For each chapter in the textbook, the study guide has a number of important features. There is a CHAPTER PRETEST to allow you to discover whether there are any overall weaknesses in your understanding of the material. The REVIEW ACTIVITIES are designed to help you master the concepts, and include working with the special features, such as the Applications and Biographical Highlights, as well as a Programmed Review of the main ideas in the chapter. The CHAPTER OBJECTIVES REVIEW provides an opportunity to check your general understanding of the key concepts in the chapter. The CHAPTER OBJECTIVE EXERCISES are designed to generate critical thinking of the applications and implications of the principles of psychology. The CHAPTER POSTTEST gives you one last chance to assess your readiness for a test. And for those who wish to go beyond the normal expectations, the USEFUL READINGS provide suggestions for studying topics in more depth. The CHALLENGE ACTIVITIES provide enriching experiences that should help you critically evaluate general psychological concepts. The CROSSWORD PUZZLES help you learn the terms and concepts that are important in each chapter. I designed and wrote the study guide to make sure it enhanced your learning experience. If you follow the study procedure outlined above, you should have no difficulty learning the material of introductory psychology.

Finally, I hope you will share my enthusiasm for and enjoyment of the study of behavior and cognition. Good luck in your exciting learning adventure.

Terry F. Pettijohn

THIRD EDITION

PSYCHOLOGY

A Concise Introduction

CHAPTER 1

THE STUDY OF PSYCHOLOGY

Although barely a century old as a formal discipline, the study of psychology has revolutionized how we look at ourselves and others. While psychologists are involved in a broad range of specialties, they share the common goal of understanding how we think and behave. To accomplish this, psychologists use a variety of scientific research methods and measurement techniques.

CRITICAL THINKING OBJECTIVES FOR CHAPTER 1

After reading chapter 1, you should be able to identify, apply, and evaluate what you have learned about the following questions:

What are the components in the definition of psychology?
What is the importance of each goal of psychology?
What is the influence of each school of thought on psychology today?
What are the subfields of psychology?
What is the advantage and disadvantage of each research method?
What is the importance of statistics in psychological research?

CHAPTER 2

PSYCHOBIOLOGY

In order to understand human behavior fully, we need to know something about the biological influences on people. Psychobiologists study the endocrine system and the nervous system and pay special attention to the functioning of the brain. Also of great interest to psychologists is how heredity and environment interact to produce the development of behavior.

CRITICAL THINKING OBJECTIVES FOR CHAPTER 2

After reading chapter 2, you should be able to identify, apply, and evaluate what you have learned about the following questions:

What is the importance of the biological response systems in behavior?
What is the role of the neurotransmitters in influencing behavior and cognition?
What are the functions of the major brain structures?
What is the importance of the peripheral nervous system in regulating behavior?
What is the importance of the endocrine glands in regulating behavior?
What are the contributions of heredity and the environment in influencing behavior?

CHAPTER 3

DEVELOPMENT

The study of human development covers the entire life span from conception through infancy, childhood, adolescence, and adulthood, ultimately ending with death. Developmental psychologists are interested in changes in the physical, cognitive, and social aspects of behavior over time.

CRITICAL THINKING OBJECTIVES FOR CHAPTER 3

After reading chapter 3, you should be able to identify, apply, and evaluate what you have learned about the following questions:

What is the importance of the three aspects of development studied by psychologists?
What is the importance of prenatal development on behavior after birth?
What is the importance of attachment in infancy?
What are the important periods of cognitive development?
What are the important tasks of adolescence?
What is the importance of family and work in adulthood?

Part I provides the groundwork for understanding the science of behavior and cognition. In this section, the research methods used by psychologists, biological influences on behavior, and life-span human development are discussed.

PART I

Foundations

CHAPTER OBJECTIVES

What You'll Learn About the Study of Psychology

After studying this chapter, you should be able to:

1. Define psychology.
2. Identify the four basic goals of psychology.
3. Outline the five major schools of thought that developed into modern psychology.
4. List five major subfields of psychology.
5. Outline the scientific method used by psychology researchers.
6. Identify the code of ethics to which psychologists adhere when using research subjects.
7. Describe the naturalistic observation research method.
8. Describe the case study research method.
9. Describe the interview research method.
10. Describe the survey research method.
11. Describe the psychological testing research method.
12. Describe the experimental research method and identify the variables and research designs in an experiment.
13. Describe the correlation research technique.
14. Describe the procedures used in descriptive statistics (central tendency, variability).
15. Identify the concepts in inferential statistics (generalization, probability, and significance).

WHAT IS PSYCHOLOGY?

THE GOALS OF PSYCHOLOGY

THE HISTORY OF PSYCHOLOGY
Structuralism
Functionalism
Behaviorism
Gestalt Psychology
Psychoanalysis
Current Approaches to the Study of Psychology

SUBFIELDS OF PSYCHOLOGY

METHODS OF RESEARCH
Ethical Considerations in Research
Naturalistic Observation
The Case Study
The Interview Method
The Survey Method
The Testing Method
The Experiment
Correlation Research

MEASUREMENT IN PSYCHOLOGICAL RESEARCH
Descriptive Statistics
Inferential Statistics

We have all watched television shows in which the victim picks the criminal out of a lineup. And many of us have been asked to recall details of certain events to help someone solve a problem. Do we always remember our perceptions correctly? Or are our recollections of what we hear and see influenced by other variables? Research by psychologist Elizabeth Loftus of the University of Washington has focused on these questions, and her findings are reported in her 1979 book, *Eyewitness Testimony*.

Loftus was interested in what subjects could remember about an incident, and how their memory could be influenced by outside factors. College students served as subjects in experiments in which films of automobile accidents were shown. Loftus then tested the accuracy of the students' recall and examined how the questions asked of the students might influence their answers.

In one study, 100 students were shown a film of an automobile accident and then were asked to fill out a questionnaire about the accident. One group was asked several key questions that began with "Did you see a . . . ?" while the other group was asked key questions that began with "Did you see the . . . ?" The only difference was the "a" or "the" in the questions. Do you think that would make a difference in how the subjects responded?

Loftus found that the subjects that were asked the "the" questions (for example, "Did you see the broken headlight?") were much more likely to answer yes (they would say that they did see the broken headlight, even if

Although barely a century old as a formal discipline, the study of psychology has revolutionized how we look at ourselves and others. While psychologists are involved in a broad range of specialties, they share the common goal of understanding how we think and behave. To accomplish this, psychologists use a variety of scientific research methods and measurement techniques.

1

The Study of Psychology

it did not appear in the film). For example, 15 percent in the "the" group reported they saw a nonexistent item, whereas only 7 percent of the "a" group reported seeing a nonexistent item. Perhaps this is because we use "the" when we know something exists, while "a" is used in a more general way.

Loftus showed other subjects a film of a different automobile accident, and again asked questions afterward. The key question here was "About how fast were the cars going when they _____ each other?" Different verbs were substituted for each group. When "smashed" was used, subjects reported that the cars were going about 41 miles per hour, but when "contacted" was used, the subjects only reported the cars were going 32 miles per hour. Other intermediate speeds were given when the key word was "collided," "bumped," or "hit." The particular question asked elicited a different estimate of speed, even though all subjects saw the same film.

Research on eyewitness testimony is important because it shows that our memory is not perfect, but rather is constantly being modified according to the new information we receive from our environment. What we perceive and what we remember can become even more crucial in trials by jury, where a person can be falsely identified as a criminal due to faulty perceptions or memories. Research such as Loftus's helps us understand the importance of careful investigation of eyewitness testimony. We discuss memory in chapter 7, "Human Memory," and we explore eyewitness testimony and courtroom behavior in chapter 16, "Applied Psychology."

FIGURE 1.1 Eyewitness Testimony
Different witnesses often remember events differently. The questions witnesses are asked about an accident can influence their recollections of what they saw.

WHAT IS PSYCHOLOGY?

The experiments Loftus performed typify the scientific approach in psychology. Rather than just casually noting that memory seems to be influenced by outside factors, Loftus investigated the problem in a series of scientific experiments. The scientific approach in the study of behavior is an important characteristic of psychology.

Psychology is the science of behavior and cognition. Behavior is generally defined as anything you do, especially if it can be observed. Psychologists often study behaviors such as eating, talking, writing, running, or fighting, precisely because they can be observed and recorded. Psychologists study the behavior of people and animals in a variety of settings.

Cognition includes mental processes like dreaming, thinking, remembering, or problem solving. These cognitive activities are usually not directly observable, and are often studied through reports provided by human research subjects. Cognitive behavior is often included in the general concept of behavior.

Another area of scientific study is the biological, or physiological, processes that often accompany both behavior and cognition. Brain wave activity during dreaming or thinking, heart rate during strong emotion or fighting, or blood chemistry changes during eating are examples of physiological processes.

While some psychologists may focus on one area, many study psychology from all three perspectives. Since the behavioral, cognitive, and physiological processes are usually interconnected, many psychologists include all three when they discuss concepts in psychology. In this book behavior includes observable actions, cognitive activities, and their physiological processes.

Psychology is a fascinating discipline that touches every aspect of our lives. Over the last century it has evolved from a fairly narrow field that emphasized immediate experience into a diverse discipline with a variety of goals and procedures. As you explore the science of behavior and cognition, you should develop a better understanding of why people do the things they do.

THE GOALS OF PSYCHOLOGY

As stated earlier, psychology is defined as the science of behavior and cognition. As a science, psychology shares goals and scientific methods with other sciences, such as biology, chemistry, sociology, and anthropology. Scientists begin with a body of knowledge and then proceed systematically to investigate a topic to add to that body of knowledge. Scientists use a variety of research methods, including observation, survey, test, and experiment. These research methods allow scientists to reach the goals of description, prediction, control, and explanation. The ultimate aim for psychologists is to understand behavior and help people.

As an example of this aim, many clinical and counseling psychologists are involved in helping people with emotional problems. Others, called experimental psychologists, are engaged in research to discover the basic principles of behavior, using a wide variety of subjects: monkeys, rats, children, and very often students. Still other psychologists are busy applying research findings to

FIGURE 1.2 Goals of Psychology
Psychologists are interested in describing, predicting, controlling, and explaining behavior. A familiar social activity is sitting down to dinner with one's family. This common ritual raises many questions of interest to the psychologist. For example: What motivates people to eat? Does eating with others cause people to eat faster than eating alone? How can parents encourage children to eat properly? Will people act more politely if they have more time to eat?

people's everyday problems. Consumer psychologists study purchasing behavior, including what type of advertisements influence people most. Educational psychologists help make teaching in the classroom more effective. And social psychologists are involved in reducing prejudice and aggression.

While most psychologists try to understand and help people, some experimental psychologists (called comparative psychologists) study and often compare the behavior of animals, including fruit flies, rats, and monkeys. Why? Because animal research can suggest new techniques for helping people. For example, behavior modification techniques that are discussed in chapter 6, "Learning," are currently used in schools and mental hospitals but were first developed in animal studies. And producing what looks like helplessness in dogs, discussed in chapter 12, "Adjustment and Health," has led to recent therapies for relieving depression in humans. While some psychologists hope the results of animal behavior research will be directly applicable to human experience, others study animals solely to provide additional information about the behavior of animals.

Psychology seeks to understand behavior through meeting four basic goals: *description, prediction, control,* and *explanation.*

Description is important in any science. It helps psychologists understand basic patterns of behavior. Description of behavior allows them to develop theories, or assumptions, about the behavior. It also helps to fill in the gaps of what we know about behavior. Child development, discussed in chapter 3, "Development," is an area of psychology that describes the stages of motor development in babies and has enabled psychologists to formulate a theory of normal motor development. This helps people identify possible problems in babies who do not develop in the normal sequence.

Psychologists often make predictions about behavior; these are based on the descriptions they have obtained. For example, psychologists have described many situations where people exhibit certain behaviors in order to receive reinforcements (or rewards). We discuss reinforcement in chapter 6, "Learning." After observing that reinforcements encourage people to modify their behavior, you might develop a theory predicting that people would increase a particular behavior if rewarded. Then you could test this prediction by making further observations. As an example, you might find that when you smile, people are nice to you. You could then predict that if you smiled more, more people would be nicer. You could easily test your prediction by keeping a record of your observations.

After psychologists verify predictions they can control behavior to a certain extent. Once you conclude that the frequency of a given behavior increases after a reward, you are in a position to control (modify) behavior

by giving or withholding rewards. For example, you could control the frequency with which your dog sits up and begs by offering the dog biscuits as a reward. When you stop giving biscuits, the dog will probably decrease begging behavior.

People sometimes have a difficult time understanding the issue of control. They might mistakenly think that psychologists want to control millions of people with secret "mind-bending" techniques. This is not true; psychologists study control in a different sense. Actually, you are controlled by others and you control others all the time, each and every day. Remember the person who smiled at you yesterday? What did you do in return? Very likely, you smiled back. That was control. When you place an order in a restaurant, you are controlling another person. Psychologists are interested in learning about control so that they can help people gain control over their own actions. For instance, psychology may be able to help you overcome your shyness (discussed in chapter 12, "Adjustment and Health") so you will gain enough confidence to be in control of a situation.

The fourth goal of psychology is explanation. By describing, predicting, and controlling behavior, we gain insight into the forces that motivate people. Then we can begin to explain why people engage in various activities. For example, hunger has been explained as motivated behavior in some studies that are discussed in chapter 9, "Motivation." The conditions that cause and alleviate hunger are described and predicted, as well as the behaviors that control it. You feel hungry both because your body needs food for energy and because you have learned to eat at certain times of the day.

THE HISTORY OF PSYCHOLOGY

People have always been interested in the behavior of other people. We can trace some of the philosophical ideas in psychology back to the early Greeks. For example, Aristotle and Plato debated whether human ideas are *innate* or need to be experienced. Philosophers have always been interested in the nature of people. In the seventeenth century the British philosopher John Locke described the human mind as a blank slate (*tabula rasa*) upon which could be written all of life's experiences.

Other influences on early psychology came from biology and physics. Charles Darwin was a naturalist whose observations while on a worldwide voyage were published in *The Origin of Species* in 1859, in which he also outlined his theory of evolution. Darwin's influence on psychology included both his method of naturalistic observation of behavior and his theory of evolution. In his theory of evolution, Darwin suggested that animals

BIOGRAPHICAL HIGHLIGHT

WILHELM WUNDT

Wilhelm Wundt, the son of a Lutheran clergyman, was born in 1832 in a small German village called Nekarau. He was a solitary child who shunned the games of children in favor of books and study.

At 19, Wundt decided to study medicine, most likely as a means of entering a scientific career. His attention shifted to physiology, the field in which he lectured widely and published a number of articles during the years following his graduation. Psychology was just beginning to emerge as a distinct science, and much of Wundt's work anticipated the value of physiological methodology in dealing with psychological problems.

In 1879, at the University of Leipzig, Wundt established the first psychology laboratory. Here, he concentrated almost exclusively on psychological research, particularly on the study of human sensory experience—research that had previously belonged to the realm of physiology and philosophy. Wundt's use of a systematic methodological approach in tackling psychological problems was a landmark in establishing psychology as a science.

Wundt pursued his work with the boundless energy and enthusiasm up until the time of his death near Leipzig, two weeks after his 88th birthday in 1920.

and people show behavior that is adaptive to the environment and that helps them to survive.

A year after Darwin's book, Gustav Fechner published *Elements of Psychophysics*, in which he outlined his experimental method of measuring sensory experience. Fechner would produce a tone on a tuning fork and determine if his subject could hear it. By manipulating the conditions of the experiment, he was able to examine the relationship between the physical stimulus and sensory experience. His experimental approach was important for the new science of psychology.

These early developments finally led to what is now known as psychology. The formal history of psychology can be best described by the "schools of thought" that guided psychologists in their actions. There are five major historical schools that we will discuss: structuralism, functionalism, behaviorism, Gestalt psychology, and psychoanalysis.

Structuralism

The science of psychology had its formal beginning in 1879 when Wilhelm Wundt (1832-1920), a German physiologist, set up a laboratory at the University of Leipzig to study consciousness.

FIGURE 1.3   E. B. Titchener
Edward Titchener (1867–1927), a British psychologist who studied under Wilhelm Wundt, came to Cornell University in New York in 1892 to study and teach structuralism. Titchener defined psychology as the study of the human normal, adult mind. His empirical approach to psychology was important to the new science.

The school of thought associated with Wundt and his student E. B. Titchener is called structuralism, or the science of the structure of the mind. Wundt studied the conscious experience of the mind through introspection. Introspection was a method in which specially trained subjects reflected on their immediate experience of some stimulus. First they would be shown an apple. What would come to mind? Red, round, shiny, slender green rod on top, brown spot, small? Next the subjects might be shown a peach or a pear, and the procedure would be repeated.

Through careful recording of immediate conscious experience, Wundt believed he could discover the structure of the human mind. Although his definition of psychology did not survive, Wundt's important contribution to the field was his strict reliance on a systematic method of research in his efforts to determine the conscious elements of the mind.

An American, G. Stanley Hall (1884-1924) also studied under Wundt. Hall was an active psychologist,

and among his many accomplishments were establishing the American Psychological Association in 1892 and founding the first American psychology journal, *The American Journal of Psychology*, in 1915. He was especially interested in psychological development, and published research on childhood, adolescence, and aging.

Functionalism

If you think structuralism doesn't sound much like modern psychology, you're right. Many people didn't see the relevance of studying the elements of the mind. One of these people was William James (1842-1910). In 1890 he published *Principles of Psychology*, in which he expressed his ideas of what psychology should be.

William James was the first American-born psychologist. He was greatly influenced by Darwin's work on evolution and believed that psychology should explain the function of consciousness as it influences behavior.

BIOGRAPHICAL HIGHLIGHT

EARLY BLACK PSYCHOLOGISTS

KENNETH B. CLARK

The first black American to earn a Ph.D. in psychology was Francis Cecil Sumner, who was born in Arkansas in 1895. Sumner studied under G. Stanley Hall at Clark University, and received his degree in psychology in 1920 (Houston, 1990). After graduating from Clark University, Sumner taught at Wilberforce University in Ohio before accepting the chair of the psychology department of Howard University in Washington, D.C., in 1928. He was interested in the psychology of religion, and remained at Howard University until his death in 1954.

The first black female psychologist was Beverly Prossor, who earned her Ph.D. in 1933 from the University of Cincinnati.

Charles Henry Thompson earned his doctorate in educational psychology in 1925 from the University of Chicago. During the next 50 years, he served as a faculty member and administrator at Howard University. Thompson served as editor of the *Journal of Negro Education* for 30 years, and did much to promote black psychology before his death in 1975.

Kenneth B. Clark, a social psychologist, was born in 1914. After attending Howard University, he earned his Ph.D. from Columbia University in 1940. Clark became interested in the areas of self-concept and racial identification. In a 1939 classic study, he and his wife found that black preschoolers preferred white dolls to black ones. He taught at City College of New York City from 1942 until 1975 when he retired. He served as president of the American Psychological Association, and in 1987 was presented APA's gold medal award for contributions by a psychologist in the public interest.

FIGURE 1.4 John Dewey
John Dewey (1859–1952) greatly influenced American thinking as an educator, philosopher, and psychologist. While at
the University of Chicago, he argued that psychology
needed a unifying principle. Dewey believed that behavior
and consciousness could not be studied as separate enti-
ties, but should be understood in terms of the individual's
adaptation to the environment. This approach to psychology
became known as functionalism. Dewey later made significant contributions to education.

FIGURE 1.5 William James
While he believed that a goal of psychology was the study of
consciousness, William James (1842–1910) rejected the
notion that this could be accomplished by structuralism's
attempts to reduce the mind to elements. He regarded
consciousness as an ongoing process in continuous interaction with the environment. In addition to consciousness,
his numerous interests included the learning of habits, the
development of emotions, the awareness of self, and religion. James was the first to set up a laboratory in 1875 at
Harvard University to demonstrate psychological principles
to his students.

The ideas of William James paved the way for the
school of functionalism, which described psychology as
the study of the adaptive properties of consciousness and
behavior. Important functionalists included John Dewey
(1859-1952) and James Angell (1869-1949) from the
University of Chicago, and Edward Thorndike (1874-
1949) and Robert Woodworth (1869-1962) from Columbia University. Dewey's 1896 paper on the reflex arc
is often considered to be the formal beginning of the
functional school of psychology. The concept of the
reflex arc was also considered a unifying principle of
psychology because as the complete nervous path that is
involved in a reflex, it unified the mind and body.
Thorndike's book, *Animal Intelligence* (1898), is also
considered a major work in the school of functionalism.

Functionalists used not only introspection to study
behavior, but also used tests, surveys, and experimental
techniques (Benjamin, 1988). In studying children and
animals as well as adults, the key question they asked
was, "What function does the specific behavior have?"
Psychologists in the school of functionalism studied topics
such as thinking, memory, consciousness, animal intelligence, learning, and motivation. They were also interested in applying psychological concepts in schools,
businesses, and homes.

Behaviorism

Some psychologists felt that functionalism did not go
far enough in getting away from the structural study of
the mind. In 1913 another American psychologist, John
B. Watson (1878-1958), became the founder of the
school of thought called behaviorism. Watson believed
that psychology should be the science of overt behavior.
He rejected the ideas of introspection and mental processes. Behaviorists concentrated on the objective measurement of observable behavior. They believed that
psychology should be a "hard" science, like physics or
chemistry.

The early behaviorists went to an extreme with their
ideas. They limited psychology to the study of the observable behavioral response given by an organism to a
stimulus. For example, a sudden loud noise causes a
person to respond by giving a little involuntary jump. The
behaviorists believed all behavior was determined by
stimuli in the environment.

Psychology is still considered the science of behavior. Of course, the concept of behavior has been broadened to include the unseen cognitive processes, such as

thinking, which lead to observable behavior. All psychologists—not just behaviorists—study behavior. Since its formation by Watson, the school of behaviorism has been extremely influential in psychology. But other schools of thought helped to broaden its outlook.

Gestalt Psychology

At about the same time that behaviorism was becoming the dominant force in American psychology, another movement was taking place in Germany. The Gestalt psychology school of thought moved away from the analysis of individual elements or parts. It did not accept structuralism's goal of studying the parts of the mind or behaviorism's goal of studying parts of behavior.

Max Wertheimer (1880-1943) is usually regarded as the leader of the Gestalt school along with Wolfgang Köhler (1887-1967) and Kurt Koffka (1886-1941). They believed that people are more than the sum of their parts and that we cannot understand the whole by studying only the parts. The German word "Gestalt" means "whole," and Gestalt psychology's goal was to study

FIGURE 1.6   Important Dates in Psychology

1859	Darwin publishes *Origin of Species*
1860	Fechner publishes *Elements of Psychophysics*
1879	Wundt sets up psychology lab; structuralism
1885	Ebbinghaus publishes *On Memory*
1890	James publishes *Principles of Psychology*
1892	Hall founds American Psychological Association
1896	Dewey publishes paper on reflex arc concept; functionalism
1898	Thorndike publishes *Animal Intelligence*
1900	Freud publishes *The Interpretation of Dreams*; psychoanalysis
1905	Binet and Simon publish first intelligence test
1912	Wertheimer publishes paper on Gestalt ideas; Gestalt psychology
1913	Watson publishes paper on behaviorism; behaviorism

BIOGRAPHICAL HIGHLIGHT

JOHN B. WATSON

John B. Watson was born in 1878 in a rural community outside Greenville, South Carolina, where he attended the local country schools near his parents' farm. At 16 he entered Furman University, where he earned an M.A. degree.

Watson received his Ph.D. in experimental psychology at the University of Chicago in 1903. His research was on the sensory cues used by rats in learning to run through a maze. He remained at Chicago for 5 years.

In 1908 he began teaching at Johns Hopkins University, where he remained until 1920, when a highly publicized divorce forced him to resign. Watson was the driving force for the school of behaviorism, and his approach can be seen in a popular quote: "Give me a dozen healthy infants, well-formed, and my own specified world to bring them up in and I'll guarantee to take any one at random and train him to become any type of specialist I might select—doctor, lawyer, artist, merchant-chief, and yes, even beggarman and thief, regardless of his talents, penchants, tendencies, abilities, vocations, and race of his ancestors" (1924, p. 82). In 1921 Watson entered the business world and soon became vice president of an advertising agency. He married his former laboratory assistant and continued to write popular articles on psychology for some time. He died in 1958 at the age of 80.

FIGURE 1.7 Max Wertheimer
A founder of Gestalt psychology, Max Wertheimer (1880–1943) began his research in perceptual studies in Germany. He and his colleagues, Wolfgang Köhler and Kurt Koffka, believed that the whole person has to be studied, rather than just individual parts, in order to gain a complete understanding of human behavior. Wertheimer was also interested in creative thinking and problem solving, especially in educational settings.

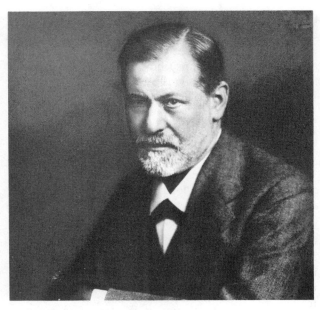

FIGURE 1.8 Sigmund Freud
An Austrian physician, Sigmund Freud (1856–1939), developed the theory of psychoanalysis to explain personality and to treat people with psychological problems. Although his important book on dreams was published in 1900, he did not make an impact on American psychology until the 1930s. Freud wrote on many topics, including personality development, human sexuality, therapy techniques, and adjustment.

perception, learning, problem solving, or personality as a whole (Hothersall, 1990).

The Gestalt school has had its greatest influence in the area of perception. Stop reading for a moment and think about someone you know. Do you think about his or her nose, eyes, each strand of hair, the ears, each separate tooth? Or do you have a complete image of the whole person? The Gestalt psychologists argue that we perceive the entire person.

Psychoanalysis

The last major historical influence on psychology was psychoanalysis. At approximately the same time that the behaviorism and Gestalt schools of thought were being formulated, a young Austrian physician named Sigmund Freud was beginning to use hypnosis as a method of treating people with emotional problems.

Freud found that people who were hypnotized were able to recall hidden feelings about others, especially sexual feelings and hostility toward their parents. This led him to formulate his psychoanalytic theory, which concentrates on the unconscious motivations often expressed in dreams or "slips of the tongue" (accidently

saying something you don't want to). In other words, Freud believed that past experiences of which a person is unaware significantly influence current behavior.

Psychoanalytic theory had its major impact on concepts of personality and on therapy techniques in psychology. It helped broaden the behavioristic notion of psychology to include unconscious motivations as well as observable behavior.

Current Approaches to the Study of Psychology

Today, psychology does not have one dominant school of thought. As previously discussed, it has been influenced by a variety of viewpoints and approaches. Psychologists now are more likely to have an eclectic approach to the study of behavior and cognition, combining theories and methods from a variety of sources. The current major approaches to the study of psychology include the biological, humanistic, psychoanalytic, cognitive, and behavioral.

The Biological Approach Understanding the biological processes that underlie behavior is an important objective in today's psychology. The past several

FIGURE 1.9 Approaches to Psychology

Approach	Goal Is to Understand:
Biological	Biological processes that underlie behavior
Humanistic	Human potential
Psychoanalytic	Unconscious motivation
Cognitive	Mental processes
Behavioral	Fundamental causes of behavior

decades have seen an increased emphasis on understanding the function of behavior, as evidenced by behavior genetics studies. The brain and nervous system help us interpret perceptions, coordinate actions, store information, and make decisions. There are biological explanations of motivation, personality, social interaction, memory, and psychological disorders.

The Humanistic Approach   Some of the ideas of the Gestalt psychologists have come to be represented in what is known as humanistic psychology. These psychologists stress that people are unique and complex organisms and emphasize that each person has a capacity to reach his or her maximum potential. Humanistic theories are especially important in the fields of personality, motivation, and psychotherapy.

The Psychoanalytic Approach   Freud's theory of psychoanalysis has continued to influence the way we think of ourselves. Psychoanalytic theory emphasizes unconscious motivation and the influence of sexual and aggressive drives on behavior. It has its major impact in the fields of personality, psychological disorders, and therapy.

The Cognitive Approach   Cognitive psychology is the approach that includes the study of mental processes, such as thinking, perception, memory, and problem solving. Because of their emphasis on consciousness, the schools of structuralism and psychoanalysis strongly influenced cognitive psychology. Today, cognitive theories are important in virtually every area of psychology.

The Behavioral Approach   Many of the ideas from the schools of behaviorism and functionalism are evident in the current behavioral approach to understanding why we act as we do. Although many psychologists utilize behavioral theories, today behavior is defined very differently from the way it was originally; it now encompasses cognitive processes like thinking and feeling as well as directly observable behavior.

As we study the findings and applications of today's diverse psychology, keep in mind how psychology as a science has developed from a great variety of methods and approaches.

SUBFIELDS OF PSYCHOLOGY

There are over 100,000 psychologists in the United States today (Pion, Bramblett, & Wicherski, 1987). About one-third of these people are engaged in teaching and research in colleges and universities, and another one-half of them are involved in providing mental health services in hospitals, counseling centers, or in private practice. Still others are employed in businesses, schools, the military, and even the government. The field of psychology attracts men and women from a wide variety of races and ethnic backgrounds.

With over 70,000 members, the American Psychological Association (APA) is the largest professional organization for psychologists. Its members include both academic scientists (who teach and conduct research) and clinical practitioners (mainly those who diagnose and treat individuals with psychological disorders). The APA has 47 divisions (including the newest divisions of peace psychology and group psychotherapy), each of which represents a different interest area in psychology. In 1988, the American Psychological Society (APS) was formed by psychologists with primarily an academic or scientific orientation. There are also many smaller specialty organizations to which psychologists belong.

The question of what psychology is today might be answered by describing some of the different specialty areas, or *subfields*, of psychology. They best illustrate the diversity that exists within psychology. Here we review eight of the major subfields in psychology.

Clinical Psychology   "What do you do?" is a question I'm commonly asked. When I respond, "I'm a psychologist," the other person often says, "Oh, I'd better watch what I say or you'll analyze me." This attitude reflects the fact that the largest single group of psychologists (over 40 percent) is in clinical psychology (Pion, Bramblett, & Wicherski, 1987). Many professionals in clinical psychology work in institutions that care for and treat people who need help—mental hospitals, homes for people who are mentally retarded, prisons, mental health clinics, juvenile courts, university health centers, and child guidance clinics. Like medical doctors, some clinicians have private practices and treat persons with abnormal behavior problems. Others may teach in schools and universities. Clinical psychologists evaluate mental and

FIGURE 1.10   Divisions of the APA

1. Division of General Psychology
2. Division of the Teaching of Psychology
3. Division of Experimental Psychology
5. Division on Evaluation and Measurement
6. Division on Physiological and Comparative Psychology
7. Division on Developmental Psychology
8. Division of Personality and Social Psychology
9. The Society for the Psychological Study of Social Issues
10. Division of Psychology and the Arts
12. Division of Clinical Psychology
13. Division of Consulting Psychology
14. Society for Industrial and Organizational Psychology
15. Division of Educational Psychology
16. Division of School Psychology
17. Division of Counseling Psychology
18. Division of Psychologists in Public Service
19. Division of Military Psychology
20. Division of Adult Development and Aging
21. The Society of Engineering and Applied Psychologists
22. Division of Rehabilitation Psychology
23. Division of Consumer Psychology
24. Division of Theoretical and Philosophical Psychology
25. Division for the Experimental Analysis of Behavior
26. Division of the History of Psychology
27. Division of Community Psychology
28. Division of Psychopharmacology
29. Division of Psychotherapy
30. Division of Psychological Hypnosis
31. Division of State Psychological Association Affairs
32. Division of Humanistic Psychology
33. Division of Mental Retardation
34. Division of Population and Environmental Psychology
35. Division of the Psychology of Women
36. Psychologists Interested in Religious Issues
37. Division of Child, Youth, and Family Services
38. Division of Health Psychology
39. Division of Psychoanalysis
40. Division of Clinical Neuropsychology
41. Division of American Psychology—Law Psychology
42. Division of Psychologists in Independent Practice
43. Division of Family Psychology
44. Society for the Psychological Study of Lesbian and Gay Issues
45. Society for the Psychological Study of Ethnic Minority Issues
46. Media Psychology
47. Exercise and Sport Psychology
48. Peace Psychology
49. Division of Group Psychology and Group Psychotherapy

Note: There is no Division 4 or Division 11.

The American Psychology Assocation is the largest professional organization of psychologists in the United States; its divisions indicate the diverse interests of its members.

emotional problems, administer and assess personality tests, and treat patients who have behavior problems, using psychological techniques such as psychotherapy. We discuss behavior problems in chapter 13, "Psychological Disorders," and psychotherapy in chapter 14, "Therapy."

It is important to distinguish between the clinical psychologist and the psychiatrist. The clinical psychologist obtains a bachelor's degree in psychology and then goes on to graduate school. After about 2 years, he or she receives a master's degree in clinical psychology, and after approximately another 2 or 3 years of study, earns the Ph.D. (doctor of philosophy) degree, the customary degree for psychologists. The clinical psychologist will then spend a year in an internship, working under the supervision of other psychologists, before beginning to evaluate or treat people independently.

The training for a psychiatrist is quite different. Psychiatrists are physicians, like your family medical doctor, and as such can prescribe medication. Psychiatrists go to medical school and obtain an M.D. (doctor of medicine) degree. They then specialize in the treatment of abnormal behavior. Psychiatrists often see the patient's behavior problems as stemming from medical causes and thus often use medical treatments, like drug therapy, along with psychological therapy. Psychiatry, then, is a branch of medicine and is not a subfield of psychology.

Counseling Psychology   Counseling psychology is the subfield in which psychologists help people to adjust to emotional or personal problems that are generally less severe than those treated by the clinical psychologist. Counseling psychologists may help high school students choose a career, prisoners reform, or a wife and husband discuss problems in their marriage. Like clinical psychologists, counseling psychologists assess and treat people with behavior problems, but will usually refer them to clinicians or psychiatrists if the problems seem too severe. We will discuss the topic of adjustment in chapter 12, "Adjustment and Health."

School Psychology   Some psychologists focus on helping students. Those in school psychology are responsible for administering and interpreting intelligence or aptitude tests. They also consult with teachers and students about academic and emotional needs. And they place students in appropriate educational programs.

Educational Psychology   Other psychologists who work in schools are in the subfield of educational psychology. School systems and colleges hire them to study the effectiveness of textbooks, classroom organization, methods of teaching, and the design of tests. Some educational psychologists conduct research on learning and methods of education while also teaching at colleges or universities.

Social Psychology   Have you ever noticed that you perform some tasks better in front of an audience than when you are by yourself or with close friends? This phenomenon, called *social facilitation*, is one of the many topics that social psychologists are studying. The subfield of social psychology focuses on how people influence other people in areas such as attitudes, aggression, liking and loving, helping, and prejudice. For example, Kenneth Clark, a social psychologist, studied how prejudice is learned by children. In a 1939 study with his wife, Mamie, he found that black children preferred light-skinned dolls over dark-skinned ones. Clark concluded that prejudice is learned by minority as well as majority children through the process of socialization. Using similar methods, personality psychologists study how the characteristics of an individual develop and are related to how the individual behaves.

Industrial Psychology   Improving working conditions is an important concern of those in the subfield of **industrial-organizational psychology**. They engage in a variety of tasks, including increasing communication within an organization, consulting with management to improve employee satisfaction, developing employee training programs, and counseling workers on career choices. Engineering psychologists help design machines and equipment for efficient use by people. And consumer psychologists are interested in why people purchase particular products. We explore industrial psychology further in chapter 16, "Applied Psychology."

Developmental Psychology   Behavioral, cognitive, and personality changes that occur in individuals over time are the concern of those in the subfield of developmental psychology. Since the greatest changes in humans occur most rapidly during childhood, many developmental psychologists specialize in child development. They study the development of the person—his or her likes, fears, and abilities. Psychological development doesn't stop at adolescence, and there has been a trend to study development from a life-span approach, including infancy, childhood, adolescence, and adulthood. We cover developmental psychology in chapter 3, "Development."

Experimental Psychology   The last group of psychologists we describe here falls into the broad area of experimental psychology. Experimental psychologists research the fundamental causes of behavior. They investigate questions such as: Why do people dream? Why do we forget? Why do people go on roller coasters? How can animals identify one another? What is the effect of alcohol on aggression? Why do people experience optical illusions? Experimental psychologists provide much of the information that is used by other psychologists, who apply the research findings to practical situations.

Currently, experimental psychology can be divided into cognitive psychology, which studies cognitive processes in humans, and psychobiology, which studies biological processes in animals. Cognitive psychologists are interested in topics such as perception, memory, thinking, problem solving, language, and intelligence. The description of Loftus's work in the beginning of this chapter is an example of research in cognitive psychology. Psychobiologists who study the physiological processes involved in animal behavior are called physiological psychologists. They might study how the nervous system and brain are involved in motivation, learning, perception, or social behavior in animals. Comparative psychologists are psychobiologists who study the behavior of animals in a variety of situations. They might be interested in how heredity influences social behavior, or how behaviors of different species of animals function to help the animals survive.

This brief overview of the subfields should help you understand the great diversity that exists in psychology today. Even within a field of specialization, not all psychologists spend their time doing just one thing. For example, academic psychologists often divide their time among teaching, research, and service activities. Psychologists are thus flexible enough to meet the demands placed upon them by students, the community, and their profession. It is their professional research to which we turn next.

METHODS OF RESEARCH

Research is sometimes divided into basic and applied categories. Basic research is research conducted to obtain information for its own sake. Many experimental psychologists research topics that may provide valuable information for future problems but do not solve immediate problems. Applied research is conducted to solve a practical problem or pressing question. The industrial psychologist who wants to determine the best approach for a television advertisement is conducting applied research.

Research methodology is an important part of psychology. You may be wondering, "Why should I study research methods if I'm not going to major in psychology?" Actually, there are a number of good reasons for learning about research methods. Barbara and Robert Sommer (1991) point out that almost all occupations are concerned with information about human behavior. Schools want to attract students. Businesses want to increase profits. Parents want to help children. Manufacturers want to sell products. Studying research methods will help you understand how psychologists obtain the information they use to develop theories about behavior.

You can also gain the skills necessary to evaluate claims made by others. For example, when an advertisement claims "no other product is better than ours," does it also mean that all products are the same as the one being advertised? It might, but this fact is not always obvious to the consumer. You might also be surprised to learn that you already use some of the research methods employed by psychologists.

Psychology researchers utilize the scientific method. First, you start with a problem. Let's assume you are interested in the effects of color on emotional expression. Next, you develop a hypothesis, or prediction about observable events. You might predict that students taking a test of emotions that is printed on yellow paper would score higher on positive emotions than students taking the same test printed on blue paper. Then, you test this hypothesis by having two groups of subjects take the same test, some on blue paper and some on yellow paper.

After you collect the information (*data*), you interpret it. In the example we are using here, you would record the scores for students with yellow and blue tests. Finally, you draw your conclusions. You might find the test scores of students with yellow tests showed they were happier and more enthusiastic, while students with the blue tests rated sadder and more apathetic. If so, you have some evidence to support your hypothesis.

Psychologists, like all scientists, need to communicate the results of their research to others. One useful way is to publish the research in scientific journals, as discussed in the following Application.

APPLICATION

Publication of Psychological Research

How can we find out about the research psychologists conduct? The research results are communicated to others in a variety of ways, including discussions with colleagues, interviews with the media, presentations at psychological conventions, and publication in professional journals and books.

Psychologists are able to keep informed by attending conventions and learning about the latest research findings. In the United States, the American Psychological Association's annual convention is the largest in the discipline. In addition, there are several regional conventions.

The communication method that reaches the widest audience and provides a permanent record is publication in scientific journals. Many journals, including several by The American Psychological Association, publish psychological research. You might want to browse through some psychology journals to become familiar with the style of writing and the research in which psychologists are currently engaged.

A research article is organized so that its four major sections correspond fairly closely to the steps of the scientific method.

The introduction section provides background information on the problem and includes a statement of the hypothesis being tested. The literature review included in the introduction is a good place to find detailed information on a topic. All of the articles described in the introduction are included in the reference section at the end of the article.

The methods section includes information on the subjects, apparatus, and procedures. A description of the subjects used in the research is included in enough detail so that the reader is aware of any unique characteristics. The specifics of materials and any experimental apparatus used are given so that the study may be replicated. The actual procedures followed are carefully enumerated.

The results section is where the actual data are summarized, often in graphs or tables indicating the outcomes of the statistical tests.

The last major section is the discussion, in which the study's conclusions are explained, as well as its relevance and implications.

Although research articles in scientific journals are usually written for other scientists, students can obtain a great deal of information on current research trends by reading them. If you can't find psychology journals in your library, ask your instructor about finding them.

Ethical Considerations in Research

Psychologists have a very strict code of ethics when dealing with human or animal subjects. Researchers typically must submit a proposal of their planned research study on humans to a "human subjects committee," which reviews the methodology to ensure it is ethically sound. The human subjects committee is concerned that the research does not embarrass or cause pain in unsuspecting subjects. For example, if not told the nature of a study on sexual attitudes beforehand, some subjects might find the questions asked them objectionable. The human subjects committee would ensure that information collected is treated confidentially and professionally.

Human subjects are usually asked to sign a consent form that explains the general purpose of the experiment and informs them of the possibility of any stress or pain. The researcher has the ethical responsibility of protecting subjects from mental and physical harm. Unless alternative arrangements are agreed to beforehand, the responses of the subjects are strictly confidential, and the researchers may not disclose names or the scores of individual subjects.

The American Psychological Association has published a set of ethical principles for research (APA, 1990). The ultimate responsibility rests with the individual investigator. Sometimes *deception* must be used in a specific experiment, in which case the researcher must take extra precautions to ensure the welfare of the subjects. If

FIGURE 1.11   The Scientific Method

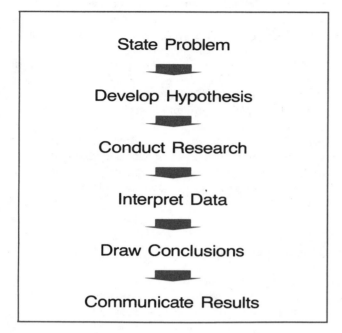

State Problem

Develop Hypothesis

Conduct Research

Interpret Data

Draw Conclusions

Communicate Results

deception is necessary, the subject must be debriefed when the study is over. In debriefing, the experimenter carefully explains the true purpose of the study and answers any questions.

Very strict guidelines also exist for dealing with animal subjects in research. Many standards and safeguards exist for the humane treatment of animals, such as the Federal Animal Welfare Act. The APA's 1990 statement, "Ethical Principles of Psychologists," contains a section on the care and use of animals. It specifies that all research must be in compliance with laws and regulations, researchers must be properly trained, and every effort must be made to minimize any distress of research animals.

Psychological research on animals has resulted in many improvements for both animals and humans (Miller, 1985). Benefits include our increased understanding in such areas as biofeedback for the control of high blood pressure and stress, conditioned taste aversion to help cancer patients who have lost their appetite, and behavior modification to help people control alcohol, drug, and tobacco abuse.

Despite these benefits, advocates for animal rights have argued that psychological research on animals is cruel and inhumane. However, reviews of animal experimentation in psychology have not turned up extreme cruelty. Psychologists are motivated to provide good care for their research subjects so mistreatment doesn't confound their data. Johnson (1990) pointed out that psychologists who study animals need to continue their research so that they can continue to help us understand both animal and human behavior.

Although there is great diversity in the subject matter of psychology, there are a limited number of research methods used in most subfields. The major research methods reviewed here include: naturalistic observation, case study, interview, survey, test, experiment, and correlation.

Naturalistic Observation

How many times have you attended a social event with other people? A party, dance, or picnic? A circus, zoo, or school event? While you were there, did you observe what people were doing? Some people were quiet, while others were very talkative. Were couples holding hands? Were people yelling, fighting, or comforting one another? If you noticed the behavior of people in any of these settings, you were using the research technique of observation. Naturalistic observation is simply the objective recording of what you see and hear when watching people or animals in their natural environment.

The library is a fascinating place to conduct naturalistic observation research. In their 1975 study, Fisher and Byrne observed students sitting alone at a library table. In an earlier research study, it was reported that males prefer to sit *across* from people they like, while females prefer to sit *next* to those they like. Fisher and Byrne reasoned that if people have a preference for sitting with friends, they might be upset if strangers were in their preferred space. They were testing the idea that males are more vulnerable to an invasion by strangers from the front and females are more vulnerable from the side. In their study, they found that males built barricades out of their books and placed them in front of themselves to protect their privacy and keep intruders away. Females, however, placed book barricades to the side of themselves. The next time you are in the library, conduct an observation of your own and see if you come up with the same results.

Comparative psychologists (or animal behaviorists) make extensive use of observation in their studies. A classic study was published in 1971 by Jane van Lawick-Goodall, who spent years in Tanzania observing chimpanzees. Through her research, she discovered that chimpanzees used simple tools in getting food. Before her findings, it was believed that only humans used tools for food-gathering. This sort of observation allows psychologists to understand better the behavior patterns of different animals.

Naturalistic observation involves recording information about subjects in their natural environment. In one such observation several psychologists, who were studying obesity, went into restaurants and observed the eating habits of normal and overweight patrons (LeBow, Goldberg, & Collins, 1977). They found that overweight people tend to eat faster and take larger bites. This information is now being used to help people lose weight. Christensen (1991) explained that observations of naturalistic behavior are extremely important because they provide an accurate picture of life outside the laboratory.

The Case Study

Often psychologists want to know what led to a particular behavior or event. The case study, or scientific biography, is a reconstruction of a person's life to discover the background in order to shed light on the present. For instance, a case study may be conducted on a person who is showing signs of severe depression to help discover where the problem began and why it developed.

Case studies are especially useful to clinical psychologists, who need to evaluate a client's problem and then decide upon an appropriate treatment. It's much easier if the psychologist knows the specific experiences the client has had in his or her lifetime that may have led up to the problem. Information on childhood, school, employment, and relationships with his or her parents and friends is valuable in gaining insight about the client. Information is collected in a systematic, scientific manner (as described at the beginning of this section).

Abraham Maslow developed a theory of personality called *self-actualization*, which he based partially on intensively researched case studies of individuals he considered to be self-actualized. Self-actualization, which is the state of having reached your full potential, is discussed in chapter 11, "Personality."

Although the case study provides a great deal of information about a particular person, one of its weaknesses is that the information is usually only pertinent to that one person and cannot usually be used to help others. Another weakness is the difficulty of retracing a person's life.

The Interview Method

In an interview the subject interacts with the psychologist by responding to verbal questions. The interview is designed to obtain information about a person from his or her behavior as well as from the responses to the interviewer's questions. Some interviews are *structured*, in which standardized questions are asked. Other interviews are *unstructured*, in which the person discusses general topics with the interviewer.

Interviews are used by a variety of psychologists. Clinical psychologists may use an interview to assess the personality of a client so they can select the proper treatment. School psychologists interview students to obtain information concerning their interests and attitudes. Industrial psychologists use the interview to select or evaluate employees.

The interview takes a great deal of time. However, it allows the trained interviewer to obtain extensive information about a topic. One of the most famous research programs employing in-depth interviews was the sexual-behavior research conducted in the 1930s and 1940s by Alfred Kinsey and his coworkers. They successfully interviewed hundreds of people about their sexual attitudes and practices, and used the detailed information to develop a profile of sexual behavior in America.

The Survey Method

Many times psychologists need a great deal of information in a relatively short period of time. The survey, in the form of interviews or written questionnaires, is designed for this need. A survey has questions that the respondent can usually answer briefly. If proper sampling techniques are used, a researcher can often get an accurate picture of how people feel about an issue.

Imagine you need to survey the students in your school about their opinions concerning the athletic program. How could you make sure you really had a true school opinion? One way, of course, would be to survey the entire school. But this may be impractical, so you could survey a sample of students by randomly selecting names from the school registration list. This will help assure that there is no bias in your procedure, and will cut down on time.

What do surveys measure? Just about everything. The Gallup poll is famous for surveying people's presidential preferences. It is especially publicized during election campaigns. The Nielsen ratings measure people's opinions on television show preferences. Other surveys may have questions on eating habits, sexual preferences, religions, incomes, career goals, educational backgrounds, recreational activities, or ideas for tax reforms. Consumer psychologists use surveys to determine which products will succeed. Social psychologists use surveys to obtain information on attitudes and beliefs. A major survey that is conducted once every 10 years is included in the U.S. census.

Research with a survey obtains relevant answers to important questions very quickly. However, one weakness of surveys is that you must rely on impersonal answers that might not be totally honest. For example, a subject may not reveal prejudices or unpopular views in a survey. Still, the survey is a popular research method in the social and behavioral sciences.

The Testing Method

The testing method can also be used to collect and compare information about people's behavior. However, it also has the weakness of having to rely on the honesty of the test taker for accurate information. You are certainly familiar with tests given in school. In addition to the regular academic tests of ability, you undoubtedly have taken achievement tests, such as the Metropolitan Achievement Test or the Stanford Achievement Test. You might also have been given the Strong-Campbell Interest Inventory by your school counselor. Tests often used for admission to college are the SAT and ACT.

Psychologists use many types of psychological tests to measure people's abilities, interests, personality, and intelligence. School psychologists may use an intelligence test to help place a student at the correct educational level. Clinical psychologists give personality tests to help assess a person's emotional problems. A test of anxiety may give some insight into why you are having trouble when you take academic tests. Developmental psychologists use motor skills tests as indicators of a child's developmental readiness to enter school. If used correctly, tests can be very useful tools. They can help predict the best alternative for future action. We review the requirements for a good test in chapter 8, "Language and Intelligence."

Unlike many of the research methods we have just reviewed, the next method, the experiment, permits researchers to exercise a great deal of control over the objects of their study and allows replication (duplication) of any experimenter's successful procedures by others.

The Experiment

Psychologists often want to know specifically what causes a particular behavior. They may conduct an experiment in which conditions can be carefully controlled. The experiment allows psychologists and other scientists to infer cause-and-effect relationships among conditions, or *variables*, of interest. Many experiments are conducted in a laboratory so that extraneous, irrelevant conditions can be excluded and the variables of interest can be precisely manipulated and measured.

There are many variables that are taken into consideration when designing an experiment. Environmental variables include such things as temperature, lighting, color of walls, amount of space available, and time of day. Subject variables include age, sex, background, experience, intelligence, personality, and ability. Most of these variables are not of prime interest, and the psychologist tries to control them so that they will not influence measurement of the condition of interest. However, some

of these variables are what the experiment is all about, and the psychologist carefully manipulates them so that their effects on some particular behavior can be measured.

Independent and Dependent Variables   In an experiment, a psychologist is usually interested in the relationship between two specific variables. The independent variable is the condition that is manipulated by the experimenter. It is a stimulus that is expected to cause a response. The dependent variable is the behavior or response outcome that is measured. The behavior depends upon the independent variable. These two variables form the basis of an experiment, so it is essential that you understand them.

A few examples will help you grasp the concept of independent and dependent variables. A social psychologist predicts that alcohol will decrease aggression. Alcohol is the independent variable and aggression is the dependent variable. A child psychologist wants to know whether a reward of candy will affect the time required to toilet train a toddler. The independent variable is reward and the dependent variable is toilet training. An experimental psychologist hypothesizes that the amount of space available will affect social contact time in gerbils. The independent variable is space and the dependent variable is contact time.

Experimental and Control Groups   In many experiments, there are two groups of subjects. Subjects who receive the independent variable are in the experimental group, while subjects who do not receive the independent variable are in the control group. Notice that the only difference between the two groups is the presence or absence of the independent variable. They are treated identically in every other way. And the dependent variable is measured exactly the same way in both groups.

Experimental Designs   Psychologists need to control extraneous variables, that is, all of the conditions that are not of interest in a particular experiment. There are several experimental designs used by researchers to control extraneous variables. Here we discuss two popular designs: the between-subject experiment and the within-subject experiment.

In the between-subject experiment, subjects serve in only one condition (either the experimental group or the control group). One type of between-subject experiment uses *matching*, in which the experimental and control groups are "matched" on as many variables as possible. For example, both groups might be given a pretest to make sure they each contain subjects with similar IQs, personalities, or ability levels. In many situations it is not possible to match all variables for the experimental and

FIGURE 1.12   Psychological Experiment

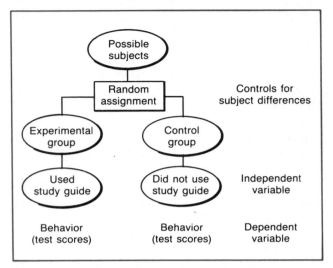

In a typical between-subject experiment, subjects are randomly assigned either to the experimental group or to the control group. The experimental group receives independent variable treatment (in this case, a study guide), and no specific treatment is given to the control group. A comparison is then made between the behaviors of the two groups.

control groups. Experimenters may then use *random assignment* to assign subjects to groups, and assume that differences in individual subjects will cancel each other out with a large sample size.

Another way to control extraneous variables is to have each subject serve as his or her own control. When the same subjects serve in both the experimental and control groups, it is a within-subject experiment design. Let's assume that I am interested in whether or not the use of a study guide influences student test performance. I could test one class of students twice: once after no one used a study guide (control condition) and again after everyone used a study guide (experimental condition). The scores could be compared to determine the effect of the independent variable. There could be several sources of confounding in this design. For example, the tests might not be equivalent, and when the subjects take the second test they have already had the experience of taking a test. An alternative would be to use the within-subject procedure of counterbalancing, in which subjects are exposed to both the experimental and control conditions, but half receive the experimental condition first, and the rest receive the control condition first. When using counterbalancing, the experimental group scores are compared to the control group scores to determine whether significant differences exist. Since everyone has been exposed to both conditions, *order effects* can be examined to determine whether receiving the independent variable first or second makes a difference.

Control of Bias Psychologists are also concerned about the possibility of experimenter or subject bias in an experiment. Robert Rosenthal and Lenore Jacobson (1968) conducted an experiment that demonstrated the possibility of experimenter bias in the classroom. The researchers went into an elementary school in the autumn and gave the students an intelligence test, which they disguised as a test that could identify those students who would do exceptionally well during the school year.

Rosenthal and Jacobson picked certain students at random and told the teachers that these students would "bloom." The researchers then returned in the spring and readministered the intelligence test. They found that those students that the teachers had been told would do the best actually did make the highest gain in intelligence scores. This phenomenon has been called expectancy. This effect may not always be present in experiments, but experimenters should be aware of the possibility.

Subject bias can also affect the outcome of an experiment. When subjects believe the experiment requires or demands a certain way of behaving, they may react according to the demand characteristics of the experiment. Assume you were a subject in an experiment to assess the effects of caffeine (independent variable) on reading speed (dependent variable). If you were given a dose of caffeine (experimental group), would you have a tendency to expect that you would read faster? If so, it is because of the demand characteristics of the experiment. Possibly both you and the experimenter would expect this result. One way to avoid expected behavior is to use the blinding technique, in which the assignment of a subject to the experimental or control group is unknown to the subject (resulting in a single-blind experiment) or to both the subject and experimenter (resulting in a double-blind experiment).

When the experiment involves giving a drug, the group assignment can be hidden from subjects by giving them a placebo. A placebo is an inert substance, such as a sugar pill or an injection of saline, that has no effect on behavior; but because subjects may think that a placebo is real and should have an effect, expectancy and demand characteristics lead to biased behavior. In the caffeine experiment, for example, half of the subjects (the experimental group) would receive caffeine and the other half (the control group) would receive a placebo.

The experiment is one of the most powerful methods that psychologists can use to infer cause-and-effect relationships. Some experiments can become quite complex, with several independent and dependent variables being tested simultaneously. The basic purpose of the psychology experiment, however, is to gain a better understanding of behavior by exerting control over stimuli that lead to responses.

FIGURE 1.13 Correlations

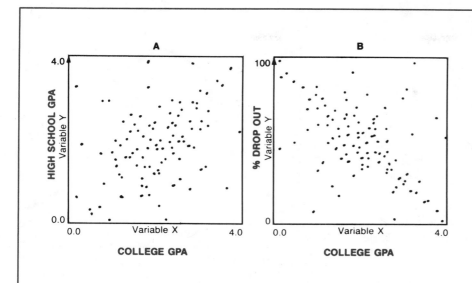

Researchers use the correlation technique to determine the degree of relationship between two variables. In graph **A**, the scatter plot demonstrates a positive correlation between the high school and grade point averages (GPA) of college students; as their high school GPAs increase, their college GPAs also increase. Graph **B** shows a negative correlation that indicates a decrease in the dropout rate of college students as their GPAs increase.

Correlation Research

Some researchers are interested in the relationship between two variables. For example, you might want to know whether a person with high grades in high school will also do well in college. Or you might be interested in the relationship (correlation) between watching violence on television and aggressive behavior. As we discuss in chapter 2, "Psychobiology," psychologists are often interested in the relationship between genetically related people for characteristics such as intelligence, personality, and abnormal behaviors. The technique of correlation can be used to determine the degree of relationship that exists between two variables.

The correlation coefficient is a statistical measure of relationship ranging from −1.00 (a perfect negative relationship) to 0.00 (no relationship) to +1.00 (a perfect positive relationship). The closer the correlation coefficient is to 1 (either positive or negative), the stronger the relationship is. For example, a correlation coefficient of +.89 indicates a very strong positive relationship between two variables, whereas −.17 suggests a very weak negative relationship between two variables. Take measurements of two variables and plot them on the vertical and horizontal axes of a graph, making a scatterplot. If one variable increases as the other one does, a positive relationship exists. There is likely to be a positive correlation between high school and college grades: thus, the higher your high school grade average, the higher your college grades will be. There is also likely to be a positive correlation between amount of time spent studying and test scores. Can you think of other variables that are likely to be positively correlated?

If one variable decreases as the other one increases, a negative correlation exists. There is probably a negative correlation between grade average and school dropout rate: as grade average increases, the dropout rate decreases. There is usually a negative correlation between the loudness of a sound and the distance to the source of the sound: as the distance decreases, the loudness of the sound increases. If absolutely no correlation exists, the two variables are completely independent. We would expect there to be no correlation between a person's height and grade average. Likewise, no correlation should exist between a person's age and his or her intelligence.

The research and statistical method of correlation helps psychologists make predictions. For instance, if all we knew about a student was that he or she had an extremely high grade point average in high school, we could predict fairly accurately that the student would be successful in college. Since there is a positive correlation between height and weight, if all I knew was that a person was tall, I would predict that the person also weighed more than another person who was short.

Correlation does not, however, imply a cause-and-effect relationship. It only tells us that as one measure changes, the other one will also. For example, let's assume the population of a town is growing. As the number of churches in the town increases, the number of criminals also increases. Does this statement mean that churches turn people into criminals? Of course not. In this case, the number of both churches and criminals increases as the population increases. Correlation allows psychologists to gain insight into how different behaviors are related.

MEASUREMENT IN PSYCHOLOGICAL RESEARCH

Psychologists use a variety of measurement techniques in collecting and analyzing research data. Two measurement terms are so important that they are described here and referred to throughout the textbook. We want our measurements always to be *valid* and *reliable*.

Validity refers to the degree that you actually measure what you intend to measure. A valid intelligence test would actually measure intelligence. A valid personality test would actually measure personality.

Reliability is the consistency of a measurement. It is the degree to which a person's score at one time is the same as when the measurement is repeated. A reliable intelligence test would yield consistent scores from one test time to the next. We want our measurements to be *both* valid and reliable. It is important to note that although a measurement could be reliable without being valid, it could not be valid without also being reliable.

I might tell you that I have just invented a new test to measure intelligence. It's very simple. Just write down your height. According to this test, you are assigned 2.5 intelligence points for every inch of height. So anyone 6 feet 6 inches tall would have an intelligence score of 195. This "pretend intelligence test" would not be valid (because it measures height rather than intelligence), but it would be reliable (because your height would not change significantly from one time to the next).

Measurement techniques help psychologists efficiently collect and analyze data on behavior. There are two classes of analysis techniques that you should be familiar with: *descriptive statistics* and *inferential statistics*.

Descriptive Statistics

Descriptive statistics are techniques that help summarize large amounts of information (Gravetter & Wallnau, 1992). An instructor might wish to tell a colleague about the recent test scores in her class. She might start out, "On the last test, students received scores of 95, 63, 90, 78, 82, 77, 85, 91, 72, 85, 92, 81, 85. . . ." I strongly suspect that before she had the opportunity to list all of the scores from the class, her colleague would be gone. This is not a very efficient method of communicating information. Descriptive statistics could help her summarize the scores for a meaningful conversation.

Frequency Distribution A researcher can organize scores into a frequency distribution that shows the number of times each score occurs, so that the scores can be interpreted. If the instructor had 100 test scores, she

FIGURE 1.14 Normal Curve Distribution

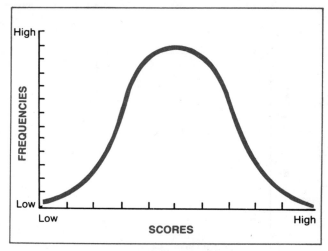

A normal curve has about as many low scores as high scores, with the highest frequency of scores occurring in the middle range.

would take each possible score and count how many times it occurred.

Next she would show the scores in a frequency distribution on a graph called a *frequency polygon*. All of the possible scores would be given on the horizontal axis (the abscissa) and the frequency of each score would be indicated on the vertical axis (the ordinate). A point would be placed on the graph for each score's frequency and a line drawn to connect the points. A graph allows people to understand a great deal of numerical information quickly.

Often when a large number of scores are plotted on a graph, scores begin to fall into a bell-shaped distribution called a normal curve. A normal curve has about as many low scores as high scores, with the highest frequency of scores occurring in the middle range. A variety of measurements tend to fall into a normal curve, including height, weight, and intelligence scores (see also Figure 8.17, p. 196).

To summarize a set of data using descriptive statistics, we need to calculate measures of *central tendency* and *variability*.

Central Tendency Measures of central tendency give a number that represents the entire group or sample. Instead of repeating all of the scores that her students earned on their test, the instructor could state one number that represents all of the scores in the distribution. Since distributions of scores tend to be grouped toward the middle, a number that represents this middle range will likely be representative of the majority of scores. The statement "men are about 69 inches tall" suggests that 69 inches represents all of the heights of men. This may be interpreted in several different ways, using three common measures of central tendency: the *mean*, *median*, and *mode*.

The most commonly used measure of central tendency is the mean. The mean is simply the arithmetic average. All scores are added and the total is divided by the number of scores. For example, the mean for the 13 test scores provided above would be 82.8. To obtain the mean, you need to first find the sum of the scores, which is 1,076. Then divide 1,076 by 13, the number of scores, to obtain the mean of 82.8. Usually, when people talk about an average score, they are referring to the mean.

The median is the middle score when the scores are arranged from the lowest to the highest with 50 percent of the scores falling below the median and 50 percent above it. The median of the above test scores is 85. There are 6 scores below and 6 scores above the middle score of 85. If there are an even number of scores, the median is determined by adding the two scores in the middle and dividing by two.

The mode is the most frequent score in a distribution. In the test score example above, the score of 85 occurs three times and thus is the mode. The mode is most useful when the number of scores is high.

In distributions such as the test score example, where one mode clearly exists, it is called a unimodal distribution. In some distributions, two modes are present and the distribution is referred to as a bimodal distribution. For example, if a teacher gives a test and many students do well and many others do poorly, the bimodal distribution will have two modes, one high and one low. In this case the mode is a better measure to use than the mean, which would suggest everyone performed averagely.

Variability   Measures of variability communicate how dispersed or spread out the scores are in the data. A measure of central tendency, such as the mean, is important because it is a number that is representative of the entire group. But this is only part of the picture. For instance, the mean of the test score distribution above is 82.8. However, the mean by itself does not tell you how much the scores varied. Did everyone score in the low 80s? Or were some scores in the 40s and others in the 90s? A measure of variability will show how spread out the scores are. The commonly used measures of variability are the range and the standard deviation.

The range is the simplest measure of variability to calculate. It is merely the highest score minus the lowest score. For the above test scores, the range is 32 (95 minus 63). This tells us how far apart the scores are. A small range indicates that everyone scored similarly. A large range indicates dissimilar scores. If in the above test score data, the mean was 83 and the range 5, you would know that everyone scored in the high 70s or mid-80s.

FIGURE 1.15   Calculation of Standard Deviation

Raw Data

Scores (n)	d	d²
95	12.2	148.8
63	−19.8	392.0
90	7.2	51.8
78	−4.8	23.0
82	−0.8	0.6
77	−5.8	33.6
85	2.2	4.8
91	8.2	67.2
72	−10.8	116.6
85	2.2	4.8
92	9.2	84.6
81	−1.8	3.2
85	2.2	4.8

Formula for Calculating Standard Deviation

$$SD = \frac{\text{sum of } d^2}{n - 1}$$

d = deviation scores; the subject's score minus the mean
n = the number of scores in the distribution
SD = standard deviation

Results

Mean of scores = 82.8
Sum of d² = 935.8
Standard deviation (SD) = 8.8

However, if the mean was 83 and the range 32, you would know some scored in the high 90s while others probably scored in the 60s.

The range conveys a great deal of information about a group of scores. But its weakness is that it is based on only two scores (the highest and the lowest) and can easily be influenced by one extreme score. Perhaps in the above example, all of the scores were in the low 80s except one score which was 50, producing a range of 32. One deviant score produced a range which was really not representative of the majority of the scores. A more complex, but often more informative measure of variability is the standard deviation.

The standard deviation is a measure of variability that describes how scores are distributed around the mean (Couch, 1987). The standard deviation is calculated from all of the scores, not just the two most extreme ones. To calculate the standard deviation, first the mean of the distribution is obtained. Then the difference between each score and the mean is determined. These difference scores are squared and the squared difference scores are added together. The result is then divided by the number of scores minus 1. And finally, the square root of this result is obtained. This is the standard deviation. A distribution with a large standard deviation consists of scores that are spread out, whereas a small standard deviation describes a distribution with scores more similar to one another.

The concept of the standard deviation helps us understand the properties of the normal curve. In a true normal curve, about 68 percent of the scores lie within a standard deviation above or below the mean (34.13 percent above and 34.13 percent below). Over 95 percent of scores lie within two standard deviations of the mean, and over 99 percent lie within three standard deviations.

As we learn in chapter 8, "Language and Intelligence," scores from the general population approximate the normal curve. With a mean score of 100 and a standard deviation of 15, 68 percent of the IQ scores lie between 85 and 115, and 95 percent lie between 70 and 130 (two standard deviations). The Scholastic Aptitude Test (SAT) has been constructed so that it has a mean of 500 and a standard deviation of 100. Thus 68 percent of the SAT scores lie between 400 and 600, and 95 percent of the scores on the SAT lie between 300 and 700 (two standard deviations).

Sometimes there are more scores at the high or low end of a distribution. When this happens, we say the distribution of scores is *skewed*. Let us hope that when your instructor gives a test, the scores are skewed at the high end of the distribution.

Inferential Statistics

Psychologists employing the experimental method want to draw proper conclusions from their research. A problem with research methods like the experiment is that they deal with a limited number of subjects. Psychologists want to be sure that their results can be generalized to a much larger number of subjects. Inferential statistics are techniques that help researchers make generalizations about a finding based on a limited number of subjects.

All of the individuals from the large experimental group that the subjects were selected from are called the population. The actual subjects make up the sample. In Figure 1.12 we saw an experiment that examines the effects of using a study guide (the independent variable) on student test scores (the dependent variable). Is the experimenter only interested in the sample of students who were actually involved in the experiment? No, the experimenter wants to generalize from the sample to all students in a similar situation. But since all students cannot be tested, the researcher needs to rely on inferential statistical techniques to provide the answers.

Although the actual calculation procedures are technical, what is important for you to know is that tests of significance are inferential statistical techniques for determining whether the difference in scores between the experimental and control groups is really due to the effects of the independent variable or just due to random chance. Some tests that psychologists use include the chi-square test, the t-test, and analysis of variance.

The concept of probability is important in inferential statistics. A test of significance that shows $p < .05$ indicates that the outcome (the difference between experimental and control groups) has a probability (p) of occurring by random chance less than five times per hundred and researchers arbitrarily conclude that the effect of the independent variable is significant (real). This means that the probability that the outcome is due to a real effect of the independent variable is 95 percent. When a statistically significant effect is found, it is concluded that the independent variable made a real difference between the experimental group and the control group. Psychologists then have confidence that research has helped in understanding human behavior. ■

We have seen in this chapter that psychology is a diverse field of study. As shown in the opening discussion of eyewitness memory, the common denominator in all of psychology is the fact that psychologists study behavior and cognition scientifically. Loftus approached the problem of eyewitness memory by systematically studying the variables that influence memory of observed events. In a relatively brief period of time, psychology has developed into a relevant discipline that touches many areas of everyday life. We turn next to the area of psychobiology to discover how biology influences our behavior.

CHAPTER REVIEW

What You've Learned About the Study of Psychology

1. Psychology is the science of behavior and cognition. Psychologists study easily observable behaviors, mental processes, and physiological reactions in humans and animals.
2. The ultimate aim of psychology is to understand behavior. Psychologists seek to understand behavior through four basic goals: description, prediction, control, and explanation.
3. Five major schools of thought help trace psychology's formal history. The first psychology laboratory was set up in 1879 by Wilhelm Wundt at the University of Leipzig to analyze the elements of the human mind through introspection (this school was called structuralism). William James of Harvard University influenced functionalism, which included the study of overt behavior as well as conscious experience. In 1913 John Watson excluded everything except overt behavior, in the school of behaviorism. Gestalt psychologists studied whole or complete perceptions rather than individual elements. Psychoanalysis, under the leadership of Sigmund Freud, broadened the viewpoint of psychology to include consciousness once more. Today's approaches to the study of psychology include the biological, humanistic, psychoanalytic, cognitive, and behavioral perspectives.
4. The American Psychological Association has numerous divisions that represent the different subfields and interest areas in psychology. Some of the subfields include clinical, counseling, school, educational, social, industrial, developmental, and experimental psychology.
5. Psychologists utilize the scientific method of research, in which hypotheses are tested, data are interpreted, and results are published. Basic research is conducted to obtain information for its own sake, whereas applied research is conducted to help solve a practical problem.
6. Psychologists have a strict code of ethics when dealing with human or animal subjects. Researchers have the responsibility of protecting subjects from mental and physical harm.
7. The research method of naturalistic observation involves the objective recording of what you see and hear when watching people or animals in their natural environment.
8. The case study is a reconstruction of a person's life in order to shed light on the present.
9. In the interview research method, the subject interacts with the psychologist by responding to verbal questions. Interviews can be structured or unstructured.
10. In the survey research method, questions are presented to the respondent. Research with a survey allows psychologists to obtain a great deal of information in a brief time.
11. Psychologists use many types of psychological tests to measure people's abilities, interests, personality, and intelligence.
12. The experiment allows us to infer cause-and-effect relationships among variables of interest. The independent variable is the condition that is manipulated by the experimenter. The dependent variable is the behavior or response measured. Subjects who receive the independent variable form the experimental group, while those who don't are in the control group. In order to control extraneous variables, psychologists can match groups or use random assignment of subjects. When different subjects are used, the design is between-subject; when the same subjects serve in experimental and control groups, the design is within-subject. Expectancy and demand characteristics can be controlled through the blinding technique.
13. The research technique of correlation can be used to determine the degree of relationship that exists between two variables.
14. Descriptive statistics are techniques that help summarize large amounts of information. Measures of central tendency (such as the mean, mode, and median) give a number that represents the entire group or sample. Measures of variability (such as the range and the standard deviation) communicate how dispersed the scores are.
15. Inferential statistics are techniques that help researchers make generalizations about a research finding based on a limited number of subjects. If a statistical test shows that the outcome (difference between experimental and control groups) has a probability of occurring by random chance less than five times per hundred, the effect of the independent variable is said to be significant.

CHAPTER OBJECTIVES

What You'll Learn About Psychobiology

After studying this chapter, you should be able to:

1. Define psychobiology.
2. Identify the parts of a neuron.
3. Describe the neural impulse and the functioning of the synapse.
4. Identify the major functions of the central nervous system (spinal cord and brain).
5. Describe the major structures of the brain.
6. Describe the research findings on cerebral hemisphere functioning.
7. List three research methods used to study the brain.
8. Compare the functions of the somatic nervous system and the autonomic nervous system.
9. Identify the functions of the hormones produced by four important endocrine glands.
10. Describe the basic principles of genetics.
11. Explain how heredity influences behavior.
12. Outline three research methods used in behavior genetic research.

Have you ever wondered what your brain is made of? The human brain is extremely complex and difficult to study. We know that the top layer of the brain consists of two parts, called hemispheres, but until fairly recently, we did not understand how the two hemispheres of the brain functioned together.

In the early 1960s, the mystery of the brain began to be revealed. Neurosurgeon Philip Vogel had a patient who suffered from severe and uncontrollable epilepsy. In an attempt to reduce the patient's severe seizures, Vogel cut the neural fibers that connected the two hemispheres. The operation was a success: the patient's seizures were drastically reduced in intensity and frequency.

Because of his previous "split-brain" work with cats, Roger Sperry was invited by Vogel to study the psychological effects of cutting the connection between the two brain hemispheres. Sperry had shown that when the neural connections between the hemispheres were cut in cats, information obtained with one eye was not transferred to the other side of the brain. Now he was interested in studying human split-brain patients who had the neural connections between the hemispheres cut in order to treat their epilepsy.

Sensory information travels to the brain hemisphere opposite the side of the body it enters. For example, our eyes are connected to our brains in such a way that the left field of vision is received initially only by the right hemisphere of the brain and the right field of vision only by the left hemisphere. With the normal brain connection (called the corpus callosum) intact, the information is quickly transmitted to both hemispheres.

But what happens when the information is not allowed to cross to the other hemisphere? Sperry (1968)

In order to understand human behavior fully, we need to know something about how biology influences people. Psychobiologists study the endocrine system and the nervous system and pay special attention to the functioning of the brain. Also of great interest to psychologists is how heredity and environment interact to produce the development of behavior.

2

Psychobiology

devised an apparatus that allowed him to present visual stimuli to the right or left side of a screen placed in front of a subject, or to place objects into the right or left hand of the subject (outside the field of vision). Sperry and his colleague Michael Gazzaniga found that when they presented different information to each hemisphere in the split-brain epileptic patients, normal functioning broke down. For example, if you place an object, like a pencil, in the right hand, the information is received by the left hemisphere, which also has the language ability to name it. But when the object is presented to the left side of the visual field or placed in the left hand, the split-brain patient can't say what it is. This is because the right hemisphere has received the information and can't transmit it to the part of the left hemisphere that controls the production of language.

Although the right hemisphere does not control speech, it can recognize words. If a word is shown only to the left visual field, the patient cannot say what the word is. However, such patients can write the word with the left hand. If asked what they just did, the patients cannot tell you, because the language center, located in the left hemisphere, has not received the information from the right hemisphere.

Sperry's research has helped psychologists understand better how each hemisphere functions and interacts under normal conditions. This allows psychologists to help stroke victims who have lost function of part of the brain, as well as gain insight into the complex operations of the human brain in normal individuals. This understanding is valuable whenever we want to study how people learn, remember, think, or solve problems.

FIGURE 2.1 Cerebral Hemisphere

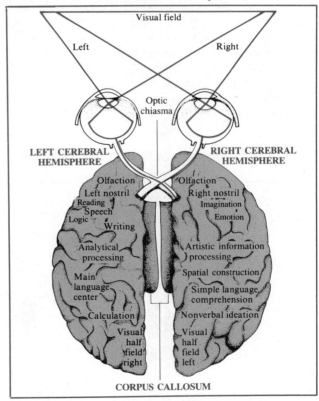

The cerebrum consists of two distinct hemispheres connected by the corpus callosum. The corpus callosum is a bundle of neurons that keeps each hemisphere informed about what is happening in the other one. Each hemisphere controls somewhat different functions, as shown in this diagram of the brain.

WHAT IS PSYCHOBIOLOGY?

Sperry's dramatic demonstration of how the brain's two hemispheres function is a good illustration of the biological basis of behavior. However, it isn't necessary to study split-brain patients in order to demonstrate that biology influences behavior.

Think about the last time you went to class. Perhaps you were a bit late and your heart was racing as you took your seat. Then the instructor called on you, and, as you responded, you noticed your hands were sweating. Your behavior depended on your being able to hear the instructor, be aware of your physical environment, speak, move, recall information, and recognize signs of emotional nervousness. To behave appropriately, you relied on various biological response systems. By biological response systems, we mean the parts of your body that gather information, process it, make decisions based on the assimilated information, and act on these decisions.

The biological response systems include your sense organs, nervous system, muscles, and endocrine glands. It was the interplay between your eyes, ears, brain, and muscles that allowed you to respond in the classroom. And your endocrine system was partly responsible for your sweaty hands and racing heart. (We discuss the endocrine system later in this chapter.)

Our biological response systems play a major role in our behavior. In fact, along with the genes, they form the biological basis of human behavior and constitute a subfield of experimental psychology called psychobiology, biological psychology, or physiological psychology. It is in this part of psychology that we study the sense organs, nervous system, muscles, endocrine gland system, and heredity—all of which influence our responses to the world around us.

It is important to study psychobiology now because an understanding of how biology influences behavior will help you understand better many other complex topics later. For instance, knowing how the nervous system works helps us understand how thinking develops in a child or how a person remembers learned information. Similarly, genetics teaches us how our biological heritage influences the way we think and behave in a wide variety of situations. The importance of research on the brain is recognized by the U. S. Congress, which passed a resolution declaring the 1990s the "Decade of the Brain."

THE NEURON

The human nervous system helps us respond with appropriate behavior to stimuli in the environment. It communicates information throughout the body. Specifically, the human nervous system carries messages about the environment from our *sense organs* to our brain, where the messages are analyzed and decisions made. Then the nervous system carries messages about these decisions to our muscles and glands, so we can respond

FIGURE 2.2 Biological Response Systems

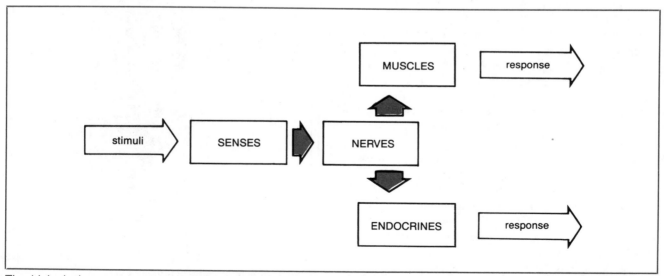

The biological response systems are the parts of the body that gather information, process it, make decisions on the information, and then act on them. A stimulus enters through the sense organs and is carried through the nervous system to the brain, where it is interpreted. The brain then directs the muscles and endocrine glands to respond.

FIGURE 2.3   Neuron

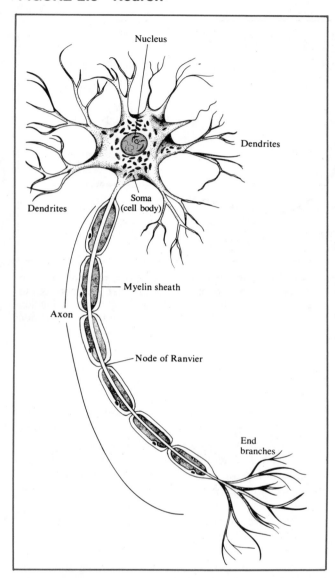

A neuron is a specialized cell that carries messages throughout the body. Its major parts include dendrites, a cell body, and an axon. Sometimes the axon is covered with a myelin sheath so information can be carried more quickly over long distances.

with the appropriate behavior. The human nervous system is made up of billions of tiny nerve cells called neurons.

Structure of the Neuron   The neuron is the basic unit of the nervous system. It is a specialized type of cell that conducts messages throughout the body. Like all cells, the neuron has a cell body, or soma, that contains the nucleus and cytoplasm. The genetic material is contained in the nucleus, and the normal cellular metabolism occurs in the cytoplasm. The cell membrane encloses the entire cell. The neuron has short, finger-like projections extending from the cell body called dendrites. These receive incoming information from other neurons.

Each neuron has one axon, a tail-like fiber projection along which messages are conducted. The place at which the axon leaves the cell body is called the axon hillock. Axons may project up to several meters. For example, an axon from an individual neuron may travel down the length of a giraffe's neck, a distance of 3 meters. Larger axons are often covered by a protective substance called a myelin sheath. The myelin sheath is not a continuous covering, but consists of segments with small gaps, called nodes of Ranvier. The fatty myelin helps insulate axons so information can travel through them quickly and will not be interfered with by neighboring axons. A lack of myelination—which occurs, for example, in multiple sclerosis—results in severe disruptions in sensory and muscle functioning. At the end of the axon are the terminal buttons, or end branches.

Types of Neurons   The body has three types of neurons: sensory neurons, interneurons, and motor neurons. When you hear your instructor ask you a question in class, sensory neurons, or afferent neurons, carry the information from your ears to your brain. Interneurons, or association neurons, carry the information throughout your brain so you can interpret the sensory information and think about what action to take. When you decide how to respond, motor neurons, or efferent neurons, carry the information to your muscles so you can talk.

The axons of neurons outside of the brain and spinal cord run together in bundles called nerves. Thus, sensory neurons form sensory nerves and motor neurons form motor nerves. These form the peripheral nervous system, which will be discussed later in this chapter. Next we focus on how neurons function.

The Neural Impulse

Neurons are able to receive and carry messages throughout the body because these cells have two unique properties—irritability and conduction. Irritability is the characteristic that allows a neuron to change in response to stimulation. Conduction is the ability to carry a message—actually an electrical impulse—along the length of a neuron. When a stimulus irritates the dendrites of a neuron, the dendrites conduct the information to the cell body, and then the impulse travels down the axon. This process, conduction of a neural impulse, is basically electrical in nature.

The neuron might be compared to an electrical battery, because it contains both positive and negative

FIGURE 2.4 Neural Impulse

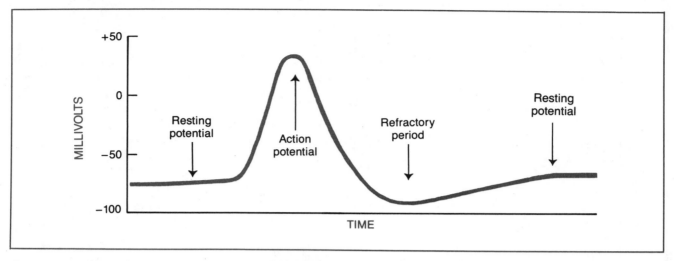

Conduction of a neural impulse along a neuron is an electrical process. The normal electrical charge of a neuron in resting potential is −70mV. When the dendrites are stimulated, the cell membrane allows positive ions to enter. As soon as the electrical charge reaches about −50mV, the neuron fires and creates a condition called an action potential. During an action potential, the charge briefly goes to +40mV before dropping back to −90mV during the refractory period, and then to −70mV, the resting potential.

particles called *ions*. The normal electrical charge of a passive neuron is called its resting potential (Pinel, 1990). In this state of polarization, there are more negative ions (such as chloride) inside the neuron and more positive ions (such as sodium and potassium) outside. The resting potential (electrical charge) of a neuron is −70 millivolts (mV).

When a stimulus irritates the dendrites of a neuron, the cell membrane becomes permeable and lets the positively charged particles pass through to the inside of the neuron to meet the negative ions stored there. Any change in which the internal electrical charge becomes more positive is called depolarization. As soon as the electrical charge reaches about −50 mV, the neuron *fires* and an electrical charge called the action potential is created, which travels down the length of the axon. During an action potential, the electrical charge briefly goes to about +40 mV before becoming negative again.

According to a principle called the all-or-none law, a neuron only fires when the stimulus is above a certain minimum strength, called the threshold, and when it fires it always fires at full strength. This is similar to the way a smoke alarm operates: a small amount of smoke won't set off the alarm, but when a sufficient amount does set it off, there is no increase in the alarm's duration or loudness even if there is a lot more smoke. After firing, there is a brief period of time, called the refractory period, during which the neuron cannot fire again. During the refractory period the electrical charge drops to nearly −90 mV before returning to −70 mV, the resting potential.

The Synapse

For information to get from one neuron to the next, it must cross the synaptic cleft of the synapse, the space between the axon of one neuron (called the presynaptic neuron) and the dendrites of the next (called the postsynaptic neuron). The synapse is typically very tiny, about 30 nanometers wide (or 30 billionths of a meter).

Synaptic Transmission Unlike the electrical communication within a single neuron, communication between neurons involves a chemical reaction. When the electrical neural impulse reaches the terminal buttons of the axon of a presynaptic neuron, it causes the synaptic vesicles to release a chemical substance, called a neurotransmitter, into the synapse. The chemical neurotransmitters cross the synapse and combine with receptor chemical molecules of the dendrites of the postsynaptic neuron, where they may either initiate or inhibit a new neural impulse. If neurotransmitters did not sometimes act to inhibit neural impulses, our nervous system would be a chaos of neurons firing at the same time.

Neurotransmitters We are learning that neurotransmitters play a key role in controlling behavior, and understanding how they work has become a vital part of physiological psychology. Nearly a dozen neurotransmitters have been extensively studied, with many other substances suspected of serving in this capacity (Pinel, 1990). Let's take a look at the major classes of neuro-

FIGURE 2.5 Synapse

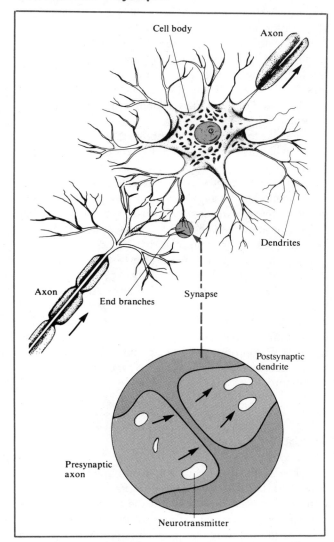

The synapse is the space between the axon of one neuron and the dendrites of the next. When the electrical neural impulse reaches the terminal buttons of the axon, it causes the release of a chemical neurotransmitter into the synapse. This neurotransmitter crosses the synapse and causes the dendrites of the next neuron to react.

transmitters: acetylcholine, monoamines, amino acids, and neuropeptides.

One of the first neurotransmitters to be identified was acetylcholine, which is involved in the activation of muscles as well as in arousal, memory, and motivation. Recent research suggests that the severe memory disruption in persons with Alzheimer's disease is due to the degeneration of brain neurons that use acetylcholine (Marsh & colleagues, 1990).

The monoamine neurotransmitters include serotonin, dopamine, and norepinephrine. Serotonin is produced in

the brain stem and is involved in sleep, sensory experiences, and mood. Research has suggested serotonin is involved in some types of hallucinations, and recently this neurotransmitter has been implicated in the psychological disorder called obsessive compulsive disorder, discussed in chapter 13, "Psychological Disorders" (Zohar & Insel, 1987).

The neuromuscular breakdown symptomatic of Parkinson's disease is associated with low levels of the neurotransmitter dopamine in the brain. Dopamine is involved in a variety of functions, including movement, learning, reinforcement, and attention. High levels of dopamine have been implicated in the serious psychological disorder of schizophrenia (discussed in chapter 13, "Psychological Disorders").

Levels of norepinephrine in the brain are associated with wakefulness, arousal, memory, and emotion. Low levels of norepinephrine are associated with depression; thus antidepressant drugs raise the level of norepinephrine in the brain (discussed in chapter 13, "Psychological Disorders").

The amino acids that function as neurotransmitters include glutamate, aspartate, glycine, and GABA (gama-aminobutyric acid). Glutamate (or glutamic acid) is a principal excitatory transmitter in the brain's cortex. This is why you may feel dizzy after eating oriental food containing monosodium glutamate. Aspartate is also an excitatory neurotransmitter, and is found chiefly in the thalamus and spinal cord. Glycine is an inhibitory amino acid found mainly in the spinal cord and hindbrain. A reduction in the level of glycine can result in severe convulsions. GABA is an important inhibitory neurotransmitter found throughout the central nervous system. Recent research suggests that GABA is involved in anxiety reactions (Breir & Paul, 1990).

A number of neuropeptides, short chains of amino acids, are currently suspected of functioning as neurotransmitters or as neuromodulators—substances that modify the sensitivity of neurons to neurotransmitters (Iversen, 1987). Some of the prominent neuropeptides include cholecystokinin (involved in regulation of eating), vasopressin (involved in learning), substance P (involved in pain regulation) and the endorphins (involved in pain regulation, reinforcement, emotion, and memory). The term "endorphin" comes from "endogenous morphine," or morphine produced by the body. Some of the endorphins (the enkephalins) are produced throughout the brain and spinal cord, while others (beta-endorphin and dynorphin) are primarily found in the limbic system (Sweep & Wiegant, 1989). The endorphins appear to be a major discovery in understanding behavior, because they are involved in some of the most fundamental psychological processes. In later chapters, we will further discuss the role of endorphins in pain (chapter 4, "Sensation and Perception"), reinforcement (chapter 6, "Learning"), and memory (chapter 7, "Human Memory").

THE CENTRAL NERVOUS SYSTEM

Imagine that you're sitting in class trying to concentrate on a discussion as your thoughts wander. You remember how pleasant it was to see the person you date. Then you suddenly snap to attention as you hear your name called; you've been asked to define a term written on the chalkboard. Fortunately, you remember the definition. Next, the lights are turned off to show a slide. When the lights come back on, you blink and cover your eyes to protect them from the bright light. After class, while walking toward the door, you decide to ask your friend to go to the big soccer game with you. In order to understand what's happening behind these scenes, or inside us, we need to review some of the basic functionings of our nervous system.

Our nervous system is divided into two parts. The peripheral nervous system transports messages from the sense organs to the spinal cord and brain, and carries information from the spinal cord and brain to the muscles and glands. The central nervous system includes the spinal cord (which controls simple reflexes and serves as a relay network between the brain and the peripheral nervous system) and the brain (which interprets and stores information from the sense organs, decides what behaviors to exhibit, and sends appropriate messages through the spinal cord and peripheral nervous system to the responding muscles and glands). Most of the behaviors involved in the narrative above would have been accomplished through the working of the central nervous system.

Thanks to the part of your brain that controls muscle coordination, the *cerebellum,* you were able to sit in your chair. You remembered a pleasant event from the past because that memory was stored in the *cerebral cortex* of your brain. You were also able to think about future events because of the cerebral cortex. When your teacher called your name, you became alert because of a network of neurons in your brain, called the *reticular formation,* that affects arousal. You were able to understand what you saw on the board because of the *occipital lobe* of your brain, which analyzes visual information. And you could plan to ask someone to go to the soccer game because of a part of your brain called the *hypothalamus,* which controls motivation. Although these things involved the brain, it is appropriate to begin our discussion of the central nervous system by reviewing the functions of the spinal cord.

FIGURE 2.6 Human Nervous System

The human nervous system can be divided into the central nervous system (brain and spinal cord) and the peripheral nervous system (autonomic nervous system and somatic nervous system). The peripheral nervous system receives messages from the sense organs and carries information to the muscles and glands. The central nervous system interprets and stores information from the sense organs and sends messages via the peripheral nervous system to the muscles and glands.

The Spinal Cord

The spinal cord, housed in the spinal backbone, consists of bundles of neurons that form a communication link between the brain and the peripheral nervous system. One important function of the spinal cord is to serve as the pathway along which neural impulses from the sense organs travel up to the brain and other neural impulses from the brain travel down to the muscles and glands. Most of the peripheral nerves connect with the central nervous system through the spinal cord, and thus are called spinal nerves.

Besides serving as a pathway for neural impulses, the spinal cord controls certain types of reflexes. A reflex is an automatic movement that occurs in direct response to a stimulus. Spinal reflexes need not directly involve the brain, but rely rather on the neural pathways in the spinal cord for their activation. You are probably familiar with a number of reflexes. In the classroom scene above, you blinked your eyes when the lights were turned on because the pupil of the eye automatically contracts when exposed to bright light. Another reflex you are probably familiar with is the "knee jerk," in which the lower leg swings forward quickly when an area just below the knee is tapped. Reflexes enable people to respond quickly to potentially painful or dangerous situations.

FIGURE 2.7 Diagram of Spinal Reflex

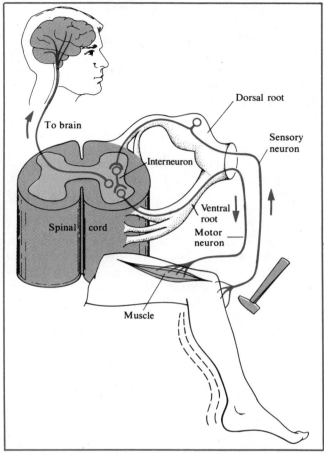

In the knee-jerk reflex, the lower leg swings forward quickly when an area just below the knee is tapped. In order for this reflex to occur, a message travels through a sensory neuron to the spinal cord, where an interneuron carries it to a motor neuron, which sends the information to the leg muscle and causes the movement.

FIGURE 2.8 The Human Brain

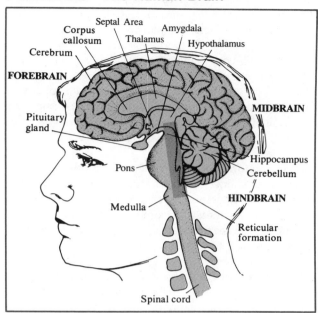

The major structures of the brain are shown here. The hindbrain structures—the medulla, pons, and cerebellum—help regulate basic body activities, including heart rate, breathing, and coordination. The reticular formation only allows relevant information to enter the higher brain centers. The limbic system includes the hypothalamus, thalamus, and hippocampus. The hypothalamus regulates motivation and emotion and the thalamus primarily relays sensory information to the cerebrum, the part of the brain that allows humans to think and store information. The hippocampus is involved in memory processing.

The Brain

The brain has always attracted the attention of psychologists because its physiological activity governs most behaviors. Made up of billions of neurons, the human brain is more intricate than any computer. All of the behaviors described earlier in the classroom scene, apart from the blinking reflex, were controlled by the brain. It is the center for "higher" mental functions, such as thinking and memory. It processes the messages carried to it by the peripheral nervous system and the spinal cord, makes decisions about what responses are necessary, and sends directions to the muscles to carry out the appropriate behavior. The brain can best be understood by examining its three major divisions: the hindbrain, the midbrain, and the forebrain. Keep in mind,

however, that it is the interaction of many brain structures that controls behavior.

The Hindbrain The hindbrain connects the spinal cord with the rest of the brain. It controls the basic life-support functions of the body, such as breathing and heart rate. The hindbrain consists of the medulla, pons, cerebellum, and reticular formation.

The medulla, the part of the hindbrain that directly connects the spinal cord with the brain, helps regulate basic bodily functions, such as breathing and heart rate. The medulla is where a number of peripheral nervous system cranial nerves, which include sensory and motor nerves, enter the central nervous system. Lying just above the medulla is the pons, which, through the cranial nerves, plays a role in controlling such behaviors as eating and making facial movements. Next to the medulla is a convoluted structure known as the cerebellum, which controls body balance, movement, and muscle coordination, allowing us to walk and run without tripping.

The reticular formation is a network of neurons extending from the medulla up to the higher brain centers found in the forebrain. This structure, sometimes called the *reticular activating system (RAS)*, acts as a gate, allowing relevant sensory information such as that involved in arousal or sleep to enter the brain. When your instructor calls your name, your reticular formation stimulates the higher brain centers that allow you to become alert. When you are sleeping, your reticular formation prevents most environmental stimuli from entering your brain. All of the structures in the hindbrain work together and are influenced by other parts of the brain.

The Midbrain   The midbrain is a relatively small region that connects the hindbrain with the forebrain. Although the midbrain appears to function mainly as a relay station for messages coming into the brain, it also contains structures that play a role in seeing, hearing, and movement.

The Forebrain   The forebrain is the largest and most complex part of the brain. It not only influences many of the basic life-support functions controlled by the midbrain and hindbrain, but is also responsible for such uniquely human higher-level behaviors as thinking and speaking. The major structures of the forebrain include the thalamus, hypothalamus, and cerebrum.

The Limbic System   James Papez (1937) proposed the theory that the hypothalamus and related structures formed a circuit for emotional behavior. Paul MacLean (1949) later revised the theory and named the circuit the limbic system. Located in the most primitive part of the forebrain, called the rhinencephalon, it is a collection of structures that influences motivation and emotional behaviors such as sex, aggression, fear, pleasure, and pain. The structures usually included in the limbic system are the thalamus, hypothalamus, amygdala, mammillary bodies, fornix, and septal area.

The function of the limbic system was discovered accidently in 1954 by James Olds and Peter Milner, who were testing the effects of electrical stimulation on the reticular formation in rats and placed an electrode in the septal area by mistake. This part of the limbic system produces a pleasurable sensation when stimulated. When the rats learned that they could control the electrical stimulation and thus the pleasure by pressing a lever, they pressed it thousands of times per hour. Electrical stimulation of the brain (ESB) has a potent reinforcing effect, which means the subject will repeat whatever behavior led to the pleasurable sensation. The reinforcing effects of ESB have been found in a variety of animals, including humans. Recent research suggests that ESB involves endorphin synapses (Wise & Bozarth, 1984).

The Thalamus   The thalamus is an important relay station for sensory information, including visual,

auditory, tactile (touch), pain, and temperature stimuli. Messages from these sense organs are channeled into the thalamus, and from there are carried into specific parts of the forebrain for interpretation and action.

The Hypothalamus   An important part of the limbic system is the small structure called the hypothalamus. It is involved in the motivation of such behaviors as eating, drinking, sex, sleeping, and regulating temperature. It influences the pituitary gland, which regulates biochemical reactions in the body. The hypothalamus also influences the part of the peripheral nervous system that regulates the internal body organs. We discuss some of the specific motivated behaviors influenced by the hypothalamus in chapter 9, "Motivation."

Other areas in the limbic system are also important in a wide variety of behaviors. The hippocampus is important in learning and memory. The *amygdala* and *septal area* are involved in fear, aggression, and other social behaviors. Research has shown that reward sites for ESB are located throughout the brain, but are especially concentrated around the medial forebrain bundle, a tract that runs through the limbic system.

Behind the thalamus is the *pineal gland,* a small structure that apparently is influenced by light-dark cycles and helps regulate reproductive behavior in some animals through the release of the hormone melatonin. Its role in human behavior is unclear, although there is evidence that it is involved in reproduction, sleep, and mood (Levinthal, 1990).

The Cerebrum   The cerebrum, the largest part of the forebrain, consists of two distinct structures called hemispheres. As discussed in the opening story, the two hemispheres are connected by the corpus callosum, a bundle of neurons that keeps each hemisphere informed about what is happening in the other. Basically, the left hemisphere controls the right side of the body and the right hemisphere controls the left side. For proper motor coordination, each hemisphere must know what the other is doing. An activity involving both sides of the body, such as crossing our hands or tying our shoes, would be difficult if our two cerebral hemispheres were not connected.

The outermost layer of the cerebrum, the cerebral cortex, is the part of the brain that renders humans unique. Here is where messages from our sense organs are interpreted and stored, and where decisions about behavior are made. The cerebral cortex has distinct sections, or lobes, that control different activities. When you are in the classroom remembering past events or giving the answer to a question, you are using the frontal lobes of your cerebral cortex. Your occipital lobes allow you to interpret what you see in the environment. When

FIGURE 2.9   Lobes of the Cerebral Cortex

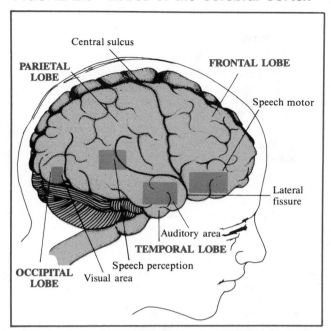

The cerebral cortex is divided into four distinct sections, or lobes. The frontal lobe controls thinking and motor coordination. The occipital lobe interprets visual information. The temporal lobe perceives speech and hearing. The parietal lobe receives sensory information.

you hear your instructor talking, your temporal lobes are operating. And your parietal lobes are responsible for interpreting somatosensory senses such as touch, pain, and temperature.

Although each lobe of the brain is primarily responsible for one main function (frontal lobes, movement and memory; occipital lobes, vision; temporal lobes, hearing; and parietal lobes, somatosensory senses), much of the area of the cerebral cortex is involved in multiple sensory or motor functions. These association areas of the brain help integrate information for successful adaptation. For example, when you think about a dog, you utilize a variety of association areas. You remember the sound of the dog's bark, the feel of her fur, the sight of her body, the image of her running, and the features of her face.

Cerebral Hemisphere Functioning   In general, each hemisphere of the cerebrum controls the opposite side of the body: the left half controls the right side of the body and the right half controls the left side. But the two hemispheres are not totally redundant in function. When the *corpus callosum*, the neural bundle connecting the two hemispheres, is cut, people appear to function pretty much as they did previously, but in fact there are subtle dysfunctions. As described in our opening story, the classic research in this area was done by Roger Sperry (1968), who studied epileptic patients whose corpus

FIGURE 2.10   Testing Split-Brain Subjects

This figure illustrates the difficulty a split-brain subject has in integrating information between the two hemispheres of the brain. The subject with a split brain sits in front of a divided visual display screen. In the first step of the test, the image of a spoon is shown on the left side of the screen, and the image of a fork is shown on the right. When asked what image has been presented, the subject responds "a fork," because the left, verbal hemisphere has received that image, and can also name it. In the next step of the test, the subject is asked to pick up in the left hand the object that was presented. The subject picks up the spoon, since the left hand is controlled by the right hemisphere, and that hemisphere saw a spoon. But, when asked to name the object that has just been picked up, the subject incorrectly identifies it as "a fork," because the visual and tactile information received in the right hemisphere cannot cross the severed corpus callosum into the left, verbal hemisphere.

callosum had been severed in order to reduce the frequency of seizures.

Sperry received a Nobel Prize in 1981 for his work on what he termed the *syndrome of hemisphere decon- nection*, popularly known as split-brain research. You will remember that he discovered that only information presented to the right side of the body enters the left hemisphere, where the speech center allows the patients to verbalize the information. Information presented to the left side of the body enters the right hemisphere, where it is interpreted so the patient can write the information with the left hand.

Research such as Sperry's has shown that the left hemisphere tends to be the more logical, analytical, and verbal half, exerting greater control over manual dexterity, reading, language, and understanding speech. The right hemisphere tends to process nonverbal information

ROGER SPERRY

Roger Sperry was born August 20, 1913, in Hartford, Connecticut. He was rewarded with a Nobel Prize in physiology and medicine in 1981 for his more than 40 years of research on the brain. The prize was given specifically for his work on the "split-brain," in which he discovered that the two cerebral hemispheres of the brain have distinct functions. The left, usually the dominant side, is involved in reasoning, language, writing, and reading, while the right, or less dominant side, is more involved in nonverbal processes, such as art, music, and creative behavior.

Sperry received his Ph.D. from the University of Chicago in 1941. He did his early research at the Yerkes Primate Laboratory and the National Institute of Health before joining the staff of the California Institute of Technology in 1954 as Hixon Professor of Psychobiology. He originally studied cats, and found that the corpus callosum, or nerve bundle connecting the two cerebral hemispheres, was necessary for the transfer of information from one side of the brain to the other.

Sperry next began to study epileptic patients whose corpus callosum had been severed to prevent seizures. His technique, which he termed "hemisphere deconnection," has contributed valuable information to the treatment of various brain disorders.

and is more concerned with emotion, imagination, and artistic information (Gazzaniga, 1989). For most people, the left hemisphere is viewed as the more dominant.

In the past 2 decades, great strides have been made in our understanding of how the brain functions. Much of the recent research emphasizes how the two hemispheres work together to create consciousness. A study by Fabbro, Brusaferro, and Bava (1990) illustrates how the hemispheres function. They tested the notion that the right hemisphere is more musical and artistic. The study compared young teenage musicians with adult expert musicians. Subjects were given a hand-tapping task under disruptive conditions. The young musicians showed more left hand disruption, suggesting a right-hemisphere specialization for music. The experts, however, showed more disruption with the right hand, suggesting more left-hemisphere involvement after formal academic training. This research shows the complexity of brain functioning and the difficulty of drawing simple conclusions.

Under most conditions, in the person with the brain hemispheres connected, information about the environment is sent from the sense organs through the peripheral nervous system to both hemispheres of the brain, so that the brain can make a decision and send the appropriate response message back through the peripheral nervous system to the muscles and glands. Therefore, it is incorrect to say that a normally functioning person is totally "left-brained" or "right-brained." In most cases, both hemispheres work together to produce our conscious experience (Gazzaniga, 1987).

Methods of Studying the Brain   Psychologists have developed a variety of techniques to study the brain so that they can better predict, control, and explain behavior. One early method was proposed by Franz Gall, who in the early 1800s measured the bumps on people's skulls and tried to relate them to various behavior characteristics. While this method, called phrenology, never produced significant results, it did set the stage for later methods of identifying the functions of particular parts of the brain.

In the 1930s it was discovered that if the frontal lobes were disconnected from the rest of the brain, violent or extremely emotional mental patients became calm. This procedure, called prefrontal lobotomy, was for a time popular in treating severe behavior problems. However, studies showed that prefrontal lobotomy had negative side effects: lobotomy patients showed little emotion, had no social inhibitions, and had trouble solving problems. Because of these behavioral side effects, and because of the ethical

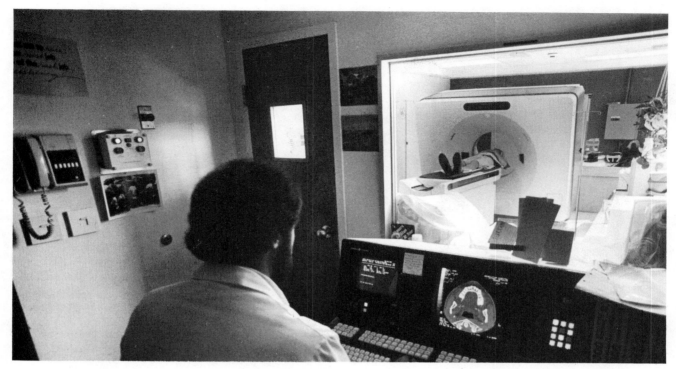

FIGURE 2.11 CAT Scan
The CAT scan technique involves taking a series of X rays of the brain from various angles. The patient remains still while the CAT apparatus rotates to obtain the X rays (visible on the control panel screen, above). A computer is then used to generate a slice through the brain from any angle desired, and to identify brain damage.

implications in cutting out part of a brain, lobotomies are no longer performed to treat mental disorders. Currently, the most common biological method for treating mental disorders is drug therapy. (See chapter 14, "Therapy.")

An important technique now used for studying the brain involves the *electrical stimulation* of specific areas. In our discussion of the limbic system, we mentioned the discovery of pleasure centers in the brain by Olds and Milner. Using ESB with rats, they found that when an electrode, which is an extremely thin insulated wire, was inserted into the brain and a very weak electrical current was sent through the electrode, the rats increased the frequency of whatever behavior had preceded the ESB.

Another demonstration of the effects of brain stimulation on behavior was described by José Delgado (1969). Delgado implanted an electrode in the brain of a bull, and then entered the bull ring armed with a radio transmitter. When the bull charged toward him, Delgado pressed a button, causing the bull to stop and turn away, thus demonstrating the brain's control over behavior.

Electrical stimulation of the human brain can be used to help people with behavior problems, as demonstrated by the research of Wilder Penfield (1975). Penfield used brain stimulation to locate malfunctioning areas of the brain. His purpose was to find the areas of the brain that cause a type of epilepsy in which a number of neurons begin to fire wildly. When the area was located,

the malfunctioning part was removed. In the course of such brain surgery, Penfield discovered that stimulating areas of the cerebral cortex could produce vivid memories (although later research hasn't always been able to validate the accuracy of the memories).

In addition to stimulating the brain electrically, psychologists can also record the brain's electrical activity. In the technique called electroencephalography (EEG), electrodes are attached to the scalp to record general brain-wave patterns. We discuss how EEG helps researchers understand sleep in chapter 5, "Sleep and Consciousness." An extension of the EEG technique is the EEG imaging procedure. In EEG imaging, electrodes are placed on the scalp and the wires are connected to a computer. Then the activity of the brain can be measured while the person responds to stimuli (Fishman, 1985).

Brain researchers now have several computer techniques to study brain activity. The CAT scan (computerized axial tomography) uses a series of X rays to reveal brain abnormalities. A method known as the PET scan, or positron emission tomography, has been developed to examine brain activity during particular behaviors or mental activities (Raichle, 1983). The patient is given an injection of radioactive glucose. Then the PET scan records the gamma rays produced by the radioactive glucose as it is used by the brain cells. Marsh and colleagues (1990) recently used PET to identify brain

FIGURE 2.12   Electrical Brain Stimulation
José Delgado implanted an electrode in the brain of a bull and stopped the bull from charging by giving him an electrical signal.

changes in individuals who had been diagnosed as having Alzheimer's disease.

Another approach to studying brain activity is MRI (magnetic resonance imaging), which uses magnetic fields to study chemical activity of brain cells. Recording the electrical activity of the brain in this way allows scientists to locate parts of the brain involved in specific behaviors, detect neural damage, and study states of consciousness such as sleep and dreaming. For example, MRI was recently used to study brain abnormalities in depressed patients (Zubenko, Sullivan, Nelson, & Belle, 1990).

Technology is quickly advancing our ability to study the functioning of the brain. With the newer methods of brain study, scientists are beginning to understand what the brain is doing when a person is in different states of consciousness, is solving problems, or is remembering previously learned experiences.

THE PERIPHERAL NERVOUS SYSTEM

On your way home from school, you are confronted by a large, snarling dog with its teeth bared. Immediately you feel "butterflies" in your stomach, you begin to breathe faster, and your heart speeds up. You can almost feel the blood flowing away from your inner organs toward your muscles, preparing you for what is called a "fight or flight" response. You begin to feel more energy

as blood sugar is released. Then you breathe a sigh of relief as you see the dog's owner take it away. When you sit down to rest, your breathing begins to slow down and your heart rate decreases. After you feel relaxed, you get up and proceed home, thinking about what you will be eating for dinner.

While you were having your encounter with the snarling dog, your whole nervous system was active. Up to this point, we've concentrated only on the central nervous system—the part that allows us to interpret sensory information, think, remember things, and make decisions. Another branch of the human nervous system, the peripheral nervous system, carries messages from the sense organs to the central nervous system, and from the central nervous system to the muscles and glands. It includes all of the nerves outside the brain and spinal cord. The nerves that connect to the spinal cord are called spinal nerves; those that connect to the brain are called cranial nerves. The peripheral nervous system consists of two major divisions—the somatic nervous system and the autonomic nervous system.

The Somatic Nervous System

The somatic nervous system might be regarded as more "external," since it involves the sense organs and the skeletal muscles, both located close to the outside surface of the body. The sensory division of the somatic nervous system carries messages from the sense organs, whereas the motor division relays information that directs primarily the voluntary movements of the skeletal muscles. When you first encountered the snarling dog, it was the somatic nervous system part of your peripheral nervous system that carried the information from your eyes and ears to your central nervous system. Also, it was your somatic nervous system that carried the directions to the skeletal muscles of your legs, enabling you to turn around and walk the other way. Without your somatic nervous system, you would not be aware of your external environment and you could not respond appropriately to changes in it.

The Autonomic Nervous System

The autonomic nervous system is more of an internal system, connecting the central nervous system to the endocrine glands, the muscles controlling the heart, and the primarily involuntary smooth muscles controlling the other internal organs, such as the stomach, intestines, liver, and lungs. The autonomic nervous system is very important in emotion, and we'll be referring to it in chapter 10, "Emotion."

The autonomic nervous system is further divided into two branches: the *sympathetic nervous system*, which is more active in emergencies, and the *parasym-pathetic nervous system*, which is more active under normal circumstances. When you are calm and quiet, the parasympathetic nervous system causes your heart rate to slow down, your blood pressure to drop, and breathing to become normal. It also activates the stomach and intestines so that normal digestion can occur. The primary neurotransmitter found in the parasympathetic nervous system is acetylcholine, whose effects mainly inhibit muscle action. The parasympathetic system can be thought of as the maintenance system that is in control during relaxation. Your parasympathetic nervous system was dominant as you began to walk home from school and were not yet in any danger from the dog.

When you suddenly saw the snarling dog in your path, your sympathetic nervous system caused the increase in heart rate, blood pressure, and breathing. Your eyes dilated to take in more information, blood was redirected from your stomach to your limbs so you could fight or flee, and your adrenal glands secreted a chemical called adrenaline to provide you with extra energy. The sympathetic system utilizes norepinephrine as its main neurotransmitter, which helps to explain the sympathetic nervous system's excitatory effects on the muscles and glands. Often activated in emergency situations, the sympathetic nervous system is especially important when you are under stress.

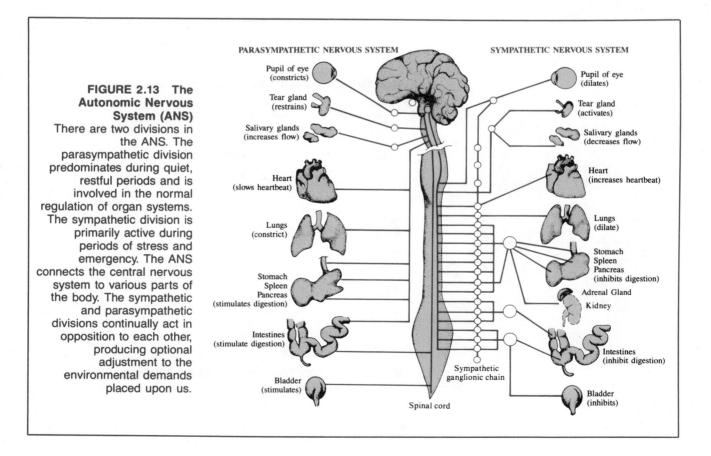

FIGURE 2.13 The Autonomic Nervous System (ANS) There are two divisions in the ANS. The parasympathetic division predominates during quiet, restful periods and is involved in the normal regulation of organ systems. The sympathetic division is primarily active during periods of stress and emergency. The ANS connects the central nervous system to various parts of the body. The sympathetic and parasympathetic divisions continually act in opposition to each other, producing optional adjustment to the environmental demands placed upon us.

Although our description implies a simple division of labor, we must remember that neither part of the autonomic nervous system acts in isolation. The sympathetic and parasympathetic divisions continually act in opposition to each other, the sympathetic arousing and parasympathetic relaxing the body. Behavior is the end result of the interaction of both parts, along with the other biological response systems.

THE ENDOCRINE SYSTEM

The autonomic nervous system works closely with the endocrine (or ductless) glands to maintain homeostasis, or biochemical stability inside the body. Endocrine glands help provide you with the extra energy you require when faced with an emergency, and regulate the energy you use when you're relaxed. Although the endocrine glands are also a communication system, unlike the nervous system they secrete hormones directly into the bloodstream to produce a slower but more generalized control over internal physiological processes and, ultimately, behavior. Hormones help regulate the body's biochemical activity, enabling us to make appropriate responses to environmental situations.

The Pituitary Gland   The pituitary gland, located near the hypothalamus at the base of the brain, is sometimes called the "master gland" because some of its hormones stimulate other endocrine glands into action. The pituitary gland secretes the growth hormone, which helps regulate growth, and the antidiuretic hormone (ADH), which causes the kidneys to retain water.

The Thyroid Gland   The thyroid gland secretes thyroxin, a hormone that helps determine the rate of *metabolism*, which is the biochemical process that produces energy for the body's maintenance. The condition resulting from an underactive thyroid, called hypothyroidism, results in sluggishness, sleepiness, and weight gain. On the other hand, if the thyroid gland produces too much thyroxin, a person will become easily excitable, have excess energy, and lose weight.

The Adrenal Glands   Located over the kidneys, your adrenal glands help the body react to stress by regulating short-term energy use. The inner part, or adrenal medulla, secretes adrenaline, a hormone that works with the sympathetic nervous system to bring about the arousal necessary to produce the "fight or flight" response required in an emergency, such as when you encountered the snarling dog. The outer part, known

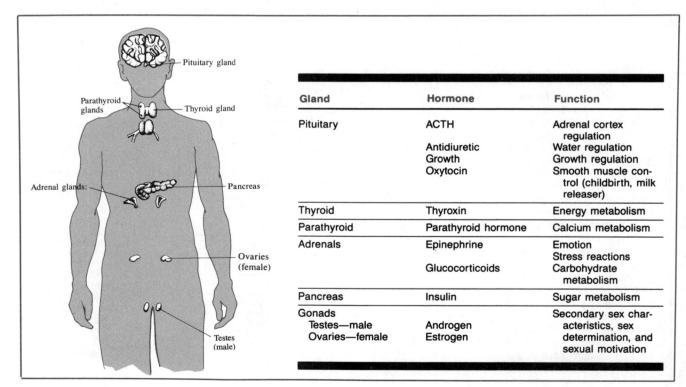

Gland	Hormone	Function
Pituitary	ACTH	Adrenal cortex regulation
	Antidiuretic	Water regulation
	Growth	Growth regulation
	Oxytocin	Smooth muscle control (childbirth, milk releaser)
Thyroid	Thyroxin	Energy metabolism
Parathyroid	Parathyroid hormone	Calcium metabolism
Adrenals	Epinephrine	Emotion Stress reactions
	Glucocorticoids	Carbohydrate metabolism
Pancreas	Insulin	Sugar metabolism
Gonads Testes—male Ovaries—female	Androgen Estrogen	Secondary sex characteristics, sex determination, and sexual motivation

Labels: Pituitary gland, Parathyroid glands, Thyroid gland, Adrenal glands, Pancreas, Ovaries (female), Testes (male)

FIGURE 2.14   Endocrine System
The endocrine glands secrete hormones directly into the bloodstream to control physiological processes. This figure shows the major endocrine glands and some of the activities regulated by them.

as the adrenal cortex, produces steroid hormones that help provide energy and regulate the balance of salt in our system. The adrenal cortex of each gland also secretes sex hormones.

The Gonads   The reproductive glands, or gonads, are ovaries in the female and testes in the male. They are involved in sex determination and development, secondary sexual characteristics, and sexual motivation. Ovaries secrete estrogen and testes secrete androgen. Each individual has hormones of both sexes, but females have a predominance of estrogen, and males of androgen. Estrogen produces female characteristics, such as breasts and wide hips, while androgen produces male characteristics, such as facial hair and low-pitched voices.

Hormones may play a role in premenstrual syndrome (PMS), as shown in the Application that follows.

APPLICATION

Hormones and Premenstrual Syndrome

Many women experience distinct changes in their physical and psychological functioning just prior to menstruation. During the past decade, an increasing amount of attention has been given to the symptoms of premenstrual syndrome (PMS), or what is termed *late luteal phase dysphoric disorder* in the diagnostic manual of the American Psychiatric Association (APA, 1987). There is a great deal of controversy over the existence, cause, and treatment of PMS. Here we focus on the possible role of hormones in this syndrome.

Symptoms that sometimes occur just before or during menstruation in women are both physical and psychological. Physical symptoms include headaches, backaches, constipation, fluid retention, uterine cramps, and tender breasts. Psychological symptoms include feelings of irritability, stress, fatigue, depression, anxiety, low sex drive, impatience, and a general negative mood. Estimates of the number of women experiencing these symptoms vary from 10 to 80 percent. There are no differences in reported symptoms of black or white women in America (Stout, 1986). Cross-cultural research suggests cultural expectations play a major role, since in some societies these symptoms are not as often experienced (Gottlieb, 1988).

Although the exact cause of PMS is not yet known, biological theories include gonadal hormone imbalance, adrenal hormone abnormality, hypoglycemia, vitamin deficiency, or endorphin neurotransmitter abnormality (Alberts & Alberts, 1990). The female gonads, the ova-ries, produce estrogen and progesterone. An increase of estrogen facilitates the development of an egg cell from the ovary. Estrogen production increases during the first half of the menstrual cycle, and then tapers off prior to menstruation. Levels of progesterone increase gradually and peak during the second half of the menstrual cycle. Progesterone prepares the uterus for pregnancy. Both estrogen and progesterone levels drop off just prior to menstruation, perhaps causing PMS. Some research has found estrogen treatments reduce PMS symptoms, but other studies have not found a significant difference between subjects receiving estrogen treatments and subjects receiving a placebo.

Sex hormones affect neurotransmitters, including serotonin, GABA, and the endorphins. One hypothesis is that PMS is caused by a significant decrease in beta-endorphin just prior to menstruation (Giannini, Martin, & Turner, 1990). Remember the endorphins are related to mood, which may explain the shift to a negative, irritable mood prior to menstruation.

At the present time, we do not know the cause of PMS. Treatments vary widely, and include such suggestions as reducing the intake of sugar, salt, and caffeine, increasing the B vitamins, taking hormonal supplements, engaging in meditation, and exercising. Although estimates vary, most researchers think that only about 10 percent of women experience incapacitating symptoms (Gottlieb, 1988). More research is needed before we can understand better the cause and evaluate treatments of this problem.

In summary, hormones secreted by the endocrine glands play an important role in behavioral responses. Hormones enable the body to respond appropriately to environmental stimuli. Some hormones produce short-term changes, but most produce long-term physiological reactions in the body.

HEREDITY AND BEHAVIOR

The biological response systems, including the sense organs, nervous system, endocrine system, and muscles, permit us to respond appropriately and immediately to environmental stimuli. It is, however, our heredity that determines the ultimate structure of our biological response systems, as well as their functioning ability. Heredity is the natural capability of individuals to develop the characteristics possessed by their ancestors.

FIGURE 2.15   The DNA Molecule

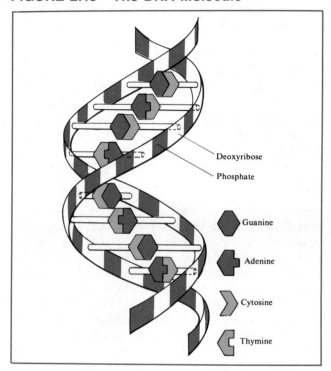

Genes are made of organic molecules called deoxyribonucleic acid (DNA). Watson and Crick discovered that
DNA has a double helix pattern that determines the code
that directs the formation of biochemicals. The biochemicals produced will, in turn, ultimately produce the characteristics of the individual.

In the study of heredity, called <u>genetics</u>, scientists
study the laws that determine how traits are passed along
from parents to offspring. Psychologists study genetics in
order to understand better how behavior is influenced by
heredity and the environment.

Basic Genetic Principles

The <u>gene</u> is the basic unit of heredity. The complete set
of genes inherited by an individual from parents is called the
<u>genotype</u>. The genotype interacts with the individual's physi-
cal environment to produce the <u>phenotype</u>, which is the
sum of observable characteristics of the individual: the
phenotype includes sex, eye and hair color, height, weight,
and intelligence, as well as personality characteristics
such as shyness, aggressiveness, and strength—in fact, all
the attributes that determine the unique individual.

Genes control the development of chemicals called
proteins and enzymes, which in turn are involved in the
biochemical reactions that ultimately produce the organs

FIGURE 2.16   Sex Determination

At the time of conception, the 23 chromosomes from the
egg combine with the 23 chromosomes from the sperm to
produce a zygote, or fertilized egg cell, which then has 46
chromosomes. **(A)** Two of these chromosomes determine
sex. **(B)** If an X chromosome is inherited from both parents,
the offspring will be a female. If an X is inherited from the
mother and a Y is inherited from the father, the offspring will
be a male.

and biological response systems that make up an individual. Genes control <u>maturation</u>, or the physical growth of
the individual. However, all the effects of genes are
achieved through an interaction with the individual's
environment. We discuss maturation in chapter 3, "Development."

Plate 1   Sperm Penetrating Egg

A sperm spends several hours in the female reproductive tract undergoing a process called capacitation, which enables it to penetrate an egg. Here we see a sperm approaching an egg. Although several hundred sperm reach an egg, only one penetrates it. The egg then produces a hard protein covering to prevent penetration by other sperm.

Plate 2   6-Week-Old Embryo (Rear View)

At 6 weeks, the embryo is just over half an inch long. As shown in this photograph, the arms and legs are just beginning to grow, and the head area is extremely large compared to its size after birth. The embryo is shown here in the amniotic sac, which is filled with fluid to protect it.

Plate 3   4½-Month-Old Fetus Sucking Thumb

At about 4½ months of prenatal development, the fetus is about 10 inches long and weighs approximately 9 ounces. As shown in this photograph, the fetus shows the reflexive movement of sucking its thumb. This activity appears remarkably similar to thumb-sucking in neonates.

Plate 4 Photograph of the Human Eye

The human eye is sometimes compared to a magnificent living camera. The pupil, the dark circle in the center of the colored iris, automatically adjusts to let in the proper amount of light. The visual image is then focused by the lens, which lets the proper image fall on the back of the eyeball, where the visual receptors (rods and cones) are located.

Plate 5 How the World May Look to Someone With Red-Green Color Blindness (Right)

The top photograph is in full color; the bottom photograph shows what the same scene looks like to a person with red-green color blindness.

Plate 6 Test for Red-Green Color Blindness (Below)

Color blindness can be tested by asking a subject to identify a number within the circle. If the subject is color-blind, he or she is unable to differentiate the dots and identify the number. This is an example of what such a color blindness test might look like, although the colors shown here may vary from those used in an actual test.

Plate 7 Negative Afterimage

Stare at the center of the green, black, and yellow flag for 1 minute, and then look at the blank white space. You should see a negative afterimage resulting in the familiar red, white, and blue American flag. The opponent-process theory of color vision suggests that the receptors respond to one of each pair of opposing colors, so that when you stare at one color, your reaction to that color is weakened and the opposite color appears in the white space.

Plate 8 Color Spectrum

The human eye responds to wavelengths of between 380 and 760 nanometers (from violet to red). When white light is passed through a prism, it breaks down into the visible color spectrum shown here. Isaac Newton first demonstrated this process. One easy way to remember the colors is to use the mnemonic Roy G. Biv (red, orange, yellow, green, blue, indigo, and violet).

Plate 9 Complementary Colors

The colors of the visible spectrum are arranged here in a circle in which complementary colors are placed directly opposite each other.

Plate 10   The Human Brain

This photograph shows the human brain from above. Note how the cortex (outer layer) of the brain is divided into two hemispheres. The grooves shown are called fissures and the places between the fissures are called gyri. The convoluted structure of the brain's cortex allows it to have significantly more surface area than if it were smooth.

Plate 11   PET Scan

The Positron Emission Tomography (PET) technique allows scientists to view brain activity while the subject is engaged in mental activity. The subject is given an injection of radioactive glucose. The PET scan records the areas of the brain that are actively utilizing the radioactive glucose for energy. In this image, the subject on the left was asked to listen subjectively to sequences of musical notes, and the subject on the right was asked to analyze differences in the musical notes.   Note that the subjective experience was focused in the right hemisphere, whereas the analytical experience was focused in the left hemisphere.

Plate 12   CAT Scan

The Computerized Axial Tomography (CAT) technique uses a series of X rays taken along an axis to reveal brain structures and abnormalities. The subject is given an injection of a radioactive substance that is absorbed by brain tissue, providing an outline of the structures. Here is shown a CAT scan of a normal human brain.

Plate 13   MRI

The Magnetic Resonance Imaging (MRI) technique uses magnetic fields to study chemical activity of brain cells. The magnetic field causes the nuclei of the brain cells to line up. This allows scientists to measure brain activity in subjects engaged in mental activity.

Genes are composed of organic molecules called deoxyribonucleic acid (DNA). It was only in 1953 that James Watson and Francis Crick found that DNA has a double helix pattern (like a spiral staircase) that allows the gene to transcribe its message and direct the formation of biochemicals that can be utilized to produce ultimately the characteristics of the individual. Genes can be thought of as locations along chromosomes (from the Greek word for "colored bodies"). Chromosomes are slender bodies found in the nucleus of every cell.

Normally, every cell in the human body (except the sex cells) has 23 pairs of chromosomes, for a total of 46 chromosomes. The sex cells, however, only have 23 chromosomes. At the time of conception, the 23 chromosomes from the egg combine with the 23 chromosomes from the sperm to produce a zygote, or fertilized egg, which then has 46 chromosomes. Thus, with an equal number of chromosomes from our mother and father, we have 46 chromosomes in every body cell.

Twenty-two of the pairs of chromosomes are called autosomes, which carry genes that regulate various bodily processes and characteristics, such as eye color, intelligence, and height. Since each chromosome of a given pair comes from a different parent, two forms of a particular gene are possible. Using eye color as a simplified example, one form of the gene (B) might result in brown eyes, whereas another form (b) results in blue eyes. If a child received a B gene from each parent, she would probably have brown eyes, and if she received a b gene from each parent, she would likely have blue eyes. But if the child received a B gene from one parent and a b gene from the other one, she would probably end up with brown eyes. Geneticists say the B form of the gene is dominant, whereas the b form is recessive. It takes only one dominant gene for the phenotype to be reflected but it takes both recessive genes to produce a recessive trait. An individual with both genes identical is said to be homozygous for the gene, whereas the individual with two different genes is said to be heterozygous. Even though the phenotype of a heterozygous person reflects the dominant gene, he or she still carries the recessive gene, which could be passed along to offspring.

One pair of chromosomes is called the sex chromosomes, because the genes located on this pair are responsible for determining the sex of the person. If you are a female, you have two X chromosomes; if you are a male, you have one X chromosome and one Y chromosome. When the sex cells are formed, in a process called meiosis, eggs always carry an X chromosome, whereas sperm can carry an X or a Y chromosome. Therefore, at conception it is the sperm that determines the sex of the offspring genetically. If an X chromosome from a sperm combines with the X chromosome from the egg, the offspring will be a female. On the other hand, if a Y chromosome from a sperm combines with the X chromo-

FIGURE 2.17   Heredity

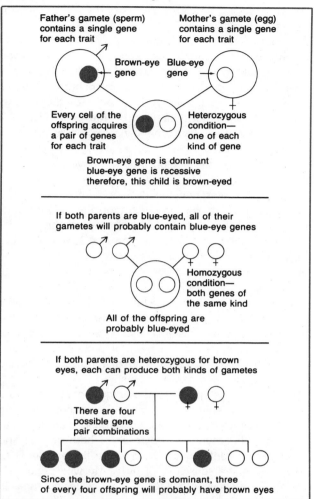

Heredity is the tendency of individuals to develop some of the same characteristics as their ancestors. This simplistic figure demonstrates how eye color is likely to be inherited.

some from the egg, the offspring will be a male. The sex chromosomes also contain many other genes that control processes other than the determination of sex.

Behavior Genetics

The study of how heredity influences behavior is called behavior genetics. The term behavior genetics might suggest to you that behavior is inherited directly from parents. Actually, the only things biologically passed on from parents to offspring are the nuclei of the egg and sperm containing the genes. Thus, it is technically incorrect to say "You inherited your father's eyes" or "You inherited your intelligence from your mother." What you really inherited were the genes that ultimately influenced the physiological reactions necessary for you to develop eye color or intelligence.

The interaction of hereditary and environmental influences is necessary for any physical trait or behavioral characteristic to occur. For example, an individual who inherited the genes for the physical trait of brown eyes will probably develop brown eyes because of the various physiological reactions directed by the genes. But the person might also have the gene for albinism, which results in a lack of coloration, including a lack of eye color. Therefore, the person may not have brown eyes, even if the genes for brown eyes are present. This example illustrates that the development of a physical trait such as eye color depends upon the interaction of heredity and the physiological pathways of the internal body environment. Obviously, the development of behavioral traits can be even more complex as the external environment interacts with the body's physiological pathways.

How do genes influence behavior? Exactly the same way they influence physical characteristics—through the biological response systems. Genes influence behavior indirectly through the biochemical pathways that ultimately result in the functioning of muscles, endocrine glands, nerves, and sense organs.

Because each person has a unique set of genes, or a unique genotype, and we each have experiences that are different from other people's, the variability among people (their phenotype) is the result of both genetic and environmental influences. To illustrate these influences, let's look at the sensation of taste. My wife prefers six spoonfuls of sugar in her tea, while I prefer no sugar in mine. What could have caused this behavior difference? It is very likely that learning played an important role in my wife's preference for sweetened tea, as her early experience included many more sweet foods than mine did. Research has also shown, however, that there are genetic differences in the distribution of taste buds on the tongue and in the ability to perceive tastes. Genes affect the production of the hormones that help regulate the utilization of food energy sources such as sugar. This helps to explain why my wife is much slimmer than I am, even though she loves sweets.

Genes also influence behavior through their control of the development of the nervous system. This may be better understood by reference to an abnormality in the body's chemistry that can produce mental retardation. Phenylketonuria (PKU) occurs when the body is not able to convert a chemical found in some food proteins into harmless by-products. The chemical, phenylalanine, instead becomes a brain poison called phenylpyruvic acid that results in severe mental retardation. PKU is caused by a single recessive gene that prevents the normal biochemical reactions in the body.

Researchers have discovered that when the condition is detected early enough and the child is placed on a phenylalanine-free diet, intellectual development will proceed normally (Ozanne, Krimner, & Murdoch, 1990). For instance, phenylketonurics (individuals who have PKU) are warned not to eat any food that is sweetened with NutraSweet, since it contains phenylalanine (Holder & Yirmiya, 1989). Note the warning on the label the next time you see a product containing NutraSweet. Fortunately, a simple test for PKU is now routinely performed on newborns in the hospital.

The point here is that the gene that causes PKU must interact with the nutritional and biochemical environment to produce its effect. When the environment is changed (in this case, the diet), the behavior resulting from the interaction (in this case, intellectual functioning) can be changed.

The influence of heredity on behavior is an extremely important concept that will be discussed throughout this book. Some relevant topics include biological constraints on learning (chapter 6, "Learning"), heredity and intelligence (chapter 8, "Language and Intelligence"), instinct, sociobiology, and motivation (chapter 9, "Motivation"), heredity and personality (chapter 11, "Personality"), and heredity and abnormal behavior (chapter 13, "Psychological Disorders"). I hope that this partial list convinces you that behavior genetics is an important part of today's psychology.

Animal Studies   Psychologists believe that by understanding how heredity and the environment affect behavior, they will be better able to help people with behavior problems. However, basic research is often performed using animals. Two important research methods used in animal behavior genetics are inbred strain comparisons and selective breeding (Plomin, DeFries, & McClearn, 1990).

Researchers produce inbred strains by mating animals that are closely related genetically (such as brother-sister) over a number of generations. Eventually the offspring become more identical to one another genetically, and are then said to belong to an inbred strain. The inbred strains can be used to test whether genetic differences affect behavior. If two genetically different inbred strains of animals are reared in identical environments, any differences in behavior should be due to the genetic differences of the strains. For example, Badiani, Castellano, and Oliverio (1991) recently found that different inbred strains of mice react differently to stress. This suggests that genetic differences in neurotransmitter functioning may explain stress reactions.

Inbred strains can also be used to test the influence of the environment on behavior. If groups of animals from the same inbred strain are reared in different environments, any behavior differences in the groups should

FIGURE 2.18   Genetic/Environmental Interaction

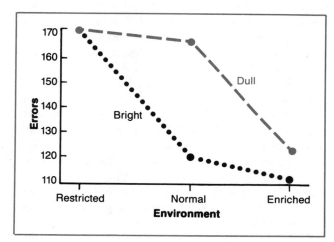

In their experiment, Cooper and Zubek (1958) found that the maze-solving ability of selectively bred bright and dull rats was modified when the animals were raised in either an enriched or restricted environment. This demonstrates that behavior is the result of the interaction of both genetic and environmental influences.

be due to environmental influences (or more precisely, to the interaction of heredity with the environment).

Another important animal research technique is selective breeding, in which similar animals are mated over many generations. Because they have similar genes, if you continue to mate the most similar animals, eventually you will obtain strains of animals that are different from the original population. In their 1965 book, Scott and Fuller explain that dogs have been bred selectively for ten thousand years, resulting in the wide variety of specialized breeds we have today. Wimer and Wimer (1985) review the types of animal behaviors that have been bred selectively, including activity, learning, emotionality, aggression, and even alcohol preference.

In a classic selective breeding study, Robert Tryon (1940) selected rats for their ability to find their way in a maze. He mated the animals that made the fewest errors in finding their way in the maze (maze bright) together and the ones that made the most errors (maze dull) together. Then he mated the most similar offspring for 21 generations. After seven generations, Tryon had developed two genetically different lines of rats.

Another classic behavior genetic study was conducted by Cooper and Zubek (1958). For their experiment, they used selectively bred rats who had been bred from a maze-bright group and some from a maze-dull group. Since the maze-bright and maze-dull rats were reared in identical environments, the difference between the two groups could only be attributed to heredity. Cooper and Zubek placed the rats from both groups in

either a restricted environment (in an empty cage with gray walls) or an enriched environment (in a cage, with designs on its walls, that contained objects such as ramps, mirrors, swings, balls, slides, and tunnels).

When raised in restricted environments, the dull rats made many errors as usual, but the bright rats also made many errors. And when raised in the enriched environment, both groups made few errors. Since the genotypes did not change, it seems clear that the changes in behavior were caused by the changes in environment. Cooper and Zubek argued that heredity and environment always interact to produce final behavior. (See Figure 2.19.)

Human Studies   Although with animals it is possible to use selective breeding and inbred strain comparisons to estimate genetic and environmental influences on behavior, it is obviously more difficult to conduct behavior genetic research in humans. Researchers do not produce people from specified matings, but must find subjects in the population. Nor is it possible to conduct experiments with human beings with the same rigidity as it is with animals, since we cannot isolate people to ensure a uniform environment.

Psychologists can study the effects of heredity and environment on human behavior in studies of twins and adopted children (Plomin, DeFries, & McClearn, 1990). Twins are a natural phenomenon that allows behavior geneticists to study some effects of heredity and environment. Nonidentical (fraternal) twins, called dizygotic twins, are the result of two separate eggs fertilized by two sperm at about the same time, and are no more genetically related than any two siblings. Identical twins, called monozygotic twins, result from one fertilized egg that splits into two shortly after fertilization. Therefore, monozygotic twins are genetically identical.

Since monozygotic twins have identical genotypes, any differences between them should be due to environmental influences (more accurately, to interactions between genotype and environment). Results of research with twins are especially informative when the twins are reared in different environments. Occasionally, each of a pair of twins is adopted and raised by a different family. Studies of twins indicate that characteristics that make up intelligence, personality, and some behavior disorders are more similar in monozygotic twins than in dizygotic twins; this suggests a significant genetic contribution to these behaviors (Plomin, 1989).

A review of studies of twins and their intelligence (Loehlin & Nichols, 1976) concludes that monozygotic twins are significantly more similar than dizygotic twins. Data from over 6,000 pairs of twins indicated that the degree of relationship, or correlation, between heredity and intelligence for all dizygotic twins was .62. (Remember from chapter 1, "The Study of Psychology," that correlation is a statistical measure of relationship ranging from 0, no relationship, to 1.00, identical as measured.) Since dizygotic twins have half of their genes in common, this figure (.62) might not have been surprising. The correlation for the monozygotic twins was .86, which is less than the expected 1.00 for a perfect relationship. Because monozygotic twins are genetically identical, the less-than-perfect correlation is due in part to environmental influences on intelligence. This study shows again that heredity and environment interact to produce behavior. We discuss heredity and intelligence further in chapter 8, "Language and Intelligence."

Genetic influences have been discovered in many behavior disorders, such as depression, alcoholism, schizophrenia, and anxiety (Crowe, 1990). In each case, the genotype predisposes the individual to react in a way that will vary according to environmental influences. For example, a person with a genetic predisposition to alcoholism could not become an alcoholic if alcohol were unavailable to her or him.

In adoption studies, comparisons can be made between children and their adoptive parents as well as between children and their biological parents. As we discuss in chapter 8, "Language and Intelligence," there have been a number of important studies of adoption that show a genetic influence on behavior. For example, the Texas Adoption Project found that the IQs of 300 adopted children were more similar to the IQs of their biological mothers (.28 correlation) than to those of their adoptive mothers (.15 correlation) who reared them

from birth (Horn, 1983). There are some problems with some adoption studies (for example, selective placement, in which adoptive children are placed in homes that are similar to their biological parents' homes), and more research needs to be conducted. But adoption studies do emphasize the importance of heredity in behavior development.

Behavior genetics is receiving increasing attention from psychologists because the biochemical pathways controlled by genes are now conclusively known to have an effect on human behavior. Genes always interact with the environment to produce the biological response systems necessary for behavior. Genes influence the muscles, endocrine glands, nervous system, and sense organs. And these biological response systems all work together to allow us to adapt to the changing demands of our environment. ■

Great strides are being made in the field of psychobiology. From Sperry's pioneering studies of the brain to today's research on the role of the brain in memory and thinking, researchers have always been fascinated with human potential. This chapter has described the fundamentals of the biological effects on behavior. As you will see throughout this book, heredity, the nervous system, the endocrine glands, and the sense organs play a major role in what you and I do and think. In the next chapter, we continue to apply the biological approach to psychology when we examine the development of the person from birth through death.

Drawing by Chas. Addams: © 1981 The New Yorker Magazine, Inc.

Separated at birth, the Mallifert twins meet accidentally.

CHAPTER REVIEW

What You've Learned About Psychobiology

1. Psychobiology is the field that studies the biological basis of behavior. The biological response systems include the sense organs, nervous system, muscles, and endocrine glands.

2. The neuron is a specialized cell that functions to conduct messages (neural impulses) throughout the body. The neuron has a cell body (soma), dendrites (which receive messages from neurons), and an axon (which carries messages to the next neuron).

3. The neural impulse, the process of conducting electrical information along the length of the neuron from the dendrites to the axon, is possible because of the neuron's properties of irritability and conduction. The space between neurons is called the synapse. Neurotransmitters are chemicals released from the axon that travel across the synapse to stimulate the dendrites of the next neuron.

4. The central nervous system (CNS) consists of the spinal cord and the brain. The spinal cord consists of nerve bundles that serve as the pathway along which neural impulses from the sense organs travel to the brain and neural impulses from the brain travel to the muscles and glands. The spinal cord also controls certain reflexes. The brain processes and stores information, makes decisions about what responses are necessary, and sends orders to the muscles and glands to carry out the behavior.

5. The hindbrain controls the basic life-support functions of the body, such as breathing (medulla), eating (pons), muscle coordination (cerebellum), and arousal (reticular formation). The midbrain is a relay station for sensory information going to the higher brain centers. The forebrain receives sensory information (thalamus), regulates motivation and emotion (hypothalamus, a part of the limbic system), and is responsible for the higher-level mental processes (cerebrum).

6. The largest part of the forebrain consists of two cerebral hemispheres connected by the corpus callosum. In general, each hemisphere controls the opposite side of the body. Research on hemisphere deconnection shows that the left, usually dominant, side is logical, analytical, and verbal and exerts greater control over manual dexterity, reading, language, and understanding speech. The right hemisphere processes nonverbal information and is concerned with emotion, imagination, and artistic information. The outermost layer of the cerebrum, the cerebral cortex, is where sensory information is interpreted and stored.

7. Psychologists use a variety of methods to study the functions of the brain, including electrical stimulation of the brain (ESB), EEG brain-wave recordings, CAT scans, PET scans, and MRI.

8. The peripheral nervous system includes all the nerves outside the brain and spinal cord. The somatic nervous system carries messages from the sense organs to the central nervous system and relays information from the central nervous system that directs primarily the voluntary movements of the skeletal muscles. The autonomic nervous system connects the central nervous system with the endocrine glands and the primarily involuntary internal organ muscles. It is divided into the sympathetic nervous system, more active in emergencies, and parasympathetic nervous system, which functions more in normal circumstances.

9. The endocrine glands work to maintain homeostasis, or biochemical stability within the body, by secreting hormones directly into the bloodstream. Hormones help regulate a variety of processes, including growth (pituitary gland), metabolism (thyroid gland), reaction to stress (adrenal glands), and sexual motivation (gonads).

10. Heredity is the natural capability of individuals to develop the characteristics possessed by their ancestors. The study of heredity is called genetics. The gene is the basic unit of heredity. Genes lie along chromosomes, which are slender bodies found in the cell nucleus. Human cells have 46 chromosomes: 22 pairs of autosomes and one pair of sex chromosomes. The complete set of genes for an individual is called the genotype. It interacts with the environment to produce the phenotype, the observable characteristics of an individual.

11. Behavior genetics is the study of how heredity influences behavior. Genes influence behavior indirectly through the biochemical reactions that ultimately result in the functioning of sense organs, nervous system, muscles, and endocrine glands (the biological response systems). Behavior is the result of the interaction of heredity and the environment.

12. Behavior genetic research methods used with animals include comparison of inbred strains (genetically identical animals) and selective breeding. Human behavior genetic research methods include studies of monozygotic (identical) or dizygotic (nonidentical) twins and adoption studies.

CHAPTER OBJECTIVES

What You'll Learn About Development

After studying this chapter, you should be able to:

1. Define development.
2. Describe the changes that occur during prenatal development.
3. Outline the sensory capabilities of the newborn infant.
4. Identify the variables that influence the development of motor behavior during infancy (reflexes, maturation, and readiness to learn).
5. Outline personality development during infancy.
6. Describe the sequence of attachment and explain how attachment develops.
7. Describe the development of social behavior in childhood.
8. Identify the concepts presented in Piaget's theory of cognitive development and describe the periods in the theory.
9. Outline Kohlberg's theory of moral development.
10. Outline physical development in adolescence.
11. Identify major areas of personality and social development in adolescence.
12. Describe Erikson's psychosocial theory of development.
13. Outline physical development in adulthood.
14. Identify the major milestones of adult personality and social development.
15. Outline cognitive development in adulthood.
16. Outline the psychological stages of dying.

WHAT IS DEVELOPMENT?

PRENATAL DEVELOPMENT AND BIRTH

INFANCY
Sensory Development
Motor Behavior Development
Personality Development
Attachment

CHILDHOOD
Social Development
Freud's Theory of Personality Development
Piaget's Theory of Cognitive Development
Kohlberg's Theory of Moral Development

ADOLESCENCE
Physical Development and Puberty
Personality and Social Development
Erikson's Psychosocial Life-Span Approach

ADULTHOOD
Physical Development
Adult Personality and Social Development
Cognitive Development in Older Persons
Psychological Stages of Dying

Children think in different ways than adults do. This is sometimes difficult to grasp if you do not spend a great deal of time with children. For example, if you show a child in kindergarten four pennies and ask whether four pennies that are arranged close together make more or less than four pennies that are spread apart, chances are good that the child will tell you the ones that are spread apart are more. By the second grade, however, a student usually has no trouble seeing that the number of pennies is the same in each case. This is the type of observation that Swiss psychologist Jean Piaget spent over 60 years of his life exploring.

Trained as a zoologist, Piaget became interested in the behavior of children as they solved problems in their environment. He began by observing his own children and questioning them about their thoughts and behaviors. Piaget believed that cognitive (intellectual) development occurred in children because their developing mental structures were challenged by events they observed in the environment. In order to overcome these challenges, children have to develop more complex cognitive structures.

One of the best-known studies of Piaget is on conservation, the ability to recognize that properties of objects do not change even though their appearance may. For example, the kindergarten child who is about 5 years old does not understand conservation: he or she focuses on one feature of an object and excludes all other characteristics. As in the example above, if a child has four pennies grouped close together, he or she thinks there are fewer pennies than when they are spread out. But by the second grade (about 7 years old), the child begins to show conservation and realizes that four pennies are equal to four pennies whether they are spaced out or close together.

The study of human development covers the entire life span from conception through infancy, childhood, adolescence, and adulthood. Developmental psychologists are interested in changes in the physical, cognitive, and social aspects of behavior over time.

3
Development

FIGURE 3.1 Conservation of Volume

In a classic experiment conducted by Piaget, children were asked to judge the volume of liquid contained in beakers of varying shapes and sizes. When the liquid from one short beaker was poured into a tall beaker, children in the preoperational period judged there was an increase in the volume of liquid. Only children who had reached the period of concrete operations, and therefore understood the principles of conservation, realized that the volume of liquid in the tall beaker was the same as that in the original beaker.

A typical conservation study focuses on the child's ability to conserve liquids in glass containers. The child is shown two identical glass beakers that have been filled to the same level with juice (or other liquid). The experimenter tells the child that one of the beakers is the child's and the other one belongs to the experimenter. When asked if they both have an equal amount of juice, the child responds positively. Next the experimenter pours the juice from one of the beakers into a third beaker that is tall and thin. The child is then asked who has more to drink. If the child responds that they both have the same amount, he or she shows a knowledge of conservation. If

the child says that the person with the tall thin beaker has more, he or she has not yet learned how to conserve.

Piaget tested different types of conservation, such as the conservation of number, volume, mass, and length. Although each child develops conservation at a different time, in all cases it is due to development of cognitive skills. Especially important in elementary school are the experiences that help students think. For example, counting, sorting, explaining, observing, and manipulating are necessary for cognitive development. Conservation is just one of the many cognitive abilities that Piaget studied in children.

WHAT IS DEVELOPMENT?

Piaget's research on conservation is important because it demonstrates the child's developing ability to reason or to think logically rather than to be fooled by his or her senses.

Development includes the changes in the physical, cognitive, and personality-social characteristics of the individual over time. *Physical development* includes the changes of the bodily features such as weight and height, refinement of motor behavior, and the physiological changes that accompany processes such as puberty and aging. *Cognitive development* refers to the changes in thinking, memory, language, and problem solving. *Personality and social development* includes the changes that occur in an individual's personality, social functioning, and emotions. Changes in development can be described as quantitative, in which easily measured changes (such as a change in height) occur, or qualitative, in which the characteristics being measured become more complex. For example, vocabulary growth is evidenced by a larger number of words being used by a child (quantitative), whereas language development is shown by a greater complexity in the sentence structures the child uses (qualitative).

Developmental psychology is the study of physical and mental growth and behavioral changes in individuals from conception to death. This approach to the study of development, which we use in this book, is usually referred to as *life-span development*.

Developmental psychologists haven't yet determined exactly in what proportion heredity and environment are involved in the development of human behavior. Maturation is the genetically controlled process of growth that results in orderly changes in behavior; it triggers changes in the capacity to function, rather than just quantitative changes (for example, the physical development of the sexual organs must take place before sexual reproduction becomes possible). Learning, the relatively permanent change in behavior that results from experience, is a factor that is presumed by some psychologists to have the most influence on development. For some traits, such as height, it would appear that the genetic influence is stronger than environmental influences. For other traits, such as shyness, it would appear that learning has the greater influence. Most scientists agree that maturation and experience interact to focus and shape development.

The study of development touches almost every other area of psychology, and will help you understand better many of the topics discussed later. We begin our survey of development by examining prenatal development.

PRENATAL DEVELOPMENT AND BIRTH

Development begins at *conception*, when a sperm fertilizes an egg cell to produce a *zygote*, a fertilized egg cell. Prenatal development is the growth of an individual from conception until birth. Psychologists are interested in prenatal development because during the months before birth the various components of the biological response systems (the sense organs, nervous system, muscles, and endocrine glands) begin to grow and develop.

As soon as the egg cell is fertilized, it starts to divide. This zygote stage lasts about 2 weeks. As the zygote divides, it travels down the fallopian tube to become attached to the wall of the uterus.

The embryonic stage lasts from the time the zygote becomes attached to the uterus to about 8 weeks after conception. During this time, three distinct layers of cells form. The *ectoderm*, or outer layer, eventually will form the sensory system, nervous system, and skin. The *mesoderm*, or middle layer, will form the muscles, blood, and bones. And the *endoderm*, or inner layer, will become the digestive tract, many internal organs, and the endocrine system. It should be obvious that if anything should go wrong at this point in prenatal development, it could have severe consequences.

The first 3 months of pregnancy, called the first trimester, are considered a *critical period* because during this period external stimuli can affect the pregnancy drastically. The mother must be especially careful not to contract contagious diseases such as German measles, take drugs other than those prescribed by her doctor, or have excessive X rays taken, for any of these outside stimuli could disrupt normal development. For instance, recent research has shown that cigarette smoking during pregnancy can result in premature birth of the baby. It may be that nicotine and other chemicals can penetrate the placenta to affect the fetus. Infants born to women who drink alcohol excessively during pregnancy may have fetal alcohol syndrome (FAS). FAS infants often have brain defects and are retarded; they are usually underweight at birth (Randall & colleagues, 1990). Infants born to mothers who are users of heroin or cocaine may suffer from inhibited growth and have withdrawal symptoms. Similarly, children born to mothers who have taken the antibiotic drug streptomycin may be deaf. Even high doses of certain vitamins, such as A and D, can cause problems in offspring. The AIDS virus has recently been found to infect unborn children (Diamond & colleagues, 1990).

Sexual differentiation occurs during the 7th week of gestation. Up to this time, all embryos have identical reproductive structures. If the XY chromosomes are

FIGURE 3.2   Summary of Prenatal Development

FIRST MONTH: Fertilization occurs
Zygote implants itself in the lining of the uterus
Rapid cell division occurs
Embryonic stage lasts from 2 weeks to 8 weeks
Cells differentiate into three distinct layers:
 the ectoderm, the mesoderm, and the endoderm
Nervous system begins to develop
Embryo is ½ inch long

SECOND MONTH: Heart and blood vessels form
Head area develops rapidly
Eyes begin to form detail
Internal organs grow, especially the digestive system
Sex organs develop rapidly and sex is distinguished
Arms and legs form and grow
Heart begins to beat faintly
Embryo is 1 inch long and weighs $\frac{1}{10}$ ounce

THIRD MONTH: Head growth occurs rapidly
Bone formation begins to form rapidly
The digestive organs begin to function
Arms, legs, and fingers make spontaneous movements
Fetus is 3 inches long and weighs 1 ounce

FOURTH MONTH: Lower parts of the body show rapid growth
Bones are distinct in X rays
Reflex movement becomes more active
Heartbeat detected by physician
Sex organs are fully formed
Fetus is 7 inches long and weighs 5 ounces

FIFTH MONTH: Mother begins to feel reflex movements
A fine, downy fuzz covers the entire body
Vernix (a waxy coating) collects over the body
Ears and nose begin to develop cartilage
Fingernails and toenails begin to appear
Fetus shows hiccups, thumb sucking, and kicking
Fetus is 12 inches long and weighs 14 ounces

SIXTH MONTH: Eyes and eyelids fully formed
Fat is developing under the skin
Fetus is 14 inches long and weighs 2 pounds

SEVENTH MONTH: Cerebral cortex of brain develops rapidly
Fetus is 16 inches long and weighs 3 pounds

EIGHTH MONTH: Subcutaneous fat is deposited for later use
Fingernails reach beyond the fingertips
Fetus is 17 inches long and weighs 5 pounds

NINTH MONTH: Hair covering the entire body is shed
Organ systems function actively
Vernix is present over the entire body
Fetus settles into position for birth
Neonate is 21 inches long and weighs 7 pounds

FIGURE 3.3 Sensory Development in Neonates
Newborn infants have much better sensory systems than was previously assumed. Infants only a few days old prefer a sweet smell to a sour smell. They turn away from unpleasant odors.

present, at this time the undifferentiated gonads become testes, which produce the male hormone testosterone. Testosterone causes the male reproductive system to develop; without it the female reproductive system develops (Wachtel, 1983). Developmental psychologists are interested in the biology of sexual differentiation because of the possibility that a variety of social behaviors are influenced by hormone levels in prenatal development.

The fetal stage lasts from about 8 weeks until birth. During the fetal stage the various structures develop and become refined. The fetus can suck its thumb, kick its arms and legs, and even hiccup. During this stage the fetus grows tremendously both in length and weight. (See Figure 3.2.)

Ordinarily, miscarriages due to abnormality of the uterus or some genetic disorder are possible between conception and about 13 weeks. Women who are concerned about the possibility of genetic abnormalities can undergo amniocentesis, a procedure in which cells in the amniotic fluid are examined for chromosomal damage. A new prenatal test, called chorionic villi sampling (CVS), analyzes a sample of embryonic tissue for defects. This procedure can be used during the first trimester of pregnancy (Kolata, 1983). A more common testing procedure is ultrasound, in which extremely high-pitched sound waves are bounced off the embryo or fetus to produce a picture. Ultrasound can help determine the

position of the fetus, identify structures, and monitor heartbeat when a medical problem exists.

During the last months of prenatal development, the fetus usually turns upside down in the uterus so that it is born headfirst. Because of the risks to the baby involved in the use of many pain-reducing drugs, many women prefer to have *natural childbirth*, in which drugs are used only if necessary. At approximately 9 months after conception, birth occurs, and the fetus becomes a newborn baby, or neonate. At birth, most neonates weigh about 7 pounds.

INFANCY

Infancy is usually defined as the first 2 years of life. During this period the neonate develops from a tiny and seemingly helpless being into a small, achieving child. In this section, we examine sensory development, motor behavior development, personality development, and attachment.

Sensory Development

Do you remember being born? Of course not; and because babies can't talk, psychologists find it difficult to understand what it's like to be a newborn baby. Until fairly recently, people thought that the senses were not well developed in babies. Early American psychologist William James once remarked that the infant's world is full of "booming, buzzing confusion."

Actually, the infant's senses appear to be much more developed than was once thought. Right after birth, the ear canals are filled with amniotic fluid, but within a few days hearing is fairly normal. Neonates will turn their heads toward sounds very early in life. DeCasper and Fifer (1980) found that 3-day-old infants preferred their own mothers' voices to the voices of unfamiliar women, suggesting that even young infants recognize meaningful sounds. They don't, however, show a similar preference for their fathers' voices.

It had been assumed that the senses of taste and smell were poorly developed in the neonate. Evidence has shown, however, that infants only a few days old can discriminate different tastes and different odors. Rosenstein and Oster (1988) found that neonates responded to sweet solutions by smiling and sucking, whereas they produced gagging reactions to bitter solutions. Ganchrow, Steiner, and Daher (1983) reported that neonates wrinkled their noses and stuck out their tongues when a cotton swab containing the odor of rotten eggs was

FIGURE 3.4   Infant Visual Preference

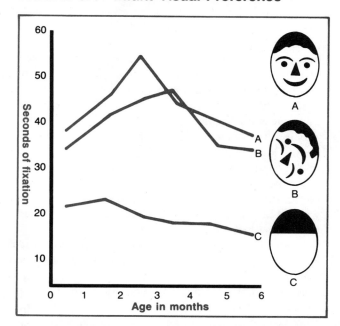

Fantz demonstrated that very young infants prefer complex visual stimuli, especially when the stimuli resemble the human face. After 3 months, infants spend more time looking at the face (after Fantz, 1961).

placed under their noses. However, the subjects smiled and licked their lips when the odor was of strawberries or bananas.

Some research has focused on odor recognition in infants, an ability that may be biologically useful. Aidan MacFarlane (1977) found that 1-week-old infants preferred the smell of their own mother's breast milk over the smell of another mother's milk. Researchers have found that breast-fed (but not bottle-fed) infants preferred their mother's underarm odor to the underarm odor of other mothers, suggesting that odors might be involved in attachment formation (Cernoch & Porter, 1985). And recent research also indicates that mothers can recognize their own newborn infants through odor cues alone (Kaitz & colleagues, 1987).

The visual sense ability of newborns is also more developed than you might expect. Neonates are near-sighted and can focus best at objects that are about 9 inches in front of them (Banks & Salapatek, 1983). A classic study by Fantz in 1961 demonstrated that young infants showed a strong preference for complex visual stimuli, especially when they resembled the human face. Langlois and her colleagues (1991) found that 6-month-old infants prefer attractive adult faces over unattractive ones, irrespective of sex or race of the stimulus (the attractiveness of the faces was determined independently by adult volunteers). Recent research suggests that in-

fants can sometimes imitate the facial expressions of adults (Kaitz & colleagues, 1988). Kellman, Gleitman, and Spelke (1987) reported that infants can perceive objects in motion. This suggests that the visual perception of newborns is better than believed previously.

Such studies on sensory capabilities of neonates suggest that infants are much more prepared to attend to information in their environment than was often assumed hitherto. The practical implication of this information is that infants can begin learning about their environment immediately after birth.

Motor Behavior Development

When we brought our first baby home from the hospital, Terry was very small and fragile. I soon found out, however, that he was anything but completely helpless. Although he definitely needed the care of adults, he was genetically programmed to show certain reflexes, use his senses, and mature and grow in a systematic fashion.

Reflexes   Babies are born with a number of re-flexes that help them adapt to their environment. As described in chapter 2, "Psychobiology," a reflex is an automatic response to a stimulus that does not necessarily involve direct higher brain functioning.

The rooting reflex occurs when you touch a baby's cheek. The baby turns his or her head to search for the source. This is extremely adaptive for survival, since it prepares the baby for nursing. By turning toward the source, the baby is more likely to find the mother's nipple.

If anything touches the baby's lips, the baby immediately begins to show the sucking reflex. This is a reflex that is readily apparent to anyone who has watched a baby eat. The *swallowing reflex* occurs automatically when something is put in the baby's mouth.

The Moro reflex, or startle reflex, occurs when something in the environment changes quickly. When a loud noise, for example, is heard, the baby quickly extends both arms and brings the feet close to the body. The Babinski reflex occurs when the bottom of the baby's foot is stroked. The baby first spreads out the toes and then curls them in. Since it is known when in the infant's development these reflexes normally disappear, they can be used to test for neurological development (Capute, 1984).

Motor Development   As defined earlier, matura-tion is the genetically controlled process of growth that results in orderly changes in behavior. The sequence, timing, and patterning of these changes are largely independent of experience and training. For instance,

FIGURE 3.5 Motor Development

Infants follow a fairly predictable pattern of motor development. The various stages leading to walking begin with the infant lifting its head, and then continue with rolling over, sitting, and standing. When the infant is a little over a year of age, he or she is usually able to walk alone.

human babies vary greatly in the rate at which they mature, but they all go through pretty much the same sequence of stages. The development of the muscular and neural structures necessary for these successive stages is dependent upon maturation. Thus babies usually turn over before they sit, sit before they crawl, and pull themselves up before they walk.

The various steps that lead to the human baby actually walking generally follow this description from Frankenburg and Dodds (1967). During the first month babies begin to lift their heads, and by 2 months they can easily lift their heads high. By about 3 months they can roll over. At about 4 months babies can sit with support, and by 6 months they can sit by themselves. At 6 months they can stand when helped, and by about 9 months, they can walk with help. Around 11 months they can stand alone well, and at about 12 months they can walk alone.

The sequence of motor development follows a fairly predictable pattern. This allows psychologists to devise *developmental norms* that describe the developmental rate for a typical person. While norms are useful for diagnosing possible problems of development, they are not rigid rules that every child follows.

Readiness to Learn In some cases, maturation appears to be largely responsible for the development of particular behaviors. For example, walking develops at a predictable rate regardless of environmental factors. Hopi Indian babies, for instance, develop motor skills as quickly as other children, even though Hopi infants are carried on their mothers' backs and have less opportunity to practice such skills as turning over, sitting, and pulling themselves up (Dennis & Dennis, 1940).

In other cases, maturation provides only the readiness to learn, and the environment plays a more crucial role in behavioral development. Readiness to learn refers to the fact that babies cannot learn until their muscles and neural structures are developed enough. Infants cannot walk at 2 months of age because their muscles and nervous systems are not yet ready.

At what age do you toilet train children? The correct answer is, "When they are ready." You cannot teach children something until they are mature enough, physically and mentally. Maturation determines the readiness to learn. For toilet training, the muscles and the brain must be mature enough for children to learn to control their sphincter muscles. For many children, this is around 2 years old.

But what happens when the environmental experiences do not occur once maturation produces readiness to learn? There is evidence that for some animals critical periods exist, during which particular behaviors should ideally be learned. If learning does not occur at that time, the individual has great difficulty learning and may never be able to master the behavior. Critical periods have been noted in the social development of animals such as birds, sheep, and dogs. For example, if a dog has not been house-trained by 6 months of age, chances are it will never make a good pet (Scott, 1968). To date, no conclusive evidence for critical periods exists for humans. However, critical periods have been suggested for human behaviors such as attachment and language acquisition. Additional research is necessary to determine the exact nature of these periods.

Personality Development

Each individual's personality is unique. A person's distinctive temperament usually begins to become apparent soon after birth, and influences such as birth order and sex roles contribute to the development of personality.

Temperament Different tendencies in temperament or ways of responding to the environment may begin to appear as early as the first days of life. Alexander Thomas and Stella Chess (1986) identified some of the

FIGURE 3.6 Temperament
Infants differ in a wide variety of characteristics, including their level of activity, irritability, adaptability, and their social preference. Their individual temperaments are apparent soon after birth.

basic categories of temperament, including activity level, rhythmicity, distractibility, approach, adaptability, intensity, attention span, quality of mood, and threshold of responsiveness. Susan Gennaro and her colleagues (1990) reported that premature infants tended to be rated as more difficult than full-term infants, but found no differences in races or sexes. Although the importance of these tendencies for later personality development is unknown, it is clear that individual differences are present at birth.

At one time it was believed that young infants could only show undifferentiated excitement. Recent research by Izard and his colleagues has begun to explain the range of emotional expressions present in very young infants. In one study (Izard & colleagues, 1980) facial expressions of infants from 5 to 9 months old were recorded and played back for college students. The students were able to identify emotions such as joy, fear, sadness, anger, and surprise. Although we cannot be absolutely sure that the infants experienced these emotions, they were able to show expressions similar to those used by adults. Termine and Izard (1988) found that 9-month-old infants looked at their mothers more when the mothers showed joy than when the mothers showed sadness, suggesting that infants can perceive different emotions at an early age. We discuss emotion further in chapter 10, "Emotion."

Some evidence does suggest that early temperaments are influential later in life. Adam Matheny and his colleagues (1985) reported that emotional activity of neonates remained stable for the first 9 months of life. Some research suggests that infants who are shy tend to continue to be shy throughout life (Caspi, Elder, & Bem, 1988). Thomas and Chess (1986) argued that an infant's temperament influences the way others will act toward him or her. It might be easier to show affection to an

infant who enjoys being cuddled than to one who is upset upon contact with adults. Reid, Loeber, and Patterson (1982) showed that children who were more likely to be abused were ones who made extra demands on their parents. For example, premature, retarded, or hyperactive infants were more likely to suffer from child abuse.

Birth Order Psychologists have looked at the relationship of birth order to personality characteristics. Firstborn children tend to be high achievers and more intelligent than later-born children. In one study, Falbo (1982) examined college students who were born first, middle, last, or were only children. He found firstborns to be more competitive and have higher self-esteem than those born last. It has been found that only children had more of a sense of control and more self-understanding than children with siblings (Mellor, 1990).

Other psychologists have found that firstborn children tend to be more cooperative and helpful, especially in their relationships with adults. Children born later tend to be more friendly, social, and outgoing, which helps to increase their popularity among peers. Some of the differences among first- and later-born children are due to parental behaviors. Firstborn children (and only children) have more time to interact with parents, even if only for a year or two.

Sex Roles Among the personality differences that appear very early in life are characteristics associated with sex roles. From birth on, we are "labeled" according to our sex. In fact, often the first thing the doctor says is "It's a boy" or "It's a girl."

Many parents treat boys and girls differently, even as infants. Girls are often handled gently, while boys are played with more actively. Beverly Fagot (1985) argues that parents may not be fully aware of the subtle ways in

FIGURE 3.7 Sex Roles
From birth on, we are labeled according to our sex. Children often learn their sex roles by imitating their parents. This little girl is playing mommy, behaving just like her own mother.

Social Demands Usually by the age of 18 months, infants are faced with their first clearly defined *social demands*, and must learn to cope with an increasing number of these over the next few years. There are things they should do and things they should not do. For example, they must not handle certain objects. They must eat without making a mess. They must use a fork instead of their fingers. They must use a toilet instead of soiling their pants. And they must put their toys away. These social demands will contribute to later personality and social behaviors as the children grow older.

Attachment

Perhaps you have been the first baby-sitter that an 8-month-old baby has had. You know the parents and have seen the baby on several occasions. She is happy and seems very contented while sleeping in her mother's arms. But as soon as the parents leave, she wakes up, and upon seeing you, screams for hours until they return. The baby has obviously not yet become attached to you!

Attachment is the process in which the individual shows behaviors that promote proximity or contact with a specific person (Ainsworth, 1979). According to British psychiatrist John Bowlby (1982), the primary function of attachment behaviors is to help maintain an affectional bond or association with a specific person and prevent separation from that individual.

What behaviors are shown by babies that might produce interaction with the mother? They cry, which usually brings the mothers to see what is wrong. The babies smile, and the mothers "have" to smile back, thus creating more intense interactions between mothers and babies. Babies vocalize when they get a little older. The cooing of little babies is fascinating to adults, who often vocalize back. Babies also show sucking and clinging behavior, which tends to keep the mothers in close contact. Bowlby points out that these behaviors all seem well adapted to promote the formation of attachment.

Schaffer and Emerson (1964) studied attachment in babies and identified four phases in attachment development. When first born, the neonate is in what might be called the asocial phase. Social stimuli are not distinguished from nonsocial ones. The neonate responds to people or mobiles or pictures that are interesting. This phase is actually the period before real attachments are formed.

Within a few weeks after birth the baby begins to prefer humans to objects. This is the beginning of the indiscriminate attachment phase. Babies like people to hold and rock them, but usually they are not too particular about who the people are.

At about 6 or 7 months, an infant becomes attached

which they encourage or discourage particular patterns of behavior. They may show approval of a male infant's boisterousness, while expressing disapproval of the same high spirits in a female, perhaps by withholding affection or some reward. An interesting study by Parke and Sawin (1980) found that fathers tend to be more affectionate toward infant daughters, and mothers toward their infant sons. The implication is that sex-role development begins very early in life.

Parents also tend to give their children culturally defined "sex appropriate" toys, such as cars and trucks for their sons and dolls for their daughters. And parents serve as models for their children's behavior, often perpetuating traditional sex-role behavior. These early influences, although often unconscious, continue to reinforce society's traditional sex-role behaviors. Children begin to develop gender identity, or the inner sense of being male or female, from their early experiences with their parents (Huston, 1983).

to one specific person, usually the mother. This is the specific attachment phase. He or she becomes distressed when the mother leaves him or her alone or even just leaves the room. About a month later, a baby begins to show fear of strangers, called *stranger anxiety*. He or she demonstrates this by crying when someone unfamiliar approaches him or her.

The multiple attachment phase usually occurs by about 10 or 11 months of age. Here the baby begins to form attachments to people other than the primary caretaker (often the mother), such as the father, brothers or sisters, and others regularly seen by the baby. By 18 months attachment to a variety of people is fairly strong. The process of forming attachments continues throughout life. Mary Ainsworth (1989) indicates that attachment bonds are formed between infants and parents, and siblings; later the same thing occurs with lovers, friends, and relatives.

A frequently used measure of attachment is Ainsworth's (1978) strange situation procedure. It consists of eight phases during which the infant is increasingly stressed. It begins with an introduction to an unfamiliar room, followed by periods in which a stranger enters the room and tries to interact with the infant while the mother leaves the room and later returns. These separations and reunions provide opportunities to measure attachment. Although Ainsworth's strange situation procedure has become the standard measure of attachment in infants, it is not without its critics. Field (1987) summarized research that suggests a more complex testing procedure, which measures meaningful attachment situations, is needed.

Ainsworth (1978) has identified three types of infant-parent attachment. The first type is avoidant attachment, in which infants avoid their mothers when reunited in the *strange situation procedure*. The majority of infants (65 percent) fall into the second type, called secure attachment, in which infants actively seek contact with their mothers. The third type is called ambivalent attachment, and is characterized by infants who seek contact but resist once the contact is made. These attachment types may be used to explain later social behavior. For example, if the infant shows anxiety in avoidant attachment, he or she may have problems forming social relationships later in life.

Does the mother's behavior affect the attachment of the baby? A number of studies suggest that the behavior of the mother is indeed important in the infant's development of attachment. Russell Tracy and Mary Ainsworth (1981) showed that in an unfamiliar situation, mothers who tended to kiss their babies were more likely to have anxious babies, whereas mothers who tended to hug and cuddle them were likely to have more secure babies.

For a long time, it was assumed that babies form an attachment to their mothers because the mothers most often feed them. Food is rewarding, and since the mother

FIGURE 3.8 Attachment and Separation Anxiety
At about 6 or 7 months of age, infants become attached to one specific person, usually the mother. Whenever the mother is absent they show separation distress by crying and exhibiting great anxiety, even in the presence of other familiar persons.

usually gives the food, she becomes associated with the reward. While he was conducting research at the University of Wisconsin, Harry Harlow noticed that isolated baby rhesus monkeys spent a great deal of time clinging to pieces of cloth in their cages. This suggested to him the importance of contact comfort in attachment formation.

Harlow (1958) designed an experiment in which an isolated baby monkey had two surrogate (substitute) "mothers": a wire mother and a cloth mother. These mothers consisted of a wire cylinder with a wooden head on top. In addition, the cloth mother had a soft terrycloth cover wrapped around it. Either "mother" could feed the baby by way of a milk bottle inserted in a hole in the body. Harlow was able to vary which surrogate mother fed each baby monkey. Harlow found that the baby monkeys spent most of their time on the cloth mother, even when they were always fed by the wire mother! Thus it appears that contact comfort is more important in attachment formation than is feeding.

Contact comfort also appears to play an important role in human attachment. Most parents touch and hold infants a good deal of the time. Hunziker and Barr (1986) had parents hold their infants at least 3 hours a day, and found that these babies cried significantly less than infants whose parents held them less.

FIGURE 3.9   Contact Comfort in Monkeys
Harlow found that infant rhesus monkeys preferred the cloth-covered surrogate mothers to the wire ones, even when the infants were fed only by the wire mothers. Harlow called this preference contact comfort.

Until fairly recently, attachment to fathers has not received much attention (Feldman, Nash, & Aschenbrenner, 1983). Fathers have been assumed to be the primary providers for the family, whereas mothers have been seen as the primary caretakers of the children. Even though fathers often spend less time interacting with infants than mothers do, infants develop attachment to both parents (Parke, 1981). It appears that the quality of the father's interaction with the infant is more important than the number of hours. In one study (Bridges, Connell, & Belsky, 1988), data from year-old infants indicated that their attachment to mothers and fathers are different. Their reactions to their fathers predict how the infants will respond to strangers. The researchers suggest that fathers teach children social skills for dealing with nonfamily individuals.

One force that keeps the infant trying to maintain contact with its parent is the distress experienced by the infant when separated from the parent (Scott, 1971). During the course of a normal day, the infant experiences numerous separations, and with each reunion after being separated the attachment grows stronger. If separation distress does not occur, attachment may not develop

normally. This may help to explain the developmental disorder called *autism*, characterized by severe withdrawal in which the child does not differentiate between social and nonsocial stimuli.

Attachment is vitally important in the development of a child's self-concept and his or her ability to interact with others. For example, children raised in institutions where there is little contact comfort tend to become withdrawn, frightened, and despairing. Children raised in abusive or neglectful environments have a tendency to become abusive themselves. On the other hand, children who form secure attachments to their parents usually are more mature than others of the same age, are outgoing and responsive with other children, and approach life with a sense of trust.

CHILDHOOD

Childhood is usually considered to be the period of development roughly between 2 and 11 years. Socially, the child becomes less dependent on his or her parents and more responsive to peers. Cognitive development proceeds rapidly as the child nears the end of the childhood period. In this section, we discuss social, cognitive, and moral development.

Social Development

During childhood the infant's sheltered environment and relatively narrow circle of human contacts gives way to a wider world in which ever-increasing numbers of people influence the growing child in various ways. Each child's social development is shaped by factors such as identification with his or her parents, the playing of social roles, peer pressure, and friendships.

Identification   Overcoming their earlier self-centeredness, children of 4 or 5 begin to identify with their parents. They see themselves as being like their parents and begin to imitate the parents' characteristic ways of behaving. Through this process of identification, children adopt the attitudes, values, and behaviors of their parents. The child begins to imitate his or her same-sex parent carefully as he or she learns expected sex-role behaviors. It is at this age that you see boys acting like "daddy" or girls dressing up like "mommy." Jerome Kagan (1971) suggested four processes that result in identification in children: children want to be like their parents, believe they are similar to their parents, experience emotions similar to their parents, and behave like their parents.

Several early studies, such as Clark and Clark's 1939 study of the preference of black children for a white doll over a black one, suggest a poor self-concept in black children. Jeanne Spurlock (1986) pointed out that more recent research (since the civil rights movement) suggests a much more positive self-concept. More emphasis has recently been placed on increasing ethnic awareness among black children through family and school programs (Lee & Lindsey, 1985).

It is in this way that the development of self-concept begins. It moves from more external traits and behaviors to more internal personality characteristics in childhood. Eleanor Maccoby (1980) found that young children focus on the external characteristics of their name, age, home, family, friends, and favorite activities. Older children begin to emphasize the internal qualities of emotions, cognitive abilities, and personality. Eventually, as we will see later in this chapter, the question of self-identity becomes a central theme during adolescence.

Early Social Influences   From the ages of 6 to 10, the influences upon children's personality and social development expand to a wide range of sources beyond the immediate family. Schools, churches, clubs, and the mass media all exert influences. Children in elementary school learn to play social roles. They may become leaders, followers, bullies, cowards, peacemakers, mischief-makers, or clowns. Children in this age group tend to show increasing signs of independence and even rebellion in their relationships with parents, teachers, and other adults. They also continue to develop appropriate gender identities.

During this period children come under the strong influence, and even pressure, of other children their own age. They become especially sensitive to the behavior of peers toward them, and carefully observe how these peers judge their behavior. They might feel that they have to take an electronic game to school to play during recess because "all" the other children have similar games. Or they feel that if they don't have a certain brand name athletic shoe, no one will like them at school. If children feel accepted by their peers, they will become confident and engage in more positive, social behavior. On the other hand, if they feel rejected, they may become aggressive and disruptive (Dodge, 1983). A review by Parker and Asher (1987) found that children who have low acceptance by peers and exhibit aggressiveness tend to have difficulties later in life, including the tendency to drop out of school and to adopt criminal behavior.

Friendships   From early infancy on, it is very evident that people are social beings. Even young infants appear interested in other people. Friendships tend to first develop when children are 3 to 4 years old. Selman and Selman (1979) interviewed people from 3 to 45

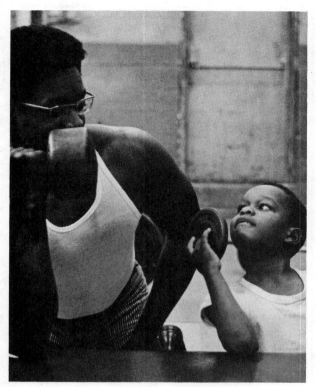

FIGURE 3.10   Identification in Childhood
Through the process of identification, children learn the attitudes, values, and behaviors of their parents. As shown in this photograph, the child begins to imitate his or her same-sex parent carefully.

years old to describe the development of friendships. Very young children are likely to view friendship as a convenience and label any other children they play with as friends. Around 9 years of age, children define friends as children who do what they want them to. Between 6 and 12 friendship is based more on reciprocal cooperation. My 10-year-old son Tommy plays whatever his friend wants to, as long as he then gets to do what he wants. Finally, older children develop friendships that tend to be mutually satisfying and interdependent.

Freud's Theory of Personality Development

Freud theorized that from birth to adolescence children go through five developmental periods called psychosexual stages. Each stage focuses on an area of the body that is of prominent concern to the individual at that particular time. During the first, or *oral stage*, the baby gets pleasure mainly from sucking. During the second and third years, the baby goes through an *anal stage*, in which the first restrictions on impulses are experienced during the process of toilet training. Around the age of 4,

BIOGRAPHICAL
HIGHLIGHT

JEAN PIAGET

Jean Piaget was born in Neuchâtel, Switzerland, in 1896. His father was a professor of medieval literature. As a child, he became absorbed in philosophy and zoology, and wrote his first scientific article, on the albino sparrow, at the age of 10. After graduating from the University of Neuchâtel in 1918 with a degree in zoology, he turned to psychology, going to Zurich to pursue his studies. There he met Theodore Simon, who invited him to work on the development of intelligence in a grade school in Paris.

Trained as a zoologist, Piaget had the skills necessary to begin observing children. He found that children make certain types of errors when solving problems, depending upon their age. He concluded that their thinking is qualitatively different from adults', and thus it is important to understand children from their own viewpoint.

Because of his extensive work studying the development of intelligence, he has had an important impact on developmental psychology. He believed that cognitive development occurred because of the child's unsatisfactory experiences in solving problems. His observations led him to develop his famous theory of cognitive development.

Piaget was a prolific writer and produced numerous books and articles. He continued to teach and write until his death at 84 in 1980.

the *phallic stage* begins and the child starts to find pleasure in stimulating the genitals. From the age of 6 to puberty, there is a *latency stage* during which the child appears to have little need for erotic satisfaction. As sexual maturity is reached, the *genital stage* begins, in which the individual can begin to relate in a positive sexual way toward other people.

Freud considered these stages crucial in the development of a healthy personality. The child's experiences during these stages form the foundation for the development of many personality traits that continue into adulthood. For instance, according to Freud, such traits as disorderliness, cruelty, and destructiveness may develop as an expression of anger in reacting to punitive and repressive toilet-training tactics during the anal stage. Irregularities and difficulties in passing from one stage to the next, can, according to Freud, result in prolonged and serious emotional disorders. Unfortunately, Freud's theory is difficult to test, and thus remains largely unconfirmed. We discuss Freud's personality theories further in chapter 11, "Personality."

Piaget's Theory of Cognitive Development

As we discussed in our opening story, children do not think the same way adults do. Long before children develop a measurable intelligence, before they can read or write and take intelligence tests, they have already begun to show the ability to think and handle ideas. This cognitive activity was intensively studied for over 60 years by Swiss psychologist Jean Piaget (1896–1980).

Piaget believed that cognitive development occurred in a child because the developing mental structures were challenged by events that the child observed in his or her environment. In order to overcome a challenge, the child has to develop more complex cognitive structures or schemes. A scheme may be thought of as a unit of knowledge that the person possesses, or a mental picture of the world. At the simplest level, a newborn has reflexive schemes for grasping, sucking, and swallowing. Eventually, the child coordinates these schemes so that he or she can think through a series of actions and imagine the consequences of those actions. For example, your schemes allow you to realize that when you open the refrigerator, you will find food.

Piaget studied the ways in which children acquire certain concepts and organize ideas, and he outlined the predictable and orderly periods of intellectual development. The progress of these periods depends upon the child's constantly increasing adaptability to new situations. For Piaget, motor development and exploration of the environment are the foundations for later logical thought.

Two processes are fundamental to cognitive development: assimilation and accommodation. Assimilation is the process by which the child integrates new stimulus events into already existing schemes. For example, the child might assimilate a new breed of dog into the existing scheme of dog.

Children try to incorporate any new stimulus into their already existing schemes of the world. However, sometimes the child cannot assimilate a new stimulus into existing schemes and must instead use accommodation. Accommodation is the process of creating a new scheme or changing an existing scheme to make room for a new stimulus event or experience. The child accommodates a cat by creating the new scheme of cat. According to Piaget, the interaction and balance of the processes of assimilation and accommodation, called *equilibration*, are responsible for moving the child through the periods in the child's intellectual development (Piaget, 1960).

Sensorimotor Period   During the first 2 years of life infants learn to differentiate themselves from their environment. In this sensorimotor period they spend a great deal of time learning to coordinate sensory experiences with motor activities. They learn to coordinate looking, tasting, touching, and hearing with sucking, reaching, and grasping. Newborn infants spend much of their time looking around. As they grow older, they explore their world, touching everything they can. This exploration is important, since the only way they can learn to coordinate their senses and their muscles is to try things out. During this period infants go from trial and error reflexes to more deliberate manipulation of the environment.

During the sensorimotor period infants also learn object permanence. Until about 8 months old, infants will not look for an object if it is removed from sight. They act as if it ceases to exist. Once they have developed object permanence, the ability to realize that objects continue to exist even though they can no longer see them, they will search for the missing object. When you place a pillow over their rattle, infants with object permanence will

simply lift the pillow and find the rattle. Piaget considers this to be an important step for infants; it explains why they enjoy playing peekaboo. This information tells us the infants are beginning to use images.

Preoperational Thought Period   From roughly 2 to 7 years of age, children pass through the preoperational thought period, when they acquire language and learn to represent their environment with objects and symbols (Wadsworth, 1984). In the early part of the preoperational stage, children are learning to use symbols and mental representations of the world. They enjoy playing with stuffed animals or dolls because they can believe the playthings are real animals or friends, a concept called animism. An example of animism occurs when children say that the sun is sleeping for the night.

Children have vivid imaginations at this age. Given a few *Ninja Turtles* figures and a place to play, children can become heroes and villains. This is also the age when children sometimes develop imaginary playmates. They will play and talk to their imaginary friends and sometimes even bring them to dinner.

Children in the preoperational thought period are egocentric. This means that they see themselves as the center of their universe. They focus on their own pleasures, pains, and desires, and are unaware of those of other people (Flavell, 1986). They see the world from one perspective—theirs. This is the reason that children at this age might point to your left hand and say it is your right, especially if you are facing them when you ask the question.

In the latter part of the preoperational thought stage, children can group objects into classes according to their similarities. However, they cannot yet give a clear account of the features common to a class of objects. Although they show intuitive thought and can work out problems in a fairly orderly fashion, they have trouble reversing their reasoning and tracing their thinking back to its starting point. Eventually, however, they proceed to the next period.

FIGURE 3.11   Object Permanence
During the sensorimotor period infants learn that an object continues to exist even when they can no longer see it. If an infant, such as the one shown in the photo, has not yet developed object permanence, he or she quickly loses interest in an object that has been hidden from view.

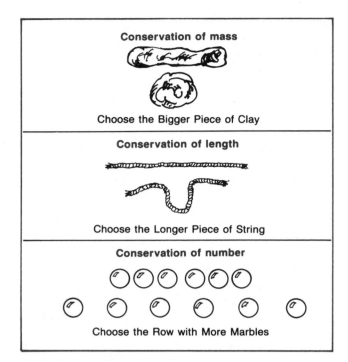

Conservation of mass

Choose the Bigger Piece of Clay

Conservation of length

Choose the Longer Piece of String

Conservation of number

Choose the Row with More Marbles

FIGURE 3.12 Conservation
Conservation is the ability to recognize that properties of objects do not change even though their appearance might. Piaget and other researchers have demonstrated conservation of mass, length, and number, as well as volume. Children in the concrete operations period of development, from about 7 to 11 years of age, begin to demonstrate an understanding of conservation.

Concrete Operations Period   From about 7 to 11 years, children's ability to solve problems with reasoning, as well as their ability to think symbolically with words and numbers, greatly increases. They can now solve problems of classification, in which objects are ordered into hierarchies of different classes. For example, they understand that 10 pennies equal a dime, that 10 dimes equal a dollar, and that a dollar is equal to 100 pennies. They can also order objects in a series, using increasing size or some other simple property as a criterion (Piaget & Szeminska, 1952).

If you place two same-sized balls of clay in front of a child in the preoperational period (before about 7 years old) and ask which is bigger, he or she will say they are the same. Now, if you roll one out into a long snakelike form and ask again, the child will probably say that the snake is bigger than the ball. This demonstrates that a child in the preoperational thought period does not show conservation (Piaget, 1967). Conservation is the ability to recognize that properties of objects do not change even though their appearance does. Its emergence marks the beginning of logical thought. Probably the most famous conservation experiment (discussed in our opening

story) focuses on the amount of liquid in two beakers (conservation of volume).

Children in the concrete operations period develop conservation. They are now able to see that the mass of clay is the same in both the ball and the snake forms. They can also attend to both height and weight and thus realize the volume of liquid stays the same when placed in beakers of different sizes. Also children can conserve numbers and realize that the number of items stays the same whether the items are grouped together or spread apart.

Children at this age are able to decenter, or realize that their way of looking at the world is only one perspective. They can understand other people's point of view. They also show reversal, the ability to work a problem backwards. If asked to make the snake into a ball, they will have no trouble reversing the process and rolling it back into a ball. Despite these cognitive abilities, children in the concrete operations period still rely on what they see. They cannot yet effectively deal with abstract reasoning. If, for example, you ask them, "If A is greater than B, and B is greater than C, is A greater than C?" they will not be able to solve the problem. This ability appears in the last period proposed by Piaget.

Formal Operations Period   At about age 11, adolescents begin to understand how abstract scientific, moral, religious, and political ideas work, and to see their logical implications. They also begin to understand hypothetical relationships (if X were to happen, then Y would follow) and the logic of systematic experimentation and hypothesis testing. Although people are in the formal operations period throughout the rest of their lives, Piaget considered that the basics of formal operations are mastered by about age 15.

Instead of starting with only the information available to their senses, like children in the concrete operations period, adolescents in the formal operations period begin with possible hypotheses, or guesses, which can be tried out in the head rather than worked out with objects in the environment (Phillips, 1981). Adolescents and adults in the formal operations stage are able to approach a problem by thinking through several possible solutions and discarding unworkable ideas until they arrive at a workable one.

Piaget's work on cognitive development has taught us that children and adults think differently—a fact that adults engaged in educating or rearing young children should not forget. Children are now viewed as developing individuals and not simply as "miniature adults," as they once were. With a knowledge of Piaget's periods, the teacher or parent has a better grasp of the intellectual capabilities of children.

Criticism of Piaget   Piaget's work has greatly contributed to our understanding of children. However, the theory has been criticized by a number of researchers. John Flavell (1982) argued that cognitive development is more gradual than discontinuous. The ages indicated in Piaget's periods may be higher than they should be. For example, Gelman and Gallistel (1978) found that nursery school children were capable of demonstrating some degree of number conservation. Bovet and colleagues (1986) point out that methodological differences might explain some age differences. When younger children who could conserve were asked to justify their answers, they gave nonconservation responses. Experience probably also affects how children respond in research studies. Flavell (1985) found that 2½- to 4-year-old children may be able to decenter under some conditions. Presumably, future research will refine our knowledge of how children think.

Kohlberg's Theory of Moral Development

Cognitive development is also involved in moral reasoning. Lawrence Kohlberg (1969, 1985) studied the development of the awareness of ethical behavior, or moral development. Kohlberg, who based his theory on Piaget's early research, proposed that the way a child reasons about right and wrong develops according to a specific pattern. Kohlberg's theory consists of six stages arranged on three levels of moral reasoning.

Kohlberg's Level I, preconventional morality, is a period in which moral reasoning is based largely on expectation of rewards or punishments. Level I has two stages. In stage 1, the child obeys rules in order to avoid being punished. In stage 2, the individual conforms to society's rules in order to receive rewards. At Level I, behavior is guided largely by the tendency to seek pleasure. Children under the age of 10 are generally in Level I.

Kohlberg's Level II, conventional morality, is a period in which moral reasoning is based largely on conformity and social standards. In stage 3, the individual behaves morally in order to gain approval from other people. Stage 4 is characterized by conformity to authority to avoid censure and guilt. By the time a person is 13 years old, he or she is likely to be at Level II.

Kohlberg's Level III, postconventional morality, is the highest level of moral thinking and is based largely on personal standards and beliefs. In stage 5, the individual is concerned with individual rights and democratically decided laws. In stage 6, the individual is entirely guided by his or her own conscience. According to Kohlberg, some people never reach Level III in their moral development.

There is considerable evidence that supports Kohlberg's theory of moral reasoning. It appears that the stages develop in the order suggested by him. Indeed,

FIGURE 3.13 Examples of Postconventional Morality Martin Luther King, Jr., and his role model, Mahatma Gandhi, both demonstrated the level of moral thinking and behavior that Kohlberg described as postconventional. In stage 5 of this level, the individual is concerned with democratically determined laws and in stage 6 with his or her own conscience determining universal ethical values.

research on a variety of cultures supports the basic theory, although there is controversy over the link between moral reasoning and moral behavior (Blasi, 1980). Just because an individual is at the postconventional morality level does not automatically mean that he or she will behave in a particular manner. As you might imagine, many variables influence the actual behavior of a person. Other concerns focus on the generality of the results of Kohlberg's research, which was based only on males.

Nancy Eisenberg and her colleagues (1987) examined how moral judgments are made in social situations in which one person's wants conflicted with another's wants. They studied groups of children for 7 years to determine how prosocial moral judgment developed. She agreed with Kohlberg that reasoning became more sophisticated with age. Adolescent girls were more sympathetic and concerned for others in their moral reasoning than were boys, and the empathy of older girls tended to lead them to share. This prosocial research extends Kohlberg's emphasis on cognition by demonstrating the importance of emotion in moral reasoning and social behavior.

ADOLESCENCE

Most psychologists agree that adolescence begins at puberty. For males, that is approximately age 13; for females, about age 11. Psychologists don't agree on when adolescence ends and adulthood begins, but it is usually sometime between 18 and 21. Adolescence is, in a very real sense, a transition from dependence to independence and ends when the individual achieves adult status. We will review briefly some of the significant developmental changes that occur in adolescence. Then we will view a life-span psychosocial theory by Erikson that helps us understand how this transition period fits into the development of human behavior in general.

Physical Development and Puberty

Although there is a great deal of variation among individuals, adolescence is closely associated with the onset of puberty, or the maturation of the sexual and reproductive systems and the development of secondary sex characteristics. During adolescence many other physical changes also occur, such as the growth spurt.

Adolescent Growth   Both boys and girls experience a growth spurt during adolescence that significantly increases their height and weight. For girls, the growth spurt begins between 8 and 10 years old and peaks at about age 13 (Tanner, 1981). Boys begin their growth spurt between 10 and 12 years old, with a peak at about age 14. Both sexes may gain about 12 pounds during this period. Height increases during adolescence, with females reaching adult height by about age 17, and males reaching adult height by about age 20.

Female Sexual Development   Girls typically become sexually mature a year or two before boys. Menarche, or the onset of menstruation, is an obvious sign of puberty. Many North American girls experience menarche when they are between 12 and 14 years of age, with the range being from 10 to 18 years old. The development of secondary sex characteristics, such as breasts, pubic hair, and broadened hips, occurs about this time. Breast development begins about age 11, and pubic hair appears at about age 12.

Sexual development is also accompanied by psychological changes. Although most girls view menarche as a sign of their womanhood, many have reservations and concerns about menstruation (Grief & Ulman, 1982). Until they get used to their new physical appearance, many girls worry about how others view them. Research on girls who mature early is not entirely conclusive. For example, in some cases early maturation means that girls are looked down upon, or even teased, by peers (Brooks-Gunn & Peterson, 1983). But later, in high school, the early-maturing girls are often more popular.

Male Sexual Development   In boys, the testes and penis begin to grow at about 12 to 13 years of age. Pubic hair appears shortly thereafter. By the time he is 15, a male can usually produce sperm. Secondary sex characteristics for males include development of beards, lower voices, broadened shoulders, and pubic hair.

In general, boys who become sexually mature early seem to have fewer problems than those who mature later. They are more popular, often because of their superior athletic ability, and they tend to have higher self-respect than later-maturing boys. Other studies show that these earlier-maturing boys continue to have higher self-respect (Jones, 1965). Early-maturing boys often become leaders and have positive self-images.

Personality and Social Development

Stanley Hall (1916) conceived of adolescence as a time of "storm and stress." Although adolescence usually is accompanied by some problems, Conger and Peterson (1984) point out that it is not necessarily as stressful a period as has been suggested in the past. Practically everyone in our culture encounters some problems during adolescence, whether related to sex, self-consciousness, parental controls, morality codes, or conformity to social norms. Adolescents also have to begin thinking about adulthood, of who they are, and of the need to make decisions about the future.

Cultural standards play a large part in the life of the adolescent. Some cultures have elaborate "rites of passage" ceremonies that may bring adolescents immediate and complete adult status, both in their own eyes and those of their society. Other cultures (such as ours) leave the adolescents more or less on their own, and they achieve adult status only gradually. In fact, in American society, full maturity can be defined only vaguely in terms of age, leaving home, earning a living, getting married, or rearing children.

Identity Development   According to Erik Erikson, the successful adolescent is one who has answered the question, "Who am I?" Identity is a major goal in adolescence. Onyehalu (1981) believes that much of the identity crisis in our youths today is the result of conflicting demands made upon them by society. Adolescents are in a transition period between childhood and adulthood. They are sexually mature but are expected to refrain from sexual encounters. They are intelligent thinkers, but are not allowed to make important decisions concerning future careers and families.

James Marcia (1980) defines identity in adolescence as the internal organization of drives, abilities, and beliefs of an individual. Like Erikson, Marcia believes crisis and commitment are important in identity formation. During crisis, the individual struggles with the pressures to achieve personal organization in values and beliefs, whereas during commitment, the individual decides to take action according to his or her beliefs. Marcia defines four possibilities of identity status for adolescents. Adolescents who make a commitment to values and roles without struggling with personal ideas have the status of foreclosure. Those who are struggling with identity issues but have not made a commitment are experiencing a moratorium. A failure to make a commitment or struggle with identity results in an identity diffusion. Finally, adolescents who have struggled with values and beliefs and have made a personal commitment have reached identity achievement.

Carol Gilligan (1983) has studied sex differences in identity formation. She has suggested that males form their identities as separate individuals based on individual achievement, whereas females are more likely to develop their identities based on social responsibilities and relationships. These sex differences in identity formation may help explain some of the difficulties men and women have when interacting at this stage of their lives.

Family Relationships   As adolescents develop a sense of identity, they also strive for more independence. The reaction of parents to this independence often determines the relationships within the family. Parents and adolescents must learn to deal with concerns about communication, control, autonomy, responsibilities, authority, and styles of interaction (Knox, 1985). Some conflict within the family appears to be inevitable. For instance, Steinberg (1988) reported that puberty is associated with increased adolescent autonomy and parent-adolescent conflict. But it is worth noting that the majority of adolescents have overall positive relations with their parents. Many continue to rely on family for advice and guidance (Wilks, 1986).

Friendships   Individuals who have similar interests, personalities, and temperaments are likely to become friends. Hays (1985) investigated the development of friendships in college students and found that over the

course of time, the amount of time spent with friends and the intimacy level of friendships increased. Hays suggested that male friendships may develop more from shared behavioral activities, whereas female friendships may develop from verbal communication. The nature of friendship changes over the course of adolescence. Young adolescents often belong to a small group of same-sex friends. Over time, the groups become mixed-sex, and then in later adolescence dating predominates.

Adolescent Sexual Relationships   During adolescence, the practice of dating helps individuals develop interpersonal skills and facilitates mate selection in anticipation of marriage or cohabitation. The age at which individuals engage in their first premarital sexual activity decreased through the 1970s; more recently it has apparently leveled off, in part because of the fear of becoming infected with AIDS. Although it is difficult to measure accurately, some data suggest that 60 percent of white males engage in sexual intercourse by the age of 18 and 60 percent of white females by the age of 19. Sixty percent of black males engage in sex by the age of 16, and 60 percent of black females by the age of 18 (Hoffeth & Hayes, 1987). Along with increased sexual activity has come increased teenage pregnancy. Recent reports indicate approximately 10 percent of adolescent girls become pregnant by the age of 18.

Serious Adolescent Problems   Although all adolescents experience problems, some are affected by extreme stress and have severe problems. We discuss some of these problems in more detail in later chapters, but mention them here because of their impact on adolescents. One serious problem, which is increasing significantly, is adolescent suicide. Over 5,000 teenagers commit suicide each year. Although there are a variety of reasons for suicide, many victims feel depressed and worthless (Brent, 1989). Drug abuse is a dangerous problem in adolescence. Although alcohol and marijuana are the most common drugs, cocaine and other illegal drugs are also being used. Adolescent females especially may experience *anorexia nervosa*, a disorder in which they will starve themselves because they believe themselves to be overweight. And delinquency and crime have increased in recent years. Still, as mentioned earlier, most individuals are able to deal successfully with adolescence and become healthy adults.

Erikson's Psychosocial Life-Span Approach

An important theory in developmental psychology was proposed by Erik Erikson (1963). Erikson took a life-span approach to development, in which he described

FIGURE 3.14 Erikson's Stages of Psychosocial Development

Age	Stage	Developmental Task	Resolution
0–1 year	Trust vs. Mistrust	Feel secure	Hope
2–3 years	Autonomy vs. Doubt	Gain independence	Will
4–5 years	Initiative vs. Guilt	Explore environment	Purpose
6–11 years	Industry vs. Inferiority	Manipulate objects	Competence
Adolescence	Identity vs. Role confusion	Form positive self-concept	Fidelity
Young adulthood	Intimacy vs. Isolation	Form social relationships	Love
Middle adulthood	Generativity vs. Self-absorption	Develop concern about world	Care
Old age	Integrity vs. Despair	Achieve personal fulfillment	Wisdom

eight stages that take a person from birth to death. In each stage, the person faces a crisis, and if it is successfully met, the person then progresses to the next stage. If at any of the stages the individual does not develop the required capacity, there will be problems of varying degrees of severity later on.

Stage 1 is *trust versus mistrust*. During the first year of life, infants should develop a sense of trust. They are completely dependent on others, and it is hoped that they will learn that others will help them and will do them no harm. If infants are loved, they will develop trust for the future. But if their life is uncertain, they will develop fear and suspicion of others.

Stage 2 is *autonomy versus doubt*. During the second year of life, children have the potential to develop a sense of autonomy, a knowledge that they have the freedom and capability to take certain actions quite independently of those around them. How children respond to and take responsibility for toilet training can be an important aspect of developing autonomy. If others are critical, they may develop doubts about their independence.

Stage 3 is *initiative versus guilt*. At the "play stage," the third through fifth years, children should develop a sense of initiative. They should develop the power to begin projects on their own, and to do so guided by their developing conscience. They often imitate the actions of their parents in this stage. If parents punish initiatives, the child may develop guilt feelings and loss of self-confidence.

Stage 4 is *industry versus inferiority*. In school, children have to learn industry, competence, and persistence at activities. During this period, which runs roughly from 6 to 11 years, they must learn that they are members of society, who must cooperate with others and channel aggression in acceptable ways (such as in sports). They must develop confidence in their own abilities. If they do not master the tasks given them, or if they are too severely criticized, they will experience a sense of failure and feelings of inferiority.

Stage 5 is *identity versus role confusion*. This stage encompasses adolescence, from around age 11 to 18. As noted above, according to Erikson adolescents face the

problem of personal identity, the question of "Who am I?" They may imitate other people, including parents, friends, or even teachers. If the behaviors they imitate are conflicting or contradictory, they may face an "identity crisis," and then they must modify or discard their imitations. In this stage, adolescents must begin to decide what they want to do in life.

Stage 6 is *intimacy versus isolation*. The theme of young adulthood is intimacy, the challenge of integrating one's whole life with that of someone else. The most common occasion for sharing deeply in someone else's life is marriage. If a person does not learn to relate intimately with someone else, he or she may face isolation and loneliness throughout life.

Stage 7 is *generativity versus self-absorption*. In middle adulthood, the challenge is one of establishing goals, commitments, and lasting attachments that permit reasonable productivity. The adult is concerned for his or her family and with contributing to the world at large. The alternative is self-absorption and stagnation, where the person feels that his or her own life is the only thing that matters.

Stage 8 is *integrity versus despair*. In later adulthood and old age, individuals must learn to accept life as it was lived, with its disappointments as well as its joys, and thereby face death bravely in this final stage. If unable to do this, they face the despair of believing they are no longer useful and may have indeed missed life altogether.

While it is important to remember that Erikson's "psychosocial" theory of development is only one way to think about development, it allows a view of the entire life span. In recent years, psychologists have become more interested in the life-span approach to development.

ADULTHOOD

Development does not stop when we become physically mature. During adolescence, we complete our education and plan what we want to do with our lives. Then during adulthood we are able to carry out our adolescent plans (or develop new ones). One way to view adulthood

FIGURE 3.15 Developmental Theories

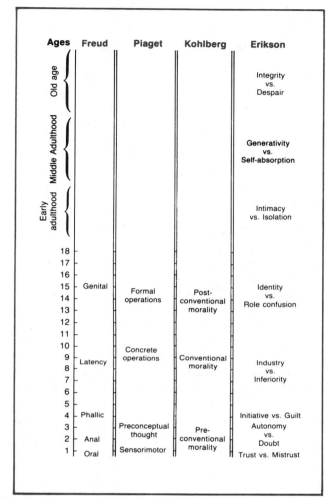

Freud, Piaget, Kohlberg, and Erikson all have developmental theories that propose an orderly sequence to some aspect of human behavior. Freud's psychosexual development theory focuses on areas of the body important at different ages. Piaget's cognitive development deals with the thinking abilities of the individual. Kohlberg's theory of moral development outlines various stages in the awareness of ethical values. Erikson's psychosocial theory relates to the social development of the individual from birth through old age.

is to divide it into early (ages 18–45), middle (ages 45–65), and late (ages 65–death) stages (Levinson, 1986). In this section we will survey physical, social, and cognitive development, and review the psychological stages of dying.

Physical Development

Early Adulthood Early adulthood might be characterized as the "prime of life." The body is at its physical peak during the early twenties. Muscle strength is maximum, and the sense organs are functioning well. The current trend for adults to exercise and maintain proper nutrition is an excellent means of prolonging this youthful fitness. Many adults are becoming more conscious of the effects of diet, drugs, and exercise on health and longevity (Taylor, 1991).

Middle Adulthood Physical aging becomes noticeable during middle adulthood. During the 40s, the hairline begins to recede, and by 50 many people have grey hair. The skin is not as flexible as it once was and wrinkles begin to appear. The cardiovascular system becomes less efficient at pumping blood. By 50, the breathing capacity is 75 percent of what it was in early adulthood (Skalka, 1984). The sense organs begin to decline in efficiency during this period. The leading causes of death in middle adulthood are cardiovascular diseases and cancer. Menopause, or the end of menstruation, occurs in women who are about 50 years old.

Late Adulthood During late adulthood, the aging process accelerates, and people experience a variety of physical deteriorations. Wrinkling of the skin continues, and hair loss is accelerated. Many people lose their teeth and require dentures in old age. There is general deterioration of the cardiovascular, respiratory, and muscular systems. And the sense organs gradually become less effective.

Theories of Aging The study of late adulthood and aging is called gerontology. There are many theories of aging. Some theories suggest that the body just wears out over a period of time. The immunity theory focuses on stress and the accumulated effects of illness and contaminants in our environment. Eventually, the body loses its ability to protect itself from stress and disease. Some of the most promising research has concentrated on cellular aging.

Hayflick (1980) found that human body cells are programmed to reproduce themselves a finite number of times. He took cells and let them reproduce until they eventually died. He found that most human cells die after about 50 doublings under ideal conditions. But Hayflick believes that most cells probably never reach their maximum because of physiological changes that take place in the cell. Perhaps we will be able to extend the human life span by discovering how cellular aging occurs.

Adult Personality and Social Development

Personality is not automatically "set" by the time the individual attains full physical maturity at adulthood.

Stevens and Truss (1985) found that between ages 20 and 40, people increase their need of achievement, autonomy, and dominance, and decrease their need of affiliation. However, the need for order and endurance remained stable. As an adult, the individual must face and learn to cope with many situations that are likely to influence his or her personality, such as marriage, career, rearing children, retirement, and the prospect of old age and dying.

Levinson's Life Structure Theory Yale psychologist Daniel Levinson (1986) has developed a comprehensive theory of adult development. Through a series of intensive interviews with men (1978) and women (1987), Levinson proposed a theory based on a series of stages that adults go through as they develop. At the center of his theory is the life structure, the underlying pattern of an individual's life at any particular time. An individual's life structure is shaped by the social and physical environment. Many individuals' life structures primarily involve family and work, although other variables such as religion, race, and economic status are often important. Levinson's four "seasonal cycles" include preadulthood, early adulthood, middle adulthood, and late adulthood.

Levinson (1978) originally studied 40 adult males between 35 and 45 years of age. Early adulthood is entered when men begin careers and families. After an evaluation of themselves at about age 30, men settle down and work toward career advancement. Then another transition occurs at about age 40, as men realize

some of their ambitions will not be met. During middle adulthood, men deal with their particular individuality and work toward cultivating their skills and assets. Finally, the transition to late adulthood is a time to reflect upon successes and failures and enjoy the rest of life.

More recently, Levinson (1987) interviewed 45 women between the ages of 35 and 45 years of age. One-third were homemakers, one-third college instructors, and one-third businesswomen. In general, he found that women go through the same type of cycles that men do. However, the life stages of women tend to be tied closer to the family life cycle. Adult personality has only recently been studied in depth, and more research will undoubtedly provide additional insights into how personality develops in adulthood.

Marriage and Family Much of our adult life centers around family and work. As Erikson pointed out, the main theme of young adulthood is intimacy, in which the individual finds another person to share life with, often through marriage. According to recent statistics, 95 percent of Americans get married. Although marriage is chosen by the vast majority of individuals, it is important to remember that there are alternative life-styles, including remaining single, cohabitation, and homosexuality.

There are many reasons for marrying, including commitment, intimacy, companionship, love, happiness, sex, and children (Brehm, 1992). The first several years of marriage are spent in the practical pursuits of getting established and getting to know one another. Children are a major responsibility of married couples. The birth of a first child turns a husband and wife into a father and mother. And with each additional child, the social structure of the family becomes increasingly complex. As the children grow, the financial burden becomes greater. The following Application traces the stages of parenthood.

APPLICATION

Developmental Stages of Parenthood

Erikson pointed out that raising children can serve as an important function of adulthood. Generativity involves helping the next generation, and this can be done through parenthood. Some research has focused on the developmental stages of parenting. In her book, *Between Generations: The Six Stages of Parenthood* (1981), psychologist Ellen Galinsky described how adults develop through the interaction with their children. She based her theory on interviews with over 200 parents.

Husband and wife become father and mother at the birth of their first baby. This is the beginning of the first stage, the *parental image stage,* during which the mother and father form their images of themselves as parents.

FIGURE 3.16 Family
With the joy of parenthood come added responsibilities—both emotional and financial.

They have a desire to be perfect, but often experience heavy demands that were unexpected.

The *nurturing stage* occurs during infancy, when attachment occurs and relationships with spouse, infant, and other people are challenged and determined. Often heavy demands are made upon parents at this time, as they establish their roles.

During the *authority stage*, when offspring are between 2 and 4 years of age, adults face questions of their effectiveness as parents. The young child is beginning to develop independence and more demands are made on a parent's time. Often a second child is born, adding to the stress of the family.

The *integrative stage* extends from preschool through middle childhood. As children develop more autonomy and social skills, parents are required to set realistic goals, motivate their children, develop effective communication skills, and establish authority.

The fifth stage, the *independent teenage stage*, is the time when adolescents wrestle with identification, responsibility, and maturity. Parents must provide support for their adolescents, while maintaining authority and responsibility.

Finally, the *departure stage* occurs when the adolescent leaves home. At this time, parents evaluate their past performance and prepare for the future relationship with their offspring.

The important point of Galinsky's theory is that parenthood develops as the children grow and that the adult's self-concepts are shaped through interactions with children at each stage. When parents are aware of and can achieve their goals, they will be happy and satisfied. If not, they will be frustrated, stressed, and depressed. Therefore, it is critical that people understand and prepare for the developmental stages of parenthood.

When the children leave the home, it is often a major transition for parents, but it usually eases the financial burden, and the parents find that they have time to pursue other interests. For many couples, this later period is the happiest time of their lives (Mudd & Taubin, 1982). However, some couples may find that they have drifted apart over the years. Holmes and Boon (1990) provide suggestions to rekindle romantic love, such as finding time to share enjoyable activities, improving communication, working on physical attractiveness, and learning to compromise on disagreements.

Sometimes the relationship cannot be repaired and the couple decide to divorce. Divorce can, of course, occur at any time, and the causes are extremely varied. It often produces a major disruption of family life and requires a great deal of effort to adjust to it. Nearly half of the marriages in the United States and Canada end in divorce today, although most people eventually remarry (Glick, 1989).

Work   An occupation is extremely important in adulthood. Most people go through several stages in selecting a career (Tiedeman & O'Hara, 1963). In the exploration stage, young adults think about various work options. In the crystallization stage, career choices are narrowed down in preparation for the actual career choice. In the induction stage, workers enter the new job.

Whatever the job—homemaker, accountant, secretary, teacher, mother, or laborer—people need to be engaged in some worthwhile activity as adults. As Erikson suggested, a major task of adulthood is generativity, or being productive. Being satisfied in one's work is very important. Positive evaluation and promotion will help people feel that they are leading useful, productive lives.

A topic of increasing interest to psychologists is women in the workplace. Currently, about 65 percent of women over 16 work in jobs outside of the home. Over 50 percent of mothers with young children have jobs that require day-care services for the children (Glick, 1989). Some of the influences on women entering the workplace include the fact that more women are graduating from college and have more access to once male-dominated professions. Dual-career families often have more money, but sometimes also experience more stress (Moen, 1982).

FIGURE 3.17   Women in the Workplace
Erikson indicated that a major task of adulthood is generativity, or productivity. Some women have found satisfying work in what traditionally have been considered masculine fields.

Retirement   A major transition period occurs when a person retires. Retirement reminds us once again that we are getting older and will die eventually. It often signals a drastically different financial picture for the family. And it usually means a major reorganization of the person's time and activities.

Cox (1984) described several factors important in adjustment to retirement. Personality and life-style will influence how easily a person can make the transition to retirement. A person dependent upon others for motivation may experience difficulty in managing his or her time in retirement. The person who adapts quickly to changes should enjoy the challenge of retirement. People who have hobbies and family interests outside of the workplace generally enjoy the excess time on their hands more than people who have devoted all of their energy to their job.

Robert Atchley (1985) has proposed a model of retirement that includes six phases. In the *preretirement phase*, the worker becomes aware that retirement is approaching. The *honeymoon phase* occurs immediately after the actual event and is normally characterized by enjoyment of one's free time. During the *disenchantment phase*, the retiree begins to feel depressed about life and the lack of things to do. Often the person then goes through a *reorientation phase* of developing a more realistic attitude toward effective use of time. During the *stability phase*, the retirement routine is established and enjoyed. The *terminal phase* occurs when illness or disability prevents the retiree from actively caring for himself or herself.

Cognitive Development in Older Persons

Are most old people wise or senile? Many cultures respect their elders for having the wisdom to solve important problems. Other cultures sometimes portray old people as forgetful, incompetent, and feebleminded. Evidence suggests that intellectual capacity does not automatically deteriorate once you're past the age of 60. Intelligence is a complex concept. Hertzog (1989) points out that some areas appear to remain stable with age (vocabulary and general information), while other areas decline somewhat (short-term memory and problem solving).

There are problems with the testing methods used to measure intelligence in adults. For example, it is difficult to compare people born and reared at different times. Also, older people are at a disadvantage on subtests of intelligence that require quick reactions. Horn and col-

FIGURE 3.18   Retirement
A major transition period in someone's life occurs when he or she retires. Proper preparation ensures that a retired person will continue to lead a productive, although different, life. Many retirees have hobbies and family interests to which they can devote their time and energy.

leagues (1981) suggested that biological processes result in a gradual decline in <u>fluid intelligence</u> (ability to solve novel problems), but have little if any effect on <u>crystallized intelligence</u> (verbal reasoning and comprehension of cultural concepts). It is also important to remember that people often act the way they think they should. According to one view, it is possible that some decline in cognitive ability may be due to older people's belief that they are expected to be less intelligent, or it may be due to their lack of motivation to perform well on tests (Hertzog, 1989). At any rate, there are many very capable older people in our society, and with the influence of medical science extending life expectancy, this trend is likely to continue. We will discuss the concept of intelligence further in chapter 8, "Language and Intelligence."

A problem of growing concern for older individuals is <u>Alzheimer's disease</u>, a degenerative disorder of the brain that results in irreversible memory loss. Along with the memory loss are other symptoms, such as intellectual and personality deterioration. Many patients lose the ability to perform more than simple body functions (Reisberg, 1983). Alzheimer's disease (sometimes called senility) often occurs in the elderly, but may occur in people as young as 40. The exact cause of Alzheimer's disease is not known, but it appears that a decrease in the neurotransmitter acetylcholine plays a role. To date, treat-

ment has been ineffective in preventing the inevitable intellectual decline in Alzheimer's disease patients.

Psychological Stages of Dying

Ultimately, the final stage of life is the process of dying. Erikson's last psychosocial stage is integrity, where the person learns to accept life and feel satisfied with its accomplishments. Recent research has shown that fear of death decreases with age. Dorothy Rogers reported in 1980 that almost 20 percent of young adults were afraid of death, compared to less than 2 percent of those over 65.

Psychiatrist Elizabeth Kübler-Ross (1969, 1981) proposed a theory that describes the stages terminally ill people usually go through as they prepare to die. While all the stages are not experienced by everyone, they do provide a basis for thinking about this last stage of life.

The first stage is *denial*. The person believes the doctor made a mistake and that it is not possible that he or she could actually be dying. The second stage is *anger*. When people realize they are dying, they become angry and resentful of all those around them. The anger is replaced by the third stage, *bargaining*. The person tries

FIGURE 3.19 Cognitive Activities in Older Persons
Many older people stay intellectually alert in old age by continuing to seek new information and participating in programs designed to challenge their knowledge and problem-solving skills.

FIGURE 3.20 Kübler-Ross's Stages of Dying

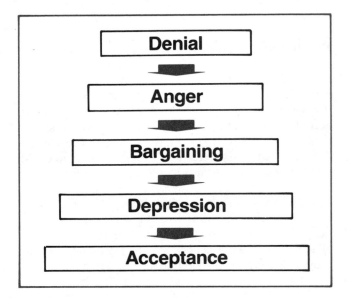

to buy time by bargaining with doctors, family, and God. Typically, those who are dying say that if they survive, they will work harder, go to church, be faithful, and so on. Finally, they recognize the inevitable fact that they are going to die and go into the fourth stage, *depression*. Eventually the dying person may reach the last stage, *acceptance*. He or she accepts death as part of life, and then is able to make the necessary preparations for death, quietly.

E. Mansell Pattison (1977) argued that there are so many individual differences in dying that it is not possible to identify specific emotional stages. He suggested three phases that the terminally ill go through. The *acute phase* occurs when an individual realizes that he or she will die. The *chronic living-dying phase* involves a host of emotions, including fear, loneliness, pain, and sorrow. Eventually the *terminal phase* is reached when the individual withdraws from people and life.

The hospice movement provides an alternative for the terminally ill to spend their last days in the loving company of their family (Holden, 1980). A hospice is an organization that helps the person and the family with social needs, as well as medical attention. Psychologists are becoming involved in learning more about dying so

that they can help others successfully meet the challenges of this last stage in life.

Based on a concept originally developed in England, a hospice is a center established for the care of dying patients and their families. The program provides supportive services, including physical, psychological, social, and spiritual aid for people who are dying.

According to Holden (1980), hospices serve several important functions. Medical personnel help make patients physically comfortable by providing pain medication. Psychological personnel provide support for patients by helping them feel secure. This support might be in the form of talking to patients or helping them get their legal and social affairs in order. Finally, hospices provide support for the bereaved through counseling or pastoral care. ■

This final stage of life marks the end of our brief survey of developmental psychology. As indicated in our opening story on cognitive development in children, development changes over time and is due to the interaction of heredity and the environment. We have spanned the human life cycle from prenatal development through adulthood. As you read through the rest of this book, keep in mind the developmental stages that people go through in life. We turn next to how people know about the outside world, through sensation and perception.

"Why did you cut my squash in half, Mommy? Now I have TWICE as much to eat."

CHAPTER REVIEW

What You've Learned About Development

1. Development includes the changes in the physical, cognitive, personality, and social characteristics of the individual over time. Developmental psychology is the study of physical and mental growth and behavioral changes in individuals from conception to death.

2. Prenatal development includes the growth of an individual from conception until birth. Stages in prenatal development include the zygote stage, the embryonic stage, and fetal stage.

3. The first 2 years of life are defined as infancy. Overall, the infant's senses appear to be much more developed than was once thought. Within a few days of birth, the neonate's hearing is normal. Infants can discriminate different tastes and smells. Infants prefer complex visual stimuli, especially ones that resemble the human face.

4. Infants are born with reflexes, or automatic responses to stimuli, including the rooting reflex, Moro reflex, and Babinski reflex. The sequence of motor development follows a fairly predictable pattern. Readiness to learn states that children cannot learn until they are mature enough to be able to use their muscles.

5. Temperament tendencies, or ways of responding to the environment, begin to appear as early as the first days of life. Sex-role differences (masculinity and femininity) also appear early in life. By the age of 18 months the infant is faced with social demands.

6. Attachment is the process in which the individual shows behaviors that promote contact with a specific person. Infants go through the phases of asocial, indiscriminate, specific, and multiple attachments. Ainsworth identified avoidant, secure, and ambivalent types of infant-parent attachment. Approaches to attachment focus on separation distress and contact comfort.

7. Childhood is the period between the ages of 2 and 11 years. Friendships begin to develop when children are about 3. At about 4 years, children begin to identify with their same-sex parents. From about 6 years, children are also influenced by peers, schools, churches, and the mass media. Freud's psychosexual stage theory of personality includes the oral, anal, phallic, latency, and genital stages.

8. Piaget's theory of cognitive development emphasizes the processes of assimilation (integrating new information into existing schemes) and accommodation (creating schemes for new information). In the sensorimotor period, the infant coordinates sensory experiences with motor activities. In the preoperational thought period, the child acquires language, is egocentric, and learns to represent the environment with symbols. In the concrete operations period, the child develops conservation, decentration, and reversal. In the formal operations period, the adolescent is capable of abstract logical thinking.

9. Kohlberg studied moral development, or development of the awareness of ethical behavior. In Level I, preconventional morality, moral reasoning is based on expectations of rewards or punishments. In Level II, conventional morality, moral reasoning is based on conformity. In Level III, postconventional morality, moral reasoning is based on personal standards.

10. Adolescence is the period of development between the onset of puberty and about 18 or 21 years. Both boys and girls experience a growth spurt during adolescence. At puberty (about age 11 in girls, age 13 in boys), adolescents are capable of reproducing.

11. A major goal in adolescence is the development of a personal identity. Parents and adolescents deal with concerns such as communication and independence. Adolescents develop friendships and date members of the opposite sex as they develop interpersonal skills.

12. Erikson's psychosocial theory of development includes eight major stages. In infancy, we develop a sense of trust. In early childhood, we develop autonomy. In middle childhood, we develop initiative. In later childhood, we develop industry. In adolescence, we develop identity. In early adulthood, we develop intimacy. In middle adulthood, we develop generativity. In later adulthood, we develop integrity.

13. The body is at its peak physically during early adulthood. Physical aging becomes noticeable during middle adulthood. There are several theories that focus on the aging process.

14. Our society does not have a rigid definition of adulthood. We become adults when we leave home, get a job, get married, or have children. Much of adult life centers around family and occupation. Major transitions occur when a person gets married, works, has children, and retires.

15. During adulthood, cognitive development may continue indefinitely, but consists of elaborations on themes already developed. Intellectual capacity does not deteriorate automatically in later adulthood.

16. The last stage of life is the process of dying. Kübler-Ross described five stages that people go through in the process of dying, including denial, anger, bargaining, depression, and acceptance.

CHAPTER 4

SENSATION AND PERCEPTION

Everything we experience in our environment comes to us through our senses. Psychologists study how the sense organs receive sensory input, how this information is then carried through the nervous system to the brain, and how perception, the interpretation of sensation, occurs. Much attention has focused on the sense of vision, but psychologists are also interested in the perceptual systems of hearing, smell, taste, and the skin and body senses.

CRITICAL THINKING OBJECTIVES FOR CHAPTER 4

After reading chapter 4, you should be able to identify, apply, and evaluate what you have learned about the following questions:

What is the distinction between sensation and perception?
What are the methods used to measure sensation?
What are the structures of the eye?
What are the Gestalt rules of perceptual organization?
What are the two theories of hearing?
What is the theory of olfaction?
What is the role of endorphins in pain?

CHAPTER 5

SLEEP AND CONSCIOUSNESS

Consciousness has long been an area of interest for psychologists. Much of the research has been conducted on altered states of consciousness, such as sleep, hypnosis, and meditation. The information learned about sleep and dreaming has practical consequences. And practical, too, is the study of the effects of drugs on behavior.

CRITICAL THINKING OBJECTIVES FOR CHAPTER 5

After reading chapter 5, you should be able to identify, apply, and evaluate what you have learned about the following questions:

What are the types of consciousness?
What are the two types of sleep?
What are the most serious psychoactive drugs?
What are the uses of hypnosis?
What are the effects of meditation?
What are the effects of sensory deprivation?
What are the uses of biofeedback?

Part II provides an overview of the role perception plays in our lives. The areas covered include sensation, perception, and altered states of consciousness.

PART II

Perceptual Processes

CHAPTER OBJECTIVES

What You'll Learn About Sensation and Perception

After studying this chapter, you should be able to:

1. Define sensation and perception.
2. Describe transduction and sensory adaptation.
3. Differentiate between absolute and difference thresholds.
4. List the major structures and function of the eye.
5. Compare the two major theories of color vision.
6. Define perceptual constancy and identify four types.
7. Describe Gestalt principles of perceptual organization.
8. Identify monocular and binocular cues used in depth perception.
9. Identify four different types of apparent motion.
10. Define visual illusion and list six examples.
11. Outline the functioning of the ear.
12. Compare the two major theories of hearing.
13. Outline the process of sound localization.
14. Describe the sense of smell.
15. Describe the sense of taste.
16. Describe the skin sense of pressure.
17. Outline the gate-control theory of pain and the role of endorphins in controlling pain.
18. Describe the skin sense of temperature.
19. Describe kinesthesis and the vestibular sense.

While visiting the Grand Canyon during a vacation, Eleanor Gibson of Cornell University noticed a group of small children playing. She worried about their safety and wondered if very young children could perceive the danger of falling off the cliff. Because she was an experimental psychologist interested in perception, Gibson decided to test depth perception in her laboratory.

One question that Gibson was interested in was whether infants have an innate sense of depth perception, or if they must learn to be careful when around places where they could fall and hurt themselves. This "nature or nurture" question is important in psychological research.

Gibson and her colleague, Richard Walk (1960), devised a "visual cliff" to study perception of depth in infants. The visual cliff consisted of a large sheet of heavy glass supported by legs a foot or so off the ground. A board was laid across the center of the glass, creating two equal sides. On the "shallow" side of the apparatus, a checker-patterned cloth was placed immediately under the glass to provide a solid-looking surface. On the "deep" side, the cloth draped down to and across the floor, creating the illusion of a large drop-off from the board. Since the glass extended on both sides, the subjects were always safe and could not actually fall off the cliff. If an infant was able to perceive depth, he or she would be expected to stay on the shallow side, whereas if the infant did not show depth perception, he or she would be expected to go to either side indiscriminately.

Everything we experience in our environment comes to us through our senses. Psychologists study how the sense organs receive sensory input, how this information is then carried through the nervous system to the brain, and how perception, the interpretation of sensation, occurs. Much attention has focused on the sense of vision, but psychologists are also interested in the perceptual systems of hearing, smell, taste, and the skin and body senses.

4

Sensation and Perception

In one experiment 38 infants between the age of 6 months and 14 months of age were tested for depth perception on the visual cliff. Each infant was placed on the center board and observed. If the infant did not immediately crawl to a side, his or her mother went to the deep side and called the infant. Then the mother went to the shallow side to coax the infant to crawl over to her.

Twenty-seven of the subjects crawled off the center board. All of them crawled to their mother when she was on the shallow side of the visual cliff, but only three would crawl on the deep side. Some of the infants moved away from their mother when she was on the deep side, while others just stayed on the center board and cried.

Gibson concluded that infants show depth perception as soon as they can crawl (by 6 months of age). Even at this young age, infants have a well-developed visual sense. Many of the subjects looked down at the deep side and then backed up. Some of them touched the glass on the deep side, but refused to place their weight on it.

Does this experiment prove that depth perception in infants is innate? No, since the subjects were 6 months old when tested and may have learned to avoid heights during that time. It does suggest that visual perception is important in infancy and is developed at a very early age. Certainly, when infants are ready to crawl, they have developed enough visual perception to allow them to navigate.

Gibson's research on depth perception illustrates the typical approach to studying sensation and perception. It

is important to develop a hypothesis that can be tested through a carefully designed experiment.

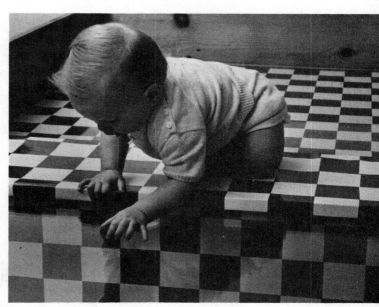

FIGURE 4.1 Visual Cliff
Depth perception in animals and human infants is tested using a visual cliff. One side of the table top is clear glass, with the checkered cloth running down the side and across the floor several feet below it so that a cliff is simulated. Both humans and animals hesitate to cross this end of the table even when encouraged to do so. Experimenters use this information as evidence of the importance of depth perception.

WHAT ARE SENSATION AND PERCEPTION?

Our world is filled with a wide variety of environmental stimuli that we are aware of through the processes of sensation and perception. Although it is difficult to distinguish sensation from perception, psychologists tend to view sensation as a physiological process and perception as a cognitive one.

Douglas Bloomquist (1985) defined sensation as the passive process through which stimuli are received by sense receptors and transformed into neural impulses that can be carried through the nervous system. It is the first stage in becoming aware of the environment. Sense receptors are physical structures at the end of the nervous system directly affected by environmental stimuli. Everything we experience in the environment comes to us through our sense receptors, or senses.

Perception is a more active process in which the sensory information is carried through the nervous system to the brain and is organized and interpreted (Matlin & Foley, 1992). Perception involves other cognitive processes, such as memory and thinking and an ability to form meaning through the sense processes. One distinction that we will use in this chapter is that the study of sensation focuses on sense activity, whereas the study of perception emphasizes what we actually experience.

At any one moment we experience a vast array of sensory stimuli. Since we cannot attend to all of the stimuli in our environment simultaneously, we must select and pay attention to only a limited number. Through experience we have learned to attend to the sensory data relevant to our purposes. As drivers, for instance, we pay close attention to other cars, bends in the road, street signs, and stoplights; as passengers we can afford to ignore these things. This process, called selective attention, is extremely important to our survival, since it allows us to concentrate on the most important aspects of the environment. Selective attention is determined, in part, by motivation.

Expectancy is another important variable in perception. If I were to say to you, "Get ready, get set, . . ." what would you fill in the blank space with? You would respond with "go" because you expected it to be there. *Perceptual expectancy* can be thought of as the culmination of all our experiences that directs us to perceive the world from a unique perspective. How we perceive the world depends upon our previous learning experiences, our culture, and our biological makeup.

SENSORY PROCESSES

A basketball game is a sensational experience—for all our senses. Even before we enter the court, we hear the noise: the sounds of the crowd laughing, talking, and shouting contend with the sounds of bouncing balls, announcements over the loudspeaker, and the band playing. As we enter, we see people everywhere—spectators making their way to their seats and the teams practicing their shooting. If we take the time to sort them out, we may detect several distinct odors: cigarette smoke, popcorn, the smell of people, and the smell of a gymnasium. At a basketball game, not even our sense of touch is spared as we bump into people on the way to the bleachers. Our sense of taste is tested by drinks, popcorn, hot dogs, gum, and candy. And after a while, we may begin to feel warm as the game gets exciting and we enthusiastically cheer for our team.

Overview of the Senses

Each of our senses is designed to receive a particular type of information. Before we review each of the senses

FIGURE 4.2 Perceptual Expectancy

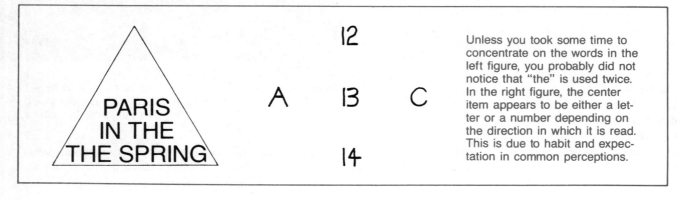

Unless you took some time to concentrate on the words in the left figure, you probably did not notice that "the" is used twice. In the right figure, the center item appears to be either a letter or a number depending on the direction in which it is read. This is due to habit and expectation in common perceptions.

FIGURE 4.3   The Human Senses

Sense	Stimulus	Sense Organ	Receptor	Perception
Vision	Light waves	Eye	Rods and cones	Sights
Hearing	Sound waves	Ear	Organ of corti	Sounds
Smell	Volatile substances	Nose	Olfactory epithelium	Odors
Taste	Soluble substances	Tongue	Taste buds	Tastes
Pressure	Light pressure	Skin	Nerve endings	Pressure
Pain	Deep pressure	Skin	Nerve endings	Pain
Warm	Temperature	Skin	Nerve endings	Warmth
Cold	Temperature	Skin	Nerve endings	Cold
Kinesthesis	Muscle movement	Tendons, joints	Golgi tendon organs	Movement
Vestibular	Gravity	Inner ear	Semicircular canals	Balance

The senses provide us with critical information about internal and external events. The study of sensation is a search for correlations between physical events acting on living organisms and the behavior or experiences that they evoke.

in detail, a brief overview of the human senses may help you understand the general processes of sensation and perception. The 10 senses discussed in this chapter include vision, hearing, smell, taste, pressure, pain, warmth, cold, kinesthesis, and the vestibular sense.

Vision is a very important sense in humans. The stimulus for vision is light, and the sense organs are the eyes. Hearing, or audition, depends on sound, and the sense organs are the ears. Smell and taste are called the chemical senses because the sensory stimulation of the receptors involves contact with chemical substances. The sense organs for smell are located in the nasal passages; and the taste receptors, the taste buds, are found in the tongue.

The somatic, or body senses include the skin senses of pressure, pain, warmth, and cold and the proprioceptive senses: kinesthesis and vestibular. The skin senses are sensitive to stimuli on the body surface. Pressure receptors are located just below the surface of the skin and respond to a slight touch. Pain receptors are located more deeply under the skin and are stimulated by stronger pressure. The skin senses of warmth and cold are sensitive to changes in temperature. The proprioceptive receptors are located within the body and allow us to respond to changes in body movement and position. Kinesthesis is the sense of bodily movement, whereas the vestibular sense helps us maintain our balance.

Transduction and Sensory Adaptation

As we saw in the basketball game example, people have a variety of senses that help them perceive the environment so they can respond appropriately. Sensation is the first step in the sequence. As we saw in chapter 2, "Psychobiology," the senses are the biological response systems that must originally receive stimuli. Sensation is the process in which stimuli are received by the sense receptors and transformed into neural impulses

that can be carried through the nervous system. The sensory stimulus is some form of physical energy that excites the sense receptor.

Transduction   The process of changing the stimulus energy from the environment into neural impulses that travel through the nervous system is called transduction. The receptors in each of the sense organs are specialized structures that are sensitive to a particular type of physical energy, such as light waves, sound waves, pressure, temperature, or chemical reactions. The receptor is a biological transducer. Once the sense receptors are stimulated, they transform the energy into electrical neural impulses. All neural impulses are the same and follow specific nervous system routes to the areas of the brain where the electrochemical information is perceived and acted upon.

Sensory Adaptation   Imagine that you have just come home from a vacation and your house smells musty from being closed up. You start to open a window to air out the house, but stop first to look over the mail that has accumulated during your absence. After reading a couple of letters, you suddenly realize the house no longer smells musty even though you haven't yet opened the windows. But when you go out to the car to bring in the rest of your luggage and come in again, you notice the musty smell once more. You've just discovered the phenomenon of sensory adaptation.

Sensory adaptation is the tendency of the sense organs to adjust to continuous, unchanging stimulation by reducing their functioning. In other words, a stimulus that once caused a sensation may become less effective. Your different senses vary quite a bit in their capacities to adapt. The smell receptors adapt to a new odor within a few minutes, often so completely that the odor is no longer detectable (as in our example of the musty house). The sense of hearing shows less adaptation; for instance, we are all familiar with the experience of having to shout to make ourselves heard over the sound of a jackhammer or loud music, which goes to show that our sense of hearing has not adapted to the new loud sound level. Visual adaptation is a very slow process, partly because our gaze continually moves about our environment.

Sensory adaptation is important for our survival. If we paid total attention to every stimulus in our environment, we would not be able to concentrate on important tasks. For example, you might be in a classroom that has a fluorescent bulb flickering, a closed-in odor, or a ventilator fan humming. Sensory adaptation lets you ignore all of these ambient stimuli so that you can do the most important task—concentrate on the class discussion.

Measurement of Sensation

Psychophysics is the area of psychology that compares the physical energy of a stimulus with the sensation reported by a subject. A stimulus must have a certain minimum energy before it can be detected by a sensory receptor. Some of our senses seem to have extremely low thresholds. For example, Galanter (1962) reported that we are capable of perceiving the wing of a bee falling on our cheek. And we can detect one drop of perfume diffused throughout an average-sized apartment.

Absolute Threshold   When we ask the question, what is the minimum light intensity we can see, or the minimum sound pressure we can hear, we are asking about the absolute threshold of these senses. The absolute threshold is the minimum amount of physical energy required to produce a sensation. To determine the absolute threshold, experimenters can use the *method of constant stimuli*, in which a subject is presented with stimuli of various intensities and is asked to report their presence or absence.

In an experiment to determine absolute threshold for hearing, for example, a subject would be in a soundproof room and the experimenter would present sounds of different intensities, from sounds so soft that the subject could not possibly hear them to sounds so loud that there could be no doubt that they would be heard. In between these extremes lies the absolute threshold. It is usually accepted that the absolute threshold is the level that produces a response sensation 50 percent of the time.

We use absolute thresholds all the time. We might use a detectable amount of perfume or after-shave, but not enough to upset those around us. When talking to someone in the library, we whisper in order to keep the sound below the absolute threshold of the other students but above the absolute threshold of the person we are talking to.

FIGURE 4.4   Absolute Threshold

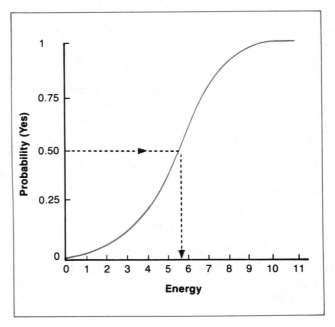

In order to determine an absolute threshold, the experimenter presents a stimulus at a variety of intensity levels and asks the subject whether the stimulus was presented. The point at which the subject responds affirmatively 50 percent of the time is the absolute threshold, as shown on this hypothetical graph.

Difference Threshold   When we ask, what is the minimal change in sound pressure or in brightness that we can detect, we are asking about the difference threshold of these senses, or their discriminative capacity. The difference threshold is the minimum amount of physical energy change required to produce a difference in sensation. The difference threshold is often called the just noticeable difference (JND). In the *method of limits*, the experimenter determines the difference threshold by presenting stimuli of greater or lesser intensity than the original. The subject has to report whether the test stimulus is greater than or less than the original stimulus.

FIGURE 4.5   Common Difference Thresholds

ITEM	QUALITY	PERCENTAGE
solutions	saltiness	8%
lights	brightness	8%
sounds	intensity	5%
objects	weight	2%
sounds	frequency	0.3%

A noticeable difference will normally be detected by someone if the qualities of the items vary by the given percentages.

FIGURE 4.6   The Visible Spectrum

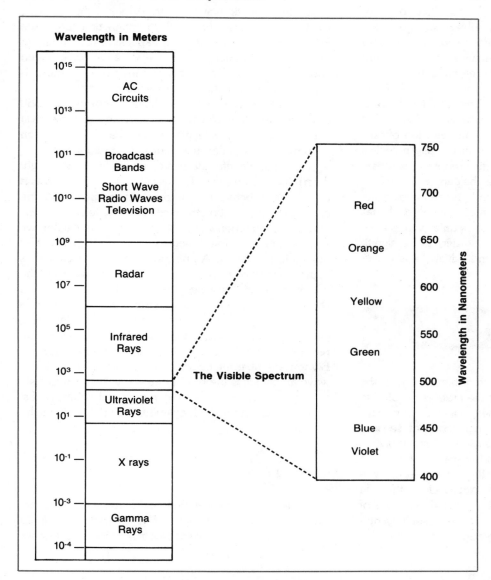

Visible light is only a small part of the electromagnetic spectrum. The human eye responds to wavelengths of between 380 and 760 nanometers, but a wider range exists, including X rays and radio waves. The colors of the visible spectrum range from violet to red.

When someone asks you to turn down the volume on the television, you go up to the set and turn the knob; but, before you get back to your seat, the other person may complain that you didn't reduce the volume. Of course you did; but from where the other person is sitting the adjustment was not enough to reach the difference threshold.

In 1834 Ernst Weber noticed that the difference threshold depends upon the intensity of the original stimulus. He found that a strong stimulus requires a larger change in intensity for a difference to be noticed than does a weak stimulus. For example, if the television volume is loud, it will take a greater change to reach the just noticeable difference than if the volume is very soft to begin with. Weber's Law states that the difference thresh-

old depends on the *ratio* of the intensity of one stimulus to another, rather than on an absolute difference.

Signal Detection Theory   Psychophysics depends exclusively on subjective reporting of sensation. To help overcome the problem of guessing by subjects, the signal detection theory was developed (Green & Swets, 1966). Signal detection theory approaches the subject's behavior in detecting a threshold as a form of decision-making.

In each trial of a signal detection test, two sets of two probabilities are possible: the sensory stimulus can be presented or withheld, and the subject can report perceiving the stimulus or not. If a stimulus is presented and the subject says yes, the trial is a "hit." If no stimulus is presented but the subject still says yes, it is a "false alarm" and might indicate that the subject is motivated to guess. If a stimulus is presented and the subject says no, it is a "miss" and gives information on the subject's ability to detect the stimulus. Finally, if no stimulus is presented and the subject says no, it is a correct rejection. From these data, it is possible to plot a subject's responses when the intensity of the stimulus is varied. The resulting curve is called the *receiver operating characteristic (ROC)*, and provides additional information on the detection of sensory thresholds. By including the subject's psychological characteristics as well as the subjective reporting of sensation, signal detection theory has helped psychologists learn more about how sensation and perception operate. Recent research using a signal detection approach has found the perceptual sensitivity of people with schizophrenia (a severe psychological disorder) to be significantly lower than that of healthy individuals (Mussgay & Hertwig, 1990).

VISION

Most people rely more on vision than on any of the other senses. A larger portion of the brain is devoted to vision relative to the other senses, and we often trust visual information more than other types of sensory information (hence the common saying, "seeing is believing"). Have you ever noticed that the speech of actors in a movie appears to come from the front screen, even though the theater's speakers are placed along the side walls? This is due to visual capture, the dominance of vision over hearing. Visual capture is one reason psychologists have studied vision so thoroughly.

The stimuli that affect vision are light waves, a type of electromagnetic wave energy. Visible light is only a small part of a spectrum of electromagnetic energy (see Figure 4.6). The human eye is capable of responding to electromagnetic energy with a wavelength of between about 380 and 760 nanometers (nm). (A nanometer is one billionth of a meter.) The electromagnetic spectrum also includes energy with wavelengths shorter than 380 nm (such as ultraviolet rays, X rays, and gamma rays) and energy with wavelengths longer than 760 nm (such as infrared rays, radar, television, and radio waves).

The wavelength and wave amplitude of visible light determine what we see. The wavelength of light waves is the distance between any point in a wave and the corresponding point on the next cycle. Wavelength determines our experience of hue, which is the color we actually perceive. Psychologists refer to the purity of a hue as its *saturation*. A hue from a single wavelength is high in saturation, whereas one that results from the mixing of several wavelengths is low in saturation. The shortest wavelength produces the color of violet. As wavelengths get longer, the hue changes to indigo, blue, green, yellow, orange, and at the longest wavelength, red. (You might have memorized the mnemonic Roy G. Biv to remember the colors of the visible spectrum.) The wave amplitude is the height of a wave. Wave amplitude primarily determines our experience of brightness. Essentially, the higher the amplitude, the brighter the light.

The Eye

The human eye is sometimes compared to a magnificent living camera. It has a fine lens that can focus images viewed from as close as a few inches to a distance

FIGURE 4.7   The Human Eye

The eye contains complex structures that convert light waves into neural impulses carried by the optic nerve to the occipital lobes of the brain, where they are interpreted as vision. The image enters the eye through the cornea and then passes through the pupil opening in the iris. The lens focuses the images on the retina where the sense receptors, rods and cones, are located. The image is reversed and upside-down because light rays travel in a straight line and are striking the curved surface of the retina. Images are most sharply seen when they fall on the fovea and not seen at all when they fall on the blind spot.

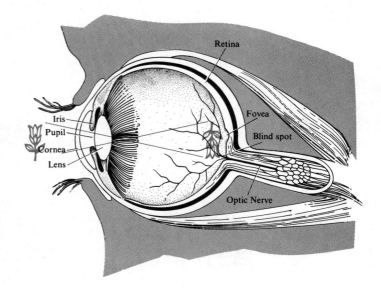

of many miles. It has a mechanism (the pupil) that automatically adjusts to changing light intensities, and a remarkably sensitive and constantly available "film" (the retina).

Light rays enter the eye through the cornea, the tough outer membrane that covers the eyeball and holds it in shape. The rays then pass through the opening in the *iris* (the colored part of the eye). This opening is the pupil, which contracts or expands automatically, controlling the amount of light getting through. The rays are focused by the lens, which flattens out for more distant objects and thickens for those closer. The focused images fall on the retina at the back of the eyeball. In the retina lie the sense receptors for vision: the rods and cones.

Rods and Cones The rods and cones are so named because of their shapes (Sterling, 1983). Rods respond to differences in brightness, so they are most

important for seeing in dim light. The rods are most sensitive to light waves in the 500 nm range, or to blue and green light. They contain a chemical pigment called rhodopsin that breaks down into substances that stimulate the neurons sending visual messages to the brain. Vitamin A is involved in the chemical process of rebuilding rhodopsin, lending support to the notion that, within limits, consuming foods like carrots is good for vision (Coren & Ward, 1989).

The cones respond to hue, or color variations, so they are most important for color vision in bright light. Unlike the rods, which are primarily distributed around the outside edge of the retina, the cones are clustered more in its middle, particularly in an area called the fovea. Images are seen most sharply when they fall on the fovea, and this is the area we try to aim at an object when we focus on it. Although the cones respond to all color variations, they are most sensitive to wavelengths in the 550 nm range, or to green and yellow light. Some fire departments are beginning to paint their fire engines lime yellow so people can more easily see them.

Have you noticed what happens when light intensity changes rapidly, as when you go from a dimly lighted room into a brightly lighted one? You are dazzled by the light at first, but your eyes soon adapt. Your pupils contract, letting less light into the eyes, and in a short while the cones begin functioning efficiently again. Upon reentering the dimly lighted room, it then takes a while for dark adaptation to occur. Dark adaptation takes place in two stages. Cones adapt as much as they can (remember cones are for color vision) in about 10 minutes, while rods

FIGURE 4.8   The Human Retina

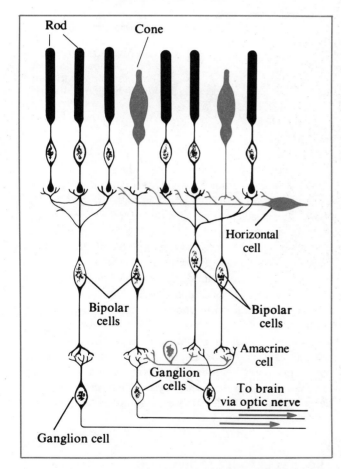

In the retina lie the rod and cone sense receptors for vision. The cones of the fovea, the area of greatest visual sensitivity, have their own direct paths through bipolar cells with single endings. Outside the fovea, larger bipolar cells with multiple endings collect signals from a number of sensors.

FIGURE 4.9   Dark Adaptation

In an experiment on dark adaptation, subjects are placed in total darkness after being in bright light. They are then asked to identify the weakest light they can. The longer they stay in the darkness, the weaker the light they can see. The typical curve for the threshold drops rapidly, flattens out, then drops again. The first curve represents cone adaptation, and the second curve represents rod adaptation (after Hecht & Shlaer, 1938).

reach dark adaptation in about half an hour (Hecht & Shaler, 1938). In dark adaptation, the eye receptors adjust to the dimmer levels of light for optimum vision.

Optic Nerve The retina also contains several other types of cells: bipolar, ganglion, horizontal, and amacrine cells (Masland, 1986). Light causes the rods and cones to send electrical energy to the bipolar cells, which then pass on neural impulses to the ganglion cells. The horizontal cells and amacrine cells interconnect the neurons in the retina (Linberg & Fisher, 1986). The axons of the ganglion cells come together at the eye's blind spot to form the optic nerve. You cannot see objects focused on the blind spot. In the eye, there are about 120 million rods and 6 million cones, which converge on about 1 million optic nerve fibers. This means that many rods or cones send information to the same neurons. An exception is the 100,000 or so cones directly at the fovea, which are connected one-to-one with optic nerve fibers (which helps explain why vision is best here).

Information from each side of the visual field ultimately reaches the opposite hemisphere of the brain, but first it follows a rather complicated pathway (see Figure 2.1, p. 27). Stimuli from the right visual field travels through the lens to the retina on the left half of each eye, and information from the left visual field goes to the right half of each eye. The optic nerve from each eye consists of two nerve fibers, carrying information from each half of the retina. The nerves from the retina on the same side of each eye join at the optic chiasma. Then the optic tracts travel to the thalamus of the brain and eventually reach the occipital lobes, where the sensation of vision is interpreted. Images from the left half of each eye go to the left hemisphere of the brain, and images from the right half of each eye go to the right hemisphere. But ultimately the visual information from the right visual field ends up in the left hemisphere and information from the left visual field ends up in the right hemisphere.

FIGURE 4.10   Blind Spot Demonstration

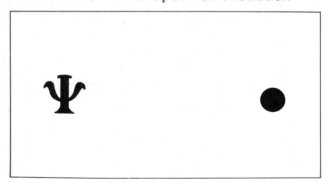

Close your right eye and look at the spot on the right. Move the book slowly up to your face. The symbol on the left will disappear when it is focused on your blind spot.

FIGURE 4.11   Snellen Eye Chart

Visual acuity is typically measured with the Snellen eye chart. A person with normal vision can read the row of letters marked with a star at a distance of 20 feet. This sample is reduced for illustration purposes.

Visual Acuity

The ability to discriminate fine details when looking at something is visual acuity. One of the most popular ways of measuring visual acuity is with the *Snellen eye chart.* This measurement is often called the 20/20 test because a person with normal vision can stand 20 feet from the chart and easily identify the row of letters fourth up from the bottom (starred in the figure above). A person whose eyes cannot be corrected with glasses to 20/200 is usually considered legally blind.

In the visual impairment of myopia (nearsightedness) the eyeball is unusually long, so the image is focused in front of the retina. Glasses can be used to see normal to long-range stimuli in the environment. In hyperopia (farsightedness) the eyeball is unusually short and the image is focused beyond the retina. Glasses permit close-up work, such as reading.

Theories of Color Vision

Our world is filled with a richness in all the color variations. How are we able to see the many colors in our environment? There are various theories of color vision, and they all agree on the importance of the cones in producing all the colors we see. The disagreement among theories of color vision is on the nature of the complex processing that allows the cones to send correct messages to the brain.

There are three types of cones, each of which is most sensitive to a particular wavelength producing either red, green, or blue colors. But if there are only three different receptors, how is it we see so many colors? In 1807 an English physicist, Thomas Young, proposed that the eye sees color because of a combination of these three colors. He showed how mixing red, green, and blue lights in different amounts could produce all colors in the spectrum.

Later, the German physiologist Hermann von Helmholtz extended the theory by suggesting that three different types of receptors are responsible for the colors red, green, and blue, and when different combinations of receptors are stimulated, different colors are produced. The Young-Helmholtz theory is called the trichromatic theory of color vision, since it depends on three basic color receptors.

Shortly after Helmholtz, physiologist Ewald Hering proposed the opponent-process theory of color vision. Hering believed that yellow is also a basic color. He argued that while there are three types of color receptors, rather than being only sensitive to one color, each type of color receptor responds to opposing pairs of colors: blue-yellow, red-green, and black-white. Each receptor can respond to one color at a time, but can combine with the other receptors to produce the colors in the visual spectrum.

Which theory is correct? The debate is still going on, but it appears that both theories may be partially correct. Researchers have identified three types of cones in the human retina (MacNichol, 1964). One type of cone is most sensitive at about 450 nm, one is most sensitive at about 540 nm, and the third somewhere around 577 nm. This information provides some support for the trichromatic theory in initial physiological visual processing.

Other evidence supports the opponent-process theory in perceptual visual processing. If you were to look at an American flag that is yellow instead of blue, black instead of white, and green instead of red, for about a minute, and then stare at a white space, you would see a great red, white, and blue American flag. This is known as a negative afterimage, because it is the reverse of the original colors, as suggested in the opponent-process theory. Hering's theory also does a better job of explaining color blindness.

Color Blindness While most of us can see the wide variety of colors in the world, some people see only shades of gray. If you have normal color vision, you are a trichromat, and if you can see only light and dark, you are totally color-blind, or a monochromat.

It is more common to be partially color-blind, or a dichromat. Color blindness is determined genetically, is sex-linked, and occurs mostly in males (in the United States 10 percent of men are color-blind, while only about 1 percent of women are) (Gouras, 1985). The dichromat lacks one of the three types of cones. For example, if the red-green complement of cones is missing, he will be unable to distinguish red and green and will see all colors as yellow or blue. Among men, about 7 percent of the population suffers from red-green color blindness. A few individuals have blue-yellow blindness and see all colors as red or green. Although many animals, including dogs, are monochromats, there are very few cases of total color blindness in humans.

VISUAL PERCEPTION

As we discussed earlier, most people rely more on vision than on any other sense. Because vision is so important for humans, and so much work has been done in this area, in this section we review visual perception in great detail. Many of the principles that apply to visual perception also hold true for the other senses.

The sensory properties of objects differ from moment to moment depending on such factors as the amount of light reflected by them and the distance and angle at which we view them. We are not slaves to such variations in sensory stimulation, however. Regardless of momentary change, the perceptions we experience appear pretty much the same to us from one moment to the next.

Perceptual Constancy

Perceptual constancy is the tendency to perceive objects in a consistent manner despite the changing sensations that are received by our senses. Visual constancy plays an important role in helping us adapt to our environment successfully. Can you imagine the chaos that would result if you could not identify your friends because they wore different clothes each time you saw them? Visual constancy allows us to focus on the permanent features of objects rather than the changing retinal images.

Brightness Constancy A sheet of white paper seen in the bright sunlight reflects a very different amount of light than the same sheet of paper seen later that night in a softly lighted room. Yet we perceive the paper as having the same whiteness in each case. This is an

FIGURE 4.12 Brightness Perception

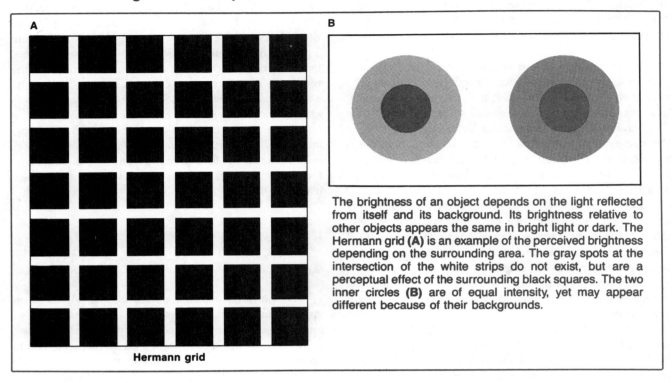

Hermann grid

The brightness of an object depends on the light reflected from itself and its background. Its brightness relative to other objects appears the same in bright light or dark. The Hermann grid (A) is an example of the perceived brightness depending on the surrounding area. The gray spots at the intersection of the white strips do not exist, but are a perceptual effect of the surrounding black squares. The two inner circles (B) are of equal intensity, yet may appear different because of their backgrounds.

example of brightness constancy, our ability to see objects as continuing to have the same brightness even though light may change their immediate sensory properties. Psychologists have determined that an object will exhibit brightness constancy as long as both the object and its surroundings are in light of the same intensity. If the background brightness differs from the object, brightness constancy is not maintained. For example, if the background is lighter than the object, the object appears darker.

Color Constancy Although you probably do not notice, the illumination of the environment determines what color you perceive. For example, if you took a color photograph (without flash or filters) of an outdoor scene, it would be more red at daybreak and more blue at midday. Photos taken under fluorescent lights are greenish, while photos taken with tungsten light (in your home) are yellowish. The different colors result from the different wavelengths of the illuminating source. However, we do not normally notice the subtle changes in color. Color constancy is the perceptual tendency to see familiar objects as the same color consistently, regardless of the illumination. This is why we tend to see our blue shirt as blue, irrespective of the circumstances.

Shape Constancy Is there a rectangular door nearby? Does it look rectangular at all times? Unless you

FIGURE 4.13 Shape Constancy

Even when we look at an object from different angles, we perceive it to have the same shape, due to shape constancy.

stand directly in front of it, chances are good that more often a door appears to be a trapezoid rather than rectangular, because of the angle from which you view it. Yet we usually perceive most doors as rectangular. Shape constancy allows us to perceive familiar objects as having a permanent shape, even if we look at the objects from different angles. In a movie theater, if we are forced to sit very close to the screen or far off to one side, the actors and objects we see at first may look distorted. After a short time, however, we partially make up for this distortion and see the scenes in normal perspective (Cutting, 1987).

FIGURE 4.14 Size Constancy

As the distance of an object from us increases, its retinal image becomes smaller. We tend to correctly perceive the object as being farther away, rather than changing in size. Sometimes our perceptions can be fooled, as in this figure, where the silhouettes are really the same size, but, because of the changing background, we interpret the one on the right to be taller.

Size Constancy   Generally, we perceive a familiar object as remaining the same size even though the image it casts on the retina may vary. As a person walks away from us, the retinal image of that person becomes smaller and smaller, yet in reality he or she is not perceived to be any smaller. Here again, cues other than the retinal size of the image determine how objects appear to us. Size constancy is the process in which we adjust the retinal image by taking into account the apparent distance of an object.

Research has shown that young children are more likely than are adults to judge the size of distant objects on the basis of the size of the retinal image. The younger child usually takes fewer cues into account, and, of course, has had fewer perceptual experiences. Recent research suggests that size constancy is present in infancy, but is not always used by young children (Slater, Mattock, & Brown, 1990). Even in an adult, however, size constancy can be violated in two-dimensional pictures, in which objects actually the same size appear to be different.

You may have visited an amusement park fun house that utilized the research findings of perception psychologists: Balls appear to roll uphill and people appear to shrink before your eyes. The Ames room is a specially constructed room that, due to size and shape constancy, looks normal. Actually, the walls and windows are trapezoidal and one corner is much farther away from the observer than the other. When two people stand in the corners, one person looks small while the other appears a giant, and when a ball is rolled straight, it appears to go uphill. Perceptual constancy demonstrates that the brain is actively involved in the process of perception.

Perceptual Organization

In chapter 1, "The Study of Psychology," we described the Gestalt school of psychology. A number of German psychologists, including Max Wertheimer, Kurt Koffka, and Wolfgang Köhler, were disturbed with the way structuralism and behaviorism broke things down into elements. They argued that people view the whole or complete picture, not merely parts. The greatest influence of Gestalt psychology has been in the field of perception. The rules of perceptual organization discovered by the Gestaltists earlier in this century and published by Koffka in 1935 are still valid today.

Read the following sentence quickly and count the number of *f*s in it. "The field of psychology is full of fascinating facts." How many *f*s did you find? Most people will say four. Try counting them again. Gestalt psychologists would argue that the reason you did not count six *f*s is because you were looking at the sentence as a whole and were not breaking it down into individual units.

FIGURE 4.15 The Ames Room
The Ames room is specially constructed to appear normal even though one corner is much closer to the viewer than the other. This results in the perception of the people in the corners as disproportionate in size relative to their age.

BIOGRAPHICAL HIGHLIGHT

MAX WERTHEIMER

WOLFGANG KÖHLER

KURT KOFFKA

Gestalt psychologists were interested in studying the whole rather than the fragments suggested by structuralism and behaviorism. In 1910 the three founders of Gestalt psychology met in Frankfurt, Germany, where they started their study of perception.

Max Wertheimer was born in Prague, Germany, in 1880. His parents wanted him to become a musician, but he chose psychology. He obtained his Ph.D. from the University of Würzburg in 1904. He taught at several universities in Germany until Hitler came into power. Then he fled to the United States and became a professor at the New School for Social Research in New York, where he remained until his death in 1943.

Wolfgang Köhler was born in Revel, Estonia, in 1887 and grew up in Germany. He obtained his Ph.D. from the University of Berlin in 1909 and then went to the University of Frankfurt, where he met Wertheimer and Koffka. In 1913 he went to the Canary Islands, where he was the director of a research station on ape behavior. Köhler applied the Gestalt principles to study insight learning by chimpanzees. In 1921 he went to the University of Berlin. In the 1930s he fled to the United States and became a professor at Swarthmore College. Köhler died in 1967.

Kurt Koffka was born in Berlin, Germany, in 1886. He earned his Ph.D. from the University of Berlin in 1908, and then went to the University of Frankfurt, where he met the other Gestalt founders in 1910. In 1927 he became a professor at Smith College in the United States. Koffka was especially interested in studying the laws that govern our perceptions of the environment. He was the chief spokesman for the Gestalt movement. Koffka died in 1941.

Therefore, the *of*s were not of major consideration, and you probably didn't count their *f*s. In a sense, the *of*s were part of the background of the sentence.

Figure and Ground   An important rule of perceptual organization is the figure-ground relationship. When we look at a scene, we tend to separate a main figure from a background. Familiar shapes and objects are usually seen as figure and the surrounding space is seen as ground. Often the figure is distinctive and solid, while the ground is vague and formless. And often the figure is seen as being in front of the ground.

Sometimes it is difficult to identify the figure-ground relationship. In a reversible figure scene, the figure and ground appear to reverse themselves. One of the most famous ambiguous reversible figures is the Rubin vase (vase-profile), in which the figure can either be a vase in the middle or two profiles on either side.

While many figure-ground relationships are visual, we also tend to perceive figure-ground relationships with our other senses. In hearing, for example, when we are at a noisy party talking with someone, that person's voice becomes the figure and all the rest of the talking becomes the background. In olfaction this might occur when we visit a friend in the hospital and smell a fresh bouquet of roses; the other odors fade into the background.

FIGURE 4.16   Figure-Ground Relationship

Do you see a vase or two facial profiles? Normally there is one figure that stands out from the background, but in the Rubin vase-face figure shown here the figure and ground are reversible.

FIGURE 4.17 Closure

Through the process of closure, we are able to close the gaps in an image and see a triangle resting on top of three circles rather than three circles with notches in them. The angles of the triangle are called subjective contours (after Coren, 1972).

Closure   The Gestalt psychologists discovered that people have a tendency to group stimuli according to certain rules or principles. The law of Prägnanz states that this grouping, or association, of separate sensory stimuli into a whole pattern provides structure for our perceptions, and occurs whenever possible.

What would you call a circular form made out of dashed lines? A circle, of course. Why? You filled in the gaps and provided the missing spaces for yourself. Closure is the principle of filling in the gaps to perceive a complete form. Closure allows us to see a whole stimulus even when part of it is out of view. For example, you recognize a house as a house, even if bushes and trees block your view partially.

Continuity   The principle of perceiving a line as continuing on its course is called continuity. The lovable alien in *E.T.* wanted to help the boy with the fake arrow in his head because continuity made the arrow appear to go through the boy's head. Continuity helps to explain the success of camouflage. We see the background objects in a scene as continuing, even if something foreign is blocking part of our view, and thus tend to ignore the camouflaged foreign object. (See the following Application for a more in-depth discussion of perceptual organization and camouflage.)

APPLICATION

Camouflage

Many animals blend in with the background of their environment to hide them from predators. This is called camouflage, and is often an effective tool to aid in survival. Camouflage is effective in part because of the Gestalt laws of perceptual organization.

If coloration and patterns are very similar, it might be difficult to separate figure from ground. Thus, we tend not to be able to see the animal in its natural habitat, and focus instead on other objects in the environment.

The principle of continuity is an important part of camouflage because it encourages us to perceive lines as continuing in a natural progression. When an animal blends into the background, continuity helps us see the background lines and shapes as continuing, often through the animal. A "walking stick" or an inchworm on a tree branch illustrate this. Expectancy is also important, and when we expect to see a forest or prairie, we tend to do so, often ignoring the animals that might also be contained there.

Coloration is often very important in helping animals hide in an environment to elude their predators or until they are ready to attack their prey (Gotmakr, 1987).

Many animals are colored in such a way as to make them easily blend into the background. If the animal were significantly different from the background of its habitat, then we could easily identify it. But the spotted fawn in the forest, the fish in the water, or the polar bear in the snow all blend in so well which it is difficult to detect them. Some animals can even change colors to blend in better with the environment. One example of this is the chameleon, which can change from brown to green depending on its surroundings.

Coloration helps the animal blend in, and, combined with expectancy, continuity, and figure-ground effects, results in effective camouflage. If people practice and become more observant, they can improve their detection of camouflage.

FIGURE 4.18 Perceptions According to Gestalt Principles

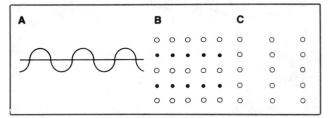

A. Continuity. When one shape is interrupted by another, we perceive the original form as continuing and complete the whole image in our minds.
B. Similarity. When all of the stimuli are equally spaced we group similar ones together. Here we perceive distinct rows of circles and rows of dots.
C. Proximity. Spacing influences whether we see rows or columns. Here we perceive columns rather than rows because the stimuli in the columns are closer together.

Similarity We tend to perceive similar stimuli as being together. Thus, in rows of black and white circles, the black ones are perceived as one line and the white ones are perceived as another. Similarity is the principle of organization in which similar stimuli are perceived as a unit.

Proximity Stimuli close to one another are perceived as belonging together. Proximity is the principle in which stimuli next to one another are included together. For example, lines that are near each other are perceived as a unit. People standing close together are perceived as a group.

Common Fate The principle that groups together stimuli or objects that are moving together is common fate. Thus, we see a flock of birds, a group of cross-country runners, or a collection of lines converging together as units.

Depth Perception

Think for a minute about walking down a street. It's relatively easy to judge the distance between buildings, even though the path might not be straight. This is partially possible because of depth perception, which is the ability to judge the distance to an object. We can even perceive depth in two-dimensional pictures. What are the cues we use to judge depth? Is depth perception innate or do we learn to perceive it correctly? Some of the cues work when we use only one eye, and are called monocular cues; others need both eyes, and are called binocular cues. Both types require the brain to interpret the images received on the eye retina.

Monocular Depth Cues Monocular depth cues only require one eye to detect distance. There are a number of monocular depth cues that help us turn two-dimensional retinal sensations into three-dimensional visual perceptions. Some of these include interposition, size perspective, linear perspective, texture gradient, aerial perspective, and motion parallax.

When one object partially blocks our view of another, we assume that this overlap is due to the first one being closer. Interposition helps us realize that a tree in front of the library is closer to us than the library itself is. Yonas (1984) found that infants as young as 7 months can judge distance on the basis of interposition.

Perspective refers to changes in the appearance of objects or surfaces as the distance from the perceiver increases. The monocular depth cue of size perspective helps us recognize that the smaller an object becomes, the farther away it is perceived to be. We normally interpret distance by the relative size of one object to another. In the school's parking lot, for example, the closest cars appear larger, so we perceive the smaller cars as being farther away. We also use the cue of familiar size, in which our past experience and knowledge about an

FIGURE 4.19 Interposition
When one object partially blocks the view of another, we perceive the blocking object as being closer.

FIGURE 4.20 Linear Perspective
The lines along this road converge, indicating a greater distance in the middle of the photograph than at the bottom.

object helps us to judge its distance (Fitzpatrick, Pasnak, & Tyer, 1982).

Parallel lines, as they become more distant from the observer, appear to converge. The convergence of railroad tracks in the distance is an example of <u>linear perspective</u> often used in drawings to illustrate distance. We interpret the converging lines as being farther away from us, a three-dimensional perception even though the drawing is two-dimensional.

As we stand on grass, we might notice that the individual blades of grass near our feet can be identified, but as we look farther away, the texture becomes blurred and we just see green. <u>Texture gradient</u> is an important depth cue because many surfaces, such as buildings, sidewalks, and floors, have texture. <u>Aerial perspective</u> is a depth cue in which we use brightness, color, and detail to determine distance. On a hazy day, buildings appear to be farther away than on a bright sunny day. Also, objects close to us appear bright and clear, objects that are farther away often have *shadows* (Cavanagh & Leclerc, 1989).

As we walk down a street, we notice that people and objects close to us appear to move by faster than objects farther away. Buildings in the distance do not seem to move within our field of vision at all. <u>Motion parallax</u> causes us to perceive that telephone poles at the side of the road are flying by when we're riding in a car, while the distant scenery or the moon appears to be standing still relative to us. It is one of the important monocular depth cues (Rivest, Ono, & Saida, 1989).

Binocular Depth Cues   While we have many cues for judging depth that depend on only one eye, for even greater accuracy at judging depth we have <u>binocular depth cues</u> that depend on both eyes working together. The principal binocular depth cues are retinal disparity and convergence.

A very important binocular cue for depth is <u>retinal disparity</u>. Our eyes are about 5 cm apart. This means that they receive slightly different (disparate) sensations, which must be combined by the brain for normal vision. Look at an object in your room with only your left eye. Then close your left eye and look at the object with your right eye. The object will appear to move to the right, especially if you hold your index finger out at arm's length while you are looking at the object.

How does retinal disparity help in depth perception? Try the above demonstration outdoors, while looking at a distant object. What happens now? The object will seem to shift its position very little; the image it creates on the retina is more similar in each eye. Therefore, the less retinal disparity we have, the greater the distance of the object we are looking at.

Retinal disparity has been used to create the feeling of depth in 3-D movies. If a scene is photographed simultaneously by two cameras close together, and the viewer wears special glasses that permit the image from each camera to go to one eye only, a three-dimensional effect is obtained. Retinal disparity has also been suggested as one of the problems in some children with learning disabilities. It is possible that some children have difficulty interpreting the disparate images presented by the eyes. Until the brain matures to a point where it can correctly interpret these images, the child may be confused by them.

When we look at objects in our immediate environment, our eyes have to converge, or move inward toward one another, to focus on the objects. The kinesthetic sensations produced by the muscles of the eyeballs send this information to the brain. The brain interprets the amount of <u>convergence</u> as a cue to depth. The farther away an object is, the less convergence we experience. Distant objects do not create any convergence at all. Putting all of these monocular and binocular depth cues together allows us to be fairly precise in judging the distance between us and objects in our environment.

Development of Depth Perception   As described in our opening story, depth perception has been studied in infants with the use of the <u>visual cliff</u>, developed by Gibson and Walk in 1960. The visual cliff is a device that appears to have a solid support on one (shallow) side and a cliff drop-off on the (deep) other. Actually, a large sheet of heavy glass is on top of both halves so the subject cannot fall. A variety of infant animals have been tested on it, including chickens, goats, kittens, pigs, and puppies. Newborn animals stayed on the shallow side, indicating that depth perception is innate in these infants.

Human infants as young as 4 months of age have been tested on the visual cliff. Even at this age, most of the babies appear to have depth perception, since they stay on the shallow side (Granud, 1986). This research strongly suggests that depth perception is important in humans, and is either innate or developed at an early age. Infants younger than about 4 months cannot crawl and therefore cannot effectively be tested on the visual cliff.

Perception of Motion

As we look out of our window, we see people and cars moving by. How do we know that the people are moving? The perception of movement is a complex process that involves the visual receptors in the retina, the eye muscles, and the interpretation by the brain of the visual sensations provided by the environmental stimuli.

Generally, we are fairly adept at detecting real motion, or movement that is actually created by objects in motion. Sometimes, however, we perceive movement when in fact there is none. Apparent motion has interested psychologists since the Gestalt psychologists first studied it. Let's look at several types of apparent motion.

Induced Motion   Have you ever seen the sun go behind a cloud? If so, you experienced induced motion. Actually, the sun is relatively stationary and the clouds move through the sky. But we see the sun as the central figure and the clouds as background, so we often incorrectly perceive that the sun is doing the moving. The tendency to see the figure move against the background is so strong that sometimes we misinterpret what is happening. Another example of induced motion can occur if we are in a car waiting at a stoplight and the car

FIGURE 4.21   Induced Movement

How many times have you said that the sun went behind the clouds on a sunny day? Actually, the clouds went in front of the sun, but we tend to induce movement in the figure (the sun) rather than the ground (the clouds).

next to us begins to move forward. We will likely try to put on our brakes as we feel the car we are in moving backward. Because our car is the figure, we induce movement to it, rather than the car next to us.

Phi Phenomenon   One type of apparent motion occurs when we look at a neon sign with arrows that seem to move. This is an application of what Wertheimer called the phi phenomenon. If we are in a darkened laboratory room and see two lights alternately turning on and off, we will perceive a single source of light that seems to jump between the two points. Of course, the lights have to be a certain distance apart, and the second one has to be turned on at the right time to achieve the effect. The phi phenomenon is an example of an illusion, or misinterpreted sensation.

Stroboscopic Motion   We all are familiar with the movement produced in stroboscopic motion. This is the basis for movement that occurs in motion pictures. What we see is a series of still pictures, each one just slightly different from the previous one. The pictures are presented in rapid succession, and we perceive smooth, coordinated movement. Part of the explanation for stroboscopic motion (as well as for the phi phenomenon) is the afterimage that remains briefly after the stimulus is gone (Farrell, Pavel, & Sperling, 1990). Thus, the last image is still in the nervous system and brain as the next one is received. The Gestalt principle of closure helps us fill in the gap and produces a smooth motion from individual still pictures.

Autokinetic Motion   If we stare at a small spot of light in a dark room for a few minutes, it will appear to begin to move around. Although the light is stationary, we see it move randomly back and forth in the darkness. While we don't know the reason for this positively, the autokinetic effect may be caused by the eye muscles moving to keep the eyes moist.

Visual Illusions

An illusion is an incorrect perception that occurs when sensation is distorted. Although many of our illusions are visual, they are not limited strictly to the sense of sight. The study of illusions helps psychologists understand better how we process perceptions.

In our discussion of depth perception we have, in effect, already discussed many illusions in this chapter. Constancy can create powerful illusions. For example, in monster movies, a small "monster" close to the camera gives the false perception of bigness. The Ames room is sometimes called the distorted-room illusion. Monocular depth cues are used to create an illusion of depth in a two-dimensional painting or photograph. Likewise, the apparent motions of the autokinetic effect and stroboscopic motion are illusions of movement, as is the movement we see in a motion picture. Certain patterns, such as a moiré pattern, make lines in a figure appear to move. There are many illusions that have been studied extensively in psychology; here we sample only some of the more interesting and familiar ones.

Impossible Figures   Our brain is able to take sensation that is two-dimensional and produce perception that is three-dimensional. Sometimes, a figure can be drawn that contains information that is incompatible with the processing system. Impossible figures demonstrate the complexity of perception; they are figures that logically cannot exist. One of the best known is the three-pronged figure in which the middle prong disappears at one end.

FIGURE 4.22   Impossible Figures

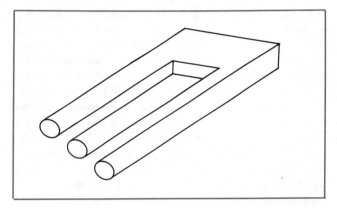

As shown here, sometimes a figure can be drawn that contains information that is incompatible with the visual processing system. This three-pronged figure above only has two sides at the opposite end; the triangle below looks plausible at first, but would be impossible to construct.

FIGURE 4.23   Reversible Figure

Do you see a beautiful young woman or an ugly old woman in this figure? The young girl is looking to the side, whereas the old woman is looking forward. We tend to organize complex stimuli into meaningful relationships.

Reversible Figures   Closely related to impossible figures are reversible figures. Reversible figures present ambiguous information that can be interpreted in more than one way. One well-known reversible figure is the Rubin vase-face figure mentioned earlier. Most of us alternate between making the vase the dominant foreground (with the profiles in the background) and vice versa. We lack the cues to confirm which perception is correct.

Another example of a reversible figure is a drawing of a person's face that can be either a beautiful young woman or an ugly old woman. The young woman is looking to the side, whereas the old woman is looking forward. The nose of the old woman is the chin of the young woman, and the eye of the old woman is the ear of the young woman. The drawing is ambiguous enough that we again alternate between the two perceptions. The Necker cube is a drawing of a cube designed so that it is difficult to determine which side is toward the observer. As we look at the front side of the cube, it appears to shift from the front to the bottom of the cube. Usually, the more we look at reversible figures, the more ambiguous they appear.

Müller-Lyer Illusion   One of the most popular illusions is the Müller-Lyer illusion (see next page). In this one, two lines of equal length appear to be different lengths due to the wings or arrows at the ends of each line. When the end lines point back toward the line, the line appears shorter than when the end lines point out away from the line. Because the end lines pointing away from the line tend to produce an illusion of depth, we

FIGURE 4.24   Visual Illusions

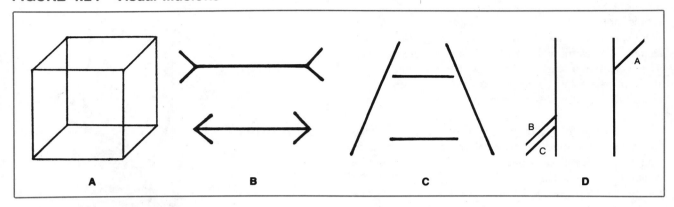

A. In the Necker Cube illusion, one side appears to shift from the front to the back of the cube.
B. In the Müller-Lyer illusion, the two horizontal lines of equal length appear to be different lengths due to the wings at the ends of each line.
C. In the Ponzo illusion, the two horizontal lines of equal length appear to be different lengths due to the linear perspective of the converging lines.
D. Does line A continue to line B or to line C? In the Poggendorff illusion, a line that is partially blocked tends to look displaced on one end.

perceive this line as longer (Pressey & Martin, 1990).

One application of the Müller-Lyer illusion occurs when looking at the corner of a room. When viewing it from within the room, the ceiling and floor lines appear to flair out forming a "v" shape, giving the illusion of a taller wall. When viewing the corner from outside the room, the ceiling and floor lines appear to form the shape of arrowheads, giving the illusion of a shorter wall.

Ponzo Illusion   Another well-known illusion is the Ponzo illusion. Here the two converging vertical lines are likely to be interpreted as two parallel lines receding into the distance, much as railroad tracks might. The two horizontal lines are of equal length, but because of linear perspective, we tend to perceive the top line as longer since the background (the converging lines) makes it appear farther away from us.

Poggendorff Illusion   The Poggendorff illusion involves both physical and cognitive factors (Coren & Porac, 1987). Look at a straw in a glass of water. As the straw emerges from the water, it looks as if it is bent. The Poggendorff illusion is found in a variety of everyday situations. For example, if the middle part of a pencil is covered by an index card, one end of the pencil might look displaced, or if the architectural lines of a building are partially blocked from view by its pillars or columns, the lines might not appear to match up perfectly. The Poggendorff illusion is not always seen, since the principle of continuity often allows us to compensate.

The Moon Illusion   When we look at the moon on the horizon, it looks larger than it does when it is high in the sky. Although many explanations have been suggested for the moon illusion, probably the best is the 1962 theory by Kaufman and Rock. They propose that when we view the moon on the horizon, we compare it to the objects on the terrain, such as houses, trees, and telephone poles. Next to these, it is large. But in the sky, what do we compare it to? Since there are no familiar objects in the sky to compare to the moon, it appears smaller. The moon is actually the same size in both cases. Try this: in a sheet of paper, cut a hole just large enough through which to see the moon on the horizon. Later on, when the moon is higher in the sky, look at it through the same hole. In both cases, the view of the moon will fit the same-sized hole.

HEARING

The stimuli that affect our sense of hearing are sound waves. These are rapid changes in air pressure caused by a vibrating object, such as vocal cords or a guitar string, in contact with the air. Sound waves in the air are similar to ripples on the water caused by a pebble dropped into a still pond. One cycle of a sound wave includes a peak of highest pressure and a valley of lowest pressure.

Sound waves vary in three ways, each with a distinct sensory effect: frequency, amplitude, timbre. They vary in frequency, that is, the number of cycles of sound pressure per second measured in hertz (Hz), which

FIGURE 4.25 Sound Decibel Scale

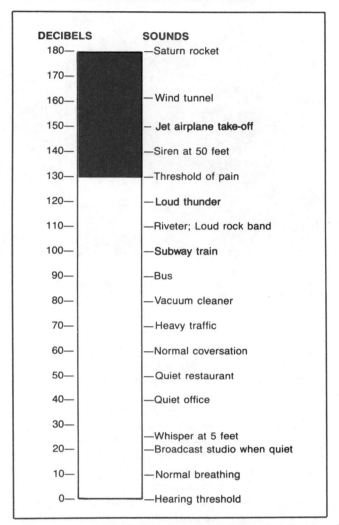

DECIBELS	SOUNDS
180—	—Saturn rocket
170—	
160—	—Wind tunnel
150—	—Jet airplane take-off
140—	—Siren at 50 feet
130—	—Threshold of pain
120—	—Loud thunder
110—	—Riveter; Loud rock band
100—	—Subway train
90—	—Bus
80—	—Vacuum cleaner
70—	—Heavy traffic
60—	—Normal coversation
50—	—Quiet restaurant
40—	—Quiet office
30—	
20—	—Whisper at 5 feet —Broadcast studio when quiet
10—	—Normal breathing
0—	—Hearing threshold

Loudness of a sound is measured in decibels. The threshold of hearing is defined as zero decibels. Some common sounds have intensities above the threshold of pain. Perceived loudness increases geometrically with decibels; for a 10-decibel increase, the perceived loudness doubles.

determines their pitch. The young healthy ear can hear sounds from 20 Hz to 20,000 Hz. High-pitched sounds are the result of a rapid frequency of vibration, while low frequency produces low-pitched sounds.

Sound waves also differ in amplitude, or intensity, which determines a sound's loudness. Amplitude is the height of the sound wave peak. High amplitude creates loud sounds, while low amplitude produces soft sounds. Loudness is usually measured in decibels (dB). As shown in Figure 4.25, normal conversation is about 60 dB, while a rock band can be about 110 dB. Sound above 130 dB is usually painful. You are probably aware that deafness may be caused by listening to very loud music for too long.

The complexity of the mixture of sound waves determines a sound's distinctive timbre. Two people talking at the same level of amplitude and frequency sound different because each voice has its characteristic timbre. The most complex pattern of sound waves we hear is *white noise*, such as the roar of the surf or the hum of an air conditioner, where all the frequencies are jumbled together. The simplest sound is a single pure tone, like that produced by a tuning fork.

The Ear

Sound waves are first received by the pinna of the *outer ear*, which "collects" them and directs them into the auditory canal. The waves then hit the eardrum or tympanic membrane, stretched across the inner end of the auditory canal, and cause it to vibrate. The three bones of the middle ear (called the *hammer*, the *anvil*, and the *stirrup*), carry these vibrations to the cochlea, a spiraled organ in the inner ear that looks something like a snail. Sound vibrations entering the cochlea create waves in the fluid it contains. These waves cause a delicate partition, the basilar membrane, to change its shape. Low frequencies cause an indentation in the basilar membrane near the base of the cochlea, and high frequencies an indentation near the other end at the top of the spiraled cochlea.

FIGURE 4.26 The Human Ear

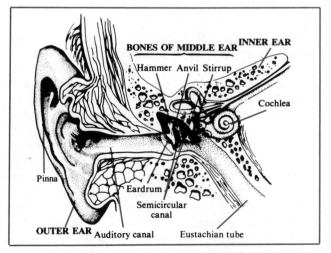

The ear is divided into three major components, the outer ear, middle ear, and the inner ear. The outer ear collects sound waves and transmits them to the bones of the middle ear. There they are amplified and received by the cochlea in the inner ear, which vibrates and moves sound waves from the organ of Corti through the auditory nerve to the temporal lobes of the brain. The utricle and saccule in the inner ear contribute to the vestibular sense.

When the basilar membrane is deformed by a traveling sound wave, the organ of Corti is also displaced. This organ contains the auditory receptors, a collection of hair cells. Above it is the *tectorial membrane*. The fluid in the cochlea pushes the basilar membrane up so that the hair cells brush against the tectorial membrane. This action triggers neural impulses in the auditory nerve that carry messages up to the *temporal lobes* of the brain.

Hearing Processes

The process of audition is nearly as remarkable as the process of vision. We can determine sounds as faint as the gentle wind rustling the branches of a blue spruce or as loud as a rock band in concert. We can recognize the individual voices of our friends and acquaintances. The physics of sound waves, namely frequency, amplitude, and timbre, and the biological structure of the ear are well understood. However, the process of transmitting and understanding sound impulses has not yet been completely explained.

Theories of Hearing   The two basic theories of the process of hearing are the frequency and place theories.

The frequency theory of hearing (first proposed by Rutherford in 1886) states that the frequency of vibrations at the basilar membrane determines the frequency of firing of neurons that carry impulses to the brain. The problem with this theory is that nerves cannot fire as fast and continuously as the frequency of many sound waves. Therefore, the *volley principle* was proposed by Wever (1949). This states that individual neurons fire in sequence, thus increasing the total frequency of impulses it is possible to send to the brain.

Hermann von Helmholtz (the same person who developed the trichromatic theory of vision) proposed the place theory of hearing in 1863. Helmholtz suggested that the sensation of pitch is determined by the place on the basilar membrane that is stimulated. The nerves attached to the basilar membrane are sensitive to different frequencies and send out different impulses from different locations. More recently, Georg von Békésy (1960) expanded the place theory by suggesting the *traveling wave principle*, which states that sound waves traveling through the cochlea move the basilar membrane at a location that vibrates at the particular pitch. There are problems with both the frequency and place theories of hearing, and further research will be needed to unravel some of these questions.

Hearing Impairment   There are two basic types of deafness: conduction deafness and nerve deafness.

FIGURE 4.27   Noise
Exposure to noise or any loud sound over a long period of time can result in hearing loss.

The former usually involves problems with structures in the outer or middle ear; the latter is a more serious condition resulting from damage to the inner ear or auditory nerve.

How many times have you been told not to put anything smaller than your elbow into your ear? My grandmother would always tell us that, and I found it pretty funny until I discovered that a ruptured eardrum can cause a loss of hearing called conduction deafness. Conduction deafness results from a structure in the outer or middle ear not functioning properly. This type of deafness can be congenital (from birth), or it may be caused by damage to the ear from an injury or infection. Temporary conduction deafness could result from a head cold or a buildup of wax. Fortunately, many people with conduction deafness can be helped with a hearing device that helps conduct sounds to the inner ear, where they can be transformed into nerve impulses and sent to the brain.

A more severe problem occurs when the inner ear or auditory nerve is damaged or missing. Nerve deafness could result in the loss of ability to hear high-frequency sounds, or in the total loss of hearing. Often nothing can be done when nerve deafness occurs, since a hearing aid cannot make a nonexistent neuron fire. Prolonged exposure to extremely loud noises, such as factory noise or very loud rock music, can cause nerve deafness. The aging process or excessive reliance on certain drugs may also contribute to this problem. Zimbardo and his colleagues (1981) suggested that hearing loss could sometimes lead to paranoid behavior, especially if the person were unaware of the loss. If you cannot hear what others are saying, you might think they are whispering behind your back and thus become suspicious of everyone.

Auditory Perception

Earlier we learned that auditory information is carried from the ears through the auditory nerves to the brain, where it is interpreted. Each ear is connected with the brain through a separate auditory nerve. Thus, sound received only by the left ear is carried only to the left side of the brain. Sound delivered only to one ear is referred to as monaural.

The higher brain auditory centers are designed to process binaural information from both ears. We use binaural cues to help us judge the location of a sound source. Sound that reaches one ear slightly before the other ear serves as a cue for the location of the sound. For instance, if a friend who is standing to your left calls your name, you will hear it first in your left ear and then in your right ear. In addition, your friend's voice will appear slightly louder in your left ear, providing another binaural cue for localization. Often we are unaware that there is a difference, but we respond appropriately by turning toward the sound source.

Auditory information travels from the cochlea through the auditory nerve to the thalamus before reaching the auditory cortex in the temporal lobes of the brain. Next to the auditory cortex is a part of the temporal lobe known as the Wernicke's area, which is important in speech perception. Damage to the Wernicke's area leads to aphasia, a disorder in which a person loses the ability to understand speech. In most right-handed people, the Wernicke's area is located in the left hemisphere.

THE CHEMICAL SENSES

The senses of smell and taste are sometimes called the chemical senses because the sensory stimulation of the receptors involves contact with chemical substances in liquid or gaseous form. We know less about these senses than we do about vision or hearing, although the general processes for all of these senses are similar: a stimulus excites a receptor cell, and the energy is transformed into neural impulses and sent to the brain.

Smell

The sense receptors for smell, or olfaction, are located high in the nasal passages leading from the nose to the throat. Vapors interact chemically with the cilia of the olfactory epithelium to produce the neural impulses

FIGURE 4.28   Cross Section of a Nasal Passage

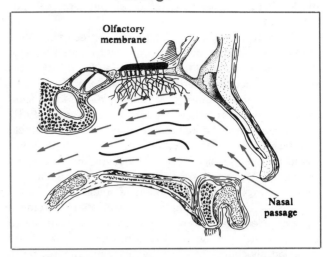

Odors enter the nasal passage and stimulate nerve endings in the olfactory membrane, the receptors for smell. The messages then travel to the olfactory bulbs of the brain.

that go to the olfactory bulbs of the brain to be interpreted and acted upon. Olfaction is dissimilar to the other senses in that the qualities smelled cannot clearly be broken down into distinct physical properties. Some research indicates that there may be seven basic forms of molecules that produce seven basic smells, which then combine to form various complex smells. The description of

FIGURE 4.29   Identifying Odors
People are able to identify a wide variety of odors easily. Researchers are attempting to discover seven basic molecules that produce basic smells. This basic list, however, has yet to be scientifically verified.

basic smells has not been definitely established, but according to Amoore (1970), it includes: camphoraceous, musky, floral, pepperminty, ethereal, pungent, and putrid odors.

One theory of smell is that the odor receptors have "holes" the same shape as the odor molecules. The odor molecules fit into the "holes" like a key fits a lock. This theory is called the stereochemical theory of olfactory coding (Amoore, Johnston, & Rubin, 1964). More recent research by Susan Schiffman and her colleagues (1981) does not support the key-and-lock explanation of smell. She tested molecular shapes of various substances and found no relationship between the shape and the odors produced. At present, psychologists do not have a theory that fully explains the perception of smell.

As we discuss in chapter 9, "Motivation," chemical signals, called pheromones, are used by some animals to communicate by olfaction. Very little research has been done on olfaction and social behavior in humans, but a study by Baron in 1981 suggests that perfume does have an effect on the perceptions of males toward the attractiveness of females. Research by Richard Doty and his colleagues (1982) has shown that both males and females can identify the gender of a person breathing through a hole in a wall (although females are better at it). Humans have the potential to utilize odors in social interactions, although it is not known to what extent they actually do.

Taste

The sense receptors for taste, or gustation, are located in our tongues. The surface of the tongue is covered with little bumps, called papillae. The walls of the papillae contain the taste buds, the actual taste receptors. Substances tasted must be soluble (able to be dissolved in liquid), so that they can penetrate the taste pores or spaces between papillae to get through to the taste buds. Anything that is absolutely dry and solid is tasteless, although our own saliva contributes to making certain "dry" foods tasty.

Despite some debate, most researchers agree that we are sensitive to four distinct tastes: sweet, sour, salty, and bitter (Erickson, 1985). We are the most sensitive to bitter, next to sour, then salty, and the least sensitive to sweet tastes. Early research suggested that taste quality depended upon the location of stimulation on the tongue. More recent research tends to support the cross fiber theory of taste, which proposes that taste quality is coded neurally by the firing pattern of receptor cells. The sensory information of taste is interpreted in the parietal cortex of the brain.

New taste buds quickly replace those killed by scalding hot cups of coffee or red-hot chili. In fact, they renew themselves completely about every 10 days. Infants have few taste buds, but the number increases to about 10,000 by the time we are adults. As we grow older, we gradually lose taste buds, which explains why older people are generally less sensitive to tastes than are young children (Cowart, 1989).

The flavor of particular foods we eat or the way we taste them is due to their smell, appearance, texture, and temperature as well as our sensitivity to taste. With the nostrils pinched tight, we often cannot tell the difference between mashed squash and mashed potatoes or between strawberry and vanilla ice cream. When we have a congested nose, food often does not taste right to us,

FIGURE 4.30 Taste Receptors

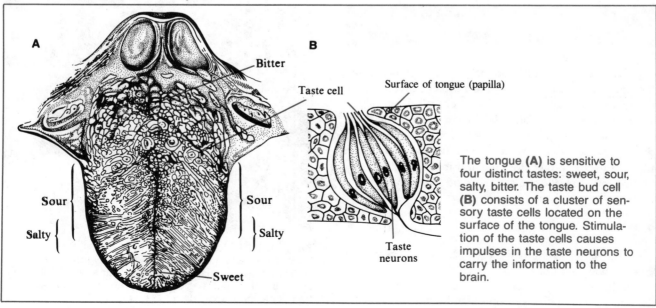

The tongue **(A)** is sensitive to four distinct tastes: sweet, sour, salty, bitter. The taste bud cell **(B)** consists of a cluster of sensory taste cells located on the surface of the tongue. Stimulation of the taste cells causes impulses in the taste neurons to carry the information to the brain.

again because we don't smell it. Appearance, texture, and temperature affect our sense of taste. Would we eat green eggs or pink mashed potatoes? Do we enjoy cold french fries as much as sizzling hot ones? Taste performs an important biological function in fueling the body, since it makes eating a very pleasurable experience. (In chapter 6, "Learning," we discuss an instance when eating is not pleasant, called conditioned taste aversion.)

THE SKIN AND BODY SENSES

We have six additional senses that provide us with valuable information. The four skin senses include pressure, pain, warmth, and cold. These sense receptors are located throughout the body under the skin and provide information about the environment. We also have two proprioceptive senses: kinesthesis, which is the sense of bodily movement that keeps us informed of the movement of various parts of the body; and the vestibular sense, which helps us maintain body balance.

Pressure, or touch, is detected by receptors located throughout the body just under the surface of the skin. Some parts of the body are more sensitive to pressure than others. For example, the belly, back, and face are very sensitive to light pressure, whereas the feet, lower legs, thighs, and fingers are much less sensitive (Weinstein, 1968).

A number of different kinds of receptors have been identified in the skin, including *free nerve endings, Pacinian corpuscles, Ruffini endings, Meissner's corpuscles, Merkel's discs,* and *hair nerve endings.* At one time it was thought that each of the skin senses had its own type of receptor. For instance, the Pacinian corpuscle is designed to detect pressure and the hair nerve endings can detect hair movement caused by light pressure. However, there is not a one-to-one correspondence between all sensations and the various skin receptors.

Our sense of touch, or our haptic sense, is important in helping us keep aware of stimuli in the environment. Susan Lederman and Roberta Klatzky (1990) recently examined how we use touch to manipulate and classify common objects. They found that the college students who served as subjects went through a two-stage process in haptic exploration. First the subjects used a general grasping and lifting procedure. Then they began detailed touching to identify and classify the objects. We often use the haptic sense to help us perceive the shape, size, texture, and location of objects in our environment.

Pain

Pain has always been of particular interest to both psychologists and medical scientists. The free nerve end-

FIGURE 4.31 Skin Senses

A graphic representation of a section of skin showing the various structures involved with the sensations of pressure, pain, warmth, and cold. The free nerve endings are sensitive to pressure. Meissner's corpuscles detect texture and movement on the skin. Merkel's discs keep us aware of objects. Ruffini endings and Pacinian corpuscles are located deeper in the skin and are sensitive to heavy pressure.

ings mentioned above are believed to be the receptors for pain. It is possible that the pain receptors utilize histamine as their neurotransmitter. (Histamine is the substance responsible for the misery of allergy sufferers.)

Gate-Control Theory   The current theory of how pain sensations operate is the gate-control theory of pain, first proposed by Melzack and Wall in 1965. An area of the spinal cord called the substantia gelatinosa acts as a gate that regulates the level of neural impulse transmission from the free nerve endings to transmission cells in the spinal cord. There are two types of neural fibers that interact at the substantia gelatinosa—large fast ones and small slow ones. When the neural impulses in the fast

FIGURE 4.32   Gate-Control Theory of Pain

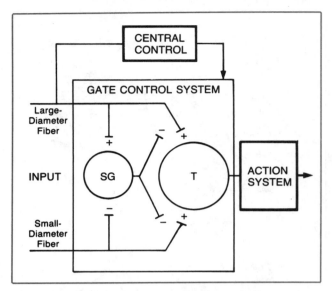

Melzack's gate-control theory argues that the fast large-diameter fibers in the substantia gelatinosa (SG) regulate the level of neural transmission (T) in the spinal cord like a gate by preventing the slow small-diameter fibers that open the gate from sending pain messages to the brain. In the diagram, + indicates closing the gate (inhibiting pain messages) and − indicates opening the gate (facilitating pain messages) reaching the brain (after Melzack & Wall, 1965).

fibers reach the "gate," they tend to close it and prevent the slower pain signals from reaching the brain. As slower fiber impulses are transmitted, they open the gate and allow more pain signals to reach the thalamus in the brain.

This would explain how we are able to distinguish between minor discomforts and major pain. In minor pain, the fast fibers are more active, allowing fewer pain signals to reach the brain. It could also dispel the mystery in the perplexing cases of phantom-limb pain, in which people who have lost an arm or a leg still feel pain in the missing limb. The theory demonstrates that what the neurons of the spinal cord allow to be transmitted to the brain is more significant than the actual sensations at the site of pain reception.

Endorphins and Pain   By identifying the mechanism of pain transmission, the spinal gate-control theory gives promise of new therapies for pain reduction. During the past decade, great advances have been made in our understanding of the endorphins, peptides produced in the brain that have a morphine-like effect on the reduction of pain. There are several types of endorphins, including leu-enkephalin and met-enkephalin. Frederickson and Geary (1982) proposed a theory in which the periaqueductal gray (PAG) area of the brainstem pro-

duces endorphins that inhibit the neurons in the spinal cord from transmitting pain. Recent research also suggests that intense stress (such as an emergency) can cause the release of beta-endorphin, a hormone that travels through the cerebrospinal fluid and could inhibit pain through the PAG circuit. This could be the mechanism that allows an injured person to conduct heroic acts without feeling pain at the time of injury (Nichols & Thorn, 1990).

Acupuncture   The gate-control theory may provide possible insights into the ancient Oriental art of acupuncture and why it may be successful in controlling pain. Through centuries of practice and tradition, practitioners of acupuncture may have discovered the areas of the body where needles can be inserted and somehow cause the pain-control gates to close. It is currently believed that acupuncture can stimulate the production of endorphins in the brain, which in turn inhibit the pain-carrying neurons of the spinal cord (He, 1987).

Temperature

Scientists believe that there are two kinds of temperature receptors in the skin (one for warmth and one for cold), but they have not been able to identify which types of skin receptors are responsible for temperature (Hensel, 1982). The skin has spots about 1 mm in diameter that respond to either warm or cold stimuli. Warmth receptors are maximally sensitive to tempera-

FIGURE 4.33   Acupuncture
The ancient Oriental art of acupuncture stimulates the body's natural painkilling substances, the endorphins. The insertion of needles in particular areas of the body may work to block pain by using the gate-control theory.

tures slightly above normal skin temperature, whereas cold receptors respond maximally to temperatures just below normal skin temperature.

An intriguing finding is that there apparently are no specific receptors that respond only to hot temperatures. Sherrick and Cholewiak (1986) pointed out that when stimuli have temperatures of about 45° C (112° F), they sometimes feel cold, a phenomena called <u>paradoxical cold</u>. For example, you might turn on a hot shower and at first touch it appears cold. After a couple of seconds, however, it feels hot. Hensel (1982) pointed out that the warmth receptors stop functioning at about 45° C and the cold receptors, along with the receptors for pain, begin to function. Thus the sensation of hot might be due to the simultaneous firing of cold and pain receptors. Remember this the next time you get into a hot shower.

Skin sensitivity to temperature varies throughout the body (Stevens, 1979). The forehead is most sensitive to warmth, followed by the chest, stomach, shoulder, and arms. The chest is most sensitive to cold, followed by the arms, legs, and foreheads. People usually find an air temperature of about 22° C (72° F) as most comfortable. Hancock (1986) found that performance on a variety of tasks decreased significantly at temperatures above 29° C (85° F). Temperature can affect the way you feel and act.

Your body has the ability to maintain a normal skin temperature of 33° C, which keeps the normal internal body temperature at 37° C (98.6° F). When you begin to get cold, you shiver and the skin's blood vessels constrict so you lose less heat. Likewise, when you become too warm you sweat and the skin's blood vessels dilate to release body heat. The ability to regulate temperature is important to survival, since without maintaining normal body temperature we could not effectively function.

Kinesthesis

The sense of bodily movement, or <u>kinesthesis</u>, tells us what various parts of our bodies are doing. The kinesthetic sense enables us to know whether our foot is pointed, our stomach full, our fist clenched, or our neck tense. We use information from our kinesthetic senses to coordinate our movements. The receptors (Golgi tendon organs) are located in the tendons connecting muscles to bones, and in the linings of the joints. They are activated when muscles are stretched or contracted (Clark & Horch, 1986). These receptors are generally slow to adapt and continue to provide information over long periods of time. The sense of kinesthesis is obviously extremely valuable in everyday behaviors, such as walking, reaching, and sitting.

The Vestibular Sense

The other important proprioceptive sense is that of equilibrium or the <u>vestibular sense</u>, which helps us keep our balance, orient properly to gravity, and tell when we are being moved. For example, without seeing motion we know when an elevator starts and stops. Without this sense, we would not be able to maintain our balance as consistently as we do, or automatically adjust to "right" ourselves when thrown off balance. When we are constantly in motion, such as on a boat or in a car, the

FIGURE 4.34 Vestibular System
The semicircular canals in the inner ear help us maintain a sense of balance both in everyday life and in specialized circumstances such as ice skating, tightrope walking, and space flight.

vestibular sense is upset and we may experience motion sickness. The sense of equilibrium is different from all the other senses, because we are seldom even aware that the vestibular sense is in operation.

Hair cells in the semicircular canals of the inner ear (see Figure 4.26) are the receptors for the vestibular sense. The canals are filled with a fluid that moves when the head moves, and causes the hairs projecting from the receptors to bend, triggering nerve impulses to the brain signaling the need for reflex adjustment of the eyes and body (Coren & Ward, 1989).

Additional receptors for the vestibular sense are located in the *utricle* and *saccule* inside the inner ear. Here the hair cells form a mass and contain small solid crystals that exert gravitational pressure on these cells. Any change in this pressure "tells" the brain that we are not upright. In a weightless condition, like that of the astronauts in space, the lack of gravity affects the shape of these hairs. ■

As illustrated in our opening story, sensation and perception are essential for survival. Without sensation, we would have no idea of what the internal or external environments are like. The sensations that are received by the sense organs and sent to the brain are interpreted by a nervous system that is actively involved in the process of perception. An understanding of the processes of sensation and perception will help us understand other areas of psychology. Learning, memory, motivation, and social interaction all require that we receive and interpret environmental information. In the next chapter, we review consciousness, the awareness of the perceptions we experience.

Reprinted by permission of *Saturday Review/World* and Junco.

CHAPTER REVIEW

What You've Learned About Sensation and Perception

1. Sensation is the process through which stimuli are received by sense receptors and transformed into neural impulses that can be carried through the nervous system. Perception is the process in which the sensory information is organized and interpreted in the brain.

2. Transduction is the process of changing the stimulus energy from the environment into neural impulses that travel through the nervous system. Sensory adaptation is the tendency of the sense organs to adjust to continuous unchanging stimulation by reducing their functioning.

3. The absolute threshold is the minimum amount of physical energy required to produce a sensation. The difference threshold (or JND) is the minimum amount of physical energy change required to produce a difference in sensation.

4. The eye includes a cornea, pupil, lens, and retina. The rods in the retina are for dim light vision, whereas color vision is made possible by the cones.

5. The trichromatic theory of color vision proposes that cones are most sensitive to one of three different colors: red, green, or blue. The opponent-process theory states that cones are sensitive to pairs of complementary colors: red-green, blue-yellow, and black-white.

6. Perceptual constancy is the tendency to perceive objects in a consistent manner, despite the changing sensations that are received by our sense organs. Four types of visual constancy are brightness constancy, color constancy, shape constancy, and size constancy.

7. In the figure-ground relationship, we identify a dominant figure and an ambiguous background. Closure involves filling in the gaps to perceive a complete form. Continuity involves perceiving a line as continuing. Similarity involves perceiving similar stimuli as a unit. Proximity is the principle in which stimuli next to one another are grouped together. Common fate involves grouping together stimuli that are moving together.

8. Depth perception is the ability to judge the distance to an object. We use monocular, or one-eye, cues such as interposition, size perspective, linear perspective, texture gradient, aerial perspective, and motion parallax to help determine depth. We also use binocular, or two-eye, cues such as retinal disparity and convergence in determining depth perception.

9. Apparent motion occurs when we perceive movement when in fact there is none. Induced motion occurs when we attribute movement to a figure rather than the ground. The phi phenomenon occurs when two lights are alternately turned on and off in a dark room. Stroboscopic motion occurs when a series of still pictures are shown in rapid succession, creating smooth motion. The autokinetic effect occurs when we look at a single spot of light in a dark room and see it move.

10. An illusion is an incorrect perception that occurs when sensation is distorted. Some of the better-known visual illusions include: impossible figures, reversible figures, the Müller-Lyer illusion, the Ponzo illusion, the Poggendorff illusion, and the moon illusion.

11. The stimuli that affect our sense of hearing are sound waves that cause the eardrum to vibrate. The vibrations are carried to the cochlea, where they cause the basilar membrane to change shape. This stimulates the organ of Corti, which contains the auditory neural receptors.

12. The frequency theory proposes that the neuronal firing frequency determines sound. The place theory of hearing states that the sensation of sound is possible because of the particular place the sound waves hit in the ear.

13. Sound delivered to one ear is called monaural, whereas sound delivered to both ears is called binaural. Binaural sound that reaches one ear slightly before the other or is slightly louder in one ear serves as a cue for the location of the sound.

14. Smell and taste are called the chemical senses. The receptors for smell, or olfaction, are located high in the nasal passages leading from the nose to the throat. The stereochemical theory argues that odor receptors have holes that odor molecules fit into.

15. The taste receptors in our tongues are sensitive to four qualities: sweet, sour, salty, and bitter. It is suspected that taste qualities are coded neurally by the firing pattern of the receptor cells.

16. The somesthetic, or skin senses, include pressure, pain, cold, and warmth. Pressure, or touch, is detected by at least six types of receptors located throughout the body in the skin.

17. The gate-control theory of pain states that fast fibers inhibit and slow fibers facilitate a gate that allows pain to be transmitted through the spinal cord. Endorphins are brain peptides that have a morphine-like effect on the reduction of pain.

18. Cold receptors are responsible for the sensation of cold, whereas warm receptors are responsible for the sensation of warmth. The sensation of hot may be due to the simultaneous responding of the cold and pain receptors.

19. The sense of bodily movement, or kinesthesis, tells us what various parts of our body are doing, and we use this information to coordinate our movements. The vestibular sense helps us keep our balance and causes us to be properly oriented to gravity.

CHAPTER OBJECTIVES

What You'll Learn About Sleep and Consciousness

After studying this chapter, you should be able to:

1. Define consciousness.
2. Describe the two basic types of sleep (REM and NREM).
3. Outline the theories of the physiology and function of sleep.
4. Identify the topics that people dream about.
5. Identify four sleep disorders.
6. Define the concept of psychoactive drugs.
7. Describe the depressant drugs.
8. Identify the opiate drugs.
9. Describe the stimulant drugs.
10. Describe the psychedelic drugs.
11. Describe the techniques and uses of hypnosis.
12. Describe the effects of meditation.
13. Describe the effects of sensory deprivation/REST.

Why do we sleep? Poets and philosophers have pondered this question for centuries, and recently psychologists and other sleep researchers have provided partial answers. In 1975 Wilse Webb reported the results of a study he conducted in which people were deprived of normal sleep. He was trying to determine the effects of sleep loss on physiological processes, mental activities, and behavior. The different ways that people react to being deprived of sleep give us clues to the role sleep normally plays in everyday life.

The subjects in Webb's study were required to stay awake continuously for 51 hours from 8 A.M. the first day until 11 P.M. the third day. There were two nights in the experiment, and during one of these, subjects were to lie in bed but remain awake. During the other night the subjects remained active by using an exercise bicycle at regular intervals.

The experimenters monitored a variety of physiological measurements, including body temperature, heart rate, and brain-wave patterns. During the normal waking hours, the subjects were given a variety of tasks to complete, such as listening to a tone signal, taking tests, and playing card games.

During the first night, everyone was able to stay awake easily. Some subjects became sleepy in the early hours of morning, but were able to fight off the urge to sleep. They all remained cheerful and appeared to enjoy the experience.

By the second night, however, their moods began to change. They had trouble staying awake and, as soon as the experimenter left the room, they would try to doze off; the experimenter had to shake them to keep them awake. They became irritable and emotionally apathetic. They had trouble focusing attention on a task; they acted almost mechanically. Staying awake became a chore.

Consciousness has long been an area of interest for psychologists. Much of the research has been conducted on altered states of consciousness, such as sleep, hypnosis, and meditation. The information learned about sleep and dreaming has practical consequences. And practical, too, is the study of the effects of drugs on behavior.

5

Sleep and Consciousness

On the third day, most subjects were overcome with an urge to sleep. Many fell asleep during an activity in which they had to monitor a tone signal for a brief period of time; their mood was serious and their behavior very apathetic. When they did not have a specific activity, they would fall asleep and then deny it when they were awoken by the experimenters.

Webb reported that there were many individual variations among the subjects, but most reacted in a similar fashion. They preferred the scheduled exercise program and had real problems during the night that they were required to stay awake while lying in bed.

Webb pointed out that while the need for sleep was very strong, he did not observe any truly bizarre behaviors in these subjects. They did not have long attention spans and became extremely irritable, but they were still able to function fairly normally.

In his report, Webb also described some of the typical reactions in other sleep deprivation studies. In some cases, subjects have shown delusions about the experiment, such as thinking the experimenters were plotting against them or that the experiment was a joke. Many subjects typically have shown confusion, problems in attention, irritability, and apathy.

Sleep deprivation has some effect on performance, although less than what might be expected. Complex tasks that require constant attention tend to give subjects the most difficulty. On the other hand, short-term tasks are not greatly affected by sleep loss, especially if the subjects are motivated to do their best. Short-term memory tasks are sometimes adversely affected.

Webb also pointed out some physiological changes associated with prolonged sleep deprivation. Subjects tend to develop hand tremors, have difficulty focusing, and have an increased sensitivity to pain. Overall, autonomic nervous system activity is not greatly affected by sleep deprivation until the sleep loss is extended for more than 5 days. After reviewing the results of his own study as well as other studies of sleep deprivation, Webb concluded that while sleep is necessary for human survival, people are able to live without it for several days.

FIGURE 5.1 Dream Research
This subject is participating in dream research in a sleep laboratory at Stanford University. When his eye movements indicate that he is dreaming, the goggles flash a red light in an effort to make him conscious of his dreams while he is asleep.

WHAT IS CONSCIOUSNESS?

Webb's study of sleep deprivation is important because it demonstrates an approach to understanding this area of psychology. We all realize the importance of sleep, and yet there are many things we don't understand about its specific functions. Sleep is considered one of the altered states of consciousness we experience. Although we know what it is like to be conscious of events, ideas, time, feelings, and the world around us, trying to define consciousness is surprisingly difficult. One definition provided by Wallace and Fisher (1991) states that consciousness is the processing of information at various levels of awareness. Most definitions stress an awareness of the sensations, thoughts, and feelings that we experience.

Although philosophers have debated the nature of consciousness for hundreds of years, the modern study of the psychology of consciousness can be traced to William James, who defined consciousness as the capacity to be aware of experience and knowledge (James, 1904). In his book, *Principles of Psychology*, published in 1890, James described four major characteristics of consciousness. First, every thought is part of an individual's personal consciousness. Second, consciousness is always changing. Third, consciousness is a continuous process that cannot be broken down into segments. And fourth, consciousness selects from its environment what it will be aware of. Thus, according to James, who compared consciousness to a flowing river, our "stream of consciousness" is private, changing, continuous, and selective.

As we discuss in chapter 11, "Personality," Sigmund Freud (1900) suggested that the structure of personality includes three levels of conscious awareness. The conscious mind is what we are aware of in everyday life. The preconscious mind is where we store information we have learned. And the unconscious mind is where material is kept that is not readily available to us (such as fears and unpleasant memories).

Most introductory psychology textbooks around the turn of the century defined psychology as the study of consciousness. But then in 1919 John Watson, the founder of the school of behaviorism, effectively eliminated the study of consciousness from psychology by saying he didn't know what it meant and could get along without it. It has been only with the past few decades that psychologists have begun again to study seriously the different states of consciousness (Webb, 1981).

There are currently various theories on the function of consciousness, all of which focus on awareness. Kihlstrom (1987) suggested that consciousness allows us to pay attention selectively to certain aspects of ourselves and our environment so we can effectively think and carry out our actions. Marcel (1983) stated that con-

FIGURE 5.2 Altered State of Consciousness
People may have a need for altering their states of consciousness through deliberately engaging in exciting activities such as hang gliding, marathon running, or roller coaster riding.

sciousness allows us to pull specific ideas and events into our awareness so that we can analyze them and make decisions about our behavior. Ornstein (1986) argued that because of consciousness we have the ability to think, remember, and reason. One might say that without consciousness, the human race might not have survived.

Psychologists tend to divide the study of consciousness into waking consciousness and altered states of consciousness. The awareness of sensations and thoughts while we are awake and alert is often called waking consciousness (or conscious awareness). Much of psychology studies such aspects of behavior and cognition of the individual in waking consciousness as memory, language, thinking, problem solving, and perception. Kokoszka (1988) states that the ordinary waking state of consciousness tends to involve the left hemisphere of the brain, and is characterized by beta brain waves of alertness.

This chapter focuses on altered states of consciousness (ASC). In an altered state of consciousness, there is a redirection of attention, in which different aspects of the world occupy our thoughts and different stimuli cause us to respond. Charles Tart (1975) stated that an altered state of consciousness occurs when there is a qualitative shift (differentness) in the mental processes rather than just a quantitative shift (alertness). For example, during sleep, except for intense stimuli (the buzz of an alarm), we lose the ability to attend to much of what is going on around us.

Many of our altered states of consciousness are completely normal and occur effortlessly, such as daydreaming, sleep, and dreaming. Andrew Weil (1973) argued that people have an inborn urge to actively alter their states of consciousness occasionally. He pointed out that children around the world spin themselves to become dizzy. And, of course, many of us love those thrilling wild rides at amusement parks.

Other altered states of consciousness are obtained by more deliberate efforts. Hypnosis, meditation, and drug-induced states are voluntary altered states of consciousness that are fairly common experiences around the world. Kokoszka (1988) refers to them as differentiated waking states of consciousness, and reports that they are characterized by less mental activity and more imagery. We review the topics of sleep, drugs, hypnosis, meditation, and sensory deprivation in this chapter.

SLEEP

At about the same time every night, you look at the clock, yawn, and prepare to go to sleep. You lie in bed with the lights off and your eyes closed, waiting for that drowsy feeling to take hold and carry you off into the state in which you will spend the next 8 or so hours.

You spend approximately a third of your life sleeping. For many people, that means about 25 years. Since you sleep more or less regularly every day, you simply take sleeping for granted. Scientists are just now learning some of the many mysteries of sleep and dreaming.

In our opening story, we mentioned some of the effects of the loss of sleep. By studying sleep deprivation, we may be able to get some clues as to the functions of sleep in daily life. Let's begin with some of the measurement techniques used in sleep research.

Research on sleep often is conducted in university sleep laboratories, where variables can be monitored carefully and controlled. The subject lies in a comfortable bed while the experimenter prepares to record electrophysiological measures. Electrodes (recording devices) to measure brain waves are taped to the scalp. The record of brain-wave activity is called an electroencephalogram (EEG). Electrodes are connected also to the face and body to measure variables such as heart rate (EKG), blood pressure, temperature, eye movement (EOG), skeletal muscle activity (EMG), and respiration. Then the subject is told to relax and go to sleep. (Sleeping with all this equipment attached, of course, may take a little practice.)

During the waking state, the EEG shows two basic brain-wave patterns: alpha activity and beta activity. Alpha activity has a frequency of 8-12 Hz and is produced when a person is relaxed and resting quietly with eyes closed. Beta activity has a frequency of 13-30 Hz, and is produced when a person is alert. Resting will produce an alpha EEG, while reading this textbook should produce a beta EEG.

The Two Types of Sleep

The two types of sleep were first labeled in 1953. This was the year that Eugene Aserinsky and Nathaniel Kleitman of the University of Chicago reported that periodically during sleep the eyes moved very rapidly back and forth under the eyelids. This activity, called REM (rapid eye movement), indicated a type of sleep that was very active compared to the other more passive stages of sleep, called NREM (non REM) sleep. Up to this time, most researchers had considered sleep a totally passive phenomenon.

Stages of NREM Sleep   EEGs of the brain show that there are four distinct stages of NREM sleep. Sometimes these stages are collectively referred to as slow-wave or classical sleep, since this is the classical idea of what sleep is like. When we go to bed each night, we pass through each of the four stages of NREM sleep before going into REM sleep. We then pass through several cycles of these sleep stages before waking in the morning. The NREM stages of sleep are called Stages 1, 2, 3, and 4 (Dement & Kleitman, 1957).

Stage 1 is the transition from relaxation to sound sleep. The EEG is characterized by theta activity having a frequency of 4-7 Hz. The sleeper is drowsy and may have visual images that are more like hallucinations than daydreams. He or she can be easily awakened, and can be influenced by outside stimuli such as a ringing telephone. The EEG of Stage 2 also contains theta activity and is characterized by *sleep spindles*, which are brief bursts of 12-14 Hz waves. Stage 2 also contains *K-complexes* that are sharp rises and drops in the EEG. We spend about 50 percent of our sleep in Stage 2. Stage 3 is a transition stage from Stage 2 to Stage 4 in which we spend about 10 percent of our sleep. The EEG of Stage 3 may still contain sleep spindles, but also begins to show delta activity, which has a frequency of 1-3 Hz. The EEG of Stage 4, often called deep sleep, consists of over 50 percent delta activity. We spend approximately 15 percent of our sleep in Stage 4. It is extremely difficult to

FIGURE 5.3   EEG Sleep Patterns

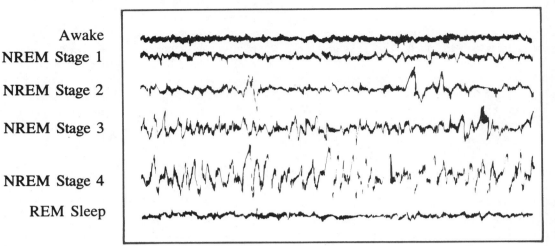

Awake
NREM Stage 1
NREM Stage 2
NREM Stage 3
NREM Stage 4
REM Sleep

Each stage of sleep can be identified by its distinctive EEG pattern. The *alpha* waves of the awake, relaxed state are quite different from the large rhythmic *delta* waves of stage 4. The REM patterns of sleep more nearly resemble the awake patterns; thus, REM sleep may be known as *paradoxical sleep.*

wake someone from Stage 4, and when we do, the person tends to be groggy and does not function fully. As we discuss later, sleep talking, sleepwalking, night terrors, and bed-wetting all occur mostly in Stage 4 sleep.

Certain characteristics are common in NREM sleep. The eyes may move slowly from side to side. The heart rate slows down and blood pressure falls slightly. Breathing is slow and regular (this is when snoring occurs). In general, muscular tension is absent and the sleeper is immobile. Watching the sleeper in NREM sleep, we would conclude that he or she is resting peacefully.

REM Sleep   Rapid-eye-movement sleep is often called dream sleep, active sleep, or paradoxical sleep, because dreaming occurs here and the characteristics of REM sleep are similar to those of the waking state. The eyes move quickly back and forth. The heart rate accelerates, blood pressure rises, breathing becomes variable, and sexual arousal occurs in both sexes (Kiester, 1980). There is peripheral twitching of the face and fingers, but the large muscles of the body are completely paralyzed by the nervous system, so that no overall body movement can take place. In general, the EEG activity is similar to the alert waking state but contains the characteristic "saw-tooth" waves of the EEG sleep patterns. Reviewing these characteristics, we conclude that REM sleep is indeed an active state of sleeping.

REM sleep is regarded as dream sleep, since most dreaming occurs in this stage. William C. Dement compiled the results of a number of studies in 1976 and reported that when subjects were awakened from REM sleep, they could recall dreams up to 83 percent of the time. However, when subjects were awakened from

NREM sleep, they reported dreaming only about 14 percent of the time. Dreams in the REM stage are often vividly recalled, while the few occurring in the NREM stages are often vague and ambiguous.

Time Patterns of Sleep   When we fall asleep, we progress through the various NREM stages to deeper and deeper sleep (Dement, 1976). Stage 1 lasts for a few minutes, followed by several minutes of Stage 2. We are in Stage 3 for about 10 minutes before we enter Stage 4. Forty minutes or so after sleep begins, we go through the stages of NREM sleep in reverse order (Stages 4, 3, and 2).

Approximately an hour and a half after first falling to sleep, we go from Stage 2 to Stage REM (or Stage 1-REM, which now takes the place of Stage 1). The first REM period might last about 10 minutes. This cycle is repeated throughout the night. During the first part of the night, we spend more time in NREM sleep, especially in Stages 3 and 4, but during the last part of the night, we spend much more time in REM sleep, with brief alternations with Stage 2. At the end of the sleep period, we might spend 60 minutes in a final REM sleep period. We usually wake from REM sleep (unless the alarm wakes us first).

Although there are wide variations, sleep researchers have found that most people show a common pattern of sleeping over their lifetimes (Roffwarg, Muzio, & Dement, 1966). The neonate sleeps up to 16 hours a day, usually in relatively short sessions distributed across the 24 hours. In the first year, nighttime sleep with several day naps becomes the norm. Between the ages of 2 and 5, children sleep about 11 hours per day, including an hour of daytime napping. Between 6 and 16 years old, the

FIGURE 5.4   Sequence of Sleep Stages

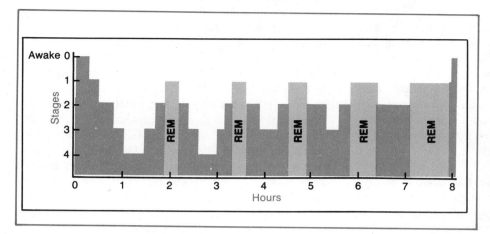

This figure shows the sequence of sleep stages for a typical night. Note that early in the night, more time is spent in Stage 4, whereas later in the night more time is spent in REM sleep. We wake naturally from this stage of sleep (after Dement, 1976).

total sleep time goes from an average of 11 to about 8 hours per night and remains at about 8 hours during most of adulthood.

As people age, they tend to have more difficulty sleeping. Webb (1975) reported that in a group of 60-year-olds the number of awakenings during the night increased significantly when compared to a group of 30-year-olds. The older group took longer to fall to sleep, woke spontaneously more often at night, and had less overall "quality" sleep. The majority of the older people also took naps during the day. Recent research suggests that women tend to be more resistant to age changes in sleep patterns than do men (Rediehs, Reis, & Creason, 1990).

In general, adults have about five REM periods each

night and spend up to 2 hours in REM sleep. This represents about 25 percent of their total sleep time. Newborn infants spend approximately 50 percent of their sleep time in REM. This drops to about 30 percent by age 2, and levels out at about 25 percent by about age 10. The level of REM sleep remains fairly constant until old age, when it declines very slightly.

Stage 4 constitutes about 18 percent of a 10-year-old's sleep, and this percentage remains constant until the early thirties, when it begins to decline. Individuals over the age of 50 may have very little Stage 4 sleep (Kelly, 1981). This helps to explain the increase in spontaneous wakings in older individuals, who often become light sleepers. Stage 2 sleep remains fairly constant across the life span.

BIOGRAPHICAL HIGHLIGHT

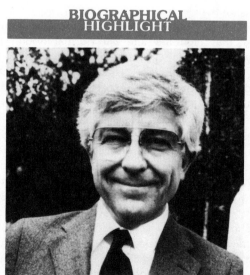

WILLIAM C. DEMENT

William C. Dement was born in 1928 in Wenatchee, Washington. He decided on a career in medicine and, as a second year medical student, was working in Nathaniel Kleitman's sleep research laboratory at the University of Chicago in 1953, when rapid eye movements were discovered. Dement first used the term REM, which is now standard nomenclature in sleep research.

William Dement earned his M.D. degree from the University of Chicago in 1955, and his Ph.D. degree in physiology in 1957. In 1963 he established the sleep laboratory at Stanford University, and in 1970 he established the Stanford University Sleep Disorders Clinic. Dement started the publication *Sleep Reviews*, and has written hundreds of scientific papers on sleep and dreaming.

Currently, Dement is professor of psychiatry at the Stanford University Medical School. As director of the sleep laboratory, he is busy researching the problems that plague millions of people when they sleep. He has contributed significantly to our knowledge of the altered state of consciousness in which we spend a third of our lives.

Theories of Sleep

Acquiring knowledge of how the brain controls sleep and developing theories about the functions of sleep has been a very slow process. Partially, this is because it is difficult to study the brain while it is functioning. The mechanisms involved are much more complicated than early researchers believed. Although we now have an idea of sleep's functions and of how the brain influences some aspects of sleep, there are many gaps that need to be filled in by sleep researchers.

Physiology Michel Jouvet has been a leading researcher in the field of neural sleep control. In 1967 Jouvet reported that NREM sleep seemed to be influenced by an area in the brain stem known as the raphe nucleus. Electrical stimulation of this area usually causes sleep, while lesions tend to eliminate sleep. Jouvet proposed that the raphe nucleus influences NREM sleep by producing the neurotransmitter serotonin (see chapter 2, "Psychobiology"), which inhibits the activity of the reticular activating system (which normally causes alertness during waking periods). While other brain systems are also involved in neural sleep control, Jouvet's theory appears useful in directing future sleep research.

The research on the brain areas influencing REM sleep is much less clear. Jouvet found that the pons area of the brain stem called the locus coeruleus is involved in REM sleep. This area inhibits muscle tone during REM sleep, as shown by Jones, Harper, and Halaris (1977), essentially paralyzing you and preventing you from acting out your dreams. Hobson and his colleagues (1974) proposed that the pontine reticular formation's gigantocellular tegmental field and the locus coeruleus connect with the higher brain structures to produce cortical arousal during REM sleep. The pons and the neurotransmitters norepinephrine and acetylcholine also appear to be involved in REM sleep. Vertes (1983) argued that it appears that REM sleep is controlled by several different brain sites, and although there is a great deal of research being conducted in this area, it is too early to draw definite conclusions.

Functions of Sleep What are the functions of sleep? One way to learn about these functions is to deprive a subject of sleep and then note changes that occur. Sleep deprivation has been used for many years by military interrogators. Recently this interrogation technique was reported by U.S. downed flyers in Iraq. Research has tended to find that sleep deprivation by itself does not produce extreme changes in mental functioning in individuals. For example, in Webb's 1975 study discussed in the opening story, subjects were totally deprived of sleep for several days. He concluded that his subjects wanted to sleep and had some trouble paying

attention to required tasks, but otherwise didn't show any bizarre or unusual behaviors. Because the EEG record indicates precisely which stage of sleep a subject is in, it is possible to deprive a subject selectively of one type of sleep at a time. A few studies have done this.

An early report by William Dement (1960) suggested that lack of REM sleep results in personality changes, increased anxiety, and irritability. Later studies failed to find any decrease in psychological functioning when subjects were deprived of REM sleep for long periods of time. In later research, Dement did, however, find a need for REM sleep. After REM deprivation, a subject often shows a rebound effect, spending much more time than usual in REM sleep.

Some studies suggest that REM sleep is involved in learning and memory. For instance, Greiser, Greenberg, and Harrison (1972) reported that REM sleep deprivation produced deficits in recall of emotionally related words. And a study by Lucero (1970) found that REM sleep in rats increased immediately after they learned a new maze.

Hartmann (1973) proposed that REM sleep is important in memory consolidation, especially when stress is involved. He compared people who slept 6 hours or less a night with people who slept 9 hours or more. In general, the "short sleepers" were happier and more energetic, while the "long sleepers" were more thoughtful and anxious. Hartmann found that both groups spent about the same time in NREM sleep, but the people who slept 9 hours or more spent much more time in REM sleep. Apparently, we need more REM sleep when we are stressed or have a need for more fantasy in our lives.

A recent theory of REM sleep by Francis Crick, the codiscoverer of the structure of DNA, runs in the opposite direction. Crick and Mitchison (1983) proposed that the function of REM sleep is to clear the brain of memories that might interfere with normal thought and memory. This is why we don't remember many of our dreams. Currently, we cannot draw any definite conclusions from these hypotheses except to say that it does appear that REM sleep is important enough to require us to experience it every night.

Most studies of NREM sleep deprivation focus on Stage 4 sleep, since it is the farthest from REM, and shows a distinctive EEG pattern. People deprived of Stage 4 sleep also tend to show a rebound effect by spending more time in Stage 4 when allowed to sleep normally, as shown in a study by Agnew, Webb, and Williams in 1964.

Some research suggests that Stage 4 sleep is important in the physical restoration of the body. Moldofsky and Scarisbrick (1976) reported that subjects deprived of Stage 4 sleep complained of muscle and joint pain. Shapiro and his colleagues (1981) reported that after strenuous physical activity such as running a marathon,

FIGURE 5.5   Changes in REM/NREM Sleep Needs Through the Life Cycle

This graph shows how the need for REM and NREM sleep declines as we grow older. At birth, REM sleep consists of about 8 hours and in old age declines to about 1 hour. NREM sleep needs decline less radically from about 8 hours at birth to about 5 hours in old age. This chart also graphically portrays the percentage of REM sleep to total sleep time in 24 hours (after Roffwarg, Muzio, & Dement, 1966).

NREM sleep increases while REM sleep decreases for several nights. Other evidence concerned with tissue growth and repair comes from a study by Sassin and colleagues (1969) that indicated that human growth hormones were released during Stages 3 and 4. Hartmann (1973) proposed that NREM sleep restores the body when it is physically injured or fatigued. The evidence is not overwhelming, but it does appear that NREM sleep could be involved in the normal physical restoration of the body. There is also some evidence that our sleep habits may be genetically determined (Webb & Campbell, 1983). Perhaps, as Webb (1974) suggested, we sleep because it conserves energy and because it is safer not to do much in the dark anyway!

Dreams

People have always been fascinated by dreams. Poets and philosophers have interpreted them either as romantic fantasies or as manifestations of the darker side of human nature. Many researchers have taken a more practical attitude toward dreams and have studied them in and out of the laboratory in order to understand their place in human lives more scientifically.

Freud's Theory of Dreams   One popular early theory of dreams was proposed by Sigmund Freud (1900), who believed that dreams were the road to the unconscious mind. He thought that conflicts that disturb us or events that we can't deal with during the day make their way into our dreams. Freud distinguished between the manifest dream content (what we remember about the dream) and the latent dream content (the actual thoughts and emotions in the unconscious dream).

In order to analyze a dream, we need to focus on each of the individual elements or symbols rather than the connections between the parts of the manifest dream. The manifest dream is really a disguised representation of our unconscious wishes (which, according to Freud, are often unacceptable in society).

Freud believed a number of processes were involved in determining a dream's content. In displacement, the emotional feelings are displaced from one object to another one. For example, your hatred for one person might be expressed as hatred for someone else in a dream. In symbolization, the latent content of a dream is converted into manifest symbols. Freud believed that dreams disguised the images they presented and so it was necessary to interpret them. A great deal of Freud's interpretation focused on sexual symbolism. For example, he suggested that the male genitals are represented

FIGURE 5.6 "The Nightmare" by Henry Fuseli

Freud's theory of dreams proposed that conflicts we can't deal with during the day find their way into our dreams. He distinguished between the manifest and latent content of dreams and proposed several processes for interpreting them.

in dreams by symbols such as sticks, posts, trees, daggers, spears, revolvers, pencils, or hammers; the female genitals by pits, cavities, vessels, bottles, boxes, and pockets. The basic problem with this approach is that a symbol might not have the same meaning for every dreamer. In fact, other researchers find significantly fewer sexual dreams than Freud did.

Dream Content Another approach to studying dream content is represented by Palumbo (1978), who suggested that dreams are a way to process the events of the day. Calvin Hall (1966) also believed that dreams are simply visual representations of daily experiences. Hall studied the dream content of thousands of subjects and found that, although individual differences occur, there are some general trends. Women tend to dream of familiar people, places, and events, while men tend to dream more of unfamiliar situations. One gender difference that occurs in a variety of cultures is that females tend to dream about males and females equally often but males dream more often (65 percent) about males (Hall, 1984). Hall cautions that any analysis of a person's dreams must be highly individualized and cannot be generalized.

College students were surveyed for their most common dreams by Griffith and his colleagues (1958). Their study found 83 percent of the students reported dreams about falling and 77 percent reported dreams in which they were being attacked. A large percentage of dreams involved school, sexual behavior, eating, being frightened, or having a loved one die. Fire was included in 41

percent of the reports, while failing an exam was in 39 percent. Other significant topics included finding money, swimming, snakes, being nude, and death. Many of these topics are probably items of concern to the student, while some of them seem unusual.

In a 1988 study, I asked over 200 college students what they dreamed about. Although many of the topics were similar to Griffith's 1958 findings (see Figure 5.7), there were some interesting differences. Falling (males 65 percent, females 86 percent) and being attacked (males 68 percent, females 89 percent), were frequently mentioned, but so were romantic situations (males 65 percent, females 86 percent), and being with family and friends (males 53 percent, females 81 percent). Sexual experiences were popular, but the older study's gender difference disappeared (in 1958—males 93 percent, females 36 percent; in 1988—males 76 percent, females 72 percent). I also found that students in 1988 appear to dream less about school, teachers, and studying (males 41 percent, females 70 percent) than in 1958.

Estimates of time that lapses during a dream indicate that dream time is about the same as real time. In one experiment, Dement used an external stimulus, a spray of water, as a marker during REM sleep. When the dreamers were awakened, they usually incorporated the external stimulus into the appropriate time sequence in the dream. They interpreted the water as rain or a shower, depending on the content of the rest of the dream. Recent research by Badia and colleagues (1990) indicates that subjects can also respond to olfactory stimuli presented during sleep. While dreams remain a

FIGURE 5.7   Common Dreams

DREAM	Percentage of Students		
	Total	**Male**	**Female**
Falling	83	80	85
Being attacked or pursued	77	77	78
Trying repeatedly to do something	71	68	75
School, teachers, studying	71	60	84
Falling, with fear	68	62	73
Sexual experiences	66	93	36
Arriving too late	64	60	67
Eating delicious food	62	57	67
Being frozen with fright	58	53	64
A loved person is dead	57	49	67
Being locked up	56	55	58
Finding money	56	61	50
Swimming	52	47	58
Snakes	49	43	55
Being on verge of falling	47	52	41
Being inappropriately dressed	46	39	54
Dead people as though alive	46	40	53
Being smothered	44	42	47
Being nude	43	48	37
Fire	41	33	50
Failing an examination	39	34	44
Flying through air	34	32	35
Seeing self as dead	33	33	34
Being tied up	30	28	34
Killing someone	26	38	11

Here are the most common dreams of U.S. college students as reported in 1958 by Griffith, Miyago, and Tago.

very private affair, psychologists are beginning to understand some of the complexities involved in the process.

Lucid Dreams   The popular movie *Nightmare on Elm Street*, in which people fight evil creatures in their dreams, was designed to entertain us. A line of recent research suggests, however, that there might be some truth in the premise that we can gain control over what we dream about.

Have you ever been aware of the fact you were dreaming? Some people report having lucid dreams, in which they seem to be aware while they are actually dreaming. Stephen LaBerge (1986) studied lucid dreaming by interacting with his subjects while they were dreaming. For example, he taught subjects eye movements to indicate they were aware that they were experiencing a dream. Some lucid dreamers report that they can alter the course of their dreams. LaBerge suggests that becoming aware of lucid dreaming could help people become more creative and better able to solve problems. It is also possible that people who have nightmares could learn to control the terrifying events to reduce the severity of the dreams (Gackenbach & Bosveld, 1989).

Activation Synthesis Theory   Recently, the activation synthesis theory of dreaming was proposed by McCarley (McCarley & Hoffman, 1981). Essentially, this view states that during REM sleep, the brain activates itself and then synthesizes the information generated into dreams. Hobson and McCarley (1977) suggested that many dreams are the interpretation of brain activity. For example, they suggest that falling is the interpretation of vestibular activity; fear or being unable to escape is the interpretation of the muscular paralysis, and running is the interpretation of the stimulation of the cerebellum that occurs during REM sleep. Hobson (1989) argued that the activation synthesis hypothesis may explain the bizarre dreams that we sometimes experience. He suggested that during REM sleep, the usual cognitive orientation in consciousness breaks down, resulting in improbable, bizarre, and confusing dreams. Although the activation synthesis theory of dreaming is interesting, it has not yet been proved.

Daydreams   In addition to the dreams we have when we are asleep, we also experience daydreams when we are awake. Daydreaming is an altered state of consciousness that occurs without effort and involves a brief escape from reality into fantasy. Daydreams can occur anywhere and at any time: while watching television or listening to the radio, or just while we are relaxing. Often, they occur when we are bored. Most people daydream every day, although the frequency tends to decrease somewhat with age.

Jerome Singer (1975) reported that daydreams include both personal fantasies that tend to be repeated and the ongoing stream of consciousness we experience moment by moment. Most daydreams are the ongoing type. They tend to include making plans, worrying, evaluating activities, and just experiencing perceptions. Research suggest that daydreams tend to be personal, and men and women tend to have similar daydreams (Klinger, 1987).

What is the purpose of daydreams? Singer suggested that some daydreams simply relieve boredom or stress. At other times, our daydreams allow us to rehearse possible future actions or evaluate possible solutions to our problems. We may also use our daydreams to develop creative thinking or provide motivation to accomplish necessary tasks. The experts seem to agree that as long as it is not excessively engaged in, daydreaming is healthy for us.

Sleep Disorders

Sleep disorders include the dyssomnias and the parasomnias (DSM-III-R, 1987). In the dyssomnias, such as insomnia and hypersomnia, the chief symptom is a disturbance in the amount and quality of sleep one obtains. In the parasomnias, such as sleep terrors, bed-wetting, and sleepwalking, the chief symptom is an unusual event that disturbs sleep.

Insomnia The high demand for sleeping pills is a symptom of the widespread occurrence of insomnia, the inability to sleep. In a recent survey, 6 percent of men and 14 percent of women reported that they suffered from this type of sleep disorder. There are many causes for, and types of, insomnia (Kripke & Gillin, 1985). Some insomniacs fall asleep easily, but dream that they are awake. Hence, when they wake up, these people feel as if they were still trying to get to sleep. Others have trouble falling to sleep because of anxiety, fear, stress, depression, or other problems. People who suffer from insomnia tend to show higher sympathetic nervous system activity, indicating that stress is often a key factor. Recent research using a sleep restricting technique (in which subjects limit their time in bed) appears successful in some people with insomnia (Friedman & colleagues, 1991). There are currently a number of behavioral therapies for insomnia (we discuss behavior therapy in chapter 14, "Therapy").

Some insomniacs suffer from a condition known as sleep apnea. They fall asleep easily, but then stop breathing and wake up gasping for air. People with sleep apnea might wake up several hundred times a night. Raymond (1986) reported that about 10 percent of men over the age of 40 have some form of sleep apnea. Obstruction of the air passage by the relaxation of the throat muscles or a malfunction in the brain might result in apnea but its cause is not completely known. It is possible that sudden infant death syndrome (SIDS), or crib death, may be caused by sleep apnea. Hales (1986) suggested that the newborn infant may not yet have the neural structure required to wake it up when breathing stops, and hence it suffocates while sleeping.

Narcolepsy A form of hypersomnia, narcolepsy is a sleep disorder characterized by inappropriate daytime attacks of sleep. The narcoleptic person unpredictably falls asleep during the day. EEG records show that the narcoleptic goes directly into REM sleep, and since this stage is associated with muscle paralysis, it can be very dangerous for the individual (Aldrich, 1990). Sometimes the attack is brought about by an intense emotion, such as laughing, surprise, or sexual arousal. One symptom of narcolepsy is the occurrence of hypnagogic hallucinations (Dement, 1976). These are very vivid dreams that occur as the narcoleptic enters a sleep attack. Often the dream is a continuation of prior waking events, creating the illusion of reality and resulting in a frightening experience.

The episode lasts for less than 15 minutes, and the person then gradually wakes up and continues with daily activities. We don't know what causes narcolepsy, but researchers suspect that it has to do with inadequate amounts of the neurotransmitter dopamine or abnormal REM functioning in the daytime (Erlich & Itabashi, 1986). Sometimes the disorder can be treated with stimulant drugs, such as amphetamines.

NREM Sleep Disorders There are several parasomnias (sleep disorders) that occur in Stages 3 and 4 of NREM sleep, including sleep talking, sleepwalking (somnambulism), bed-wetting (enuresis), and sleep terrors (pavor nocturnus). They are, for the most part, not dangerous, and are often found in children (Mahowald & Rosen, 1990). In many cases, the child eventually grows out of the behavior.

Sleepwalking (somnambulism) reaches a peak in children about 12 years old. It tends to run in families, suggesting a genetic base. An accepted treatment for sleepwalking is to make sure that the sleepwalker does not hurt himself or herself. Bed-wetting (enuresis) can have a physiological cause, but often appears to have a psychological basis. There are several behavior therapies used to treat it, such as training the child to recognize the feeling of a full bladder by having him or her wait as long as possible before urinating. Waiting until the child outgrows the problem is also a common treatment. An effective treatment developed by Mowrer and Mowrer (1938) consists of having the child sleep on a pad into which a wire mesh that is connected to a bell has been sewn. When the child wets the bed, an electrical circuit is closed, setting off the bell and waking the child. Sleep terror disorder (pavor nocturnus) occurs when children wake up screaming and terrified, but cannot recall why. It usually begins at around 4 years of age. Webb suggests that it is possible that the terror results from a rapid shift from Stage 4 sleep into waking. The best treatment seems to be to let it run its course.

The NREM sleep disorders have the common characteristic that the sleeper often does not remember them the next morning. This fits with the concept that NREM sleep is not a mentally active state of consciousness. Sleep is an interesting topic because everyone regularly experiences it. Other altered states of consciousness are experienced less frequently.

PSYCHOACTIVE DRUGS

A *drug* is any foreign chemical substance that alters the functioning of a biological system. Many substances can serve as drugs, including pain relievers, alcohol, nicotine, caffeine, antibiotics, clinical drugs, and illegal psychoactive drugs. A psychoactive drug causes changes in behavior and cognition by modifying conscious aware-

FIGURE 5.8   Drug Addiction
Drug addiction is characterized by psychological and/or physiological dependence, affecting all areas of a person's life.

ness. Psychopharmacology is the science of the effects of psychoactive drugs on behavior and cognition. Some psychoactive drugs, such as alcohol, nicotine, and opium, have been consumed for centuries. Others, like tranquilizers, are the products of recent medical research. Still others, like LSD and PCP, have appeared in the illegal marketplace within the past several decades. As indicated earlier, people have always been interested in producing altered states of consciousness through drugs.

With repeated use, a person can become psychologically and physiologically dependent upon a drug. A person has developed psychological dependence when he or she craves the drug even though it is not biologically needed by the body; it often involves learning that the effect of the drug is pleasurable or effective in helping to cope with problems. Some drugs cause physical dependence, or addiction, a condition in which the habitual user's body becomes biochemically dependent upon the drugs.

Physical dependence is characterized by tolerance and withdrawal. The habitual use of some drugs leads to tolerance, in which larger and larger doses of the drug are required to produce the same effect. If the dependent person stops taking the drug, he or she will experience withdrawal symptoms, which are very unpleasant physical reactions. For example, with heroin the withdrawal symptoms include vomiting, diarrhea, loss of appetite, anxiety, and sweating; with alcohol they can include

nausea, insomnia, and sometimes hallucinations and seizures. In this section we will review the major types of psychoactive drugs. These are usually divided into five categories based on how they influence behavior (Julien, 1992) and include depressants, opiates, stimulants, psychedelics, and the antipsychotic drugs. Psychologists are interested in the kinds of experiences produced by various drugs, the kinds of behavior associated with drug taking, and the nature of dependence on drugs. They are also interested in types of therapy for abusers of drugs, as well as the use of drugs in the treatment of mental disorders. We discuss the therapeutic use of drugs in chapter 14, "Therapy."

Depressants

Depressants (or sedative-hypnotics) are central nervous system-affecting drugs that have a sedative, or sleep-inducing, effect. The general group includes alcohol, anesthetics (such as ether), barbiturates, and antianxiety tranquilizers (such as Librium and Valium). In small amounts, depressants produce tranquilizing effects. In high doses, they can induce sleep, and in even higher doses, coma and death.

It is important to note that the effects of depressants are additive. Thus, if you are taking barbiturates, and also take alcohol, you will become extremely sleepy. All of the depressants produce feelings of excitement when given in very small doses, because they affect inhibitory, before excitatory, synapses in the brain. Depressants operate on the arousal-sleep circuits in the brain (Julien, 1992).

Alcohol   Alcohol is the most frequently used depressant drug available today. In cultures throughout the world, ethyl alcohol is widely accepted as a legal intoxicant. While it varies widely in concentration, from less than 6 percent in beer to about 50 percent in hard liquor, what is important is the absolute amount in the bloodstream. Alcohol is quickly absorbed into the bloodstream from the stomach and intestines. It is then metabolized in the liver, where it is converted to carbon dioxide and water (Julien, 1992).

Alcohol appears to affect individuals in different ways, depending upon personality and expectation. In a 1979 experiment using dogs, I found that alcohol increased or decreased aggression, depending on the dominance status of the subject. Although people often assume otherwise, Miller and Gold (1988) showed that alcohol depresses human sexual responsiveness. Alcohol in large doses disrupts REM sleep, motor coordination, thinking, and perception, and therefore has a disastrous effect on automobile driving. There are over 10 million alcoholics in the United States, with psychological and

FIGURE 5.9   Alcohol Abuse
Alcohol is a widely used intoxicant that is quickly absorbed into the bloodstream. It affects physical coordination and perception. An estimated 40 percent of all Americans will be involved in an alcohol-related accident during their lives.

social problems ranging from depression and loss of family life to physiological problems such as liver disease and memory loss.

Of major concern is fetal alcohol syndrome (FAS), in which infants born to women alcoholics have congenital malformations. FAS babies often have brain defects, problems in speaking, retardation, and are premature and underweight at birth (Overholser, 1990). Much research is needed in the area of fetal alcohol syndrome.

Barbiturates   The barbiturates are drugs that can be used for mild sedation (Amobarbital), anesthesia (Methohexital), and as a treatment for insomnia (Nembutal or Seconal) or anxiety (Phenobarbital). They relax the muscles, produce a state of euphoria, and, with increasing doses, induce sleep. Research indicates that barbiturates interfere with the arousal neurotransmitter norepinephrine (Kolb & Whishaw, 1985). They are

highly addictive, with both physical dependence and tolerance developing in the user. Overdoses of barbiturates can end in coma or death.

Antianxiety Tranquilizers   The first benzodiazepine, chloridiazepoxide (Librium), was marketed in 1960. Librium and Valium (diazepan) are among the most widely prescribed drugs in this country as antianxiety minor tranquilizers, useful for treating anxiety, psychological pressure, and sometimes insomnia. The benzodiazepines facilitate GABA neurotransmission (Zorumski & Isenberg, 1991). Excessive use of these depressant drugs can produce symptoms such as disorientation and aggression. The additive effects of benzodiazepines and alcohol are severe disruptions of visual and motor coordination needed for driving.

Opiates

Opiates or narcotic analgesics refer to drugs whose effect on the body is similar to morphine, the *analgesic* (pain-relieving) ingredient derived from the opium poppy plant. Opiates include naturally occurring drugs such as codeine, morphine, and heroin, and synthetic drugs such as methadone, Darvon, and Demerol. Methadone has been used to treat dependence on morphine. The medical uses of narcotics include relief of pain, treatment of diarrhea, and suppression of coughing.

Opiates affect the central nervous system, eyes, and gastrointestinal tract. Julien (1992) reviewed evidence that suggests that narcotics are able to relieve pain by depressing the pain receptors in the brain and spinal cord. It appears that opiates act similarly to the natural pain-relief substances, the endorphins (see chapter 4, "Sensation and Perception").

Heroin and other illegally used opiates can produce a sense of pleasant euphoria and well-being and can initially increase sexual interest (Abel, 1984). The user quickly develops a tolerance and addiction, however, and must take increasingly larger amounts to achieve the same feeling. Heroin addiction is often associated with criminal behavior because the addict needs large amounts of money to continue to buy enough of the drug to support the habit.

Stimulants

Stimulants are drugs that increase central nervous system activity and behavior speed, and produce feelings of alertness or even euphoria. They can help us stay awake when necessary, but often a cycle of arousal-depression develops, producing overall negative effects. Stimulants include common drugs such as caffeine and nicotine, and stronger drugs such as amphetamine and cocaine. The clinical antidepressants we discuss in chapter 14, "Therapy," are also classified as stimulants.

Caffeine   Probably the most widely used stimulant in our society is caffeine. Whether you drink a cup of coffee in the morning to get going, drink tea or Coke at lunchtime, or eat a chocolate bar in the afternoon, you are getting a dose of caffeine. Julien reports that, in general, caffeine increases glucose production in the cells, which provides more energy and speeds up bodily activities. It affects the cerebral cortex of the brain, producing mental alertness. With frequent doses, the user may experience insomnia, agitation, anxiety, and rapid breathing.

It appears that caffeine is physically addictive, and many people develop psychological dependence on it (thus needing their "morning coffee" to wake up). Withdrawal symptoms (headaches, irritability, and nausea) are produced if the user stops taking caffeine. There is currently concern about the effect of caffeine on a pregnancy, although definitive answers have not yet been procured. All the major cola companies are now marketing no-caffeine colas to attract people who are concerned with their intake of caffeine.

Nicotine   Nicotine is a stimulant contained in the tobacco of cigarettes. It is absorbed by the lungs and distributed by the bloodstream. In general, nicotine has many of the same effects as caffeine. Nicotine appears to stimulate neurons sensitive to acetylcholine.

One side effect of nicotine is that it reduces muscle tension, which might be why people claim it relaxes them. Nicotine induces psychological and physical dependence. Withdrawal symptoms include headaches, nausea, irritability, and insomnia. It is now known that nicotine affects the fetus during pregnancy, resulting in increased probability of miscarriages and premature babies. Despite health hazards and the surgeon general's warning on all cigarette packages that smoking is dangerous to people's health, many people still continue to smoke. However, due in part to the program established by former surgeon general C. Everett Koop, there is an increasing awareness of the dangers of smoking, as evidenced by "no smoking" areas in public areas.

Amphetamine   Amphetamine is a much stronger stimulant than caffeine or nicotine, producing arousal of the central nervous system and increasing internal bodily processes such as heart rate and breathing. Large doses can lead to restlessness, insomnia, shaking, and sometimes *amphetamine psychosis,* which is characterized by marked changes in personality. Structurally, amphetamine is similar to the neurotransmitter norepinephrine,

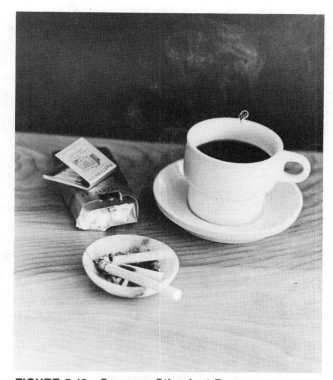

FIGURE 5.10   Common Stimulant Drugs
Coffee and cigarettes contain stimulants that affect behavior. Caffeine and nicotine are both central nervous system stimulants.

and some psychologists believe research with amphetamine abuse may lead to insights into causes of abnormal behaviors. Amphetamine's trade name is *Benzedrine,* and its close derivatives are *Dexedrine* and *Methedrine.*

During the past several decades, amphetamines and other stimulants, such as Ritalin and Cylert, have been used to treat *attention deficit disorder* (hyperactivity) in children. These children are hyperactive in the classroom and cannot focus their attention on the curriculum. When given stimulants, their attention and concentration improve. This effect was once thought paradoxical, but research on hyperactivity and attention has demonstrated that stimulants make sense. The actual reason is not known, but some researchers believe that it is possible that hyperactive children have brains that are developing at a slower-than-average rate, and the stimulant speeds up the brain functioning so the children can concentrate. Amphetamines are sometimes used to treat the sleep disorder narcolepsy. Amphetamines also suppress appetite, but because people quickly develop a tolerance, they are not effective as diet pills. Although there are some valid medical uses of amphetamines, they are also widely used illegally.

Cocaine   Cocaine is a powerful stimulant derived from the leaves of the South American coca plant. Cocaine was identified as the active ingredient in coca leaves in 1844. In the late nineteenth century it was often used in medicine, and many claimed it had great beneficial effects (including Sigmund Freud, who used it to relieve depression). Although recent Coca-Cola commercials advertise their product as "the real thing," Coca-Cola has not contained cocaine since 1900, when the medical world decided that it wasn't as beneficial as first believed (Musto, 1991).

A popular way of taking cocaine, or "coke," is to snort it by inhaling it through a straw into the nose. It can also be ingested, injected, or smoked. A recently introduced potent form, called crack, comes in pellets and is smoked in a pipe. Crack is made by mixing baking soda and water with the crystalline form of cocaine and heating it. Crack cocaine has become extremely popular in recent years because it is relatively inexpensive and produces its effects quickly (Johnson & colleagues, 1989).

Cocaine produces stimulant effects similar to amphetamines. It increases heart rate and breathing, causes dilation of the pupils of the eyes, and constricts blood vessels. Cocaine is an effective local anesthetic, numbing nerve endings with which it comes into contact. Psychologically, cocaine causes an increased state of alertness, a feeling of energy, and a general sense of euphoria. Side effects include sweating, anxiety, irritability, and occasional hallucinations. Unlike amphetamines, cocaine produces effects that last a short time, often only minutes; then withdrawal symptoms occur, including depression and a desire for more of the drug. Like amphetamines, cocaine produces its effects by increasing the utilization of the neurotransmitter norepinephrine in the central nervous system. Recent research suggests that some of the reinforcing effects of cocaine are due to its action at serotonin sites in the brain (Wold & Kuhn, 1991).

Antidepressant Drugs   As we discuss in chapter 14, "Therapy," the antidepressant drugs are used to treat depression. Like other stimulants, they increase the levels of neurotransmitters, including norepinephrine and dopamine. Two major classes of antidepressants include MAO inhibitors (which include Parnate, Nardil, and Marplan) and the tricyclic antidepressants (which include Tofranil, Norpramin, Elavil, and Adapin). A new antidepressant drug, Prozac, increases the level of serotonin. Because these drugs do not produce euphoria in healthy individuals, there is little recreational abuse of them (Julien, 1992).

Psychedelic Drugs and Marijuana

The psychedelic drugs are sometimes referred to as hallucinogens because at high doses they result in hallucinations, but they also have other effects on behavior

and perception. They may excite the nervous system, producing a change not only in the user's emotional feelings, but also in his or her perceptions of the external world. Psychedelic drugs vary widely in their effects, which seem to depend on the taker's expectations and the settings in which the drug is experienced. The most common hallucinogens are LSD (lysergic acid diethylamide), mescaline (which is derived from the peyote cactus), and cannabis (source of both marijuana and hashish). Although marijuana is not truly a hallucinogen, at high doses it can cause psychedelic experiences, and is included in this section.

Hallucinogens   The effects of drugs such as *LSD* and *mescaline* include brightly colored visual illusions and vivid dreamlike thoughts, a sense of existing outside the body, a sense of unity between the body and objects in the environment, and intense emotions ranging from feelings of well-being to terror. The social and physical setting seems to have an important role in determining whether the "trip"—an altered state of consciousness that generally lasts from 6 to 14 hours—is a pleasant or a bad experience. Partially due to unfavorable publicity, including studies suggesting that taking LSD might produce genetic defects in one's offspring, usage has declined sharply from its peak in the late 1960s.

Research has linked the action of LSD to a decrease in the effectiveness of serotonin neurons in the brain (Jacobs, 1987). In chapter 2, "Psychobiology," we learned that the neurotransmitter serotonin is involved in sleep and perception. Apparently, sensory information is incorrectly interpreted when LSD is present. The perceptual changes are usually visual and tactile. Tolerance to LSD rapidly develops, but there does not appear to be evidence of physical dependence.

A drug that became popular in the 1970s is phencyclidine hydrochloride (PCP), often called "angel dust." PCP was developed as an anesthetic in 1956, but, because of its side effects of producing disorientation and delirium, it was declared unfit for humans. It was approved, however, as a veterinary anesthetic. PCP acts like a hallucinogen, and can have dangerous and unpredictable effects on people.

Marijuana   An ancient and still very popular drug (reports of its effects date back to about 2700 B.C.), marijuana is a mixture of the leaves and flowers of the cannabis sativa plant. This plant grows throughout the world, especially in tropical regions, and its active ingredient is *THC* (delta-9-tetrahydrocannabinol). Marijuana contains a fairly low dose of THC, whereas hashish is much more potent. People who use marijuana illegally do so for a variety of reasons. Some believe that it increases their awareness and creativity, while others take it with friends to increase sociability and a feeling of

FIGURE 5.11   Major Psychoactive Drugs

Drug Classification	Slang terms often used	Chemical or trade name	Medical uses	How taken usually	Immediate effects of use	Physical dependence	Psycho-logical dependence
DEPRESSANTS							
Alcohol	booze, juice	ethyl alcohol	antiseptic	swallow	reduce anxiety	yes	yes
Barbiturates	blue devils, barbs, candy	Seconal, Nembutal	sedation, anxiety relief	swallow, inject	euphoria, reduce anxiety	yes	yes
Antianxiety Tranquilizers		Librium, Valium, Dalmane	anxiety relief	swallow	none	yes	yes
OPIATES							
Codeine	schoolboy	Methyl-morphine	cough, pain	swallow	euphoria	yes	yes
Morphine	white stuff	Morphine sulfate	pain relief	swallow, inject	euphoria	yes	yes
Heroin	horse, smack	Diacetylmor-phine	pain relief	swallow, inject	euphoria	yes	yes
Methodone	dolly	Dolophine amidone	pain relief	swallow, inject	aid in withdrawal	yes	yes
STIMULANTS							
Caffeine	caffeine	caffeine	migraine headache	swallow	alertness	yes	yes
Nicotine	smoke	nicotine	emetic	smoke, chew	alertness, relaxation	yes	yes
Amphetamine	speed, bennies	Benzedrine	narcolepsy, hyperactivity	swallow, inject	alertness, active	yes	yes
Cocaine	coke, crack, snow, dust	cocaine	anesthesia	inhale, inject, smoke	excitation	yes	yes
Anti-depressants		Tofranil, Nardil, Prozac	relieve depression	swallow	none	?	?
PSYCHEDELICS							
LSD	acid, trips	lysergic acid diethylamide	none	swallow	sensory distortion	no	no?
Mescaline	mesc	3, 4, 5 trimeth-oxyphenethy-lamine	none	swallow	sensory distortion	no	no?
PCP	angel dust	phencyclidine hydrochloride	veterinary anesthesia	swallow	disorientation	no	no?
Marijuana	pot, grass	Cannabis	glaucoma	smoke, swallow	euphoria, relaxation	no	yes?
ANTIPSYCHOTIC DRUGS							
Thorazine		chlorpro-mazine	treat psychosis	swallow, inject	relaxation	?	?

FIGURE 5.12 Effects of LSD on Artistic Drawing
LSD causes changes in perception. These drawings illustrate its effects. The first was done before the drug was taken.

warmth. Some people take it because they are curious, or because they hope it will help them escape from problems. The most common psychological effects of marijuana include a sense of well-being, feelings of relaxation and happiness, an altered perception of time and space, and a vivid awareness of sensations. Some research has shown that with moderate doses of marijuana, subjects tested in laboratory settings showed impairment of short-term memory and of the capacity for complex thinking. Higher doses result in confusion, hallucinations, and feelings of panic (Miller & Branconnier, 1983).

The effects of marijuana appear to be highly subjective, individual, and dependent upon the expectations of the user. When it is used in social settings, its effects might be described as mildly mood-altering. Marijuana use does not appear to develop physical dependence, but tolerance for the drug has been noted. Many claims have been made pro and con about marijuana; confirmation of these claims must await further research.

Antipsychotic Drugs

The last category of psychoactive drugs is the antipsychotic drugs, or major tranquilizers. As we discuss in chapter 14, "Therapy," the antipsychotic drugs appear to alter the functioning of dopamine in the brain, and are used to treat severe disruptions of psychological functioning called the psychoses. Psychotic patients who have been treated with antipsychotic drugs act calmer and less anxious than they had been. Chlorpromazine (trade name Thorazine), which helped to create a dramatic change in the way psychotic patients were treated, was marketed in the United States in 1955. These drugs are not usually used for recreational purposes.

HYPNOSIS

Hypnosis is an altered state of consciousness that is characterized by heightened suggestibility. Hypnotism involves producing a dreamlike trance in people through the use of verbal suggestion. Hypnosis was once thought to be a form of sleeping (the word hypnosis comes from the Greek word for sleep), but recent evidence from EEG experiments indicates that the brain-wave pattern of the hypnotized person resembles various types of wakefulness rather than sleep. It should be mentioned that not everyone considers hypnosis an altered state of consciousness; some suggest it is simply a normal state in which the subject is extremely motivated to comply with requests from others.

In the late 1700s a Viennese physician, Franz Anton Mesmer, demonstrated a technique called animal magnetism, in which magnetized rods in a tub of water generated an electrical current that produced seizures in patients. Mesmerism later became known as hypnotism as the emphasis shifted to producing an altered state of consciousness through verbal suggestion. In the latter part of the nineteenth century, French physician Jean Charcot thought hypnosis was a way to help people relax. Sigmund Freud utilized hypnosis as one way to view the unconscious mind (the other way was through dreams). However, he decided that hypnosis was not as effective as other methods, and thus abandoned its use.

Techniques and Susceptibility

There are many techniques used to induce hypnosis; most of them have several features in common. The setting should be one that relaxes the subject and eliminates any fears. Usually there is something on which the subject focuses attention. It can be an object (such as a watch on the end of a chain) or a repetitive sound. The hypnotist repeatedly gives the subject the suggestion that he or she feels comfortable and is relaxed; the hypnotist tests the depth of the state of hypnosis.

Several hypnotic susceptibility tests are available, such as the Stanford Hypnotic Susceptibility Scale and the Barber Suggestibility Scale. These tests have various tasks such as having subjects close their eyes, lower their hand, and react to a posthypnotic suggestion. There is a wide variation in individuals' susceptibility to hypnotism, and psychologists have not yet identified a distinct "hypnotizable" personality. When people are hypnotized, their altered state of consciousness is characterized by an extraordinary increase in their normal openness to the influence of suggestion. Ernest Hilgard (1987) reported that the best subjects for hypnosis are those who have good imaginations and the ability to fantasize.

Theories of Hypnosis

There are several theories of hypnosis, including the trance theory, the sociological role theory, and the task-motivation theory (Wallace & Fisher, 1991). According to the *trance theory*, hypnosis involves an altered state of consciousness in which the subject is in a heightened state of suggestibility (Hilgard, 1979). Hilgard suggested in his *neodissociation theory* that consciousness can be split into several streams of thought that are partially independent of each other. The hypnotized subject is not aware of all of the events happening in each of the levels of consciousness.

Sarbin and Coe's (1979) *sociological role theory* states that hypnotized subjects are in a normal state of consciousness and are trying to meet the role expectations set up by the hypnotist and society. Barber (1969) also argued in the *task-motivation theory* that hypnotism is not an altered state of consciousness but rather is a normal state of consciousness in which the subject is motivated to attend to the suggestions of the hypnotist. As you can see, there is no agreement on one theory of hypnosis.

Uses of Hypnosis

Hypnosis has been used for a variety of purposes, such as to control pain, change behavior, improve memory, and modify perception. In the 1800s hypnosis was used as anesthesia for surgical patients, but with the advent of anesthetic drugs, hypnosis was no longer used for this purpose (although it has been successfully used since then to reduce pain during childbirth). Hilgard and Hilgard (1983) suggested that hypnosis allows the individual to divide consciousness into two levels, and that under hypnosis the pain is not experienced at a conscious level of awareness.

One of the most common uses of hypnosis has been in controlling everyday behavior problems such as smoking and obesity. By providing suggestions that smoking or overeating is bad for health and encouraging a positive self-image, hypnotists are able to help people change unwanted habits. Anderson (1985) found that using hypnosis to control obesity was most successful when subjects were shown to be good subjects for hypnotism when measured on the Stanford Hypnotic Susceptibility Scale and when hypnosis was used along with other behavior modification techniques; otherwise there was a tendency by some individuals to revert to their undesirable habits.

Fears and problems of stress have been treated successfully with hypnotic techniques. John, Hollander, and Perry (1983) reported that subjects with fears (such as a fear of snakes) can be hypnotized to reach the subconscious level of awareness from which their fears stem. When hypnotized, the subjects are taught to relax in the subconscious level and get over their fear. Pekala & Forbes (1990) argued that hypnosis can help individuals deal with stress and tension. They also pointed out that just being relaxed produced some of the same effects as treatment during hypnosis did to some subjects.

Hypnosis has also been used to help individuals remember past events. Psychologists have hypnotized witnesses to help them remember details of a crime. Although witnesses sometimes make up information (or are influenced by the hypnotist's suggestions), this procedure has produced valuable information (McMaster, 1990). It is interesting to note that in a recent study by McConkey and Kinoshita (1988) subjects who were hypnotized were able to recall significantly more pictures, which they had been shown a week earlier, than subjects who were not hypnotized. Although we don't yet understand how hypnosis works, this altered state of consciousness continues to intrigue psychologists.

MEDITATION

For perhaps thousands of years, people in the Eastern world have been altering their awareness by means of meditation. And in recent years, hundreds of thousands of individuals in Western industrialized nations have become regular meditators. Meditation is the practice of some form of relaxed concentration that can block distracting sensory stimuli. Goleman (1977) reported that by focusing their attention on a single sound, sight, movement, or thought, accomplished meditators can refresh themselves emotionally and even physically.

Effects of Meditation   Studies of meditators have reported that meditation can produce a wide variety of psychological and physiological effects. A number of studies have found that meditation can enhance self-esteem and confidence in subjects (Orme-Johnson, 1987). It appears capable of reducing stress, anxiety, high blood pressure, and can help individuals control asthma, insomnia, or excessive fears.

Some of the physiological changes that can occur during meditation were described in a comprehensive study by Wallace and Benson (1972). They found that transcendental meditation was able to help individuals reduce oxygen consumption, increase electrical resistance of the skin, decrease the heart rate, and increase the EEG alpha-wave activity. Wallace and Benson pointed out that these changes do not occur in hypnosis.

Types of Meditation   There are several forms of meditation, including Zen, yoga, and TM (transcendental meditation). *Zen* is the oldest form of meditation. The meditator usually begins by counting his or her breaths. Then the individual focuses on breathing, trying to eliminate all other stimuli. With practice, the Zen meditator may be able to produce an altered state of consciousness.

In *yoga* meditation, the individual alters his or her state of consciousness by modifying autonomic processes such as heart rate, blood pressure, and digestion. The yoga meditator assumes a particular position such as the lotus, focuses on a visual object, and repeats a word or phrase called a mantra. Again, these procedures may allow the yoga meditator to produce an altered state of consciousness by blocking out environmental stimuli.

Transcendental meditation, or TM is a form of yoga in which the subject repeats a specific mantra (sound) over a period of time, while trying to block out all other stimuli. The person practicing TM can take any comfortable position (unlike yoga in which the lotus position is usually assumed). The goal of all meditation is to block out distractions in normal awareness to get in touch with the real self.

Evaluation of Meditation   Herbert Benson (1975) studied individuals who practiced TM and concluded that most of the effects of meditation can be achieved by producing a "relaxation response." A number of other studies have also concluded that meditation does not produce an altered state of consciousness, but rather a relaxed state in which physiological arousal is significantly

FIGURE 5.13   Meditation
In meditation the subject concentrates on blocking out distracting stimuli and focuses on one specific thought or image. This can reduce physical and emotional tension.

lowered (Shapiro, 1985). Relaxation techniques are widely used in therapy to treat a variety of fear and anxiety problems, as we discuss in chapter 14, "Therapy."

David Holmes (1984) did not find any significant differences between people who practiced TM and individuals who rested quietly. Changes in heart rate, blood pressure, and respiration were similar in both groups. The question of whether meditation produces an altered state of consciousness or a state of extreme relaxation has not yet been conclusively answered, but psychologists do recognize its benefits in dealing with stress and anxiety.

APPLICATION

Biofeedback

The biofeedback approach to altering consciousness usually involves the use of a device that permits the individual to monitor and influence one or more bodily processes that are not normally subject to voluntary control. Essentially, the person is responding to his or her own internal biological cues.

Neal Miller was one of the pioneers in this field. He reported the results of an experiment (Miller & Banuazizi, 1968) in which rats learned to increase or decrease their heart rates when rewarded for doing so. Miller (1973) also conducted research on the ability of humans to control various "involuntary" internal biological functions.

In a typical biofeedback session, a person is taught to recognize the effects of the autonomic nervous system on bodily functions. For example, the subject might monitor his or her own blood pressure by listening to a machine that buzzes when blood pressure increases, then beeps when blood pressure decreases. The subject tries to become aware of the bodily feelings that accompany the higher and lower blood pressure. With practice, the subject can raise or lower blood pressure at will, even without the monitoring device. This is accomplished by learning to control the tension in the skeletal muscles (McGuigan, 1984).

One commonly practiced form of biofeedback uses an EEG monitoring device that permits a person to generate alpha brain waves of 8 to 12 cycles per second. By generating such brain waves to the exclusion of all others, a person can enter a type of consciousness known as the alpha state, which is characterized by a relaxed, tranquil, composed, yet fully aware state of mind. Another form of biofeedback is electromyographic, or EMG relaxation. In one procedure, the subject focuses on the muscles in the forehead and attempts to reduce the tension activity in these muscles (Friedlund, Fowler, & Pritchard, 1980). A number of studies have shown that

FIGURE 5.14   Biofeedback
In a biofeedback session, a subject is taught to recognize the effects of the autonomic nervous system on bodily functions.

EMG biofeedback is about as effective as relaxation training for relieving headaches.

People have been taught to gain conscious control over a wide variety of processes, including their own heart rates, blood pressure, temperature, and other bodily functions. The biofeedback method is gaining acceptance as a therapeutic technique for treating emotional, behavioral, psychosomatic, and even organic problems. Tension headaches, vomiting, anxiety, and even ulcers, can be treated through biofeedback (Roberts, 1985).

SENSORY DEPRIVATION

Early Deprivation Research   When we are deprived of the normal stimulus information from our environment, does our brain rest or does it make up for the lack of stimulation by creating its own? This basic question has been studied through research on sensory deprivation, in which the normal environmental sensory stimuli available to an individual are reduced drastically.

In 1951 a group of researchers headed by Donald Hebb began experimenting with sensory deprivation at McGill University in Montreal. The original intent of the research, as described by Woodburn Heron (1957), was to learn more about the brainwashing techniques used on prisoners in some countries. The researchers were interested in the effects of deprivation on behavioral and perceptual processes.

McGill University male college students volunteered for experiments in which all they had to do was remain in a room until they decided to withdraw from the study. For this, they were paid $20 per day, during which time they were required to lie quietly on a bed for all 24 hours. Their sensory inputs were severely restricted. They wore special goggles through which only diffused light could penetrate. Cardboard cuffs and cotton gloves restricted their sense of touch. A special pillow and the steady hum of an air conditioner in the background impaired their hearing. Essentially, the normal and varied sensory input was cut off for the subjects.

The students had great difficulty concentrating during the experiment. As time went on, many of them showed extreme mood swings. Much of the time they were irritable, but sometimes they were very happy. After longer periods of isolation, some subjects reported seeing images as though they were dreaming while they were awake. Occasionally subjects also reported hearing sounds, such as music or singing. Most subjects were restless while they lay on the bed with nothing to do and were able to remain in isolation for only 2 or 3 days. Heron (1957) concluded that a varied sensory input is essential for human beings, and that without it, the brain produces its own stimulation.

REST Peter Suedfeld (1980), of the University of British Columbia, argued that the term *sensory deprivation* suggests that all of the senses are totally prevented from receiving stimulation. Actually, the McGill studies only restricted sensory stimulation, and hence Suedfeld prefers the term Restricted Environmental Stimulation Technique (REST) as an alternative (Suedfeld & Coren, 1989).

In the 3 decades since the original studies at McGill, increasing numbers of researchers have found positive uses of REST. Suedfeld and Baker-Brown (1986) reported that REST was effective in helping cigarette smokers break their smoking habit. Barabasz and Barabasz (1989) reported that REST is useful as an adjunct to hypnosis when treating people suffering from pain. Suedfeld and Kristeller (1982) reviewed other applications of REST, which include weight reduction, drug abuse treatment, and stress management. Apparently this technique can be used to alter consciousness and treat a variety of health problems. ■

It is important to remember that the study of consciousness—whether it is the waking state or an altered state—is extremely subjective, since we must rely on the subjects for much of our data. People sometimes have trouble understanding altered states of consciousness such as sleep because they are such a normal part of our everyday existence. However, as reported above, research is helping people sleep better and relax more fully, and is helping psychologists treat a variety of problems.

Drawing by Henry Martin; © 1983 The New Yorker Magazine, Inc.

"This concludes the conscious part of your day. Good night."

CHAPTER REVIEW

What You've Learned About Sleep and Consciousness

1. Consciousness is the processing of our sensations, thoughts, and feelings at various levels of awareness. Waking consciousness is the awareness of sensations and thoughts while we are awake and alert. In an altered state of consciousness there is a redirection of attention.

2. There are two types of sleep: REM, or rapid-eye-movement sleep, and NREM, or non-rapid-eye-movement sleep. In REM sleep, the heart rate accelerates, the eyes move rapidly about, breathing becomes variable, and the EEG is similar to the waking state. In NREM sleep, the heart rate and breathing slow down and muscular tension is absent. When we sleep, we pass through the four stages of NREM sleep and then come back to REM.

3. NREM appears to be influenced by serotonin produced in the raphe nucleus. REM is influenced by the locus coeruleus, and is affected by norepinephrine and acetylcholine. One theory suggests that REM sleep is involved in memory, whereas NREM sleep helps with physical growth and tissue repair. A recent theory proposes that REM sleep clears the brain of memories that interfere with thought and memory.

4. Everyone dreams each night, mostly during REM sleep. Early theories of dreaming suggested that dreams are where our unconscious conflicts reside. Current theories suggest that dreams are extensions of our everyday experiences. In one survey people reported dreaming about falling, being attacked, school, sexual behavior, eating, being frightened, or having a loved one die. The activation synthesis theory of dreaming suggests that dreams are the interpretation of brain physiological activity.

5. Insomnia is the inability to sleep. In sleep apnea, the person immediately awakens because he or she can't breathe. Narcolepsy is an inappropriate daytime attack of sleep. Other sleep disorders occur in NREM sleep and include sleep talking, sleepwalking, bed-wetting, and night terrors.

6. A psychoactive drug causes changes in behavior and cognition by modifying conscious awareness. Psychological dependence occurs when a person craves the drug. In physical dependence, or addiction, the habitual user's body becomes biochemically dependent upon the drug. Psychoactive drugs include depressants, opiates, stimulants, psychedelics, and the antipsychotic drugs.

7. Depressants (or sedative-hypnotics) are drugs that have a sedative effect. In large doses, alcohol disrupts motor coordination, thinking, and perception. Infants born to women alcoholics might have congenital malformations. Barbiturates are used for mild sedation, anesthesia, and as a treatment for insomnia or anxiety. Antianxiety minor tranquilizers are useful for treating anxiety, psychological pressure, and sometimes insomnia.

8. Opiates (or narcotic analgesics) are drugs whose effect on the body is similar to morphine. Opiates include naturally occurring drugs such as codeine, morphine, and heroin, and synthetic drugs such as methadone, Darvon, and Demerol. Medical uses include relief of pain, treatment of diarrhea, and suppression of coughs.

9. Stimulants are drugs that increase central nervous system activity and produce alertness or euphoria. Caffeine is probably the most widely used stimulant in our society. Nicotine produces effects similar to caffeine. Amphetamines have been used to treat sleep disorders and hyperactivity. Cocaine is derived from the coca plant. Antidepressant drugs treat depression.

10. The psychedelic drugs excite the nervous system, producing not only a change in emotional feelings, but also in the user's perceptions of the external world. They are called hallucinogens because at high doses they can result in hallucinations; they include LSD, mescaline, and PCP. Marijuana, derived from the cannabis plant, produces changes in time perception, attention, and mental organization.

11. Hypnosis is an altered state of consciousness characterized by heightened suggestibility. Techniques require a subject to relax and focus attention on something such as an object or repetitive sound. The best subjects are those who have good imaginations and the ability to fantasize. Hypnosis has been used to control pain, change behavior, improve memory, and modify fears and stress.

12. Meditation is the practice of relaxed concentration. It appears to be capable of reducing anxiety, increasing resistance to anger and depression, and improving a person's self-esteem and sense of well-being.

13. In sensory deprivation, or REST, the normal environmental sensory stimuli are drastically reduced. Recently, REST has been used to treat a variety of stress and health problems.

CHAPTER 6

LEARNING

Experimental psychologists have contributed significantly to discovering how we learn. They have paid particular attention to the association of stimuli and responses and the effects of reinforcement and punishment on behavior. Psychologists have also studied cognition and the biological constraints on learning.

CRITICAL THINKING OBJECTIVES FOR CHAPTER 6

After reading chapter 6, you should be able to identify, apply, and evaluate what you have learned about the following questions:

What are the components of the definition of learning?
What are the basic principles of classical conditioning?
What is the schedule of reinforcements?
What is the importance of cognitive learning?
What is the value of the continuum of preparedness?

CHAPTER 7

HUMAN MEMORY

How do we remember things? Why do we sometimes forget to do things? Psychologists are interested in how information is entered, stored, and retrieved from our memory systems. Recent attention has focused on how information proceeds from sensory memory to short-term and long-term memory stores. Practical suggestions for improving our ability to learn and remember are some of the benefits of the study of memory.

CRITICAL THINKING OBJECTIVES FOR CHAPTER 7

After reading chapter 7, you should be able to identify, apply, and evaluate what you have learned about the following questions:

What is the distinction between learning and memory?
What is the importance of the three processes of memory?
What are the important stages of memory?
What are the theories of forgetting?
What are the most useful memory enhancement techniques?
What is the importance of the theory of memory consolidation?

CHAPTER 8

LANGUAGE AND INTELLIGENCE

Part of what makes us unique is our ability to use language to communicate and to use thought to solve problems. The cognitive processes of language and thought are involved in intelligence. A number of important theories of intelligence have been proposed, and a variety of IQ tests have been developed to measure it.

CRITICAL THINKING OBJECTIVES FOR CHAPTER 8

After reading chapter 8, you should be able to identify, apply, and evaluate what you have learned about the following questions:

What are the areas of cognitive psychology?
What are the theories of language development?
What are the types of concepts?
What are the theories of problem solving?
What are the components in the definition of intelligence?
What are the important intelligence tests?
What are the roles of heredity and environment on intelligence?
What are the levels of mental retardation?

Part III surveys learning and the cognitive areas of psychology. In this section, learning, memory, language and thought processes, and the concept of intelligence are covered.

Learning and Cognitive Processes

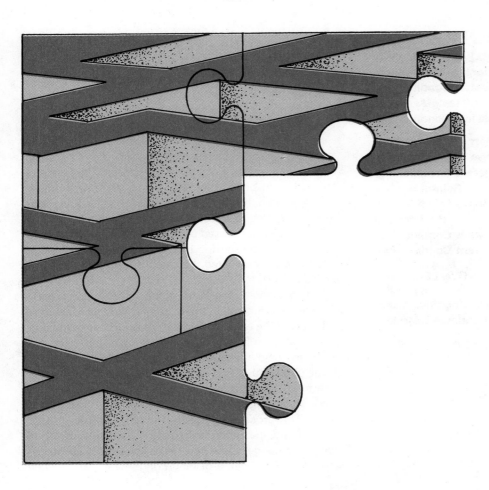

CHAPTER OBJECTIVES

What You'll Learn About Learning

After studying this chapter, you should be able to:

1. Define learning.
2. Identify the types of stimuli and responses involved in classical conditioning.
3. Outline the basic principles of classical conditioning.
4. Describe how taste aversions might be acquired through classical conditioning.
5. Identify three applications of classical conditioning in everyday life.
6. State Thorndike's law of effect.
7. Define shaping and describe an example.
8. Outline the basic principles of operant conditioning.
9. Define reinforcement and describe the major schedules of reinforcement.
10. Contrast and give examples of the different types of reinforcement (primary and secondary reinforcement, positive and negative reinforcement).
11. Describe the procedures of aversive conditioning (escape conditioning and avoidance conditioning).
12. Define punishment and list the variables that contribute to its effectiveness.
13. Identify three applications of operant conditioning in everyday life.
14. Compare classical conditioning and operant conditioning.
15. Describe the major forms of cognitive learning (insight, latent learning, and observational learning).
16. Outline the biological constraints on learning (instinctive drift, imprinting, and the continuum of preparedness in learning).

Can you imagine two pigeons playing Ping-Pong together? Harvard psychologist B. F. Skinner reported on a demonstration of this unlikely behavior. Skinner found in 1962 that, under the proper circumstances, pigeons are capable of learning fairly complex, sophisticated patterns of behavior, including how to play the game of Ping-Pong.

The Ping-Pong table was about 8 inches wide, 16 inches long, and 8 inches high. (See Figure 6.1.) It was constructed so that a pigeon could approach the edge of the table and peck at the ball. The surface was sloped slightly toward the edges that so that the ball would roll to a player. A trough at each end of the table would catch the ball if a player missed it, and the falling ball would trip a switch that caused food to be provided to the other pigeon. Wires prevented the pigeons from jumping onto the table itself.

In a pigeon Ping-Pong game, the human experimenter starts the ball in the middle of the table. The ball rolls toward the edge of one side. Each bird is expected to peck at the ball as it approaches and send it to the opposite side of the table. If it succeeds in causing the ball to roll off the other end of the table, that bird is rewarded with food. However, if an opponent pecks the ball and successfully returns it, the first pigeon must peck at it again. This procedure continues until one player misses the ball and the other bird gets the food reward. How could Skinner get these pigeons to learn the skills necessary to play the game of Ping-Pong?

6

Learning

Experimental psychologists have contributed significantly to discovering how we learn. They have paid particular attention to the association of stimuli and responses and the effects of reinforcement and punishment on behavior. Psychologists have also studied cognition and the biological constraints on learning.

He began by working with one pigeon at a time. First, he motivated a pigeon by making sure it was hungry. Then he glued a Ping-Pong ball to the edge of the table and gave the pigeon a little food whenever it pecked at the ball. In the beginning the pigeon did not show very much pecking behavior, but after receiving food for pecking, this behavior gradually increased in frequency.

When the bird had learned to peck consistently, Skinner unglued the ball so it could move about. The food reward was given only when the pigeon was able to drive the ball a certain distance. Gradually, the distance the ball had to travel before the pigeon received food was increased. Then Skinner began to delay giving food until the ball went to the opposite side of the table. Although the pigeon's behavior occasionally deteriorated, Skinner was able eventually to train the bird to continue to peck even if it did not immediately receive the food reward.

Finally, Skinner had trained pigeons to the point that they were ready to play an actual "game" of Ping-Pong. In a typical game, the pigeons were able to return the ball five or six times before scoring a point. The pigeons worked hard to peck at the ball until they received food. They watched the ball as it came toward them, and usually got in the correct position to send it back.

Through the gradual shaping of behavior by using a food reward, Skinner was able to teach the pigeons the fairly complex (for a pigeon) game of Ping-Pong. Using similar procedures, Skinner was able to get a variety of animals and people to learn numerous complex behaviors. The procedures he developed are being used in schools, mental hospitals, and homes to help people learn more efficiently. The shaping technique is a very powerful tool used by psychologists today.

FIGURE 6.1 Operant Conditioning
Harvard psychologist B. F. Skinner was able to shape the behavior of pigeons so that they pecked at a Ping-Pong ball in order to get food. Eventually, the pigeons were able to play a modified version of Ping-Pong. Shaping animal behavior is a technique of operant conditioning.

WHAT IS LEARNING?

From the moment we wake up until the moment we fall asleep, most of what we do involves learning. We get up, shower, dress, eat, walk, study, talk, listen to music—all because we have learned how to perform these behaviors. In fact, learning is so important in our lives that we would find it difficult to think of situations that do not involve learning in some way.

Psychologists usually define learning as the relatively permanent change in behavior or behavioral ability of an individual that occurs as a result of experience. There are several features of this definition we ought to discuss. First, learning involves a relatively permanent change. This refers to the fact that the individual's behavior is modified and continues to remain different in the future. The term *relatively permanent* distinguishes learning from temporary changes in behavior caused by motivation, fatigue, or drugs. For example, when we are tired, we behave differently than usual (perhaps we go to sleep or become sloppy in our work), but this is a temporary change and thus does not reflect learning. Likewise, motivations such as hunger or thirst might temporarily alter our behavior, but after we have eaten or have had a drink, we revert to our former behavior. Learning only includes relatively long-lasting changes.

Second, learning involves a change in the individual's behavior or ability to exhibit a behavior. There is some variation in the emphasis of different perspectives; the behavioral viewpoint focuses on the actual change in behavior and the cognitive perspective emphasizes the change in the ability to exhibit the behavior. Often a distinction is made between learning and *performance*. The actual behavior that is observed is called performance, whereas learning is inferred from the behavior. Performance can be thought of as the combined result of learning and motivation. Let's assume that you read this chapter and know the definition of learning when you go to class. But even though you have learned the definition, you do not show it until motivated to do so (perhaps when taking a test). How does your instructor know you have learned the information? He or she observes your performance on the test and infers from your behavior that learning has taken place. Although we often talk as if performance and learning were equivalent, there is a difference. Typically, you learn much more than you exhibit (unless motivated to do your best).

Third, learning results from behavioral experience in the environment. In order to learn, we need to perceive events in our environment and to associate or connect those events with our behavior. For instance, through our experience of eating in restaurants, we learn that certain ones serve better food than others and we continue to eat in the better ones. We learn how to play basketball by practicing until we become good players. By watching television programs, we learn that certain programs are more entertaining than others and continue to watch the more entertaining ones. Experience in the environment is necessary for learning to occur, and thus behavioral changes caused only by physical growth, maturation, or injury are not examples of learning.

Most psychologists study an individual's behavior in terms of specific actions, which are called responses. If we looked at an individual in isolation and ignored his or her surroundings, we would not make much headway in understanding behavior. Clearly, we must also consider the individual's *environment*, the events taking place outside the body. Only in relation to the environment do an individual's movements—taking a pill, kissing a baby, eating a meal, or writing a letter—become meaningful responses. Like behavior, environment must also be broken up into useful units, which psychologists call stimuli. Environmental stimuli cause us to give particular responses. The red traffic light that signals a driver to stop his or her car at an intersection is an example of a stimulus.

The pigeons in our opening story had to learn how to play Ping-Pong. Their modified ability to play can be seen in the change from random pecking to pecking the ball in a way that would score a point. This change came about because they experienced a food reward when they showed the expected behavior. They continued to show the learned behavior in later Ping-Pong matches, thus demonstrating that the learning was relatively permanent.

Learning involves forming associations between the events in the environment (stimuli) and our behavior (responses). Many theorists argue that reinforcement, or reward, is necessary for learning to take place, whereas others suggest that reward provides the motivation to exhibit what has been learned. We will discover many variables that influence learning as we go through this chapter.

CLASSICAL CONDITIONING

Picture in your mind a research laboratory in Russia. The year was 1904 and the researcher was the Russian physiologist Ivan Pavlov, who had recently won the Nobel Prize for his work on the digestive process in dogs. He had been measuring saliva and other internal secretions produced by dogs when they eat and digest their food.

Pavlov discovered that his dogs began salivating before he fed them. In fact, upon careful observation, he

FIGURE 6.2 Classical Conditioning

The apparatus pictured is similar to that used in Pavlov's famous early experiments on conditioning. Pavlov trained dogs to salivate at the sound of a tone. In classical conditioning, the conditioned stimulus (CS, a tone) is presented just before the unconditioned stimulus (US, food). After several pairings, the conditioned stimulus evokes the conditioned response (CR, salivation).

found that the dogs were salivating when they saw the experimenter, the food dish, or even when they heard footsteps coming into the lab. Pavlov decided to study this anticipatory response in its own right, and by doing so, greatly influenced the future of psychology.

He conducted one famous experiment in which he produced the sound of a tone by ringing a bell just prior to administering food to a dog. At first, the dog showed no particular reaction to the tone. But after several trials in which the dog heard the tone just before being fed, it began to salivate in response to the bell alone. What had originally been a neutral stimulus now caused the dog to salivate. The dog had learned to interpret the sound of the bell as a signal that it was about to be fed.

Pavlov did not stop here. He gave the dog a number of trials in which he only produced the sound of the bell (and no food was given). When the bell alone was used as a stimulus, after several trials the dog's salivation response declined drastically. Pavlov found, however, that when he then gave the dog a rest for a day or two, again it quickly responded only to the bell for several more trials before stopping (Pavlov, 1927).

Pavlov conducted a large number of experiments in dogs to study the associations of responses and stimuli. For neutral stimuli, he presented lights, and sounds of buzzers, bells, and metronomes. He usually followed one of these stimuli with food (meat powder) but also used a weak acid solution, or even a mild electric shock. The subject responses measured were often salivary, but also included flexing the leg (after a shock). Pavlov referred to these responses as "reflexes," and was interested in how the physiological pathways in the brain that produced the newly acquired reflexes were formed.

Pavlov gave the name *conditioning* to the formation of this new bond or association between a neutral stimulus and the response. Today, this type of learning is called classical conditioning, or sometimes Pavlovian or respondent conditioning. The term conditioning is usually used to signify a relatively simple form of learning that is often studied scientifically. Learning, on the other hand, is a much broader term that incorporates conditioning as well as other forms of acquiring new behaviors (Houston, 1991).

Ivan Petrovich Pavlov, shown here on the right (with a white beard), was born in 1849 in Ryazan, Russia, at the beginning of one of the most fertile intellectual eras in Russian history.

In accordance with his father's wishes, he attended the local theological seminary until a growing interest in the natural sciences led him to rebel against his intended career. He went on to obtain a medical degree from the Imperial Medicosurgical Academy in 1879. He then studied physiology in Germany briefly before being appointed professor of pharmacology at the St. Petersburg Institute of Experimental Medicine in 1890.

He won the Nobel Prize in 1904 for his research on the physiology of digestion. At this time, he began research on conditioned reflexes in dogs, thus becoming the pioneer in classical conditioning. Pavlov spent the rest of his life studying conditioning, which he believed was a useful research method for studying physiology. He engaged in research actively until his death at the age of 87 in 1936.

BIOGRAPHICAL HIGHLIGHT

IVAN PETROVICH PAVLOV

FIGURE 6.3 Example of Classical Conditioning
In everyday life, a loud noise is often an unconditioned stimulus (US) that elicits a startle response, which is an unconditioned response (UR). A balloon, by contrast, is typically a neutral stimulus (NS), eliciting no special response. If the sight of an overinflated balloon precedes the loud noise of it bursting, the balloon becomes a conditioned stimulus (CS). The next time a balloon is seen, it might elicit a startle response, which is now a conditioned response (CR).

Classical Conditioning Terminology

We begin by discussing four important terms in classical conditioning: unconditioned stimulus, unconditioned response, conditioned stimulus, and conditioned response. The unconditioned stimulus, or US, is any stimulus that provokes an automatic or reflexive reaction in an individual. Examples of common unconditioned stimuli include: loud noises, a pin-prick, and an object rapidly approaching you. The particular response elicited by the US is called the unconditioned response, or UR. Examples of unconditioned responses include: tensing the body in response to hearing a loud noise, jumping in response to being pricked by a pin, and ducking in response to an object being thrown at you. In Pavlov's original experiment, the US was food, and the UR was the dog's salivation. The term *unconditioned response* refers to a behavior that does not have to be learned as a response to a stimulus in the present situation. It may be a genetically programmed reflex, or it may have been previously learned. The important point is that the subject automatically shows the unconditioned response when presented with the unconditioned stimulus.

If the US is repeatedly presented immediately after some neutral stimulus, such as Pavlov's bell, the neutral stimulus alone will become sufficient to elicit the re-

sponse. The originally neutral stimulus is then called the conditioned stimulus, or CS. The newly learned response to the CS is the conditioned response or CR.

I like to think of classical conditioning as "stimulus substitution," in which the US is replaced by the CS, and the response stays about the same. Although this particular interpretation is somewhat simplistic, it will help you grasp the general idea of classical conditioning. The CR, for our purposes, is essentially the same as the UR, although it is important to remember that they are elicited by two different stimuli (Houston, 1991). Thus, to understand classical conditioning we must identify which kind of stimulus elicited the response. If the stimulus previously caused the response, it is the US, and if the stimulus was just learned, it is the CS.

A famous experiment was conducted in 1920 by John Watson and his assistant, Rosalie Rayner. Although not strictly pure classical conditioning, it exemplifies the principles we are discussing. Watson was interested in how human emotions were learned. He tested an 11-month-old baby named Albert for reactions to a variety of stimuli, including a white rat, a rabbit, masks, and a ball of cotton. "Little Albert's" response was positive to all of these things, and he readily touched them when given the chance. In order to produce a fear response, when Albert reached out to touch the rat (CS), Watson produced a loud, unpleasant noise (US) behind the child by striking a hammer on a steel bar. Albert, not surprisingly, responded by crying (UR). After five or six trials, the mere sight of the rat alone (CS) caused Little Albert to burst out in tears (CR). Watson had conditioned Little Albert to associate a loud noise with one of the stimuli, the white rat. Watson suggested that many emotions, both positive and negative, are learned through classical conditioning.

Classical conditioning is involved in *every* aspect of our lives. For instance, you probably still associate the smell of certain foods with your enjoyment of a particular occasion in your life. You feel warm and tingly when you see that special someone. And hearing your special song on the radio brings back happy memories. Classical conditioning is indeed involved in a wide variety of situations.

Basic Principles of Classical Conditioning

To understand how classical conditioning works, it is necessary to identify and examine its basic principles. These include acquisition, extinction, spontaneous recovery, stimulus generalization, stimulus discrimination, and higher order conditioning.

Acquisition A great deal of research has examined the variables that have an impact on the acquisition

FIGURE 6.4   Little Albert Experiment

John B. Watson in his experiment with Little Albert, an 11-month-old baby (*above*), studied how emotions are learned. He presented **(1)** a white rat (CS) and **(2)** a loud noise (US) to Little Albert. After several pairings, **(3)** Albert showed fear (CR) of the white rat. Later, **(4)** Albert generalized the fear to stimuli that were similar to CS, such as a beard. *Below:* the youngster reacts to the scarecrow in a manner that is similar to Little Albert's generalized fear.

of classical conditioning (Klein, 1991). The <u>interstimulus interval</u> between the CS and US is an extremely important variable. For classical conditioning to take place effectively, the CS usually comes first, followed by the US usually within half a second. Pavlov discovered in 1927 that the timing of the CS was a crucial factor in conditioning. If the CS was presented at the same time as the US, too long after it, or too long before it, it had little or no effect on the dog's behavior.

There are several procedures in classical conditioning that vary the temporal relationship of the stimuli, including forward delayed conditioning, forward trace conditioning, simultaneous conditioning, and backward

conditioning. Overall, the forward delayed conditioning procedure is the most effective, followed by forward trace conditioning and then simultaneous conditioning (Sherman, 1978). Backward conditioning is not very effective, and indeed can sometimes lead to opposite effects.

In <u>delayed conditioning</u>, the presentation of the CS precedes the onset of the US, and the termination of the CS is delayed until the US is presented (either at the US onset or during the presentation of the US). In Watson's study, the rat (CS) was presented before the loud noise (US) and remained in view of Little Albert until the loud noise was presented.

In many situations, the CS is a discrete event that is presented and terminated before the US is presented. Examples of discrete events include the noise of a gun being fired, the flash of a strobe light, one ring of a telephone, and the sound of an automobile horn. This is the procedure of <u>trace conditioning</u>, which can be very effective if the interstimulus interval is very brief. Pavlov used trace conditioning when he produced the tone once and then one second later presented the food. Even though trace conditioning is often used, it is not as effective as delayed conditioning.

Although Pavlov restricted his own research to dogs, other investigators have studied classical conditioning in many animals as well as in people. In many situations, the optimum time interval between the CS and US is about one-half to 2 seconds (Klein, 1991). However, there is variability among species and the particular response being conditioned. For example, in conditioned taste aversion, discussed later in this chapter, the successful interstimulus interval can be hours rather than seconds.

In <u>simultaneous conditioning</u> the CS and the US are presented at exactly the same time. Pavlov found that conditioning was very weak when the tone and food were presented together. One explanation is that there is no time for the subject to anticipate the US and thus the CS does not take on the properties of the US.

In the procedure sometimes called <u>backward conditioning</u>, the US is presented and terminated before the presentation of the CS. If Pavlov had presented the food and then, after the dog ate, presented the sound of the bell, the tone alone would not elicit much salivation, since it no longer signals that food is imminent. Backward conditioning is controversial because many psychologists argue that it does not work.

In the above examples, it is assumed that the CS is originally a truly neutral stimulus. Often, however, both stimuli have meaning to the subject, and the labeling of them is arbitrary. What usually happens is that the first stimulus (called the CS) takes on the properties of the second stimulus (called the US). This can be demonstrated with a simple illustration. Suppose you have a child who loves honey and hates medicine. Your child is sick and must take medicine, so you decide to use

FIGURE 6.5 Temporal Relationships

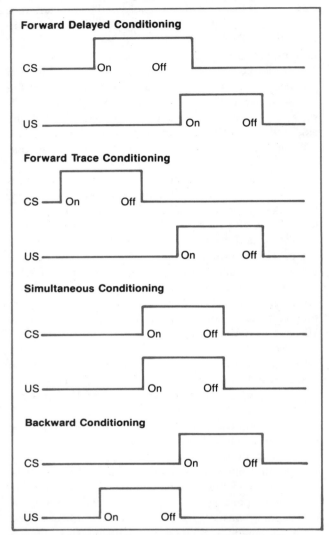

In classical conditioning, the conditioned stimulus (CS) presented immediately before the unconditioned stimulus (US), is known as forward delayed conditioning. If the CS is presented and terminated before the US is presented, the procedure is known as forward trace conditioning. Sometimes the CS and US are presented at exactly the same time and the process is known as simultaneous condition-ing. When the CS is presented after the US, it is referred to as backward conditioning.

FIGURE 6.6 Classical Conditioning Paradigm

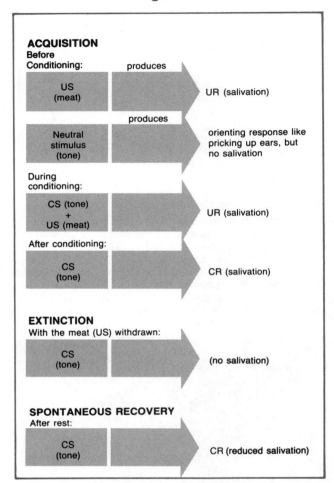

Before conditioning, the unconditioned stimulus (US) of meat elicits the unconditioned response (UR), or salivation from the dog. The neutral stimulus (NS), the sound of a tone, elicits an orienting response, but does not cause the dog to salivate. During conditioning, the conditioned stim-ulus (CS), the tone, is presented immediately before the US. After several pairings, the tone (CS) alone elicits the condi-tioned response (CR). During extinction, when the US (meat) has been removed, the CS (tone) becomes less and less effective in eliciting the CR. In spontaneous recovery, after a rest period, the CS is again briefly able to elicit the CR.

classical conditioning to accomplish your task. Which would you give first, the medicine or the honey? Think about it very carefully, because if you do the wrong thing, your child will come to hate honey as well as the medicine.

If you give honey (CS) first, and then medicine (US), your child will come to hate (CR) honey. However, if you give the medicine (CS) first, and then the honey (US), the medicine will become associated with the

honey, and after a couple of pairings, the medicine alone will be liked (CR), or at least tolerated.

The CS becomes stronger as the number of condi-tioning trials containing the US increases (Adams, 1980). That is, if you only pair the CS and US once or twice, the CS alone will not be as effective as it would be if you paired the stimuli a half-dozen times. Pavlov needed to have a number of pairings before the bell alone would elicit salivation.

FIGURE 6.7 Acquisition, Extinction, and Spontaneous Recovery of Classical Conditioning

During acquisition, the conditioned stimulus and unconditioned stimulus are paired. A short interstimulus interval and a large number of conditioning trials result in effective acquisition. During extinction, the conditioned stimulus is presented by itself. The more often the conditioned stimulus is presented by itself, the less effective it becomes in producing the conditioned response. A conditioned response may reappear after extinction if the CS is withheld for awhile and then presented later (after Pavlov, 1927).

Extinction I once had a guinea pig who loved lettuce. Within a few weeks, she would squeal every time the refrigerator door was opened, because she often received lettuce shortly thereafter. The guinea pig had become classically conditioned to squeal (CR) at the sound of the refrigerator door being opened (CS). Then the price of lettuce went up and I no longer fed her any. What do you suppose happened? She squealed for a while, but then the squealing became weaker and died out altogether. The squealing had been extinguished.

Extinction is the elimination of a CR by presenting only the CS without the US. Pavlov found that when the bell was rung by itself without any meat powder following it, the dog salivated less and eventually stopped altogether. The US is sometimes referred to as the reinforcement, and thus we say that extinction occurs when reinforcement is withdrawn.

Spontaneous Recovery Extinction does not necessarily stop the CR permanently. If the subject is given a rest in which the CS is withheld, a later presentation of the CS alone may bring on at least some of the old CR, although it is likely to be weaker and disappear fairly quickly. This sudden reappearance of a CR after extinction is called spontaneous recovery. This occurs even though the US has not been presented after extinction began.

I went on a vacation and took my guinea pig with me. When we arrived home, I happened to open the refrigerator and the guinea pig squealed loudly and clearly, even though she had not had any lettuce for a long time. Likewise, Pavlov found spontaneous recovery in his dogs. After he had extinguished their response to the sound of the bell, they were returned to their home cages. The next morning, they spontaneously recovered, and salivated at the sound of the bell, even though it had not been re-paired with meat powder.

Stimulus Generalization After Little Albert had been conditioned to fear a white rat, Watson and Rayner discovered that he began to cry when shown other furry objects—a rabbit, a dog, a fur coat, and even a mask of Santa Claus. He was exhibiting the principle of stimulus generalization. That is, once the CR (crying) was conditioned to the CS (rat), stimuli similar to the CS became sufficient to elicit the CR. The greater the similarity between the new stimulus and the original CS, the stronger the CR.

Once Pavlov had the dog responding to the sound of a bell, he tried other signals and found that sounds similar to the tone would also elicit the CR. For example, Pavlov found that the sound of a buzzer or the clicking of a metronome would also cause the dog to salivate.

The phenomenon of stimulus generalization has been observed and well documented in both animal and human studies. It seems that many of our fears are learned through classical conditioning and stimulus generalization. For example, an individual who is bitten by a large dog may later find that he or she is not only fearful of all large dogs but of small dogs and other similar animals as well.

Stimulus Discrimination If organisms were to generalize their learned responses to one particular type of stimulus to all remotely similar stimuli, the result would be a vast array of unadaptive behaviors. We usually learn to limit our responses to relevant stimuli. Indeed, the capacity for adaptive living depends upon how well we learn to recognize and respond to the critical features of the environment. This process is called stimulus discrimination and is important in successful adjustment.

Pavlov also identified this phenomenon in his dogs. Once a dog had been conditioned to the sound of a bell, through stimulus generalization, it would also salivate in response to the clicking sound of a metronome. But then if the metronome was never followed by the US, whereas the bell always was, the CR to the metronome would soon cease to occur. The dog would learn to discriminate between the two stimuli, never salivating to the one but always to the other.

Discrimination learning is important in our everyday lives. Reading would be extremely difficult if we could not discriminate between similar letters, like *b* and *d*. We learn to respond to people on the basis of individual behavior and personal characteristics, not stereotypes.

Higher Order Conditioning The potential complexity of the role of classical conditioning in our lives has one final principle. Pavlov and his colleagues discovered that a CS could sometimes work as a US. If still another neutral stimulus was constantly presented before a particular CS, it too would bring on a CR. For example, they injected a dog with morphine, which produced vomiting. After that, the dog would vomit at the mere sight of a needle, thus exhibiting a CR. They then found that various stimuli occurring before the sight of the needle— the smell of alcohol, the box containing the needle, or even the sight of the laboratory—might be sufficient to elicit the CR.

In higher order conditioning, the CS is paired with a new neutral stimulus, which takes on the properties of the CS. Higher order conditioning is not the same as stimulus generalization. It is no longer a question of responding to stimuli similar to the original CS. Rather, the individual is now responding to stimuli that are totally unlike the original CS but associated with it in time. Thus, the victim of a dog bite may subsequently develop fears and apprehensions that will cause him or her to avoid the street in which the event took place.

Higher order classical conditioning is a common phenomenon. It is often successfully used in advertising. For example, you probably have seen model/actress Brooke Shields in an advertisement for blue jeans or Michael Jackson in a commercial for a popular soda. Consumers presumably have learned to respond positively to these stars and thus will also respond favorably to the advertised product. Another example is the development of test anxiety. Let's assume that as a child when you went to school (CS) you were threatened by a bully (US) and became very upset (UR). School then caused anxiety (CR). If you were then given a test in school, the test would become associated with school, and through higher order conditioning also elicit anxiety. Of course there are many ways that test anxiety can develop, such as having people tell you that you will probably fail a test or actually failing a test yourself.

Conditioned Taste Aversion

Do you have a particular type of food that you do not like? Do you know why? For many people, conditioned taste aversion (CTA), might be due to situations where they become ill (often with the stomach flu) after eating a meal that contained something new. One example is my "Big Mac Attack," which I experienced as a graduate student. I loved Big Macs from McDonald's and often treated myself to them in the evening. One night, I woke up in terrible pain, and eventually found myself in the hospital awaiting surgery for kidney stones. After I recuperated from the operation, I headed for McDonald's, only to find that every time I started to eat a Big Mac, I felt nauseated. I had developed a conditioned taste aversion. The kidney stone was the US, the severe stomach pain was the UR, the hamburger was the CS, and the stomach pain was the CR. Luckily, I learned about extinction, and the taste aversion eventually disappeared. But for awhile, the "Big Mac Attack" slogan had special meaning for me.

It is difficult to look in a journal dealing with animal learning and not find an article on conditioned taste aversion. Many animals, as well as humans, have been quick to learn to avoid particular tastes and odors when the tested substance is followed by stomach distress (Braveman & Bronstein, 1985). Ilene Bernstein reported finding conditioned taste aversion in children with cancer who were undergoing chemotherapy. She believes that studying CTA might help prevent the dangerous loss of appetite experienced by many chemotherapy patients (Bernstein, 1985).

People who use poison to get rid of rats often discover an interesting set of events. Upon introduction, the new poison is extremely effective and kills many rats. However, shortly afterward, the poison seems ineffective because the rats will not eat it. This phenomenon, sometimes called bait shyness, is an example of conditioned taste aversion (Garcia, 1989). Rats are nibblers—they nibble a little of a variety of foods. When a rat nibbles on

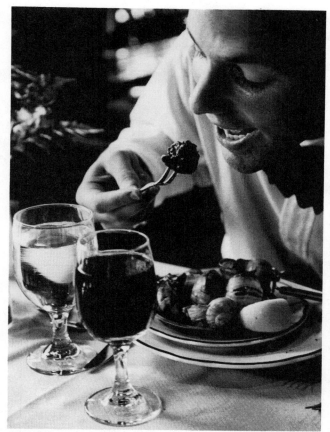

FIGURE 6.8 Conditioned Taste Aversion (CTA)
We encounter CTA when we become ill after eating a particular food. If you enjoyed eating escargots, but later became sick, you would probably dislike the appearance of snails the next time, and would avoid eating them. CTA has likely helped in our survival as well as the survival of other species.

the poison, it is likely to become very sick. If it survives, it has learned to avoid substances tasting like the poison.

John Garcia and his colleagues first tested taste aversion in the laboratory in 1955. They allowed rats to drink sweetened water and then produced gastrointestinal distress, or a stomachache, by giving them X-irradiation. They found that when given the opportunity a few days later to drink the sweetened water, the rats refused. The X ray (US) that caused the stomachache (UR) had been associated with the sweetened water (CS), so that it also came to be associated with illness (CR).

A study that I completed in 1981 shows that conditioned aversion can also be formed in social situations. I paired two gerbils together for 5 minutes and then had one of them, by injection of lithium chloride, experience a stomachache. When placed together again 2 days later, the gerbil who had had a stomachache appeared to be afraid of the other gerbil. He had learned to avoid another animal because he associated it with the stom-

achache. This research suggests the possibility of liking or disliking others due to classical conditioning.

Conditioned taste aversion differs from regular classical conditioning in several respects. CTA often occurs in one trial, requiring only one pairing of the CS with the US instead of several. The interstimulus interval for CTA can be hours rather than seconds. There is currently a scientific debate going on to determine whether CTA is a unique form of learning or a special case of classical conditioning. At any rate, you should be aware of the possible effects of conditioned taste aversion in your everyday life.

Applications of Classical Conditioning

By this time, you will recognize that classical conditioning plays an important role in our lives. The principles of classical conditioning have been used to help improve the human condition. The applications of classical conditioning in treating behavior problems are discussed in detail in chapter 14, "Therapy," and several examples of therapies involving classical conditioning are provided here.

Classical conditioning has been used in predation control. Because they like to eat sheep, coyotes are a problem to sheep farmers. We could kill the coyotes, but this approach would probably not be appropriate. Instead, Gustavson and Gustavson (1985) described a study in which they conditioned some coyotes not to eat the sheep. They took sheep meat (CS) and sprinkled it with a chemical (US) that would produce a stomachache (UR) in the coyotes. After the coyotes ate the treated meat, they avoided the live sheep (CR), at least temporarily. This humane application of conditioned taste aversion might be used to control other predators as well.

Classical conditioning can be used also to help people reduce fears. Counterconditioning involves pairing the stimulus (CS) that elicits fear with a stimulus (US) that elicits positive emotion (UR). For example, a person who is afraid of snakes but loves chocolate ice cream is shown a snake and then given the ice cream. While the person is busy eating the ice cream, classical conditioning helps associate the snake with good feelings.

Some evidence suggests that classical conditioning may be involved in drug tolerance (see Chapter 5, "Sleep and Consciousness," for a discussion of drug tolerance). After repeatedly taking a drug, it is sometimes necessary to increase the dosage to obtain the same effect. For example, after being given repeated doses of morphine to reduce pain, patients often require larger doses. Siegel and colleagues (1982) argue that cues such as the needle used to administer the drug elicit negative feelings that tend to work against the normal effects of the drug. Siegel also suggests that an essential component in the treatment of drug addiction is to reduce the conditioned responses produced by positive cues associated with taking the drug. Siegal argued that drug overdose can occur when the drug is taken in a new location that doesn't have all of the associated cues, such as the familiar furniture in a room. Although a lower dose of the drug would have been effective, the individual may take the usual increased amount, resulting in an overdose.

Classical conditioning appears to be involved both in the formation and elimination of our emotional reactions. You might try to keep a list of the stimuli in your environment that elicit responses from you. Then put to work the principles of classical conditioning to help you understand how you learn the many emotions you experience.

OPERANT CONDITIONING

About the time Pavlov was experimenting with conditioned reflexes in dogs, an American experimental psychologist, Edward L. Thorndike, was observing trial-and-error learning in cats. In a typical study, he placed a hungry cat in a small cage and left some food outside the cage, in full view of the cat. At first, the cat moved restlessly about. Then it began clawing at the bars of the cage and at the objects in it. Eventually, after about 3 minutes of trying, the cat pulled the right string or pushed

FIGURE 6.10 Instrumental Conditioning

A single cat learning to escape from a Thorndike puzzle box

Thorndike studied trial-and-error learning in cats by placing them in cages and observing them escape. In successive trials, it took less time for the cats to escape from the puzzle box (after Thorndike, 1898).

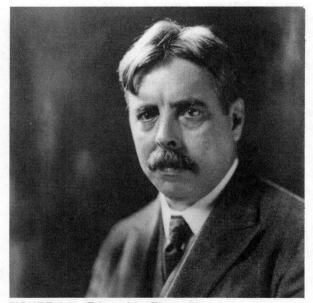

FIGURE 6.9 Edward L. Thorndike

An early American psychologist who conducted research in the area of instrumental learning, Thorndike proposed the law of effect, which states that a response that produces satisfaction will be repeated.

the right knob, the door of the cage opened, and the cat rushed out and pounced on the food. Thorndike then put the cat back in the cage and let it try again. In each successive trial, the cat took less time to find the right way to get out of the cage. After 20 trials, the cat could escape within 10 seconds (Thorndike, 1898).

The cat had definitely learned something, but classical conditioning did not fit this situation. Pulling and pushing were not reflexes but rather voluntary responses; there was no unconditioned stimulus that automatically elicited them. Thorndike called this form of learning instrumental conditioning, stating that the individual is instrumental in emitting, or producing, a response.

To explain this form of learning, Thorndike proposed his law of effect: Any response that produces satisfaction in a given situation becomes associated with that situation, and when that situation occurs again, the response is more likely to be repeated. Conversely, a response that brings discomfort in a certain situation will be less likely to occur when the situation arises again (Thorndike, 1932). The law of effect applies to learning responses that affect (or change) the environment, which in turn affects the individual. The effect these responses have on the environment determine whether they will be repeated or not.

The person who probably did the most to shape the direction of the form of conditioning called operant conditioning was the well-known behaviorist, B. F. Skinner. He named the behavior that comes to be controlled by its consequences, or effects, *operant behavior* because its function is to operate on the environment. He called the behavior Pavlov studied "respondent behavior," because the reflexes are elicited responses to preceding stimuli. In contrast to the respondent behavior, the operant behavior is first emitted more or less as a random act. This behavior becomes learned, or operantly conditioned, only when it is regularly followed by reinforcement. *Reinforcement* is any event that increases the probability that the behavior preceding it will be repeated. Reinforcement can generally be thought of as a reward.

Shaping (Successive Approximation)

Assume that you are a psychologist and your task is to get Little Tommy to wear his glasses. Tommy is 4 years old and does not like his glasses because his sisters laugh at him and call him names when he wears them. How would you help Tommy wear his glasses willingly?

After you are finished with this chapter, here is what you might do. First, ask Tommy's mother not to feed him before bringing him to the session. And make sure that he loves Reese's Pieces. (What little boy doesn't love E.T.'s favorite candy?) Prepare the treatment room by taking everything out except one table in the center. Place the glasses on the table. When Tommy's mother drops him off, tell her to wait in your office, on another floor.

Bring Tommy in and lock the door. He might cry and try to escape. You do nothing. Eventually he looks at you. You run over and give him a Reese's Piece. He cries some more; again you do nothing. Then he stands up and takes a step toward the table on which his glasses have been placed. He is rewarded with one Reese's Piece. He stops and looks around. Nothing. When he takes two steps toward the table, one Reese's Piece. He moves back to the door. Nothing. He takes two steps forward, placing him where he was before. Nothing. Finally he walks over to the table. A Reese's Piece (or maybe two). He stands there. Nothing. Then he reaches out toward the glasses. A Reese's Piece. Then he stands there. Nothing. Eventually, he picks up the glasses and puts them on. Two Reese's Pieces. He may take them off but when he puts

FIGURE 6.11 Shaping (Successive Approximation)
This killer whale was taught to perform tricks by trainers who consistently reinforced the kind of behavior that approximated the desired trick. This is an example of shaping, a technique that works on humans as well.

them back on he gets a Reese's Piece only if he keeps them on for 10 seconds. Then 30 seconds. Then 1 minute. Then 5 minutes.

When he reaches this point (which might take more than one session), you bring Tommy's mother back and give her the candy. She continues to reinforce him with the candy as long as he wears the glasses. You also arrange for his mother and sisters to say nice things to him and to include him in activities that he finds reinforcing. Eventually, other reinforcers take the place of the candy, and he will continue to wear the glasses because with them he can see better.

You have been using shaping with Tommy. Shaping, or successive approximation, is a gradual process that begins with the reinforcement of some behavior that approximates, or gets closer to, the final behavior desired (Skinner, 1953). When that response has been conditioned, reinforcement is withheld until the subject emits a response just a little closer to the goal desired. With careful giving and withholding of reinforcements, the subject can gradually be made to perform complex responses that he or she would never perform in an "uncontrolled" environment.

This technique really works. Many animal trainers regularly make effective use of shaping, as do some sports coaches. As illustrated in this chapter's opening story, Skinner used shaping techniques in the laboratory, where he got two pigeons to play a form of Ping-Pong. In fact, this basic approach to conditioning is so successful that it has become popular with psychologists in helping people in educational settings as well as in mental institutions.

Can you think of other situations in which shaping might occur? A second-grade teacher helping students write? A friend of yours getting you to go to a movie? An instructor helping students give correct answers on tests? Or a parent helping a child overcome shyness? Shaping is a very common phenomenon in our lives.

Basic Principles of Operant Conditioning

In operant conditioning, it's "what comes afterward that counts." Much of our everyday behavior is based on its effects, as Thorndike pointed out with his law of effect: if we do something and we get rewarded, we will do it again. If we do it often enough, we will form a habit.

Acquisition Shaping is a very effective way to help subjects acquire or learn a behavior through operant conditioning. But we often do not need to be shaped to learn a behavior. We discover what gets reinforcement through trial-and-error learning, as did Thorndike's cats.

Much of the early basic work on operant conditioning was done with *mazes* and Skinner boxes (or operant chambers). In maze learning, a subject has to travel through the maze before being reinforced. In Skinner boxes, we train a subject, most commonly a rat or a pigeon, who finds itself in a box (or a cage) that features a depressible bar (or other manipulative device) and a cup that presents food pellets (or other reinforcers). The Skinner box was designed by B. F. Skinner to study operant conditioning in animals.

First, the experimenter checks the operant level of the behavior being studied. The *operant level* is the rate at which the subject makes the desired response without getting direct reinforcement from the experimenter. In this instance, the operant level, or *baseline,* is the rate at which the subject—let's suppose it is a rat—depresses the bar without getting food. The experimenter then turns on a mechanism that dispenses food into the cup as soon as the rat presses the bar. Typically, the rat will be moving about the Skinner box more or less randomly. Sooner or later, it will probably push down on the bar, immediately receiving a food pellet. Later, the same thing happens again. If the rat has not eaten for some time, it soon begins to press the bar faster and faster until it reaches the

FIGURE 6.12 Reinforcement: The Skinner Box
Reinforcement is used to teach a rat to press a bar by rising on his hind legs and bending forward. This is accomplished by strengthening the animal's natural behavior each time he comes close to the bar.

maximum rate at which the food pellets may be dispensed. The rat is undergoing operant conditioning. If the rat didn't by chance touch the bar, the experimenter could always use the technique of shaping.

In order for the acquisition of operant conditioning to occur, the subject must be motivated to want whatever is used as *reinforcement.* If reinforcement is food, then the subject should be hungry. It is important that reinforcement follows the response because the response then occurs more frequently. We discuss the concept of reinforcement more fully later in this chapter.

Extinction In operant conditioning, extinction is the withholding of reinforcement. As we discussed earlier in classical conditioning, when there is no reinforcement (the US in classical conditioning), the frequency of the behavior decreases and often eventually disappears altogether. For example, when a rat operantly conditioned in a Skinner box is in extinction, at first its behavior may become more variable and more frequent. Fairly soon, however, the rat depresses the lever less and less, and eventually no longer shows the bar-pressing behavior.

What do you do when you do not receive reinforcement for your behavior? What if you studied hard for your tests, but continually failed them? Or you worked all week and then found there was no paycheck? Chances are good that you would stop studying or stop working (at least at that job).

B. F. SKINNER

Burrhus Frederic Skinner is probably the most famous, influential, and controversial figure in contemporary American psychology. He was born in the small railroad town of Susquehanna, Pennsylvania, in March 1904. After graduating from Hamilton College in 1926 with a degree in English, he tried writing, but eventually gave it up, because he felt he had nothing important to say. He became interested in psychology and earned his Ph.D. from Harvard University in 1931.

He taught for several years at the University of Minnesota and Indiana University. During this time he wrote two of his most important books, *The Behavior of Organisms* (1938) and a novel, *Walden Two* (1948), which is an account of a utopian society run in accordance with operant principles. Skinner returned to Harvard in 1948, where he remained until his death in August 1990.

B. F. Skinner made numerous contributions to the science of behavior. He strongly influenced the area of learning that he named operant conditioning. His Skinner box is now a standard apparatus for the experimental study of animal behavior. Much of his work involved the study of how reinforcement schedules influence learning and behavior. His *Beyond Freedom and Dignity* (1971) is a nonfiction examination of his utopian society, in which he explains why we must understand how we control behavior in everyday life. In his 1987 book, *Upon Further Reflection*, Skinner presented his views on issues ranging from world peace and evolution to education and old age.

There are many factors involved in the extinction rate. The stronger the original learning, the longer you will continue to respond. As we discuss later in the chapter, the number of reinforcements, the delay of reinforcement, and the schedule of reinforcement are all important factors. You might even create some internal reinforcement when the observable reinforcement is absent. For example, you could tell yourself you really enjoy working, and do it just for fun. Sooner or later, however, you will decrease your response rate when your behavior is no longer followed by reinforcement.

Spontaneous Recovery Spontaneous recovery, the occurrence of behavior that had been extinguished, can appear after a rest period. Rats that have been on extinction in Skinner boxes will begin to press the lever again when placed back in the Skinner box after a rest period. Likewise, after a break, you might be ready to try hard again in your studies the next semester.

Generalization and Discrimination Many fathers have found, to their dismay, that when their young children learn to say "daddy," they begin to call all men

by that name. Individuals tend to emit similar responses to stimuli that are similar to ones that have in the past led to reinforcement. This is stimulus generalization. If we find that we enjoy a particular kind of food, chances are very good that we will go to all of the restaurants that specialize in serving it.

The child who calls the man next door, as well as the mailman, "daddy" soon learns that the name applies only to one man. Through the process of stimulus discrimination, the parents selectively reinforce the child only when he or she calls the father "daddy." Likewise, if we find that one hamburger restaurant is consistently better than another, we will begin to eat there exclusively.

Generalization and discrimination also occur when a pigeon is in a Skinner box. A pigeon who has learned to peck at an illuminated red disk (with food as a reinforcer) will continue to peck at the disk, although at a lower rate, when the color of the disk is changed from red to orange. If, however, the pigeon receives no food after pecking at the disk while it is orange, it will soon cease pecking. If, when the disk turns red again, the pigeon begins pecking, we say that the pigeon is showing stimulus discrimination.

FIGURE 6.13 Stimulus Discrimination
Behavioral psychologist B. F. Skinner has observed that a pigeon can learn to distinguish between stimuli (red disk and orange disk) in order to receive reinforcement (food).

Reinforcement

Reinforcement is any event that increases the probability that the behavior that precedes it will be repeated. If a behavior is immediately reinforced, we will show the behavior again. Food is a reinforcer when we are hungry. Water is a reinforcer when we are thirsty. Money, praise, and attention can all serve as reinforcers in the right circumstances. Reinforcement is most effective if it is given immediately after a behavior. If it is delayed, its power is diminished.

Schedules of Reinforcement Continuous reinforcement, in which every correct response is reinforced, quickly produces a high rate of responding. However, continuous reinforcement provides little resistance to extinction. When the rat, for example, no longer gets any food pellets, the rate and number of bar presses fall off rather quickly. Resistance to extinction is the most common measure of the "strength" of a conditioned operant response.

When resistance to extinction is the measure of response strength, one would think that the more times the response has been reinforced, the greater the number of responses after reinforcement is discontinued. But an operant response can be made even stronger if it is not

always reinforced during conditioning. This partial reinforcement produces a response that takes longer to extinguish than continuous reinforcement does and is called the partial reinforcement extinction effect. Flaherty (1985) argued that the partial reinforcement extinction effect is important in nature since it motivates animals to continue to seek goals even when they have experienced several unsuccessful attempts. Recent research (Pittenger & Pavlik, 1988) has also found the partial reinforcement extinction effect in humans. Who will go on spending dimes longer, the person operating a slot machine that reinforces him or her only occasionally, or the person operating an out-of-order pay phone, which has previously always provided reinforcement?

You might think of schedules of reinforcement as being on a continuum. On one end is continuous reinforcement, where reinforcement is given after every response. At the other end is extinction, where no reinforcement is given. In between is intermittent, or partial, reinforcement, where reinforcement is given after some of the responses. Partial reinforcement schedules are based on two properties: the ratio of unreinforced responses to reinforced responses, and the time interval between reinforced responses. Ferster and Skinner (1957) describe the four basic partial reinforcement schedules: fixed ratio, variable ratio, fixed interval, and variable interval.

FIGURE 6.14   Schedules of Reinforcement

These are typical rates of pigeons responding under different partial reinforcement schedules. "Ratio" refers to number of responses before reinforcement occurs; "interval" refers to time periods before reinforcement occurs. Short diagonal lines indicate occurrence of reinforcement (after Skinner, 1961).

In the fixed ratio (FR) schedule, a certain number of responses must be made before reinforcement is given (Ferster & Skinner, 1957). For instance, reinforcement might be given after every three responses. A good example in industry is piecework, where the worker must produce a certain number of items for a certain amount of money. FR results in a fairly high rate of continuous responding. There is just a little *scallop* effect between reinforcements. If you know the instructor only calls on you after you have raised your hand 10 times, you will pause immediately after being called on, and begin to increase hand raising as you approach the next reinforcement.

The second partial reinforcement schedule is the variable ratio (VR) schedule. Here the number of responses required for reinforcement to occur varies. There is an overall average, but for each trial, the number changes. An example of variable reinforcement is the slot machine used in gambling establishments. The machine provides reinforcement, but you can never tell when it will occur. Thus, your response rate is steady and high, with no scalloping effect on a cumulative response curve. Other examples are the salesperson who continues to work hard because he or she never knows when the next reinforcing customer will come along, or the person who buys a lottery ticket each week in the hopes of hitting it big someday.

In the fixed interval (FI) schedule the subject receives reinforcement for the first response shown after a given time interval (Ferster & Skinner, 1957). For example, in a FI 2-minute schedule, the subject is reinforced once every 2 minutes. After a reinforcement is given, no further responses are reinforced until the 2 minutes have elapsed. Then the next response is reinforced. The fixed interval schedule is probably the most common everyday form of reinforcement. For instance, people work hard to receive a weekly paycheck. Students study to receive a test grade at the end of the semester. And children are "good" all week to receive their allowance.

In a fixed interval schedule, the subject tends to rest immediately after a reinforcement and then increases frequency of responding just before the next reinforcement occurs. Think about your study behavior. Chances are good that right after an exam you relax awhile, and increase your study activity as the time for the next exam draws near. If you made a graph of the behavior, you would see that the fixed interval schedule results in a characteristic scalloping effect in a cumulative response curve.

In the variable interval (VI) schedule, the subject is reinforced for the first response given after a particular time interval, which is changed for each trial (Ferster & Skinner, 1957). One trial may have a 2-minute interval, the next a 4-minute interval, and the third a 1-minute interval. There is an overall average time interval, but each trial is different.

FIGURE 6.15   Example of Variable Ratio Schedule of Reinforcement
A slot machine provides reinforcement, but the gambler can never be sure whether the next bet will pay off. This results in a high rate of response.

An example of the variable interval schedule might be an instructor who gives unannounced quizzes. At the beginning of the semester, the students are told that there will be six quizzes, on the average of one every 3 weeks, but that they can be given at any time. What would your study pattern be under these circumstances? You would probably study at a fairly steady pace throughout the semester. Another example of the VI schedule is calling someone on the telephone. Success in reaching your friend is dependent upon an interval of time that varies from one incident to the next. If your friend does not answer, you wait a while and try again. The variable interval schedule produces steady responding, but sometimes at a fairly low rate.

Primary and Secondary Reinforcement   Psychologists distinguish between primary and secondary reinforcement. Primary reinforcement is effective without having been associated with other reinforcers. Food is a primary reinforcer for a hungry person. Water is a primary reinforcer for a thirsty person. Food and water satisfy basic physiological needs and serve as reinforcers without being paired with other reinforcers.

FIGURE 6.16 Reinforcement in Everyday Life

Reinforcement		
	Potential Primary Reinforcers	Potential Secondary Reinforcers
Usually Positive	Food Water Sex Sleep Sensory stimulation	Money Tokens Esteem Grades Status Approval
Usually Negative	Shock Pain Extreme temperatures Loud noise Physical pressure	Low self-esteem Ridicule Exclusion Violation of personal space

There are many types of reinforcement in everyday life. Primary reinforcers are effective without having been associated with other reinforcers. Secondary reinforcers are effective only when associated with primary reinforcers. Positive reinforcers strengthen a response when they are presented. Negative reinforcers strengthen the behaviors that caused them to be removed.

FIGURE 6.17 Reinforcement and Punishment

STRENGTH OF PRECEDING BEHAVIOR		
	Increased	Decreased
Present Stimulus **PROCEDURE**	**POSITIVE REINFORCEMENT**	**POSITIVE PUNISHMENT**
Remove Stimulus	**NEGATIVE REINFORCEMENT**	**NEGATIVE PUNISHMENT**

The definition of reinforcement and punishment depends upon whether an event is presented or removed after a response is made, and whether the subject's responding increases or decreases. Any event that increases responding is called reinforcement and any event that decreases responding is called punishment; any event that is presented is called positive and any event that is removed is called negative. Each square defines one possibility: for example, if a subject's rate of responding increases after an event is presented, we say that positive reinforcement has occurred.

Secondary reinforcement is effective only after it has been associated with a primary reinforcer. For instance, what can you do with money? It's dirty, often smells, and is sometimes difficult to carry around. Why is it reinforcing to find a 20-dollar bill? Obviously, it is valuable to you because it is associated with other reinforcers, such as food. Money is a secondary reinforcer. Other examples of conditioned secondary reinforcers include praise and attention.

We learn about secondary reinforcers through the process of classical conditioning. Would you work hard for a poker chip? Studies have shown that chimpanzees, children, and adults will all work for poker chip tokens, if the tokens can later be cashed in for food or other objects of value. Higher order conditioning may take place when the token (a *conditioned reinforcer*) is traded for money, which is traded for a gift coupon, which is traded for a hamburger.

Positive and Negative Reinforcement As we learned earlier, Thorndike's law of effect states that any response that produces satisfaction in a given situation becomes associated with that situation, and when that situation occurs again, the response is more likely to be repeated. Reinforcement can thus be thought of as something satisfying or pleasant to the individual that causes the individual to repeat the behavior preceding the reinforcement. The discussion so far has concentrated primarily on positive reinforcement, which occurs when a pleasant stimulus such as food is presented and strengthens the response it follows. But much of our behavior is controlled by negative reinforcement, which occurs when an aversive stimulus is removed and the preceding behavior is strengthened (Skinner, 1953). Have you ever felt pain from having a stone in your shoe? When you removed the painful stone, you felt relief and experienced negative reinforcement. Escaping from a hot, crowded room, removing a splinter from your finger, and running away from someone who is yelling at you are all examples of negative reinforcement.

Many students have difficulty distinguishing between these two terms (McConnell, 1990). Remember that reinforcement always increases the likelihood that the behavior will occur again. Think of positive as presenting and negative as removing. Then, essentially, as far as the individual is concerned, positive reinforcement means he or she is presented something pleasant that increases a response, and negative reinforcement means something unpleasant is removed and that also increases a response. Although somewhat simplistic, this will help you differentiate the two terms in a given situation. Both types of reinforcement lead to an increase in behavior.

Aversive Conditioning

Negative reinforcement occurs when a response leads a subject to escape or avoid stimuli that are annoying, unpleasant, uncomfortable, or painful. Such escape or avoidance is called aversion. Psychologists studying how aversive responses can be used to control behavior have used mainly two types of procedures: escape conditioning and avoidance conditioning.

Escape Conditioning   In escape conditioning the subject is presented with an unpleasant stimulus from which he or she must learn to escape. For example, if a particularly traumatic scene appears during a movie someone is watching, he or she might escape (at least visually) by closing his or her eyes. If this works, the person will escape even faster the next time a scary scene appears.

In the laboratory, psychologists sometimes use mild electric shocks to condition a subject. A rat learns very quickly to escape from an electrified floor by running up a pole to a safe platform. Leeming and Little (1977) studied escape conditioning in houseflies. The experi-

FIGURE 6.18 Aversive Conditioning
Behavior can be modified by aversive conditioning. To make smoking unenjoyable this therapist gives a slight electric shock to the smoker each time he takes a puff from his cigarette. The smoker can see in the mirror opposite how his hand shakes at each shock. He has also been surrounded by cigarette butts and the smell of tobacco that add to his unpleasant experience.

menters placed the houseflies in a tube that was divided into two sections. One section was lighted and hot, while the other was dark and cool. The houseflies quickly learned to escape from the hot section to the cool section.

Avoidance Conditioning   In avoidance conditioning the subject learns to avoid an unpleasant stimulus by responding appropriately before it begins. Perhaps we have had very poor service in a particular restaurant and thus avoid that establishment thereafter. We learn to avoid getting traffic tickets by following established rules of the road and being harmed by locking our cars in high-crime areas.

In a classic laboratory experiment, a dog was placed in a cage made up of two compartments separated by a small hurdle. A light came on and a few seconds later the dog was shocked. The dog needed very little training to learn that it could avoid the shock by jumping the hurdle into the other compartment just after the light came on and before the shock began (Solomon & Wynne, 1953). Once learned, avoidance behavior is very persistent; when the warning stimulus occurs, the avoidance behavior is likely to be repeated.

What happens if an animal cannot escape or avoid an unpleasant stimulus? Seligman and Maier (1967) conducted a study similar to that of Solomon and Wynne, except that the dogs were restrained and could not escape the shock. After a few shocks, the dogs gave up even trying to escape. Learned helplessness is a phenomenon observed in humans as well as animals. Its possible relationship to depression is discussed in chapter 12, "Adjustment and Health."

Punishment

Punishment decreases the likelihood that the behavior preceding it will be repeated. It is, in many ways, the opposite of reinforcement. Although not always called positive and negative punishment, you can think of punishment in these two distinct forms (McConnell, 1990). You can present something unpleasant (positive punishment) or you can remove something pleasant (negative punishment). Skinner (1953) described punishment as either presenting a negative reinforcer or withdrawing a positive reinforcer. In either case, if the preceding behavior decreases, this is defined as punishment (Skinner, 1988).

The presentation of something unpleasant after a behavior will lead to a decrease in the behavior. Scolding a child, assessing a fine, and shocking a rat are examples of positive punishment. The removal of something pleasant after a behavior will usually also lead to a decrease in the behavior. Taking away a teenager's car keys, with-

FIGURE 6.19 Punishment
Prison as a form of punishment is meant to decrease undesired behavior, but the overcrowded and sometimes inhuman conditions of prison life can have negative effects. The resentment inmates may have for unusually bad prison conditions may increase, rather than decrease, undesired behavior.

holding visiting privileges, and keeping a child inside school during recess are examples of what is meant by negative punishment. Often, when people speak of punishment, they are referring to positive punishment.

The effectiveness of punishment varies widely, and is often dependent upon the characteristics of its presentation (Schwartz, 1984). In particular, proximity, consistency, and intensity are important variables. *Proximity* is the closeness of the aversive stimulus to the punished behavior. The closer the punishment follows the behavior, the more effective it is. For example, let's assume you want to housebreak your new puppy. Unless you catch it in the act of misbehaving, you will not be very effective. If, after leaving it alone all afternoon, you arrive home to discover that it has excreted, scolding will most likely have the effect of teaching it to run away from you when you open the door. *Consistency* means always following the behavior with punishment. *Intensity* refers to the strength of the punishment. Usually more consistent and intense punishment results in a more effective reduction in the undesired behavior.

Punishment might have undesirable side effects. Azarin (1959) has shown that aggression is often pro-

duced by intense punishment. There are ethical considerations in the use of some punishments such as imprisonment or electrocution for certain crimes. Anthony Burgess suggested in his 1963 novel, *A Clockwork Orange*, that violence and crime might effectively be controlled if a society is willing to accept the side effects, including resentment, hate, and the tendency to aggress.

There is an ongoing debate on the use of punishment to control behavior (Landers, 1988). Some clinical psychologists support the use of aversive stimuli such as electric shock to treat severely mentally retarded or autistic individuals who do not effectively communicate with others. Recently, an electric shock device called the Self-Injurious Behavior Inhibiting System was introduced to help parents and clinicians reduce head-banging behavior in autistic children. On the other hand, some states have banned the use of aversive stimuli in therapy. B. F. Skinner released a statement in which he argued that brief and harmless stimuli that suppressed self-destructive behavior in autistic children might be justified. However, Skinner and others urged the exploration for nonpunitive alternatives such as reinforcement.

It is important to note that reinforcement and punishment are defined by their consequences. If it increases behavior, it is reinforcement; if it decreases behavior, it is punishment. As an illustration, imagine that there is a disruptive student in a classroom. The instructor constantly yells at the student. Is this reinforcement or punishment? If the student quiets down, it is punishment. But if the student increases the disruptive behavior, it is reinforcement. Perhaps the student feels ignored, and this is the only way to get noticed. Regardless of the motivation of the student, it is the consequence of events that defines the procedure either as reinforcement or punishment.

Applications of Operant Conditioning

Operant conditioning has become a very influential area of psychology, because it has successfully provided practical solutions to many problems in human behavior. Operant principles discovered in the laboratory are now being employed to improve teaching techniques so that even slow or unmotivated students can learn faster and better. Behavior modification is the application of operant conditioning techniques to modify behavior. It is being used to help people with a wide variety of everyday behavior problems, including obesity, smoking, alcoholism, delinquency, and aggression. For example, people with the eating disorder anorexia nervosa have been helped to gain weight, and animals such as primates have been trained to assist physically disabled individuals by feeding and caring for them. It has been successfully used in child rearing, in school systems and in mental institutions. The following Application reviews how operant conditioning is used to learn with computers.

APPLICATION

Computers and Programmed Learning

Operant conditioning has been used in developing programmed learning. According to B. F. Skinner (1958), the purpose of programmed learning is to manage human learning under controlled conditions. Typically, a textbook or machine presents the material to be learned in a series of very small steps, called frames. Each frame contains some information and a statement with a blank that the student fills in. The student then uncovers the correct answer (by moving a paper down the page) before going on to the next frame. Each frame introduces a new idea or reviews material covered earlier. The agreement between the uncovered answer and the student's own response reinforces correct responses, making it likely that they will occur again. Moreover, shaping is employed, in that the frames start from the student's initial knowledge and in small steps proceed to the final knowledge. The student is therefore usually correct and continues to be reinforced, which keeps him or her at the task until completion.

The principles of programmed learning have been incorporated into a method of instruction that is usually called Personalized System of Instruction (PSI). PSI is a self-paced instruction format where each student works his or her way through the course material, which is broken down into small steps. Each student must "master" the material in one unit through a quiz before moving on to the next unit. Because of active student participation, small steps, immediate feedback, and reinforcement, PSI can be very effective (Reiser, 1984; Gage & Berliner, 1988).

Currently, the principles of programmed learning are being applied to a form of education called computer assisted instruction (CAI). The computer can be used to present learning material and help students learn through a variety of techniques such as multiple-choice quizzes, fill-in-the-blank, simulations, and personality tests (Pettijohn, 1985).

The advantages of the computer are that it can be continuously available, provide immediate feedback, and allow students flexibility in studying and testing (Quintanar, Crowell, & Pryor, 1982). With the advent of microcomputers, programmed learning is becoming an attractive way to implement in the classroom some of the basic principles of operant conditioning (Kulik, Kulik, & Gangert-Drowns, 1985).

FIGURE 6.20 Computer Assisted Instruction
The principles of operant conditioning and programmed learning are currently being applied to the educational technique of computer assisted instruction. The computer is used to present learning material and then test the student's knowledge. Studies show this procedue to be effective in helping a student learn.

Some therapeutic uses of behavior modification are explained in detail in chapter 14, "Therapy." One example is the token economy method of behavior modification, which we describe here. A classic study was conducted in a mental hospital with psychiatric patients who had difficulty performing expected behaviors (Ayllon & Azrin, 1968). The researchers chose a number of simple grooming behaviors, including face washing, hair combing, teeth brushing, bed making, and dressing properly. The researchers first recorded baseline, or normally occurring, frequencies of the behaviors. Then they gave the patients a token every time the proper behavior was performed. The tokens could be exchanged for food and personal items at the hospital drugstore. The patients significantly increased the frequency of the desired behaviors when they were reinforced with tokens.

Another practical application of reinforcement was suggested by David Premack in 1965. The Premack Principle states that of any two responses, the one that is more likely to occur can be used to reinforce the response that is less likely to occur. People prefer doing certain things more than others. For example, a child might prefer to play outside rather than practice the piano. A parent could then use the playing response to reinforce (and increase) the occurrence of piano practice by promising more play time only after practice was finished. Likewise, a child is more likely to watch television than

FIGURE 6.21   Behavior Modification
Operant conditioning techniques are often used to modify behavior in school learning, child rearing, or animal training. One of the most frequent techniques is to give the subject reinforcement after a desired response has been given.

perform household chores. Thus, television watching could be used to reinforce doing chores. If a student likes going to the movies more than studying, he or she could use going to the movies as a reinforcer to increase study behavior. Or if someone enjoyed talking on the telephone more than reading a book, he or she could use telephone conversation as a reinforcer for reading. The Premack Principle is used regularly by many people, even if they are not aware of it (Allison, 1989).

It has even been suggested that the principles of operant conditioning can be used efficiently to control a society. B. F. Skinner, in his 1948 novel, *Walden Two*, presented a utopian society guided by operant conditioning principles. His 1971 book, *Beyond Freedom and Dignity*, caused a controversy by presenting his ideas on how operant conditioning could be utilized in an actual society. Although most people are not willing to accept Skinner's utopian ideal, the principles of operant conditioning are being applied in our everyday lives.

Comparison of Classical and Operant Conditioning

Classical and operant conditioning share many of the same basic principles and procedures. For example, Kimble (1961) has pointed out that the basic principles of acquisition, extinction, spontaneous recovery, and stimulus generalization are common to both types of learning.

There are several differences, however, between classical and operant conditioning (Houston, 1991). Although a basic feature of operant conditioning is reinforcement, classical conditioning relies more on association between stimuli and responses. A second distinction is that much of operant conditioning is based on voluntary behavior, while classical conditioning often involves involuntary reflexive behavior.

Klein (1991) pointed out that these distinctions are not as strong as they once were believed to be. For example, Neal Miller (1978) has demonstrated that involuntary responses, such as heart rate, can be modified through operant conditioning techniques. It now appears that classical conditioning does involve reinforcement. And many classical conditioning situations also involve operant behavior. For example, let's assume that Tina was conditioned to fear rats in the same way that Little Albert was. She would first learn to associate the rat with the loud noise through classical conditioning. Then presentation of the rat would produce a fear reaction and Tina would learn to escape from the aversive stimulus through operant conditioning (negative reinforcement). This is sometimes called the *two-factor theory* of avoidance conditioning (Mowrer & Lamoreauz, 1942).

Perhaps the best distinctions are the particular procedures developed by the psychologists in each area. Current approaches to learning emphasize the general phenomenon of learning, rather than the uniqueness of each approach.

COGNITIVE LEARNING

Classical and operant conditioning are both examples of association learning. Another type of learning relies more on cognitive processes. Cognitive learning proposes that the learner utilizes mental structures and memory to make decisions about behaviors. The types of cognitive learning include insight, latent learning, and observational learning.

Insight

Learning by insight is one type of cognitive learning, as we discuss in chapter 8, "Language and Intelligence." In a classic 1927 experiment, Gestalt psychologist Wolfgang Köhler observed a chimpanzee trying to reach a bunch of bananas hung just out of reach. The animal jumped at the bananas several times, but soon stopped and looked around the cage. Then, after a minute or so,

FIGURE 6.22 Insight Learning
With no clues to a solution, the chimpanzee must decide how to reach the bananas. Through insight he solves the problem by stacking the boxes to reach the food.

the chimpanzee stacked a couple of boxes together, climbed up, and easily reached the bananas.

Köhler called this an example of insight, or sudden perception of the relationship of the cognitive elements necessary to solve a problem. In this situation, there was no gradual shaping of the response with reinforcement. Köhler argued that cognitive processes allowed the animal to learn the solution to the problem without having to try alternatives through a trial-and-error approach.

Epstein and colleagues (1984) replicated Köhler's banana problem with pigeons. Because moving boxes and eating bananas were not usual behaviors for pigeons, the researchers, by using a food reward, first trained the birds to push a box and then to jump on it and peck at a picture of a banana. What happened when the pigeons were placed in a new cage with a box and a banana hung too high to reach? Like Köhler's chimpanzees, the pigeons found that they couldn't reach the banana from the box in its original location. They waited awhile, and then solved the problem by pushing the box to a new location under the banana. The researchers argued that the pigeons showed insight when solving the problem.

Latent Learning and Cognitive Maps

Cognitive factors are also central to latent learning. Latent learning occurs when an individual acquires knowledge of something but does not show it until motivated to do so. Edward Tolman, in his 1932 book, *Purposive Behavior in Animals and Men*, suggested that purpose was important for learning. He argued that understanding was the key to learning, and reinforce-

ment was only necessary to motivate an individual to perform the behavior that was learned.

In one experiment (Tolman & Honzik, 1930), three groups of rats were run through a complex maze on 17 consecutive days. One group never received food reinforcement upon reaching the end of the maze and performed poorly throughout the experiment. The second group always received reinforcement and continued to improve (by choosing fewer blind alleys) throughout the study. The third group did not receive reinforcement for the first 10 days, but were always reinforced the last 7 days of the experiment. This group did poorly the first 10 days, but as soon as they began to receive reinforcement, they did as well as the group that was always reinforced. Tolman argued that this third group had learned the maze, but had not shown it until motivated. They showed latent learning.

Tolman (1948) suggested that the rats had developed a cognitive map or mental representation of the maze. Cognitive maps help us learn in a goal-oriented way. For example, if a person were driving somewhere and the road was closed, he or she could rely on a cognitive map of the streets to help decide on an alternate route. A cognitive map is similar to the concept of scheme used by Piaget in his theory of cognitive development (see chapter 3, "Development").

Gary Allen (1987) recently demonstrated the ease with which we develop cognitive maps in learning routes. He took slides of the sights during a walk through a neighborhood. The series of slides were shown in sequential order to one group of subjects, while another group was shown the same slides in random order. Allen then asked the subjects to judge distances from the beginning of the walk to various locations along the

FIGURE 6.23   Cognitive Maps

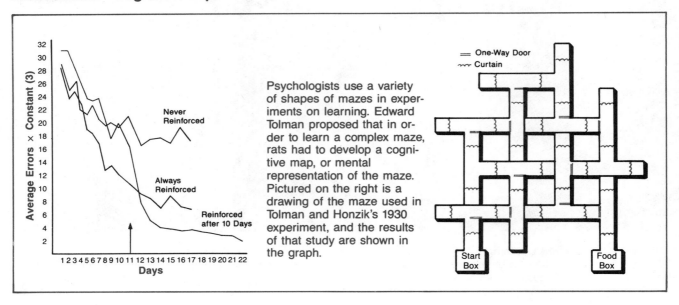

Psychologists use a variety of shapes of mazes in experiments on learning. Edward Tolman proposed that in order to learn a complex maze, rats had to develop a cognitive map, or mental representation of the maze. Pictured on the right is a drawing of the maze used in Tolman and Honzik's 1930 experiment, and the results of that study are shown in the graph.

route. He found that the group who viewed the slides in random order did almost as well as the subjects who had seen the correct sequence. How could the "random sequence" subjects be so accurate? Allen suggested that they were able to form a cognitive map from the overlapping information in the slides. They remembered parts of the route that overlapped and developed a cognitive map of the entire route. We tend to be able to develop cognitive maps of our surroundings easily, especially when the information is important to us.

Observational Learning

Another form of cognitive learning is observational learning. Social psychologist Albert Bandura (1977) argued that reinforcement is important in learning. But, like Tolman, Bandura held that reinforcement is largely involved in motivation rather than in the learning process itself. As a cheerleader, my daughter Karen carefully observes her coach and then imitates her actions. The learned cheers are then performed at a game when reinforcement is provided by the spectators. This approach is called *social learning theory*.

One of the best-known studies by Bandura is the 1961 experiment in which he and his colleagues looked at the influence of observational learning on aggression in children. Nursery school children observed adults interacting either passively or aggressively with an inflated life-sized doll. The children were able to imitate the adult role model of aggressive behavior, especially when the

behavior was reinforced. Although not absolutely conclusive, a number of research studies have shown that when children observe violence in television shows, they behave more aggressively. But when nonaggressive role models are available, children can easily learn to behave in socially cooperative ways (Gelfand & Hartmann, 1980).

Bandura (1986) suggested that many kinds of behavior are learned through observation. Children often acquire appropriate behaviors and gender roles such as dressing up like Mommy, shaving like Daddy, or cooking, through observation and *imitation* of their parents. Often the behaviors are neither reinforced nor explained to the children, but parents serve as models whom their children observe and from whom they learn.

In order for observational learning to be effective, four steps must occur (Bandura, 1977). First, we must pay attention to the role model. We tend to do this most often when we are motivated and believe the behavior has some relevance to us. This might help to explain why students sometimes have difficulty learning academic course concepts but can readily learn sports activities or memorize the latest popular songs. Second, we must store our observations in our memory system. Third, we must be able to remember what we have learned when we are motivated to behave in the appropriate fashion. And fourth, our behavior must be reinforced if we expect to repeat it with any regularity.

Cognitive learning is involved in many day-to-day situations. We use insight to solve problems and utilize what we have observed to make decisions about our behaviors. We discuss the role of cognitive learning in a variety of applications throughout this book, including the areas of problem solving and thinking (chapter 8), motivation (chapter 9), personality (chapter 11), and social behavior (chapter 15).

THE BIOLOGICAL CONSTRAINTS ON LEARNING

There is no doubt that conditioning plays a role in teaching both humans and animals various forms of behavior. The manipulation of stimuli, responses, and reinforcements influences learning in natural settings and experimental environments alike. This is why whales and porpoises can be made to perform so beautifully in oceanarium shows, why even people with severe mental disabilities can learn to function fairly normally, and why computer-assisted instruction has proven so effective in school classrooms. Do these successes of learning theory mean that conditioning can be used to train any animal (or person) to perform any behavior? Although some learning theorists have argued exactly this, recent evidence indicates that there are biological limits on what an individual can learn.

Instinctive Drift   Instinctive drift, the process in which conditioned behavior moves toward more instinctual behavior, is an example of the biological limits on learning. For instance, Keller and Marion Breland (1961) easily trained a raccoon to pick up coins and deposit them in a container in order to get a food reward. But the animal soon began holding on to the coins and eventually just rubbed and handled them instead of depositing them. Although the raccoon had been successfully conditioned, there appeared to be a limitation on the strength and lasting power of the learning process. Raccoons have a strong natural instinct to handle and wash their food before eating. This instinctual "washing" behavior proved to be stronger than the operantly conditioned action of placing the coin in the container. The concept of instinct is described in more detail in chapter 9, "Motivation," where we also discuss the related subjects of species-specific behavior and ethology.

Imprinting   Instinctive influences on learning have forced psychologists to take a close look at how biology prepares the individual for learning during development. Newborn ducklings, and some other animals, learn to follow their mothers—or any moving object—11 to 18 hours after hatching (Hess, 1959). This form of early learning in a *critical period* is called imprinting. A critical period is a brief time during which an individual is very sensitive to changes in the environment and will be

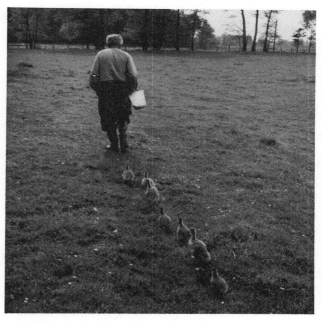

FIGURE 6.24   Imprinting
This is a form of learning in which very young animals learn to follow their mothers. Most imprinting occurs in birds, and takes place within 18 hours of hatching. Ethologist Konrad Lorenz demonstrated that young geese will imprint on any moving stimulus by acting as the stimulus himself. These geese preferred Lorenz to their natural mother even at a later time.

greatly influenced by them. And if certain learning that normally takes place in that period does not occur, the individual can have a hard time learning it later. After being imprinted, the ducks will continue to follow the object in the future. Some of the most influential work on imprinting was conducted by the Nobel Prize recipient, Konrad Lorenz. Among his most memorable studies was one in 1937 in which he allowed goslings to imprint on him instead of the mother goose—and they followed him around wherever he went.

Imprinting is highly adaptive for the species. The babies need to stay close to the mother for protection, and to learn species identification. Psychologists are not sure whether or not imprinting takes place as part of the attachment process in humans. At any rate, imprinting is a good example of how heredity influences learning and behavior.

Continuum of Preparedness   Martin Seligman (1970) has proposed a continuum of preparedness in learning, which helps place the biological constraints on learning in perspective. According to Seligman, animals are biologically prepared to associate some stimuli and responses more readily than others. At one end of his continuum is *prepared learning*, such as conditioned taste aversion, where the association is formed after one pairing. In the middle is *unprepared learning*, where the subject can learn but only after a number of trials. Examples might include rats pressing a lever in a Skinner box, or people learning to spell words. At the other end of the continuum is *contraprepared learning*, where the subject cannot learn, or does so only after many trials. An example would be teaching a dog to yawn for food.

The concept of preparedness can help explain some of the research findings in the field of emotion. Seligman reported in 1972 that fears in people usually involve animals or danger, which could be due to our evolutionary past, when it was important for *Homo sapiens* to learn to escape or avoid dangerous predators. We have already discussed the case of Little Albert quickly learning to fear a rat. Another study done a few years later (Bregman, 1934) found that, although it was easy to get children to fear animals through classical conditioning, it was not possible to get them to fear inanimate objects.

Earlier, we examined conditioned taste aversion, and saw how quickly the subjects were able to associate taste with stomachache. A study in 1966 by Garcia and Koelling demonstrates the importance of the animal's preparedness in determining whether learning successfully occurs. The researchers compared the ease with which rats could associate internal (taste) and external (noise and light) stimuli with internal (poison-induced stomachache) and external (electric shock–induced pain) consequences. All of the rats first drank salty water in the presence of clicking noises and flashing lights (each lick produced a click and a flash of light). Half of the subjects drank water with lithium chloride (a salt that produces a stomachache) whereas the rest drank water with a harm-less salt, but received an electric shock. Later, half of each group was given pure water in the presence of noise and lights, while the other half received plain salt water in quiet surroundings. Significantly, rats that had been poisoned preferred to drink the pure water in the presence of clicks and lights, and rats that had been shocked drank significantly more of the salty water in the quiet conditions. Thus, the rats tended to associate internal stimuli with internal consequences and external stimuli with external consequences. Some animals are more prepared to associate certain stimuli and responses than others.

Psychologists are discovering that before they plan an experiment the biological constraints on learning must be considered. Both the species being studied and the particular responses and reinforcers used must be carefully matched to increase the likelihood of success. By studying the biological constraints on learning, psychologists understand better the complex process of learning. ■

By now, you should be aware of the importance of learning in your life. The techniques of operant and classical conditioning can be used in a variety of ways, from training pigeons to play Ping-Pong to modifying human behaviors. Everything you do and think involves learning in some way. Because learning is basic to our individual behaviors, we refer to the principles and applications of learning throughout the rest of our text. We next turn to the topic of memory, the process of storing what we learn for later use.

"PERHAPS, DR. PAVLOV, HE COULD BE TAUGHT TO SEAL ENVELOPES."

CHAPTER REVIEW

What You've Learned About Learning

1. Learning is the relatively permanent change in behavior or behavioral ability of an individual that occurs as a result of experience.

2. In classical conditioning, described by Ivan Pavlov, the unconditioned stimulus (US) is a stimulus that provokes an automatic response, the unconditioned response (UR). If the US is repeatedly presented following a neutral stimulus, the neutral stimulus becomes the conditioned stimulus (CS) and gains sufficient power alone to provoke the conditioned response (CR). The CS is presented first, and takes on the properties of the US.

3. When the conditioned stimulus is presented by itself, after a while the conditioned response is extinguished. If the subject is given a rest during extinction, the subject will show spontaneous recovery and respond again briefly to the conditioned stimulus. Once a CS becomes effective, other similar stimuli also elicit the conditioned response, a process called stimulus generalization. In stimulus discrimination, the subject learns to respond only to a stimulus that is paired with the US.

4. Conditioned taste aversion occurs when an individual experiences stomach distress after eating something. This phenomenon, sometimes called bait shyness, is a unique form of classical conditioning because it can occur with one trial and the interstimulus interval can be hours rather than seconds.

5. Applications of classical conditioning include treating behavioral problems, controlling predators, reducing fears, and treating drug addictions.

6. Thorndike's law of effect states that any response that produces satisfaction in a given situation becomes associated with that situation. When that situation occurs again, the response is more likely to be repeated.

7. Shaping is the gradual process of reinforcing successive behavior approximations to achieve some goal. Examples include training an animal, treating behavior problems, helping students learn, and treating shyness.

8. In operant conditioning, extinction is the withholding of reinforcement. After a rest period, spontaneous recovery may occur. Stimulus generalization is responding to stimuli that are similar to ones that have been reinforced. Stimulus discrimination is learning to respond only to stimuli that lead to reinforcement.

9. Reinforcement is defined as any event that increases the probability that the behavior preceding it will be repeated. In continuous reinforcement, every correct response is reinforced. In partial reinforcement schedules, the subject is reinforced after some responses and not others. The four schedules of partial reinforcement are fixed ratio, variable ratio, fixed interval, and variable interval.

10. Primary reinforcement, like food, is effective without having been associated with other reinforcers. However, secondary reinforcement, such as money, works only after it has been paired with primary reinforcers. Positive reinforcement is anything that, when presented, strengthens the response that precedes it. Negative reinforcement is anything that, when removed, strengthens the response that precedes it.

11. Negative reinforcement occurs when a response leads to escape or avoidance of stimuli that are unpleasant. In escape conditioning, the subject is presented with a stimulus from which he or she must learn to escape. In avoidance conditioning, the subject learns to avoid an unpleasant stimulus by responding appropriately before it begins.

12. Punishment decreases the probability of the behavior preceding it being repeated. Punishment can consist of presenting something unpleasant (such as a scolding) or removing something pleasurable (such as the car keys). Effective punishment depends upon a variety of variables, including proximity, consistency, and intensity.

13. Behavior modification, programmed learning, and token economies are useful in child rearing, school systems, mental institutions, and animal training. The Premack Principle states that of any two responses, the one that is more likely to occur can be used to reinforce the response that is less likely to occur.

14. Classical and operant conditioning share many of the same basic principles, including acquisition, extinction, spontaneous recovery, and stimulus generalization. While a basic feature of operant conditioning is reinforcement, classical conditioning relies more on association between stimuli and responses. Much of operant conditioning is based on voluntary behavior, while classical conditioning often involves involuntary reflexive behavior.

15. Cognitive learning proposes that the learner utilizes mental structures and memory to make decisions about behaviors. Insight involves the sudden perception of the relationship of the cognitive elements necessary to solve a problem. Latent learning occurs when an individual acquires knowledge of something but does not show it until motivated to do so. In observational learning, the individiual observes another performing a task.

16. There are biological constraints on what can be efficiently learned. Instinctive drift is the process of learned behavior moving toward innate patterns. Imprinting is a form of learning in birds, occurring within hours after hatching, which involves following a moving object. The continuum of preparedness states that animals are prepared to associate certain stimuli and responses, but unprepared to learn other associations.

CHAPTER OBJECTIVES

What You'll Learn About Human Memory

After studying this chapter, you should be able to:

1. Define memory.
2. Outline the memory processes of encoding, storage, and retrieval.
3. Describe the iconic and echoic sensory memory stores.
4. Identify the processes of attention and pattern recognition.
5. Identify the variables that influence encoding in short-term memory.
6. Describe the characteristics of short-term memory.
7. Compare maintenance and elaborative rehearsal.

8. Compare the three types of long-term memory.
9. Define the concept of metamemory.
10. Identify three procedures used in verbal learning and memory.
11. Identify three measures of memory retention.
12. Compare the three theories of forgetting.
13. Identify five techniques for memory improvement.
14. Identify the steps of the SQ5R study technique.
15. Describe the biological basis of memory.

The scientific study of remembering verbal materials began with the German psychologist Hermann Ebbinghaus. He became interested in the process of human memory and developed procedures to measure it objectively, contributing significantly to the study of human memory. His major book, *On Memory*, published in 1885, is still read today.

Using himself as a subject, Ebbinghaus memorized lists of unrelated words and later tested himself to find out how many he could remember. At first, he worked with ordinary German words. But some words were more familiar and had more associations for him than others, and were thus easier to remember. So he decided to make up new words that would be equally unfamiliar to him and that would have no associations. These *nonsense syllables* (or trigrams, as they are also called) usually consist of a consonant, a vowel, and a consonant. For example, such "words" as DAJ, FUP, and CIN might be chosen as nonsense syllables for someone who speaks English. They can be pronounced, but have no literal meaning in the language of the person using them.

Ebbinghaus created over 2,000 nonsense syllables that he used to test his memory. His basic method of testing memory (called serial learning) required him to memorize a list of about 15 nonsense syllables until he could repeat it without making any mistakes. He read each word at a specified rate set by a metronome until he finished the list. Then he would try to recall the list perfectly. If he could not recite it without errors he read the list again and retested himself.

In order to determine how much he forgot within a given period of time, he would wait and then retest himself. Inevitably he would forget some of the items on the list. So next he would relearn the list until he could again recall it perfectly.

154

How do we remember things? Why do we sometimes forget to do things? Psychologists are interested in how information is entered, stored, and retrieved from our memory systems. Recent attention has focused on how information proceeds from sensory memory to short-term and long-term memory stores. Practical suggestions for improving our ability to learn and remember are some of the benefits of the study of memory.

7

Human Memory

FIGURE 7.1   Ebbinghaus's Forgetting Curve

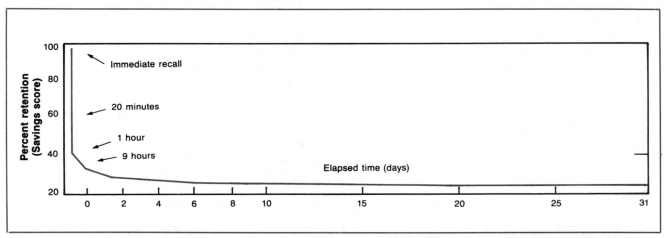

Ebbinghaus demonstrated that a greater rate of memory loss occurs in the first hour after learning than in a 31-day period of time.

In order to assess the amount of forgetting that occurred, Ebbinghaus developed the "memory savings" measure. He took the number of times he needed to repeat the list until he could recall it perfectly during the first session and subtracted from it the number of times he took to memorize the list during the second session. This difference was called the savings. If the savings score was converted to a percentage (by dividing the savings by the number of times needed during the first session), it served as a comparative measure of memory. For instance, if learning took 12 times during the first session and 6 times during the second, there was a savings of 50 percent, meaning that 50 percent of the material had been forgotten.

Ebbinghaus was especially interested in the amount of material that was forgotten at various time intervals after the original learning took place. In his classic study, he learned a list perfectly and then relearned it after a period of time elapsed (from 20 minutes to 31 days). The dependent variable was the savings score.

He found that the forgetting curve was steep immediately after learning, and slowed down over time. After 1 hour about 50 percent of the material had been forgotten, but by 6 days the loss had leveled off. Eventually, forgetting stopped altogether. Ebbinghaus thought perhaps the memory became permanent and did not weaken after a certain period of time. (See Figure 7.1.)

Ebbinghaus also found that when a person memorizes a list of unrelated words, he or she is most likely to remember those occurring near the beginning and end of the list, while the words in the middle are quickly forgotten. For example, you can immediately recall the first or last item on a grocery list, but you probably have more difficulty remembering the items in the middle. The findings of Ebbinghaus have led to extensive research in the area of memory.

WHAT IS MEMORY?

After reading about Ebbinghaus and his experiments, you may be wondering what the difference is between learning and memory. Actually, the two terms are not easily distinguished. In order to remember something, you must learn it in the first place, and the only way to test learning is to measure what is remembered.

In the last chapter, we defined learning as the relatively permanent change in behavior or behavioral ability that occurs as a result of experience. Thus, learning can be thought of as the acquisition of new information or behavior skills. Memory involves storing the information that is learned so it can be retrieved and used at a later time. The process of memory overlaps the processes of perception (perceiving the stimuli that are being learned), learning (acquiring associations among stimuli), and consciousness (being aware of certain information at any point in time).

In order to have a memory of something, one needs to acquire (or learn) the behavior (or information), retain it until it is needed, and then be able to retrieve it. When psychologists study memory, they are interested in the *retention* level, which is simply the amount of information accurately stored after learning has taken place. Retention is measured by asking a person to retrieve previously learned information. *Forgetting*, or retention loss, is the part of the original learning that cannot be retrieved.

There has been a long history of attempting to describe the stages that our memories go through as they are being stored. For example, William James (1890) viewed *primary memory* as part of our conscious awareness, and *secondary memory* as the part of the mind where knowledge is stored until it is needed. This model was reintroduced in the 1960s as the information-processing approach to memory. As we discuss later in this chapter, an expanded version of this model, which includes sensory memory, short-term memory, and long-term memory, is currently dominant in psychology.

Brewer and Pani (1983) proposed that our memories consist of three distinct types of information: personal, generic, and skill. Personal information includes our specific experiences; generic information includes general knowledge we have gained not associated with a particular experience, such as our attitudes about school, our knowledge of VCRs, or our vocabulary; skill information includes behavioral and cognitive abilities, such as riding a bicycle or solving a crossword puzzle.

In chapter 6, "Learning," we made a distinction between learning and performance, indicating that learning was inferred from the actual performance of an individual. In the same way, we cannot know what an individual remembers until the person demonstrates it by retrieving the selected information. Psychologists use the techniques of recall, recognition, and savings as measures of memory retention. We begin this chapter with a look at the processes involved in our memory system.

BIOGRAPHICAL HIGHLIGHT

HERMANN EBBINGHAUS

Hermann Ebbinghaus was born in 1850 to Lutheran merchants in Barmen, Germany. At the age of 17 he entered the University of Bonn, where he developed an avid interest in philosophy. However, his studies were temporarily interrupted in 1870, at the outbreak of the Franco-Prussian War, when he enlisted in the Prussian army. He resumed his studies a year later, and received his Ph.D. in 1873.

In 1885, the year of the publication of his most important book, *On Memory*, he was appointed professor of philosophy at the University of Berlin. Several years later, he accepted a position at Breslau, where he remained until his death in 1909.

Ebbinghaus's contributions to psychology are numerous. In addition to founding two psychology laboratories in Germany, he also founded and edited a major journal that did much to advance psychology in its early days. His famous work on memory set a precedent for experimental psychology. Ebbinghaus helped to bring clear and precise experimental techniques to the science of psychology.

He was highly popular as a lecturer, and his sense of humor, informal style, and personal charm endeared him to students and colleagues alike. He died of pneumonia in Breslau at the age of 59.

MEMORY PROCESSES

What if someone asked you the name of the author of your psychology textbook? You might give one of three responses: "I never learned it," "I completely forgot," or "I can't quite remember." These three responses correspond roughly to the three basic components of our memory system: encoding, storage, and retrieval.

The first step is encoding, the process of putting information into our memory system (Klatzky, 1984). If we don't learn or experience something first, we cannot remember it at a later time. The stimuli that we perceive or are aware of must be transformed in some way into data that can be deposited into our brain's memory banks. Essentially, encoding is the process in which the nervous system develops a representation of the stimuli that we perceive.

There are a number of variables that influence the effectiveness of the encoding process. We must perceive the event and pay attention to its characteristics. We should be motivated to remember, and find the information meaningful or relevant to our lives. And if we practice or rehearse the information, the likelihood of successfully remembering it increases significantly.

Once we have encoded the information, we need to store it. If we don't store it, then it's forgotten. The second step, storage, is the process that retains information in our memory system for some length of time. The processes of encoding and storage are not easily distinguishable, since each depends upon the other for successful memory to take place.

Although we might prefer our stored memories to be like a video recording that can be played back perfectly, research has demonstrated that our memory is a dynamic process that is continually changing to accommodate new information (Loftus, 1980). It is believed that three sepa-rate memory stores exist, with memories being transferred among the three.

The third step in memory process is retrieval, pulling information out of the memory system. We don't know what is stored until we retrieve it. Sometimes the information is adequately stored, but not easily accessible at that moment. For example, have you ever taken a test and gone blank on some of the questions, only to remember them completely as soon as you leave the classroom? The test answers were in your memory but you had difficulty retrieving them. The success of retrieval obviously is closely tied to the effectiveness of encoding and storage. For this reason, the distinction among these processes is not always clear.

STAGES OF MEMORY STORAGE

One useful way of approaching memory is to distinguish between processes and structures (Atkinson & Shiffrin, 1971). As we just discussed, memory processes—including encoding, storage, and retrieval—help us place information into our memory systems, keep it there, and then pull it out when needed. Memory structures are concerned with the stages of memory storage. For example, what the capacity of memory is, what the duration of storage is, how information is stored and organized, and what form the information takes are questions concerning memory structures. Psychologists consider the three memory stores (sensory, short-term, and long-term) to be cognitive structures of the mind.

Currently, memory theories are dominated by the information-processing theory of memory. Information-processing theory relies on mathematical and computer models to describe the flow of information through the memory system. There are numerous models of memory

FIGURE 7.2   Information Processing Theory of Human Memory

ENCODING   **STORAGE**   **RETRIEVAL**

Currently, the area of human memory is dominated by the information processing theory, which compares the way our memory works to the way a computer works. In both instances, information is encoded into the system, is stored for some period of time, and ultimately is retrieved so that it can be used.

available and we cannot hope to describe them all. One of the most popular is the *separate-storage model*. Atkinson and Shiffrin (1971) developed a model that contains three memory stores: sensory register, short-term store, and long-term store. Since many information-processing theories have these three memory storage structures, we will use this as the basis for our discussion of the storage process.

Sensory Memory

A stimulus from the environment persists for a brief time in our perceptual-nervous system even after it has been terminated. For example, when a photographer uses a flash, you tend to see "light flashes" immediately afterward (even though the actual flash is no longer being used). The perceptual persistence of a stimulus after its termination in the environment is called a stimulus trace.

Sensory memory refers to the memory store that sensory information first enters in the memory system. The stimulus trace information in sensory memory is in a relatively raw form, waiting until it can be processed further. The sensory register, or sensory memory, is crucial to the correct functioning of our memory system. We are exposed to an enormous number of sensory stimuli (sights, sounds, smells, tastes, and touches) every moment we are awake. We need to be able to keep the relevant stimuli in our system until we decide which are important and therefore process them further into a more permanent form.

Sensory memory has several important characteristics that distinguish it from the other memory stores (Matlin, 1989). The information in sensory memory is a fairly accurate representation of the environmental stimuli but is unprocessed. Sensory memory has a very large capacity, but maintains itself for a very brief time, less than one second. Although a few studies have examined other senses, most have focused on visual and auditory sensory memory.

Iconic Memory   Visual sensory memory, the brief persistence of visual stimuli, is referred to as iconic memory. An icon is a particular visual perception, such as our memory for a letter or word immediately after we have seen it. George Sperling ran a classic experiment in 1960 that demonstrated the major characteristics of sensory memory. He was interested in determining how much people could see in a brief exposure to the stimuli.

Prior research indicated that when people are presented a number of letters for a very brief time, they often reported that they had seen more than they could remember. Following is an array of letters typical of what Sperling used in his research project. Glance at it for 50

FIGURE 7.3   Sperling's Sensory Memory

Sperling (1960) found that when subjects were asked to recall a portion of an array of letters immediately (partial report), they were able to remember significantly more than when they tried to remember the entire array (whole report). This suggests that the capacity of sensory memory is large but short-lived; it decays in less than 1 second.

milliseconds ($^{1}/_{20}$ of a second) and try to recall as many items as possible.

```
X  B  R  G
F  S  L  C
Z  N  T  P
```

When the stimuli are presented for a brief time and then the subject is immediately requested to remember as many items as possible, it is called the *whole report* procedure.

If you are like most of Sperling's subjects, in the whole report procedure you could remember a mean of 4.3 items out of the 12 presented. This is a measure of your immediate memory span. You would also have a tendency to forget the items while you were writing them down, indicating the brief time span of sensory memory.

Sperling next told subjects that he was going to ask them to give a *partial report*, that is, recall a specific row. He indicated which row by means of a high (top row), medium (middle row), or low (bottom row) auditory tone. If, immediately after presentation of the items, he indicated a particular row, he found that subjects could recall 3 or 4 items from the row. Sperling concluded the subjects actually had a memory for a mean of 9.1 of the 12 items. He also found that if he delayed asking for a partial report by one second, the subjects' scores dropped down to about the level of the whole report (4.6 items). Thus, Sperling demonstrated that iconic memory has a large capacity but a very brief (less than 1 second) time span. (See Figure 7.3.)

Echoic Memory   The brief persistence of auditory stimuli after the sound itself has ended is called echoic memory. A classic study was reported by Darwin, Turvey, and Crowder (1972) that tested echoic memory. Subjects wore headphones that could present three different three-item auditory sequences (such as J 3 H or 4 T F) simultaneously (one sequence to the left ear, one to the right ear, and one to both ears). After hearing the stimuli in the whole report condition, subjects were asked to recall all of the stimuli, and in the partial report they were asked to recall either the left, middle, or right sequence as indicated by a visual marker.

When asked to recall all nine items, subjects typically could remember about half (4.2). As was the case with iconic memory, the subjects performed better in the partial report condition (a mean of 4.9 items immediately after the presentation). Also like the iconic memory study, the mean number of items recalled decreased with a delay of the partial report cue, to a rate of about 4.3 items with a delay of 4 seconds.

Crowder (1982) suggested that echoic memory typically lasts about 3 seconds. Why is echoic memory longer than iconic memory? It could be because speech requires more time than vision. For instance, we might be able to see a dozen letters in 50 milliseconds (msec), but it would take longer to listen to someone reading them to us. It therefore is necessary to keep sounds in sensory memory long enough to hear a complete phrase so that it makes sense to us.

Some researchers suggest that there might be two distinct phases of echoic memory. Cowan (1988) proposed a first phase that lasts about 300 msec, during which the sensory information exists as an unanalyzed afterimage. The second phase lasts 2 to 3 seconds and contains partially analyzed sensory information. Further research will be needed to clarify the issue of the proposed additional phase of memory storage, as most scientists accept the idea that sensory memory contains only unprocessed sensory information.

Attention and Pattern Recognition   Two processes that help us begin to analyze the raw, unprocessed sensory information in sensory memory so it can be transferred to short-term memory include attention and pattern recognition. Attention is the process of focusing on certain stimuli. When we pay attention to certain sensory stimuli in sensory memory, they can be processed further (Anderson, 1990). Attention functions as a gate that determines what we have available to remember. As we discuss in chapter 8, "Language and Intelligence," a condition in which the individual cannot pay attention is called attention-deficit hyperactivity disorder (ADHD). A schoolchild with this condition has a difficult time concentrating and can create behavioral problems in the classroom.

Once we select information from sensory memory through attention, the next processing step is pattern recognition. In pattern recognition we compare the selected information with the information already permanently stored in our memory. When we see an *A*, we compare the distinctive features of this stimulus with template patterns in our memory in an attempt to identify it. We are able to recognize a wide variety of sensory stimuli in this fashion. Research has shown that the context in which we experience a stimulus and our motivation and expectations can influence pattern recognition. After we pay attention to sensory information and analyze it through pattern recognition, we are able to transfer it into our short-term memory.

Short-Term Memory

Information is placed in short-term memory (STM) when the individual attends to a stimulus. There are various terms used for this stage of memory, including working memory, immediate memory, active memory, and primary memory (Baddeley, 1986). Essentially, short-term memory is where we hold the information we are aware of at any particular moment. In a way, it is our consciousness, and is important in a variety of tasks (such as thinking, reading, speaking, and problem solving). We use our short-term memory when we remember a phone number we just looked up, when we decide what to purchase at the grocery store, and when we have a conversation with another person.

Encoding in STM   Encoding involves placing information into the memory system. Do we encode into memory everything we see? Many stimuli bombard our senses, and we must use pattern recognition and selective attention to screen out irrelevant information while focusing on significant stimuli. We tend to remember information that we have an interest in and are motivated to learn. For example, in a textbook we most easily remember practical material or information that is interesting to read. Two important variables in encoding information are meaningfulness and chunking.

Meaningfulness refers to the informational value of the material. High-meaningful material is encoded more easily than low-meaningful material. Read the following letters and then, without looking, try to recall them in order: T—HED—OGS—AW—TH—ECA—T. How well did you do? This string of letters had very little meaning for you. However, we can increase the meaningfulness of these letters dramatically by rearranging the grouping. Here are the same letters again. THE—DOG—SAW—THE—CAT. This time you should have no trouble remembering the letters, because they are arranged in meaningful units

FIGURE 7.4   Chunking

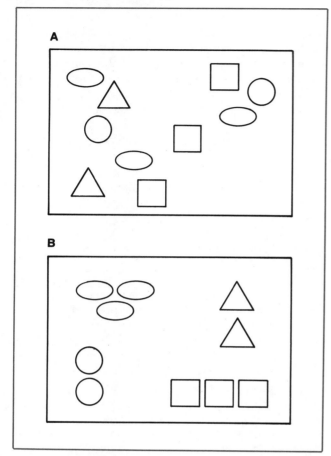

If you look at picture **(A)** for a few seconds, you will probably have trouble remembering how many figures you saw. But if you were to look at picture **(B)** for the same amount of time, you should be able to recall them. Although there are as many figures in B as in A, they are grouped, or *chunked,* in B, and are thus easier to count and remember.

(words). Whenever possible, we should try to remember information in a meaningful way.

Another reason you did better the second time is a phenomenon called chunking. This is the encoding process of combining stimuli (we combined the letters into five words). It has been found that our ability to remember items presented a short time earlier is restricted to about seven pieces of information. Chunking may help us improve our memory because each chunk may contain more information. For example, XHNQC represents five chunks, the same number as the word groups presented in the earlier dog-and-cat example (but the dog-and-cat sentence contains significantly more information). A practical application of chunking is to reduce your study notes to fewer phrases, so you will do better on tests.

Information Code in STM   When discussing sensory memory, we stated that the sensory stimuli accu-

rately reflected the environmental stimuli. That is, visual information was coded visually and auditory information was coded acoustically. What code is used in short-term memory? Research suggests that we are most likely to use an acoustic code, storing information in terms of how it sounds. For example, assume we just looked up the zip code for a friend who lives in Pinckney, Michigan, and learn that it is 48169. How would we store it in our short-term memory until we could write it down? Chances are good that we will repeat the number over and over again, and, by rehearsing its sounds, store it in STM.

Some individuals are capable of using a visual code in short-term memory. A small number of children (about 5 percent) have such good visual memories that they are said to have photographic memory, or eidetic imagery (Haber, 1980). In one study, Haber presented a picture to children who studied it for 30 seconds and then were able to answer extremely detailed questions about the picture. The subjects reported that they could still "see" the image of the picture. This ability usually declines with age, and adults rarely possess it.

Capacity of STM   The storage capacity of short-term memory is severely limited. Sometimes it is said that STM is the bottleneck of information flow. Earlier we mentioned that we could remember about seven chunks of information. George Miller (1956) was so impressed by this finding (and the fact that Ebbinghaus had earlier reported the same results), that he called it the magic number 7. Most people can remember 7 (± 2) items of information for a short time. This is why we can easily remember a telephone number of seven digits for the short time it takes to place the call after looking up the number.

The digit-span memory test is often used to test short-term memory. Following is a list of numbers. Read it once slowly, and then write down as many of the numbers as you can remember.

1 8 7 9 1 9 1 3 1 4 9 2

Most people remember about five to nine numbers. Do you remember how you can increase your memory of these numbers? Try the date of the first psychology laboratory, the founding of the school of behaviorism, and Columbus's first voyage to the Americas. These are three dates: *1879, 1913,* and *1492.* Now I bet you can easily remember all 12 items (since now they are in three chunks of information).

Some memory researchers have suggested that memory capacity is determined by the number of items that can be processed in 2 or 3 seconds, rather than the number of chunks. Other research indicates that as the size of the chunk increases, fewer chunks can be held in memory. For example, Zhang and Simon (1985) found that when items are encoded on the basis of sound, we can hold seven items in STM. But when the items are encoded on the basis of meaning, we can only hold about three chunks of information. Although additional research is needed to clarify this area, we can conclude that the capacity of STM is definitely limited.

Retrieval in STM We are able to retrieve information from our short-term memory quickly. Saul Sternberg (1966, 1969) conducted a series of experiments to determine whether people scan items in short-term memory all at once (*parallel processing*) or one at a time (*serial processing*). In one study, he presented a display of from one to six different digits to a subject for 1.2 seconds. Then he presented a test digit and the subject had to decide whether the test digit was included in the display just shown. If parallel processing occurred, the length of the display should not influence the reaction time, but if serial processing occurred, the reaction time should increase with an increase in the length of the display.

Sternberg found that it took a minimum of 397.2 msec (each second contains 1,000 msec) to respond when one item was in the display and increased by 37.9 msec with each additional item. This indicated an average scanning rate (without responding) of about 27 digits per second. An interesting finding was that the reaction time was about the same whether the response was a "yes" or a "no." In other words, subjects did not stop responding when they found a match, but continued searching the entire display in their memory. This process is called an exhaustive search. Thus, Sternberg con-

cluded that people perform an *exhaustive serial search* when retrieving information from STM. He argued that it is more efficient to search our STM exhaustively than it is to stop searching before reaching the end. (See Figure 7.5.)

Duration of STM A classic experiment was conducted in 1959 by Lloyd and Margaret Peterson to determine the duration of short-term memory. They presented subjects with a nonsense syllable followed by a number. When the subjects heard the number, they were to immediately count backward by threes until told to stop. Then they were to give the nonsense syllable. Sounds easy, right? Try it on a friend. For instance, try BEQ and 409. Then in 18 seconds ask for the letters. Chances are good that your subject will not be able to remember the syllable letters after this amount of time. In the Peterson and Peterson study, fewer than 10 percent of the nonsense syllables could be remembered after 18 seconds. This finding is sometimes called the Brown-Peterson effect because Brown (1958) discovered the same phenomenon at about the same time. (See Figure 7.6.)

Rehearsal There is a way to keep information in the short-term memory store for a much longer time. The Atkinson-Shiffrin model of memory (1971) includes a rehearsal buffer in the short-term memory store. Rehearsal may take two forms—maintenance or elaborative rehearsal (Craik & Watkins, 1973). Maintenance rehearsal is simply repeating the material over and over again without thinking about it. We would use mainte-

FIGURE 7.5 Sternberg's Short-Term Memory Experiment

Sternberg (1969) found that the time to scan information in short-term memory increased as the number of items increased. This suggests that we use serial processing to scan short-term memory.

FIGURE 7.6 Peterson and Peterson's Short-Term Memory Experiment

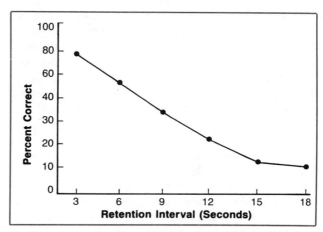

Peterson and Peterson (1959) found that a nonsense syllable was quickly forgotten if subjects could not rehearse it. This suggests our short-term memory retention time is less than 30 seconds.

FIGURE 7.7 Observation and Encoding

Only one of these pennies is the real thing. Can you pick it out? (after Nickerson & Adams, 1979).

nance rehearsal if we wanted to remember a phone number long enough to make the call.

Theoretically, it is possible to keep information indefinitely in short-term memory through maintenance rehearsal. At one time it was believed that maintenance rehearsal contributed to the transfer of information from short-term memory to long-term memory, but more recent evidence suggests that maintenance rehearsal alone does not effectively facilitate transfer, no matter how often it occurs. For example, Nickerson and Adams (1979) found that less than half of the people they asked could identify a penny correctly from a group of very similar models. Just looking at pennies does not help us permanently store the information.

Apparently, some organization is necessary for transfer of information into long-term memory. For instance, you have undoubtedly made many telephone calls, rehearsing the numbers and perceiving the letters on the phone. Which two letters of the alphabet are missing? Like most people, you probably don't know. Exposure to stimuli alone is ineffective, and therefore as you study, just going over your notes by rote will not significantly affect your test score. Greene (1987) pointed out that maintenance rehearsal strengthens the information about the item itself rather than associations with other items, and thus any positive results are seen more on recognition tests rather than recall tests. Elaborative rehearsal is thinking about the meaning of the material and trying to form associations with information already in memory. Elaborative rehearsal is much more effective because it involves a deeper level of processing (Craik & Lockhart, 1972). Rehearsing information correctly helps to encode it into long-term memory.

Long-Term Memory

Through elaborative rehearsal, you are able to encode information so that it enters long-term memory. The key to encoding in long-term memory is to organize the material and make it meaningful. In a sense, long-term memory incorporates the best of both sensory and short-term memory stores: its capacity is fairly unlimited as to amount of material and length of time, and it appears to be relatively permanent. We continue to add information to our long-term memory throughout life. Some of this information, such as our name, is always readily available. Other information, such as the name of our kindergarten teacher, is available only part of the time.

Depth of Processing Closely related to elaborative rehearsal is the concept of depth of processing. As described by Craik and Lockhart (1972), the depth-of-processing approach does not incorporate separate memory stores, but rather views memory as having different levels of depth. Information that is irrelevant or incidental will not be remembered as well as information that is meaningful and that the subject is motivated to learn. Meaningful material can be processed more deeply.

Hyde and Jenkins (1969) tested the idea of depth of processing in an experiment employing three groups of subjects. The first group was told to try hard to remember a list of words, and they did quite well. The second group was told to check to see whether the words in the list contained the letter *e*. This procedure is irrelevant to memory and should result in "shallow" processing. In-

FIGURE 7.8   Three Stages of Memory

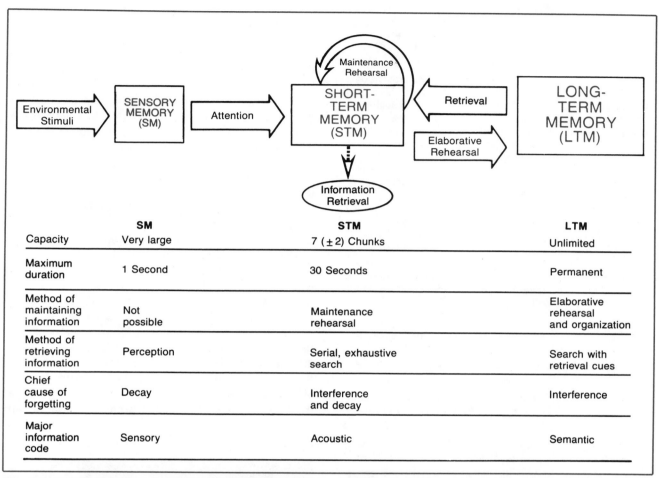

	SM	**STM**	**LTM**
Capacity	Very large	7 (± 2) Chunks	Unlimited
Maximum duration	1 Second	30 Seconds	Permanent
Method of maintaining information	Not possible	Maintenance rehearsal	Elaborative rehearsal and organization
Method of retrieving information	Perception	Serial, exhaustive search	Search with retrieval cues
Chief cause of forgetting	Decay	Interference and decay	Interference
Major information code	Sensory	Acoustic	Semantic

The flowchart for this theory of memory indicates that all incoming information first passes through Sensory Memory (SM) before it enters Short-Term Memory (STM). There it can be maintained by rehearsal and either successfully encoded for storage in Long-Term Memory (LTM) or forgotten. In retrieval, the information passes from LTM back to STM, where it enters our consciousness. A summary of the characteristics of each stage of memory is included beneath.

deed, they found the subjects in this group did rather poorly. The third group was also not told to try to remember the words, but to rate each word for its pleasantness or unpleasantness. This task involves searching the memory for other associations and thus encoding the meaning of the word. The researchers found that this deep processing procedure did result in memory as strong as that of the group that was instructed to try hard to remember. When we want to remember something, we should try to think about its meaning and its association with similar information. We could incorporate deep processing into our study routine for improved performance.

Procedural, Semantic, and Episodic Memory

Endel Tulving in 1972 distinguished between two types of long-term memory—semantic memory and episodic memory. Then in 1985 he expanded his theory to include three long-term memory systems. He proposed a classification scheme in which procedural memory is the most basic, semantic memory is intermediate in complexity, and episodic memory is the highest memory system. Some researchers consider semantic and episodic memory to be types of *declarative memory*.

Procedural memory is the most basic type of memory, and involves the formation of associations between stimuli and responses, as when animals or humans learn to respond behaviorally in adapting to their environment (Tulving, 1985). Remembering how to ride a bicycle, how to eat a lobster, or that you were sick after eating tomato soup would involve procedural memory.

Semantic memory has the additional characteristic of allowing the individual to develop mental models of the environment. Whereas procedural memory results in

FIGURE 7.9   Episodic and Semantic Memory

CHARACTERISTIC	EPISODIC MEMORY	SEMANTIC MEMORY
Source	Sensation	Comprehension
Units	Events	Facts, Ideas
Organization	Temporal	Conceptual
Reference	Self	Universe
Registration	Experiential	Symbolic
Temporal	Present	Absent
Affect	More affect	Less affect
Vulnerability	More chance of disruption	Less chance of disruption
Access	Deliberate	Automatic
Queries	Time? Place?	What?
Reports	Remember	Know
Development	Later in life	Early in life
Amnesia	Affected	Unaffected

Tulving proposed that episodic and semantic long-term memory differed in several important aspects. This chart shows that comparison.

overt behavior, semantic memory can involve cognitive activities. Knowledge that is used in everyday experience, such as 2 plus 2 equals 4, it's dark at night, or add an *s* to form the plural of a word, are examples of semantic memory. Access to information is automatic in semantic memory, and retrieval often involves answering the question "what?"

Episodic memory, according to Tulving, is the highest memory system, and provides the additional characteristic of retaining knowledge about personal experiences (Tulving, 1985). Sometimes called autobiographical memory, it includes events that have personal meaning for us. Remembering that we had chicken for dinner last night or that we saw a movie with our friends Ella Jean and Don last week are examples of episodic memory. Like semantic memory, this form involves cognitive activities. However, episodic memory is more personal, involves a time frame, and retrieval often involves answering the questions "when?" and "where?" In amnesia (a form of forgetting), the individual still possesses general facts and comprehension (semantic memory), but cannot remember personal information (episodic memory). You might think of semantic memory as a dictionary and episodic memory as a diary.

Occasionally, an event is so major in importance that it leaves a vivid impression in episodic memory and significantly more details than usual about it can readily be retrieved. This type of memory is called a flashbulb memory (Brown & Kulik, 1977). For example, what were you doing on January 28, 1986, when you heard the tragic news about the *Challenger* space shuttle explosion? Chances are good that you can recall many details about your experiences that day.

In a study of flashbulb memory, Reynolds and Takooshian (1988) asked people where they were on a specific date 19 months earlier. They found that even where there was no major event, all of the subjects were able to give a general description and 54 percent gave detailed descriptions of that specific day. Some of this kind of research suggests that flashbulb memories are only examples of episodic memory, and are not produced by any special mechanism (McCloskey, Wible, & Cohen, 1988). Research continues to explore the variables that determine the effectiveness of our memories.

Retrieval in LTM   As defined earlier, retrieval is the process of pulling information out of our memory system. There is a difference between episodic and semantic memory in retrieval success rate: episodic material is more difficult to retrieve than are semantic memories. There is usually no need to remember all of the details of our personal life. What did you eat for dinner a week ago last Tuesday? It was probably important then, so you wouldn't eat the same thing the next day, but now more than likely it is not of any great consequence.

How should you proceed to try to remember a personal event (episodic memory)? A study by Whitten and Leonard (1981) suggests that you should start with the most recent experience and work backwards. They asked college students to recall the name of a teacher from each of the 12 grades of primary and secondary

FIGURE 7.10   Flashbulb Memory

An extraordinary event usually imprints itself in our memory with such sudden clarity that we can vividly recall a great deal of detail about it many years later. Do you remember where you were and what you were doing when the space shuttle *Challenger* exploded on January 28, 1986?

school. One group was asked to come up with names randomly, one group was asked to start with grade one, and one group was asked to start with grade 12. Those who started with grade 12 did the best. The study also demonstrated that remembering one item can help in remembering a contiguous item, thus showing the importance of association in our memory system.

The importance of association is shown in what Brown and McNeil (1966) call the tip-of-the-tongue phenomenon: the closer you come to recalling a name or a word, the more accurately you can remember the number of syllables and some of the letters (often the first or last). What was the name of your kindergarten teacher? If you cannot recall it, you might say, "I can picture her, but I can't get the name yet. . . . It rhymes with spoon. It's on the tip of my tongue. I know it. Moon. No, it's Kuhn. Mary Kuhn. Yes, I remember her well."

Organization of information in long-term memory significantly increases the success of retrieval. Sometimes events and experiences are well organized, but often we must produce our own organization scheme. In subjective organization, the individual organizes information in some type of order. Tulving (1962) gave subjects lists of unrelated words and asked them to recall as many as possible. Those who created an organizational framework by creating associations among words were able to remember significantly more than those who tried to recall the words randomly. A useful suggestion is to organize your course material to facilitate retrieval on tests.

Sometimes when we attempt to retrieve information from long-term memory we cannot remember all of the details. Reconstructive memory involves combining the actual details of an event with other information that tends to fill in the gaps. For example, suppose you were asked to describe your 10th birthday party. You probably can remember some details, but not everything. In an effort to reconstruct the event, you will, perhaps, remember your brother was sick that year and couldn't attend. Because he normally attended you might use that detail to reconstruct the rest of your party.

Eyewitness Testimony An important application of reconstructive memory is the area of eyewitness testimony. As we discussed in the opening story in chapter 1, "The Study of Psychology," Elizabeth Loftus (1979) found that memories of eyewitnesses were influenced by assumptions and social variables. For example, in one study subjects saw a short film of an automobile accident and then were asked questions about it. Some of the subjects were asked how fast the car was going when it passed a barn along the road, while others were asked how fast the car was going along the road (no mention of the barn). When questioned later, over five times as many subjects who had been asked the first question replied that they remembered seeing the barn

BIOGRAPHICAL HIGHLIGHT

ELIZABETH F. LOFTUS

Elizabeth F. Loftus was born in 1944 in Los Angeles. Her mother was a librarian and her father a doctor. Her interests include both mathematics and psychology, which helps to explain her double major at the University of California at Los Angeles. Then she went on to obtain her Ph.D. in psychology from Stanford University in 1970.

Loftus's early research centered on learning and problem solving with computers. Eventually, she became interested in how human memory functions and coauthored several books on memory. She wanted to become involved in more socially relevant kinds of research and got her chance in 1974 with a grant to study the effects of leading questions on witnesses' memory of traffic accidents.

In her 1979 book, *Eyewitness Testimony* (which won a 1980 National Media Award, Distinguished Contribution), she described her theory of how perceptions can modify human memory. Leading questions can have a permanent effect on the memory of a witness. This research helped her to become one of the nation's leading legal consultants in the area of eyewitness testimony in trials.

Elizabeth Loftus is professor of psychology at the University of Washington. She has written several books with her husband, Geoffrey Loftus. Her interests continue to focus on understanding how the human memory is shaped by perception and experience.

than those who had been asked the second question with no mention of the barn. Just the fact that the barn had been mentioned caused the subjects to incorporate it into their memory. Loftus points out that many times we supplement our recollection of events with sensible but possibly false information.

In another study, Loftus and her colleagues showed subjects slides of the events leading up to an automobile accident. Slides for two groups were identical except for one slide in which half of the subjects saw a stop sign and the other half saw a yield sign. Next, subjects were asked a series of questions that included the assumption that there was either a stop or yield sign. They were later shown pairs of slides and asked to identify the one they had previously seen. Of those subjects who had been asked questions that matched the kind of sign they had seen, 75 percent correctly chose the slide they had seen before. But of those subjects who had been asked questions mentioning a sign they had not seen, only 41 percent correctly chose the slide they had seen before. Thus, our memory of what we have seen can be altered by inaccurate information.

Loftus (1983) pointed out that, during an interview, inaccurate or false information could be given to a witness, thereby causing the witness to reconstruct an unreliable account of the incident. Loftus (1984) suggested that the accuracy of a witness's memory is especially a problem when the witness is identifying a member of a different race, since some people have difficulty distinguishing features of members of another race and therefore are more likely to make inaccurate identifications.

Metamemory   Metamemory refers to the knowledge of one's own memory ability (Cavanaugh & Perlmutter, 1982). People appear to have a fairly good idea about how well they are able to remember things. If your psychology instructor asked you if you knew his or her birthday, you would not have to think too long before indicating you do not have that information stored in your memory. Likewise, you would probably be able to predict that it would be more difficult to memorize a list of Chinese words than a list of English words. Metamemory is concerned with how much people know about their memory systems and how accurately people can predict how difficult a memory task will be.

Children are often unable to predict how well they will remember things. Yussen and Berman (1981) reported that 7-year-old children overestimated the number of words that they could remember from a list. Schneider and Sodian (1991) tested a group of children both at 4 and 6 years of age on tasks requiring memory of clusters of objects. Although there was an improvement over the 2 years, the children had difficulty predicting how they would recall at both ages. Merfo and Ryan (1990) recently reported that fourth-grade students who were better readers had more efficient metamemory skills than those who were poor readers, although all of the students had difficulty in the memory tasks.

Research indicates that metamemory is well established by college age. Leal (1987) asked her university students to predict their performance prior to taking examinations. She found that the students were able to assess their exam readiness adequately. Intons-Peterson and Fournier (1986) reported that college students used external memory aids (taking notes or asking someone else) more than internal memory aids (mental rehearsal or imagery) to prepare for an exam. The students appeared to be able to evaluate and select effective strategies for remembering. Research by Hertzog, Dixon, and Hultsch (1990) found that older adults both predicted they would do worse and actually did perform at a lower level on recalling word lists and narrative text material compared to younger adults.

FORGETTING

The opposite but equally important factor in the process of remembering is, of course, the process of forgetting. It would probably be annoying, if not impossible, to think abstractly, to rationalize, or to organize material to function effectively, if we were not able to forget some of the insignificant material that enters our memory every day. Forgetting refers to the apparent loss of memory. Here we discuss the methods of studying and measuring forgetting and review its major theories.

Verbal Learning and Memory

As discussed in our opening story, a significant amount of learning and memory involves language— learning to respond to, or with, words or symbols. The study of verbal learning, pioneered by Ebbinghaus, focused on learning associations between verbal units and the time it takes to forget the associations. Three basic procedures used in studying verbal learning and memory are serial learning, free recall, and paired-associate learning.

Serial Learning   In serial learning the stimuli are always presented in the same order, and the subject has to learn them in the order in which they are presented. We used serial learning when we learned the letters of the alphabet or months of the year.

Ebbinghaus read a list of nonsense words at a steady pace (such as LOQ, BAJ, NUR, SEB, and CIV). When

FIGURE 7.11 Serial Position Effect

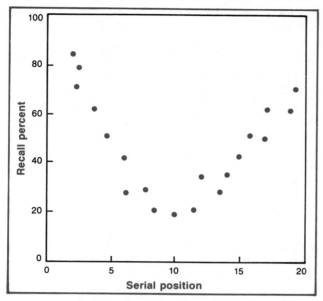

In experiments in which subjects were shown a list of words for a brief time, they tend to recall the words at the beginning and the end of the list better than the words in the middle.

he thought he knew the entire list, he tried to reproduce the items in the correct order. If he could not remember the list perfectly, he repeated the procedure until he could.

As mentioned in our opening story, a common finding is that items at the beginning and end of the list are remembered better than those in the middle. This is called the serial position effect. Remembering items in the beginning of the list is due to the primacy effect, whereas the recency effect is used to explain remembering items at the end of the list.

Free Recall   In free recall, the order of presentation of the stimulus items is varied on each trial, and the subject can learn and remember the items in any order. An example of such a list would be the names of people invited to a party. Free recall is often used to study how people organize their memory and what strategies are used to retrieve information. As we mentioned earlier, people tend to use subjective organization when learning unrelated stimuli.

Paired-Associate Learning   In paired-associate learning, the subject is presented with a series of pairs of items (for example red-bike, girl-horse, tree-dog). In subsequent trials, he or she is given any of the first items of the pair (the stimulus) and attempts to produce the second item (the response). You might use paired-associate learning in learning vocabulary words of a foreign language.

FIGURE 7.12 Paired-Associate Learning Task

QEW	GUX
QEW-ZAJ	GUX-PIW
KEZ	WUJ
KEZ-FUH	WUJ-BOF
QOS	DAQ
QOS-MIF	DAQ-ZUY
XAJ	CEJ
XAJ-NUX	CEJ-KOJ

In this test of memory, a series of pairs of nonsense words is first presented to the subject until he or she can remember them all. On subsequent trials, the first syllable (stimulus) is presented alone, and the subject must remember the second syllable (response).

Measures of Retention

After Ebbinghaus learned a list of nonsense syllables, he would wait a given length of time and then test for forgetting. In order to test the amount of forgetting that has taken place, psychologists commonly use three measures of retention: recall, recognition, and savings.

Recall   In recall (reconstruction), the subject is required to retrieve learned information from memory. In *free recall* the subject can remember the information in any order without any cues. In *cued recall*, the subject is helped by cues or aids to remembering. For example, in serial recall, each item acts as a cue for the next one. Research suggests that we tend to organize our memories, and provide our own cues if none are given. If we were asked to recall the 10th letter of the alphabet, very likely we would start at the beginning and count off letters until we reached the letter *j*. We would provide the cues we needed to retrieve the correct response from our memory. Some very common types of recall tests used in school include the essay test, short answer test, and fill-in-the-blank test.

Recognition   A second measure of memory retention is recognition. In recognition the subject is required to identify items that were previously learned and ignore new items that are used for distraction. A true-false or multiple-choice test is a good example of a test of recognition. Subjects often do better with recognition tests than with recall tests. The recognition test requires that you do only one task—identify the correct item. The recall test requires two tasks—first you must retrieve the item from memory and then you must identify it as being the correct one. You engage in recognition tasks every day. For example, you use recognition when you pick your coat out of many from the coatrack, or when you identify a friend.

The difference between recall and recognition is nicely illustrated in a study conducted by Bahrick, Bahrick, and Wittlinger (1975) to test the memory of high school graduates for the names and faces of their former classmates at times ranging from 3 months to 48 years after graduation. The subjects who had graduated 48 years earlier were able to recall only 6.8 percent of their classmates' names, but could recognize 71.0 percent of their faces.

Maggie Bruck pointed out that in Bahrick's study subjects were required to recognize photographs of classmates taken during high school, but in many situations we need to recognize individuals as they appear now. Bruck, Cavanagh, and Ceci (1991) had subjects who had graduated 25 years earlier match high school yearbook photographs of their former classmates with current photographs of the same individuals. The subjects were able to match the yearbook and current photographs correctly 49 percent of the time (control subjects who were not classmates made accurate matches 33 percent of the time). So it appears that we are able to recognize faces after long periods of time, even when the faces change with age.

Savings A third measure of retention is savings (relearning), in which the subject first learns a task and then is required to relearn it at a later time. Ebbinghaus used the savings technique in the research described in our opening story. The number of trials or amount of time needed to relearn the material is subtracted from the number of trials or the time it originally took to learn it and the difference is divided by the original number of trials or time it took to learn. The result is called the

FIGURE 7.13 Nonsense Syllables

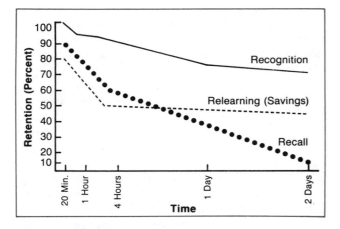

Three measures of retention of nonsense syllables are compared here. Although there is substantial forgetting for all three measures, recognition produces the best retention curve, followed by savings, and then recall. (After Luh, 1922.)

percent savings score. For example, someone might take 18 trials to learn a list of words the first time, but only 12 trials to relearn it 2 weeks later. This is a savings of $33^1/_3$ percent ($18 - 12 = 6$; $6 \div 18 = .333$ or $33^1/_3$ percent). Much of what we learn seems to be forgotten, but we often find that it is relatively easy to relearn it, indicating that some of it has still been retained. An important implication of this is that while you will forget much of what you learn in school, once you learn it, it will be easier to relearn it at a later time.

Theories of Forgetting

Sometimes we can remember things that happened to us as children, while at other times we seem to forget what happened to us yesterday. Are memories permanent, or do they tend to fade with time? And if memories are permanent, why can't we retrieve needed information whenever we want to? Forgetting refers to the apparent loss of memory. There are several major theories of forgetting, including decay, interference, and motivated forgetting (repression).

Decay According to the traditional theory, sensory impressions and acquired knowledge of facts leave memory traces that fade away with time or decay through disuse. This is a commonsense theory, and is believed by many people. But there is very little experimental evidence that decay occurs to memories in our long-term memory store. We already know that we tend to forget things after a time, but not all memories fade away like photographs in old newspapers or unused paths in a forest. Sometimes we can recall a fact today that we could not remember yesterday. And, under hypnosis or through electrical brain stimulation, we can sometimes remember occurrences from our past that we are unable to recall while fully conscious and alert. Decay might operate in short-term memory, where information fades within 30 seconds if not rehearsed, but that does not seem to be the case with long-term memory. We need another theory to help explain the unavailability of material in long-term memory.

Interference Most psychologists currently believe that once information is properly encoded and stored in long-term memory, it is relatively permanent. The reason we cannot retrieve information at one time but can at another is because of interference from other information that was also learned. The interference might come from information learned before (proactive interference) or after (retroactive interference) the information being tested for. Whereas decay appears to be a problem of storage, interference is a problem of retrieval.

FIGURE 7.14 Procedures to Test for Interference

	STEP 1	STEP 2	STEP 3
PROACTIVE INTERFERENCE			
Experimental Group	Learn List A	Learn List B	Recall List B
Control Group	Rest	Learn List B	Recall List B
RETROACTIVE INTERFERENCE			
Experimental Group	Learn List A	Learn List B	Recall List A
Control Group	Learn List A	Rest	Recall List A

The chart above illustrates the procedures for testing the effects of proactive and retroactive interference on memory. If the experimental group's recall performance is not as good as the control group's performance, then interference has occurred.

In proactive interference, information learned earlier interferes with retrieval of information learned later. If you already speak French when you begin studying Spanish, you probably will experience some difficulty in remembering newly learned Spanish words because your knowledge of French interferes with your memory of the corresponding Spanish words.

To test for the effects of proactive interference in the laboratory, psychologists have subjects in the experimental group learn List A, while subjects in the control group rest (and thus do not learn the list). Then both groups are required to learn List B, a new list of items. Finally, after a given period of time, both groups are tested for retention of List B. If proactive interference took place, the experimental group that had previously learned List A will not be able to remember List B as well as the control group, because List A items interfere with remembering List B items. (See Figure 7.14.)

In retroactive interference, newly learned information interferes with the memory of previously learned information. After you have studied Spanish until you are fairly fluent, and have meanwhile neglected your French, you might find that when reaching for a French expression you only remember the Spanish translation.

Psychologists test for the effects of retroactive interference by first having both the experimental and control group learn List A. Then the experimental group learns List B while the control group rests. Finally, after a given period of time, both groups are tested for the memory of List A. If retroactive interference took place, the experi-

mental group that had recently learned List B will not be able to remember List A as well as the control group. The newly learned material interferes with the earlier learned material. (See Figure 7.14.)

Interference theory sounds reasonable, and helps account for the fact that some of our memories last an extremely long time. However, much of the work on interference has been on nonsense syllables or unrelated words, and its applicability to everyday situations is not yet fully known. One recent study by White (1989) found that rare events could be remembered better over time than more common events, suggesting the importance of interference (especially proactive interference) in our difficulty recalling episodic events. Psychologists are still investigating why interference occurs at some times with some memories, but not at other times (for example, during a test, but not afterwards).

Underwood (1983) suggested that, in addition to interference, the inability to retrieve long-term memories can be due to the lack of an appropriate environmental stimulus. According to Underwood, we use memory attributes, or critical features of an event, when we encode the experience. We also use memory attributes when we retrieve the memory. For example, when my family and I recently visited the campus of Michigan State University, a flood of memories of when I asked my wife to marry me rushed through me. The sights and sounds of the university campus served as memory attributes of the event. Paying attention to memory attributes might help prevent forgetting from occurring.

Motivated Forgetting   One last theory we cover suggests that sometimes we forget because we want to. Motivated forgetting (repression), is a term used by Freudian psychologists (*see* chapter 11, "Personality") for the process of forgetting something that is anxiety-arousing. Although repression is often a personality problem, it can result in a loss of memory. For example, let's assume that you have a dentist appointment this afternoon. Although your dentist is always careful, there is still some pain involved in having your teeth drilled and this causes you to be anxious. The Freudian psychologist might suggest that you could become so involved in other activities that you forget to go to the dentist. In this situation, you might be motivated to forget your appointment.

Psychologists do not agree on any one theory of forgetting. Ongoing research on memory processes promises to help shed more light on the processes of memory and forgetting.

IMPROVEMENT OF MEMORY

Most people complain at one time or another that their memory is not as efficient as they would like it to be. Part of the problem is likely to be the techniques used to encode, store, and retrieve information, rather than the memory system itself. In this section, we will look at several methods for improving memory.

APPLICATION

Improving Your Memory

This chapter contains many suggestions for improving your memory. In addition, there are a number of excellent "help" books available that give practical advice to people who would like to be able to remember things better. One of the more popular books currently out is a paperback by Laird Cermak called *Improving Your Memory*. Cermak's book is a nontechnical review of practical suggestions to help you improve your memory, including attention, organization, mediation, imagery, and mnemonics.

The first suggestion is to increase *attention* in order to focus on the information we want to remember. You've heard it said again and again, but you must pay attention if you want to remember better. When reading, focus on the material and don't let your mind wander. When listening to a lecture, concentrate on the information and don't daydream. Attention brings information into our short-term memory.

Organization is important in memory improvement, and is usually considered essential for retrieval of information. Organization in putting information into the system saves time in trying to retrieve it later. In some ways, memory can be thought of as a filing cabinet, and an organized filing system saves the individual time and frustration in finding particular information. The key is to associate new information with information already in the system. The key organizational techniques include mediation, imagery, and mnemonics.

Mediation helps you organize and remember material by making words, sentences, or other connections out of the information. For example, you could insert a word between two words you are trying to remember. If you needed to remember milk and bread you might insert the word white. Then you can associate both white milk and white bread.

Imagery is the technique of making mental pictures of the material to be remembered. It is important to make the images as vivid or bizarre as possible. For example, with milk and bread, you might picture a huge water fountain made out of a loaf of bread, with milk flowing out of it.

The third technique for organizing material in memory is *mnemonics*. A mnemonic sometimes combines mediation and imagery, but uses an already existing organization scheme. A mnemonic is like a peg on a pegboard in that it allows you to hang information on the peg. For example, you might already know "one is a bun," "two is a shoe." Then you imagine milk flowing out of a big bun and bread stuffed into a shoe. The key to all of these memory techniques is to personalize them and make them work for you. Good luck!

Memory Enhancement Techniques

Psychologists have developed a number of procedures to enhance memory. For example, practice activities, mnemonic techniques, and other special strategies or forms of organization all serve as effective tools to help memory.

Practice Activities   Suppose you have a week to learn a fairly important role in a play, but your schedule allows you only 14 hours to memorize all the lines. You want to know what pattern of learning would best enable you to have those lines down cold by the end of 7 days. Should you work on them in two stretches of 7 hours each? Or should you devise some other schedule? Psychological research suggests that massed practice, or "crash" learning of as much material as possible in long continuous stretches, would *not* be the ideal method. The most effective method would be distributed practice, in which the memorization process is spaced out over an extended period of time. Underwood (1983) explained that less interference is likely when you use distributed practice than when you try to learn all at once.

In most situations, we will remember material longest and most accurately when we have overlearned it. Despite the way it sounds, overlearning does not mean too much learning. Rather, overlearning means that the material has been rehearsed over and over again following its initial learning. Of course, it is always helpful if the material we are trying to learn interests us. But in every case, the more we rehearse beyond the first "perfect" performance, the longer we will be able to remember the material that we have learned.

A memory lasts longest when the material is familiar, and *review* following learning helps to keep the material familiar. Students who regularly review assigned reading and lecture notes generally do better than those who study the material only when assigned or just before an exam.

To remember written or verbal material, even material whose content need not be learned word for word, it helps a great deal to actually recite, or repeat from memory, the material just read. This active *recitation* or elaboration has a far greater effect on long-term memory than does mere passive reading, even when the material is clearly understood in the first reading.

In general, the better we encode and store information, the easier it will be to retrieve. This chapter contains a number of useful encoding suggestions for improving memory, including chunking, selective attention, and depth of processing.

Mnemonic Techniques   Examples of chunking, organizing, and logically relating the components of material to be recalled may be encountered in various learning experiences. What they have in common is the need to reduce the information to be remembered to the most manageable and, therefore, the most memorizable form.

Mnemonic techniques are strategies for improving memory by organizing and encoding information to aid memory performance (Bellezza, 1981). One mnemonic technique is to combine items to be remembered into words or *phrases*. For example, to learn the colors of the spectrum, you might remember the name "Roy G. Biv," which should help you remember red, orange, yellow, green, blue, indigo, and violet.

Imagery is important in a number of mnemonic techniques (Bellezza, 1981). A mnemonic that utilizes imagery is the pegword technique, which typically starts with a rhyme or series in which the key words serve as "pegs" to associate with other items to be remembered.

(See Figure 7.15, next page.) Another technique, used originally by Greek orators, is the method of loci (places). You first memorize a series of familiar locations, such as the rooms in a house, buildings on a street, or even parts of the body. For example, you might take a mental walk through your house and come up with *living room, dining room, kitchen,* and *bedroom*. Once you have these places learned, you are ready to memorize the new words. You pair a word with a location, and form a vivid image. For example, if you had a grocery list, you might have items such as milk, bread, eggs, and steak. Your images might include milky white living room furniture, a huge table made out of bread in the dining room, fried eggs as burners on your stove, and a huge cow sitting in your bed. In order to remember your grocery list, you then go through the sequence of rooms, recalling the vivid images you formed in each room. (See Figure 7.16, page 173.)

One way to improve encoding of material for easier retrieval is to employ a device that logically relates and organizes the components. In this way, a person can easily learn an apparently complex list that could go to infinity: 0, 2, 5, 7, 10, 12, 15, 17, 20, 22, 25, 27, 30, . . . Can you come up with a rule that organizes these numbers? Use this formula: Beginning at zero, add two, then add three, then add two, then add three again, and so forth. Instead of trying to memorize the entire list, you have greatly simplified your task by reducing it to merely two actions (adding two and then three alternately) which can be readily learned. You are no longer memorizing an imposing list of items, but organizing the items by finding the relationship between the items and remembering that relationship.

Henry Ellis (1987) described a memory strategy called ARESIDORI, which he said was a mnemonic code for the important variables in improving memory. ARESIDORI stands for attention, rehearsal, elaboration, semantic processing, imagery, distinctiveness, organization, retrieval, and interest. We have discussed these concepts and variables throughout this chapter.

What do memory experts use to enhance their own memory abilities? Park, Smith, and Cavanaugh (1990) surveyed a group of memory research psychologists and found that the technique they most used and recommended for remembering was to write things in lists and notes! This suggestion was followed by general memory techniques (such as organization or rehearsal). The least recommended strategies were the formal mnemonic techniques (such as pegword or method of loci). The researchers suggested that although formal mnemonic techniques are effective in certain situations, they require a significant investment in time and energy to use correctly. Thus, while you should try to incorporate the suggestions for improving your memory included in this chapter, it is also wise to carry pen and paper.

FIGURE 7.15 Pegword Mnemonic Technique

Rhyme with Pegwords	Words to Memorize	Pegwords	Visual Image
	1. steak	bun	
One is a bun			
Two is a shoe			
Three is a tree			
Four is a door	2. milk	shoe	
Five is a hive			
Six is sticks			
Seven is heaven	3. eggs	tree	
Eight is a gate			
Nine is a line			
Ten is a hen			
	4. bread	door	

Imagery and association are involved in many mnemonic devices. In the pegword mnemonic technique, you first memorize the short rhyme. Then, using these words as pegs, you create a visual image of each of the words you to wish to remember.

Context and Memory Psychologists have found that remembering is easier when we do it under conditions that are similar to those that we originally learned in. If possible, study under conditions similar to those that will exist in the test situation. For example, study at a desk, rather than lying on the floor. Study under quiet conditions, rather than with the radio playing. Ideally, you should study in an environment that is as similar as possible to the environment in which you will take the test. And while you are taking the test, think about the environment in which you studied to retrieve information through context associations.

State-dependent learning refers to the phenomenon that we remember best when we are in the same state of consciousness that we were in when we originally learned the material (see chapter 5, "Sleep and Consciousness"). A number of studies have demonstrated that if a person learns while in a drug-induced altered state of consciousness, he or she will remember it most efficiently when in the same state. Of course, this also means that information you learn when in waking consciousness will be recalled best when you are in waking consciousness. Sometimes other influences (such as envi-

ronmental cues) will outweigh the effects of state-dependent memory. Try to study when you are alert and in the same state of waking consciousness that you will be in when taking a test.

A related phenomenon is the finding that emotional mood states can influence memory. Bower (1981) reported that subjects who were either sad or happy when they learned material recalled the information significantly better when they were later in the same mood. Bower suggested that this is why we are able to remember more negative experiences when we are depressed. Thus, you need to think positively when you are studying for and taking your exams.

SQ5R Study Technique

Much of the material in this chapter can be applied immediately as you study in school. A particularly good technique for organizing some of these principles of learning and memory is the SQ5R study technique, based on the SQ3R study technique originally developed by Francis Robinson (1970). As you learn to use this

FIGURE 7.16   Method of Loci Mnemonic Technique

Location	Intend to Remember	Visual Image
Living room	Bread	
Kitchen	Eggs	
Bedroom	Meat	

Another technique to remember a list is the method of loci. You first memorize a series of familiar locations, such as rooms in your house, and combine them with the items you want to remember. Finally, you form a visual image of these combinations.

technique, you should find you are able to identify the parts of this chapter that apply to the various steps of the study formula. Here we describe the SQ5R study technique, which differs from the original SQ3R technique in the addition of two steps, record and reflect, that were suggested by Pauk (1984). SQ5R study technique stands for survey, question, read, record, recite, review, and reflect.

The first step in studying is to *survey*. If you are reading a chapter of a textbook, you should quickly glance through the entire chapter, noting the headings, style, length, and general format. This step focuses your attention on the material and helps prepare you for effective studying.

Question simply means to look at the chapter and ask yourself questions about it. What does a heading mean? What are the important points in the chapter? What does a word mean? You make up questions about the chapter by quickly looking through it. The questions are designed primarily to motivate you to study the material carefully. In this book, you could turn the chapter objectives into questions. Again, the question step prepares you for effectively studying the material.

A critical step is to *read*. It's important that you actively read the material paragraph by paragraph. Read for a purpose, even if the purpose is just to find out what is in the chapter. Read to answer the questions you have developed. Carefully note important terms, including the italicized or underlined words and phrases. Your main job in reading is to obtain the main ideas and important details. Active reading is important for effectively remembering what you have studied.

After actively reading a paragraph, you should *record* the main ideas. You can underline key words and phrases, write the main ideas in the margin, or write a brief summary in your notebook. Recording the main ideas of what you read forces you to read the textbook actively and provides you with a written outline to study later.

The fifth step is to *recite*. Recitation means recalling what you have read. It is rehearsing the main ideas and important details in your memory. You can simply recall the information, but a better technique is to organize it and form associations to other ideas you have already remembered. Recitation is an excellent way to discover what you can remember about the chapter material.

The next step of the study formula is to *review*. Reviewing the material helps to keep it fresh in your mind. Essentially you quickly reread the chapter to make sure you have covered it all. Then you recite the information to yourself and read over any notes you have taken. If you review regularly, you should have no problems when the big test comes.

The last step of SQ5R is to *reflect* on the ideas you have learned. Here is a chance to think critically about the issues raised, the points presented, and the conclusions drawn. Take time to organize the information and develop associations with your existing knowledge. Reflect on examples and applications of the concepts encountered. Evaluate the ideas and decide which point of view is correct. This will help you remember and be able to use the information you learn from your book.

BIOLOGY OF MEMORY

We can reasonably assume that our memories have a biological basis in our brain. And yet the vast amount and complexity of information we must encode and store seems to defy any simple explanation. Psychologists have been trying to discover the biological basis of memory for some time.

Karl Lashley (1950) spent many years trying to identify the engram, or memory trace, in the brain that holds specific memories. He conducted many experiments in which he trained rats and then destroyed parts of their brain. He concluded that memory is not stored in any one specific part of the brain and that the degree to which memory is hurt depends on the amount of brain destroyed (called the law of equipotentiality). In other words, memory depends on the size of the total brain and not on any specific location.

At about the time that Lashley was concluding his research efforts, Donald Hebb (1949) presented his biological theory of memory consolidation. Consolidation is the neural process of making memories more permanent. As new material is learned, neurons in a particular circuit are stimulated and fire. With rehearsal or practice, the circuit is repeated over and over, and through this consolidation procedure, the chemical events at the synapses change into a permanent record of the information. While all the details have not yet been worked out, many psychologists accept that a process similar to the one Hebb proposed is probably responsible for the biology of memory (Alkon, 1989).

Some research has been used to test Hebb's theory of consolidation and gain new information on the biology of memory. One line of research concentrated on disrupting the repeating electrical circuits. Chorover and Schiller (1965) gave rats electroconvulsive shock at various times after they had been trained. The researchers found that the shock produced retrograde amnesia, or forgetting of the information, when administered a brief time after learning took place. In other research studies, electrodes have been implanted in specific areas of the brain to test the effects of electrical stimulation at particular locations immediately after learning has taken place. Several brain areas have been suggested as potential memory processing sites, including the hippocampus, the midbrain reticular formation, and the frontal cortex.

It is likely that different brain sites are involved in different types of memories (procedural, semantic, and episodic). Richard Thompson (1985) suggested that the cerebellum plays an important role in procedural memory. In classical conditioning experiments in which rabbits were taught to blink their eyes when a stimulus was presented, the neural circuits in the cerebellum were activated.

The hippocampus, amygdala, and thalamus are involved in the development of semantic and episodic memory (Mishkin & Appenzeller, 1987). Many researchers and clinicians have reported that patients with damage to the hippocampus are not able to form new memories (Squire, 1987). Recently, Squire and his colleagues (in press) used the PET scan technique to study brain activity in subjects who were trying to recall a list of words. They found that, in addition to the hippocampus, the visual cortex and the frontal cortex were involved in memory retrieval.

Another line of research has concentrated on the neurochemistry of memory. In an experiment with rats, James McGaugh (1983) found that the hormone epinephrine significantly increased the rat's memory of a maze. Other studies have found that the adrenal hormone ACTH and the pituitary hormone vasopressin aid the memory of rats in learning tasks (Messing & Sparber, 1985).

Scopolamine, a drug that decreases the level of the neurotransmitter acetylcholine, impairs memory in rats. Humans who were given a dose of scopolamine also showed temporary memory deficits (Beatty, Butters, & Janowsky, 1986). Likewise, drugs that temporarily increase levels of the brain neurotransmitter acetylcholine tend to help improve human memory (Bartus & colleagues, 1982). Unfortunately, there are side effects, and so this is not at present a feasible way to improve memory.

Information on how memory operates has been obtained from studies of brain-related memory deficits. A topic of great interest is Alzheimer's disease, a disorder in which the individual gradually loses all memory. Research on this brain degenerative disorder (Davies, 1985) suggests that it is caused by a deficiency of acetylcholine. This research gives insight into the role acetylcholine plays in memory and also may provide a lead in the treatment of Alzheimer's disease.

Although progress has been made, there is still much to discover about the biology of memory. However, it is likely that the specific chemical code will eventually be broken. ∎

Drawing by Fisher; © 1983 The New Yorker Magazine, Inc.

"The matters about which I'm being questioned, Your Honor, are all things I should have included in my long-term memory but which I mistakenly inserted in my short-term memory."

The study of memory, begun with Ebbinghaus, continues today to provide a rich array of information about human memory. This chapter can be very useful to you if you apply the principles discussed to everyday life. You can only retrieve information that you have properly encoded and stored. While some people seem naturally to have better memories than others, research has clearly shown that memory can be improved through practice and utilization of the memory techniques. Can you now remember the name of your kindergarten teacher? How about the three measures of retention in memory? You will probably be able to find out shortly how much of the memory chapter you remember. Do you remember when your next test is scheduled?

CHAPTER REVIEW

What You've Learned About Human Memory

1. Memory involves encoding and storing information that is learned so it can be retrieved and used at a later time. The amount of information accurately stored is called the memory retention level.

2. Encoding is the process of putting information into the memory system. Storage is the process that retains information in the memory system over time. Retrieval is the process of pulling information out of the memory system.

3. Information processing theory is a model of memory that includes three memory stores: sensory memory, short-term memory, and long-term memory. Sensory memory refers to the memory store that sensory information first enters in the memory system. It has a large capacity, but maintains unprocessed information for a brief time, about half a second. Visual sensory memory is called iconic memory, and auditory sensory memory is called echoic memory.

4. Attention is the process of focusing only on certain stimuli. In pattern recognition we compare the information selected through attention with the information already permanently stored in our memory.

5. Important variables in encoding in short-term memory include meaningfulness (informational value) and chunking (combining stimuli).

6. We tend to store information in short-term memory the way it sounds (acoustic code). The capacity of short-term memory is about seven (plus or minus two) chunks of information. If you attend to a stimulus, it can be transferred into short-term memory, where it can be held for up to 30 seconds before it decays. We use a serial, exhaustive search to retrieve information from short-term memory.

7. Maintenance rehearsal (repeating information without thinking about it) can keep information in short-term memory for a longer time. If you use elaborative rehearsal (thinking about the meaning of the information) you can transfer information into long-term memory, where it can remain indefinitely.

8. The key to encoding in long-term memory is to organize the material and make it meaningful. Procedural memory involves the formation of associations between stimuli and responses. Semantic memory can involve cognitive activities, such as knowledge used in everyday experience. Episodic memory involves knowledge of personal experiences, and is the highest form of long-term memory.

9. Metamemory refers to the knowledge of one's own memory ability.

10. Verbal learning is learning to respond to (or with) words or symbols. Three basic verbal learning procedures developed by Ebbinghaus include: serial learning, free recall, and paired-associate learning.

11. Retrieval is the process of pulling information out of memory. Psychologists commonly use three measures of retention: recall, recognition, and savings.

12. Forgetting refers to the apparent loss of memory. Decay refers to the fading of the memory trace, especially in sensory or short-term memory. Interference theory suggests that memory is permanent, but we can't remember something because of other competing information learned before (proactive interference) or after (retroactive interference) the information being tested for. Motivated forgetting, or repression, is a term used by Freudian psychologists for the process of forgetting something that is anxiety-arousing.

13. There are many techniques that can be used to improve memory, including distributed practice, overlearning, review, active recitation, encoding techniques (chunking, selective attention, depth of processing, organization), mnemonic techniques (phrases, method of loci), and retrieval techniques. Mnemonic techniques are ways of improving memory by combining and relating chunks of information.

14. SQ5R stands for survey, question, read, record, recite, review, and reflect—the five steps in this study technique, which you can learn easily and utilize in your current studies.

15. The biological theory of memory consolidation suggests that memory becomes more permanent over time due to chemical changes at the neuron synapses. Memory involves various brain sites, including the hippocampus and thalamus.

CHAPTER OBJECTIVES

After studying this chapter, you should be able to:

1. Define cognition and identify the topics in cognitive psychology.
2. Define language and describe the structure of language (grammar).
3. Outline how language develops in infants and children.
4. Compare the two major theories of language development.
5. Explain how language and thought are related.
6. Define concept formation and identify the types of concepts.
7. Identify three theories of problem solving.
8. Outline effective problem-solving strategies and identify three variables that can interfere.
9. Outline the area of creativity.

What You'll Learn About Language and Intelligence

10. Define the concept of intelligence.
11. Outline the major theories of intelligence.
12. Identify the characteristics of tests.
13. Describe the development of the Stanford-Binet Intelligence Scale.
14. Describe the Wechsler Intelligence Scales.
15. Outline the genetic influences on intelligence.
16. Outline the environmental influences on intelligence.
17. List the levels of mental retardation and identify the major causes of mental retardation.
18. Describe intellectually gifted people.

Lewis Terman spent over 40 years devising and studying intelligence tests. He adapted the first test of intelligence for Americans in 1916, and spent a lot of his time examining intelligence in children. He was concerned about the misperceptions that many people had about intellectually gifted children, and in 1921 set out to dispel some of the myths people had about children with very high intelligence.

Around 1920, children who were intellectually gifted were perceived by many people to be abnormal. These gifted children were thought to be bookworms who were sickly, physically weak, and social failures.

From over 250,000 children suggested by teachers in California schools as being gifted, Terman selected 1,528 children with the highest IQs. The mean IQ of the children was 150 (and ranged from 135 to over 190). There were 857 boys and 671 girls in the group, and their ages ranged from 8 to 12 years.

The Terman Gifted Group was studied extensively. As Terman suspected, the group was very healthy, mentally and physically. They tended to be taller, stronger, healthier, and more socially outgoing than their classmates. During high school they became leaders, participated in sports and school activities, and were judged to be very well adjusted. And, of course, they did well academically in school, especially in science and mathematics.

What would happen to these gifted individuals when they grew up? Terman decided to conduct a long-term study of the group. He observed them for 40 years and published his findings in a series of books called *Genetic Studies of Genius*.

The Terman Gifted Group continued to be successful when they reached adulthood. Over 70 percent of them obtained college degrees, and many obtained post-

Part of what makes us unique is our ability to use language to communicate and to use thought to solve problems. The cognitive processes of language and thought are involved in intelligence. A number of important theories of intelligence have been proposed, and a variety of IQ tests have been developed to measure it.

8

Language and Intelligence

FIGURE 8.1 Chess Team in Harlem, New York
Most psychologists would agree with Margaret Matlin that cognition involves the acquisition, storage, retrieval, and utilization of knowledge. Here, members of the Raging Rooks, the chess team from Adam Clayton Powell, Jr., Junior High School in Harlem, New York, use cognition in a practice game. In 1991 the team tied for first place in the National Junior High Chess Championship sponsored by the United States Chess Federation.

graduate education. They tended to enter prestigious occupations, including law, medicine, education, and science. Over 40 percent of the men became lawyers, doctors, engineers, business executives, or college professors. Although fewer women pursued careers, of those who did, 65 percent were also professionals. The gifted individuals tended to earn significantly more money than average. The overall conclusion was that this group of people was highly successful in life.

Lewis Terman died in 1956, but other researchers have continued to study this group of gifted people for the past 70 years. This long-term research study demonstrates that individuals with high intelligence are likely to become robust members of the community.

WHAT IS COGNITION?

Terman's research project is among many that were designed to determine the effects of intelligence on adaptation. Intelligence, the capacity to learn and behave adaptively, is one of the topics studied in cognitive psychology. Other areas of cognitive psychology include perception, attention, memory, language, thinking, concept formation, problem solving, and artificial intelligence (Anderson, 1990). In this chapter, we focus on language, thinking, problem solving, and intelligence.

What is cognition? Most psychologists would agree that cognition involves the acquisition, storage, retrieval, and utilization of knowledge (Matlin, 1989). Examples of cognition include learning something and placing the information in our memory system, communicating through language by manipulating mental symbols, and solving problems or acting intelligently by utilizing information that we have previously learned and stored in memory.

The cognitive areas of language, thinking, problem solving, and intelligence are closely interrelated, and each of these processes is largely dependent on the others. *Language* is a form of communication utilizing manipulation of symbols to convey meaning to others or to oneself. Language can help us communicate with other people and can also help us think. *Thinking* can be defined as the cognitive or mental activity of manipulating symbols. For humans, thinking usually involves language. We use thinking to make decisions and solve problems. *Problem solving*, along with thinking, enables us to act intelligently. *Intelligence* is defined as the capacity to learn and behave adaptively. Intelligence utilizes the ability to communicate through language, and can be improved through practice solving problems.

As we discussed in chapter 1, "The Study of Psychology," cognition plays a major role in psychology. In fact, we defined psychology as the science of behavior and cognition. Historically, psychology began with a strong cognitive orientation (Wundt's school of structuralism involved the study of conscious experience through introspection). However, during the early part of this century, behaviorists effectively eliminated cognition as an area of study in psychology. It was not until the 1960s that psychology began once again to incorporate cognitive processes into its theories and methods. The information-processing theory that was borrowed from computer science provided the ideal theoretical perspective for the study of cognitive processes (see chapter 7, "Human Memory"). Now there are very few areas in psychology that do not include a cognitive approach.

Not all psychologists, however, support the pervasive influence of cognitive processes in psychology. Be-

haviorist B. F. Skinner (1987) accused cognitive scientists of loosely defining terms, speculating about internal unseen processes, and misusing terms such as storage (arguing the brain is not an encyclopedia or museum). He argued that the cognitive psychologists went too far and were not as productive as they could be. Thus, he proposed letting psychology become a behavioral science again.

Cognitive psychologists would respond that although the actual activities of cognition cannot be observed directly, cognitive processes are an important force in our lives.

LANGUAGE

One of the ways we differ from lower animals is in our advanced ability to learn and utilize language. Other animals have developed communication systems, and recently some primates have been taught the rudiments of language. But only we humans, with our complex brain and higher mental functioning, have developed the complex system of communication called language.

The Structure of Language

Language is the principal means of communication for human beings. It allows us to manipulate symbols to convey meaning to others or to ourselves. It also allows us to represent ideas and objects that are not restricted to the present. We can talk about the past and future, as well as the present.

Psycholinguistics is the psychological study of how we convert the sounds of language into meaningful symbols that can be used to communicate with others. Psycholinguists are concerned with the cognitive processes involved in the acquisition and use of a language.

Grammar   You can find most of the words in the English language in an unabridged dictionary. But no one would ever try to publish a list of all the sentences it is possible to make from those words, since their number is probably infinite. Yet almost every time you hear a sentence you understand it, even if you have never heard it before. Since you could not have learned the meaning of the sentences beforehand, how do you understand it?

The answer is that you understand the rules of the language. This set of rules, called grammar, can be used again and again, to produce and understand innumerable sentences. Every fluent speaker of a language is familiar with its grammar, a general term that includes the rules

FIGURE 8.2 Phonemes in American English

Vowels			
ee as in h*ea*t	*ah* as in f*a*ther	ʌ as in t*o*n	*au* as in sh*ou*t
ı as in h*i*t	*aw* as in c*a*ll	*uh* as in th*e*	*ei* as in t*a*ke
ε as in h*ea*d	*U* as in p*u*t	*er* as in b*i*rd	*ou* as in t*o*ne
ae as in h*a*d	*oo* as in c*oo*l	*oi* as in t*oi*l	*ai* as in m*i*ght

Consonants			
t as in *t*ee	*m* as in *m*e	*sh* as in *sh*ell	*zh* as in gara*g*e
p as in *p*ea	*n* as in *n*o	*h* as in *h*e	*l* as in *l*aw
k as in *k*ey	*ng* as in si*ng*	*v* as in *v*iew	*r* as in *r*ed
b as in *b*ee	*f* as in *f*ee	*th* as in *th*en	*y* as in *y*ou
d as in *d*awn	θ as in *th*in	*z* as in *z*oo	*w* as in *w*e
g as in *g*o	*s* as in *s*ee		

The basic speech sounds in a language are called phonemes. The numbers of phonemes vary in different languages and in different dialects within a language (after Denes & Pinson, 1963).

for the sounds (phonemes), structure (syntax), and meaning (semantics) of a language.

Basic Units of Language Language consists of basic speech sounds that are called phonemes. The *m* sounds in mother, music, and memory are all similar and thus represent one phoneme. Some languages have as few as 15 phonemes, while other languages have as many as 85 (Bourne & colleagues, 1986). The English language contains about 40 different phonemes. As many students soon discover, it can be extremely difficult to learn a foreign language that contains phonemes not found in their native tongue.

Phonemes are combined into morphemes, the smallest meaningful units of a language. Many morphemes are words, like *swim*, *teach*, and *hit*. Other morphemes are prefixes or suffixes that must be combined with other morphemes to form meaningful words. For example, the suffix *er* can be added to the word *teach* to form the new word *teacher*. The 40 phonemes in the English language can be combined to produce over 100,000 morphemes, which can be combined to produce over 500,000 words in the English language.

Syntax A subset of the rules of grammar, which governs the order of words in sentences, is called syntax. The rules of syntax help structure the language by regulating the ways in which nouns and verbs can combine to form phrases, which in turn form sentences. By providing such a structure, syntax helps us determine the meaning of language.

For example, try to decipher this sentence: "Ran Tom house quickly the into." You should be able to reorder the words to form the sentence the proper way: "Tom quickly ran into the house." Actually, there are 720 potential word orders in this sentence, but only one is (in all likelihood) correct. We learn syntax early in childhood, and can usually tell when something is wrong, even though we might not be able to explain the formal rules (Chomsky, 1965).

Semantics The study of the meaning of language is called semantics. Psychologists are trying to identify how we learn to put words together to make meaningful sentences. There are several theories of semantics. The learning theory views meaning as simply associations to words that we have learned.

More recently, the information-processing approach suggests that people process words using semantic memory. Apparently we learn the rules of semantics at a very young age.

Psycholinguists distinguish between surface structure and deep structure of sentences. The surface struc-

FIGURE 8.3 Transformational Grammar Rules

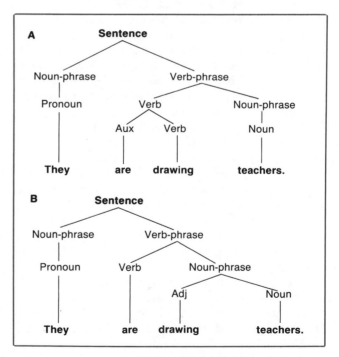

We use language rules to convert ideas into meaningful sentences. As shown here, the same sequence of words can have different meanings. In **A**, some people (they) are drawing pictures of the teachers. In **B**, the teachers (they) are identified as "drawing teachers' (after Chomsky, 1965).

ture is simply the sequence of morphemes we hear or see in a sentence. The deep structure is the actual meaning of the sentence. "Mommy kissed Karen" and "Karen was kissed by Mommy" have different surface structures, but both have the same deep structure, or meaning. Psycholinguist Noam Chomsky (1968) has proposed that we are able to relate the surface and deep structure of sentences through transformational grammar rules. These rules allow us to take ideas (deep structures) and convert them into meaningful sentences (surface structures).

When we wish to communicate something verbally, we begin with a meaningful thought, select phrases to express the idea, and produce speech sounds that make up sentences. This process is called top-down processing by psycholinguists. When we want to understand language produced by someone else, we reverse the process and use bottom-up processing. Here we listen to the speech sounds and interpret the sounds as meaningful words that fit together in sentences that convey meaningful thoughts and ideas.

Language Development in Children

Newborn babies often begin producing sounds within minutes of their birth. Historically, it was thought that babies made random noises right up until they began to talk. However, Kaplan and Kaplan (1971) described four distinct stages of sound production occurring during the first year of life. The first stage occurs when babies begin to *cry* at birth. The second stage begins at about the end of the first month, when babies *vocalize*. At around 6 months, babies begin to *babble*, the third stage. This babbling may contain sounds from many languages other than the one the babies will eventually acquire. In the fourth stage, starting at about the end of the first year of life, some sort of patterned *speech* can emerge.

Research has shown that babies are more aware of their early environment than was previously believed. Shortly after birth, infants react differently to the sound of their mother's voice than to that of an unfamiliar woman (DeCasper & Fifer, 1980). It has also been reported (Delack, 1976) that babies babble differently depending on the environment, for example if they are in their cribs or with their mothers.

By about one year of age, babies say their first word, often "Mama" or "Dada." During the second year, babies develop their vocabulary by adding one word at a time. They use one word to communicate the meaning of a complete sentence (*holophrastic speech*) at this stage. Children say "juice" to mean "I would like some juice to drink, please." Most parents quickly learn what the child's words mean and respond appropriately (if not, the child usually communicates displeasure by crying or acting frustrated).

FIGURE 8.4 Vocabulary Development

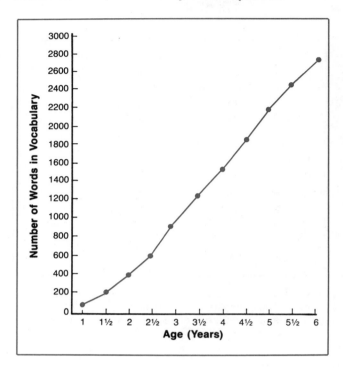

Children learn the basic structures of their language by age 3 and acquire a fairly extensive vocabulary by age 6 (after Smith, 1926).

The next stage in language development, telegraphic speech, begins at about 2 years of age, when children begin to use two-word sentences, like "my ball" and "Karen sleeping." They tend to include important words and leave out the rest. Even at this stage, children show an innate understanding of syntax, allowing them to construct grammatically correct sentences. For example, they are likely to say correctly, "drink juice" rather than "juice drink" to indicate that they are thirsty.

Later, at 3 or 4 years of age, their sentences become longer and more complex. For instance, instead of "Cara play," the child now says "Cara plays with me." At this age, children begin using the past tense and a variety of words. The size of their vocabulary grows rapidly, and by the time children enter school at the age of 5, they generally have a vocabulary of several thousand words.

Theories of Language Development

How do children acquire the language of their culture? Children everywhere learn to produce all the fundamental structures of their language within the first 3 years of life and have a vocabulary of several thousand words by about age 5. Children exposed early in their development to two different languages can easily learn to speak both fluently and with no foreign accent in either.

As a person grows older, however, it becomes more and more difficult to learn to speak a foreign language with fluency. In fact, it is extremely difficult for, say, an American in his or her thirties to learn to speak French as well as a Parisian does, even after years of living in Paris. Yet that American's 5-year-old daughter will catch up with her French playmates in a matter of months. This is happening in our country with Southeast Asians and other immigrants. Their children are able to pick up the English language very quickly at school and from friends, while their parents find it very difficult to learn English. Today some schools are making use of this early ability to learn a foreign language and offering a second language in elementary school, instead of waiting until later.

Besides the *critical period hypothesis*, which states that if a person doesn't learn to speak during childhood, he or she will never learn to speak fluently, there are two major theories of language development—learning and biological.

Learning Theory Because infants and children need to be around other people to develop language normally, many psychologists have emphasized the role of learning in language development. B. F. Skinner (1957) emphasized *reinforcement* in his theory of language acquisition. He argued that parents reinforce chil-

FIGURE 8.5 Noam Chomsky
Chomsky proposed that children are biologically programmed to understand and acquire language. His revolutionary theories caused many learning and developmental psychologists to reexamine their methods and assumptions.

dren for producing sounds that are recognizable as language. Through the process of shaping and reinforcement, children eventually learn which sounds and words will get them what they want.

Imitation also plays an important role in language development. Children try to imitate the words and phrases their parents use most frequently (Heibeck & Markman, 1987). Many times, the children will repeat sentences they have heard others make, often in a simplified version. For example, "The bus will be coming soon" becomes "Bus coming." Children acquire the essence of language rules ("He goed to the store" and "My foots hurt") rather than pure imitation of complex sentences. Parents reinforce the structure of sentences and eventually the grammar is learned.

Biological Psycholinguistic Theory As psycholinguists developed a better understanding of the complexity of adult language performance, it appeared unlikely that a small child could learn all the required rules of language in just a couple of years through reinforcement or imitation alone. Many psychologists currently accept Chomsky's psycholinguistic theory (1965) that children are biologically programmed to acquire language. Chomsky believes children are born with an internal language acquisition device (LAD) that allows them to interpret the adult speech that they hear and to make their own sentences with the correct rules of grammar.

An interesting demonstration that children are acquiring rules as they master language comes from a study by Jean Berko (1958), who tested 4- to 7-year-old children to see whether they knew rules of sound change. The mere fact that a child correctly uses the plurals of nouns or the past tense of verbs does not prove that he or she knows the rules of grammar, since those particular forms may have been learned by imitation. On the other hand, suppose you show the child a picture with two objects and then ask that the following sentence be completed aloud: "This is a wug. Now there is another one. There are two of them. There are two _____." If the child correctly pluralizes the nonsense syllable ("wugs"), he or she knows the rule.

Berko also found that children successfully applied rules to nonsense syllables to form the past tense and the possessive: "This is a man who knows how to mot. He is motting. He did the same thing yesterday. What did he do yesterday? He _____." "This is a niz who owns a hat. Whose hat is it? It is the _____ hat."

Psychologists recognize the importance of environmental factors, while also realizing that biology plays an important role in language development. Further research may help unravel the complex relationships that exist between biological and learning influences on language development.

FIGURE 8.6 Test for Learning Syntax

This is a wug.

Now there is another one.
There are two of them.
There are two _____.

Wugs are imaginary figures Berko (1958) used in her experiments to test young children's ability to acquire the rules of grammar.

Primate Language Studies The animal communication research that has been most controversial is that dealing with the ability of primates to learn and use language. Several early studies that tried to teach chimpanzees to talk resulted in failure. Then in 1966 Beatrix and Allen Gardner of the University of Nevada began their study of language in a chimpanzee named Washoe. The Gardners concluded that chimpanzees could not learn to talk because their vocal apparatus was not capable of making the proper sounds. So they decided to teach their chimpanzee, Washoe, how to communicate using a nonvocal language—the American Sign Language—that was developed for communication with the deaf. The American Sign Language uses complex hand gestures and has its own distinctive rules of grammar.

Washoe learned the correct sign gestures at about the same rate as young children do. The Gardners did not speak around Washoe, but used signs to "tell" her what they were doing. Many activities and objects that might interest the young chimpanzee were introduced, just so the Gardners could sign about them. They also tried to be as responsive as possible to Washoe's signing: to answer her questions, to sign something more on any topic she initiated, to fulfill her requests. Gradually, Washoe learned the signs, and eventually she had a vocabulary of 132 signs (Gardner & Gardner, 1969).

The amazing part of Washoe's language ability is not that she learned to "sign" the names of objects, but that she was able to use these signs to communicate. Washoe began spontaneously to combine the signs to make grammatically correct sentences. For example, one day when she wanted to play with Allen Gardner, she signed "Gimme tickle." She was also able to combine signs in meaningful ways. For example, when a window was open, she combined two signs to say "open window." Often, when she had been scolded for disobeying, she said "come hug—love sorry."

The Gardners discovered that the development of language communication in Washoe was similar to the language development in human children. Washoe didn't just memorize names of objects—she actively learned and used the rules of the language (Gardner & Gardner, 1978). Since Washoe, there have been a number of other studies of language in nonhuman primates.

David Premack (1971) taught a chimpanzee named Sarah to communicate using plastic symbols with a variety of shapes to develop sentences. Among the other primates in similar studies are Lana, a chimpanzee who can communicate with the use of a symbol keyboard connected to a computer (Rumbaugh, 1977), and Koko, a gorilla who communicates with sign language (Patterson, 1978).

These studies demonstrate that primates can learn symbols for words. But do they use language in the same way as people do? Herbert Terrace (1979) tried to teach sign language to his chimpanzee, Nim. After 5 years, Terrace concluded that while Nim could learn to imitate his trainer, he could not acquire the rules of grammar and develop complex sentences spontaneously. Terrace

FIGURE 8.7 Primate Use of Sign Language
Susan Nichols has a conversation with the chimpanzee, Washoe, using American Sign Language. According to the Gardners, Washoe has learned word signs and has acquired an elementary grammar.

(1985) argued that apes do not understand the act of naming objects, but only acquire the words demonstrated by others.

However, other psychologists argue that Terrace's methods differ from other studies and that primates do generate unique sentences (De Luce & Wilder, 1983). For instance, Fouts and Bodamer (1987) reported that Washoe spontaneously uses sign language when communicating with other chimpanzees who have also been taught to sign. Fouts and colleagues (1989) found that Washoe taught her adopted son Loulis over 50 signs. Researchers currently disagree on the interpretation of the data.

More recently, research on Kanzi, a pygmy chimpanzee, has revealed the most advanced language abilities in a nonhuman primate (Savage-Rumbaugh, 1990). Kanzi apparently uses symbols for concepts by pushing geometric shapes on a keyboard. His trainers reported that he produced creative solutions to problems and even described future actions (which he then carried out). By no means has the controversy on primate language been settled, but we can conclude from these studies that primates can learn at least the rudiments of language.

THINKING

What comes to mind when you think about thinking? Do you envision a writer hard at work, or someone with a wrinkled forehead concentrating on a test? Thinking includes a wide variety of cognitive, or mental, activities: a student trying to remember an answer on a test, an employee contemplating asking the boss for a raise, a young child deciding whether to have chocolate or strawberry ice cream for dessert, or a man searching for lost car keys.

Psychologists cannot directly observe thinking, so it must be inferred from what a person does. As we discussed earlier, thinking is part of the area of cognitive psychology. Thinking can be defined as the cognitive or mental activity of manipulating symbols. For humans, thinking usually involves language, but can also involve mental images (Richardson, 1983).

Language and Thought

Does the language we speak influence the way we think and the way we perceive the world around us? Benjamin Lee Whorf (1956) thought so. Most people believe that reality exists in much the same form for all people of sound mind. And all languages are similar in that they all have to deal with that reality by providing names for objects, qualities, actions, and relationships.

Whorf proposed in his linguistic relativity hypothesis that the perception of reality differs according to the language of the observer. More precisely, he contended that the world is experienced and conceived of in different ways in different cultures and that language is the cause of these differences. For example, he argued that Eskimos have a half dozen words to describe snow (such as slushy snow, hard-packed snow, falling snow, and melting snow) compared to our one general term. Hence it follows that Inuit (Eskimos) should actually perceive snow conditions differently than non-Inuit. Martin and Pullum (1991) recently pointed out that Eskimos do not have any more words for snow than other cultures. For example, we have terms such as blizzard, slush, and flurries.

While Whorf's linguistic relativity hypothesis has not received strong support recently, there is little doubt that language has an effect on our thinking and behavior. By knowing what a word means, you may increase your attention to the term and look for examples of it. For instance, now that you know the definition of shaping (from chapter 6, "Learning"), you may be more alert to find examples of shaping in your environment. It is also possible that language shapes our attitudes. Sexism and prejudice may be easier to learn with the language we use. For example, when a language uses masculine words such as *policeman* instead of *police officer*, or *mailman* instead of *mail carrier*, to refer to occupations available to both men and women, a sex-role stereotype is created that could affect our thinking and our behavior. The relationship between language and other cognitive processes, like thinking and memory, is extremely complex, and will require much more research to obtain definitive answers.

Concept Formation

Psychologists use the term concept formation, or concept learning, to refer to the development of the ability to respond to common features of categories of objects or events. A concept refers to a set of features with one or more properties in common. Concepts allow us to classify objects and events. In learning a concept, we must focus on the relevant features and ignore those that are irrelevant (Bourne & colleagues, 1986). For instance, paperbacks and hardcover editions are all books. But we must also discriminate on the basis of relevant features: a stack of papers is not a book. What is the crucial feature of a book? Usually it is the presence of a binding. Most concepts, however, cannot be formed on the basis of a single critical feature.

Types of Concepts   Cognitive psychologists have identified two general types of concepts: natural, everyday types and formal, systematic types. We use language to identify natural concepts intuitively in everyday life. For example, fruits, birds, or fish are natural concepts because each category includes objects that have similar characteristics.

Natural concepts are important to us in a number of ways. Being able to utilize concepts helps improve our memory, as we can easily form associations and categorize things we want to remember; we do not have to constantly relearn what objects are each time we encounter an unfamiliar one. For example, we recognize an automobile as a transportation vehicle regardless of the particular model.

Formal concepts have clear and unambiguous rules that specify exactly which attributes or features define the category. *Rules* let us know how the features must be combined for a particular concept. For example, the concept of male dogs includes the rule that the animal must be a dog and must be a male. Solso (1988) described five types of formal concepts defined by rules that psychologists have studied: affirmative, conjunctive, disjunctive, conditional, and biconditional. The *affirmative rule* is the easiest to learn, as it includes all instances of an attribute. For example, all males would include every single male animal or plant.

Many concepts are defined by the *conjunctive rule*, in which objects or events must have two or more distinct features to belong to the class in question. For example, the Greek philosopher Plato defined "human being" with the conjunctive concept, "animals having two legs and no feathers."

Other concepts are defined by the *disjunctive rule*, in which any one of two or more different features define the concept. The concept of a strike in baseball is disjunctive. A swing missing the ball, the failure to swing when the ball passes directly over the plate, or a hit landing outside the baselines (foul ball) all qualify sep-

arately as strikes. As you might expect, disjunctive concepts are generally harder to learn than conjunctive ones.

The *conditional rule* states a specific situation to define a concept. For example, "if the stimulus is round, then it must be white." (Note that if white, it could be any shape, and thus this rule applies only in one direction.) The *biconditional rule* extends the condition in both directions. For instance, "if it is round, then it must be white, and if it is white, then it must be round."

Learning Concepts   Most of the words we use refer to concepts and not to particular things. Proper nouns such as "William James" and "California" are exceptions. In learning some of their first concepts, children commonly focus not on names but on the functions of objects. For example, a spoon is something to eat with, and a pan is something to cook in. Other early concepts are based on groupings of objects that are similar in some respects: liquid things, moving things, or soft things.

Several theories have been proposed to explain how we learn concepts. The stimulus-response *association theory* was proposed by Clark Hull (1920). He argued that we learn to associate a particular response (the concept) with a variety of stimuli that define the concept. For instance, we associate the concept "dog" with all of the characteristics of dogs (four legs, fur, tail, and so on) and are able to generalize the concept to unfamiliar dogs.

The *hypothesis testing theory* was proposed by Jerome Bruner and his colleagues (1956). Bruner believed that we develop a strategy of testing our hypotheses about a concept by making guesses about which attributes are essential for defining the concept. While this tends to be the method used by subjects in an experiment, it might not be appropriate in everyday life (perhaps because we often use natural concepts rather than formal concepts in everyday life).

Eleanor Rosch (1978) suggested that the natural

FIGURE 8.8   Types of Concepts

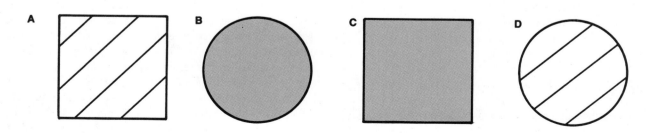

If the figures (above) are defined by the two categories, square and striped, then **A** represents a conjunctive concept. If the figures are defined by a category of either square or striped, then **A, C,** and **D** represent a disjunctive concept. Find the figure defined by the conjunctive concept of colored and square.

concepts in everyday life are learned through examples rather than abstract rules. Her *exemplar theory* proposes that we learn the concept of dog by seeing a wide variety of dogs and developing a *prototype* of what the typical dog is like. Busemeyer and Myung (1988) studied prototype learning in college students by presenting a series of exemplars and asking the subjects to reproduce the prototype. This type of study allows researchers to gain an understanding of the concept learning process.

Over the years, everyone is faced with an infinite number of complex stimuli. How we choose to group and sort them into concepts will depend upon our experiences with the environment, interests, beliefs, and values. Consider the concept "job." To one person it may mean an unpleasant task, while to another it is a means of achieving fulfillment. Concept formation is a form of thinking that helps us to understand better the world we live in, as well as ourselves.

PROBLEM SOLVING AND CREATIVITY

A chimpanzee sees a bunch of bananas suspended from the ceiling, well out of his reach. He stands up and makes a grab for them, but cannot get close. He then moves a box to a spot underneath the bananas, climbs on it, and reaches up. Still, he cannot quite make it. Finally, he takes another box, sets it on top of the first one, climbs on top of them, and takes the bananas. He has solved a problem.

Our 20-month-old son followed the same procedure in problem solving. He wanted a cookie from the cookie jar on the kitchen counter. After looking around, he pushed a chair over to the counter, climbed onto it, and then proceeded to help himself to several cookies.

We have a *problem* whenever difficulties get in the way of achieving a goal. Throughout our lives, we are continuously faced with problems that we must solve. Some problems are simple, such as deciding what clothes to wear for the day. Other problems are much more complex, such as deciding upon a career or a marriage partner.

Theories of Problem Solving

As you might imagine, there are many ways to approach problem solving. Generally, psychologists have studied problem solving from one of three viewpoints: *learning, insight,* and *information processing.*

Learning Theory The earliest approach to problem solving was based heavily on learning theory and emphasized the role of *trial and error.* As we discussed in chapter 6, "Learning," Edward Thorndike studied trial-and-error learning in cats early in this century. As the cats attempted to escape from the puzzle boxes, they learned to show particular types of behaviors. Through trial and error and association of reward with behavior, the cats solved problems.

People also use trial-and-error learning in solving problems. My computer programming skills are minimal, and so when a program I am working on does not run properly, I change each statement randomly until I learn what works. Have you ever had a radio not work? Chances are that you used trial and error to remedy the situation. Perhaps you checked for loose wires or weak batteries, or made sure the switches were properly set. Trial-and-error learning is often used when we don't have other information to guide us.

Insight Theory Trial-and-error learning is different from the method used by the chimpanzee to get the bananas mentioned above. The chimp demonstrated a far greater degree of *insight* in his situation, a sudden grasping of the means necessary to achieve a goal. Sometimes when we face a difficult problem, we become frustrated and feel we will never find the solution. Then, suddenly, we see things in a different light, and the solution is so easy it amazes us.

The Gestalt psychologist Wolfgang Köhler described his experiments on the insight approach to problem

FIGURE 8.9 Insight in Problem Solving
Gestalt psychologist Wolfgang Köhler studied learning by insight. Here the champanzee appears to think about the problem of getting fruit into his cage and then solves the problem by using the sticks together. By insight, the subject gains a sudden perception of the relationship of the cognitive elements necessary to solve a problem.

solving in *The Mentality of Apes* (1925). Köhler presented animals with problems that could not be solved by simple trial-and-error learning. In one study, a chimpanzee named Sultan was trying to obtain a banana that was out of his reach. There was a short stick in the cage and a longer stick out of his reach outside the cage. Sultan first tried to get the banana with the short stick, but failed. He sat for a while looking around the cage. Then, quite suddenly, he rushed over, used the short stick to pull the longer stick into his reach, and then quickly used the longer stick to pull in the banana. Köhler cited this as an example of insight. Psychologists don't know how insight operates, but do realize that it can be a useful approach to problem solving.

Information Processing Theory The third approach cognitive psychologists have used in recent years employs the terms and concepts of *information processing* in analyzing problem solving. The emphasis in information processing is on the active role of the problem solver in (1) formulating the problem, (2) transforming it in ways that facilitate its solution, (3) laying out a strategy for solving it, and (4) using the information or feedback that he or she receives while proceeding through the successive stages toward the solution.

The information processing approach to problem solving often makes use of flow charts and computer simulation. A flow chart is a diagram showing the possible choices at each step in solving the problem. This helps the problem solver visualize the choices and understand the potential outcomes. Computer simulation is the procedure in which the computer is programmed to approximate some event or activity.

The goal of artificial intelligence (AI) is to simulate human cognition with a computer. AI pioneer Alan Turing (1950) argued that the laws governing the thinking process could be simulated through a computer. Computer programs of artificial intelligence are used in perception, memory, language, and problem solving (Anderson, 1990). For example, computers have been programmed to play chess by determining strategies and outguessing opponents (in a fashion similar to what humans do).

All three approaches have validity because there are many kinds of problems and many ways of solving them. Human problem solving involves both trial and error and insight. Threading a needle requires few insights, but may take several unsuccessful attempts before finding the one that works. Solving a riddle, however, usually involves a sudden insight, the so-called "aha" reaction. However, insight itself requires past experience, which may have been largely trial and error. Sometimes solutions are a result neither of sudden insights nor of trial and error, but of understanding some general principles and applying them systematically to the problem. Writing a computer program or solving an algebra problem are two examples of this kind of problem solving that cognitive theorists find especially interesting. Still other problems are solved not

FIGURE 8.10 A Flow Chart in Information Processing

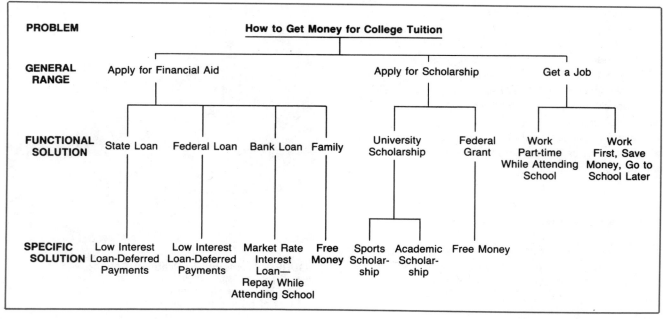

Much as a computer processes information in a logical step-by-step fashion, a flow chart can aid in the solution of a complex problem by visualizing the stages of decision-making.

by insight, trial and error, or understanding, but by the rote application of memorized rules. Some students who barely pass their courses may employ this process.

Problem-Solving Effectiveness

Our success in solving problems is influenced by several factors. One of these is perception. Unless we properly perceive the problem and what is relevant to its solution, we will be unable to solve it. Another factor is motivation. As you would expect, increased motivation improves problem solving—but only up to a point. Very intense levels of motivation actually interfere. You can be so anxious to achieve something that your anxiety prevents you from succeeding. And for humans, language is perhaps the most valuable and important tool involved in solving problems. Its use mediates between the problem and the solution. For most problems, the use of language is indispensable in the organization of thoughts leading to a solution.

Stages in Solving Problems   Psychologists believe people generally go through three or four steps in solving problems. The insight approach to problem solving includes the steps of preparation, incubation, illumination, and verification.

In the first stage, *preparation*, we study the problem carefully and collect information that might be used to solve it. We consider as many possible solutions as we can.

When we have exhausted all the possibilities, we need to go into the second stage of problem solving, called *incubation*. We need to rest from the problem and let our brain continue to sort out the possibilities. Some psychologists suggest that sleep is a good incubating activity.

Sometimes the *illumination* stage is called the "aha" phenomenon. Suddenly we get an insight into a very likely solution to the problem. It's as if a light bulb in our brain is suddenly illuminated.

In the last stage, *verification*, we test out the solution that seems most likely. If correct, then the problem is solved. If not, then we go back to the preparation stage and collect more facts that could lead to new hypotheses or ideas.

A more general theory of problem solving (Bourne & colleagues, 1986) includes the steps of preparation, production, and evaluation.

In the *preparation* step, we become aware of the problem and try to understand all sides of it. We often try to obtain additional information about the problem so we can feel comfortable working on it.

In the *production* step, we consider as many solu-

tions as possible. This may require obtaining additional information or applying a solution strategy to the information we have.

Finally, in the *evaluation* step, we evaluate the appropriateness of our solutions. If successful, we have solved the problem. If not, we go back to preparation and production to try again.

The IDEAL program for solving problems was proposed by Bransford and Stein (1984). They suggested that the steps in problem solving include the following: *Identify* the problem that you are going to solve. *Define* the problem by collecting all of the available information. *Explore* all of the possible strategies for solving the problem. *Act* on the strategy most likely to solve the problem. And *look* at your solution and evaluate the effectiveness of your strategy.

Strategies   A good aid in solving a problem is prior practice in solving similar problems. Psychologists' best guess about what occurs during such practice is that the problem solver develops strategies and plans for attack. Consider how a novice might play Twenty Questions. When told that the object is animal, his first question might be "Is it a dog?" His second question might be "Is it a cat?" The experienced player has developed a more successful strategy of starting with the most general questions (for example, "Is it human?" or "real?" or "live?" or "a whole animal?") before narrowing down to more specific questions.

Two important strategies in problem solving are algorithms and heuristics. With an algorithm, or random search strategy, every possible solution is tried until the correct one is found. For example, the three letters in the anagram NFU would be rearranged until the correct solution, FUN, is found. Sometimes algorithms can be used efficiently in computer programs, but they are often confusing. People do not use algorithms too often in everyday problem-solving situations, partly because they don't work for some problems and partly because they usually take an extremely long time. Even computer programs used in artificial intelligence research do not often utilize algorithms (especially when heuristics are available).

A heuristic is a rule-of-thumb problem-solving strategy in which a person selectively tests solutions most likely to be correct (Matlin, 1989). For example, we would most likely try a vowel in the middle to produce FUN, without having to try all of the other solutions. Heuristics are quick solutions, but they sometimes do not work (as when they prevent us from trying new ideas).

This strategy might involve a means-end analysis, in which we evaluate the difference between the current situation and the desired outcome. For example, in a chess game, we test what the outcome of various moves might be before we actually make a move.

FIGURE 8.11 **Nine-Dot Problem**

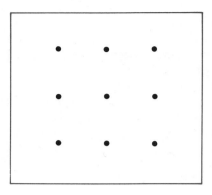

Scheerer (1963) said that people maintain assumptions that interfere with problem solving. Connect all nine dots with four straight lines without lifting your pencil from the paper or without going through any dot more than once. Solution on page 190.

Learning to Learn A well-known experiment with monkeys by Harry Harlow (1949) illustrates the advantages of prior problem-solving experience. Harlow first taught the monkeys to choose which of several objects concealed food. Each monkey had to select from among a triangle, a circle, and a square. Eventually, the monkeys learned that the food was always underneath the triangle, no matter what its position in relation to the other objects. When Harlow changed the location of the food to, say, the circle, the monkeys took much less time to learn to uncover the circle than they had taken to learn to uncover the triangle. The "skill" in this problem-solving situation transferred quickly because of prior experience with the original problem. Harlow calls this learning to learn.

Mental Sets Previous practice and experience with solving problems sometimes hinders future problem solving. This frequently occurs when the new problem appears on the surface to be similar to the familiar one, but actually requires a different solution. Difficulty arises because we tend to develop mental sets, that is, our thinking becomes standardized and we approach new problems in fixed ways, and, as a result, other possible approaches do not occur to us.

What are the missing letters in the following series?

A E F H ? ? ?

If you studied these letters closely, you will notice that these letters of the alphabet are all made up of straight lines (the ones omitted have curved lines in them). Thus, the ones that would come next would be I, K, and L.

Now, with that experience, find the missing letters in this series:

O T T F ? ? ?

This series should be more difficult for you because you are probably attempting to solve it by examining physical characteristics of alphabet letters. If so, you have formed a mental set. In this case, that information was irrelevant to the solution of the new problem. These are the first letters in the numerical counting series (one, two, three). Therefore, the missing letters are F, S, and S, for five, six, and seven.

While mental sets can interfere with problem-solving effectiveness, remember that sometimes learning to learn can overcome this difficulty. Let's try one more series of letters:

M T W T ? ? ?

If you were now thinking of words that began with these letters, you probably recognized the days of the week. The missing letters are F, S, and S for Friday, Saturday, and Sunday. The important point is to be aware of the potential for mental sets to occur.

Functional Fixedness When we habitually use an object in a certain way, we often do not think of new uses for it that could help solve other problems. Its function has become fixed. Such functional fixedness is a

FIGURE 8.12 **The Two-String Problem**

This problem requires the subject to tie two hanging strings together although one cannot be reached while the other one is held. Insight comes when the subject realizes that an object can be attached to one string and then that string can be swung like a pendulum. This enables the subject to grasp both strings and tie them together.

FIGURE 8.13   Water-Container Problems

Problem No.	Capacity of Containers			Obtain Exactly These Amounts of Water
	Container A	Container B	Container C	
1	21	127	3	100
2	14	163	25	99
3	18	43	10	5
4	9	42	6	21
5	20	59	4	31
6	23	49	3	20
7	10	36	7	3

Using the capacity of the containers A, B, and C, find a method of measuring out the exact amount of liquid called for in the column to the right (after Luchins, 1942). Solution on following page.

special case of a mental set that interferes with successful problem solving. Several studies indicate that the longer we use an object in a certain way, the less likely we are to find new uses for it. A common table knife, for example, is normally used for eating. When we want to attach the leads from an antenna to a television set, its possible use as a screwdriver may not occur to us, especially if we have at hand a "real" screwdriver. The same sort of functionally fixed thinking led to the design of the first automobiles, which strongly resembled horse-drawn carriages. There are, of course, limits as to how fixed our uses are: a shovel is something we dig with, but most of us would not hesitate to use it to kill a poisonous snake that happened to slither our way while we were digging a hole.

Confirmation Bias   A major obstacle to effective problem solving is confirmation bias, the tendency to selectively seek information that confirms our hypothesis. An effective problem-solving strategy is to try to find cases that disprove our hypothesis. But instead we only seek proof, limiting our knowledge. Peter Wason (1968) asked subjects to discover the rule that applied to a three-number series, such as 2, 4, 6. Most subjects said "increase by 2" and tried other series of numbers that did increase by 2, such as 1, 3, 5 or 8, 10, 12. These are examples of the rule. But most subjects were surprised to find that the rule was not "increase by 2," but rather "increase in magnitude." They should have tested the rule by trying to disprove it rather than trying to prove it. For example, 1, 2, 3 or 8, 9, 10 would have also been positive examples, and would have forced the subjects to rethink their hypothesis.

Creativity

Since creativity involves coming up with new or unusual responses to familiar circumstances, it is closely related to the ability to solve problems (Greeno, 1989). Psychological research on creativity has focused primarily on two areas: measuring creativity in people and identifying the personality traits of people who are recognized as highly creative.

Measurement of Creativity   Guilford (1967) distinguishes between *convergent thinking*, coming up with the single correct response, and *divergent thinking*, coming up with new and unusual responses. Intelligence tests typically measure convergent thinking, whereas divergent thinking is more involved in creativity.

There are a number of creativity tests, including the *Divergent Production Test* and the *Remote Associates Test*. In general, creativity tests ask the person to do such things as make up an ending for a story, name as many uses as possible for common objects, elaborate on drawings of simple geometric forms, or come up with words related to a series of other words. For example, you might be asked to list all the uses of a knife you can think of in

FIGURE 8.14   The Candle Problem

Using only a candle, thumbtack, and a box of matches, how would you mount the candle on a wall or bulletin board? (after Duncker, 1945). Solution on following page.

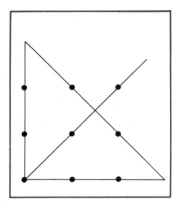

Solution to the nine-dot problem for Figure 8.10 (after Scheerer, 1963).

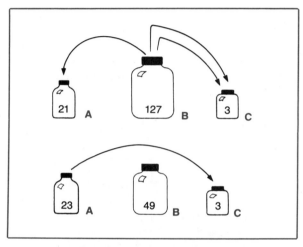

The solutions to the water-container problems in Figure 8.13 involve the formula B − A − 2C = desired liquid as shown in the top drawing. A mental set in solving problems 1–5 usually prevents the easier solutions to problems 6 (A − C) as shown in the bottom drawing and problem 7 (A + C) (after Luchins, 1942).

The solution to the candle problem in Figure 8.14 involves the ability to perceive that materials can be used in an unusual manner. The box, for example, need not be used as a container. This illustrates how functional fixedness can interfere with the solution to a problem.

one minute. Responses are scored for originality (how unique or different your answers are from others), usefulness (how relevant and practical your answers are), and quantity (how many different responses you came up with).

Research on the measurement of creativity has produced mixed results. Although results tend to be reliable, there is little evidence of validity outside of the test situation (Anastasi, 1988). And many psychologists question whether in fact the tests tap all that is involved in creativity. In general, the skills measured by intelligence and creativity tests tend to overlap (Sternberg & Davidson, 1982). People with higher intelligence generally tend to be more creative than people with lower intelligence.

Characteristics of Creative People In addition to being related to intelligence, creativity is influenced by a variety of other factors. Although there is no one particular personality profile for all creative people, there are some tendencies that have been observed. Teresa Amabile (1983) reviewed much of the research on the influences on creativity in people. She concluded that creative people tend to enjoy doing things because of internal motivation. They tend to have the freedom to choose their own activities and live in a stimulating and exciting environment. Creative people often tend to be independent and don't need external motivation, that is, social approval, when solving problems.

Amabile (1987) suggested several things that could increase creativity in children and adults. It is important to provide a stimulating environment for children, in which they are encouraged to be independent thinkers. Parents and educators should emphasize children's strengths and expose them to cultural diversity. Adults can increase creativity by learning to relax, having freedom of choice in making decisions, reducing stress, and receiving encouragement from employers, family, and friends. Research is continuing in an attempt to understand the environment in which people can best express creativity.

DEFINITION AND THEORIES OF INTELLIGENCE

Intelligence is a factor by which most people identify themselves or their behavior. They say, "I wish I were as smart as you," or "That was a stupid thing to do." But attempts at defining intelligence have been difficult, if not confusing and controversial. Is it one specific ability, or several? Is it innate or learned? Is it static or changeable? Definitions of intelligence have often been derived from theories of intelligence, and these in turn may have been derived from measurements of observed behavior that indicate the components of intelligence.

Definition of Intelligence

Although everyone seems to have an idea about what intelligence entails, not all definitions are the same. In 1982 Robert Sternberg reported on his attempts to discover what psychologists and laypersons with no expertise in psychology think about intelligence. Through surveys, he found that when academic experts define intelligence, they usually speak of the abilities to verbalize, solve problems, and achieve goals. Laypersons, on the other hand, usually associate intelligence with verbal ability, practical problem-solving ability, and social competence. Although there was a great deal of overlap, Sternberg found that the psychologists stressed motivation ("works hard," "is persistent," "gets involved") whereas the laypersons emphasized social-cultural aspects ("sensitivity to other people," "is honest with self and others").

Intelligence is a difficult concept to study, partially because we cannot observe it physically and partially because it is such a common term that in everyday language it is often misused (Green, 1981). Sometimes, a circular definition of intelligence is used: Intelligence is what is measured by intelligence tests, and intelligence tests measure intelligence. While this definition doesn't spell out the characteristics of intelligence, it is possible to discover them by examining intelligence tests themselves. Most stress verbal skills, quantitative skills, and problem-solving skills, the same characteristics that many think of when describing intelligence.

David Wechsler, the creator of a number of intelligence tests, considers intelligence to be the capacity to understand one's world and the resourcefulness to cope with the challenges of that world (Wechsler, 1975). Thus, you are intelligent if you know what is happening around you and if you are able to meet the challenges of your environment. For example, people in business are considered intelligent if they understand the financial world and are successful in making a profit. Students are considered intelligent if they understand the course material and are able to earn above-average grades.

A similar approach is to define intelligence as the skills necessary for success in a culture (Vernon, 1979). Intelligence is a culture-bound concept in that the particular skills necessary for success vary by culture. Verbal and mathematical skills are important in American culture, but speed and accuracy in throwing a spear might be more valuable in a hunting culture.

Sternberg (1986a) suggested that while the particulars may be debated, there appears to be a consensus on what kind of behavior is considered intelligent. Sternberg stated that the ability to learn from experience and the ability to adapt to the environment are essential ingredients in a definition of intelligence, and thus we define intelligence as the capacity to learn and behave adaptively.

Theories of Intelligence

Over the years, a large number of formal theories of intelligence have been proposed. Here we review some of the most influential ones: Charles Spearman's g factor, Louis Thurstone's seven primary factors, J. P. Guilford's model, Howard Gardner's theory of multiple intelligences, and Robert Sternberg's triarchic theory.

Spearman's Factor Theory Students who do well in one class usually have few problems with other classes or in participating in extracurricular activities. Charles Spearman (1904) proposed a theory of intelligence that included a general factor, g, that gave a person the ability to achieve success in a wide variety of intellectual tasks. But Spearman also noted most people were best in one or two particular areas, and so he included specific factors s that allowed a person to excel on particular tasks. For example, students who have trouble in psychology may excel in mathematics. The combination of the g and s factors provides the specific intelligence level of an individual.

Thurstone's Primary Mental Abilities Louis Thurstone (1938) believed that intelligence was determined by seven primary mental abilities rather than one general unknown factor. The seven abilities include verbal comprehension, verbal fluency, numerical ability, spatial visualization, memory, reasoning, and perceptual speed, and were incorporated in Thurstone's *Primary Mental Abilities Test*. The different abilities of an individual would explain why someone might excel in mathematics but do poorly in history. However, Thurstone later found that people who do well in one area also do well in others, suggesting that there may be some general factor underlying the various abilities. For example, verbal comprehension and reasoning were highly correlated, and could be considered what Spearman called the g factor.

Guilford's Model of Intelligence One of the most sophisticated theories of intelligence was proposed by J. P. Guilford (1967, 1982). He suggested that there are three separate dimensions interacting in intelligence: contents, operations, and products. Contents include information a person is thinking about. Operations are the actions of a person. Products are the result of thinking about the information. Through a statistical technique, Guilford was able to determine five types of contents, five types of operations, and six types of products. If these three dimensions are thought of as sides on a cube (see following page), it can be demonstrated that 150 different mental abilities might determine intelligence.

Gardner's Theory of Multiple Intelligences Howard Gardner (1983) proposed a *theory of multiple intelligences*, which stated that, rather than one general

FIGURE 8.15   Guilford's Model of the Structure of Intelligence

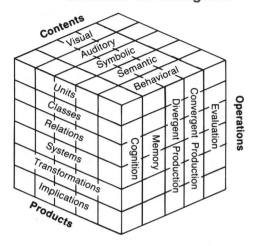

This model proposes that intelligence consists of 150 independent abilities that result from the interaction of five types of contents, five types of operations, and six types of products (after Guilford, 1982).

intelligence, there exist several different kinds of intelligences. He suggested seven types of intelligence, including linguistic, musical, logical-mathematical, spatial, bodily-kinesthetic, social sensitivity, and personal awareness. Like Thurstone, Gardner believes that these intelligences can interact to produce a unique personality. However, he argues that each kind of intelligence is independent. Thus, someone who is considered mentally retarded on an IQ test might be able to be outstanding in musical ability. Researchers have not yet determined the relationships among the kinds of intelligence or how they interact to produce adaptive behavior.

Sternberg's Triarchic Theory of Intelligence
Yale University psychologist Robert Sternberg (1985, 1986a) recently proposed the triarchic theory of intelligence. After studying theories and tests of intelligence, he concluded that intelligence was a much broader concept than what was previously assumed. The triarchic theory consists of three parts: componential, experiential, and contextual subtheories of intelligence.

The *componential subtheory* deals with the relationship of intelligence to the internal world of the individual. A component is a mental process. Metacomponents are processes that we use in planning and evaluating the behaviors that we exhibit. Performance components are the cognitive processes used when we actually solve problems. Knowledge-acquisition components are important whenever we learn something new. These form the core of the theory, and are used when gaining experience in new situations and solving problems.

There are two components to the *experiential subtheory*: the ability to deal with novel, unfamiliar tasks and situations, and the ability to process information automatically. We are able to perform complex verbal and mathematical mental tasks efficiently only because much of the procedure is automatic. For instance, reading requires operations that can be done without conscious thought. An inability to automatize cognitive processing results in less intelligent performance.

The *contextual subtheory* includes the components of adaptation, environmental selection, and environmental shaping. To be intelligent, one must adapt to the environment and, at the same time, be able to decide when to select a different environmental situation. For instance, it is important to adapt to the work environment, but if the values of the company we work for are incompatible with our own, the intelligent thing to do would be to change jobs if possible. When we can't adapt to our environment, and it is not possible to select a new one, intelligence helps us shape our present environment. In the work example, we might try to convince our boss to view things differently.

Sternberg (1986) argued that existing intelligence tests do not measure all of the intellectual skills included in the triarchic theory. The ideal test of intelligence would be one that takes components, experience, and context into consideration. Sternberg's triarchic intelligence theory was presented here in detail because it is currently considered to be a major contribution to the field, and will continue to be influential in the future.

MEASUREMENT OF INTELLIGENCE

Do you remember the different tests you've taken throughout your school career? Some were designed to predict how well you would do in the future, while others measured how much you knew at the time. While both kinds of tests measure your abilities, they have different functions. Psychologists are interested in both aptitude and achievement tests.

Characteristics of Tests

Aptitude tests are designed to predict what a person can accomplish in the future with proper training. The General Aptitude Test Battery is commonly used to test the ability of people to achieve success in a wide number of occupations. These tests measure such concepts as musical potential, athletic ability, writing potential, or general intellectual capacity.

Many colleges require high school students to take the Scholastic Aptitude Test (SAT) or the American College Test (ACT) prior to admission. The SAT and ACT are multiple-choice tests that measure verbal and mathematical abilities of students. The basic idea is that knowledge gained in high school and expressed on the test should be a fairly good predictor of how well students will do in college. As such, they are predictive tests, but also rely on measurement of the achievement of the test takers.

The SAT was first given in 1941, and although the questions are continually changed, they have been designed to remain equivalent. Thus, it is possible to compare the scores of students who take the test each year with previous years. In the 1960s and 1970s the SAT scores dropped significantly. This has been attributed partially to the fact that in the 1960s more students who were not as academically prepared took the test to get into college (Astin & Barber, 1982). Zajonc (1986) proposed that the decline was due to the large number of postwar babies born in the 1940s and 1950s, since as the number of children in a family increase, the family's resources must be spread out and each child would have a slightly lower IQ than in only-child families (we discuss Zajonc's theory later in this chapter). He also predicted that as families became smaller in the 1960s, the scores would increase in the late 1980s (which is what happened).

Achievement tests are designed to measure what a person can do at the time the test is given. A final examination that measures how much of the material you have mastered in a course such as this one is an example of an achievement test. Undoubtedly, you have taken many achievement tests in school.

Intelligence tests are usually aptitude tests designed to measure a broad range of mental capabilities. These tests are often used to predict future academic success. Alfred Binet devised the first real intelligence test for this purpose. Actually, aptitude tests depend to a certain degree on the achievement and knowledge of the test taker. Achievement and aptitude tests could be thought of as a continuum, with intelligence tests closer to the aptitude end.

What makes a good intelligence test? Originally, Binet developed the intelligence test to predict future academic success. The value of an intelligence test to predict achievement depends on several important factors: validity, reliability, standardization, objectivity, and practicality.

Validity, as discussed in chapter 1, "The Study of Psychology," refers to the degree to which a test actually measures what it is intended to measure. A valid intelligence test would measure intelligence, not memory, speed, guessing ability, or vocabulary. Reliability is the degree to which a person's score at one time is the same

at a different time. A reliable intelligence test would yield consistent scores from one time to the next.

Standardization is the process of obtaining a norm, or sample of scores representative of the population, and is necessary in interpreting a particular subject's score. For example, if a friend of yours tells you that he or she received a score of 179 on a test, how would you know whether this was a good score? It would help if you knew that the test contained a possible 200 points, the mean score was 125, and the range for the class was 75 to 190.

Psychologists standardize tests so that they can interpret individual test results. The first step is to define the population serving as the standardization group. For example, we might wish to know how an individual compared to other adult Americans, and so we would standardize the test on the adult population of the United States. Or a population might include all high school seniors in Canada. After the population is identified, we need to obtain a norm, or representative sample, that will allow us to describe what the entire population is like.

An intelligence test should be objective. Objectivity assures that a test's results are not affected by the personal feelings and biases of the examiner. Ideally, a test should be constructed so that any qualified person can administer and score it, and obtain the same results as any other scorer.

An intelligence test should also be practical. Practicality provides that a test can be administered easily and scored in a reasonable amount of time. Chances are good that psychologists would not be interested in a new test requiring five people to administer and 16 hours to complete.

Tests that are valid, reliable, standardized, objective, and practical meet the general requirements for use. Developing intelligence tests that meet all of these requirements is a difficult task.

Intelligence tests can be divided into individual or group tests, depending on the method of administration. Originally, only individual tests were used. However, during World War I the United States Armed Forces needed to test many individuals quickly. A group intelligence test, the Armed Forces General Classification Test, was developed for this purpose. We discuss two important individual intelligence tests next.

The Stanford-Binet Intelligence Scale

Alfred Binet was the director of the psychological laboratory at the Sorbonne, Paris, when he was asked by the French government to devise a test that would predict which children could most benefit from special education classes. Binet and his colleague, Theodore Simon, published the *Binet-Simon Intelligence Scale* in 1905. This test consisted of 30 items of varying difficulty that were

BIOGRAPHICAL HIGHLIGHT

Alfred Binet was born in 1857 in Nice, France. He received a doctorate in 1894, based on his research on the nervous system of insects. In 1894 Binet was appointed director of the psychology laboratory at the Sorbonne. He spent the next several years studying topics such as handwriting, hypnosis, perception, and thinking. In 1895 he started an important journal, *L'Annee Psychologique*.

Around 1900 he began publishing research on thinking that he had been conducting on his two daughters. In 1904 he was asked to help identify students in the Paris school system who needed special education because of their low level of intellectual functioning. Binet and his colleague, Theodore Simon, published the first intelligence scale in 1905.

Binet and Simon tested mentally retarded children and set guidelines for the degree of retardation. They decided that a child with a mental age of less than 2 years would be called an idiot. An imbecile had a mental age of between 2 and 7 years, while a moron had a mental age above 7. This type of classification is still used today, in a modified form.

During the next several years, Binet spent much of his time testing children and revising the intelligence test, first in 1908 and again in 1911, the year of his death. Binet's early work on intelligence testing has stimulated an enormous amount of research in this area of psychology.

ALFRED BINET

---

used to measure the functioning level of Paris schoolchildren.

Binet knew that reasoning and problem-solving ability increased with age. He tested children of different ages to determine the ability of each age level. This led him to establish the concept of mental age—what the typical child of a given chronological age (counted in years) can do. For example, a child who does what a typical 5-year-old can do has a mental age of 5, and a child who can do what a typical 10-year-old can do has a mental age of 10. If a 10-year-old child can do only what the typical 5-year-old can do, the 10-year-old has a mental age of 5 and could probably benefit from special educational training. School systems now had a test that would identify those children not working at their own chronological age level.

German psychologist William Stern developed the concept of the intelligence quotient (IQ) as an index of intelligence. An IQ is simply the ratio of a person's mental age to chronological age. It describes the performance of an individual relative to that of others of the same age. The individual's mental age (in years and months), as determined by the test, is divided by the individual's chronological age and the result is multiplied by 100 to eliminate fractions. In mathematical terms,

$$IQ = MA / CA \times 100.$$

Lewis Terman of Stanford University revised Binet's test and in 1916 published what is known as the Stanford-Binet Intelligence Scale for American subjects. The Stanford-Binet Intelligence Scale has been revised several times since 1916 to reflect current knowledge and word usage. It takes about 45 minutes to administer to a child and up to 1^{1}/2 hours to test an adult. The scoring system has also been changed so that an intelligence score is no longer simply a ratio of MA to CA. Now the examiner begins with the test nearest the person's mental age. If the subject passes all the items on this level, he or she is tested at the next level. The highest level at which all items are passed is called the *basal age*. To this is added a score for items passed at still higher levels. The overall intelligence score on the SBIS is now referred to as the composite standard age score. The average score is still 100, with a standard deviation of 16. This distribution of intelligence scores forms a *normal curve.*

When Terman revised Binet's original intelligence test, he standardized it based on a sample composed mainly of middle-class white Americans. Obviously, this did not represent the entire American population. It was not until 1972 that the Stanford-Binet Intelligence Scale was standardized based on a representative sample of young Americans that included a diversified range of races, nationalities, economic, and social classes. It is also

FIGURE 8.16   Examples From the Stanford-Binet Intelligence Scale

See Age 12 in the chart to the right.

It is possible to gauge a person's mental age by the presence of certain abilities. It is assumed that a person is able to solve more complex problems as he or she gets older.

AGE	TASK
2	**Comprehension.** Child is shown a large paper doll and asked to point to various parts of the body.
3	**Pattern analysis.** Child is shown a bridge built of three blocks and asked to build one like it.
4	**Opposite analogies.** Fills in the missing word when asked: "Brother is a boy; sister is a _____. "In daytime it is light; at night it is _____." **Reasoning.** Answers correctly when asked: "Why do we have houses?" "Why do we have books?"
5	**Vocabulary.** Defines words such as *ball, hat,* and *stove.* **Pattern analysis.** Can copy a drawing of a square.
6	**Quantitative.** Is able to give the examiner nine blocks when asked to do so.
8	**Memory for sentences.** Listens to sentences and then repeats them exactly.
9	**Rhymes.** Answers correctly when asked: "Tell me the name of a color that rhymes with Fred"; "Tell me a number that rhymes with free."
12	**Verbal absurdities.** Tells what is foolish about statements such as, "Bill Jones's feet are so big that he has to put his trousers on over his head."
14	**Inference.** Examiner folds a piece of paper a number of times, notching a corner with scissors each time. Subject is asked the rule for determining how many holes there will be when the paper is unfolded.
Adult (15 years and older)	**Verbal relations.** Can describe the difference between "misery and poverty," "character and reputation." **Memory for digits.** Can repeat series of digits forwards and backwards (that is, in reverse order) after they are read aloud by the examiner.

interesting to note that with these revisions, the norms have had to be readjusted to take into account the fact that over the years, people are doing better on the test (and hence raising the performance of the "average" test taker).

The fourth edition of the Stanford-Binet Intelligence Scale was published in 1986 and represents an extensive revision of the earlier test (Anastasi, 1988). The content has been significantly broadened, and now includes 15 separate tests in four areas: verbal reasoning (vocabulary, comprehension, absurdities, verbal relations); quantitative reasoning (quantitative, number series, equation building); abstract/visual reasoning (pattern analysis, copying, matrices, paper folding and cutting); and short-term memory (bead memory, memory for sentences, memory for digits, memory for objects). Some of the tests are designed for particular age groups, and so no one is given all 15 tests. The typical administration might include 8 to 13 tests (Walsh & Betz, 1990). The fourth edition was standardized based on a sample of 5,000 people from 47 states, ranging in age from 2 to 23 years.

The Wechsler Intelligence Scales

With the Stanford-Binet Intelligence Scale one score represents global intelligence. Another approach is represented by the tests of David Wechsler, who published the Wechsler-Bellevue Intelligence Scale in 1939 and the widely used Wechsler Adult Intelligence Scale (WAIS) in 1955. Wechsler, who was a psychologist at Bellevue Hospital in New York, had several reasons for developing a new test of adult intelligence. The Stanford-Binet Intelligence Scale was originally designed for children and depended heavily on verbal skills. The 1981 revision of the Wechsler Adult Intelligence Scale (WAIS-R) was standardized for 1,880 Americans from 16 to 74 years old. This sample represented the general population in sex, race, age, and geographical distribution (Walsh & Betz, 1990).

The WAIS-R is divided into subscales that measure verbal skills (information, digit span, vocabulary, arithmetic, comprehension, and similarities) and performance skills (picture completion, picture arrangement, block

FIGURE 8.17 IQ Score Distribution

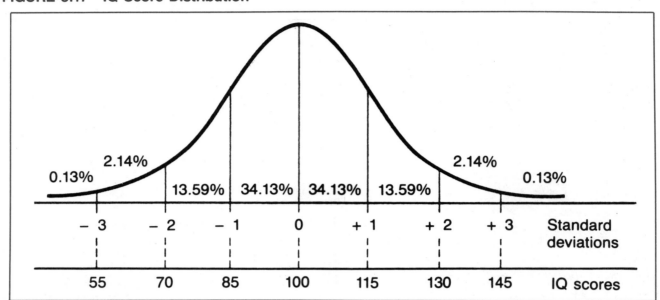

The distribution of scores from the WAIS-R forms a normal curve; most individuals fall into the middle categories.

design, object assembly, and digit symbol). The subscales are standardized with a mean of 10 and standard deviation of 3 so that the subject's strengths and weaknesses can be compared easily. Wechsler's intelligence tests give a Verbal IQ, a Performance IQ, and a Full Scale IQ (combined). Each scale has a mean of 100 and a standard deviation of 15.

Wechsler used the *deviation IQ*, which measures the extent to which a subject's score is different from the average score of 100 for a particular age group. Approximately 67 percent of the scores fall between 85 and 115, and about 95 percent fall between 70 and 130. Because of the deviation IQ it is possible to compare the IQ scores of people of different ages.

Wechsler has developed intelligence measures for children also. The 1991 revision of the Wechsler Intelligence Scale for Children (WISC-III) is used for ages 6 through 16, and the 1989 revision of the Wechsler Preschool and Primary Scale of Intelligence (WPPSI-R) is used for ages 4 through 7. Differences between the performance and verbal scores on the WISC-III can be used to help diagnose certain childhood disorders, such as dyslexia and other learning disabilities. Scores on the Wechsler scales correlate fairly well with the Stanford-Binet Intelligence Scale.

Although the Stanford-Binet and the Wechsler Scales are by far the most popular tests of intelligence, there are many other instruments, including the *Kaufman Assessment Battery for Children*, the *Cognitive Abilities Test*, and the *Otis-Lennon School Ability Test*.

INFLUENCES ON INTELLIGENCE

If you take a minute to list all of the possible influences affecting a person's intelligence, you probably will come up with items such as diet, school, friends, training, community, relationships, and experiences. These might be grouped together under the general heading of environment. You might also include factors such as parents, instinct, personality, nature, ancestors, and family. These might be grouped together as biological and, especially, genetic influences. Intelligent behavior, like all behavior, is the result of the interaction of heredity and environment.

While it seems logical to assume that heredity and environment both contribute to intelligence, the degree to which each contributes is controversial and has wide-reaching implications for education and society. If intelligence is determined almost exclusively by heredity, as some claim, then nursery school, special education, and enriched environments will not have a significant impact on the intellectual growth of children, and we should not spend money on programs such as these. If, on the other hand, environment plays a significant role in determining intelligence, we may need to undertake massive revisions in the structure of the educational system to succeed in producing the maximum intelligence in each member of society. Because of the controversial nature of intelligence testing, it is important to review carefully what we do know about the genetic and environmental determinants of intelligence.

Genetic Influences on Intelligence

We pointed out in chapter 2, "Psychobiology," that we are limited when investigating heredity and human behavior. Much of the information we have on the contributions of heredity to intelligence comes from studies of the correlation between IQ and the degree of genetic relatedness.

Genetic Relationship and IQ Correlation   In general, the closer the genetic relationship, the higher the correlation (measurement of the relationship between two variables) between individual IQs. A large number of studies were reviewed in 1981 by Bouchard and McGue, who found the highest IQ correlations between identical twins (sharing 100 percent of their genes) who were reared together in the same environment. Nonidentical twins (sharing 50 percent of their genes) were found similar to normal siblings (also sharing 50 percent of their genes). Unrelated people reared apart show virtually no correlation of IQ.

Much of the research on human heredity and intelligence has been done on twins. In 1976, when Loehlin and Nichols reviewed data from over 6,000 pairs of twins, they found a correlation of .62 in the IQs of nonidentical twins and .86 in the IQs of identical twins. In IQ studies, the more similar the IQs, the higher the correlation. So this data means that identical twins have IQs that are more similar than the IQs of nonidentical twins. This evidence strongly supports the notion that heredity significantly influences intelligence in people.

FIGURE 8.18   Identical Twins Reared Together
Monozygotic, or identical, twins not only share 100 percent of their genes, but also often share extremely similar experiences. As a result, they tend to have very similar IQs.

FIGURE 8.19   Samples of Questions Based on the WISC-III

Block design

Object assembly

Information
1. How many wings does a bird have?
2. How many nickels make a dime?
3. What is steam made of?
4. Who wrote *Paradise Lost*?
5. What is pepper?

Comprehension
1. What should you do if you see someone forget his book when he leaves his seat in a restaurant?
2. What is the advantage of keeping money in a bank?
3. Why is copper often used in electrical wires?

Arithmetic
1. Sam had three pieces of candy and Joe gave him four more. How many pieces of candy did Sam have altogether?
2. Three men divided eighteen golf balls equally among themselves. How many golf balls did each man receive?
3. If two apples cost 15¢, what will be the cost of a dozen apples?

Similarities
1. In what way are a lion and a tiger alike?
2. In what way are a saw and a hammer alike?
3. In what way are an hour and a week alike?
4. In what way are a circle and a triangle alike?

These drawings and questions are simulated examples taken from the Wechsler Intelligence Scale for Children (WISC-III).

FIGURE 8.20   Genetic Relationship and IQ

Relationship	Correlation
Monozygotic twins	
Reared together	.86
Reared apart	.72
Dizygotic twins	
Reared together	.60
Siblings	
Reared together	.47
Reared apart	.24
Parent/child	.40
Foster parent/child	.31

In general, the closer the genetic relationship between two individuals, the higher the correlation between their IQs. Identical twins who were reared together have the highest IQ correlations (after Bouchard & McGue, 1981).

Unfortunately, some of the twin data had to be discarded. The British psychologist Cyril Burt reported what was considered to be the most complete study of separated twins. His research showed extremely high correlations between the separated twins, no matter what conditions the individual twins had been reared in. After Burt's death, it was discovered that much of his data—and indeed, even his colleagues—did not exist (Hearnshaw, 1979).

There have been other problems with twin data. Twins that had been separated early in life were difficult to find, and when they were found, it was discovered that they often had been reared in similar environments, by relatives or by adoptive parents who were similar to the biological parents. However, a number of recent studies have continued to report a high correlation between IQs of pairs of twins (Bouchard, 1984). Wilson (1983) reported IQ correlations of .88 for identical twins and .54 for nonidentical twins at 15 years of age in 500 pairs of twins in the Louisville Twin Study.

Adoption Studies   Adoption studies are another type of research in human behavior genetics. A number of studies have shown that the correlation between the IQs of adopted children and their biological parents was much higher than the correlation between the IQs of children and their adoptive parents. For example, a study called the Texas Adoption Project has reported IQ correlations between children and their biological mothers of .28 and between children and their adoptive mothers of only .15 (Horn, 1983). In the Minnesota Adoption Study, Scarr and Weinberg (1983) also found a stronger correla-

tion between the IQ scores of adopted children and their biological parents (.40) than between children and their adoptive parents (.13). On the basis of studies like these, most psychologists agree that heredity does play a significant role in determining intelligence.

APPLICATION

Education and Learning Disabilities

You probably are aware of the term *learning disability (LD)* from elementary school. The term, which became popular in the 1960s, usually refers to any of a variety of learning problems experienced by a student. The problems do not include retardation, emotional disturbances, or physical handicaps, but rather include situations in which students do poorly in school, even though adequate teaching is provided and the intellectual capacity of the students is above normal. Kirk and Gallagher (1986) estimated that between 2 percent and 4 percent of students have severe learning disabilities, and many more have some degree of difficulty with learning in school.

Students with a learning disability have problems with at least one of the following: understanding written material, understanding mathematical concepts, listening, writing, and speaking (Warner, 1988). Essentially, these students have a weakness in their ability to learn. Academic skills problems include academic skills disorders, language and speech disorders, and attention-deficit hyperactivity disorder.

In the academic skills disorder of *developmental reading disorder*, or *dyslexia*, the student has difficulty learning to read written words adequately. The student has a normal intelligence level, but is not able to interpret visual information. He or she turns letters around; for instance, a *b* becomes a *d*. This is also called *mirror reading*. The student with dyslexia may also transpose letters in words. This results in oral reading that is characterized by slowness and substitutions of words. Dyslexia is usually detected in early elementary school. In mild cases, reading therapy can completely eliminate the problem, whereas in more severe cases, the person exhibits symptoms throughout life.

Other *academic skills disorders* include developmental arithmetic disorder and developmental expressive writing disorder. The chief characteristic of *developmental arithmetic disorder* is significant impairment in the development of arithmetic skills that interferes with normal academic or daily activities. The student (who is typically identified by the third grade) often has problems understanding mathematical concepts and operations, remembering steps in solving equations or following sequences, and learning the basic mathematical formulas. A student who has *developmental expressive writing disorder* has great difficulty with spelling, grammar, punctuation, and organization. His or her writing skills are significantly worse than what is expected for the particular grade level and experience.

Language and speech disorders include a broad range of language-processing problems. In *developmental articulation disorder*, the student fails to articulate speech sounds correctly at the appropriate age. Often certain sounds are omitted, substituted, or misarticulated. Speech therapy almost always provides complete recovery. Impairment in development of speaking is called *developmental expressive language disorder*, and is characterized by difficulty in acquiring new vocabulary words, in using simple grammatical structure, and in using limited sentence structure. Impairment in the development of language comprehension is called *developmental receptive language disorder*. It varies in severity, and might include difficulty in understanding sentence structures or in processing auditory information. Many children with this problem can eventually acquire normal language skills.

Attention-deficit hyperactivity disorder (ADHD) is characterized by inattention, impulsiveness, and hyperactivity (DSM-III-R, 1987). The symptoms often become worse in situations that require sustained attention, such as listening in the classroom or working on school assignments. Inattention results in not completing tasks or appearing not to listen to others. Impulsiveness is shown when the individual interrupts others, fails to wait his or her turn, and fails to completely understand an assignment before beginning. Hyperactive behavior results in the individual having difficulty remaining quiet, moving excessively, fidgeting, and constant manipulating of objects. Attention deficit disorder (ADD) can also occur without hyperactivity (Lahey & Carlson, 1991).

In school, ADHD is most characterized by *excessive motor activity*. Often the student (usually a male) has low self-esteem, experiences depression and underachieves. The problem often begins before age 4 but is usually not recognized until the child begins school. Sometimes the treatment includes administrating stimulating drugs, such as Ritalin, caffeine, or amphetamines. Barkley (1987) described ADHD as a neuromaturational delay and argued that a variety of assessment methods should be used when deciding the severity and treatment of the problem.

Rita Buchoff (1990) discussed how teachers can help students with ADHD in the classroom. She suggested that teachers should give explicit instructions, ensure that rules are followed carefully, provide opportunities for the students to achieve success to increase their self-esteem, and work with parents to develop an individualized educational program.

The goal in working with students with learning disabilities is to help them maximize educational opportunities. In many school systems, learning disability specialists are able to suggest special techniques for students to use when studying. For example, students with reading problems might listen to taped textbooks, or have someone read the textbook to them. Word processors can help students with writing problems improve spelling and organization. Those who confuse oral and written information are encouraged to tape-record lecture notes. If they have difficulty taking tests, study skill training can often help. Students often do better when they gain confidence, and these kinds of techniques may help them gain it.

Race and Intelligence   One of the most controversial issues in the relationship of heredity to intelligence concerns the issue of race. It is a fact that blacks score an average of 15 points lower on IQ tests than do whites (Reynolds & colleagues, 1987). While there have been many explanations for this finding, Arthur Jensen (1969) caused a controversy in the academic community by suggesting that intelligence was due nearly exclusively (80 percent) to hereditary factors. Let's take a look at the facts to try to understand what conclusions might be reached concerning race and intelligence.

As reported above, the correlation for IQs of identical twins reared together is .86, suggesting that heredity largely accounts for the similarity. There are other possible interpretations of the data. For example, the .86 correlation for identical twins reared together is actually determined by both genetic and environmental factors. These twins not only share identical genes, but they also share nearly identical environments. It could be argued that environment is contributing much more than the .14 figure first suggested by the data.

Keep in mind also that these correlations are for group data, and tell us nothing about individual scores. Indeed, there is more variation within a particular race than between two races. Thus, we cannot make a prediction about an individual from this group data.

Since, until recently, most intelligence tests were standardized for white, middle-class people, it is no wonder that other races do not score as well as whites. Indeed, it could be argued that the earlier versions of intelligence tests were invalid for measuring intelligence of blacks (Houston, 1990). The intelligence tests themselves could be biased. A number of attempts to construct a truly culture-fair intelligence test have shown only moderate success, and we are left with less than ideal testing instruments.

Recent studies have suggested that environmental differences that exist between races are extremely important in IQ determination. For instance, data from the Minnesota Transracial Adoption Study reported by Scarr and Weinberg (1983) found that when black children were adopted by white families at an early age, their IQs were more similar to the white IQ average of 110, compared with an average of 90 for black children reared in the black community. However, the black adopted children still scored 6 points below the white children in the same family. Scarr and Weinberg concluded that genetic differences between the races cannot be used exclusively to explain IQ differences.

New IQ data from over 10,000 cases were reviewed by Plomin and DeFries (1980). The new data suggest a heritability of around .50. Differences in the sample size, data collection techniques, IQ test revisions, and representativeness of samples help account for the lower heritability figure. Thus, while psychologists recognize the importance of heredity, it alone does not adequately explain differences in IQ. Heredity operates within an environment—the topic to which we now turn.

FIGURE 8.21   Environmental Influences on Intelligence
Environment can have both a positive and a negative effect on intelligence. A stimulating and secure environment can significantly improve IQ.

Environmental Influences on Intelligence

Psychologists also agree that environmental factors are important in determining intelligence. But determining what exactly in the environment is crucial for high intelligence is a difficult task.

Measurement of Environment and IQ   One line of research examines differences in IQs of identical twins reared in different environments. Since these twins share identical genes, any differences found could be attributed to the environment. Bouchard and McGue found in their 1981 review of twin studies a correlation in IQs between identical twins reared together of .86 and a correlation between identical twins reared apart of .72. Theoretically, both correlations ought to be 1.00 if heredity were the only factor, since the genes are identical. The lower correlations would seem to be due, then, to environmental influences. When reared in different homes, the different environmental experiences produce a correlation of only .72. Even when reared together, each twin has different personal experiences, resulting in a correlation of .86 and demonstrating the influence of the environment.

A great many studies show the importance of environment on intelligence. Remember the study by Cooper and Zubek (1958) from chapter 2, "Psychobiology," in which genetically identical rats showed differing maze-learning performance depending on whether they were reared in an enriched or restricted environment? Other studies have found diet to be important. Stock and Symthe's 1963 study of children in South Africa found that malnourished children had IQs that were an average of 20 points lower than children who were fed a well-balanced diet.

The family setting appears to be an extremely important environmental variable. Harold Skeels (1966) demonstrated the importance of adult interaction when young orphan children of low IQs were placed with institutionalized mentally retarded adult women who gave the children much attention. The IQs of these children jumped almost 30 points within 2 years, while a control group of children who remained in the orphanage actually dropped. Studies have shown that middle-class families are more likely than lower-class families to provide extensive verbal interaction with children, thus increasing the probability of higher IQs (Bradley & Caldwell, 1984).

The Colorado Adoption Project is a study of 200 adoptive families and 200 control families. In a preliminary report, Plomin and DeFries (1983) reported that environmental family influences were extremely important in the early development of cognitive abilities.

Robert Zajonc, a social psychologist at the University of Michigan, looked at the data collected on almost 400,000 young men in the Netherlands, and concluded that intelligence declines with family size as well as birth order. It seemed that the larger the family, the lower the

IQ of the children, and that later-born children tended to have lower IQs than early-born children.

Zajonc and Markus (1975) constructed a theoretical model to explain the influences of family size on intelligence. Essentially, the model proposes that with every new child the family's potential intellectual environment is reduced. Zajonc explains that the family's average score decreases because the resources of the parents are spread out over the increased number of children. Not everyone agrees with Zajonc's results. Other researchers have pointed out that social class, cultural expectations, and economic factors may be much more influential on intelligence than family size.

Another important influence on intelligence involves what we expect of an individual. For example, if a student is expected to do well, he or she probably will, and if a student is expected to fail, he or she probably will fail. In chapter 1, "The Study of Psychology," we described the Rosenthal and Jacobson (1968) experiment in which school children were administered an IQ test, which was disguised as an "intellectual blooming test." Those randomly chosen students who the teacher believed would bloom actually did increase their scores significantly on the second IQ test. Of course, expectancy also works the other way. If you come from a minority group, a lower social class, or, for whatever reason, if the teacher does not expect you to do well, chances are that you will perform poorly.

We learn from these studies that environment has a significant effect on intelligence. But it is very difficult to measure environmental influence, and the effects seem to be complexly interwoven. As we have seen, psychologists have been interested in the influences on intelligence for a long time.

What can we conclude about the effects of heredity and environment on intelligence? At the present time, we cannot design and measure the relevant variables in a way that will answer the question specifically. We can conclude that both genetic and environmental influences are extremely important in the determination of intelligence. Since our genes are set at birth and are immutable, it makes sense to concentrate on improving the environment to maximize individual success.

Environmental Enrichment Programs   A number of researchers have investigated methods of increasing intelligence through environmental enrichment programs. Recall Skeels's study in which orphanage children improved IQ scores when transferred to a mental institution that provided stimulation and individual attention. Angoff (1988) suggested that most children from impoverished homes can significantly increase performance on later intelligence tests if they receive early enrichment intervention.

FIGURE 8.22   Head Start Program
Children who experience the Head Start program generally become better students. A stimulating preschool environment improves their social and intellectual development.

Within the past couple of decades, preschools have become popular in the United States. Three- and four-year-old children are sent to preschool a couple of hours a day for a couple of days a week. The expectation is that the preschool will provide opportunities for the children to develop socialization skills, motivation, confidence, and knowledge that will translate into better performance in later years. Although the effects are generally not dramatic, there is some evidence that some programs can enhance the intelligence of school children (Zigler & Berman, 1983).

The Head Start program is a large-scale preschool for four-year-old children from disadvantaged backgrounds. Like most preschools, Head Start emphasizes socialization as well as academic skills. Although there are varying degrees of success in Head Start programs around the United States, the increased attention to the importance of nutrition and early environmental enrichment has generally paid off by producing a greater number of better students (Lazar & Darlington, 1982).

An example of an enrichment program designed to help elementary and secondary school children improve cognitive skills is Feuerstein's (1980) instrumental enrichment program. The program is designed to help students through a series of exercises, such as comparisons of objects, that promote abstract reasoning. Sternberg (1986a) argued that improving intellectual skills is an important objective for educators today.

THE EXTREMES OF INTELLIGENCE

As mentioned earlier in the chapter, the distribution of IQ scores falls into a bell-shaped or *normal curve*. Most individuals fall toward the middle, with fewer and fewer getting very high or very low scores. Wechsler designed the deviation IQ so that 95 percent of IQ scores fall between 70 and 130. The extreme lower 2½ percent and upper 2½ percent of cases are considered extremes of intelligence—mental retardation and intellectual giftedness.

Mental Retardation

Usually, an individual who scores below 70 on an IQ test, has problems in adaptive behavior (such as language skills and social competencies), and experiences these problems prior to age 18 is considered mentally retarded. Tests of adaptive behavior include the *Adaptive Behavior Scale* and the *Vineland Social Maturity Scale*. It is estimated that about 3 percent of Americans are mentally retarded.

Levels of Retardation Not everyone classified as mentally retarded is affected to the same degree. The range goes from individuals who are extremely slow learners to individuals who are incapable of doing anything for themselves. As mentioned in the biographical highlight, Binet originally classified the mentally retarded as morons, imbeciles, and idiots. If you have ever heard jokes using these labels, you will understand why they were changed to reflect more descriptive terms.

The DSM-III-R (1987) divides the mentally retarded into four classifications: mild, moderate, severe, and profound. Individuals in the mild retardation classification have IQs of between 50 and 70. This classification comprises the largest group (85 percent of all mentally retarded individuals) and includes within it a great deal of variability. Adults who are mildly retarded may have a

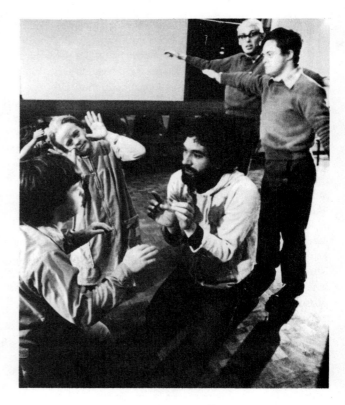

FIGURE 8.23 **Training People With Mental Retardation**
Many mentally retarded individuals can lead happy, productive lives. In a class at the Young Adult Institute in Manhattan, this adult is being trained to perform simple skills.

mental age of anywhere between 8 and 12. Some of the higher-functioning individuals can be fairly successful in family and occupation, and few of them need institutionalization. Most of these individuals, however, have difficulty dealing with abstract ideas.

Moderate retardation refers to a much smaller group (10 percent) of retarded individuals who have IQs of between 36 and 49 and a mental age of about 4 to 7. They can read and write on an elementary level, but they need constant supervision and are often placed in institutions and group homes. Some people in this category

FIGURE 8.24   Levels of Mental Retardation

	Level	Percent	IQ	Functioning Ability
The functioning ability of the mentally retarded is variable and depends on many factors (adapted from DSM-III-R, 1987).	Mild	85%	50-70	Educable
	Moderate	10%	36-49	Trainable
	Severe	3%	20-35	Custodial
	Profound	2%	0-19	Totally Dependent

work in sheltered workshops, and many are productive members of their community.

Severe retardation includes those individuals with IQs of between 20 and 35. Individuals in this group (3 percent of retarded individuals) show little language usage. Although they are dependent upon caretakers, they can learn to perform some routine tasks for themselves. Profound retardation refers to a very small number of retarded individuals (2 percent) with IQs below 20. They cannot learn even routine tasks and are totally dependent upon caretakers for their existence.

Until fairly recently, it was common to provide separate classes in school for all mentally retarded individuals. This practice did not help them as much as was expected. The Education for All Handicapped Children Act of 1975 changed this and required that children must be taught in the least restrictive environment. For the higher-functioning individuals, this means *mainstreaming* into regular classrooms as much as possible. Now the developmentally handicapped (DH) are taught in regular classrooms unless they have special needs that can best be met elsewhere.

Causes of Retardation   Psychologists are interested in researching the causes of mental retardation, treating the mentally retarded, and preventing future cases of retardation. The factors that cause mental retardation are varied, and often we do not know the cause for certain (Hallahan & colleagues, 1985). However, two general categories are identified—genetic and environmental.

Genetic causes of mental retardation include biochemical disorders, such as phenylketonuria (PKU) and chromosomal disorders. An extra chromosome number 21 (resulting in three number 21 chromosomes, rather than the usual two) can cause a form of mental retardation known as Down syndrome. Older mothers are more likely to have children with Down syndrome. As their ova (eggs) get older they are exposed to a greater volume of potential environmental hazards (such as heat or X rays), which could cause the chromosomes to remain as a pair rather than splitting normally.

Overall, it appears that general genetic factors usually result in mild mental retardation, while specific factors result in more severe retardation. For instance, there are some genes that contribute to intelligence and some that contribute to mild retardation. If two individuals with IQs of 60 were to reproduce, the genes that resulted in their particular IQs would likely produce offspring with IQs also in the 60s. On the other hand, a specific gene, such as the one that produces phenylketonuria, can cause severe mental retardation.

There are many possible environmental causes of mental retardation. During pregnancy, the use of harmful drugs, smoking, a poor diet, or infectious diseases (such as German measles or chicken pox) can be factors. Birth complications may cause brain injury to the baby, or early in life the young child may ingest poison or contract certain infectious diseases (such as meningitis).

The general family environment—such as that found in homes where children are neglected or abused or in homes where little is done to motivate children—

FIGURE 8.25 Intellectually Gifted Children
Intellectually gifted individuals tend to do well in many different areas of life. Here we see talented students rehearsing for a band concert. It is more than likely that these students are also involved in many other school and social activities.

can contribute to mild retardation. But often a specific accident, such as ingesting poison or being dropped on the head, can result in severe retardation. Remember that genetic and environmental factors interact to produce any behavior, including mental retardation.

The Intellectually Gifted

At the upper extreme of the IQ scale are the intellectually gifted individuals. A person with an IQ above 130 is usually labeled as gifted, although some psychologists and educators prefer a cutoff of 140. Teachers often refer outstanding students for consideration for inclusion in a school's gifted program. Sternberg and Davidson (1985) suggested that gifted individuals are able to effectively utilize the cognitive components of intelligence (planning and evaluating performance and learning new information).

Contrary to what many people believe, gifted individuals are not always the stereotyped "eggheads" who wear thick glasses (from reading 20 hours a day), are thin (malnourishment from skipping meals to study) and physically weak (from never lifting more than a book). Actually, people with high IQs tend to be superior in many areas, including sports, occupation, interpersonal relations, and academic achievement. A study in which gifted, general, and special learning needs students were compared found that gifted students tended to score highest both in academic and social self-concept, whereas the special learning needs students scored lowest on all measures (Colangelo, Kelly, & Schrepfer, 1987).

As described in our opening story, the most famous study of gifted children was started by psychologist Lewis Terman in 1921. He selected 1,528 children with a mean IQ of 150 and followed them as they developed into adulthood. Terman found that, as children, these individuals generally were physically healthier, better adjusted, and happier than other children (Terman, 1925).

Follow-up studies have shown that these gifted children grew up to be very successful adults (Goleman, 1980). Overall, the group was healthier, happier, more successful, and wealthier than the average person.

There has been a general trend in schools to develop programs for intellectually gifted students (Horowitz & O'Brien, 1986). Gifted children are now being challenged in and out of the classroom by enriched activities that allow them to develop their potential to the fullest. As more research is conducted in the area of giftedness, our schools will become better equipped to provide an education designed to maximize each student's intellectual capacity. ■

This chapter has pointed out that the cognitive processes of thinking, problem solving, language, and intelligence are so much a part of our everyday behavior that it is impossible to stop them. Intelligence is a difficult term to define properly, and yet, as we have shown, most people understand what is meant by intelligent behavior. All behavior, including intelligence, has genetic and environmental determinants. Intelligence influences other cognitive processes, such as learning, memory, language, and perception. We will see how these topics relate to intelligence in the chapters that follow.

"You mene I've bin spending this whol term with a defektiv reeding machin?"

CHAPTER REVIEW

What You've Learned About Language and Intelligence

1. Cognition, or mental processes, involves the acquisition, storage, retrieval, and utilization of knowledge. Cognitive psychology includes the study of the mental activities involved in perception, memory, language, thought, problem solving, and intelligence.

2. Language is a form of communication utilizing the manipulation of symbols to convey meaning. Grammar is the set of rules that determines the structure of the language required for understanding. The basic speech sounds of a language are called phonemes. Phonemes

are combined into morphemes, the smallest meaningful units of a language. Syntax is the subset of rules of grammar that governs the order of words in phrases and sentences. The meaning of language is called semantics.

3. Language tends to develop in a regular pattern. Infants begin to cry at birth, vocalize at 1 month, babble at 6 months, and speak at 1 year. During the second year, infants use one-word sentences. At about 2 years of age, children begin telegraphic speech in which they use two-word sentences. Eventually their sentences become longer and more complex, and their vocabularies become larger.

4. According to the learning theory of language, parents reinforce children for producing sounds that are recognizable as language, and children try to imitate words and phrases used by parents. According to the biological psycholinguistic theory of language, children are biologically programmed with an internal language acquisition device (LAD). A number of researchers have reported that primates can learn to use language, although others question whether these studies actually demonstrate language learning.

5. Thinking is the cognitive activity of manipulating symbols. For humans, thinking usually involves language. Whorf's linguistic relativity hypothesis states that the language of the observer influences thinking and perception.

6. Concept formation refers to the development of the ability to respond to common features of categories of objects or events. Natural concepts are used intuitively in everyday life, whereas formal concepts have clear and unambiguous rules that specify which attributes define the category. The rules include affirmative, conjunctive, disjunctive, conditional, and biconditional rules.

7. Theories of problem solving include trial-and-error learning, insight into the reorganization of the perceptual field, and information processing.

8. Most people go through the steps of preparation, production, and evaluation when solving problems. Strategies in problem solving include algorithms and heuristics. Experience is often useful in learning to solve problems, but sometimes leads to mental sets, functional fixedness, or confirmation bias, which can interfere with problem solving.

9. Creativity involves coming up with new or unusual responses to familiar circumstances, and is closely related to the ability to solve problems. Creative people tend to be internally motivated, to have freedom to choose their activities, and to live in a stimulating and exciting environment.

10. Intelligence can be defined as the capacity to learn and behave adaptively. Most intelligence tests stress verbal skills, quantitative skills, and problem-solving skills.

11. Spearman's theory of intelligence includes a general factor and specific factors. Thurstone's theory is based on seven primary mental abilities. Guilford includes 150 abilities, arranged in three dimensions: contents, operations, and products. Gardner proposed seven independent kinds of intelligence in his theory of multiple intelligences. Steinberg's triarchic theory consists of three parts: cognitive components of intelligence, experience and intelligence, and context of intelligence.

12. Aptitude tests are designed to predict what can be accomplished in the future with proper training, whereas achievement tests are designed to measure what can be done at the present time. Intelligence tests are usually aptitude tests designed to predict a broad range of mental abilities. An intelligence test should be valid, reliable, standardized, objective, and practical.

13. The first intelligence test was designed in 1905 by Alfred Binet to identify students in Paris schools who needed special education. Binet defined mental age as what the typical child of a given chronological age could do. Terman revised Binet's test and in 1916 published the Stanford-Binet Intelligence Scale. Terman used the intelligence quotient, or IQ, to refer to the ratio of mental to chronological age (IQ = MA / CA × 100).

14. Wechsler published several intelligence scales, including the Wechsler Adult Intelligence Scale (WAIS-R) and the Wechsler Intelligence Scale for Children (WISC-III). The WAIS-R measures verbal skills (information, digit span, vocabulary, arithmetic, comprehension, and similarities) and performance skills (picture completion, picture arrangement, block design, object assembly, and digit symbol).

15. Intelligence is determined in part by genetic factors. In general, the closer the genetic relationship between two individuals, the higher the correlation (relationship) between IQs. Identical twins reared together have the highest IQ correlation, and IQs of adoptive children correlate more highly with biological parents than with adoptive parents.

16. Intelligence is significantly influenced by the environment. Identical twins reared apart have lower IQ correlations than those reared together, suggesting that the environment influenced the difference. Studies show that diet, adult interaction, social class, and family size all influence intelligence.

17. Individuals with IQs below 70 who have problems in adaptive behavior are classified as mentally retarded. There are four different levels of retardation: mild, moderate, severe, and profound. Genetic causes of mental retardation include biochemical disorders (such as PKU) and chromosomal disorders (such as Down syndrome). Environmental causes of mental retardation include maternal diet, smoking, infectious diseases during pregnancy (German measles), or the child contracting infectious diseases early in life. Overall, general factors usually result in mild retardation, while specific factors result in more severe retardation.

18. At the upper extreme are intellectually gifted individuals with IQs greater than 130. Studies suggest that gifted individuals are typically healthier, happier, wealthier, and better adjusted than average individuals.

CHAPTER 9

MOTIVATION

What causes us to attend psychology class? What are our incentives for passing a test? The area of psychology that attempts to explain why we do the things we do is called motivation. Psychologists have studied motivation from a variety of approaches, including drives, incentives, arousal, and heredity. Much attention has focused on the motives of hunger, sex, curiosity, and achievement.

CRITICAL THINKING OBJECTIVES FOR CHAPTER 9

After reading chapter 9, you should be able to identify, apply, and evaluate what you have learned about the following questions:

What are the components in the definition of motivation?
What are the important theories of motivation?
What are the explanations of obesity?
What is the value of the stimulus motives?
What are the learned social motives?

CHAPTER 10

EMOTION

Although not easily understood, emotions are very important in our lives. Psychologists have developed a variety of theories to try to explain emotions. They have studied love and nonverbal emotional communication between people intensively in recent years, as well as human sexuality.

CRITICAL THINKING OBJECTIVES FOR CHAPTER 10

After reading chapter 10, you should be able to identify, apply, and evaluate what you have learned about the following questions:

What are the components in the definition of emotion?
What are the classification schemes of emotion?
What are the important theories of emotion?
What are the important theories of love?
What are the ways in which people communicate nonverbally?
What are the variations in human sexual behavior?

206

Part IV includes the theories and research into the explanation of human behavior. In this section the topics of motivation and emotion are explored.

Motivation and Emotion

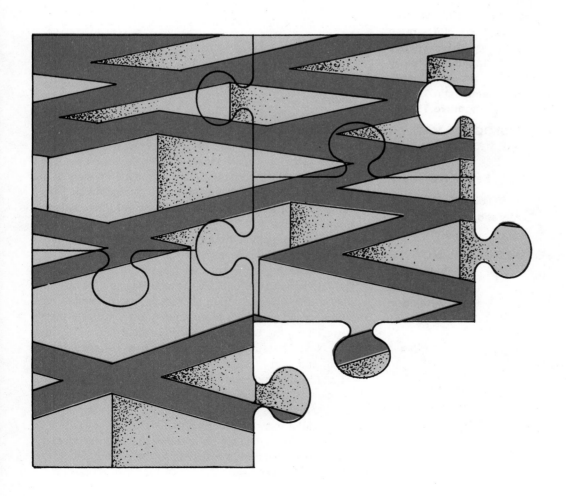

CHAPTER OBJECTIVES

What You'll Learn About Motivation

After studying this chapter, you should be able to:

1. Define the concept of motivation.
2. Describe the instinct theories of motivation.
3. Describe the drive theory of motivation.
4. Describe the incentive theory of motivation.
5. Describe the arousal theory of motivation.
6. Outline Maslow's humanistic theory of motivation.
7. Outline the cognitive theory of motivation.
8. Describe the biological motive of hunger.
9. Outline the biological motive of thirst.
10. Outline the influences on sexual motivation.
11. Identify the stimulus motive of curiosity.
12. Describe the stimulus motive of competence.
13. Describe the learned social motive of achievement.
14. Identify the learned social motive of power.
15. Identify the learned social motive of affiliation.

WHAT IS MOTIVATION?

THEORIES OF MOTIVATION
Instinct Theories
Drive Theory
Incentive Theory
Arousal Theory
Maslow's Humanistic Theory
Cognitive Theory

BIOLOGICAL MOTIVES
Hunger
Thirst
Sexual Motivation

STIMULUS MOTIVES
Exploration and Curiosity
Competence

LEARNED SOCIAL MOTIVES
Achievement
Power
Affiliation

In chapter 6, "Learning," we discussed how, with food as a reinforcer, a rat could be trained to press a lever in a Skinner box. In 1954, in the psychology laboratory of McGill University, rats in Skinner boxes were also trained to press levers; but in this experiment, instead of food, they received electrical stimulation to the brain.

James Olds and Peter Milner were interested in understanding whether the electrical stimulation of certain areas in the brain would produce behavior that would be motivated either by reinforcement or punishment.

Originally, Olds and Milner implanted an electrode (a thin piece of insulated wire) into the brain of a rat and placed the rat in a large box. Every time the rat went to a preselected corner, it was given a mild electric shock. The rat went to the designated corner several times before going to sleep.

The researchers thought, at first, the electrical stimulation was motivating curiosity in the rat; however, it quickly became apparent that pleasure was reinforcing the rat's behavior. Eventually the researchers were able to shape the subject through successive approximation so that it would go to any preselected corner, just as if they were giving the rat food as reinforcement.

Next, the subject was placed on a T-shaped platform, and every time it turned right it received a shock. The animal quickly learned to turn right. Then when the shock was given only when the rat turned left, the rat quickly reversed and always went left. The electric shock was indeed extremely reinforcing.

In order to test which areas of the brain produced the most motivation in response to the electric shock, a Skinner box was used. Instead of food being presented

What causes us to attend psychology class? What are our incentives for passing a test? The area of psychology that attempts to explain why we do the things we do is called motivation. Psychologists have studied motivation from a variety of approaches, including drives, incentives, arousal, and heredity. Much attention has focused on the motives of hunger, sex, curiosity, and achievement.

9

Motivation

FIGURE 9.1 Electrical Brain Stimulation
Olds and Milner (1954) implanted electrodes in the brains of rats and observed that lever-pressing behavior increased dramatically when the rats were reinforced with electrical stimulation of the brain.

each time a subject pressed the lever, an electric shock was delivered. In this way, motivation could be measured as the frequency of lever pressing.

The very first subject tested proved beyond doubt that electrical stimulation to the brain could produce reinforcing effects. After about 5 minutes of learning, the rat began pressing the lever once every 5 seconds. When the researchers turned the electric current off, the rat pressed the bar several times and then, without stimulation, went to sleep. When experimenters turned the current back on and gave the rat a shock, it immediately began pressing the lever again until the electricity was terminated, and then it would go to sleep once more.

Olds and Milner then began to search for the most reinforcing sites in the brain. When the electrode was placed in sensory or motor areas of the brain, the rate of lever pressing was about 25 times per hour. However, stimulation of certain areas of the brain appeared to produce a pleasurable response, with lever-pressing rates of 200 to 5,000 times per hour. Other areas apparently produced pain or distress, so that the subject pressed the lever once and never pressed it again.

After testing many areas of the brain, the researchers found the areas that appeared to produce the most pleasure from stimulation were the hypothalamus and midbrain nuclei. When electrodes were implanted in these areas, the rats pressed the lever from 500 to 5,000 times per hour. Some of these brain sites were so reinforcing that hungry rats preferred the electrical stimulation over food. Some of the subjects continued to press the lever more than 2,000 times per hour for 24 continuous hours.

The behavior of the rats with implanted brain electrodes is often referred to as self-stimulation. The work of Olds and Milner has been replicated in monkeys and has formed an important basis for understanding the brain's role in motivation. Further research by Olds and Milner as well as other experimenters has shown the brain reward circuit to include a variety of areas, such as the septal area and especially the medial forebrain bundle, a large nerve tract that runs from the brainstem to the cortex.

The discovery of pleasure centers in the brain was important in motivation research because it provided evidence that reinforcement of behavior has a physiological basis. This helped psychologists further understand the role the brain plays in motivation.

WHAT IS MOTIVATION?

In many ways motivation is central to the study of psychology. You and I are constantly engaged in purposeful or goal-oriented behavior, and underlying all such behavior are motives. Motivational concepts allow us to account for the variability in behavior, both in an individual and between individuals (Beck, 1990).

Motives arouse and direct our behavior toward some goal. There are three major categories of motives: biological, stimulus, and learned social. The *biological motives*, such as hunger, thirst, temperature regulation, and sex, have a definite physiological basis. The *stimulus motives*, such as sensory stimulation, exploration, curiosity, contact comfort, and competence, cause us to seek out sensory stimulation through interaction with the environment. They are internal and unlearned, but do not appear to have a specific physiological basis. The *learned social motives*, such as achievement, power, and affiliation, are determined largely by learning and focus on social experiences.

Motivated behavior is initiated and directed toward a goal, and varies in intensity and persistence (Petri, 1991). Motivation, then, can be thought of as the forces that initiate and direct behavior, and the variables that determine the intensity and persistence of that behavior. The *initiation* of behavior can be prompted from within the individual or from the external environment. For example, we might be hungry because of a low blood sugar level (internal cue) or because we just saw a delicious-looking dessert (external cue). Motivation also provides *direction* for our behavior. For example, when we are hungry we seek food, rather than read our textbook.

Lastly, motivation determines the intensity and persistence of our behavior. *Intensity* has to do with how strong the behavior is. For instance, if you are only a little hungry you might eat if food is readily available, but if there is no food in the immediate vicinity you would probably engage in some other behavior. On the other hand, if you are extremely hungry, you would most likely look for something to eat, doing whatever it took to obtain your goal. How motivated we are will likewise influence our *persistence*. Sometimes we will persist in obtaining a goal for a long time, while at other times we will give up after a brief try.

Psychologists often measure motivation by observing what individuals do (initiation), how they make choices (direction), how strongly they engage in the behavior (intensity), and how long they engage in it (persistence). Motivation is not observed directly, but rather is inferred from the performance of subjects (Petri, 1991). For instance, if a person selects a horror movie over a romantic comedy, we infer that the person is meeting a need by doing so.

Sometimes we can manipulate the level of motivation in others, such as when researchers temporarily deprive animals of food to increase their motivation to work for food. Parents might also motivate their children by manipulating the level of reward (praise or money) given for certain behaviors.

THEORIES OF MOTIVATION

Because motivation is so vastly complex, many approaches have been developed to try to explain it. The basic question is, *why* do we do what we do? Although many motives overlap, it is useful to study each approach separately. In this section we will survey major approaches to motivation: instinct, drive, incentive, arousal, humanistic, and cognitive.

Instinct Theories

Theories that attribute motivation to biologically determined factors, to instinctive patterns of behavior, were at one time highly influential in the United States. Instinct theories continue to be central to the work of ethologists, and sociobiologists argue that even social behavior is genetically programmed.

Instinct   Early zoologists and psychologists noticed that some behaviors of animals seemed universal and stereotyped. In other words, every member of the species showed the same behavior pattern. These observers defined instinct as a behavior that is inherited by all members of the species.

The instinct theory dominated psychology in the early years of this century. Major psychologists such as William James (1890) developed elaborate instinct theories to explain human behavior. To James, instincts were impulses that produced behaviors. He believed that although people normally expressed instincts automatically, they could modify their instincts by learning and experience. Rather than absolute responses, reflexes, or learning, he viewed instincts as tendencies to act in a given way. In fact, he thought instincts formed the biological base from which we develop habits through our experiences.

According to James, people possess all of the instincts of lower animals, plus a variety of uniquely human ones. Some of the instincts proposed by James include curiosity, shyness, modesty, fear, playfulness, sympathy, cleanliness, jealousy, sociability, and rivalry.

FIGURE 9.2 Instinct
Because primates develop more slowly than most mammals, the young of the species have developed life-saving instincts peculiar to mammals. Young primates, such as the potto pictured here, are protected during their long, helpless infancies by an innate biological drive to cling tightly to their mothers. The clinging instinct assures the infant of never being separated from the mother, who must walk about looking for food or sometimes run, climb a tree, or swing from limb to limb to escape danger.

The early instinct theories did not last very long in psychology. Kuo (1921) argued that many behaviors attributed to instinct were actually learned. He also indicated that these instincts were caused by environmental stimuli rather than by innate internal factors. Tolman (1923) argued that the major problem with the motivational concept of instinct was that it didn't really explain behavior, but rather only described it. In the 1920s American psychology became dominated by behaviorism (see chapter 1, "The Study of Psychology"). Instinct theories disappeared in the American psychological literature, but continued to flourish in the work of the European zoologists called ethologists.

Ethology The science of the behavior of animals in their natural environment is called ethology. Its focus is on inherited rather than learned behavior. The ultimate goal of ethologists is to discover how instinctive behavior evolved among related species and now improves survival. In the 1930s Konrad Lorenz and Niko Tinbergen became the leaders of this approach. Ethology grew steadily, and in 1973 the Nobel Prize for physiology was awarded to Lorenz, Tinbergen, and Karl von Frisch for their work in identifying animal behavior patterns.

The first step for the ethologist is to form an ethogram, which is a detailed description of all the behaviors shown by the species. Theories are then proposed to explain the development and adaptive function of each behavior. Experiments are next conducted to test these theories. For example, Lorenz (1965) found that newly hatched greylag geese, who normally follow the mother goose, will follow any large moving stimulus that is presented to them shortly after hatching. This process, termed *imprinting*, has the function of bonding the new bird with its mother for survival (see chapter 6, "Learning").

Many of the behaviors described in an ethogram consist of fixed action patterns (FAP). FAPs are unlearned, inherited, stereotyped behaviors that are *species-specific*, or shown by all members of a species (Alcock, 1989). Fixed action patterns are stimulated by specific cues from the environment, called releasers (sign stimuli). Releasers are especially important in social behaviors such as aggression or courtship. For example, Tinbergen (1952) reported that stereotyped courtship behavior was released in the female stickleback fish when the male stickleback swam toward her in a particular zigzag fashion.

FIGURE 9.3 Ethological Study
Ethologists study animals in their natural environment. Many ethologists study fixed action patterns, or species-specific behaviors, which are stimulated by releasers in the environment. This female stickleback fish exhibits courtship behavior that is specific to her species when the male approaches her.

FIGURE 9.4   Communication Among Bees

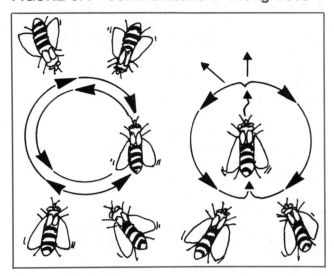

Von Frisch realized that when a bee discovers nectar, it indicates the direction and distance of the source to other bees in the hive through specific dance-like movements.

Through years of patient research, the "language" of bees was interpreted by the German ethologist Karl von Frisch (1967). When a bee finds a good supply of food, it returns to the hive and performs a dance to tell the other bees where the food source is located. Different dance movements indicate distances to the food source. For short distances, the bee does a round dance, while for longer distances, a figure-eight dance is performed that includes a particular number of tail wags (indicating precise distance). The dance also indicates direction from the hive so the other bees can easily find the food.

The ethological, or species-specific, approach to animal motivation has influenced many comparative psychologists once again to include biological concepts in their theories of the behavior of different species of animals. In fact, genetic and evolutionary principles are currently having an impact on human psychology in a controversial theory called sociobiology.

Sociobiology   Why would parents sacrifice their lives to save their children? Why do all cultures have elaborate courtship rituals and devise complex kinship rules? Is there an evolutionary basis for human behaviors such as helping, aggression, mate selection, parenting, and territoriality? According to Edward O. Wilson (1975), the answer to these questions is explained by the theory of sociobiology.

Sociobiology is the study of the genetic basis of social behavior. A key concept in this theory is that an individual is genetically programmed to show behaviors that help pass the genes on to the next generation. The

literature in animal behavior is full of observations of ritualized courtship patterns and territorial aggressive displays. There are innumerable examples in the animal kingdom of a parent sacrificing its life for its young. For instance, a mother meadowlark might flutter around as if she had a broken wing in order to distract a cat from her babies.

Sociobiology is controversial because it proposes that not only is human biology genetically based, but that human social behavior is also. Because it applies the theory of evolutionary biology to the study of social behavior, sociobiology makes some interesting predictions about human behavior (Barash, 1982). Since passing one's genes on to the next generation involves reproduction, the human endeavors of mate selection, courtship, and parenting are considered extremely important. Sociobiology predicts that people will engage in behaviors that will help them genetically.

Richard Dawkins (1976) argued that the behavior of people is motivated basically by selfishness. Even if they don't marry and have children, people still work hard to get their genes into the next generation. Each child has 50 percent of a person's genes, but each niece or nephew has 25 percent. Thus, if a person can get his or her brothers or sisters to have four children, this is considered to be genetically the same as if he or she had two children.

In courtship and mate selection, males and females have different reproductive strategies (Buss, 1989). The worst thing for a male, according to this theory, would be for his mate to become pregnant by someone else. Why? Because the offspring wouldn't be his biologically. So males want a long engagement (at least nine months) so they can be sure she is not already pregnant by someone else. A female, on the other hand, looks for someone who pampers her (and will pamper her baby) and shows a great deal of devotion. She wants protection, so she looks for a male who has status, power, and wealth. Buss (1989) tested predictions of sociobiology in 37 cultures and found general support for the theory's accuracy.

When couples do get married, who is older? Sociobiological theory would predict the male, since he matures a couple of years later than the female, takes time to acquire wealth, and is better able to protect his mate. A research study by Chris Paterson (1982) suggests men are likely to be 2 years older than their wives at marriage. When first married, with whose parents might a couple live? They often live with the husband's parents, so his parents can help keep an eye on his wife. When they move out and eventually have a baby, whose mother comes to help? Hers, because her mother is the only grandparent who knows absolutely it is her grandchild. Why do people have children in the first place? One important reason is parental pressure. A successful parent is one who becomes a grandparent, since this assures that the genes will be perpetuated into future generations. And finally, why do parents sacrifice for their children? Because the children carry the genes on into the next generation. Sociobiologists have not yet had enough time to test many of their predictions, and thus they will have to wait before they can draw firm conclusions.

Freud's Motivation Theory Freud (1915) believed that behavior is caused by internal instincts (the German word Freud used, *Treib*, can be interpreted as instinct, impulse, or drive). According to Freud, psychic energy, or libido, builds up in the personality structure called the id whenever there is a need (see chapter 11, "Personality," for a discussion of Freud's personality theory). He also believed that there are two main instincts: the life instinct and death instinct. The life instinct, or Eros, serves to help the individual and the species survive. Sex is the major expression of this life instinct. The death instinct, or Thanatos, includes aggression and destruction. Thus, to Freud, motivation is often associated with sex or aggression.

Freud proposed that instincts have four characteristics: source, impetus, aim, and object. The instinct's *source* is the bodily need that activates motivation. The *impetus* is the intensity or strength of the motivation. The *aim* of an instinct is satisfaction, which is achieved by reducing the bodily need. And the instinct's *object* is the means by which the need is satisfied. For example, we might be hungry (source) and motivated to eat (impetus). We can reduce our hunger with food (aim) and thus eat (object). Freud's theory has been criticized because it does not predict behavior, but rather only attempts to explain what has already happened. It served, however, as an early model of the drive concept, to which we turn next.

Drive Theory

The term drive was first used by Woodworth in 1918 to describe the internal forces that push us toward doing something. He argued that different drives motivate different behaviors. For instance, the hunger drive motivates eating and the thirst drive motivates drinking. Woodworth described the characteristics of drive as direction, intensity, and persistence (which we discussed earlier in this chapter). The concept of drive is often associated with the process of homeostasis.

Homeostasis If you made a graph of your hunger over time, you would find that it appears periodically (three or four times a day, counting a late-night snack), and when it does, it leads to a particular behavior (eating) that satisfies it. After reaching the goal of eating, you aren't motivated by hunger again for a while.

FIGURE 9.5 Homeostasis and Drive Reduction

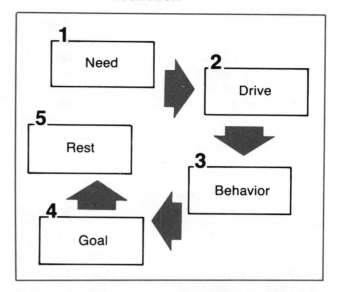

In homeostasis, a need causes a drive, which leads to behavior designed to reach a goal and then allows the individual to rest. This cycle is repeated when a new need arises.

The hunger motive follows a cycle that illustrates the concept of homeostasis. This concept was introduced by Walter Cannon in 1939 to illustrate how the internal bodily processes are maintained in a stable state of balance. The easiest example of a homeostatic mechanism is temperature. We may set the thermostat in our home on 70°. When the temperature goes below this setting, the heating system comes on. Similarly, when our body temperature rises, we perspire to cool the body, and when our body temperature drops, we shiver to warm it. Hunger and thirst are two other biological motives that operate within a homeostatic cycle.

Hull's Drive Theory The drive concept of motivation is often associated with Clark Hull's (1943) theory, since his theory was extremely influential in the development of learning and motivation theory in psychology. Hull was influenced by the concept of homeostasis and proposed that an organism is motivated to maintain it.

When there is a deviation from homeostasis, a biological need is created. This need (which often results from deprivation) produces a psychological arousal, or drive. A drive provides the energy for goal-directed behavior that will restore homeostasis and thus reduce the drive. For example, you have a biological need for water. When you go without drinking for a while, this need creates a psychological drive called thirst. Thirst leads to drinking behavior. After you reach your goal of drinking, your thirst drive is reduced and you rest until your body needs more water. This cycle of homeostasis is repeated again and again as the individual maintains internal balance. Hull's drive theory is sometimes referred to as a *push* motivation theory, since the individual is pushed by inner forces toward reducing the drive and restoring homeostasis.

Hull (1952) devised a very influential model that explained how the strength (intensity) of a behavior is related to the processes of learning and motivation. His basic formula was:

$$E = H \times D \times K$$

Originally, he theorized that the strength of a response (E) depended upon the strength of a learned habit (H) and the strength of the motivating drive (D). Eventually, he concluded that motivation as a totally internal force was inadequate, and added the concept of incentive (K) to the formula. Incentive involves external stimuli such as reinforcements. For instance, we are more motivated to perform when provided a large reinforcement rather than a small reinforcement. We turn next to a discussion of the concept of incentives.

Incentive Theory

In contrast to the push motivation theory of drive, psychologists have also proposed a *pull* theory, in which external stimuli, called incentives, pull the individual toward some goal. Sometimes there is no deprivation that causes a biological need leading to a psychological drive to restore homeostasis. Rather, we are motivated by an external stimulus, called an incentive, that pulls us toward some goal. For example, you may be tempted to eat a delicious dessert even when you are full after a big dinner. Incentives are objects or events in the environment that motivate the individual in the absence of any apparent biological need. You had no need for the dessert even though you were motivated to eat it.

Incentives can be either positive or negative. We are motivated to obtain positive incentives, whereas we are motivated to avoid negative incentives. For most of us, a positive incentive is delicious food, whereas a negative incentive is pain. There are several distinctions between drives and incentives. Drives are produced internally, and are unlearned, biological, and cyclic. Incentives, on the other hand, are produced externally, are learned, and do not depend on deprivation.

Incentive theory is similar to the motivational theory of hedonism. *Hedonism* is basically the seeking of pleasure and avoidance of pain. The theory of hedonism proposes that external stimuli motivate the individual

because they are associated with the reinforcement of pleasure or the avoidance of punishment (Petri, 1991). Incentives play an important role in motivating human behavior.

Arousal Theory

The arousal theory of motivation focuses on the level of energy necessary to regulate our overall arousal. Sometimes we need to increase our arousal level by walking, looking, feeling, or other sensory active behaviors. At other times we are already highly aroused and need to lower the arousal level by sleeping, being quiet, or engaging in other forms of relaxation. The arousal theory emphasizes the whole individual and states that in order to understand behavior we need to study how the individual regulates his or her arousal level. The fundamental principle of arousal theory of motivation is that arousal occurs on a continuum from very low levels (such as in sleep) to extremely high levels (such as in anxiety and strong emotions). Behavior is motivated as the arousal level changes, with some intermediate level of arousal usually producing the most efficient behavioral adaptation.

Optimum Level of Arousal   Donald Hebb (1955) proposed that we are motivated to maintain an optimum level of arousal. If our arousal level drops too low, we are motivated to do something to increase it. And if our arousal level becomes too high, we try to reduce it. The particular behavior is not as important as the goal of maintaining an optimum level of arousal.

Hebb suggested that sensory information from the environment provided two functions: information and arousal. When our senses are stimulated, the neural impulses are carried to both the cortex (information interpretation) and the reticular formation (arousal). The *cue function* of a sensory stimulus provides information about the environment, whereas the *arousal function* provides arousal stimulation. Hebb argued that motivation involves the arousal of the brain through the reticular formation so that the brain can interpret the sensory information and the individual can decide on direction.

The arousal theory differs from the drive theory in that in the drive theory the individual is motivated to decrease arousal by achieving some goal. In arousal theory, we sometimes increase and sometimes decrease the arousal. When we are bored, we find some excitement; we might go to an amusement park or talk to some friends to increase our arousal level. When we are overstimulated, we escape to find peace and quiet; we go off by ourselves, take a nap, or just relax to reduce our level of arousal.

FIGURE 9.6 Optimum Level of Arousal
If our overall arousal level becomes too low, we are motivated to engage in a behavior to increase it, as illustrated by this adventurous person.

Arousal and Performance It has long been noted that the relationship between arousal and performance is an inverted-U function. When there is a very low level of arousal, the individual will be asleep. As arousal levels increase, the individual's alertness also increases until a point is reached when optimum performance is obtained. Additional arousal increases lead to anxiety, disorganization, and a decreased level of performance.

To understand arousal and performance, imagine that your class is told that there will be a test next Friday, but it will not be graded. In fact, when finished you are to toss it in the waste basket. You probably would not study much nor do well on this test. Now, imagine instead that the class learns that the test next Friday is important and that it will count as a regular test. Now, you will study and do well. Lastly, imagine that you discover that the test next Friday is so important that previous grades will be thrown out, and your course grade will be based exclusively on this one test. You would probably be very anxious about this test and might not do as well as you would if it were only a regular test. Test performance is likely to be best when arousal (motivation) is moderate. At either extreme, performance declines.

The optimum level of arousal depends on the individual and the particular task, and predicts that the optimum motivation level for good performance decreases as the difficulty of the task increases (Berlyne, 1960). With a very easy task, you will need a high level of

motivation to perform well. Think of that "easy" course you're taking and how difficult it is to do all of the assignments unless you force yourself. With a task of medium difficulty, performance is best when arousal (motivation) is moderate. But with a very difficult task, the optimum arousal level is fairly low. Think of your "tough" course, and how it doesn't take much to create

FIGURE 9.7 Arousal and Performance

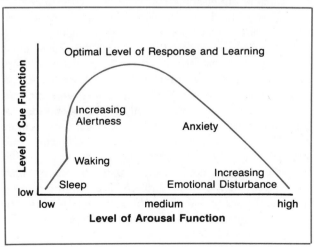

A certain amount of arousal is necessary for optimum performance, but additional stimulation leads to a decreased level of performance. This relationship is represented by an inverted U-shaped curve (after Hebb, 1955).

such a panic that you study extremely hard. Over the years the relationship between arousal and performance has come to be known as the Yerkes-Dodson Law by many psychologists. Although there has been substantial support for the inverted-U hypothesis, some researchers argue that it doesn't work under all conditions and alternatives need to be found (Neiss, 1988).

Sensation Seeking   The optimum arousal level is different for each individual. Marvin Zuckerman (1979, 1984) investigated the dimension of sensation seeking. People with high optimum levels of arousal tend to seek thrills and adventure. These people may climb mountains, drive race cars, ride roller coasters, and enjoy action movies. High sensation seekers might also be more likely to use recreational drugs, become involved in other illegal activities, or be more easily aroused sexually (Zuckerman & Como, 1983). People with low optimum levels try to keep stimulation low. They may prefer reading a good book or watching a sunset. High sensation seekers may have low levels of internal arousal, and thus depend on external stimulation to raise their internal level of arousal. On the other hand, low sensation seekers may have internal levels of arousal that are already high and thus don't require any additional stimulation.

Zuckerman (1984) developed the sensation-seeking scale to measure four characteristics of sensation seeking as a personality trait. *Thrill and adventure seeking* is the characteristic of selecting activities that involve danger and adventure. *Disinhibition* involves engaging in uninhibited behaviors such as parachuting from a plane. *Experience seeking* involves gaining a wide variety of novel experiences, such as traveling. *Susceptibility to boredom* is the tendency to avoid routine activities that can become unfulfilling.

A large number of research studies also have verified the wide variations in the sensation-seeking tendencies of people. Pedersen (1991) found that Zuckerman's disinhibition characteristic was a strong predictor of future drug use in both male and female adolescents. Arnett (1990a) reported that high school seniors who engaged in drunk driving had significantly higher scores on the sensation-seeking scale. High school juniors and seniors with high sensation-seeking scores in disinhibition and susceptibility to boredom were more likely to engage in sex without using contraception (Arnett, 1990b). Men who score high on the thrill- and adventure-seeking subscale are more likely to engage in higher-risk sports (such as rugby) rather than low-risk sports (such as running), according to Potgieter and Bisschoff (1990). Understanding the sensation-seeking tendencies of individuals may help professionals better advise people of occupations or activities in which they might obtain success.

Maslow's Humanistic Theory

Many psychologists view human behavior as being motivated by more than just strictly biological forces. One theory of human motivation, which is unusually broad in its design and appeal, is the humanistic theory proposed by Abraham Maslow, which has had an important influence on the psychology of motivation. In *Motivation and Personality* (1970), Maslow stated that a theory of motivation must take into account the whole person and should be based on a hierarchy of needs, which, if successfully satisfied, leads to the full realization of one's potential (Maslow, 1970, 1987).

Physiological Needs   According to Maslow, physiological needs include motives such as hunger, thirst, sex, exercise, and rest. A person is dominated by the physiological needs until some of them have been satisfied at least partially. Note that higher needs in the hierarchy can become stronger when physiological needs start to be met. Maslow believed that the physiological needs were adequately met in most people in our society. After that, the individual is motivated by the safety needs.

Safety Needs   Motives such as security, stability, dependency, protection, freedom from fear and anxiety, and need for structure and order are safety needs. Security, protection, and safety become dominant forces in a person's life until they can be satisfied. Children prefer routines and

FIGURE 9.8   Maslow's Need Hierarchy

This humanistic theory of motivation proposes a hierarchy of needs, which, if satisfied, leads to self-actualization, the full realization of one's potential.

BIOGRAPHICAL HIGHLIGHT

ABRAHAM H. MASLOW

Abraham H. Maslow was born in Brooklyn, New York, in 1908. He studied primate behavior at the University of Wisconsin, where he received his doctorate degree in psychology in 1934.

Early in his scholarly career, Maslow was drawn to the study of human motivation and personality. His work in this area upset strict behaviorists, whose explanations of motivation and personality failed to account for what Maslow called the whole person. His theory of the hierarchy of needs, which leads to the "self-actualized" individual, was a strong catalyst for the founding of humanistic psychology. Maslow successfully bridged motivation and personality in his theories of needs, self-actualizing persons, and peak experiences.

Maslow is considered an important figure in contemporary psychology. His career was a formidable one. For 14 years he taught at Brooklyn College, and then went to Brandeis University as chairman of the Psychology Department. In 1968 he was elected president of the American Psychological Association. In 1969 he went to the Laughlin Foundation in Menlo Park, California. He wrote two very important books: *Toward a Psychology of Being* (1968) and *Motivation and Personality* (1970). Abraham Maslow died of a heart attack in 1970.

familiar surroundings, and often experience problems when things are greatly disturbed. As we grow up, except for emergencies, the safety needs are largely met. When you feel safe and secure, you then begin to develop other social needs—the next highest level.

Belongingness and Love Needs   Motives such as love and affection are included in belongingness and love needs. As these needs dominate, we feel a desire for friends, family, and social contact. We need to belong to a group or family. Maslow suggests that when the family moves, children often have difficulties because they have many needs to be met quickly. As adults, we need to give and receive love. We can satisfy these needs through marriage, work, or social activities. If we do not satisfy the belongingness and love needs, Maslow believed that psychological problems may develop.

Esteem Needs   A high evaluation of oneself, self-respect, achievement, and recognition by others are considered esteem needs. We need to achieve competence if we want to gain other people's respect. When we earn recognition, attention, and status, we satisfy the esteem needs and feel self-confident and important. If we do not satisfy them, we tend to feel inferior and helpless.

Self-Actualization   The final need in Maslow's hierarchy is self-actualization. When the physiological,

safety, love, and esteem needs have been satisfied, the individual is motivated to reach the *growth* need of self-actualization. This refers to the attainment of the individual's special potential, to the person's becoming what he or she is capable of becoming. Self-actualization is highly individualized, since each of us has different sets of abilities. Maslow believed that self-actualization is rarely reached, and if it is, it is usually in older people who have had the time and experience necessary to achieve this level. We discuss Maslow's self-actualization theory in more detail in chapter 11, "Personality."

Although Maslow's theory of motivation has been very influential in psychology, his ideas have been broadly criticized. Many of the people he considered to be self-actualized were either friends or people who were dead. Therefore, one problem with his hypothesis is reliability. Mittelman (1991) recently argued that the individuals that Maslow studied were very open rather than self-actualized. Also, some research that tried to test the theory as a developmental model failed to support it (Goebel & Brown, 1981). Apparently, one does not necessarily move through the hierarchy as one grows older.

While Maslow's theory has been useful in helping us understand ourselves, it is important to remember that human behavior is so complex that the best way to study it is to take a thoroughly multidimensional and multicultural approach.

Cognitive Theory

The cognitive approach to motivation emphasizes thinking and perceptual interpretation. While the theory of *cognitive motivation* is currently very popular in psychology, it has been studied for many years. As we discussed in chapter 6, "Learning," Tolman (1932) proposed a cognitive theory of purposive behavior, which states that as individuals learn that certain behaviors lead to certain goals, they develop cognitive expectancies that motivate them to exhibit those behaviors.

An expectancy-value theory of motivation was developed by Julian Rotter (1954). Basically, he argued that behavior is the result of our expectations of achieving goals and the value that those goals have for us. We are motivated to maximize the value of our behavior choices. For instance, suppose you need to choose between studying for an exam or going to a movie. If passing the course is a high priority (high value) and you believe you need a good exam grade to pass the course (expectation), you will probably spend the night studying rather than going to the theater. In chapter 11, "Personality," we discuss Rotter's theory that people vary in their expectancies about the source of reinforcement. Expectancy theory is also important in achievement motivation, which we cover later in this chapter.

Attribution involves the cognitive process of determining the motives of someone's behavior. Fritz Heider (1958) proposed the *naive psychology* approach, in which a person decides the causes of behavior. According to Heider, we attribute behavior to forces within the individual (disposition forces) or forces in the environment (situation forces). *Dispositions* include ability and motivation, whereas *situations* include task difficulty and luck. As an example, you notice that the student next to you received an outstanding grade on a test. Do you attribute the performance to the person's intelligence and hard work (dispositions), or the fact that it was an easy test or the student was a lucky guesser (situation)? Heider suggested that you are probably biased toward a dispositional attribution. We discuss the current approach to attribution theory in chapter 15, "Social Psychology."

BIOLOGICAL MOTIVES

Biologically, organisms are prepared to engage in behaviors that facilitate survival. What are the biological (primary) motives? Biological motives have a definite physiological basis and are biologically necessary for survival of the individual or the species; they include hunger, thirst, body temperature regulation, avoidance of pain, and the sexual drive. Some of these motives are satisfactorily explained by the drive theory, while others need additional theories for a complete understanding. In this section we discuss the biological motives of hunger, thirst, and sex.

Hunger

It's noon, and as you look around the crowded cafeteria, you realize that many people seem to feel hungry at the same time. What motivates us to eat at certain times? Hunger is not always associated with a conscious internal sensation, and we sometimes find ourselves eating ravenously without having had any previous awareness of hunger pangs (Logue, 1991). Many times, external cues are used to signal initiation of eating behavior. When asked if they are hungry, many people consult their watches rather than their stomachs.

Peripheral Factors   When someone says he or she is hungry, the sensation most often reported is the feeling of a slight ache in the stomach. In a famous study by Cannon and Washburn (1912), a subject swallowed a balloon, which allowed the experimenters to record stomach contractions and compare them to the subject's feelings of hunger. Cannon and Washburn found a strong association between stomach contractions and feelings of hunger. However, later studies demonstrated that when it contains an inflated balloon, the stomach is actually full, and that it is otherwise fairly inactive even when it does

FIGURE 9.9   External Cues for Hunger
Although hunger has a biological basis, many times we are influenced by external cues that signal eating behavior.

FIGURE 9.10   Cannon and Washburn Experiment

Contractions as measured by volume of stomach balloon

Time in minutes

Hunger pangs

Abdominal breathing reactions

Balloon

Signal key

Pneumograph

In an attempt to measure stomach contractions during hunger, Cannon and Washburn (1912) had a subject swallow a balloon and indicate when he felt hunger pangs.

not contain food. Even when stomachs of humans and animals have been surgically removed, the subjects eat regularly. The stomach does influence the size of a meal that is eaten, probably through receptors in the stomach wall that monitor the amount of nutrients in the meal (Deutsch, 1983).

The duodenum, or initial segment of the small intestine, has been implicated as a mechanism to stop eating. Smith and Gibbs (1976) found that when fats and proteins enter the duodenum, a hormone called CCK (cholecystokinin) is released. They argued that CCK travels through the bloodstream to the brain, where a signal to stop eating is released. However, studies have reported conflicting claims on the role of CCK in stopping eating behavior through brain regulation. It appears likely that CCK influences the termination of eating in humans by inhibiting stomach muscles, thus delaying the emptying of the stomach and shortening the length of a meal (McHugh & Moran, 1985).

Several other theories that attempt to explain eating behavior involve body temperature, glucose levels, and body fat. The glucostatic theory of hunger, first proposed by Jean Mayer (1953), argued that hunger occurs when glucose metabolism in individual cells is low. Later research has shown that the liver monitors glucose levels and when glucose levels in the liver are high, eating is suppressed (Russek & colleagues, 1980). The lipostatic theory proposes that body weight regulation is due to the storage of body fat (Liebelt & colleagues, 1973). If the amount of fat in the diet is reduced, subjects increase their food intake. It is likely that there are several overlapping processes that control hunger and eating.

Brain Centers   We know that the hypothalamus is important in controlling eating behavior. In chapter 2, "Psychobiology," we learned that the hypothalamus played a key role in motivation of behavior, including eating, drinking, and sex. Two distinct areas of the hypothalamus are important in hunger. The lateral hypothalamus (LH) appears to be involved in initiating eating behavior, whereas the ventromedial hypothalamus (VMH) stops eating behavior.

FIGURE 9.11   Hypothalamus and Overeating
This rat ate itself into these proportions after experimenters destroyed the ventromedial hypothalamus, the part of the hypothalamus that stops eating behavior.

Although we are not certain how the lateral hypothalamus functions in hunger regulation, we do know that it facilitates the release of insulin and digestive secretions of the stomach (Morley & colleagues, 1985). It appears that the ventromedial hypothalamus (the satiety center) influences the cessation of eating behavior by monitoring glucose levels and other chemicals in the blood. When the lateral hypothalamus is damaged, it produces a condition called aphagia, in which the individual does not eat at all. When the ventromedial hypothalamus is damaged, it produces hyperphagia, a condition in which the individual continues to eat until he or she becomes obese.

Obesity   How many times have you heard people complain that after they go on a diet and lose weight it always comes back? Can those of us who are overweight help ourselves, or are we doomed to remain fat? The causes of obesity are complex, but psychologists are beginning to understand that the overweight person is not just someone without willpower.

Stanley Schachter (1971b) reported some interesting parallels between the behavior of rats that have a damaged ventromedial hypothalamus and obese human beings. Both obese people and VMH-damaged rats are less active, tend to eat faster, are more sensitive to taste (and eat more when the food tastes good), and are less willing to work for food. For example, in one experiment, Schachter gave people almonds to eat. When they were without shells, both obese and normal subjects ate them, but when they were in their shells, only the normal-weight subjects went to the trouble of shelling and eating

FIGURE 9.12   Amount of Effort Required to Eat

	Normal Weight (number of subjects)		Obese (number of subjects)	
	Eat	Not Eat	Eat	Not Eat
Almonds Still With Shells	10	10	1	19
Almonds Without Shells	11	9	19	1

Schachter (1971b) found that obese subjects were less willing than normal-weight subjects to shell almonds in order to eat them.

them. The obese subjects would not work to shell the almonds!

Richard Nisbett (1972) described a set-point theory of obesity. He suggested that, unlike the rat with a damaged VMH, the obese human might have a normally functioning hypothalamus. Perhaps the point at which the hypothalamus reacts to the blood sugar level is just set higher than usual, and the person eats to maintain the higher set point. Nisbett feels that perhaps the set point is determined by the number of fat cells in the body.

Obese people tend to have many more *fat cells* than do normal-weight people. Scientists believe that the number of fat cells is determined in the first couple of years of life, and is the result of heredity and early eating habits (Grinker, 1982). When you diet, you cause your fat cells to shrink, but you do not eliminate them. Then when you begin to overeat, the fat cells are enlarged, and you gain weight again.

McMinn (1984) pointed out that when a person decreases food intake, the body compensates by decreasing the metabolism rate. Thus, when you diet you actually use less energy. This can, of course, be counteracted by additional exercise with the dieting. Judith Rodin (1981) pointed out that basal metabolism slows down as we age, thus making it more difficult to lose weight in middle adulthood.

There is evidence that some overweight people eat when they feel stressed, anxious, or depressed. Wurtman (1987) suggested that it is possible that these obese people might have low levels of the neurotransmitter serotonin, and thus might be overeating carbohydrates to compensate. Wurtman reported that some people who are overweight feel anxious before eating carbohydrates and feel relaxed afterwards. Research is continuing to search for the physiological mechanisms that result in obesity.

Schachter (1971a) developed a theory of obesity in which he suggested that while overweight people are no more sensitive than normal-weight people to internal cues (stomach contractions), they are much more sensitive to external cues (time and the sight, smell, and taste of food). Although there is some debate as to the influence of these factors on obesity, Schachter's conclusions have practical implications for people trying to lose weight.

First, overweight people should shun situations in which external food cues are especially tempting. For example, they should avoid spending excessive time in the kitchen, and try not to have snack foods readily available.

Overweight people can learn to establish eating patterns similar to those of normal-weight people. Since overweight people cannot depend on cues to stop them from overeating, they can consider using smaller plates, taking smaller bites, chewing food longer, and leaving the table earlier.

In order to become more aware of external cues, overweight people can keep a food diary, including a list of what they eat, when they eat, how they feel when they eat, and under what circumstances they eat.

Sometimes people do not eat enough to maintain their health, as discussed in the following Application.

APPLICATION

Eating Disorders

Although most people eat to maintain normal or above-normal weight, some individuals have a problem with eating enough to stay healthy. Two major eating disorders are anorexia and bulimia.

Anorexia nervosa is an eating disorder in which the person becomes severely underweight because of self-imposed restrictions in eating. The problem is most often seen in young women and teenage girls as young as 14 years of age (Fosson & colleagues, 1987). Criteria in diagnosing anorexia from the American Psychiatric Association (1987) include intense fear of being overweight and loss of 15 percent of body weight without any physical problem that could account for it. Although cases of male anorexics have been reported, the vast majority of cases are female, with the disorder affecting as many as 1 percent of the female teenage population. Relatively few blacks experience eating disorders, although there may be difficulties in identifying those who do (Root, 1990).

The causes of anorexia have not been fully identified, but appear to include social, psychological, and physiological influences. Societal pressures for being thin, as portrayed in the media, appear influential and apparently affect females more than males. The anorexic believes that she is overweight even when she is extremely thin, suggesting a perceptual self-image problem (Striegel-Moore, Silberstein, & Rodin, 1986). Other causes focus on physiological mechanisms such as a malfunctioning hypothalamus, endocrine disorder, and brain tumor (Muuss, 1985).

People suffering from bulimia nervosa eat large amounts of calorie-rich food in a short time and then purge the food by vomiting or using laxatives. Young women are most likely to experience bulimia, with incidence levels of 4 to 13 percent of primarily college females (Johnson & Conners, 1987). While half of all bulimics are normal-weight individuals, the rest are anorexics. Recent data show anorexia and bulimia occur in Great Britain and Africa as well as North America (Dolan, 1991). Clinical symptoms are similar in all samples studied. Blacks are more likely to have both anorexia and bulimia simultaneously.

Johnson and Larson (1982) suggested that women with bulimia tended to be sad, lonely, irritable, passive, and emotionally unstable. A number of studies have reported people with bulimia have poor body images, high levels of anxiety, and generally suffer depression (Hinz & Williamson, 1987). A study by Davis and his colleagues (1988) found that the mood of bulimic subjects was more positive than a control group just before a normal meal, but more negative than usual just before a binge eating episode, suggesting the importance of emotions on the behavior of people with bulimia.

Psychologists are trying to understand the causes of anorexia and bulimia. Unfortunately, often the affected individuals are noticed only after the disorder has been continuing for some time. Efforts that focus on positive self-image and emotional stability appear to help, as do treatments that involve modifying the individual's behavior (Logue, 1991). Much more research needs to be conducted to discover the complex influences on these eating disorders.

Thirst

Normally we feel thirsty when our mouths and throats are dry. But this is not the whole story. Research has demonstrated the importance of the kidneys and hypothalamus in maintaining thirst homeostasis.

Cells in the lateral preoptic area of the hypothalamus called osmoreceptors are sensitive not only to the relative amount of water in the blood, but more particularly to cellular dehydration due to the amount of salt, which becomes concentrated as the body dehydrates from loss of water (Peck & Novin, 1971). An increase in the amount of salt in the blood will thus cause the anterior hypothalamus to signal the pituitary gland to secrete antidiuretic hormone (ADH), which causes the kidneys to slow down their production of urine. This restores body fluid. At the same time, the hypothalamus signals the brain's cortex to create a thirst drive to force the increased water intake needed to restore the normal salt level (Epstein, 1982).

Prolonged water deprivation also results in the stimulation of receptors in the kidneys. The kidneys then secrete the hormone renin that produces *angiotensin* in the bloodstream. This causes the kidneys to retain more water and stimulates the subfornical and cortex areas of the brain to create a thirst drive (Simpson & Routtenberg, 1973). Drinking more water then restores homeostasis.

Often we drink when we are not particularly thirsty. Kraly (1984) pointed out that we typically drink during mealtime. He suggested that perhaps food causes the

FIGURE 9.13 Thirst Homeostasis

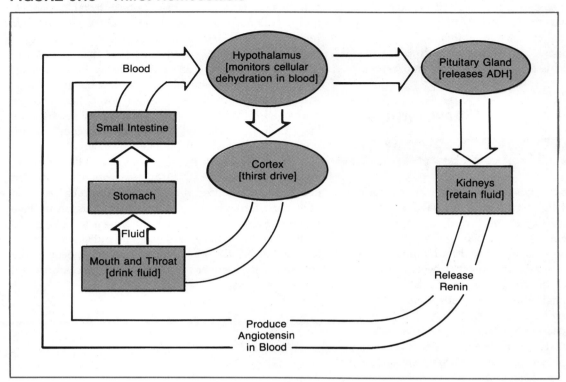

Thirst involves a variety of bodily organs and processes, including the brain, kidneys, and mouth.

gastrointestinal tract to stimulate the thirst drive. It is also likely that we learn the habit of drinking whenever we eat (Logue, 1991). Or we may drink because we have heard that health experts tell us we should drink 8 glasses of water a day. Thus, although thirst serves as an example of homeostasis, at times nonhomeostatic influences are important in thirst motivation.

Sexual Motivation

Food, water, and a moderate temperature are all necessary to keep us alive. Our drives to obtain these needs are like our drives to get enough air, to eliminate bodily wastes, to sleep, and to avoid pain. Deprivation of the goal tends to increase the drive. The longer an organism is deprived of food, the more active it becomes in searching for it (up to the point where lack of nourishment begins to slow the organism down).

Uniqueness of the Sex Drive   Sex, on the other hand, is unique. Although sex is classified as a biological drive, it is neither necessary to sustain individual life nor is it activated by deprivation. And although sex is necessary for continuation of a species, the life of an individual member of that species is not threatened by the lack of a sexual outlet.

Although the male cannot be sexually aroused for a brief period after ejaculation, and both sexes may cease sexual activity through sheer exhaustion, the sexual impulse is fairly independent of the amount of sexual deprivation. And among human beings, cognition and learning are also involved in stimulating or suppressing the motivation for sexual activity. Another way that sex is unlike the other biological drives is that individuals actively seek its arousal, since an increase in the drive is rewarding in itself. Both humans and animals will work for sexual arousal as a reward, even when there is no consummation and even though consummation produces only momentary satiation.

Animal Courtship and Mating   Although humans and other primates can be ready for sex at virtually all times, among most lower animals sexual activity is motivated largely by hormones (from ovaries or testes) plus instincts. Most commonly, when the female ovulates, her sex glands release the hormone estrogen into the bloodstream, making her sexually receptive during the period referred to as estrus.

Courtship in animals is the behavioral process whereby sexually mature individuals of a species become mating pairs. Often sensory cues in courtship attract a potential mate. Chemical odor cues often serve as sexual attractants in animals. Pheromones are chemical sub-

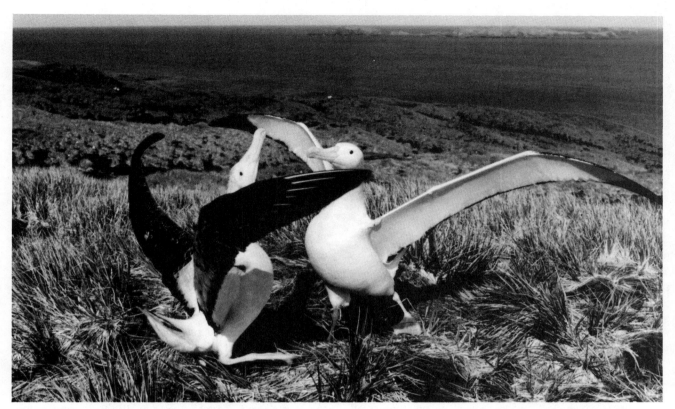

FIGURE 9.14 Animal Courtship
All male animals have certain courtship behaviors that are designed to attract a female. The wandering albatross, above left, has spread his wings and attracted a mate with his skyward screams. Now she will display her wings as they both circle each other as part of their courtship.

stances secreted by an animal that are used in communication with other members of the same species. We know that pheromones play an important role in the sexual behavior of lower animals. For example, the female cockroach produces a pheromone that attracts males from great distances. As the male cockroach approaches and his antennae touch the female, he begins to exhibit precopulatory behavior.

Among mammals, many males have scent glands that secrete pheromonal substances that attract females. For instance, deer rub their hind legs, which contain scent glands, against trees, and urine from female dogs can attract males from miles away. A number of fascinating studies have focused on pheromone effects in mice. For example, when female mice are segregated from males, they stop having regular sex cycles. But when the female mice are exposed to the odor of the urine of a male mouse, all the cycles return in synchrony. If a pregnant female comes into contact with the odor pheromone produced by an unfamiliar male, she will abort and then become sexually receptive to the new mouse.

After a mate has been found, courtship may arouse sexual motivation and synchronize the behavior of each animal so that actual mating, or copulation, can take place. Different species have evolved different behavior patterns in courtship. However, there are some common functions that courtship serves (Alcock, 1989). An animal must locate and identify a potential mate. Specific cues in the courtship pattern may differentiate closely related species, thus preventing crossbreeding and wasted energy on infertile matings. For example, different species of ducks make different head movements during courtship, and other species do not respond to these movements.

Visual or auditory cues often enhance sexual arousal. In monkeys, there is a swelling and change in coloration in the genital area of the female during estrus. And just the sound of the male cooing may provide enough stimulation for female pigeons to ovulate. Tactile stimulation may also be important in sexual motivation, as evidenced by the fact that female cats are stimulated by the male to ovulate only during copulation. This is adaptive in that it allows the cat to retain her egg until male sperm are available. In many animals, postural adjustments are required for copulation to take place. For example, in rodents such as the rat, the female must remain motionless and raise her hindquarters for the male to mount her successfully. The stereotyped court-

FIGURE 9.15 Sexual Motivation
In people, a wide variety of factors influence sexual behavior, including biological needs as well as environmental stimuli.

ship and mating activities among animals is another cue that sexual behavior is largely under biological control.

Human Sexual Motivation For human beings, sex is a very important source of motivation, but it is, literally, mostly "in the head." According to one study, college freshmen attending a lecture reported that they spent about 20 percent of their time daydreaming about sex (Cameron & colleagues, 1968). Since human sexuality is controlled by the higher brain centers that enable us to learn from experience, sexual behavior in humans is learned, even if sexual arousal and orgasm are innate.

Biological Influences on Human Sexual Motivation Men and women naturally find some people more sexually arousing than others. What motivates us to become sexually aroused? Buss (1989) argued that physical attractiveness plays an important role in the sexual attractiveness of women. The sociobiological theory proposed that physical attractiveness is related to potential reproductive success, and therefore we instinctively have certain preferences in selecting a mate (see discussion of sociobiology earlier in this chapter).

For female attractiveness, age and health are important variables (Buss, 1989). Young women who are physically healthy are more likely to be able to suc-

cessfully reproduce and raise children. Thus, according to this theory, men should be motivated to find healthy young women sexually attractive. Male attractiveness appears to depend less on physical traits and more on status in the culture, as indicated by skills and abilities. A male who has the ability to succeed is more likely to be able to provide for his family adequately, and thus a woman should be motivated to find this type of man sexually attractive.

Sex hormones are involved in human sexual motivation, although less strongly than in lower animals. In many women, sexual desire is highest just prior to ovulation, when estrogen levels are highest (Adams & colleagues, 1978). In men, sexual motivation is strongest when they are young adults and their testosterone levels are highest.

Some researchers believe that pheromones may play a role in human sexual attraction also. It is possible that human males produce a pheromone in their urine that can be detected by certain females. Research has shown that a musky substance called exaltolide can be detected by adult mature women, but not by premenstrual girls, postmenopausal women, or males of any age. And most women are most sensitive to the odor of exaltolide at the point in their menstrual cycle that they are most able to conceive (Parlee, 1983). It appears that people are sensitive to smell in sexual attraction.

The role of pheromones in human sexual behavior has also been studied. Bloom (1984) reported that people who lose the sense of smell sometimes also lose interest in sex. Morris and Udry (1978) found that when women applied perfume containing human vaginal secretions known to produce sexual arousal in monkeys, it sometimes (but not always) increased sexual activity in their husbands. Cutler and his colleagues (1986) reported that when underarm secretions of a woman were applied to the upper lip of other women, these women tended to have menstrual cycles that were synchronized to those of the donor. Further research is needed to understand better the role of pheromones on human sexual behavior.

Psychological Influences on Human Sexual Motivation We learn sexual motives and behaviors that are appropriate for our culture (Luria & colleagues, 1987). Sources of information include parents, family, friends, schools, and the mass media. Research has shown that learning is involved in what we find sexually attractive in members of the opposite sex.

Much of our motivation for engaging in specific sexual behaviors appears to be learned. Indeed, current understanding emphasizes learning in our general sexual orientation. And sexual preferences for specific physical traits in others (such as large or small breasts, or tall or short height) are learned and vary greatly among individuals (Luria & colleagues, 1987).

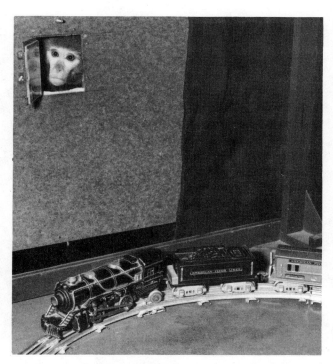

FIGURE 9.16 Exploration Motive
Butler and Harlow (1954) reported that monkeys were motivated to learn simple tasks if they were rewarded by the
novel stimulation of viewing a toy train.

Personal tastes in sexual partners and practices vary
widely, and one's preferences are culturally shaped and
may change within a lifetime (Kelly, 1992). Though it has
a basis in biology, sex plays an important role in our
psychological motivation. We discuss human sexuality, as
a part of our personality, our behavior, our emotions, and
our attitudes, in chapter 10, "Emotion."

STIMULUS MOTIVES

There appear to be certain motivating factors for
behavior that are internal and unlearned, but do not have
a physiological basis. Stimulus motives cause the individual to seek out sensory stimulation through interaction
with the environment. Stimulus motives that we cover
here include exploration, curiosity, and competence.

Exploration and Curiosity

Misty and Silver always rush around sniffing the
bushes and trees whenever they are let out in the
backyard. These two dogs are exhibiting exploration, or

sensory inspection of the environment. It's important to
know our environment, with its pleasures and its dangers.
The curiosity motive causes us to seek out a certain
amount of novelty and complexity, and with no other
apparent motivation, we seek out and explore new
environments.

Curiosity and exploration are often seen in babies.
Berlyne (1966) showed that even young babies prefer to
look at complex patterns rather than simple ones. And
babies are constantly exploring their environment, touching, tasting, looking, and listening.

As we mature, we require ever-increasing novelty
and complexity in our surroundings. We gradually lose
interest in the same situation and prefer that new elements be added, though not too many at once. Young
children will play for hours with very simple toys, but their
older brothers and sisters require more elaborate playthings. Some research suggests that our curiosity motive
remains stable as we develop (Gold & Henderson, 1990).

Curiosity is not unique to humans. Many animals
will explore a new environment with no external reward
other than the newness of what is perceived. In one study
by Butler and Harlow (1954), monkeys learned simple
discrimination tasks if they were rewarded by being
allowed to look out of a window and see a toy train.
Other experiments have demonstrated that monkeys will
work to learn how to unlock puzzles, or to open boxes,
even when there is nothing interesting inside.

Berlyne (1960) suggested that the explanation for
the curiosity motive might be simply the optimum level of

FIGURE 9.17 Curiosity Motive
Exploration and curiosity are important motivators for behavior in animals, as illustrated by these monkeys working
to unlock the boxes.

arousal tendency (discussed earlier in this chapter). We explore to raise our arousal levels, and we rest when we're too stimulated. Hebb (1966) argued that play and exploration will occur primarily when other needs are not great or demanding. Other psychologists feel curiosity might help keep track of important resources, such as food, water, shelter, and the location of friends and enemies. Whatever the answer, it is clear that we do have a need to explore the environment.

Competence

Do we engage randomly in activities in which we explore, manipulate, contact, and generally show a need for curiosity and sensory stimulation, or do our actions seem to have some purpose? A theory proposed by White (1959) suggests that we have a need to master the environment. The motivational theory of competence states that people are motivated to interact successfully with the environment. Other stimulus motives, such as curiosity and exploration, might just be ways we try to master the environment.

Even children work hard at walking, talking, and doing the basic things that will allow them to deal effectively with an increasingly complex environment. How do you feel when you have done something perfectly? Doesn't it feel great when you complete a crossword puzzle or solve a complex math problem? These feelings of competency continue to motivate us to even greater challenges. This might be why people spend hours trying to master computer and video games.

Intrinsic and Extrinsic Motivation We could say that we do things for basically two reasons: because they are fun or pleasurable (intrinsic motivation), or because they will lead to something in the environment that we want (extrinsic motivation). This could describe the difference between work and play. You might read your textbook because you enjoy it intrinsically, or you might read it to earn a good grade (extrinsic motivation) in class. Or, more likely, it is a combination of both.

A classic study by Lepper, Greene, and Nisbett (1973) with nursery children demonstrates the effects of intrinsic and extrinsic motivation. The experimenters chose children who loved to draw pictures, and told some of them to draw for fun and others to draw for a reward. They found that both groups drew good pictures, but the group that drew for the reward (extrinsic motivation) tended not to want to draw pictures later on their own. In other words, their play became work, and they only worked when rewarded. Examples of how this principle works are all around us. You may really enjoy swimming, and stay around the pool as much as possible. But when you're hired as a lifeguard, suddenly your fun becomes work, and it's not quite as enjoyable.

Expanding on White's (1959) theory of competency, Edward Deci (1975) proposed a theory of intrinsic motivation that states that we need to feel competent in controlling our environment. Intrinsic motivation causes behaviors that lead to this competency and control. We tend to do things that we enjoy and that we are good at. Our hobbies, our pastimes, our recreational outings are done largely because we find them satisfying. The rewards come from within us rather than from others.

More recently, Deci has expanded his theory of intrinsic motivation to emphasize the importance of *self-determination* (Deci, 1980; Deci & Ryan, 1985). He argued that not all extrinsic reinforcement decreases intrinsic motivation. Rewards that help people believe they have competency or self-determination can increase intrinsic motivation. Being able to determine for oneself what one does is extremely motivating. For instance, if a student receives an excellent grade on an exam for which he or she has purposively studied hard, the grade will probably encourage feelings of competency, and will likely motivate the student to continue to strive for excellence. If the student perceives the grade as an attempt to control behavior, intrinsic motivation will decrease; if it is perceived as a source of information about his or her competency, intrinsic motivation will increase.

A great deal of support for Deci's predictions has been provided by recent research studies. For instance, Curry, Wagner, and Grothaus (1990) reported that smokers with an intrinsic motivation (who were concerned about their health and their self-control) were more successful in a stop-smoking program than those with an extrinsic motivation (who were concerned with reinforcement and social influence). Vogel and Adelman (1990) reported that learning-disabled college students with high intrinsic motivation were able to graduate from college at the same rate as regular students. Participants in aerobic dance classes who perceived success in the exercise as useful information had higher intrinsic motivation than those who did not have this perception (McAuley & colleagues, 1991).

Deci believes that we need to concentrate more on intrinsic motivation and self-determination in schools and workplaces. Too often, educational and business systems depend on extrinsic reinforcement (grades or money) for control, rather than encouraging self-determination. One way to utilize intrinsic motivation is to help people do what they enjoy. For instance, instructors might have students choose individual topics to study.

LEARNED SOCIAL MOTIVES

The learned social motives are determined largely by learning and center around social experiences. Henry

Murray (1938) developed a list of human needs that are basically learned social motives. He included in his list motives such as achievement, affiliation, aggression, autonomy, dominance, nurturance, play, and understanding. Some of these motives are covered in later chapters. In this chapter the social motives of achievement, power, and affiliation are covered.

Achievement

The need for achievement, the desire to perform at some high standard of excellence, or the desire to be successful, has received considerable attention from psychologists who study learned motives. David McClelland and John Atkinson tested people's need to achieve by having them make up stories to describe what is happening in ambiguous pictures. The themes of the stories were then analyzed to identify themes involving goals and striving for success (McClelland, 1958). This test is called the Thematic Apperception Test (TAT) and is discussed in chapter 11, "Personality."

Characteristics of the Achievement Motive
Within normal limits, the need for achievement is not strongly related to ability. But people who score high on tests of need for achievement tend to do better on verbal and mathematical tests and get better grades in school. McClelland and his colleagues (1953) found that people who rank high in the need for achievement frequently have parents who demand or reward their independence as early as the second year of life. As children, for example, they are encouraged to go to bed by themselves, entertain themselves, and choose their own clothes.

McClelland (1985a) also found that the high achievers tended to assume personal responsibility for their behavior and preferred situations in which they received feedback about their performance. They also tended to be innovative in their approaches to solving problems. Veroff (1982) reported that men who scored high in achievement motivation were well adjusted in both their personal lives and their work lives.

Atkinson (1957) developed a model for understanding achievement motivation. His formula was:

$$T = M \times P \times I$$

The tendency to achieve success (T) equals the motive to achieve success (M) times the probability of success (P) times the incentive value of success (I). Thus, people who succeed must be motivated to achieve, believe there is a good chance of success, and value the achievement goal. For example, students are most likely to be successful when they are motivated to earn high grades, have a good chance of maintaining a high grade point average, and believe that high grades are important.

Fear of Failure   Research indicates that people who score low in need for achievement also tend to have a high fear of failure (Atkinson & Birch, 1978). When they have a free choice of goals, those with low need for achievement and high fear of failure scores may pick either very easy ones (thus avoiding failure) or unrealistically difficult ones (thus avoiding blame because they cannot be criticized for failing). People high in achievement motive and low in fear of failure, however, tend to choose realistically challenging goals where they run the risk of failure but also have a chance of achieving the goal.

For example, McClelland (1958) had a group of children play a ring-toss game. The children with high need for achievement tended to stand at moderate distances from the peg, while those with low need for achievement stood either very close or very far from the peg. According to McClelland, the high achiever is apparently better prepared to face failure than the low achiever, although he or she is also more realistic about evaluating the chances for success.

Fear of Success   Most of the early results in achievement motivation testing are found in research with male subjects. Female subjects don't necessarily fit the same pattern. One hypothesis developed by Matina Horner (1972) to explain the difference in achievement motivation between men and women is that, at least in our society, women have a motive to avoid success. The socialization process most women undergo in the United States creates in them the fear of negative consequences if they successfully compete in traditionally "male" achievement situations that have been defined as inappropriate for their sex. According to Horner, women are therefore faced with a conflict between their motive to achieve and their motive to avoid success. In one study, Horner asked men and women college students to complete a story about a person who was at the top of the class after first-term finals. The men wrote about "John" while the women wrote about "Anne." Only 9 percent of the men showed fear of success in their stories, whereas 65 percent of the women showed fear of success in theirs.

This conclusion has been seriously questioned by others (Zuckerman & Wheeler, 1975). Later studies showed that both men and women included more fear of success in Anne when she was in a nontraditional role (medical school) instead of a traditional role (high school). Karabenick (1977) found that a high fear of success hurt the performance of women competing with men only when the task was believed to be masculine.

Perhaps the attitude of women is more one of not wanting to reverse sex roles than of avoiding success.

Achievement Motivation in Blacks One line of research on fear of success has focused on black males and females. A 1974 study by Fleming found that 29 percent of black college women demonstrated fear of success, compared to 67 percent of black college men. In later studies, Fleming found the sex difference tended to disappear, as the sex difference among white subjects did in Horner's studies. George (1986) reported that 10th-grade black and white female students did not differ in their responses to fear of success situations, but there were differences between those from an upper-class environment and those from a lower-class home.

Psychologists are interested in the causes of racial differences in achievement motivation and academic performance. Galicki and McEwen (1989) reported that black college students are more likely to drop out of school than white students. Fordham and Ogbu (1986) argued that an important reason that some black students do poorly in school is their ambivalence toward achieving success as defined by a white culture. Fleming (1983) reported that black men who were high in fear of success tended to be very successful socially at a predominantly white college, probably because they were sensitive about being too assertive and thus had been careful to conform and "fit in" in order to be accepted by their white peers. This research demonstrates the complexity of influences on achievement motivation.

Achievement Styles One approach now being examined in achievement motivation is achievement style, or how we behave in achievement situations (Lipman-Blumen & colleagues, 1983). Three achievement styles have been identified. In the *direct style*, people face achievement situations head-on and use their own resources to gain success. The salesperson who makes many sales calls and puts in long hours has a direct style. In the *instrumental style*, people get other people to help them achieve their goals. The boss who takes full credit for the efforts of her subordinates uses the instrumental style. In the *relational style*, people obtain success through their association with other people's work. An individual who is part of a baseball team shares the success of the entire team. Research is currently being conducted to understand how these achievement styles are learned, and whether or not they change over time.

Power

The need for power involves the desire to control or exert influence (Veroff, 1957, 1982). Power is one way that we can influence others when we want something

from them. Winter (1973) found that people with a high power motive had problems establishing close interpersonal relationships, as they typically attempt to control the relationship. Fodor (1984) reported that people with a high need for power become anxious and stressed when a situation requires their leadership but they cannot gain control. They also tend to take risks, drink alcohol more often, and behave more recklessly (for example, gambling or driving a car unsafely) than those with a low need for power.

Other research indicates people with a high need for power can be very successful in life (McClelland, 1978). They become leaders and are able to exert influence to accomplish things. McClelland pointed out that leadership does not necessarily mean a dictatorship. Successful leaders are able to make others feel important and often enter careers in which they can make an impact on others.

The power motive tends to operate in a similar fashion for both men and women (Winter, 1982). However, because of differences in sex-role expectations, the expression of the motive might differ. For instance, Winter argued that men with a high need for power are more likely to fight, gamble, and take risks, whereas women are more likely to show more socially responsible behavior (such as taking action and making appropriate decisions). Most research suggests that the power motive is a fairly stable personality characteristic, learned early in life, and expressed in a wide variety of situations.

Affiliation

A person expresses his or her need for affiliation by seeking out and forming attachments to other individuals, and by working toward belonging to, and being accepted by, groups of people. The need is both a personality trait and a motive (McClelland, 1985b). As a personality trait, it remains fairly constant for each individual throughout life, although it varies from person to person. As a motive within the individual, it is a state that is aroused on some occasions much more than on others.

Individuals with a high affiliation motive are likely to be found with other people. Constantian (1981) conducted a study in which a group of students wore beepers for a week, and at random intervals were asked to report what they were doing. He found that those with a high need for affiliation were significantly more likely to be interacting with others than were those who had a low affiliation motive. Individuals with a high need for affiliation also tended to avoid competition and conflict, and hence did not often succeed in management positions. Some research suggests that people with a very high need to affiliate are less popular, more anxious about

="Learned Social Motives 229">

FIGURE 9.18 Schachter's Study of Affiliation

	Social Waiting Selection	
Experimental Condition	Together	Alone or Don't Care
High Anxiety	20	12
Low Anxiety	10	20

In his study on the relationship between anxiety and affiliation among college women, Schachter (1959) found that the need for affiliation increases under high anxiety conditions.

social relationships, and fear disapproval of others than those with a moderately high need. Crowne and Marlowe (1964) reported that individuals with a very high need for affiliation tend also to score high on the need for social approval.

The need for affiliation becomes particularly intense during periods of anxiety. This became evident in a classic series of experiments conducted by Stanley Schachter (1959). He aroused the anxiety of female subjects by getting them to believe that they were about to participate in an experiment in which they would receive severe electric shocks. The subjects were greeted by an ominous-looking "Dr. Zilstein," who told them the scientific importance of the experiment and assured them that they would receive no permanent damage from the shocks. Clearly visible to them was a sinister piece of apparatus, embedded in a maze of wires. When given a choice of waiting for their turns alone in a comfortable waiting room furnished with magazines, or with the other subjects in an empty classroom, the large majority chose to wait together, demonstrating what has been termed the need for affiliation.

Schachter gave the same choice to another group (the control group), whose anxiety had not been aroused. They were also told they would receive shocks, but they would feel only a tingling sensation. This "low-anxiety" group showed much less interest in waiting in

FIGURE 9.19 Affiliation
Most people have a need to be with others. The need for affiliation is both a personality trait and a motive for behavior.

the company of other subjects. (See Figure 9.18.) The arousal of the affiliation motive indicates that in some circumstances, at least, misery loves miserable company. Further research indicates that we choose to be with others during a frightening situation in order to see how others react, and to gauge the appropriateness of our own reactions.

People vary considerably in their need to affiliate with others, and this need affects their performance. In our society, a man who shows a need for social support may be thought to be weak, while the same apparent need may be thought charmingly feminine in a woman. The evidence indicates that all people need some social support—at least praise and assurance that they are competent and doing a good job—but that often the most seemingly independent people are the ones who received the most social support in early childhood. ■

Human behavior is extremely complex, and thus it isn't too hard to understand why any one theory of motivation cannot explain everything that we do. As discussed in the opening story, psychologists are working to discover how the brain influences our motivation. Research is also uncovering motives for biological functions such as eating and drinking as well as social interactions and personal achievement. The next time you take a break from studying, spend a minute considering the theories of motivation we have discussed in this chapter and review the possible motives for your decision to stop studying.

CHAPTER REVIEW

What You've Learned About Motivation

1. Motivation can be thought of as the forces that initiate and direct behavior, and the variables that determine the intensity and persistence of that behavior. Motives arouse and direct the individual's behavior toward some goal.

2. Instinct is a behavior that is inherited by all members of a species. Ethologists study how instinctive behavior evolved among related species and how it now improves survival. An ethogram is a description of all the behaviors shown by a species. Fixed action patterns are unlearned, inherited, stereotyped behaviors that are species-specific and are stimulated by specific cues in the environment, called releasers. Sociobiology is the study of the biological basis of social behavior. Freud proposed that behavior is caused by life instincts (sex) and death instincts (aggression).

3. Drive involves the internal forces that push us toward doing something. The drive theory of motivation suggests that a biological need (such as for food) causes a psychological drive (such as hunger). This drive motivates the individual to engage in goal-directed behavior (eating). This cycle is called homeostasis, keeping the body's internal environment in balance.

4. The incentive theory proposes that stimuli in the environment motivate the individual in the absence of any apparent biological need. These incentives, like ice cream or money, are learned, and do not depend on deprivation. We tend to approach positive incentives and avoid negative incentives.

5. Sensory information provides both an arousal and a cue function. The arousal theory suggests that we have a certain level of arousal that we try to maintain by either seeking additional stimulation or avoiding excitement. People with high optimum levels of arousal will seek thrills and adventure, whereas those with low sensation-seeking needs try to keep stimulation low.

6. Maslow's hierarchy of needs is a humanistic theory that incorporates several different types of needs. People first must satisfy physiological needs, which include hunger, thirst, and sex. Safety needs include security, stability, protection, and freedom from fear and anxiety. Belongingness and love needs include motives such as love and affection. Esteem needs include a high evaluation of oneself, self-respect, self-esteem, and the esteem of others. When these needs have been met, people are motivated by self-actualization, the full realization of one's potential.

7. The cognitive approach to motivation emphasizes thinking and perceptual interpretation. People develop cognitive expectancies when they learn that certain behaviors lead to certain goals. Attribution involves the cognitive process of determining the motives of someone's behavior.

8. Biological motives have a definite physiological basis and are related to survival of the individual or species. Hunger motivation includes factors such as stomach contractions, the release of the hormone CCK, and the monitoring of glucose levels by the liver. The hypothalamus monitors blood chemistry and influences the starting (lateral hypothalamus) and stopping (ventromedial hypothalamus) of eating. Recent work on obesity suggests that overweight people are more sensitive to external environmental stimuli and have more fat cells than normal-weight individuals.

9. Thirst is regulated by a variety of variables, including the mouth, kidneys, and the hypothalamus. Low levels of water in the body cause the anterior hypothalamus to signal the pituitary gland to secrete antidiuretic hormone, which causes the kidneys to slow down production of urine. The hypothalamus signals the cortex to create a thirst drive.

10. The sex motive is unique because it is not essential for individual survival, doesn't depend on deprivation, and allows the individual to seek its arousal. Courtship in animals is the behavioral process whereby sexually mature individuals of a species become mating pairs. In people, learning and experience are important variables in sexual motivation.

11. Stimulus motives cause the individual to seek out sensory stimulation through interaction with the environment. They are internal and unlearned, but do not appear to have a physiological basis. Exploration is the sensory inspection of the environment, whereas curiosity is the seeking out of novelty and complexity to maintain an optimum level of arousal.

12. The theory of competence proposes that people are motivated to interact successfully with the environment. Intrinsic motivation causes someone to do something for internal satisfaction, whereas extrinsic motivation causes someone to work for environmental rewards. Intrinsic motivation leads to competency in controlling the environment.

13. Learned social motives are complex human motives determined largely by learning and social experience. The need for achievement is the desire to perform at a high standard of excellence. People low in achievement need are motivated to fear failure. People high in achievement motive tend to choose goals that are more challenging.

14. The need for power involves the desire to control or exert influence. The power motive is learned early in life and expressed in a wide variety of situations.

15. The need for affiliation is the desire to seek out and form attachments to other individuals. As a motive, the need for affiliation increases during periods of anxiety and stress.

CHAPTER OBJECTIVES

What You'll Learn About Emotion

After studying this chapter, you should be able to:

1. Define the concept of emotion.
2. Describe the physiological characteristics of emotions.
3. Outline the development and classification of emotions.
4. State the James-Lange theory of emotion.
5. State the Cannon-Bard theory of emotion.
6. State the Schachter-Singer arousal-cognition theory of emotion.
7. State the Plutchik functional theory of emotion.
8. State the cognitive-motivational-relational theory of emotion.
9. State the opponent-process theory of emotion.
10. Define interpersonal attraction and identify three variables that influence liking.
11. Outline five important theories of love.
12. Describe how people communicate emotions nonverbally.
13. Outline sex determination and define gender identity.
14. Outline the human sexual response cycle.
15. Identify the major human sexual behaviors and problems.

In 1962 Stanley Schachter and Jerome Singer conducted an interesting experiment to test the influence of social and cognitive (thinking) factors on emotion. They hypothesized that the emotions we feel are due to our interpretation of the physiological arousal we experience. In other words, according to the circumstances of the situation that caused the arousal, we attribute the arousal to a particular emotion.

They designed an experiment in which they deliberately produced physiological arousal in subjects, manipulated the explanation provided to the subjects on the cause of their arousal, and created emotional situations that could be used to interpret the nature of the arousal. The research involved 136 male students at the University of Minnesota.

The subjects were told that the study was designed to test how their vision was affected by the use of vitamin supplements. All of the subjects (except the one who refused) received an injection of what they thought was a vitamin solution called "suproxin." Three-fourths of the subjects received an injection of epinephrine (adrenaline), whereas the others received a placebo (a harmless saline solution).

Epinephrine is a stimulant that produces the effects found in many emotions, including increased blood pressure and heart rate, trembling hands, flushed face, and rapid breathing. The reaction to the epinephrine generally began within 5 minutes of the injection and lasted about 15 to 20 minutes. The saline that was given as a placebo did not produce any physiological reaction in the subjects.

Schachter and Singer divided the subjects into three experimental groups (all of whom received epinephrine) and a control group (who received the placebo). The

Although not easily understood, emotions are very important in our lives. Psychologists have developed a variety of theories to try to explain emotions. They have studied love and nonverbal emotional communication between people intensively in recent years, as well as human sexuality.

10

Emotion

"epinephrine informed" subjects were told about the effects of the drug, and thus they knew the cause of the physiological arousal they experienced. The "epinephrine ignorant" group was not told anything about the effects of the drug. The "epinephrine misinformed" subjects were told that side effects might temporarily make them have an itching sensation, numb feet, and a headache. The subjects who received the "placebo" were not told anything about what to expect from the injection.

After the injection, each subject sat in a waiting room with one other person (who was actually working with the experimenters). In some cases, the experimenters' accomplice pretended to be euphoric, carrying on in high spirits by throwing wadded-up paper into a waste basket, playing with a hula hoop, or flying paper airplanes. In other cases, the accomplice acted bitter, angry, and dissatisfied with the testing situation, and complained about having to fill out a questionnaire (the subjects in this "angry" situation were asked to fill out a long questionnaire that included questions about all the food eaten in a typical day, whether the subject bathed regularly, how often the subject had sex, and how many extramarital affairs the subject's mother had). All four groups of subjects were tested in the euphoric situation, whereas only three groups were tested in the angry situation (the epinephrine misinformed group was not tested in the angry situation since it was planned as a control group).

Two psychological measures of emotion were used in the experiment. An observer recorded each subject's behavior through a one-way mirror, and each subject was asked to fill out a questionnaire on which he reported on his mood and physical reaction.

Physiologically, the subjects who received the epinephrine were significantly aroused and those who re-

ceived the placebo were not (their pulse rates actually decreased slightly). Psychologically, subjects tended to show more of the emotion presented in a particular situation (happy or angry) when they did not have an explanation for their arousal than when they did. For the euphoric situation, both in the self-report and the behavior observation, subjects in the epinephrine misinformed group showed the greatest happiness, followed by subjects in the epinephrine ignorant group, placebo group, and the epinephrine informed group. The same pattern occurred for the angry situation, although subjects were, according to the experimenters, reluctant to report anger on the self-report scale.

The epinephrine groups responded in the predicted pattern (most emotion shown by euphoric misinformed and euphoric and angry ignorant subjects, least emotion shown by euphoric and angry informed subjects), but the placebo subjects did not (they showed more emotion than the epinephrine informed subjects).

When the subjects were physiologically aroused by the drug, they labeled the emotion according to the environment. Those ignorant of the drug's true nature were guided by the situation, that is, by which type of person they were with, and labeled the emotion accordingly. Those who knew the truth about the drug identified epinephrine correctly as the source of the arousal, and hence did not display the same situational emotion as the others. Schachter and Singer concluded that we do interpret our arousal according to our environmental situation and label our emotions appropriately. This theory has come to be known as the arousal-cognition theory. Its results have not been accepted by all psychologists. We discuss some of the criticism of this experimental method later in the chapter.

WHAT IS EMOTION?

One conclusion about Schachter and Singer's research is that different emotions appear to have a similar physiological arousal base. The word "emotion" comes from the Latin term *emovere*, which means to disturb or move away. Probably because they have similar origins, emotion and motivation are similar in many ways. Emotions often accompany many of our motivations.

For a hundred years psychologists have tried to define emotion scientifically. There is no complete agreement on any one definition, partially because emotions are complex private events that are difficult to understand—in ourselves and in others.

Robert Plutchik (1980) reviewed 28 definitions of emotion that have been proposed over the past century. William James (1884) argued that emotion is the feeling of the bodily changes that take place as a reaction to something exciting occurring in the environment. Sigmund Freud (1915) stated that emotions are involved with physiological discharges that result in feelings. The behaviorist John Watson (1924) defined emotion as a hereditary pattern-reaction that involves the visceral and glandular systems. Robert Plutchik (1962) described emotion as a patterned bodily reaction brought about by a stimulus. Carroll Izard (1972) included neurophysiologi-

FIGURE 10.1 Components of Emotion
An emotion involves many things: physiological arousal, subjective feeling, cognitive interpretation, and overt behavior.

cal, motor, and phenomenological aspects in his conceptualization of emotion.

Frijda (1988) proposed several laws of emotion that emphasize the universal nature of our emotional experiences. For example, the law of situational meaning states that different emotions occur in response to different situations. The law of concern states that emotions occur in response to events that are important to an individual's goals and motives. The law of apparent reality states that emotions are caused by events the individual perceives as real. The law of change states that emotions occur in response to the individual's expected changes in favorable or unfavorable conditions. And the fact that continued pleasure loses its positive feeling is explained in the law of habituation.

We define emotion as a response to a stimulus that involves physiological arousal, subjective feeling, cognitive interpretation, and overt behavior. Psychologists have studied emotions from the four different approaches included in this definition: physiological arousal, subjective feeling, cognition, and behavior. Physiological arousal is a part of all emotions. Although there are minor differences in the physiological mechanisms involved in separate emotions, physiological processes in emotion can be viewed as a general arousal phenomenon. Usually, the stronger the arousal the more intense the emotional experience.

All of our emotions include the subjective feeling that is identified as the emotional experience. If asked what emotion you are experiencing right now, you might respond "I feel happy," "I am angry," or "I feel afraid." Scientists have difficulty studying emotions because they are such subjective experiences. Russell and his colleagues (1989) found that people from several different cultures tended to perceive emotions along two dimensions: arousal (the physiological component) and pleasantness (the subjective feeling component). Our subjective feelings are ordered along a continuum from unpleasant to pleasant.

Many psychologists believe that cognitive processes are essential to emotions, while others argue that cognition is not necessary and emphasize only the emotional experience instead. Averill (1983) suggested that cognition intervenes between the environmental stimulus and the resulting behavioral response. In other words, cognitive interpretation of the stimulus serves as the trigger for the emotional experience.

A debate on the importance of cognition in emotion is currently being conducted between two prominent psychologists. Richard Lazarus (1984, 1991a) from the University of California at Berkeley argues that cognitive interpretation is essential and must come before the subjective feeling. University of Michigan psychologist Robert Zajonc (1984) argues that feeling is universal, and cognition is independent and not necessary for the emotional experience. Zajonc states that we don't know whether animals think, but we do know that they show emotions and that much of emotional expression is nonverbal, suggesting an independence from cognitive activities. Although we will discuss the role of cognition in emotional theories, keep in mind that the issue of cognition is not yet settled.

Overt behavior can be used to infer the emotional state of the individual. Sometimes we can interpret facial expressions or behaviors (Ekman, 1985). For example, laughing is almost always an indication of a pleasant emotion. Sometimes, however, the emotion is difficult to identify from the behavior alone. For example, why do we cry? Perhaps it's because we're sad at a funeral; or it may be because we're happy at a wedding. Or it may be because we're peeling onions. Interpreting emotion depends upon our understanding of a combination of physiological, subjective feeling, cognitive, and behavioral elements.

CHARACTERISTICS OF EMOTION

As we learned in the opening story, different emotions often have a similar physiological basis. Because the physiology of emotions is the best understood component of emotion, we start our discussion here. Then we describe what is known about the development and classification of emotions.

Physiology of Emotion

You are walking home about midnight. You are all alone, and, although you know you shouldn't, you decide to take a shortcut through an empty parking lot. Halfway across, you begin to hear footsteps behind you. You turn around and see someone coming straight toward you. What physiological changes occur in your body?

The pupils of your eyes dilate so that you are able to see more of the emergency situation. The blood vessels leading to the stomach constrict and digestion falters, while those leading to the skeletal muscles dilate, assuring that enough blood will reach these muscles in case you have to fight or run. Your breathing and heart rate both increase to provide more oxygen and blood to all muscles. You sweat to reduce the heat you're generating. Your pancreas secretes the hormone *glucagon* into the bloodstream to trigger the release of sugar for extra energy. And the adrenal glands secrete the hormones *epinephrine* and *norepinephrine* so that these arousal reactions will continue as long as the emergency lasts.

FIGURE 10.2 Physiological Arousal in Emotion

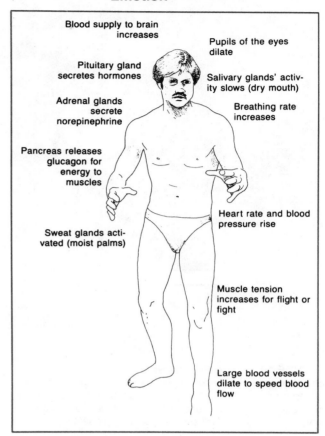

Blood supply to brain increases

Pupils of the eyes dilate

Pituitary gland secretes hormones

Salivary glands' activity slows (dry mouth)

Adrenal glands secrete norepinephrine

Breathing rate increases

Pancreas releases glucagon for energy to muscles

Heart rate and blood pressure rise

Sweat glands activated (moist palms)

Muscle tension increases for flight or fight

Large blood vessels dilate to speed blood flow

The entire body responds to an emergency situation through physiological arousal.

These physiological changes are due mainly to the action of the *sympathetic nervous system*. In chapter 2, "Psychobiology," we learned that the sympathetic nervous system produces arousal in times of emergency, while the parasympathetic nervous system tends to relax the body during normal circumstances. Both of these systems are branches of the autonomic nervous system.

Although the general physiological arousal of the sympathetic nervous system is apparently similar for different emotions, a few studies found slight variations. Ax (1953) found that during the emotional state of fear, greater amounts of epinephrine and norepinephrine are both secreted than they are during other emotions. Ekman, Levenson, and Friesen (1983) found subjects who thought about emotional states showed physiological responses that differed slightly for each emotion. For instance, heart rate increased more when the subjects posed for anger or fear than for happiness, and skin temperature increased more for anger than other emotions. Other studies have not found any differences among emotions. For example, Averill (1969) had one

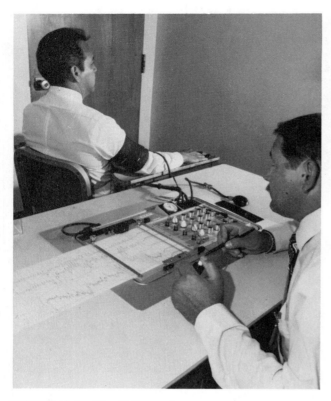

FIGURE 10.3   The Polygraph
Physiological responses such as heart rate, respiration, blood pressure, and GSR can be measured by polygraphs. Sometimes used as lie detectors, they actually measure only arousal and not the cause of that arousal.

group of subjects watch a sad movie while another group watched a comedy. There were no significant differences between groups in physiological responses to the movies. Overall, it appears that any physiological differences that might exist with emotional states are relatively minor.

The brain is also involved in emotions. The cortex is important for interpreting the emotion. The *limbic system*, especially the *hypothalamus* and *amygdala*, also plays a vital role in emotion. Paul MacLean (1968) proposed that the limbic system is involved in the emotions necessary for survival. Emotions such as fear, anger, and joy have evolved because they are related to basic survival behaviors.

Some physiological arousal reactions can be measured with a polygraph (sometimes called a lie detector). Polygraphs are instruments that record a variety of physiological responses, including heart rate, respiration rate, blood pressure, and GSR (galvanic skin response). The GSR is a measure of a change in the electrical resistance of the skin. Our skin is capable of conducting a very slight electrical current. When we feel an emotion, we are likely to sweat, and there will be a change in the current flowing across the surface of the skin. The skin conducts the electricity more readily when we sweat, thereby causing a

change in the skin's electrical resistance (GSR). The polygraph measures this change.

The basic idea is that physiological arousal is an indicator of emotion that can be registered by a polygraph. In practice, however, polygraphs are far from perfect and are not usually accepted as evidence in court cases. Part of the problem is that the polygraph cannot always distinguish between the fearful, anxious, innocent person and the guilty one. Although polygraphs can show that a person is physiologically aroused, they cannot interpret the particular cause of the arousal (Saxe, Doughterty, & Cross, 1985).

Development and Classification of Emotions

Are emotions innate or must we learn them? Charles Darwin (1872) suggested in *The Expression of Emotion in Man and Animals* that emotions are similar in animals and people and have evolved to aid in their survival. Dogs bare their teeth when they are aggressive. When people are outraged and scream at one another, they also bare their teeth. Darwin thought emotional expressions like baring the teeth are innate patterns of behavior.

Development of Emotions   Katherine Bridges (1932) was one of the first psychologists to study the development of emotions. In her naturalistic observation of 62 infants from the Montreal Foundling and Baby Hospital, she found that, beginning at birth, infants exhibit a general excitement, with both negative and positive emotions developing within a few months. As to the negative emotions, general distress appears first, with anger, disgust, and fear developing by 6 or 8 months. The positive emotions develop more slowly, with general delight becoming affection and joy during the second year of life. According to Bridges, a wide range of positive emotions are identifiable by the time an infant is 2 years old. Although this study has been influential in psychology, questions have arisen concerning the validity of generalizing the findings to home-reared infants and the reliability of the observations (Plutchik, 1980).

Carroll Izard and his colleagues at the University of Delaware (1980) have been studying the emotional expressions in very young infants. In one study, college students were able to identify the facial expressions of 5- to 9-month-old infants as joy, fear, sadness, anger, and surprise. Although it is not possible to determine whether the infants actually experienced these emotions, they were able to show expressions at this early age that were interpreted as appropriate emotions.

Learning is also very important in emotion, and many emotions appear to be learned through conditioning. In chapter 4, "Learning," we learned that the fear response was classically conditioned in Little Albert. Although many emotional expressions appear universal, differences in learning are responsible for cultural variations. One early study by Klineberg (1938) demonstrated that some of the expressions of emotion in Chinese culture are different from those in our culture. In Chinese society, sticking out your tongue indicates surprise, while opening your eyes wide can suggest anger, and clapping can indicate disappointment. Despite cultural variations, it is recognized that emotions are a part of all human experiences.

Paul Ekman has studied facial expressions of emotions. He found that people are capable of 7,000 possible facial muscle combinations, allowing a wide variety of emotional expressions. Since cultures throughout the world can correctly identify almost all the emotions being expressed facially, Ekman and his colleagues (1987) argue that emotions are biologically based.

According to Ekman (1985), lower brain stem areas produce spontaneous emotional expressions, whereas the cortex of the brain is involved in voluntary emotions. Thus, he predicted that differences between the left and right hemispheres should be apparent in voluntary but not spontaneous expressions of emotion. When he observed people who were smiling because of genuine enjoyment, their smiles were symmetrical, whereas when subjects were asked to pose, their smiles were asymmetrical, usually with an exaggeration on the left side of the face. Ekman argued that this might be one way to determine whether an emotion is real.

Classification of Emotions   No one is sure how many emotions we can actually experience. Many psychologists have attempted to draw up lists of the basic emotions. William McDougall (1921) proposed a list of seven basic instincts, each with a corresponding emotion. Some of the instincts (with their corresponding emotions) included flight (fear), repulsion (disgust), curiosity (wonder), pugnacity (anger), and self-assertion (elation). Although McDougall's theory is interesting, it was abandoned when psychology became dominated by behaviorism in the 1920s.

Today, psychologists have a number of classification schemes. James Russell (1980) proposed the circumplex model of emotion, in which emotions are arranged in a circular pattern along two dimensions (arousal and pleasantness). The emotions tend to be paired as opposites, such as happy-sad, tense-relaxed, excited-bored, and delighted-depressed.

Sylvan Tomkins (1964, 1981) proposed that there are eight basic emotions: interest, surprise, enjoyment, distress, fear, shame, contempt, and anger. These emotions are innate and expressed through bodily reactions such as facial expressions. Tomkins argued that emotions

FIGURE 10.4   Identifying Emotions
How do we identify emotions? Often facial expressions are used as clues, as suggested in this photo.

are the intensified motives that in turn are a reflection of bodily needs.

Carroll Izard (1979) proposed that there are 10 basic emotions: interest, joy, surprise, distress, anger, disgust, contempt, fear, shame, and guilt. Each basic emotion has its own neural network in the brain, its own characteristic behavioral reaction (usually involving facial expression), and its own subjective feeling. Izard suggested that the emotions we experience are innate and adaptive for the individual or species, and therefore constitute the basic motivational system for human behavior.

One of the most complete classification attempts of emotions was described by Robert Plutchik (1980). Through extensive questionnaires, he arrived at eight basic emotions: joy, acceptance, fear, surprise, sadness, disgust, anger, and anticipation. These primary emotions can combine to form secondary emotions. For example, joy and acceptance form love, fear and acceptance form submission, and anger and anticipation form aggressiveness. He placed these emotions in a circle in such a way that the emotions across from each other are opposites (for instance, joy and sadness).

In addition to combining, Plutchik stated that each basic emotion can vary in intensity. For example, grief and pensiveness are different degrees of sadness, rage and annoyance are degrees of anger, and terror and

FIGURE 10.5   Plutchik's Theory of Emotions

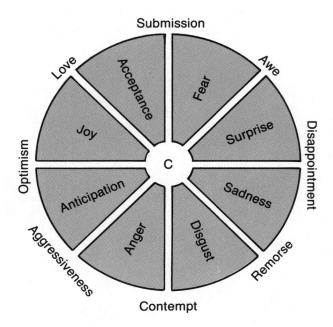

The eight primary emotions can be arranged in a circle that helps demonstrate their relationships. Plutchik explains that these primary emotions combine to form secondary and tertiary emotions. The C at the center of the circle indicates that conflict results from the mixture of the emotions (after Plutchik, 1980).

apprehension are degrees of fear. Plutchik has developed the *Emotions Profile Index (EPI)* to identify personality dispositions based on emotional responses. He has developed an elaborate scheme relating emotions to adaptive functions and personality. For instance, the emotion of fear is expressed by escape behavior, serves the function of protection, and is associated with a timid personality. The emotion of anger is expressed by attack behavior, serves the function of destruction, and is associated with an aggressive personality. Although psychologists have not completely agreed on definitions or classifications, research is continuing in this important area.

THEORIES OF EMOTION

Dozens of theories have been proposed to explain emotions. Perhaps because emotion is a private, subjective experience, or because it is such a conglomeration of potential feelings, we cannot agree on one definitive theory. Because of their historical value, several theories are notable, while a couple of contemporary concepts are gaining recognition.

The James-Lange Theory

It seems obvious to most of us that an emotion occurs before we act on it: we run away because we are afraid; we fight because we are angry; we cry because we feel sad. Working separately, William James (1884) and Carl Lange (1885) each came up with similar ideas that took the view of emotion that behavior precedes feeling. Usually called the James-Lange theory of emotion, it states that we feel sad because we are crying. Our bodies automatically react to certain environmental stimuli and we recognize these reactions (both our behavior and the physiological arousal) as making up a certain emotion that we then feel. The physiological arousal and behavior come first and the subjective experience of the emotion comes second. Thus, we are angry because we are fighting, and we are afraid because we are trembling.

If recognizing a certain emotion is just recognizing a physical state of the body, then there must be different and quite distinct physiological states for each emotion. Some research suggests that there are some slight differences in the physiological arousal for different emotions. For example, McGeer and McGeer (1980) reviewed several studies that indicated that the hormone epinephrine is secreted during anger or aggression, while norepinephrine is more likely to be secreted during fear or anxiety. Other studies have not found this difference. Indeed, as shown in our opening story, many emotions appear to have about the same physiological symptoms.

FIGURE 10.6   James-Lange Theory of Emotion
Have you ever been in an emergency situation and immediately afterward began to feel frightened? The James-Lange theory states that the feeling of fear comes after the physiological change and behavior.

WILLIAM JAMES

William James was born in New York City in 1842. He was the son of wealthy parents whose enthusiasm for their children's education sent young James traveling throughout Europe. His formative years were spent in the best schools of France, Germany, Switzerland, and the United States.

He vacillated from one interest to another, studying painting, chemistry, biology, and medicine. In 1869 he received a medical degree from Harvard University. Finally, at the age of 30, he accepted the teaching position at Harvard that launched his outstanding career in psychology.

In 1875 James established at Harvard one of the first psychology demonstration teaching laboratories in the world. Three years later, at the age of 36, he married a Boston schoolteacher and began writing his most famous work, *Principles of Psychology*, which, to his publisher's dismay, took him almost 12 years to complete.

James enjoyed great popularity as a lecturer at Harvard and was remembered by students as a vivacious personality whose extravagant sense of humor and picturesque language set him apart from the typical professor. His interests were tremendously varied: he wrote about such topics as habit, consciousness, personality, emotion, and religion.

James continued to write, lecture, and travel until his death in 1910 at his country home in New Hampshire.

Sometimes it seems that in an emergency we react swiftly at the moment and then begin feeling the emotion a few minutes later. When we see a car approaching rapidly as we cross the street, first we jump quickly to safety and then we feel fear (or anger). Members of the armed forces who have been decorated for valor under fire have expressed a similar experience: they were unafraid until later. Many scientists have previously criticized the James-Lange theory for being basically untestable.

Some recent evidence has begun to suggest that the James-Lange concept of behavior-then-emotion could have some truth in it (Izard, 1990). How do you feel when you walk briskly as opposed to walking slowly and carefully? Probably the brisk walk is accompanied by a more positive emotion (try it for yourself and see). Zajonc, Murphy, and Inglehart (1989) recently argued that facial expressions can influence the blood flow to the brain and affect the release of neurotransmitters that modify our feelings.

The Cannon-Bard Theory

One criticism of the James-Lange theory was that most emotions have nearly identical arousal. Walter Cannon (1927) and Philip Bard (1928) both proposed that when a person perceives an environmental stimulus, the thalamus in the brain reacts. According to this theory, the thalamus simultaneously sends impulses to the cortex of the brain and controls the sympathetic nervous system in its general physiological arousal. Therefore, the emotional feeling and the physiological arousal occur at the same time.

The Cannon-Bard theory of emotion has been shown to be somewhat incorrect. The hypothalamus is central to the experience of emotion rather than the thalamus, as was first proposed. However, like the James-Lange theory, it is impossible to test accurately whether the feeling occurs with or after the physiological changes. As we learned in our opening story, a theory by Schachter and Singer emphasizes cognitive factors in influencing emotions.

The Schachter-Singer Arousal-Cognition Theory

Our opening story described the classic experiment conducted by Stanley Schachter and Jerome Singer in 1962. They argued that any differences that exist in the physiological arousal of emotions are relatively minor, and that cognition plays a major role in determining emotions. The Schachter-Singer theory of emotion states that when we experience an emotion we are first physiologically aroused. Then we look for an environmental explanation for our arousal. We interpret our situation cognitively and label our arousal as an appropriate emotion.

Not all psychologists accept Schachter and Singer's results. For instance, Maslach (1979) found that subjects who were given an arousing drug always reacted negatively, regardless of the social environment. Reisenzein (1983) argued that arousal is not as important as cognition in emotional states. Leventhal and Tomarken (1986) reviewed a number of studies that could not replicate Schachter and Singer's findings. The emphasis on cognition, however, has continued to play an important role in the study of emotion.

One criticism of the Schachter and Singer study focuses on the procedure they used to eliminate certain subjects (Plutchik, 1980). For example, five subjects in the epinephrine groups were eliminated because they did not show physiological arousal, and a subject in the group that received a placebo was eliminated because of equipment failure. The experimenters have also been criticized for using heart rate as the measure of arousal, as heart rate by itself is not always an accurate measure. Even though it has been criticized, the Schachter and Singer theory of emotion has been very influential on research in this area and has helped focus attention on cognitive processes in emotion.

The Plutchik Functional Theory

Robert Plutchik (1980) described a functional theory of emotion. He perceived emotion as a chain reaction sequence: stimulus event, cognition, feeling, and behavior related to survival. For example, if you were approached by a stranger in a parking lot, the chain would include: the sight of the stranger (stimulus event), thinking of danger (cognition), experiencing fear (feeling), and running away (behavior). The outcome would provide feedback to help you deal with the situation in the future. This sequence would be followed for the emotion of fear, whose function is protection. Each primary emotion serves a particular function. Other examples include surprise (orientation), disgust (rejection), anger (destruction), and anticipation (exploration).

Plutchik suggests that emotion has evolved to ensure survival of the individual. He emphasizes the role of cognition in emotion; and states that, by thinking, the individual is permitted to predict the future, thereby improving chances of adapting to the environment successfully. He does not stress physiological arousal, perhaps since this is so similar in all situations. Plutchik's theory is an attempt to understand the function of emotions in our complex everyday world.

FIGURE 10.7 Theories of Emotion

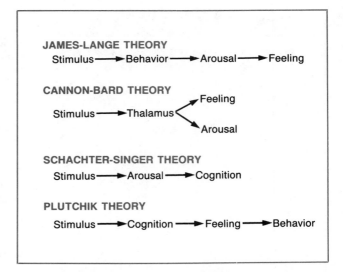

The major theories of emotion are compared here. The James-Lange theory assumes that we are first physiologically aroused and then experience the feeling as emotion. The Cannon-Bard theory states that when a stimulus activates the thalamus, physiological arousal and subjective feeling occur simultaneously. According to the Schachter-Singer theory, when physiological arousal occurs, we cognitively interpret it and label it as emotion. Plutchik's theory assumes a chain of cognition, feeling, and behavior that results in a function (along with a feedback loop).

The Cognitive-Motivational-Relational Theory

Recently, Richard Lazarus (1991b) proposed a cognitive-motivational-relational theory of emotion. The *cognitive* aspect refers to knowledge of and appraisal of one's surroundings. It includes one's beliefs about how the world operates and one's evaluation of his or her interaction with it. Cognition includes the manner in which the individual distinguishes emotions, their causes, and their consequences. As mentioned earlier in this chapter, Lazarus emphasizes the role of cognition in emotion.

The *motivational* component of Lazarus's theory refers to the fact that emotions are reactions to daily events that bring one closer to or farther from reaching goals. When an individual is helped or harmed by an action, he or she experiences an emotion. Motivation, the force that moves an individual toward a goal, becomes associated with the emotion experienced when that goal is or is not reached.

The *relational* component refers to the fact that emotions involve relationships between the individual and his or her environment. The individual learns that certain behaviors result in harmful outcomes (and are accompanied by negative emotions) and other behaviors result in beneficial outcomes (and are accompanied by positive emotions).

Lazarus suggested that there are four categories of emotion. The first category includes the negative emotions that result from harms, losses, or threats (such as anger, fear, shame, sadness, jealousy, and disgust). The positive emotions are those that result from the benefits of reaching goals (such as happiness, joy, pride, and love). The third category is what Lazarus calls borderline cases (such as hope, contentment, and compassion). The final category includes the nonemotions (such as grief, depression, frustration, disappointment, nervousness, tension, curiosity, surprise, and amazement). Lazarus argued that the nonemotions in the last category are best viewed as arousal or cognitive evaluations that could lead to emotions but are not themselves true emotions. Ultimately, a theory of emotion should explain the emotional experiences we have and predict which emotions we are likely to experience.

The Opponent-Process Theory

Richard Solomon (1980) has developed a theory of motivation/emotion that views emotions as pairs of opposites (for example, fear-relief, pleasure-pain). The opponent-process theory states that when one emotion is experienced, the other is suppressed. For example, if you are frightened by a mean dog, the emotion of fear is expressed and relief is suppressed. If the fear-causing stimulus continues to be present, after a while the fear decreases and the relief intensifies. For example, if the dog didn't move, your fear would decrease and relief that the dog didn't attack would increase. If the stimulus is no longer present, then the first emotion disappears and is replaced totally with the second emotion. If the dog turns and runs, you are no longer afraid, but rather feel very relieved.

Solomon and Corbit (1974) analyzed the emotions present when skydivers jump from planes. Beginners experience extreme fear as they jump, which is replaced by great relief when they land. With repeated jumps, the fear decreases and the post-jump pleasure increases. This theory attempts to explain a variety of thrill-seeking behaviors. It has also been proposed as a model of drug addiction. The drug originally produces pleasurable feelings, but then a negative emotional experience occurs afterwards. Eventually, the drug user takes drugs not for their pleasurable effects, but to avoid the aversiveness of withdrawal symptoms. The opponent-process theory is an attempt to link emotional states with motivation.

Although it is an intriguing idea, some researchers have not found support for the opponent-process theory. For example, Sanduik and colleagues (1985) did not find a reaction to withdrawal as predicted by the theory. Additional research is needed to test the usefulness of the opponent-process theory.

FIGURE 10.8   Opponent-Process Theory

R. Solomon views emotions as pairs of opposites. When one emotion is experienced (**A**), it triggers an opposing emotion after a period of time. With repeated stimulations (**B**), the opposing emotion becomes stronger, weakening the experience of the primary emotion and providing an aftereffect (after Solomon & Corbit, 1974).

INTERPERSONAL ATTRACTION: LIKING AND LOVING

Music and literature have immortalized one of the most potent emotions we experience—love. The area of psychology that includes liking, friendship, and love is called interpersonal attraction. Sharon Brehm (1992) viewed interpersonal attraction as the desire to approach another person and evaluate him or her positively. Interpersonal attraction has three aspects: cognitive, emotional, and behavioral. The cognitive aspect involves one's positive and negative thoughts and beliefs about another person, the emotional aspect involves one's positive and negative feelings, and the behavioral aspect involves the way one acts.

Liking

People are social creatures who have a need to be with others (see the section on affiliation in chapter 9, "Motivation"). Why are we attracted to certain people? How do we develop interpersonal relationships?

Influences on Interpersonal Attraction   Social psychologists have attempted to explain why we like certain people. In general, the research indicates three major influences: proximity, similarity, and physical attractiveness. We tend to like people who are in close geographical *proximity* to us. Our friends tend to be people in our neighborhood and people we see every day at school, work, or church. A classic study was conducted by Leon Festinger and his colleagues (1950), who measured friendship patterns among married students living in an apartment complex. They found that friendships developed between people who lived close to one another, with the person next door most likely to be a friend. One explanation of the role of proximity on liking is that we become more familiar with those people whom we see on a regular basis (Moreland & Zajonc, 1982).

Similarity research indicates that people like others who share similar values, intellectual ability, interests, and activity preferences (Wetzel & Insko, 1982). It is enjoyable to be with others who desire to do the things we like to do, and we are able to communicate more effectively with others who share our interests. Hays (1985) reported that people who enjoy doing similar things and sharing experiences are most likely to become friends. Cappella and Palmer (1990) reported that college students who held similar attitudes were significantly more attracted to one another. It seems that we like others who are reflections of ourselves, as this makes us feel comfortable.

Physical attractiveness plays a major role in whom we decide to get to know better. In general, research indicates that physically attractive people are more likely to be perceived in a favorable way and are more likely to be sought after as friends (Dion & Dion, 1987). Why is physical attractiveness important? We tend to enjoy beauty and assume that beauty is associated with goodness and positive characteristics. We also increase our status when we are associated with others who are attractive.

Theories of Interpersonal Relationships   There are several theories that focus on the development of interpersonal relationships. The social exchange theory states that we evaluate the costs and rewards of our relationships (Homans, 1961). If the rewards outweigh the costs, then we continue the relationship, but if the costs are too high we look for alternatives. Rewards might include status, information, money, emotional stability,

and enjoyment. Costs might include money, effort, or any other unpleasant aspect of the relationship.

When we are in a relationship, we value fairness. The equity theory states that people are motivated to maintain a fair balance in relationships (Walster, Walster, & Berscheid, 1978). If one person is always giving and the other always taking, it obviously is an unfair relationship, and there is some pressure to balance it. If we feel as though we do not have equity in a relationship, we are more likely to search for alternatives (such as ending the relationship).

Theories of Love

In some cases the intimacy of knowing and liking someone can develop into a more intense and passionate relationship usually defined as the emotion of love. Romantic love is popularized by songwriters and moviemakers, as evidenced, for instance, by the extremely successful movie, *Ghost*, with Demi Moore and Patrick Swayze. During the past couple of decades, social psychologists have helped us understand more about love. These findings and theories can help us understand our feelings and behaviors when we think we have fallen in love.

Fromm's Social Theory of Love   Eric Fromm (1956) believed that people are products of their social environment. He suggested that we are lonely until we can relate to other people socially. Further, of all the possible ways of relating to others, the most complete relationship is the interpersonal union that we call love.

Fromm defined love as the active concern for the life and growth of another person. He described four characteristics of love: knowledge, care, responsibility, and respect. Love grows when we understand and have concern for another person, and accept the responsibility to help him or her every way we can. We must respect other people and acknowledge their unique qualities. According to Fromm, only through unselfish giving can we experience love.

Rubin's Liking and Loving Scales   Zick Rubin presented his findings in this field in his 1973 book, *Liking and Loving*. He devised two questionnaires to measure these traits in people. The liking scale has 13 items that measure the degree of liking one person has for another. The research found that *respect* ("In my opinion, _____ is an exceptionally mature person"), *similarity* ("I think that _____ and I are quite similar to each other"), and a *favorable evaluation* ("I think that _____ is unusually well adjusted") were important factors in liking other people. Interestingly, when dating college couples were tested on

FIGURE 10.9   Rubin's Liking and Loving Scale

Liking Scale
(Sample Items)

Respect

_____ is the sort of person whom I myself would like to be.

Perceived Similarity

When I am with _____, we are almost always in the same mood.

Favorable Evaluation

It seems to me that it is easy for _____ to gain admiration.

Loving Scale
(Sample items)

Caring

One of my primary concerns is _____'s welfare.

Attachment

If I were lonely, my first thought would be to seek _____ out.

Intimacy

I feel that I can confide in _____ about virtually everything.

---

the liking scale, Rubin found that women liked their boyfriends more than their boyfriends liked them.

Rubin then looked at love in dating college couples. He found in his loving scale that there were three major components involved in the emotion of love. According to Rubin, love involves *caring* ("I would do almost anything for _____"), *attachment* ("If I could never be with _____, I would feel miserable"), and *intimacy* ("When I am with _____, I spend a good deal of time just looking at him/her"). This time, the scores for the men and the women were equal, indicating that in dating couples, love is reciprocal. Rubin also concluded that *eye contact* was one of the most valuable predictors of love. In one study, Rubin found that couples who looked into each other's eyes were more likely to remain together than those who did not look at one another. If you watch people who claim to be in love, you will probably find that they spend a great deal of time looking at one another.

Pam's Psychometric Approach   Alvin Pam, Robert Plutchik, and Hope Conte (1975) developed the "Love Scale" to measure the attitudes people have toward love. On the 40-item scale, they tested college students who were in love (but not married), who were

dating, or who were friends with someone of the opposite sex. They found five factors that were very important in interpersonal attraction: *respect* ("He/she has better judgment than the average person"); *congeniality* ("You and she get along well as a couple"); *altruism* ("You like giving gifts to her/him"); *physical attraction* ("He/she is sexually attractive to you"); *attachment* ("You feel secure with him/her").

While all five factors are important, the researchers found certain trends: they reported that physical attraction and attachment are very important in love, whereas dating emphasizes congeniality and physical attraction, and friendship requires congeniality and respect. Through tests like this one, researchers believe that we can gain an understanding of a relationship.

Knox's Attitudes Toward Love Measurement
Another research approach is the measurement of attitudes toward love as people grow older. Knox (1970) distinguished between romantic and realistic love; he stated that people believe that romantic love is mysterious and eternal and may only occur once in a lifetime. Romantic love is often characterized by excitement, arousal, and urgency. Realistic love is practical, calm, and solid. A person with a practical outlook toward love carefully weighs the options before making a commitment. Romantic and realistic love may be thought of as opposite ends of a continuum, with each individual's orientation being somewhere between the two extremes.

Knox administered his attitudinal scale to high school seniors, people married less than 5 years, and people married more than 20 years. The high school students showed a romantic orientation, while the young married adults showed a more realistic orientation to love. He reasoned that the first years of marriage forced couples to cope with everyday problems such as obtaining work to pay bills. A very interesting finding was that people married for over 20 years also showed a romantic orientation. These people presumably have overcome obstacles successfully and can now be romantic once again. Knox suggested that our attitudes toward love change as we go through life. It should be noted that Knox's research did not actually survey the same people throughout their lives and thus cannot claim a developmental trend.

Passionate Love and Companionate Love   Hatfield (1988) distinguished between passionate and companionate love. Passionate love, or romantic love, is an intense emotional experience that includes sexual desire, elation, anxiety, ecstasy, and tenderness. Physiological arousal is high and the various emotional feelings often produce confusion. Hatfield stated that passionate love rarely lasts more than 6 to 30 months in a relationship, but can lead to a more stable companionate love.

FIGURE 10.10 Love at Different Ages
People's attitudes toward love tend to change as they grow older. Knox reported that young unmarried people often have a romantic orientation toward love, which tends to become more practical after marriage. People married for many years tend to become more romantic again.

Companionate love, or conjugal love, is characterized by deep attachment, trust, respect, affection, loyalty, and familiarity. It is much less intense than passionate love, but much more enduring. Companionate love includes a long-term commitment to a relationship. Rubenstein (1983) reported that its three important components were friendship, devotion, and intellectual compatibility. Passionate love is what Knox (1970) called romantic love, whereas companionate love is what Knox called realistic love.

Falling in Love How do we fall in love? Let's put together some of the findings we have examined and describe the process. As already mentioned, proximity and similarity are important in liking someone. But the arousal of romantic love relies more on physical attractiveness. Karen Dion (1980) reported that when given a choice, people prefer others who are physically attractive. However, according to Ellen Berscheid (1983), the *matching hypothesis* best explains the process of love relationships (people tend ultimately to select someone of about the same attractiveness as themselves).

Walster and Walster (1978) suggested that in order for someone to fall in love, three conditions must be met. First, we must learn, through our culture, what love is. We are constantly exposed to films, books, songs, and stories of people in love. We thus learn what to expect when we are ready to experience this strong emotion. Second, we cannot fall in love until we have an appropriate stimulus. Our prospective love partner should meet all the requirements we set up (proximity, similarity, and physical attractiveness). And, finally, we must experience

a physiological arousal that we can label the emotion of love. As Schachter and Singer suggest, emotion is labeled according to the environmental circumstances. So if you are with someone who is attractive and if your heart is suddenly beating fast, you might very well call it love.

A study by Dutton and Aron (1974) examined the effects of anxiety and arousal on sexual attraction. Young men in Vancouver, British Columbia, were interviewed by a very attractive young woman while crossing a bridge. Some of the subjects were on a swaying suspension bridge 230 feet above a raging river. Other subjects were interviewed on a wide, solid bridge near the ground. When the interview was completed, the woman said she would be glad to explain the results of her class project in more detail when she had more time. She gave the subjects her telephone number so they could call her if they desired. Four times as many men in the high arousal (high bridge) condition actually called than those in the low arousal (low bridge) condition. The psychologists concluded that the high-bridge subjects interpreted the arousal caused by the swaying bridge as attraction to the beautiful woman.

Sternberg's Triangular Theory of Love Yale University psychologist Robert Sternberg has proposed a triangular theory of love (1986b) in which love consists of three components: intimacy, passion, and decision/commitment. The emotional component, *intimacy*, refers to the feelings in a love relationship that encourage closeness. They include respect, happiness, understanding, support, and intimate communication. The intimacy component is the core of a love relationship, and is found in a wide variety of love relationships, such as love for a parent, sibling, friend, or spouse.

The motivational component, *passion*, includes physiological arousal and is expressed by sexual desire. Other needs, such as self-esteem, affiliation, and dominance, can also contribute to passion. In a love relationship, often passion first attracts the lovers, and intimacy develops to sustain the relationship over time. In some cases, only passion is desired (for example, relationships with prostitutes).

The cognitive component, *decision/commitment*, consists of the short-term decision to love a person and the long-term commitment to continue with the relationship through good and bad times and helps to solidify it.

Sternberg (1987, 1988) proposed that the combination of these three components can determine eight different kinds of love. *Nonlove* refers to the absence of all three components, and characterizes most casual social interactions. *Liking* occurs when only intimacy is present, and characterizes friendships. *Infatuated love* results from only the passion component, and involves only the physiological arousal. It is usually associated with a short-term relationship. *Empty love* results when only the decision/commitment component is present, and can occur in a love relationship that has become stagnant without passion or closeness. In some cultures where marriages are prearranged, empty love can be the first

FIGURE 10.11 Sternberg's Theory of Love

Kind	Intimacy	Passion	Decision/Commitment
Nonlove	No	No	No
Liking	Yes	No	No
Infatuated Love	No	Yes	No
Empty Love	No	No	Yes
Romantic Love	Yes	Yes	No
Companionate Love	Yes	No	Yes
Fatuous Love	No	Yes	Yes
Consummate Love	Yes	Yes	Yes

stage as the partners begin life together. *Romantic love* results from the presence of the intimacy and passion components, and is characterized by physical attraction and an emotional bond. When intimacy and decision/commitment are present, *companionate love* results, such as in a marriage after passion has died down. *Fatuous love* results from the presence of the passion and decision/commitment components. A whirlwind romance in which a couple meets, falls in love, and gets married very quickly is an example of fatuous love. Ultimately, either intimacy develops or the relationship is terminated. In *consummate love*, all three components are present. This is for many the ideal in romantic situations, but often is difficult to maintain for long periods of time.

BIOGRAPHICAL HIGHLIGHT

ROBERT J. STERNBERG

Robert J. Sternberg was born in December 1949 in Newark, New Jersey. He attended Yale University, where he decided to major in psychology (even after earning a C in his introductory psychology course). After graduating with high honors in psychology in 1972, he entered Stanford University, earning his Ph.D. in psychology in 1975.

Sternberg has been extremely influential in psychology, especially in the cognitive area of intelligence and the emotional area of love. The APA awarded him a Distinguished Scientific Award for an Early Career Contribution to Psychology in 1981. Since then, he has received many honors in the discipline.

Sternberg recalls that he has had an interest in intelligence since he was in elementary school, when he experienced great anxiety whenever he took intelligence tests. Throughout his career he has conducted research in intelligence and thinking. His award-winning book, *Beyond IQ: A Triarchic Theory of Human Intelligence,* was published in 1985.

In addition to his work on intelligence, Sternberg has developed a theory of love, as outlined in his 1988 book *The Triangle of Love.* He felt that love was an important emotion that could be studied scientifically.

Robert Sternberg is now a professor of psychology at Yale University, where he has been since 1975.

Researchers are currently interested in refining the tests used to measure love attitudes and behaviors. Chojnacki and Walsh (1990) recently gave the Sternberg Triangular Love Scale to undergraduate students in dating relationships and found that the test was reliable but tended to have high correlations among the subscales (intimacy, passion, commitment). Hendrick and Hendrick (1989) also found Sternberg's test to have high interdependency among the subscales (in other words, the subscales tended to measure the same thing). When a variety of measures of love were analyzed, Hendrick and Hendrick found five factors involved in love: passion, love, closeness, ambivalence, secure attachment, and practicality. Further research will continue to add to our knowledge of this important emotion. Love researchers are beginning to provide practical information to people in love, as shown in the following Application.

APPLICATION

Guidelines for a Successful Love Relationship

Most of us are interested in developing and maintaining a successful relationship with the person we love. Many of the theories of love provide a glimpse of the practices that promote the continuation of a loving relationship. In his 1988 book, *The Triangle of Love*, Robert Sternberg gives many practical suggestions, including his rules for a successful relationship. Note that these suggestions can help improve any relationship, whether it is just beginning or has been in existence for decades.

Sternberg's first rule is to never take your love relationship for granted. Couples often spend a lot of attention on each other when first dating, but then tend to focus on other things (work, children, outside interests) after marriage. In order to maintain a strong relationship, it is important to always make it a high priority in your life.

Successful partners try to become aware of each other's needs and to satisfy them without being asked. When we love someone, we want to help him or her in any way possible. We care about the other person and are not afraid to show our feelings.

Sternberg points out that in a successful relationship, the partners both have a positive self-concept. They value themselves and recognize that they have something important to contribute to the relationship.

It is very important to love your actual partner, not the idealization of your partner. It is often easier to fall in love with an ideal person than a real person. The ideal person is perfect in every way, whereas a real person has flaws and shortcomings. When we love a fantasy of the ideal person, we ultimately become disappointed and

frustrated. But when we love someone for who he or she is, the relationship is based on reality. Sternberg believes this honest approach is necessary for long-term success in a relationship.

Communication plays an essential role in a successful relationship. Each partner must honestly tell the other person what he or she thinks and feels at all times. Without honest communication, the relationship loses intimacy and becomes a shell without any meaning. Your partner cannot always guess what you are feeling, so you have to let him or her know through word and deed.

Finally, Sternberg suggests that partners in a successful love relationship are actively involved in helping each other grow. They must recognize that they need to work together to improve the relationship. They must treat each other the way they want to be treated.

Sternberg argues that intimacy, passion, and commitment are essential components of a love relationship, but to get the most out of the relationship people must work at it continuously. What have you done lately to improve your love relationship? Can you think of other guidelines for people in love?

COMMUNICATION OF EMOTION

We often learn a lot about people by the way they dress, their facial expressions, and the movements of their bodies. For example, clothes can communicate a person's feelings and personality. Think of the instructor who always wears a suit, and of another who dresses more casually. Who gives the more difficult exams? When asked this question, most people believe the formal one is more strict. Actually, many psychologists feel that the real key to understanding a person's emotions is the face.

Facial Expressions

Some scientists believe that many facial expressions, such as smiling, laughing, and crying, are almost universal among cultures, and have a genetic basis. Without speaking, how do you greet someone you recognize? Chances are that you raise your eyebrows. Eibl-Eibesfeldt (1972) found this eyebrow-raising greeting present in a wide variety of cultures. Children who are born blind develop the same facial gestures as sighted children do. The idea that emotional expressions are innate can be traced to Charles Darwin (1872) who proposed that animals and humans show a common pattern that has evolved over the years. Izard (1990) stated that Darwin's

FIGURE 10.12 Facial Expressions

| | Ekman & Friesen (1969) | | | | |
	U.S.	Japanese	Brazilian	Chilean	Argentinian
	%	%	%	%	%
Happiness	97	87	97	90	94
Fear	88	71	77	78	68
Surprise	91	87	82	88	93
Anger	69	63	82	76	72
Disgust	82	82	86	85	79
Sadness	73	74	82	90	85

Ekman and Friesen (Ekman, 1973) believe that facial expressions of emotion are genetically based and universally recognized. As this chart from one of the experiments shows, people from different cultures had similar interpretations of these facial expressions. For example, 97 percent of Americans and Brazilians, and 87 percent of Japanese, interpreted the emotion in the top photo as happiness.

ideas still have a major influence on the psychology of emotion today.

In his facial feedback hypothesis, Sylvan Tomkins (1962) proposed that biological brain networks underlie each emotion and a specific facial expression is associated with it. Specifically, the facial feedback hypothesis states that changes in facial expressions can produce changes in emotional feelings. Matsumoto (1987) stated that it is not known whether the facial expressions actually cause emotional feelings or just modify the intensity of the already existing feelings.

Russell and Bullock (1985) found that young children show an ability to identify facial emotional expressions that is similar to that of adults. Later, Russell (1990) reported that preschoolers' ability to identify causes and consequences of emotions did not differ whether the emotion was expressed orally or through a facial expression.

Joseph Hager and Paul Ekman (1979) conducted a study on the recognition of facial expressions at various distances. They chose six emotional expressions that had previously been shown to be reliable: happiness, sadness, surprise, fear, anger, and disgust. Subjects were able to identify the correct emotion at distances of up to 45 meters. They predicted that happiness and surprise could be recognized at even 100 meters. Hager and Ekman argue that facial expressions can communicate emotion over long distances and that people often use this information in social encounters.

Recent research has generally supported Ekman's claim that facial expressions of emotion can be readily identified. McAlpine and his colleagues (1991) developed a series of videotaped role-playing situations that showed Ekman's six basic facial expressions of emotion. They found high agreement of subjects on identifying the emotions through facial cues and language cues. Other research found that subjects can accurately identify emotion from photographs, even when the images are extremely small and lacking contrast resolution (Wallbott, 1991).

Some researchers, however, argue that although facial expressions may be universal, the interpretation of emotion from facial expression is not always accurate. For example, Wagner and colleagues (1986) reported that subjects could reliably identify three emotions (happiness, anger, and disgust) that Ekman had found reliable but not another three (surprise, fear, and sadness). Russell and Fehr (1987) argued that the interpretation of a particular facial expression depends upon other expressions to which it is being compared. For instance, they found that a neutral face appears sad when compared with a happy face and happy when compared with a sad face.

Research on *social referencing* suggests that even infants are able to interpret facial expressions correctly and modify their behavior accordingly. Sorce and colleagues (1985) reported that when mothers stood at the deep end of a visual cliff (see chapter 4, "Sensation and Perception,"), and coaxed their infants to cross, the facial expression shown by the mother was important. Three-fourths of the infants crossed the deep end when she showed interest or joy, but very few (11 percent) crossed when the mother expressed anger and none crossed when the mother showed fear. Infants may also be influenced by the emotional expressions of other adults. In one study, Klinnert and her colleagues (1986) reported that 1-year-old infants responded correctly to the happy or fearful facial emotional expressions provided by an experimenter. When infants are confused about what to do, they utilize information provided by the facial expressions of others.

Some current researchers argue that when we smile or frown, sensory information is provided to our brain. Robert Zajonc and his colleagues (1989) recently proposed the vascular theory of emotion to explain how facial expressions might influence emotion. They suggest that changes in facial expressions influence the blood vessels of the brain that regulate brain temperature. It is possible that the veins themselves can be constricted or dilated, or the amount of air entering the nasal passages that cools the blood can be modified. Increases in brain temperature are associated with negative emotions, whereas decreases are associated with positive emotions. The brain temperature changes are proposed to lead to changes in the release of brain neurotransmitters. In one study, Zajonc and his colleagues had subjects breathe air of different temperatures, and found that the subjects experienced more positive feelings when breathing the cool air and more negative ones with the warm air. Although the details have not yet all been worked out, the vascular theory is intriguing to many psychologists.

An application of this area is that it is possible that we are aware of being happy because we smile rather than we smile because we are aware of being happy (Cacioppo & colleagues, 1988). An interesting proposal is that people might learn to control emotional feelings by controlling facial muscles. For instance, perhaps one therapy for depression might be to teach patients to smile more, thus helping them feel happier (McCanne & Anderson, 1987).

Nonverbal Communication

Because people are so accustomed to using verbal language to communicate, they often forget that there are other types of communication systems. People can communicate with one another nonverbally. In this section we discuss nonverbal communication through eye contact and body language.

Eyes: Gazing and Staring   We often tend to judge people by the amount of eye contact we have with them. Research by Kleinke and his colleagues (1974) has shown that we are more likely to look more at people we like, and consequently when the level of eye contact is high, we interpret this positively. Kleinke also found that when a male and female interact, each considers low levels of gazing as inattentiveness and high gazing as sincerity. However, males rated low-gazing females as

less attractive, whereas females rated low-gazing males as more attractive. Kleinke (1986) reported research that indicated gazing behavior served a number of functions, including providing information on attraction and attentiveness, regulating social interaction, expressing intimacy, and exerting social control.

But if we look too long (stare) at someone, it is usually interpreted negatively. An interesting study by Greenbaum and Rosenfeld (1978) found that when a person stared at drivers stopped at red lights, the drivers drove off more quickly when the light changed. Thus, although we enjoy eye contact, we try to escape from people staring at us, who make us feel uncomfortable. Eye contact is also an important measure of love, as shown by Zick Rubin (1973), discussed earlier in this chapter.

Body Language   We can convey information through the position and movement of the body. Body language can reveal emotionality, as when a person exhibits a nervous habit (biting fingernails or wringing hands). We often use *gestures*, or body movements, to accentuate what we are saying. Some people use them more than others. The clenched fist, the victory sign, the OK sign, the good-bye wave, the blowing of a kiss, and the wiping the brow in relief are all popular gestures in our culture. There are some sex differences in nonverbal behavior. In our culture, men tend to sit or stand with legs apart and hands outward, whereas women tend to keep

FIGURE 10.13   Gestures
People often use gestures to emphasize what they say or feel. Hand movements, such as those shown here, are usually recognized by people in the same culture.

legs together and hands at their sides. Women are also better at interpreting nonverbal gestures, perhaps because of their nondominant status in many relationships (Matlin, 1987).

We can also use touching as a means of communicating. Often touching conveys affection, like a pat on the back, a handshake, a kiss, or a hug; although also it can suggest power, domination, and even dislike. Crusco and Wetzel (1984) found that when a waitress briefly touched a customer on the hand when she returned change from the bill, both male and female customers left larger tips. Sometimes touching affects the sexes differently. For example, Fisher, Rytting, and Heslin (1976) stated that if they were touched by a library clerk when checking out books, female students responded positively (with positive evaluations of the clerk and library), whereas male students responded negatively. Women generally tend to respond more positively than men to touch in a variety of situations (Stier & Hall, 1984).

A little-studied nonverbal behavior is to have the tongue just slightly protruding from the mouth. Jones and colleagues (1987) found that people were less willing to interrupt others who had their tongues showing. In one situation, a sales clerk without the tongue showing was approached significantly more than another clerk who did have it showing. Perhaps this is why people often tend to avoid individuals with Down syndrome (a form of mental retardation that is often characterized by a protruding tongue and other attributes). When we make decisions about other people, we learn to recognize nonverbal cues and interpret them along with verbal information.

HUMAN SEXUALITY

Try to imagine life without sex. Our sexuality is a part of our personality, our behavior, our emotions, and our attitudes. Sexual identity becomes important as soon as we're born, as male babies are most often wrapped in blue blankets while female babies are wrapped in pink ones. As children grow older, boys tend to identify with their fathers, while girls identify with their mothers. At maturity, sex takes on new meanings. We experience new feelings, and eventually may engage in various types of sexual behavior.

Sexuality has many meanings. It may be defined as our gender identity (a sense of being male or female), our sex role (a set of behaviors appropriate for our particular sex), or the act of sexual intercourse. (See also the discussion of sexual motivation in chapter 9, "Motivation.")

Sexual Determination

Most people would agree that it's easy to determine whether a person is male or female. Just look at the way he or she dresses, walks, talks, and behaves. Sometimes, however, it is not that simple. Dr. Richard Raskind was a Newport Beach, California, ophthalmologist. He underwent a sex-change operation, and as Renée Richards became a female professional tennis player. The difficulty here is to decide whether the change in the physical appearance can determine sexual identity, or whether there must also be an internal hormonal change. The definition of sexuality is extremely complex.

Biological Determination of Sex   Sex, or gender, refers to the biological distinction of being male or female. Money and Ehrhardt (1972) described a number of biological determiners of sex. *Chromosomal sex* is the pattern of chromosomes that determine gender; males have an XY pattern and females an XX. Chromosomal sex is determined at conception when the chromosomes from the egg and sperm unite. *Hormonal sex* is the predominance of either male (testosterone) or female (estrogen) hormones in the body. After about 6 weeks, testes begin to develop and produce the male hormone testosterone if a Y chromosome is present. Without testosterone prenatally, genetic males would develop female sex structures. Or conversely, if male hormones are present prenatally (perhaps because of a drug given to the mother), genetic females might become masculinized and develop male genitals. *Gonadal sex* is the presence of either testes (in the male) or ovaries (in the female) that produce the sex cells (egg and sperm) necessary for reproduction. *Genital sex* is the physical presence of either a penis (in the male) or a vulva (in the female). *Reproductive sex* includes all of the internal organs necessary for reproduction. And *assigned sex* is the sex decided upon by doctors and parents at the birth of a baby ("It's a girl" or "It's a boy"), largely based on the appearance of the genitals. When there is a contradiction between the predominant genital appearance and other biological sex determiners, the condition is called *hermaphroditism*. Depending on their appearance, people with this condition may be raised as males or females.

Gender Identity and Sex Roles   Although biological sexual determination takes place at conception, the learned social sex role and gender identity of an individual develops at a slower rate. Gender identity is the psychological identification with a particular sex, the learned personal sense of maleness or femaleness in an individual. Gender identity is usually formed by about 2 years of age, when the child begins to master language skills.

Sex roles include the set of behaviors and attitudes that are determined to be appropriate for one sex or the other in a society. Even at very young ages, boys and girls are treated differently in our society (Tavris & Wade, 1984). They are taught appropriate behaviors for their particular sex, and are encouraged to incorporate these behaviors into their life-styles.

There are many influences on the development of sex roles. Parents or primary caregivers play an important part in influencing sex roles in children (Sedney, 1987). Parents already have well-defined concepts of sex roles, and usually communicate these concepts to even very young children. Often parents interact differently with boys (with whom they are more active) and girls (with whom they are more passive). Parents give their children sex-appropriate toys to play with, and encourage appropriate behaviors from boys and girls. Sedney stated that although some parents encourage androgyny (both masculine and feminine traits) in children, many parents still convey traditional sex roles.

As the children grow older, the peer group becomes more influential. In adolescence, males and females have fairly rigid views of appropriate sex-role behaviors, and usually coerce peers to comply with the norms. The mass media (movies, music, television, and magazines) provide additional sources of information on what is expected of each sex. By the time they are mature young adults, they have learned the cultural norms regarding sex roles and sexual behaviors. (See also the discussion of sex role stereotypes in chapter 15, "Social Psychology.")

There are several theories of the development of sex roles and gender identity, although there is not complete agreement on the issues involved. The *psychoanalytic theory*, developed by Freud, proposes that children are confused by the genital differences between males and females and tend to identify with the same-sexed parent. The *social-learning theory* argues that society reinforces certain behaviors in boys and other behaviors in girls. The child identifies with the same-sexed parent and imitates his or her behaviors (Block, 1983). The *cognitive-developmental theory* states that children naturally categorize themselves as male or female and then develop those behaviors that fit in with cognitive gender identity (Kohlberg, 1966). The *gender-schema theory* is recent and emphasizes the development of cognitions that classify behaviors as masculine or feminine. The child interprets the world from his or her gender's perspective (Bem, 1987).

John Money (1987) argued that gender identity and sex role are intertwined and cannot be separated. Gender identity is the private perception of one's sex, whereas sex role, or gender role, is the public expression of one's gender identity. Money suggested that since gender identity and gender role were so closely combined, we should use the term gender-identity/role to describe this aspect of sexuality.

FIGURE 10.14 Gender-Identity/Role
The personal sense of maleness or femaleness is a function both of biological sexual determination and learned cultural and social roles. Although attitudes toward appropriate male or female behavior are beginning to change, most people in our society still encourage stereotypical behaviors for boys and girls.

Human Sexual Response Cycle

Much of what we know about the physiology of the human sexual response comes from the work of William Masters and Virginia Johnson, who published *Human Sexual Response* in 1966. Masters and Johnson studied over 10,000 sexual responses by nearly 700 men and women. The researchers described four phases of the human sexual response cycle: excitement, plateau, orgasm, and resolution.

Excitement Phase   The excitement phase is the beginning of sexual arousal. For both sexes, heart rate, blood pressure, and breathing increase. In the male, the increased blood supply to the genital region produces penile erection. In the female, the clitoris enlarges and vaginal lubrication occurs. In both sexes, the sexual flush

FIGURE 10.15   Human Sexual Response Cycle

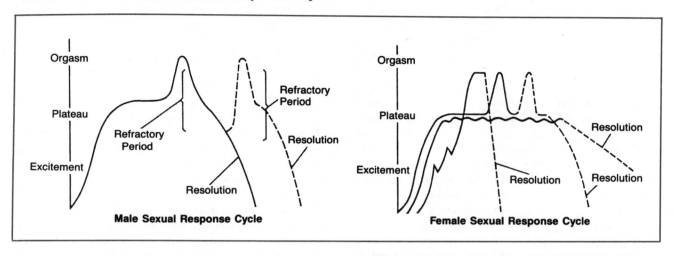

Masters and Johnson (1966) reported that the human sexual response cycle can be described in four phases: excitement, plateau, orgasm, and resolution. In the male sexual response cycle **(A)**, the dotted line shows the possibility of a second orgasm after the initial refractory period is over. The female sexual response cycle **(B)** shows several variations of sexual response. Pattern 1 shows multiple orgasm; pattern 2 shows arousal that fails to reach orgasm; pattern 3 shows some brief drops in the excitement phase followed by a rapid resolution phase.

or reddening of the chest may begin, along with erection of the nipples.

Plateau Phase   During the plateau phase, the physiological arousal becomes even more intense. Breathing, heart rate, and blood pressure continue to increase. The penis and testes enlarge even further in males. In females, the vagina and breasts swell more as the blood supply increases. In both sexes, body temperatures rise.

Orgasm   The climax of intense excitement is orgasm, during which the release of sexual tension occurs. In both sexes, there are rhythmic muscular contractions of the genitals every 0.8 seconds. In males, orgasm is accompanied by ejaculation, the sudden release of semen through the penis. Males can sometimes achieve orgasm within 5 minutes of the start of sexual activity, while females might require around 20 minutes.

Resolution Phase   The resolution phase is the time after orgasm that the body gradually returns to the unaroused state. In females, the size of the breasts, clitoris and vagina are reduced. In males, the penis loses its erection and the testes return to their normal size. In both sexes, the heart rate, blood pressure and breathing slowly return to normal levels. Some people also experience perspiration at this time.

During the resolution phase, males enter a *refractory period*, during which they are unable to have an erection or experience orgasm. There is considerable variability in the length of the refractory period, lasting from a few minutes to several hours, and it has a tendency to

increase with age. Females do not enter a refractory period and can therefore experience multiple orgasms.

Sexual arousal in people is a complex phenomenon. While the physiological response is often caused by physical stimulation of the body's erogenous or pleasurable zones (areas such as genitals, breasts, mouth, earlobes), it can also be influenced by social and cognitive factors. In fact, just thinking about sex can cause arousal in many people.

Janet Hyde (1990) pointed out that knowledge of how the human sexual response works can be valuable to people. It can help them develop good lovemaking techniques; it can be useful in treating sexual problems; and it helps us understand human behavior better.

Human Sexual Behavior

How do we know what types of sexual behavior people engage in? Since sex is usually a very private and personal affair, the main way to obtain information is through surveys and interviews. In chapter 1, "The Study of Psychology," we discussed some of the difficulties of survey research. For instance, the reliability of the data depends upon the sample, the types of questions asked, and the honesty of the people responding.

Several major research programs examined sexual behavior in America. Alfred Kinsey and his associates surveyed over 11,000 men and women in the late 1940s and early 1950s. The Kinsey Reports were one of the first major scientific efforts to study sexual behavior. About 20 years later, in 1974, Morton Hunt interviewed over

2,000 men and women to determine contemporary sexual views and practices. While neither research project was perfect (because of the limitations of survey research), they do give some insights into American sexual practices. The following information is largely from their research findings.

Masturbation   Masturbation is erotic self-stimulation to produce orgasm. There have been many myths about the evils of masturbation, but as yet no one has demonstrated any physical or mental harm. Even though masturbation was considered a deviant form of behavior in the 1940s, Kinsey reported that 92 percent of the men and 62 percent of the women had masturbated. Hunt found that the percentages were not much higher in the 1970s, but that both sexes began masturbating at an earlier age. Hunt reported that there had been an increase in the rate of masturbation in married couples; the original data from Kinsey found about 40 percent of married men and 33 percent of married women masturbated, while Hunt found the percentages to be 72 and 68 for men and women respectively. Masturbation decreases with increasing age, more so with men than women. According to Hunt, the majority of Americans do not see anything wrong either ethically or physically with masturbation.

Petting   Petting is sexual contact with another person excluding intercourse. When petting precedes intercourse, it is referred to as foreplay. Kinsey reported that 89 percent of young men and 88 percent of young women had experienced petting. Hunt reported only slight increases: 95 percent for men and 90 percent for women. In the past, petting served as a compromise for people who wanted to be intimate but did not wish to have sexual intercourse. According to Hunt, petting is not as important today as it once was, since the frequency of sexual intercourse has increased greatly for young people.

Sexual Intercourse   The number of people engaging in premarital intercourse has significantly increased over the past couple of decades. Kinsey reported that 71 percent of young men and 33 percent of young women had engaged in premarital intercourse. Hunt reported that 97 percent of men and 67 percent of women had experienced premarital intercourse. Thus, the change appears to be mainly due to the doubling of the number of women engaging in premarital intercourse. Data also indicate that people are engaging in intercourse at earlier ages than in the past (although this has recently leveled off).

Sexual intercourse with one's spouse is the main sexual outlet for married men and women. However, while the incidence of extramarital sexual intercourse has not increased greatly over the years, it continues to be engaged in by many people. Kinsey reported 39 percent of men and 20 percent of women had ever had extramarital sex, while Hunt reported 47 percent of men and 24 percent of women had engaged in this practice. What is interesting is that Hunt reported that men are tending toward extramarital sex as they grow older, while women tend to have affairs at a younger age than previously.

The frequency of intercourse usually diminishes with age, with young married couples engaging in it about three times a week and couples over 45 years old engaging in it about once a week. Hunt reported that married couples used more variety in their lovemaking than Kinsey reported earlier.

Sexual Orientation   Although the majority of people have a heterosexual orientation, some people have a homosexual orientation. A homosexual individual is a person whose sexual orientation and activities are directed toward other people of the same sex. This person is sexually aroused by people of the same sex or engages in affectional and sexual activities with them. The term lesbian refers to a female homosexual, whereas the term gay male refers to a male homosexual. A bisexual individual is sexually attracted to others of both sexes.

Kinsey reported that 37 percent of men and 13 percent of women had had at least one same-gender sexual experience, whereas about 3 percent of males and 1 percent of females were exclusively homosexual. Hunt's data showed 2 percent of men and 1 percent of women had an exclusively homosexual orientation. Because of sampling problems, it appears that Kinsey overestimated the number of people having at least one same-gender sexual experience, and that the number is more likely 25 percent for men and 10 percent for women (Pomeroy, 1972).

Although the vast majority of people feel that homosexuality is not normal (Davis & Smith, 1984), research shows that individuals with same-gender sexual orientations are often well adjusted and happy (Bell & Weinberg, 1978). There is little agreement on the causes of homosexuality. One line of research suggests that the brains of gay men are more responsive to estrogen than the brains of heterosexuals (Blake, 1985). Some recent evidence suggests that there are differences in the hypothalamus of brains of gay men. Psychoanalytic theory proposes that homosexuals have a problem in forming a gender identity with a parent. Social-learning theory suggests that early same-gender sexual experiences were reinforcing and motivated individuals to continue. An important study by Bell, Weinberg, and Hammersmith (1981) found that sexual orientation is largely determined before adolescents have had sexual experiences. Psychologists do not really understand the causes of homosexuality.

FIGURE 10.16 Same-Gender Sexual Orientation
Various theories have been proposed to explain homosexual preference, but so far none have been successful. Perhaps because same-sex behavior is not predominant in this society, many people misunderstand the physical and psychological needs of homosexuals, who prefer to be accepted as complete human beings rather than as people with particular sexual preferences.

An important point to remember about surveys on sexual behavior is that the results are suggestive of norms, but are not absolute facts. There is a great deal of variability in sexual behavior, and, since sex is usually a private matter, results of surveys cannot be totally trusted. Still, the results are presented here because they indicate the general trends in American sexual behavior.

Sexuality Concerns

Human sexuality is an important topic that researchers are now studying intensively. Here we cover three concerns of current interest in sexuality: gender-identity disorders, sexual dysfunctions, and AIDS.

Gender-Identity Disorders Gender identity is our learned personal sense of maleness or femaleness. This is ingrained in us from our earliest childhood, and most people have no difficulty with their self-perception of gender. For some individuals, however, there is an incongruence between the assigned sex and gender identity, a condition called gender-identity disorder. Most cases of gender-identity disorder can be linked back to childhood, although in rare cases the problem can develop entirely in adulthood (DSM-III-R, 1987).

In gender-identity disorder of childhood, a child experiences long-lasting and intense distress about his or her assigned sex and the desire to become the opposite sex. He or she often wants to wear clothes of the opposite sex and consistently asserts that he or she has or will have the anatomical structures associated with the opposite sex.

Sometimes a person feels trapped in the body of the wrong sex. Such a person has a gender-identity disorder of transsexualism, in which the person who has reached puberty wishes to be the opposite sex (and had this desire for at least 2 years). The transsexual often suffers from anxiety and depression. Sometimes the transsexual will undergo sex reassignment surgery to treat the problem. We do not really know much about the causes of this disorder.

Sexual Dysfunctions The term sexual dysfunction refers to problems in normal sexual behavior, usually characterized by inhibitions in sexual arousal or problems in the sexual response cycle. The DSM-III-R (1987) identifies four problem areas: sexual desire, sexual arousal, orgasm, and sexual pain. A *hypoactive sexual desire* simply means that a person has very little interest in sexual activities (a "low sex drive"). *Sexual arousal disorders* are characterized by the inability of the male to attain or maintain erection or the female to attain or maintain lubrication. (Previously, this was referred to as impotence in the male and frigidity in the female.) A persistent inability to achieve orgasm is called *inhibited female orgasm* in the woman and *inhibited male orgasm* in the man. *Premature ejaculation* refers to the problem of the male not being able to delay ejaculation until he wishes to have it. *Dyspareunia* is painful intercourse, often caused by physical problems. Remember that these problems can occur in normal healthy people and often can be successfully corrected.

Sexual Behavior and AIDS Sexually transmitted diseases have always played a role in sexual motivation and behavior (Masters, Johnson, & Kolodny. 1992). During the 1980s a deadly disease of this kind emerged. Acquired immunodeficiency syndrome (AIDS) is a fatal viral infection (HIV or human immunodeficiency virus) that can be sexually transmitted by men or women, or spread through the sharing of infected needles.

The persons at highest risk of infection include homosexual males and intravenous (IV) drug users who transmit the virus through shared needles. Women can, however, contract the disease from infected needles, or

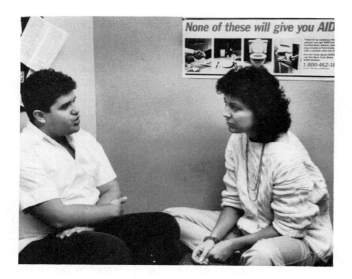

FIGURE 10.17   Sex and AIDS
The fatal disease of AIDS has been a major influence in causing psychological and physical changes in human sexual behavior.

by having sex with IV drug users or bisexual men who are infected. Unborn children can contract the disease from their mothers. Since mid-1985 blood used for transfusions has been routinely checked for the virus, but prior to that time the virus could have been transmitted to hemophiliacs and those needing donated blood in the blood itself.

Because sexual activity with an infected person is the major means of transmitting or contracting AIDS, and since AIDS is a deadly disease expanding rapidly throughout the world, many organizations have attempted to educate the public about the nature of the

disease and the means of preventing its spread. Chief among these in the United States has been the office of former surgeon general C. Everett Koop, which sent a comprehensive, informational booklet on AIDS to every household in the summer of 1988. Among others was a group of students at Dartmouth College who put together a Safer Sex kit containing a condom, a lubricant, a rubber dam, and a brochure, *Safe Sex,* published by the American College Health Association. This kit was designed to give college students the means and the information necessary to use condoms during sexual intercourse. Apart from total abstention from sex, condom use is one of the best ways to prevent the transmission of the AIDS virus.

Psychologists have begun to study the psychological aspects of this disease. They are involved in information programs aimed at preventing the spread of the disease and at allaying people's excessive fears about AIDS and how it can be acquired. Psychologists are also involved in helping patients and patients' friends and family deal with the social and psychological impacts of the disease. It is believed that the fear of AIDS will alter the sexual motivation and behavior of people for many years to come (Francoeur, 1991). ∎

Emotion is an important part of all our lives: it's what makes us human. It is also a potent source of motivation in our society. As shown in our opening story, emotion is complex and involves both biological and cognitive processes. In addition to other areas of concern, psychologists are trying to help people gain a better understanding of themselves through an understanding of their emotions. We turn next to personality, the study of the complete person.

Drawing by Tobey; © The New Yorker Magazine, Inc.

"We had that in school last week."

CHAPTER REVIEW

What You Learned About Emotion

1. Emotion is a response to a stimulus that involves physiological arousal, subjective feeling, cognitive interpretation, and overt behavior.

2. When emotion occurs, the pupils dilate, digestion stops, breathing and heart rate increase, sweating begins, and hormones are secreted. These physiological changes are due mainly to the action of the sympathetic nervous system. The cortex is important in interpreting emotions and the hypothalamus is important in coordinating motivation and emotion. Polygraphs are instruments that record a variety of physiological responses, including heart rate, respiration, blood pressure, and GSR.

3. At birth, the newborn shows only a general response, but specific emotions develop rapidly. Many emotions are shown by the time an infant is 2 years old. Emotions can be classified among a number of dimensions, such as Russell's model involving arousal and pleasantness. A recent classification scheme by Plutchik identifies eight basic emotions: joy, acceptance, fear, surprise, sadness, disgust, anger, and anticipation.

4. The James-Lange theory of emotion proposes that emotional behavior precedes the feeling (we feel sad because we are crying).

5. The Cannon-Bard theory of emotion states that when we perceive a stimulus the thalamus reacts and then simultaneously causes emotional feeling and arousal.

6. The Schachter-Singer arousal-cognition theory of emotion proposes that the emotion we feel depends upon the interpretation of our physiological arousal.

7. The Plutchik functional theory of emotion proposes that emotion occurs as a chain reaction: stimulus event, cognition, feeling, and then behavior related to survival.

8. The cognitive-motivational-relational theory of emotion proposes that emotion can best be understood by examining the individual's cognitive appraisal, motivational goals, and relationship to his or her environment.

9. Solomon's opponent-process theory of emotion states that emotions occur as pairs, and as one emotion is experienced the other is suppressed. With repeated trials, the first emotion weakens and the second one intensifies.

10. Interpersonal attraction is an attitude (involving cognitive, emotional, and behavioral components) toward other people based on the tendency to evaluate others positively. Interpersonal attraction includes affiliation, friendship, liking, and loving. Proximity, similarity, and physical attractiveness are important factors in determining whom we like.

11. Fromm described four characteristics of love: knowledge, care, responsibility, and respect. Rubin found three major components involved in love: caring, attachment, and intimacy. Pam, Plutchik, and Conte identified five factors important in interpersonal attraction: respect, congeniality, altruism, physical attraction, and attachment. Knox found developmental differences in the attitudes people have toward romantic and realistic love. Hatfield distinguished between passionate and companionate love. Walster and Walster suggested that in order to fall in love, a person must learn what love is, have an appropriate stimulus, and experience a physiological arousal that can be labeled as love. Sternberg's triangular theory of love proposes that love consists of three components: intimacy, passion, and decision/commitment.

12. We learn a great deal about people through nonverbal communication. Facial expressions can communicate many emotions, including happiness, sadness, surprise, fear, anger, and disgust. Eye contact is important, and we tend to judge people by the amount of eye contact we have with them. People convey information through body language, the position and movement of the body. We might use gestures or touching to accentuate communication.

13. Human sexuality is a part of our personality, our behavior, our emotions, and our attitudes. There are a number of determiners of sex: chromosomal sex (XX or XY chromosomes), hormonal sex (testosterone or estrogen), gonadal sex (testes and ovaries), genital sex (penis or vulva), reproductive sex (internal reproductive organs), and assigned sex (sex decided upon by doctors at birth). Gender identity is the learned personal sense of maleness or femaleness in an individual. Sex roles include the set of cultural behaviors appropriate for a sex.

14. Masters and Johnson have described the physiological basis of the human sexual response cycle. The excitement phase is the beginning of sexual arousal. During the plateau phase, the arousal becomes more intense. Orgasm is the climax of intense excitement during which the release from building sexual tension occurs. The resolution phase is the time after orgasm during which the body gradually returns to the unaroused state.

15. Kinsey's surveys around 1950 and Hunt's interviews in the 1970s provide us with an indication of the incidence of types of sexual behavior Americans engage in. The incidence of masturbation has not changed, although both sexes now begin to masturbate at an earlier age. The number of people engaging in premarital sexual intercourse has significantly increased over the past 2 decades and sexual intercourse remains the main sexual outlet for married couples. The incidence of homosexuality has remained extremely low over the years. Psychologists are studying problems in sexuality, including gender-identity disorders, sexual dysfunctions, and AIDS.

CHAPTER 11

PERSONALITY

Many psychologists have proposed theories of personality in an attempt to explain human behavior. Personality assessment is important in many areas of psychology, and a variety of methods have been developed to measure personal characteristics accurately.

CRITICAL THINKING OBJECTIVES FOR CHAPTER 11

After reading chapter 11, you should be able to identify, apply, and evaluate what you have learned about the following questions:

What are the components in the definition of personality?
What are the important goals of personality theories?
What are the major concepts in Freud's psychoanalytic personality theory?
What are the five factors of the five-factor personality theory?
What are the characteristics of the self-actualized individual?
What is the distinction between internal and external locus of control?
What are the important personality assessment techniques?

CHAPTER 12

ADJUSTMENT AND HEALTH

How much stress are you experiencing now? Stress, an unavoidable consequence of life, is anything that produces demands on people to adjust their behavior. Stress often has negative consequences, such as anxiety or burnout. Psychologists have studied a variety of adjustment techniques, some of which are more effective than others. Recently, health psychology has gained the attention of researchers in the field of adjustment.

CRITICAL THINKING OBJECTIVES FOR CHAPTER 12

After reading chapter 12, you should be able to identify, apply, and evaluate what you have learned about the following questions:

What is the relationship between stress and adjustment?
What are the important psychological causes of stress?
What are the stages of the general adaptation syndrome?
What is the distinction between Type A and Type B behavior?
What are the important defense mechanisms?

256

Part V focuses on individual differences in personality structure and adjustment to the demands placed on individuals. Personality, stress, and adjustment are covered here.

PART V

Personality and Adjustment

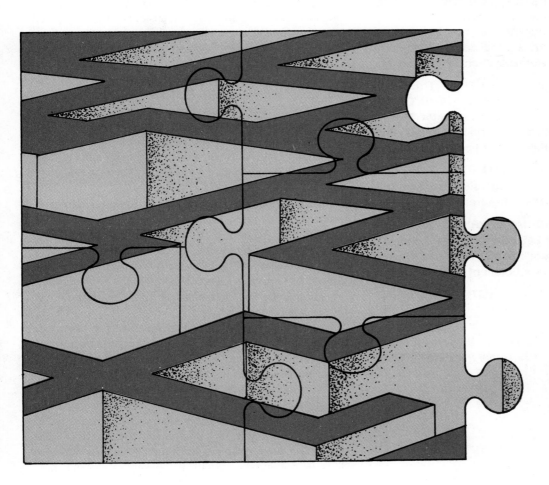

CHAPTER OBJECTIVES

What You'll Learn About Personality

After studying this chapter, you should be able to:

1. Define the concept of personality.
2. State the goals and requirements of personality theories.
3. Describe Freud's psychoanalytic theory of personality.
4. Outline Jung's analytical theory of personality.
5. Outline Adler's individual theory of personality.
6. Outline Horney's cultural theory of personality.
7. Outline Allport's trait theory of personality.
8. Outline Cattell's factor theory of personality.
9. Outline Eysenck's trait model of personality.
10. Outline the five-factor personality model.
11. Outline Rogers's self theory of personality.
12. Outline Maslow's self-actualization theory of personality.
13. Outline Skinner's behavior approach to personality.
14. Outline Bandura's social cognitive theory of personality.
15. Outline Rotter's locus of control theory of personality.
16. Describe the personality assessment methods of interview and observation.
17. Identify four major objective personality tests and two major projective personality tests.

Imagine yourself studying for a test. Would you be more likely to think "If I study hard I will earn a good grade" or "If the questions are easy I will do well"? If you answered that studying will help you earn a good grade, you probably have an internal locus of control, whereas if you answered that the chance of having easy questions will help, you probably have an external locus of control.

Julian Rotter of the University of Connecticut has spent many years investigating this dimension of personality called *locus of control*. Rotter believes that there tend to be two types of people: internal people, who believe that reinforcement is contingent upon their own behavior and that if they work hard they will be rewarded; and external people, who perceive that reinforcement is independent of their behavior and who expect to be rewarded by luck or by the control of other people.

Rotter hypothesized that the perception of reinforcement plays an important role in learning as well as in personality. According to the social learning theory, reinforcement strengthens the individual's expectancy that a behavior will be followed by reinforcement in the future. As expectancies are developed, the individual acts in certain ways that ultimately lead to the development of his or her personality.

Rotter developed a test to measure the difference between internal and external locus of control personality types. Rotter's *Internal-External Scale* took many years of revisions to reach its final form, the 29-item objective test he published in 1966. For each item, Rotter gives the subject a choice of two statements (one is indicative of an internal orientation, the other reflects an external orientation). For example, an internal item might be, "The grades I make are the results of my own efforts; luck has little or nothing to do with it." A similar external item

Many psychologists have proposed theories of personality in an attempt to explain human behavior. Personality assessment is important in many areas of psychology, and a variety of methods have been developed to measure personal characteristics accurately.

11

Personality

FIGURE 11.1   Internal-External Locus of Control

For each pair of items, select A or B according to which more closely represents your beliefs.

___1. A. Promotions are earned through hard work and persistence.
   B. Making a lot of money is largely a matter of getting the right breaks.

___2. A. The number of divorces indicates that more and more people are not trying to make their marriages work.
   B. Marriage is largely a gamble.

___3. A. When I am right I can convince others.
   B. It is silly to think that one can really change another person's basic attitudes.

___4. A. In my experience, I have noticed that there is usually a direct connection between how hard I study and the grades I get.

   B. Many times the reactions of teachers seem haphazard to me.

___5. A. I am the master of my fate.
   B. A great deal that happens to me is probably a matter of chance.

___6. A. The grades I make are the results of my own efforts; luck has little or nothing to do with it.
   B. Sometimes I feel that I have little to do with the grades I get.

___7. A. In our society a person's future earning is dependent upon his or her ability.
   B. Getting promoted is really a matter of being a little luckier than the next guy.

Internal people perceive reinforcement to be within their control, whereas external people perceive reinforcement to be controlled by outside forces. Shown here are sample test items similar to those in Rotter's locus of control scale. (The A items represent an internal locus of control, whereas the B items represent an external locus of control.)

might be, "Sometimes I feel that I have little to do with the grades I get." A subject is required to choose one of these statements. When the selections are totaled, the tester has a measure of the subject's internal or external locus of control of reinforcement. The actual score is the number of external choices selected by the subject (of 23 possible questions—6 questions are "fillers," designed to limit guessing by subjects).

Rotter tested the internal-external locus of control scale on a wide variety of subjects, including college students, prisoners, and the general population. He found that the reliability of the test scores was high (they were consistent from test to test), and so was their validity (they correlated with other measurements of personality; thus, the test seemed to measure the dimension of personality expected). His early testing found that both sexes tended to score about the same, and that blacks tended to have higher external locus of control scores than whites.

More than 600 studies investigating internal-external locus of control have been reported. Some of Rotter and his colleagues' early studies exemplify the trend in results. For instance, Rotter has shown that children from poor families tend to be external, whereas children from richer families are more internal. He found that black college students who participated in civil-rights campaigns were more internal than those who didn't. Another study reported that internal students were more successful in changing peer attitudes about fraternities, while several other studies have shown that nonsmokers tend to be more internal than smokers. People who gamble were found to be more external. One study (Doherty & Baldwin, 1985) found that during the 1970s women began to score more externally than men. The internal-external dimension demonstrates a useful method of testing personality.

WHAT IS PERSONALITY?

We often use the term *personality* without really defining it. For instance, have you heard statements such as "Carole has a terrific personality" or "Henry's personality leaves much to be desired"? Hall and Lindzey (1985) point out that we use the concept of personality to evaluate other people. We also use personality to describe people. For example, we might use statements such as "Sharon has an outgoing personality" or "Louise has an aggressive personality."

Partially because the term is used in our everyday language and partially because it is so central to our study of psychology, psychologists have a difficult time defining personality. Gordon Allport reviewed nearly 50 definitions of personality in 1961, and many more have been suggested since then. In a very real sense, personality forms a core of psychology. It is the sum total of what a person is—including his or her behaviors, thoughts, and feelings. Because of the inclusive nature of personality, psychologists have a difficult time developing an acceptable definition. In this book, we define personality as the distinctive and enduring patterns of behavior and cognition that characterize a person's adaptation to life.

Most definitions of personality are similar. Psychologist Walter Mischel (1986) defines personality as an individual's overall, stable, and distinctive patterns of behavior in responding to people and environmental events—that is, each person's characteristic patterns of behavior that are consistent across a variety of situations. Of particular concern to personality theorists are those patterns that are characteristic of the person's interactions with other people. Feshbach and Weiner (1986) also stress social interactions when they define personality as the relatively enduring behavior patterns that distinguish people, groups, and cultures.

Psychologists who study personality are more interested in understanding the fairly stable aspects of a person's behavior than the occasionally uncharacteristic acts. For example, if someone who is normally quiet and polite once swore in public, that is not really an important aspect of his or her personality. Likewise, psychologists often focus on individual differences in behavior patterns. In order to understand individual behavior, we want to know what is distinctive about the person and makes that individual different from others. Phares (1991) views personality as the characteristic pattern of thoughts, feelings, and behaviors of a person that are distinctive and enduring.

Psychologists called *personality theorists* try to discover complete and systematic explanations for people's styles of behavior. Their explanations go beyond merely categorizing people into types (although they may do that too). They are also interested in the specific events that make people act the way they do. Some of the major personality theories that explain human behavior are explored in this chapter. The other basic area of personality research, assessment of individual differences, will be covered after we discuss the major theories.

GOALS OF PERSONALITY THEORIES

There are several important goals of personality theories. One is to organize the characteristics of personality. Theories provide a structure for integrating characteristics such as aggressiveness, emotionality, intelligence, sociableness, anxiousness, and passivity. Theories identify which characteristics are most important and how they are organized in individuals. This helps us understand the relationships among our different behaviors.

Another goal of personality theories is to explain personality variability (the differences and similarities among individuals). For instance, people have different reactions to jokes, different styles of dress, and different ways of reacting under stress. We can explain some of these differences fairly easily; others not so. The personality theorist provides concepts to identify the factors that influence the development of personality and everyday behaviors in individuals, and helps us understand why everyone is unique. Houston (1990) pointed out that most personality tests focus on white personality, which is different from black personality. In the future, tests will need to incorporate more minorities in the standardization. One attempt at black personality assessment is Baldwin and Bell's (1985) *African Self-Consciousness Scale*.

A third goal of personality theories is to describe the normal, healthy personality. Personality theorists have studied normal people as well as people with problems, in the hope of determining what contributes to a healthy personality. Some of this information can be used to understand what is considered normal behavior within a culture. Theories also attempt to determine the relationship between personality characteristics and motivation. For instance, our behaviors often reflect our motives and, over time, contribute to our stable personalities.

Personality theories vary in a number of ways (Liebert & Spiegler, 1990). They may focus on the past or present, the holistic or analytical point of view, the individual versus the situation, conscious or unconscious awareness, learning versus innate knowledge, childhood experiences versus adult experiences, and degree of optimism for the human race. Personality theories have particular orientations and focus on specific aspects of personality. Try to identify the dimensions of each theory we cover in this chapter.

All of us have an implicit theory of personality that we use when we interact with others. The value of a personality theory is that it helps reduce our confusion and indecision about ourselves and other people. Understanding our own theory and being able to recognize it helps us understand ourselves and others better.

There are several requirements that a good theory of personality should meet. It should be explicit, or expressed in precise words and symbols. It should be testable, so that it can be verified scientifically. And it should be acceptable, or useful enough to get people to investigate and utilize it. Think about the functions and

requirements of good theories of personality as we review some of the major theories that have been developed over the years.

PSYCHOANALYTIC THEORIES

The first systematic and comprehensive theory of personality to incorporate unconscious influences, dreams, sexuality, and instinctual urges was proposed by Sigmund Freud. He worked to discover how the unconscious mind and the motives of sex and aggression influence human behavior.

Freud's Psychoanalytic Theory

The idea that our emotional lives are unconsciously represented in our dreams was revolutionary. The credit for it goes to Sigmund Freud, the "father" of psychoanalytic theory. Unlike most other complex theories about human behavior, Freud's ideas have filtered down through academic and professional circles to become part of the everyday thought and vocabulary of the average person.

BIOGRAPHICAL HIGHLIGHT

SIGMUND FREUD

Sigmund Freud was born in May, 1856, to a lower-middle-class family, the son of wool merchants, in the Austrian town of Freiburg. When he was four his family moved to Vienna. His parents soon recognized and encouraged young Freud's intellectual capacities. After receiving his medical degree in 1881, he began to practice medicine; shortly afterward he met a young woman whom he eventually married.

Departing from the traditional academic setting of the psychological laboratory, he began to study mental disorders by clinical observation. Initially, Freud's theories shocked his highly conservative colleagues, most of whom either dismissed him entirely or countered him vehemently with caustic criticism. Freud refused to be discouraged by his adversaries, and continued his investigations with an almost obsessive fervor, gaining the support of only a handful of men who, like Jung and Adler, were themselves destined to make major contributions to psychoanalysis.

Freud spent nearly all his life in Vienna, and, when Nazi storm troopers invaded the city in 1938, he was arrested in his home and held in captivity until his stock of unsold books could be retrieved and burned publicly. Upon his release a few weeks later, he moved to London, where he lived out the last months of his life. In September 1939 Freud died of cancer at the age of 83.

FIGURE 11.2 Freud's Psychoanalytic Theory

Personality, according to Freud, is the result of the interaction of the ego, superego, and id. The ego operates on the reality principle, which is a conscious awareness of the conflict between the id and the superego. The id contains instinctual, unconscious animal urges, and the superego contains the ethical and moral values of a person's family and culture.

Beginning his work as a medical doctor, Freud noted that his patients' reports of their dreams and thoughts, as well as their other conversational topics, seemed to form patterns that related to their emotional problems. Gradually, he developed his theory that our experiences in early childhood, especially those with sexual significance, have a lasting influence on our personalities, and are often the basis for our adult emotional problems. Freud was convinced of the importance of these early experiences; but, since many of them are usually forgotten or repressed, he concluded that we do not recognize them as the real reasons for much of our adult behavior.

Freud thought of personality as an iceberg, with only the tip showing above water. The part of personality that we are aware of in everyday life is our *conscious mind*. This is the tip of the iceberg. Below this is the *preconscious mind*, which contains information that we have learned but are not thinking about right now. Our preconscious mind contains things such as our birth date and our address. We can easily pull information in the preconscious mind into the conscious mind by concentrating. Beneath the preconscious level lies the *unconscious mind*. Material in the unconscious mind is not readily available to us. Freud suggests that our fears and unpleasant memories are repressed into the unconscious mind.

Freud's theory of personality, as described in his 1940 book, *An Outline of Psychoanalysis*, consists of three major concepts: id, superego, and ego. The id, which is present at birth, represents a person's most basic instinctual or biological drives. Freud claimed that the id operates on the pleasure principle, in which the instinctual drives unconsciously and impulsively seek immediate pleasure and consider nothing else (we discussed the motivational aspects of Freud's theory in chapter 9, "Motivation").

According to Freud, libido, or *psychic energy*, drives the id. The id contains two major instincts: the life instinct and death instinct. The life instinct, or Eros, serves to help the individual and the species survive. Sex is the major expression of the life instinct, and provides motivation for a wide variety of human thoughts and behaviors. Freud suggested that the libido was largely sexual energy motivating Eros. Eros was not limited to direct sexual motivation, but was believed to be involved in any pleasurable activity. The death instinct, or Thanatos, includes aggression and destruction (Freud, 1940). Freud did not develop the concept of the death instinct as fully as he did the life instinct.

The superego consists of societal and parental values that have been instilled in the person. It is largely unconscious and restrains the impulses of the id. It represents the person's moral aspect and is idealistic rather than realistic. The superego therefore includes the conscience (knowledge of the behaviors that are wrong) and the ego-ideal (knowledge of the behaviors that are correct).

The ego consists of a conscious faculty for perceiving and dealing intelligently with reality. It acts as mediator between the id (postponing its urges for immediate gratification) and the superego (recognizing that some of its inhibiting forces are irrational). The ego operates on the reality principle, and tries to find socially acceptable ways (according to the superego) to gratify the id. In the personality of a well-adjusted person, the ego is the dominant force.

According to Freud, an individual's personality is the result of the interaction of these three forces. In some ways, the id represents "want," the superego "should," and the ego "can." Conflict can arise when the three personality structures interact. For instance, the id demands instant gratification, whereas the ego is able to wait. Which part of your personality would be active if you were thinking of cheating on your next examination? Sometimes when the conflict is great, we utilize defense mechanisms to reduce anxiety (we discuss defense mechanisms in chapter 12, "Adjustment and Health").

In chapter 3, "Development," we reviewed the psychosexual stages proposed by Freud. Freud theorized that from birth through adolescence the individual develops through five distinct stages. Each of these stages focuses on an area of the body that is of prominent concern to the individual at that particular time. Freud's psychosexual stages include the *oral* stage, *anal* stage, *phallic* stage, *latency* stage, and the *genital* stage. Freud considered these psychosexual stages crucial in the development of a healthy personality.

During the phallic stage, children must resolve the Oedipus (for boys) or Electra (for girls) complex. The name Oedipus complex is taken from the Greek play *Oedipus Rex*, in which a young man kills his father and marries his mother without knowing who they are. According to Freud, the young boy has sexual feelings for his mother and is jealous of his father. He experiences *castration anxiety* because he is afraid his father will castrate him. To resolve this conflict, the boy identifies with his father and suppresses his sexual feelings toward his mother.

The young girl in the phallic stage goes through the Electra complex, in which she feels inferior to boys because she lacks a penis. She blames her mother for her condition and loves her father because he has a penis. This *penis envy* eventually is resolved by suppressing her feelings toward her father and identifying with her mother. Freud believed that if the Oedipus/Electra complex was not resolved, the person would have difficulty relating to members of the opposite sex as an adult.

One of the major criticisms of Freud's personality theory centers on his perception of women as inferior. Freud argued that because women do not experience castration anxiety they do not develop as strong a superego as men do. However, research has demonstrated that gender has little or no effect on the development of a conscience or a superego.

Freud attracted a close circle of followers, who joined with him to form the first psychoanalytic society. Given the distinctions between psychoanalysis as personality theory and as therapy, and considering the controversial nature of Freud's ideas, it is understandable that several members of Freud's circle, disagreeing with him on various aspects of his basic concept (especially his pessimistic view of humankind and his strong emphasis on sexuality), left the group and developed their own analytic approaches to personality and therapy. Three of the most important of these psychoanalytic theorists were Carl Jung, Alfred Adler, and Karen Horney.

FIGURE 11.3   Freud and Colleagues
Standing, left to right, are A. A. Brill, Sandor Ferenczi, and Ernest Jones; seated are Sigmund Freud, G. Stanley Hall, and Carl G. Jung.

Jung's Analytical Psychology

The personality theory of the Swiss psychologist Carl Jung is called analytical psychology. He thought that in addition to an individual personal unconscious, consisting of repressed thoughts and memories, there was also a collective unconscious shared by all humankind. Stored in the collective unconscious are universal human experiences repeated over centuries. The collective unconscious shapes our experiences, as a dried-up river bed gives shape to running water after a rainstorm. Jung called these unconscious universal ideas archetypes.

The aim of a healthy personality, Jung thought, was to achieve a kind of wholeness, in which all parts of the personality are fully developed and harmoniously integrated, rather than being fragmented as they are in most people. He called the process leading to this goal individuation. With awareness of both the bright side of our personality and its darker side, we can mediate between our animal instinct and the requirements of society, and achieve a feeling of balance, calm, and security.

The psyche includes all of the thoughts and feelings (conscious and unconscious) of an individual. According to Jung, the ego is the conscious mind, the part of the psyche that is concerned with thinking, emotion, memory, and perception. The ego is important because it provides stability in how we react to the world around us.

Jung argued that libido energy can be directed externally, called extraversion, or it can be directed inward, called introversion. The introverted person tends to be shy and withdrawn, whereas the extravert is sociable and outgoing. For each person, one of these attitudes becomes dominant and controls the ego, and the other (nondominant) attitude becomes included in the personal unconscious.

In addition to the attitudes of introversion and extraversion, Jung proposed four psychological functions to describe how people deal with the world: thinking, feeling, sensing, and intuiting. *Thinking* and *feeling* are rational functions that people use to evaluate their experiences. Thinking involves making judgments and decisions, whereas feeling is determining whether an experience is pleasant or unpleasant. *Sensing* and *intuiting* are irrational functions because they are not used to evaluate. Sensing is simply the experience produced by stimulation of the sense organs. Intuiting does not arise from external stimulation but rather from an internal source (for example, a hunch).

Jung combined the two attitudes and four functions to produce eight psychological types. The *thinking extraverted type* is objective and dogmatic. The *feeling extraverted type* is highly emotional and conforming. The *sensing extraverted type* enjoys new experiences and meeting new people. The *intuiting extraverted type* is creative and can motivate others. The *thinking introverted type* is aloof and focuses on ideas. The *feeling introverted type* tends to be quiet and shy. The *sensing introverted type* is sensitive and detached. And the *intuiting introverted type* is often eccentric and shy. Jung's psychological types form the core of a personality test called the Myers-Briggs Type Indicator (MBTI), which we discuss later in the chapter.

Adler's Individual Psychology

Alfred Adler's theory of individual psychology differed from Freud's theory in several fundamental ways. Adler's theory focused on the uniqueness of each individual person. Adler minimized the importance of the unconscious and did not subscribe to the theory that sexuality was the basis for personality or disorders. Instead, he saw human beings as motivated primarily by a *drive for superiority*. Children develop an inferiority complex because they are so little and so dependent on adults. As children develop, they encounter things they cannot do and situations in which they do not meet the standards they set for themselves. People are thus constantly striving to *compensate* for their weaknesses (a drive for superiority). Sometimes, unfortunately, they overcompensate and develop a *superiority complex*, in which they exaggerate their abilities and characteristics.

Although Adler rejected Freud's notion that childhood experiences are all-important in determining the nature of the adult personality, he believed that they contribute, along with hereditary and environmental factors, to the development of the individual's style of life—patterns of thinking and behaving that persist into adulthood. The individual's life-style directs how the person will strive for superiority.

According to Adler (1939), each person must solve life problems in the areas of interacting with other people, having an occupation, and being in love. As the person deals with these problems, he or she adopts a particular type of *life-style*. The *dominant type* typically shows no interest in other people. The *avoiding type* eschews the problems of life. The *getting type* is dependent on other people to provide for him or her. And the *useful type* interacts successfully with others. Adler's emphasis on cognitive and social processes has influenced a number of later personality theorists.

Also central to Adler's conception of personality is a human being's social nature. He believed that people are motivated by *social interest*, a capacity to love others, and a need to cooperate and work for social goals. Ideally, the individual's striving for superiority should be channeled into striving for social rather than selfish goals.

Horney's Cultural Psychology

Karen Horney was a physician trained in psychoanalysis. Like Jung and Adler, she broke with Freud, largely because of his emphasis on biological factors in personality. She believed social and cultural influences were very important influences and focused her theory on them. Horney was also distressed by Freud's views of women, and she rejected Freud's concept of penis envy. According to Horney, women envy the privileges that men enjoy in our culture, such as independence, success, sexual freedom, and strength (Horney, 1939).

Like Freud, Horney believed that early childhood was important. However, she stressed the social influences during childhood. Two basic needs in childhood include safety and satisfaction, and a failure to meet these needs may result in *basic anxiety*, a feeling of loneliness and helplessness. Children are basically helpless and need adults to care for them, but may at the same time resent their dependence and develop a hostility toward the parent. But because this hostility is not allowed in our society, and because the child is dependent on the adult, the hostility is repressed, and may ultimately lead to basic anxiety.

In order to protect oneself from basic anxiety, the person attempts to gain love from others, complies with the wishes of others, or gains power over others. These strategies may be so successful that they eventually become part of the individual's personality. Horney identified several neurotic needs, which are irrational solutions to basic anxiety, including achievement, affection,

FIGURE 11.4 Karen Horney
Karen Horney (1885–1952), a personality theorist who practiced therapy in Germany and America, disagreed with Freud's stress on the sexual influence in the development of personality. She believed that environmental and social factors were more important than sexuality and that anxiety was a stronger motivating force in human behavior than the sexual drive.

exploitation, perfection, power, prestige, and self-sufficiency.

Horney eventually proposed that rather than 10 separate neurotic needs, there were 3 *neurotic trends*, or ways of adapting. The compliant personality (moving toward people) is characterized by a strong need to be loved and needed by others. The aggressive personality (moving against people) is characterized by a need to act aggressively in a world seen as hostile. The detached personality (moving away from people) is characterized by a need to maintain distance from others. Horney's personality theory is more optimistic than Freud's, probably because she does not emphasize the biological factors, focusing instead on the social, and thus modifiable, variables of personality.

The psychoanalytic personality theories have been influential in psychology. They emphasized childhood experiences and the role of cognition. Psychoanalytic theory was the first formal type of psychotherapy available. However, psychoanalytic theory has some severe limitations (Liebert & Spiegler, 1990). The basic problem

with much of the psychoanalytic approach to personality is that it emphasizes the unconscious, and therefore is not testable. Classic psychoanalysis was sex-biased and based on biased case studies. Many psychologists were not convinced that psychoanalysis could explain completely the complexity of human personality.

A different approach is represented in the theories that try to describe personality rather than explain it. The trait theories of personality emphasize tangible qualities, rather than abstract unconsciousness.

TRAIT THEORIES

Some psychologists attempt to characterize personality through the use of traits—distinctive and stable attributes that can be found in people. Traits help to differentiate us from one another. Trait psychologists are interested in which attributes tend to occur together, indicating common underlying traits that can be identified. Typically these psychologists have based their personality theories on their observations of normal, healthy individuals.

Allport's Trait Theory

Gordon W. Allport (1961) defined personality as the dynamic organization of the psychophysical systems that determine characteristic behavior and thought of an individual. Personality is constantly changing (dynamic) and involves an interaction of biology and cognition (psychophysical). According to Allport, it is important to focus on the individual, an approach called idiographic, as each person is unique and has a distinctive personality.

In his early research, Allport referred to common traits (those shared by many people in a culture) and individual traits (those unique to a person). Later, he referred to common traits as *traits* and individual traits as *personal dispositions*.

Allport believes that individual personality can be understood through three types of hierarchical personal disposition traits: cardinal, central, and secondary. Cardinal traits are so dominant that they are expressed in everything the person does in life. For instance, the fanatical lover or the zealous religious person might represent expressions of cardinal traits. Allport believes few people have cardinal traits.

Rather than a single cardinal trait, most people have a small number of central traits. These form the core of our personality, and are developed by our experiences in life. Central traits can be measured in personality tests that include lists of adjectives. Allport (1961) asked college students to write a description of a friend, and found that the descriptions included about seven central traits.

Secondary traits are less important, situation-specific traits that help round out our personality. Things like attitudes, specific behavior patterns, skills, and preferences would be included in secondary traits. They are less dominant and are more likely to change in different situations.

Allport tried to measure an individual's traits in sufficient detail needed to classify the person and distinguish him or her from other people. He was the first personality theorist not to come from a psychoanalytic background. One criticism has been that since he took the individual approach, it is not possible to generalize from one person to another. However, his theory has been very influential in serving as a nonpsychoanalytic model of personality for other theories to follow.

Cattell's Factor Theory

Raymond B. Cattell wanted to go beyond the listing of personality traits; he wanted to understand how the traits are organized into particular clusters or patterns, and how these influence behavior. He studied under Spearman (who developed a factor theory of intelligence), and wanted to produce a mathematical model of the factors of personality. Cattell (1965) proposed the following equation to represent personality:

$$R = f(P,S)$$

FIGURE 11.5 Sixteen Personality Factor Questionnaire (16PF)

	The Primary Source Traits Covered by the 16PF Test	
Factor	**Low Sten Score Description (1–3)**	**High Sten Score Description (8–10)**
A	*Cool,* reserved, impersonal, detached, formal, aloof Sizothymia	*Warm,* outgoing, kindly, easygoing, participating, likes people Affectothymia
B	*Concrete-thinking,* less intelligent Lower scholastic mental capacity	*Abstract-thinking,* more intelligent, bright Higher scholastic mental capacity
C	*Affected by feelings,* emotionally less stable, easily annoyed Lower ego strength	*Emotionally stable,* mature, faces reality, calm Higher ego strength
E	*Submissive,* humble, mild, easily led, accommodating Submissiveness	*Dominant,* assertive, aggressive, stubborn, competitive, bossy Dominance
F	*Sober,* restrained, prudent, taciturn, serious Desurgency	*Enthusiastic,* spontaneous, heedless, expressive, cheerful Surgency
G	*Expedient,* disregards rules, self-indulgent Weaker superego strength	*Conscientious,* conforming, moralistic, staid, rule-bound Stronger superego strength
H	*Shy,* threat-sensitive, timid, hesitant, intimidated Threctia	*Bold,* venturesome, uninhibited, can take stress Parmia
I	*Tough-minded,* self-reliant, no-nonsense, rough, realistic Harria	*Tender-minded,* sensitive, overprotected, intuitive, refined Premsia
L	*Trusting,* accepting conditions, easy to get on with Alaxia	*Suspicious,* hard to fool, distrustful, skeptical Protension
M	*Practical,* concerned with "down-to-earth" issues, steady Praxernia	*Imaginative,* absent-minded, absorbed in thought, impractical Autia
N	*Forthright,* unpretentious, open, genuine, artless Artlessness	*Shrewd,* polished, socially aware, diplomatic, calculating Shrewdness
O	*Self-assured,* secure, feels free of guilt, untroubled, self-satisfied Untroubled adequacy	*Apprehensive,* self-blaming, guilt-prone, insecure, worrying Guilt proneness
Q_1	*Conservative,* respecting traditional ideas Conservatism of temperament	*Experimenting,* liberal, critical, open to change Radicalism
Q_2	*Group-oriented,* a "joiner" and sound follower, listens to others Group adherence	*Self-sufficient,* resourceful, prefers own decisions Self-sufficiency
Q_3	*Undisciplined self-conflict,* lax, careless of social rules Low integration	*Folloiwng self-image,* socially precise, compulsive High self-concept control
Q_4	*Relaxed,* tranquil, composed, has low drive, unfrustrated Low ergic tension	*Tense,* frustrated, overwrought, has high drive High ergic tension

The behavioral response (R) of a person is a function (f) of the individual's personality (P) and the situation (S). The most difficult aspect of this equation to understand is personality.

Cattell used a statistical procedure called factor analysis to determine the relationship among various personality traits. He defined a *trait* as the potential of a person to react in a certain way. Cattell used three measures to collect personality data: life records, which are observations of the person's behavior; personal questionnaires, which provide self-descriptions of personality; and objective tests, which help identify clusters of personality traits.

He started by identifying surface traits, the observable characteristics of a person's behavior and personality. Cattell noticed that surface traits tend to fall into groupings or clusters that can often be described with a single word. The identity of these trait clusters is what Cattell calls source traits, or characteristics more basic to the core of an individual's personality.

Cattell developed a personality test called the *Sixteen Personality Factor Questionnaire (16PF)* to measure source traits. With this he could develop a trait profile, or graphic representation of the source traits. We discuss the 16PF Questionnaire later in the chapter.

Eysenck's Trait Model of Personality

Hans J. Eysenck believes that biology plays a major role in personality. He used questionnaires, observations, and physiological measures of personality when developing his theory (Eysenck, 1952). His conception of personality suggests that it develops through an interaction of four sectors: cognitive (intelligence), conative (character), affective (temperament), and somatic (constitution).

Eysenck (1967) believes that personality consists of behaviors and dispositions arranged in a hierarchy. At the lowest level is the *specific response*, an isolated behavior that occurs in a single situation. For example, you might observe Ben opening the door at school for a stranger. At a more general level is the *habitual response*, a pattern of behaviors that usually occur together. For example, Ben is often observed talking with others, leading groups, organizing meetings, and smiling when others are around. Next is the *trait*, a collection of related habitual responses. Because of the habitual response shown by Ben, we could say that he has the trait of sociability. Finally, the highest and most general level is the *type*, a collection of commonly displayed traits. Eysenck would argue that Ben displays the extraverted personality type.

Eysenck (1975) proposed three major personality type dimensions: introversion-extraversion, neuroticism (stability), and psychoticism. *Introversion* includes characteristics such as pessimism, thoughtfulness, carefulness, and quietness. *Extraversion* includes characteristics such as impulsiveness, activity, excitability, liveliness, and sociability. The *neuroticism* (or emotionality/stability) dimension goes from stable to unstable, and measures stress tolerance. The unstable end of this dimension includes characteristics such as moodiness, restlessness, and anxiousness, and the stable end is characterized by calmness, leadership, and the ability to be even-tempered. The psychotic end of the *psychoticism* dimension includes characteristics such as aggressiveness, disregard for danger, solitariness, and inability to fit in with others. The traits of each dimension can be arranged along a continuum, such as when introversion-extraversion and stability-unstability are combined. For example, the stable-extraverted person might show traits such as leadership, responsiveness, and sociability, whereas the unstable-introverted person might be characterized as moody, rigid, anxious, and pessimistic.

An interesting aspect of Eysenck's theory is his suggestion that an individual's nervous system reacts to environmental stimulation in a way that influences personality. In particular, extraverts have low cortical excitation levels and therefore tend to seek outside stimulation. Introverts have high cortical excitation levels and thus tend to avoid external stimulation. Not all research supports the arousal aspect of his theory, but Eysenck's theory has been important in attempting to relate biology and personality and in utilizing the experimental approach in studying personality.

Five-Factor Personality Model

Psychologists have continued to be involved in identifying the core traits that effectively describe personality, and currently there is considerable interest in the five-factor model of personality traits. Tupes and Christal (1961) reanalyzed Cattell's data and then proposed the model, which consists of the factors of extraversion, agreeableness, conscientiousness, emotional stability (neuroticism), and openness to experience (culture). Norman (1963) argued that these five factors could adequately describe personality. Little was done with the theory until the 1980s, when a number of psychologists confirmed that these factors are central in personality (Digman, 1990).

Costa and McCrae (1980) developed a classification scheme consisting of neuroticism, extraversion, and openness (in their NEO inventory). Later they discovered substantial agreement between an updated version of their NEO scale (revised to include also agreeableness and conscientiousness) and the corresponding factors of

FIGURE 11.6   Five-Factor Personality Model

I.   **EXTRAVERSION (or SURGENCY)**
sociable, talkative, active, bold, fun-loving, spontaneous, adventurous, enthusiastic, person-oriented, assertive

II.   **AGREEABLENESS (or FRIENDLINESS)**
warm, generous, trustful, courteous, agreeable, cooperative, flexible, forgiving, cheerful, humble

III.   **CONSCIENTIOUSNESS (or DEPENDABILITY)**
conscientious, practical, cautious, serious, reliable, organized, careful, dependable, hardworking, ambitious

IV.   **EMOTIONAL STABILITY (vs. NEUROTICISM)**
relaxed, peaceful, objective, calm, unemotional, even-tempered, secure, patient, uninhibited

V.   **OPENNESS (or CULTURE, INTELLECT)**
original, imaginative, creative, perceptive, sophisticated, knowledgeable, cultured, artistic, curious, analytical, liberal

the five-factor model (McCrae & Costa, 1985). Additional support for several of the five-factor variables (extraversion, agreeableness, and conscientiousness) was reported by Peabody (1984), who also found several other possible factors. Digman and Takemoto-Chock (1981) reported support for the five-factor model when they reanalyzed six classic studies in personality. Trapnell and Wiggins (1990) found high agreement between the five-factor tests and other measures of personality. Amelang and Borkenau (1982) reported the same five factors when they tested German subjects, and McCrae and Costa (1987) again validated the five-factor model with different questionnaires and observers. McCrae and Costa (1989a) argued that strong support for the five-factor model is present, and encouraged researchers and clinicians to utilize the model in future research and assessment of personality.

Although most trait theorists agree on the "big five" structure of personality, there is disagreement on the labels for the five dimensions. For example, Digman (1988) referred to them as extraversion, friendly compliance, will to achieve, neuroticism, and intellect. Peabody and Goldberg (1989) suggested power, love, work, affect, and intellect. Goldberg (1990) recently developed a list of clusters included in each of the five factors (surgency, agreeableness, consciousness, emotional stability, and intellect). He has also developed a set of adjectives that can be used to measure people on the personality dimensions.

What are the personality traits represented by the five-factor model? By using the traits reported by McCrae & Costa (1990) and Goldberg (1990), we describe the positive aspects of the traits in each of the five factors of personality. The opposing negative aspects are not emphasized here (for example, the opposite of sociable would be unsociable).

Factor I, extraversion (or surgency) was identified as an important personality dimension in early research by both Cattell and Eysenck, and is included in McCrae and Costa's NEO inventory. Positive aspects of the traits in extraversion include terms such as sociable, talkative, active, bold, fun-loving, spontaneous, adventurous, enthusiastic, person-oriented, and assertive.

Factor II, agreeableness (or friendliness) has been examined as trust or cooperation in many studies. Traits in factor II include adjectives such as warm, generous, trustful, courteous, agreeable, cooperative, flexible, forgiving, cheerful, and humble.

Factor III, conscientiousness (or dependability or will) was first mentioned by Cattell and is similar to achievement motivation (discussed in Chapter 9, "Motivation"). Traits in the conscientiousness dimension include descriptions such as conscientious, practical, cautious, serious, reliable, organized, careful, dependable, hardworking, and ambitious.

Factor IV, emotional stability (versus neuroticism) has been identified as a basic, probably biological component of personality. Cattell referred to it as ego strength, and McCrae and Costa include it in the NEO inventory. Much of the work on this dimension has focused on the negative aspects (such as nervous, anxious, worrying, tempermental, and insecure). Positive aspects of the traits in factor IV include terms such as relaxed, peaceful, objective, calm, unemotional, even-tempered, secure, patient, and uninhibited.

Factor V, openness (or culture or intellect) is the most controversial factor. Some researchers (including Goldberg) believe that intelligence is a core part of personality, and when it is not found to be a major dimension it is because the questions do not include intelligence as a broad theme. Others (including McCrae & Costa) view intelligence as only part of the larger dimension of openness. Traits included in factor V are terms such as original, imaginative, creative, perceptive, sophisticated, knowledgeable, cultured, artistic, curious, analytical, and liberal (having broad interests).

The trait theories of personality have been very successful at guiding psychologists in the development of tests to measure personality. Traits tend to be understood readily by clients, making the test results relevant to many people. Trait theories have also been able to predict fairly accurately how well people are matched with occupations as well as personal relationships. There are, however, criticisms of trait theory. The list of traits only describes personality without explaining the influences on the individual's life. Some psychologists do not believe that personality can be classified so easily according to different traits. A more comprehensive approach to human behavior is seen in the personality theories of the humanistic psychologists.

HUMANISTIC THEORIES

Humanistic psychologists concentrate on the uniqueness of the human personality. Sometimes they are called *self* theorists because they emphasize the self (what is part of oneself and what is not). Humanistic theorists view the individual as essentially active in determining the potential course of his or her own life. Humanistic theorists tend to be optimistic, concentrating on human strengths rather than weaknesses; they stress the uniqueness of each individual, and maintain that the proper way to study a person is as a total entity that cannot be dissected into parts. We discuss the work of two representative humanistic theorists—Carl Rogers and Abraham Maslow.

Rogers's Theory of Self

Carl Rogers, who began his career as a psychotherapist, emphasized the capacities that are distinctly human in contrast to the basic drives shared by all animals. He was thus very interested in free will, responsibility, and choice. Rogers saw our basic motives as good, healthy, and positive, as discussed in his 1980 book, *A Way of Being.*

Rogers suggested that there is an inherent tendency in each of us toward self-actualization, that is, toward developing all the capacities made available to us by our heredity. He believed that under ideal conditions, our actions and feelings are determined by an innate wisdom and goodness, which, if unhampered, will result in a fully functioning person. This tendency toward self-actualization is our primary motivation and goal in life. According to Rogers, however, a healthy psychological environment is necessary for self-actualization to occur, an environment of total warmth and acceptance by others, which inspires corresponding self-acceptance.

Rogers contended that the individual *organism* interacts in the world to develop a phenomenal field, the sum total of both conscious and unconscious experiences. The phenomenal field includes everything that the individual perceives through his or her senses, such as sights, sounds, and smells, and everything that is placed in an individual's memory. A part of the phenomenal field develops as the self, the individual's perception of "I" or "me" obtained through interactions with other people.

Rogers (1971) described personality (or self) as a triangle, with real self (what you are really like), perceived self (what you perceive yourself to be), and ideal self (what you would like to be), as the sides. Central to Rogers's person-centered approach to life is the idea that every person has an innate need for a *positive self-regard*, as well as positive regard from others. To the extent that a person distorts or denies experiences (because they conflict with the need for the positive regard of others), the self-actualizing tendency is hampered, and personal growth is impaired. Congruence results when there is a fit among the aspects of self. Thus, congruence helps us become psychologically healthy and reach self-actualization. Distorted or denied experiences produce *incongruence* and conflict between the self-image and the individual's true nature. The person must spend time and effort protecting a false image of self rather than in gaining actualization. The resulting tensions can cause psychological maladjustment.

When we show unconditional positive regard toward someone, we love and accept them without conditions (that is, regardless of what they do). *Conditional positive regard* occurs when we accept another only if she or he meets our conditions (for example, if a child behaves appropriately, or if a friend doesn't embarrass us). Eventually, through conditional positive regard experiences, the individual develops *conditions of worth* (a conscience), defining what is acceptable or unacceptable about the self. A psychologically healthy person can integrate new experiences into the self-image. Even unwanted feelings such as hostility can be accepted as a part of the self without making the person feel unworthy.

According to Rogers (1961), the individual strives to be a fully functioning person by having a *good life*. There are three characteristics of the process of developing the good life. An increasing openness to experience occurs when the individual is open to feelings and events without becoming defensive. An increasing tendency to live fully moment to moment is a second characteristic. And developing trust in one's organism refers to feeling comfortable with who one is and what one is becoming. When a person is developing the good life, he or she will experience a sense of freedom.

Maslow's Self-Actualization Theory

Another humanistic psychologist, Abraham Maslow, focused his theory of personality on the psychologically healthy person. Abraham Maslow is also a leading figure in the humanistic tradition, and did much to define humanistic psychology before his death in 1970. Like Rogers, he believed that people's basic nature is good, and that the individual has an innate motive to strive toward *self-actualization*.

Maslow conceived of human beings as born with a hierarchy of needs, as we discussed in chapter 9, "Motivation." When needs on the primary level are satisfied, then needs farther up on the scale make themselves felt. Maslow's need hierarchy included physiological needs, safety needs, belongingness and love needs, esteem needs, and self-actualization. The first four are called basic needs.

Self-actualization includes another group of needs called *metaneeds*, or growth needs. Among these are the needs for knowledge, justice, truth, and beauty. The metaneeds are not arranged in a hierarchical order as are the basic needs; one can be substituted for another. Maslow (1968) proposed that the individual's personality progresses naturally with the fulfillment of the needs, steadily moving toward self-actualization. Like Rogers, he maintained that a warm and supportive environment is vital for self-actualization. Without such an environment, the individual cannot satisfy the basic needs, and because of consequent anxiety, the person will not develop the self-actualized personality.

Maslow (1970, 1987) described a number of psychological attributes that characterize self-actualized individuals. Self-actualized people are realistic, with a good grasp of what is possible. They do not frustrate themselves by working for impossible goals. They accept themselves and others for what they are. Since they have resolved inner conflicts, they tend to focus their attention on problems outside themselves. But they need privacy, for they have their own needs apart from those of others. They are autonomous and independent, able to act without orders from others or from a desire to imitate others.

Self-actualized people appreciate other people in a fresh, unstereotyped way. They form a few meaningful and intimate relationships, rather than many shallow ones. They tend to be creative, original, and have a good sense of humor. They see each new person as a unique individual, and identify with humankind, seeing themselves as part of the human experience. Their values and attitudes are democratic; they have a passion to secure equal opportunity for everyone to develop into a self-actualized person (see Figure 11.7).

Although Maslow did not conduct empirical research on his theory, other psychologists have, particularly with the *Personal Orientation Inventory* personality test (Shostrom, 1964). Generally, the characteristics that Maslow identified as self-actualization correlated highly with other tests of positive mental health and adjustment. One study (Miner, 1984) did not find Maslow's theory to be applicable to work situations; however, other research has suggested that upper-level executives were more concerned with actualization needs than were their subordinates. A study by Graham and Balloun (1973) found support for the theory in the general population. Re-

FIGURE 11.7   Maslow's Self-Actualization

- Efficient Perception of Reality
- Acceptance of Self and Others
- Spontaneity
- Problem Centering
- Need for Privacy
- Autonomy
- Continued Freshness of Appreciation
- Peak Experiences
- Identification with Humanity
- Deep Interpersonal Relationships
- Democratic Character Structure
- Strong Ethics
- Unhostile Sense of Humor
- Creativeness
- Resistance to Enculturation

Humanistic psychologist Abraham Maslow concluded that self-actualized people shared a number of common personality characteristics.

cently, Mittelman (1991) suggested that although it is difficult to replicate Maslow's original data, it is likely that many of his subjects were open-minded rather than self-actualized. Although most of us will never reach total self-actualization, this theory provides a view of the human personality that we can begin to understand and appreciate.

The humanistic approach to personality is positive and optimistic. Overall, it encourages people to become motivated to grow and improve themselves. The person-centered approach formed the core of Carl Rogers's successful type of psychotherapy (which we discuss in chapter 14, "Therapy"). It is important to note, however, that humanistic theories of personality emphasize self-actualization, a concept that is basically untestable. The humanistic theories stress the uniqueness of each person, and thus they do not provide specific predictions about individual traits. This limits their usefulness in occupational counseling, and generalization from one person to another.

BEHAVIOR AND SOCIAL LEARNING THEORIES

The last approach to personality that we review comes from the learning tradition. We discussed the basic theories of learning in chapter 6, "Learning." Learning theory in this chapter emphasizes observation, imitation, reinforcement, and punishment in the development of

FIGURE 11.8   Self-Actualization
Abraham Maslow studied the biographies of people to help him obtain case studies of those who he thought had realized their full potential, or self-actualization. Eleanor Roosevelt, Martin Luther King, Jr., and Albert Einstein might be considered examples of people who achieved self-actualization.

personality. We cover the traditional learning approach to behavior and personality, and then we discuss the cognitive social-reinforcement approach.

Skinner's Behaviorism and Personality

Behaviorists rarely speak of such "abstract" traits as aggressiveness or the need for affection. Instead they observe people and conduct research to determine what produces particular behaviors. Since moral considerations prohibit most experimentation with people's personalities, behaviorists are limited in their ability to produce theories about the human personality. Moreover, behaviorists think it is virtually impossible to conduct research that either proves or disproves any one specific theory of personality.

Behaviorists such as B. F. Skinner have generally believed that personality is defined as learned ways of behaving, which, like any behavior, follow the principles of reinforcement, extinction, generalization, discrimination, and punishment. Skinner concerned himself with the external forces operating on the individual, and did not treat the individual as an agent free to make decisions. To explain why someone strikes another person, for example, Skinner did not talk about aggressive drives, inner conflict, or an identity crisis. To explain this action, he attempted to get a history of the person's past experiences in similar situations. The individual may have learned that he or she can have his or her own way with particular types of people by striking them. With other

people, striking out may have met with negative consequences, and thus this particular behavior pattern would be ineffective.

B. F. Skinner explained his behavioristic point of view in *Beyond Freedom and Dignity* (1971): "We can no longer afford freedom, and so it must be replaced with

FIGURE 11.9   Behaviorist Approach to Personality
Behaviorists believe that personality is a learned pattern of behavior. Reinforcement is a very powerful force in shaping behavior and hence personality, according to this view. Computer-assisted instruction is one good example of how reinforcement can shape behavior. Receiving grades for schoolwork and money for work performed are other types of reinforcement.

control, control over man, his conduct, and his culture." According to Skinner, the concept of freedom is an illusion. Skinner argued that, rather than making our own decisions freely, we are controlled by our environment. We are what our past experiences and environment cause us to be. For instance, a criminal's behavior is caused by the environment. Thus the treatment of criminals must focus on changing their environment, which will in turn change their behavior (personality). Behaviorists such as Skinner argued that behavior is determined almost completely by external stimuli in the environment. Other psychologists suggest that cognition (thinking) is also very important, as we see in the next section.

Bandura's Social Cognitive Theory

Whereas Skinner's approach to personality (and indeed all of psychology) was based on reinforcement of behavior, Albert Bandura's (1977) social learning theory emphasized the role of observation and modeling. It is possible to learn and modify one's behavior by observing someone and then imitating the action, with or without reinforcement. More recently, Bandura (1989) has increased the emphasis of the role of cognition, and prefers to call his approach the social cognitive theory.

Bandura (1978) viewed the *self* as a set of cognitive structures that direct a person's perception, thinking, and behavior. Actual reinforcement is not as important as the perception of reinforcement. Thus, if a person is happy and believes his or her actions are beneficial, the person will continue exhibiting the behavior.

In his concept of reciprocal determinism, Bandura (1986) argued that the behavior, the person, and the situation interact and influence each other. People do not just respond to environmental stimuli, but rather are actively involved in influencing their own personality. For example, people are able to provide their own reinforcement when it doesn't come from other sources. Bandura argued that *self-reinforcement* produces exactly the same effects on behavior as external reinforcement. People set goals for themselves and, when their goals are reached, feel satisfaction, thus reinforcing the behaviors that led to the accomplishment of the goal. Eventually, patterns of behavior emerge that can be labeled personality.

Bandura (1982) also emphasized the concept of self-efficacy, or an individual's sense of self-worth and success in adjusting to the world. According to Bandura, people are able to judge their levels of self-efficacy through several sources of information. The most important information is *performance attainment*, as prior achievements provide evidence of the capability of the individual. When people observe others performing successfully, they receive *vicarious reinforcement*, especially if they judge themselves to be similar to the performers. If, however, the observed model has extremely high standards, most people would likely not be able to meet those same standards, and hence would have low self-efficacy and low feelings of self-worth and importance. Verbal persuasion, or being told they can achieve their goals, increases their self-efficacy. And physiological arousal caused by excitement or fear can be used as a source of positive feedback.

The social learning approach of Bandura has been influential in a number of areas of psychology, including learning, adjustment, personality, therapy, and social psychology. Many psychologists currently identify with this approach.

Rotter's Locus of Control Theory

In his social learning theory, Julian Rotter (1954) proposed that reinforcement is influential in shaping behavior and personality, but because humans are so complex, expectancies and cognitions are also involved significantly. Rotter views behavior potential as the probability that a particular behavior will be shown in a specific situation. Behavior potential depends upon two factors—expectancy and reinforcement value. Expectancy is the individual's belief that if he or she exhibits a certain behavior in a specific situation, it will result in reinforcement. Expectancy develops because of previous reinforcement in that and similar situations. Reinforcement value is the importance or value the person attaches to a particular reinforcement. For example, you will study (behavior potential) if you believe studying will lead to a reinforcement (expectancy) that you consider valuable (good grades). The preference for particular reinforcements comes from past experiences with them. The *psychological situation* results from the individual interacting in both internal and external environments. Rotter contends that behavior can be predicted only if the psychological situation is understood.

As we discussed in the opening story, Rotter has stimulated a great deal of research with his 1966 theory of internal versus external locus of control. He extended his idea of expectancy to include generalized expectancies about the control of reinforcement for a person. People tend to have either an internal or external locus of control.

People with an internal locus of control perceive that reinforcement is contingent upon their own behavior or attributes. They believe that if they work hard, they will be rewarded. They prefer situations that they have control over. Thus, internal people do not like gambling. They are less conforming and often have considerable power over their environment. They see the world as predictable and expect that consequences follow actions. If you believe that studying hard will lead to a better grade, you are likely to be labeled as internal.

People with an external locus of control tend to perceive that reinforcement is independent of their behavior, that it is controlled by external forces, by fate, or by luck. According to the external person, getting a good grade on a test depends on luck more than studying. External people cannot predict the consequences of their behavior; they tend to believe that there's nothing they can do to change things, so they give up easily.

Rotter stated that the orientation of people makes an important difference. According to him, one application of locus of control is that people cannot be helped in therapy until they begin to become internal. They must believe that their behavior does make a difference. It is possible that external expectancy actually leads to helplessness and depression, a topic we discuss in the next chapter.

Overall, behavior and social learning theories have made significant contributions to the understanding of personality. Their emphasis on behavior has led to the ability of researchers to test very specific predictions about personality and behavior. Because of the focus on learning and reinforcement, these theories have served as the core of numerous applications in clinical therapy, child rearing, educational motivation, and personal relationships. One criticism of social learning theories is their lack of attention to biological influences on personality. Researchers are now making strides toward a more comprehensive view of the influences on personality.

PERSONALITY ASSESSMENT

Psychologists have developed a number of methods to measure and assess personality. In schools and businesses, in clinics and hospitals, and as part of their counseling and therapeutic work with patients, psychologists regularly administer personality tests. Their purpose is to discover a person's characteristic patterns of behavior. They can determine from the results of personality tests what tasks a person might be assigned in a job, what kinds of courses a student might be encouraged to take, or which therapy might best serve a disturbed individual.

Any measurement of personality should meet several requirements (see chapter 1, "The Study of Psychology" for a discussion of research methods). Personality measures should be valid and reliable. Validity means that you actually measure what you intend to measure. In personality assessment, it means that you measure the subject's personality, rather than any temporary characteristics shown in the testing situation. Reliability means

FIGURE 11.10   Requirements of Personality Tests

Personality tests should be valid and reliable. **A.** Which test is more likely to be a valid personality test? **B.** Which test scores are more likely to be considered reliable?

(Answers: In **A.** the second personality test is more valid. In **B.** the first set of scores is more reliable than the second.)

consistency or repeatability; each time you measure the individual's personality, you should obtain about the same results, if the test is reliable.

In addition, personality tests, like intelligence tests, should be standardized and practical. *Standardization* is the process of determining the norms, or standards, of the population you are working with. A test is standardized by giving it to a large group that is representative of the population. *Practicality* is important in personality assessment. Most people are less interested in taking a fantastic personality test that takes 16 hours to administer than a fairly good test that can be given in 2 hours.

Personality assessment by experienced psychologists often includes an interview. But this is usually supplemented by observation and tests.

Interview

Very likely, you were interviewed when you applied for a job, talked to your academic counselor, or when someone else wanted to know how you accomplished something so well. During the interview, information about you was obtained by listening to what you said and observing how you behaved.

Interviews are sometimes classified as either unstructured or structured. In an unstructured interview no specific questions must be asked, but rather the conversa-

FIGURE 11.11   **Interview**
Interviews are often used to assess personality. In a structured interview, a specific set of questions is asked, whereas in an unstructured interview, the questions are determined by the interaction of the interviewer and subject.

tion develops in whatever direction seems appropriate. In a structured interview a set of standard questions is designed to provide the information necessary to assess personality. Both types of interview can be useful in assessing personality (Phares, 1991).

Interviews can help assess personality, but they obviously depend on the skill of the interviewer and the cooperation and honesty of the person being interviewed. The interviewer should be warm and friendly to encourage the subject to talk freely, but at the same time he or she must be objective in developing the personality assessment. Many times the person being interviewed may not want to cooperate, as in the case of criminals or the mentally ill. Especially when there is a problem with the effectiveness of the interview, the interviewer's observations are usually incorporated into the assessment.

Observation

Observation involves watching a person's behavior in everyday situations over a period of time. The ideal is naturalistic observation, where the person is observed in his or her normal environment (see chapter 1, "The Study of Psychology"). However, many times observations must be made in a clinical setting, as when psychologists are trying to diagnose behavior problems, or in other appropriate environments, such as an office during

a job interview. The observer records the subject's behavior, and then attempts to determine motivation and develop a personality description of the individual being observed.

As noted, success in observation depends upon the skill of the observer and the cooperation of the subject. The observer must interpret correctly the behavior shown by the subject. Since it is very likely that, when being observed, the subject's behavior will be somewhat different from normal, it is desirable to make observations over an extended period of time, so that the subject can relax and behave in a more normal manner.

In an attempt to standardize observations and make them more objective, psychologists have developed rating scales. A rating scale is a paper and pencil form that observers fill out in their assessment of a subject. To obtain the most accurate evaluation of a subject, several raters should be used. Ratings are used extensively in educational and industrial settings, but are also used to assess an individual's personality (Anastasi, 1988). Typically, the rating scale has a number of categories in which the characteristics shown by the subject are checked off. Self-rating scales might also be used, in which case the subject is asked to evaluate himself or herself by indicating which traits or characteristics apply. An elaborate form of a self-rating scale is the standardized objective test of personality, which we cover next.

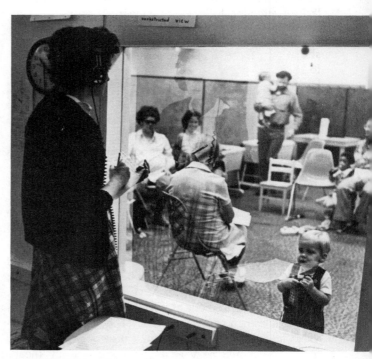

FIGURE 11.12   **Observation**
In the observation technique of personality assessment, the psychologist records the behavior of a subject and then makes an assessment of the subject's motivation and personality.

Objective Personality Tests

Objective personality tests are administered and scored according to standardized instructions. Thus, no matter where or when you take the test, it will be given and scored in the same way, assuring objectivity in administration and interpretation. There are a number of popular objective tests in use today.

Strong Interest Inventory   Edward Strong, Jr., developed a test in 1927 to help people decide which occupations they were best suited for. The original test was called the *Strong Vocational Interest Blank* and matched a person's interests and activities with those of people in various occupations. If you go to the counseling center, you may be given the current version, the Strong Interest Inventory of the *Strong Vocational Interest Blanks*, revised by Jo-Ida C. Hansen in 1985.

This 325-item personality test asks the subject to evaluate (indicate like or dislike of) a wide variety of specific activities, school subjects, amusements, occupations, and personalities. The Strong Interest Inventory (formerly called the Strong-Campbell Interest Inventory) profile includes scores on 6 general occupational scales (realistic, investigative, artistic, social, conventional, and enterprising) as well as 23 basic interest scales (interest in specific areas, such as artistic activities), 207 occupational scales (which measure the similarity between the test taker and people employed in particular occupations), and 2 special scales (academic comfort and introversion-extraversion). The Strong Interest Inventory shows that people engaged in different occupations tend to have different personalities. The differences include the kinds of hobbies engaged in, social activities enjoyed, school topics preferred, and the kind of material read. Thus, the personality of the test taker can be matched with people already in certain occupations, and the counselor's predictions for success can be guided thereby.

Minnesota Multiphasic Personality Inventory   One of the best-known personality tests is the Minnesota Multiphasic Personality Inventory (MMPI). Originally developed in 1940 by Starke Hathaway and Charnley McKinley to identify personality disorders, it is still the most widely used test for general personality assessment (Walsh & Betz, 1990). The revised 1989 MMPI-2 consists of 567 items that are answered either true or false. The scores are used to develop a personality profile on 10 basic clinical scales, 10 supplementary scales, and 15 personality content scales. The MMPI-2 items include statements such as "I believe I am being plotted against," "I do not tire easily," and "I am worried about sex matters." The subject's responses are compared to scores produced by *normal* adults, and can be used to identify a variety of personality disorders.

Research into the usefulness of the MMPI in analyzing over 1,500 normal adults was reported by Paul Costa and his colleagues (1985). They identified only nine factors dealing with normal populations represented in the test. Because of its fairly narrow emphasis on factors of normal populations, they recommended supplementing the MMPI with other tests when working with normal personalities. While there are concerns about its effective use in normal populations, the MMPI is still a very useful measure of personality. The MMPI-2 revision in 1989 was designed to correct some of these concerns. It is still too early to evaluate the success of the MMPI-2, although preliminary research reports are positive. The Application that follows describes this personality inventory and its recent revision.

APPLICATION

The MMPI-2

The MMPI-2 (Minnesota Multiphasic Personality Inventory) is the most popular objective clinical personality test in use today (Walsh & Betz, 1990). Since its conception in the early 1940s, over 5,000 studies have been published about it. What is the MMPI-2 and what does it do?

The original MMPI was developed to diagnose specific psychological disorders, such as depression and schizophrenia (a disorder of thinking and emotion that is discussed in chapter 13, "Psychological Disorders"). Starke R. Hathaway and J. Charnley McKinley, the test's developers, gave hundreds of short statements to mentally disturbed patients. They then noted which statements the patients agreed with. The basic purpose of the test was to differentiate various types of mental patients, as well as to discriminate between mental patients and normal people. The MMPI did indeed do that; certain types of people tend to give certain responses on the test. Thus, the test was used to diagnose problems by first determining who actually had them.

In July, 1989, the updated and restandardized MMPI-2 was published. Because the original MMPI was so widely used, great care was taken to improve the original while still keeping the revision compatible. The restandardization was based on a representative sample of 2,600 men and women ranging from 18 to 84 years of age. The sample included Asians, blacks, Hispanics, Native Americans, and whites. Other sample characteristics included educational, marital, occupational, and economic status. The original 550 items (with 82 reworded to eliminate sex bias and outdated topics), along with 154 new items, were included in an experimental form used in testing. Eventually, 567 items were selected for the MMPI-2 (370 items are used for the basic scales and 197

FIGURE 11.13 MMPI-2 Profiles

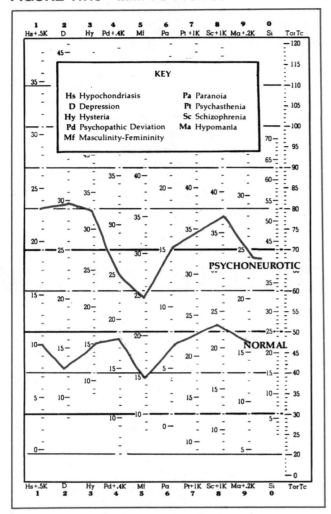

The MMPI-2 is one of the most widely used objective tests of personality. Scores from 567 true-false questions are used to develop a personality profile as shown here.

schizophrenia (form of abnormal behavior), hypomania (excitability), and social introversion (withdrawal). The MMPI-2 includes 10 supplementary scales that help diagnose clinical problems. The supplementary scales include anxiety, repression, ego strength, alcoholism, hostility, dominance, social responsibility, college maladjustment, gender-role, and post-traumatic stress disorder. There are also 15 content scales that measure various aspects of personality. They include anxiety, fears, obsessiveness, depression, health concerns, bizarre mentation, anger, cynicism, antisocial practices, type A personality, low self-esteem, social discomfort, family problems, work interference, and negative treatment indicators.

The MMPI-2 norms are much more representative of the normal population, reducing one of the major criticisms of the original MMPI. It strives to eliminate sexist language, cultural bias, and objectionable questions about sex and religion. Because the majority of questions were unchanged, it is possible to compare responses on the old and new forms. At the present time, we do not have enough research studies of the revision to evaluate its effectiveness adequately. Preliminary research suggests that the MMPI-2 will continue to be a useful tool in personality assessment.

are used for the supplementary scales). The MMPI-2 is available in booklet form, on audio cassettes, and on computers.

The MMPI-2 consists of 567 statements to which the subject responds with true, false, or cannot say. It was designed primarily for adults and has not yet been used for children. The items cover a wide range of topics, including attitudes on religion and sexual practices, perceptions of health, political ideas, information on family, education and occupation, and displays of symptoms known to be exhibited by certain groups of mentally disturbed people.

The test provides scores on 10 basic clinical scales. The scales include hypochondriasis (exaggerated concern about physical health), depression, hysteria, psychopathic deviancy, masculinity-femininity, paranoia, psychasthenia (irrational fears and compulsive actions),

California Psychological Inventory The California Psychological Inventory (CPI) is a test used to measure personality in normal populations. Harrison Gough's 1987 revision of CPI consists of 462 items that are to be answered true or false. Some of the scales of the CPI include dominance, capacity for status, sociability, self-acceptance, responsibility, self-control, femininity/masculinity, and tolerance. A sample item is similar to "I enjoy going to parties." Corporate personnel offices might use the CPI as part of their screening program for job applicants. Walsh and Betz (1990) stated that the CPI has been used in a wide variety of research and practical situations.

16PF Raymond Cattell developed the Sixteen Personality Factor Questionnaire (16PF) to measure personality traits. Originally published in 1949, it has been revised several times, the latest for the questions in 1967 and the norms for interpretation in 1986. The factor analysis statistical technique was used to identify clusters of traits that have the same underlying cause and are consistently shown by subjects.

The 16PF (Form A) consists of 187 multiple-choice questions. Examples of questions that are similar to those on the 16PF include: "People say I'm friendly. (A) true (B) uncertain (C) false" or "When with other people I am: (A) outgoing (B) shy (C) neither." The test is scored by hand or by computer, and the result is a test profile in which the score for each of the 16 dimensions is graphed on a scale of 1 to 10.

The 16PF scale has been used to assess personality in a variety of situations, such as career counseling, personnel evaluation, marriage counseling, and adjustment screening (Anastasi, 1988). Although there has been some criticism of the reliability of the test (Lanyon, 1984), it is one of the most popular personality tests available (Walsh & Betz, 1990). (See Figure 11.5.)

Myers-Briggs Type Indicator In 1962 Isabel Briggs Myers and her mother, Katherine Briggs, published the Myers-Briggs Type Indicator (MBTI) to measure scientifically Jung's 1923 Type Theory. In recent years, the MBTI has become a very popular personality test, especially in academic settings. Jung's theory included the dimension of introversion-extraversion, perception (either sensing or intuition) and judgment (either thinking or feeling). The 1985 revised test (Form G) has 126 two-choice items. The MBTI includes four dimensions that are used to generate 16 types. The four types include: introversion-extraversion, sensing-intuition, thinking-feeling, and judging-perceiving. Myers (1987) reported that different types of people tend to go into different professions. For instance, teachers and social work students had high levels of intuiting and feeling, whereas police officers and dental students scored high in extraversion, sensing, and thinking. Some recent research has questioned the usefulness of the MBTI compared to other personality tests (McCrae & Costa, 1989b).

NEO Personality Inventory Paul Costa, Jr., and Robert McCrae (1985) developed the NEO Personality Inventory (NEO-PI) to measure the five major factors in adult personality: neuroticism (N), extraversion (E), openness to experience (O), agreeableness (A), and conscientiousness (C). The personality test consists of 181 items answered on a five-point scale (strongly agree to strongly disagree). Items are similar to: "I enjoy keeping active " or "I laugh a lot." The NEO-PI has been used in research studies and has applications in clinical, vocational counseling, and educational situations (Costa & McCrae, 1985). As we discussed earlier in this chapter, the five-factor personality model is currently receiving a great deal of attention, and the NEO-PI will be useful in testing research predictions about personality traits and behavior.

Even with built-in factors to reduce lying, objective tests still depend upon the truthfulness of the answers provided by the subjects. One possible way to get around this problem is through the use of projective tests that provide ambiguous stimuli for which there are not clear-cut answers.

Projective Personality Tests

Projective personality tests present simple, ambiguous stimuli that will allow a subject to respond with projections of his or her own personality. Since there are no clear-cut correct answers, presumably this form of testing cuts down on any possible cheating. Projective tests often require subjects to form associations to inkblots or words, develop stories about situations portrayed in pictures, draw figures of people or other objects, or complete unfinished sentences (Liebert & Spiegler, 1990). If the psychologist is experienced, projective tests can provide valuable insights into personality. However, it is sometimes easy to misinterpret a response, and an inexperienced tester can misuse the information obtained.

Rorschach Inkblot Test One of the best-known projective tests is the Rorschach Inkblot Test. This test, developed by Hermann Rorschach in 1921, consists of 10 cards containing blots of ink (five black and five colored). The subject is asked to go through the cards and discuss freely what is seen. The examiner then asks questions that will help determine the assessment of personality. Rorschach's original cards are still used today. Because of the subjective nature of this kind of test interpretation, validity and reliability of this test are low. There are

FIGURE 11.14 Inkblot Test
In projective personality tests, such as the Rorschach Inkblot Test, subjects are asked to respond to relatively vague and meaningless stimuli. The assumption is that the individual's personality characteristics will be revealed through responses. What do you see in this figure?

FIGURE 11.15 Thematic Apperception Test
In the TAT, subjects are asked to make up a story about the people in the picture. The test works on the assumption that subjects will project their own personalities into the picture. Who do you think the people in this picture are and what are they thinking?

several systems that have attempted to improve objectivity in scoring. For example, one system scores responses based on location of inkblot, popularity of answer, and response content. A more recent inkblot test is the 1961 *Holtzman Inkblot Technique (HIT)*, which uses 45 cards to assess personality. Holtzman developed the HIT to overcome the deficiencies of the Rorschach. Administration of the HIT is standardized, and scoring includes examination of 22 response variables. The scorer reliability is high, and a group form of the test presented by using a slide projector produces a reliable measure. The HIT focuses on personality variables such as cognitive functioning, affective functioning, and self-concept. In general, it appears that the HIT is a useful projective test of personality.

Thematic Apperception Test Another well-known projective test is the Thematic Apperception Test (TAT), which uses pictures of people in everyday settings, rather than abstract inkblots. The TAT was developed originally by Henry Murray in 1943. Subjects are shown the pictures one at a time and are required to make up stories about the people portrayed in the pictures. It is assumed that subjects will project their own thoughts and feelings into the stories. The test contains 19 cards and

requires 2 hours of testing. Many examiners use only part of the cards.

The TAT has been used in a variety of settings. One of the most popular uses has been to measure the need for achievement, as discussed in chapter 9, "Motivation." Like other projective tests, there are problems in the TAT with the underlying assumptions, such as the assumption that the subjects always project themselves into the role of the hero in the story. John Atkinson (1981) has also shown that temporary conditions such as hunger, lack of sleep, and frustration can affect a subject's responses on the TAT significantly. Despite the problems with the TAT, it is a popular projective test of personality and has been widely used.

There are many other projective tests of personality, including word-association tests, sentence-completion tests, and picture-drawing tests. Picture-drawing tests, such as the *Draw-A-Person* or the *House-Tree-Person* test, have been especially useful in work with children, who often can't verbalize their feelings or problems adequately (Liebert & Spiegler, 1990). The major objection to projective tests is one of misinterpretation. Still, they provide a glimpse into a subject's personality. ■

In some ways personality forms a core of psychology. It is easy to see how all of the other topics covered thus far contribute to the development of personality— the distinctive, enduring patterns of behavior and cognition that characterize a person's adaptation to life. As we saw in the opening story, personality theories allow us to predict how people will react in certain situations. This chapter is also a turning point. So far, we've been discussing the variables responsible for the healthy, normal individual's behavior. In the rest of the book, we use what we have learned to understand the topics of adjustment, psychological disorders, therapy, social psychology, and applications of psychology.

"Who needs a super ego with 'Him' around?"

CHAPTER REVIEW

What You've Learned About Personality

1. Personality is the distinctive and enduring patterns of behavior and cognition that characterize a person's adaptation to life.

2. Personality theories organize the main themes of behavior, explain the differences and similarities among individuals, and define the healthy personality. Personality theories help us reduce our confusion and indecision about other people. A good theory should be explicit, testable, and acceptable.

3. Sigmund Freud's psychoanalytic theory of personality includes the conscious, preconscious, and unconscious mind. Personality is the interaction of the id, ego, and superego. The id represents a person's basic instinctual drives, which unconsciously and impulsively seek immediate pleasure. The id contains Eros (sexual) and Thanatos (aggressive) instincts and obtains energy from the libido. The superego consists of the societal values that have been instilled into a person (conscience). The ego consists of a conscious faculty for perceiving and dealing with reality.

4. Carl Jung's analytical personality theory includes not only a personal conscious, but also a collective unconscious (consisting of archetypes) shared by all humankind. The goal of a healthy personality is to achieve individuation, in which all parts of the personality are fully developed and harmoniously integrated. Jung identified eight psychological types of personality.

5. Alfred Adler's individual personality theory states that people are motivated primarily by a drive for superiority, trying to overcome a sense of weakness. Also important in this theory is people's social interest, a capacity to love others and cooperate for social goals.

6. Karen Horney believed that in order to protect oneself from basic anxiety, a person attempts to gain love from others or gain power over others. She focused on neurotic trends of adaptation.

7. Some psychologists characterize personality through the use of traits, which are distinctive and stable attributes of people. Gordon Allport distinguished among three types of traits. Cardinal traits are so dominant that they are expressed in everything the person does. Most people have a small number of central traits that are developed by experience. Secondary traits are less important, situation-specific traits.

8. Raymond Cattell identified surface traits and source traits in his Sixteen Personality Factor Questionnaire (16PF). He started by identifying surface traits, the observable characteristics of a person's behavior and personality. Surface traits tend to fall into clusters, or source traits, the characteristics more basic to the core of an individual's personality.

9. Hans Eysenck's conception of personality suggests that personality develops through interaction of cognitive, conative, affective, and somatic sectors. The personality hierarchy includes specific responses, habitual responses, traits, and types. Eysenck's types include introversion, extraversion, and neuroticism.

10. The five-factor model of personality traits includes extraversion (or surgency), agreeableness (or friendliness), conscientiousness (or dependability), emotional stability (vs. neuroticism), and openness (or culture or intellect).

11. Humanistic psychologists concentrate on the uniqueness of the human personality. Carl Rogers believed that it is important to have congruence between our real self-image and our perceived self-image.

12. Abraham Maslow's humanistic theory stresses people's innate motivation toward self-actualization. Maslow proposed that after meeting the basic needs, people work toward self-actualization. Maslow studied the characteristics of the self-actualized person.

13. Learning theories view personality as behavior patterns that are learned due to experiences with reinforcements and punishments. B. F. Skinner proposed that external stimuli almost totally determine our behavior.

14. Albert Bandura's social cognitive theory emphasizes the role of observation, modeling, and cognition. Self-efficacy is an individual's sense of self-worth and success in adjusting to the world.

15. Julian Rotter proposed that reinforcement and cognition are influential in shaping personality. Behavior potential depends on expectancy and reinforcement value. Rotter developed the locus of control theory: internal people believe that their own actions control reinforcements, whereas external people believe that their actions have no influence on reinforcement.

16. Any measure of personality should be valid, reliable, standardized, and practical. In an interview, the interviewer obtains information about a person by listening to what is said and observing behavior patterns. Interviews can be structured or unstructured. Observation can also aid in understanding personality.

17. Objective personality tests are administered and scored according to standardized procedures. The Strong Interest Inventory matches the personality of the subject with people in various occupations. The Minnesota Multiphasic Personality Inventory (MMPI-2) consists of 567 true-false items, which can be used to identify a variety of personality disorders. The California Personality Inventory (CPI) measures personality in normal populations. Other objective tests include the 16PF, the MBTI, and the NEO-PI. Projective tests assess personality by presenting ambiguous test stimuli that allow a subject to project his or her own personality. The Rorschach Inkblot Test consists of 10 cards containing blots of ink. In the Thematic Apperception Test (TAT), the subject is shown pictures and is asked to make up a story about the people portrayed in them.

CHAPTER OBJECTIVES

What You'll Learn About Adjustment and Health

After studying this chapter, you should be able to:

1. Define the concepts of stress and adjustment.
2. Identify the life changes and daily hassles that cause stress.
3. Describe the major psychological causes of stress (pressure, conflict, and frustration).
4. Describe anxiety.
5. Outline the stages of the general adaptation syndrome.
6. Describe the symptoms of burnout and identify four remedies for it.
7. Outline the problems of learned helplessness and shyness and describe how they are treated.

8. Describe five major defense mechanisms.
9. Describe the process of task-oriented coping.
10. Describe the techniques of time management.
11. Define well-being and identify three factors that contribute to a sense of well-being.
12. Identify three psychological factors that affect physical conditions.
13. Compare the Type A and the Type B behavior patterns.
14. Identify two health enhancement behaviors.

In his 1975 book, *Helplessness*, Martin Seligman described a theory to explain why some people seem to give up and become helpless. It seems that in a situation over which they have no control, people learn eventually that the responses they make will not affect the outcome. Thus, people realize that trying to respond is useless, and so they give up and ultimately become depressed.

Seligman's research on learned helplessness began in the 1960s when he and his colleagues were looking at classical conditioning in dogs. In one study the experimenters trained four dogs to associate the sound of a tone with an electric shock by placing the dogs in a Pavlovian harness, a rubberized cloth hammock. The dogs received a series of 64 shocks on the hind feet. The shocks were inescapable, and the dogs quickly learned to associate the sound of the tone with the pain of the shock.

The following day, the dogs were given an opportunity to avoid the shock. They were placed in a two-way shuttlebox that was divided by a small barrier set at the height of the dogs' shoulders. One-way mirrors allowed the experimenters to observe the subjects' performance. The experimenters sounded a tone, which was followed 10 seconds later by a shock to the side of the box that the dogs were in. Normal control-group dogs, who had not been conditioned to associate the shock with the tone, yelped and ran frantically about the box until they accidentally got over the barrier and escaped the shock. On the next trial, these "normal" dogs jumped more quickly over the barrier, and within a few trials they avoided the shock altogether by jumping as soon as the tone was sounded.

The behavior of the experimental dogs, who had previously been given the inescapable shock paired with

How much stress are you experiencing now? Stress, an unavoidable consequence of life, is anything that produces demands on people to adjust their behavior. Stress often has negative consequences, such as anxiety or burnout. Psychologists have studied a variety of adjustment techniques, some of which are more effective than others. Recently, health psychology has gained the attention of researchers in the field of adjustment.

12

Adjustment and Health

the tone, was very different. At first they ran around, but very quickly they lay down and suffered the shock. On subsequent trials, these dogs didn't even attempt to escape; they gave up the effort. Ten trials were given in the shuttlebox. None of the experimental subjects learned to escape or avoid the electric shock.

Seligman described the dogs' behavior as *learned helplessness*. Because they learned in the first part of the study that they could not escape the shock, they gave up in later experiences and didn't try to escape. They became helpless.

Seven days later, Seligman tested the four dogs again in the shuttlebox for escape behavior. One dog escaped, but the others continued to show strong learned helplessness. Then the treatment to help the dogs overcome learned helplessness began. In Phase 1, the dogs were again placed in the shuttlebox, but this time the barrier was removed. In order to escape, the dogs only had to step across a 5-inch divider. In addition, the observation window on the "safe" side was opened and the experimenter called the dog to come over. Only one dog responded to this phase of the treatment.

In Phase 2, the subjects were placed in the shuttlebox with a long leash around their necks. Now the dogs were dragged across the divider to the safe side by the experimenter. A maximum of 25 trials were given per day until the dogs began to cross over on their own accord.

One dog responded after Phase 1 (no barrier/calling). One of the dogs who required Phase 2 (forced escape/avoidance exposure) began responding after 20 trials, whereas the other two required 35 and 50 trials of Phase 2 treatment. In a follow-up test, all of the dogs continued to avoid the shock, thus indicating that they

were normal. Seligman had shown alleviation of learned helplessness in the dogs.

Seligman suggested that learned helplessness in people is acquired in a similar manner. He proposed further that this was a model of depression, and that therapy for alleviating human depression should consist of techniques, similar to that used on the dogs, that would force a person to gain control over his or her life.

FIGURE 12.1 Learned Helplessness
When people have no control over a situation, they eventually learn that their responses do not affect the outcome. This leads to what Martin Seligman calls learned helplessness.

WHAT IS ADJUSTMENT?

Learned helplessness is one of the many reactions to stress. Although we all have an idea of what stress is like, most of us find it difficult to define the concept. Some researchers define stress as a stimulus (stressor) that threatens us. Others view stress as the body's response to threats from the environment; in that context it isn't all bad. Sometimes stress is equated with anxiety as a psychological reaction to stressors.

Here we define stress as anything that produces demands on us to adjust our behavior. These demands might tax our capacities. Stress includes pressures, threats to our well-being, and other changes that require us to adjust to new situations. Lazarus and Folkman (1984) argued that cognitive appraisal is important because we must interpret an event as stressful for it to produce demands on us.

Stress can be caused by psychological or physical demands. For instance, conflict and frustration are examples of psychological demands. Physical demands might include infection, disease, or injury. In this chapter we focus chiefly on the psychological causes of stress.

How we react to the demands of stress in our lives is called adjustment. When we are threatened in some way or when excessive demands are placed upon us, we make changes in our behavior in order to protect ourselves. There are a variety of adjustment techniques, some successful and some not. To keep alert and productive we need some stress (Selye, 1980). But when excessive stress is present, we must do something to reduce it.

Adjustment can be viewed as part of a continuum of adaptation. In fact, Grasha and Kirschenbaum (1986) identified adaptation as the process we undergo when events in our lives force us to change. They argued that we tend to exhibit three kinds of adaptive responses to stress and demands in our daily lives: maladjustment, adjustment, and competence. Maladjustment occurs when we respond inappropriately to demands placed upon us. *Adjustment* occurs when we respond adequately to stress in our lives. When we behave in ways that go beyond just meeting the challenges of life to improving our lives and achieving our goals, we are exhibiting competence. Grasha and Kirschenbaum argued that maladjustment results in poor personal effectiveness and adjustment results in satisfactory personal effectiveness, but *excellent* personal effectiveness is achieved only through competence.

Adjustment is closely related to personality, because each individual adjusts to stressful demands in stable, unique ways. As in the study of personality, there are several viewpoints that contribute to our understanding of adjustment. The psychoanalytic model of adjustment emphasizes the importance of early experiences and unconscious motives, and suggests that adjustment results from the absence of internal conflict. The biological view emphasizes overall physical and psychological health, and the physiological effects of stress on our health. The learning view emphasizes the importance of environmental demands and our learned responses to meet those demands. The humanistic approach emphasizes the role of the self and the tendency toward self-actualization. And the cognitive view emphasizes the role of the mental processes of perception, memory, and thinking in interpreting stress and our adjustment to it.

Successful psychological adjustment is often associated with good physical health. The field of health psychology is concerned with understanding the psychological influences on people's health. Especially relevant are topics such as the role of stress in illness and cancer, the management of stress, and how behaviors such as exercise or diet relate to health. We begin this chapter with a look at the causes of stress, then examine how we adjust to the stressful demands in our lives, and end with a brief review of health psychology.

CAUSES OF STRESS

Stress is often unavoidable for most of us. We are aware of the negative sources of stress, but often forget about the positive sources. Hans Selye (1976) defined distress as damaging or unpleasant stress, such as the experience of anxiety or fear. We experience distress when we lose a loved one, do poorly on a test, or have a serious illness. Pleasant and satisfying experiences are due to what Selye called eustress. Examples of eustress include getting married, earning a high grade, or hitting a home run. Selye (1980) argued that stress is important in our lives, and that eustress, in particular, is necessary to motivate us to lead full lives. In this chapter we focus on adjusting to the more negative aspects of stress.

Life Changes and Daily Hassles

Even our daily routine may cause us stress, but we certainly experience stress when we make major changes in our lives. Here we compare these two types of stress.

Stress and Life Changes Getting married, receiving a big pay raise, going on vacation, graduating from school, or getting a new job can be major sources of stress for many people. In fact, much of our stress comes from change in our lives that taxes our capacities to adjust our behavior to new situations.

Psychiatrists Thomas Holmes and Richard Rahe (1967) designed the *Social Readjustment Rating Scale*

(SRRS) to study the amount and consequences of changes in our lives because of stress (see Figure 12.2). They asked subjects to rate various changes in their lives in comparison to the changes caused by marriage (which served as an arbitrary guidepost). Each of the changes was assigned a *life change unit (LCU)* value that indicated the amount of stress it was likely to cause. Holmes and Rahe found that individuals who score over 300 life change units of both positive and negative events within a year have a high probability of becoming ill.

A number of early studies suggested that a large increase in life change units may indicate stress severe enough to endanger health. For example, in a 1974 study, Rahe and his colleagues found that victims who died of heart attacks experienced an average of a 150 percent increase in LCUs during the six months prior to the attack. Perkins (1982) reported that high LCUs were associated with a range of psychological and physical problems, from heart disease to psychological disorders.

Serious criticisms have been voiced concerning the

life change approach. Monroe (1982) pointed out that this type of research is correlational, and hence there can be other explanations for the data. Perhaps the problems existed prior to the life changes and even contributed to the changes. For instance, an illness might cause poor work habits or marital problems. A number of research studies have reported that negative life changes are much more likely to be associated with stress and illness than are positive life changes (Thoits, 1983). Rice (1987) reported that some researchers do not find any relationship between life change units and illness. Taylor (1991) argued that variables such as personality, prior experience, social support, and individual differences in perception of experience determine whether life change events will contribute to illness. In summary, an understanding of the life changes and amount of stress is valuable in predicting difficulties, but the exact relationship is unknown.

Daily Hassles Richard Lazarus and his colleagues (1985) argued that rather than major life change

FIGURE 12.2   Social Readjustment Rating Scale

Life Event	Adult Group		Adolescent Group	
	Rank of Life Change Unit	Mean Value of Life Change Unit	Rank of Life Change Unit	Mean Value of Life Change Unit
Death of spouse	1	100	1	69
Divorce	2	73	2	60
Marital separation	3	65	3	55
Jail term	4	63	8	50
Death of a close family member	5	63	4	54
Major personal injury or illness	6	53	6	50
Marriage	7	50	9	50
Fired from work	8	47	7	50
Marital reconciliation	9	45	10	47
Retirement	10	45	11	46
Major change in health of family member	11	44	16	44
Pregnancy	12	40	13	45
Sex difficulties	13	39	5	51
Gain of a new family member	14	39	17	43
Business readjustment	15	39	15	44
Change in financial state	16	38	14	44
Death of a close friend	17	37	12	46
Change to a different line of work	18	36	21	38
Change in number of arguments with spouse	19	35	19	41
Mortgage over $10,000	20	31	18	41
Foreclosure of mortgage or loan	21	30	23	36
Change in responsibilities at work	22	29	20	38
Son or daughter leaving home	23	29	25	34
Trouble with in-laws	24	29	22	36
Outstanding personal achievement	25	28	28	31
Wife begins or stops work	26	26	27	32
Begin or end school	27	26	26	34
Change in living conditions	28	25	24	35
Revision of personal habits	29	24	35	26
Trouble with boss	30	23	33	26
Change in work hours or conditions	31	20	29	30
Change in residence	32	20	30	28
Change in schools	33	20	34	26
Change in recreation	34	19	36	26
Change in church activities	35	19	38	21
Change in social activities	36	18	32	28
Mortgage or loan less than $10,000	37	17	31	28
Change in sleeping habits	38	16	41	18
Change in number of family get-togethers	39	15	37	22
Change in eating habits	40	15	40	18
Vacation	41	13	39	19
Christmas	42	12	42	16
Minor violations of the law	43	11	43	12

Life change units measure stress. Research has shown that a large shift in life change units, positive or negative, can endanger a person's health. Holmes and Rahe (1967) used the scale to measure stress in adults, whereas Ruch and Holmes (1971) used it to examine the level of stress in an adolescent group. The rank of a life change unit is different for each group. Add the value of life change units for each change you have experienced during the past year to determine your level of stress.

events, much stress is produced from the *daily hassles* that routinely annoy us. Lazarus (1981) defined hassles as petty routine annoyances, aggravations, or frustrations, such as driving in traffic, preparing meals, the pressure of time, financial problems, communications problems, and making decisions.

According to Lazarus, major life events themselves do not directly cause stress as much as they create numerous minor hassles that contribute to the overall stress level. For instance, a divorce or death of a spouse, while traumatic, often modifies the life of the sole or surviving spouse in such a way as to make him or her responsible for many details of life the other person had taken care of, like making meals, washing clothes, paying bills, shopping, or maintaining the automobile. Lazarus and his colleagues found that the most frequent hassles include too many responsibilities, maintaining an attractive physical appearance, loneliness, not enough time, and job dissatisfactions.

It should be pointed out that Lazarus also found people had daily "uplifts" or satisfactions such as relating well with others, visiting, having enough money for something desired, listening to music, and sex. Research suggests that these uplifts might be able to counteract some of the effects of stress (Cohen & Hoberman, 1983). It appears that daily hassles and uplifts are important in our perception of stress, but further research is needed in order for us to predict with greater accuracy when they are likely to lead to serious life problems.

Major Psychological Causes of Stress

Here we review the major causes of stress in our daily lives. Along with physical stresses, such as illness, noise, or temperature extremes, there are three major psychological causes of stress: *pressure*, *conflict*, and *frustration*.

Pressure When we strive to meet the social and psychological demands we impose on ourselves and others impose on us, we experience <u>pressure</u>. Internal <u>pressure</u> results when we attempt to maintain self-esteem by forcing ourselves to achieve higher standards: we study harder in school, try to be more popular with our friends, attempt to solve difficult challenges, and try to look attractive. We may feel pressured because there is not enough time to finish our work, or because we want to take on more than we are capable of handling effectively. Internal pressure is important for self-improvement. With internal pressure, we try harder to achieve more. Without internal pressure, we would not be motivated to improve and try harder. But when we try too hard because of excessive pressure, the result is unhealthy stress.

FIGURE 12.3 Pressure
Excessive demands made upon us by others or ourselves can result in stress. This marine private at boot camp in San Diego is probably experiencing stress from trying to maintain a high self-esteem and trying to please others in his life.

<u>External pressure</u> results from the demands other people make on us. We try to please the people who are important in our lives. We may try to lose weight to please or attract a loved one, get high grades to make our parents proud, work hard to impress the boss, or compete to be successful so we will be admired by our friends. External pressure helps us adjust to a social environment. But when others make too many demands on us, or we find their demands too difficult to comply with, the result is stress. Sometimes different pressures act on us at the same time to produce a situation called conflict.

Conflict Conflict occurs when we experience in-compatible demands or desires (Rice, 1987). In many cases, when the conflict is not resolved, the result is stress. Psychologists generally follow the lead of social psychologist Kurt Lewin (1935), who suggested that conflict can be described by two opposing tendencies: *approach* and *avoidance*.

In <u>approach-approach conflict</u> we are attracted to two equally desirable goals that are incompatible. Choosing one goal means giving up the other one. For instance, we can take psychology *or* biology, but not both. Or we can see only one movie at a time. When we experience approach-approach conflict, we often have difficulty in making a decision. Then after the decision is made, we have doubts about it. This leads to stress that would not have existed if we did not have to make the decision.

In avoidance-avoidance conflict we are faced with two equally undesirable demands that we must choose between. With either choice we are not going to be happy. For example, we might be terrified of water, but we don't want people to laugh at us for not swimming. Because the outcome will be negative, we are bound to experience stress. Our objective is to choose the alternative that is less likely to be stressful. There is a strong tendency for us to try to escape avoidance-avoidance conflicts. For example, we might forget to bring a bathing suit to the swim party so that we can put off making a decision. Of course, this also creates its own type of stress.

In approach-avoidance conflicts we are faced with a single goal that has positive and negative aspects. We might really want to have a car, but realize we cannot afford one. We might really want to run for an office in student government, but we are afraid of the responsibility. In this type of conflict we may consider the costs and benefits carefully before making a decision, being aware that the consequences are not all positive. Or we may remain undecided and let the opportunity slip away.

Sometimes we experience conflict over two or more goals, both of which have positive and negative aspects.

This situation is called a multiple approach-avoidance conflict (or double approach-avoidance conflict when only two goals are involved). For example, perhaps your family is considering a vacation, and the ideal destination (approach) is extremely expensive (avoidance) and a second choice would not be as much fun (avoidance) but would be more affordable (approach). Typically, we must make choices among several alternatives, all possessing positive and negative features. As you can well imagine, almost anything we do will result in some stress. Conflict situations often produce frustration.

Frustration   Frustration occurs when we are prevented from reaching a goal (Rice, 1987). When we experience frustration, we must either give up the goal or find another way to attain it. In either case, stress is produced. Morris (1990) described some of the most common types of frustrations: delays, daily hassles, lack of resources, losses, failure, and discrimination.

1. *Time Delays*. We live in a society where time is important, and we get upset when we are delayed. People are frustrated when they must wait in line at a store, when a phone number is busy, or when someone is late.

FIGURE 12.4   Conflict

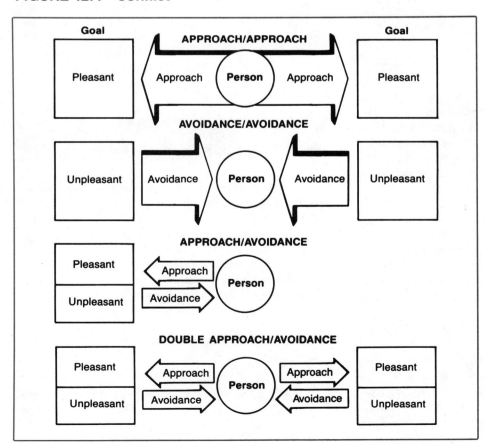

Conflict occurs, according to Lewin, when a person experiences demands or desires that are incompatible with each other. In approach-approach conflict we are attracted to two equally desirable goals. In avoidance-avoidance conflict we must choose between two equally undesirable demands. In approach-avoidance conflict we have one goal that has positive and negative aspects. And in double approach-avoidance conflict we experience two or more goals, both of which have positive and negative aspects.

FIGURE 12.5   Frustration
Many factors may block a person's goals and produce frustration and stress. They range from the loss of a relationship, to spraining an ankle in a championship game, to dropping an egg on the floor.

2. *Daily hassles.* As we discussed above, Lazarus and colleagues (1985) have identified numerous daily hassles, or routine irritations and aggravations that contribute to stress, often because they cause frustration. For instance, dropping an egg, misplacing a wallet, forgetting an appointment, or spraining an ankle all produce frustration, and ultimately increase stress level.

3. *Lack of resources.* Most people do not have enough money to purchase everything they desire. They also lack the ability always to perform their best and the capability always to succeed in everything they try.

4. *Losses.* When people lose something important, it frustrates them because it means they are deprived of goals. If they lose money or possessions, they may not be able to purchase things that they desire. If they lose someone they love, they are deprived of the future of a relationship.

5. *Failure.* Failure frustrates people. Sometimes they fail to win, to get a high grade on a test, or to impress other people. Sometimes they feel as though they have failed, even when they do better than expected, because they have such high expectations for themselves. Then their failures may produce guilt.

6. *Discrimination.* When people are unable to accomplish goals solely because of their sex, race, religion, or age, they experience frustration. For example, Houston (1990) pointed out that racial prejudice, discrimination, and bigotry have prevented many black individuals from the goals of equal opportunity, justice, and full participation in society.

Post-Traumatic Stress Disorder   The pressures, conflicts, and frustrations we have discussed so far, while capable of contributing to severe stress, have mainly been common events that occur in our daily lives. Sometimes, however, people encounter extraordinary events, such as military combat, rape, earthquakes, assault, or an accident or disaster. People who experience severe distressing events such as these may develop post-traumatic stress disorder, which is characterized by repeatedly remembering the traumatic event, avoidance of anything associated with it, and general arousal (DSM-III-R, 1987). They tend to have disruptions of sleep habits, and often become irritable and aggressive. The re-experiencing symptoms usually develop soon after the event, but may be delayed months or even years. The reaction may be mild, but is often severe, and disrupts the individual's entire life.

Some research suggests that individuals who develop post-traumatic stress disorder may tend to be more susceptible to the effects of stress. Support from family and friends is very important for the individual, who may also require professional help. Successful treatment often involves helping the individual cope with general stress and learn how to solve problems that arise (Solomon & colleagues, 1988).

REACTIONS TO STRESS

Stress in our lives is often unavoidable. As we discussed earlier, some stress is good, but often we have more stress than we can handle easily. There are many topics in psychology that deal with how people react to stress. In this section, we review some of the most common. We begin with anxiety, and next cover the general adaptation syndrome and burnout. Then we discuss several personal adjustment problems related to stress, including learned helplessness and shyness.

Anxiety

Anxiety is a difficult concept to understand. It might be thought of as a vague unpleasant feeling of fear, worry, and apprehension. The person generally has no clear idea of the real cause of the anxiety. Often he or she tends to avoid thinking about the fears because that only seems to intensify them. Anxiety is often a general emotional response to stress. It is a fear of the demands placed upon the individual when the individual doesn't know what the demands actually are.

Anxiety is usually measured by examining self-reports, observing behavior, and recording physiological activity. Self-report responses include items such as feelings of uneasiness, impulses to escape, inability to concentrate, apprehension, vague fears, and tensions. Behavioral responses include avoidance, escape, and impairment in speech, coordination, and mental activities. Physiological measurement focuses on the sympathetic nervous system, and includes responses such as increased blood pressure, breathing and heart rate, sweating, and stomach distress (Grasha & Kirschenbaum, 1986).

Psychologists distinguish between trait and situation anxiety. Trait anxiety is anxiety that is long-lasting and a relatively stable personality characteristic. Some people are more anxious in general than others. A useful diagnostic tool in measuring trait anxiety is the 1953 *Taylor Manifest Anxiety Scale.* Situation anxiety is associated with a particular situation or event. For example, most people would be anxious when skydiving for the first time, regardless of their general overall anxiety level.

Anxiety can also be thought of as an emotion with important motivational consequences. A psychologically or physically painful experience is often associated with particular cues. A later presentation of these cues may lead to anxiety and an attempt to avoid any further encounter with them. A child who has been bitten by a dog may become anxious when he comes into contact with any dog. Since the anxiety makes him avoid all dogs, he may never give himself a chance to learn that dogs can be friendly.

Children experience anxiety mainly about such external events as punishment, physical harm, withdrawal of parental affection, and sudden intense changes in sensory conditions (such as sirens, the dark, and thunder). Anxiety in adults depends less on immediate physical threat than on their general security and self-concept, interpersonal relations, social expectations, and task completion (Grasha & Kirschenbaum, 1986).

It would not be in our best interest to be free of anxiety completely, since many things that arouse our anxiety are indeed dangerous (Brodsky, 1988). The uneasiness we feel while driving in heavy traffic in an unfamiliar city keeps us alert for the unexpected. But anxiety demands our undivided attention, and too much of it will impair the performance of tasks that require attention to other things. In the next sections, we focus on the physical consequences of stress and anxiety.

General Adaptation Syndrome

Obviously our emotions, anxiety, and stress affect our behavior and performance. But they also play a central role in the preservation of good health, and are critical factors in our survival of serious injuries and illnesses. Hans Selye (1976) theorized that our emotional reactions to stress produce important physiological changes. These changes can even result in a major illness that develops and progresses independently of the initial cause of the stress.

Selye referred to the pattern in which people respond to stress as the general adaptation syndrome (GAS). He believed that the response to stress is the same whether the stress is an illness, infection, physical danger, anxiety, psychological threat, or a change in lifestyle. The GAS consists of three distinct stages: the *alarm reaction,* the *stage of resistance,* and the *stage of exhaustion.*

FIGURE 12.6   Situation Anxiety
When under stress, people often experience anxiety. This condition might include feelings of uneasiness, inability to concentrate, avoidance responses, and increases in breathing and heart rate.

The Alarm Reaction The alarm reaction is the immediate response to stress. The body prepares for an emergency situation by increasing alertness and activating the sympathetic nervous system. The alarm reaction forces the individual to realize that stress is being experienced. Heart rate and blood pressure increase, adrenaline is released, digestion slows, and blood moves away from the skin. If there is a real physical danger, the alarm reaction is extremely useful. When the danger is past, the alarm subsides and the person can then relax.

Sometimes the stresses of modern life do not pass, but remain with us day in and day out. We must always prepare for the next test or the next encounter with our employer. Our parents, friends, children, employers, classmates, and coworkers continue to place demands on us. And so the body responds by entering the second stage.

The Stage of Resistance When stress is prolonged, the body eventually builds a resistance to the effects of stress. According to Selye, people in the stage of resistance believe that they have overcome the negative consequences of stress and can handle the situation adequately. But the stress is still there and is still having negative effects on the body. The body is in high gear and reacting as if an emergency is present. In other words, even though the person appears normal on the outside, there is inner turmoil. If the stress continues, the individual enters the third stage, exhaustion.

The Stage of Exhaustion As the body continues to resist the stress, it begins to deplete its energy resources and eventually becomes exhausted. When the stage of exhaustion occurs, stress can even lead ultimately to death.

Selye has made a fairly convincing case for the idea that the causes of stress are not as important as the body's response to it. He has shown how stress can play an important role in diseases such as asthma, diabetes, arthritis, colitis, allergies, and ulcers. However, research by others has indicated that different stressors can have different effects on the body, and that different individuals respond differently to stress (Hobfoll, 1989). Thus, it appears that Selye's model is too narrow to be applied to everyone. Lazarus and Folkman (1984) pointed out that Selye did not concentrate on psychological and cognitive factors. Cognitive interpretation of a stressful situation can vary considerably from one person to the next.

Psychological Appraisal of Stress

As we discussed, Selye's model of stress did not emphasize psychological factors. Richard Lazarus has proposed a theory that does focus on psychological appraisal of stress (Lazarus, 1981; Lazarus & Folkman, 1984). According to Lazarus, whenever we face something new in our environment, we engage in primary appraisal to determine whether the stimulus event is positive, neutral, or negative. Potentially negative events are also appraised for their possible harm, threat, or challenge. Harm is the amount of damage that has already occurred, whereas threat refers to the possible future damage that could happen. Challenge is the probability of overcoming the damage constructively. For

FIGURE 12.7   General Adaptation Syndrome

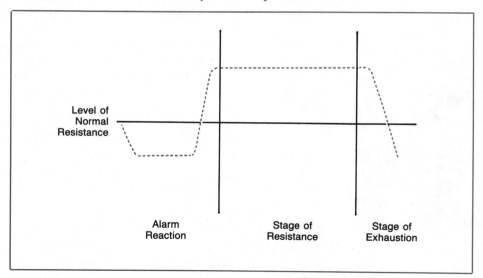

Selye noted that there is a pattern to the way in which people respond to stress. The general adaptation syndrome consists of the alarm reaction, stage of resistance, and stage of exhaustion.

Source: Adapted from H. Selye, *The Stress of Life* (New York: McGraw-Hill, 1976).

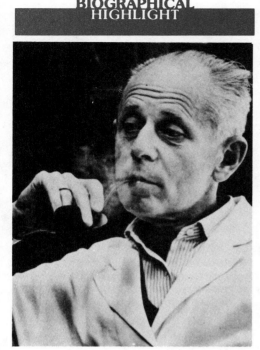

HANS SELYE

Hans Selye was born in Vienna in 1907. As early as his second year of medical school (1926), he began developing his now-famous theory of the influence of stress on people's ability to cope with and adapt to the pressures of injury and disease. He discovered that patients with a variety of ailments manifested many similar symptoms, which he ultimately attributed to their bodies' efforts to respond to the stresses of being ill. He called this collection of symptoms—this separate stress disease—stress syndrome, or the general adaptation syndrome (GAS).

He spent a lifetime in continuing research on GAS and wrote some 30 books and more than 1,500 articles on stress and related problems, including *Stress Without Distress* (1974) and *The Stress of Life* (1976). So impressive have his findings and theories been that some authorities refer to him as "the Einstein of medicine."

A physician and endocrinologist with many honorary degrees for his pioneering contributions to science, Selye also served as a professor and director of the Institute of Experimental Medicine and Surgery at the University of Montreal. More than anyone else, Selye has demonstrated the role of emotional responses in causing or combating much of the wear and tear experienced by human beings throughout their lives. He died in 1982 in Montreal, where he had spent 50 years studying the causes and consequences of stress.

example, let's assume your instructor announces a surprise quiz. Some of your classmates will perceive this as a positive opportunity to show the instructor what they have learned, whereas others will not be too concerned about it. Other students will appraise this event as potentially negative, causing harm to their grade average and threatening their future success as students.

After we complete our primary appraisal of a potential source of stress, Lazarus states that we then engage in secondary appraisal, the evaluation of the likelihood that our abilities and resources are sufficient to meet the demands placed upon us by the stressful event. Essentially, stress is experienced when the potential harm and threat are large and the ability to cope with the demands are low. For instance, if a surprise quiz is perceived as extremely harmful and threatening, and we are not able to guess well on an exam, we experience stress. Lazarus argues that appraisal is a key element in the perception of stress.

Burnout

We live in a society that constantly places demands on us. Although most of us feel that we are able to deal with stress adequately, many people are unaware that they are burning energy too fast. Burnout is the depletion of our physical and mental resources. It occurs when we have more energy going out than we do coming in. Burnout is a major concern of mental health professionals.

Unfortunately, it's the "good guys" who often experience burnout. The achiever who takes on extra assignments, the executive who works extra hours, the student who takes extra courses, the instructor who gives extra help to students, and the police officer who logs extra time are all prime candidates for burnout. Because this type of person is hardworking, others take advantage of him or her and the work load increases; so he or she continues to work hard and take on even more responsibility. Then, as we noted in the general adaptation syndrome, stress persists until exhaustion or burnout occurs.

Symptoms of Burnout   In his 1980 book *Burnout* Herbert Freudenberger described some of the major symptoms of burnout:

1. *Exhaustion.* The person feels tired and fatigued; he or she has exhausted his or her source of energy.

2. *Detachment.* The person will often use detachment as a protective device. This is true especially in the helping professions, where personal interaction on a continuous basis can be exhausting.

3. *Boredom.* The person begins to question the value of activities and friendships; he or she becomes bored with life.

4. *Impatience.* The person grows increasingly impatient with others who can't keep up; he or she becomes irritable with other people.

5. *Sense of omnipotence.* The feeling that no one else can do it is common in burnout victims. They believe they must attend to all the details themselves.

6. *Feeling unappreciated.* Burnout victims feel that other people don't appreciate all their hard work and effort.

7. *Psychophysiological problems.* The stress eventually begins to show up in symptoms such as headaches, ulcers, asthma, or heart problems. Not everyone will show all of these symptoms, but they are all indicative that burnout could be developing.

Occupation and Burnout   While burnout can occur to anyone in any situation, certain occupations are more likely to produce it. Christina Maslach has investigated burnout in caring professionals: nurses, teachers, counselors, doctors, therapists, police, and social workers. She described several occupational and demographic sources of burnout in her 1982 book, *Burnout: The Cost of Caring.* People in the helping professions often have too much contact with people. A doctor, social worker, or counselor might be seeing too many patients to provide the individualized care that they need.

Many times people in these occupations feel they do not have control over their jobs. Supervisors tell them exactly what to do. They must follow the rules, with the result that frustration develops (Veninga & Spradley, 1981). A survey of mental health workers (Shinn & colleagues, 1984) found that the most common source of stress (47 percent) was the way in which they were expected to perform their jobs (such as a high caseload of clients). Many (44 percent) complained that administrators were incompetent or didn't give them the recognition they deserved. One third of the workers felt unable to meet their own high expectations and 23 percent cited their clients as sources of stress.

Overall, men and women experience burnout about equally (Pines & Aronson, 1988). Age is an important factor, since young people burn out more rapidly than older people do. It seems that the longer you work at something, the more likely it is that you adapt to it, or else you are likely to find another job. Single people experience burnout more frequently than married people, perhaps because they don't have the same opportunities as married people to talk things out. College graduates without postgraduate education seem to experience the highest levels of burnout, perhaps because they enter their professions in the middle, where they must deal constantly with problems above and below them in the hierarchy.

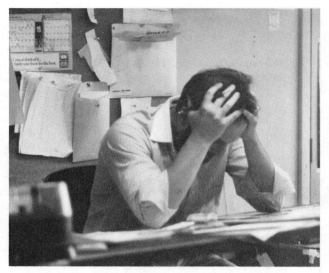

FIGURE 12.8   Burnout
When people experience too much stress for too long, they may experience burnout. This condition is especially prevalent in the helping professions. To help prevent burnout, set realistic goals and learn to relax.

Solutions to Burnout   A number of remedies have been suggested for burnout. For instance, it's important for you to set realistic goals that are manageable and yet still challenging. Know your limits and don't continue to accept additional responsibilities beyond them. It's important to escape once in a while. Take a break, relax, and enjoy yourself before you tackle the job again. It's important not to become too involved emotionally with the problems of many other people. Try to help others as much as possible, but try to remain professional. Experts now realize that social support groups are important aids in relieving tension in the helping professions. Whether in informal coffee hours or professional conferences, talking to others with similar responsibilities helps you and me feel better. And finally, many people in the helping professions are learning specific techniques of relaxation to help them deal with potential burnout. We need to understand better the relationship between stress and performance, as shown in the following Application.

APPLICATION

Stress and Performance

We usually assume that it's important to reduce stress to prevent burnout. It is important to note that while burnout is the more commonly discussed extreme of stress, the opposite might also occur. Rustout is defined as the situation when the demands placed on the individual are much less than the capacity of the individual. Rustout can be just as bad as burnout.

In chapter 9, "Motivation," we discussed the theory of optimal arousal, which states that performance is best when the arousal level is medium. This concept has been applied by Walter Gmelch in his 1982 book, *Beyond Stress to Effective Management*. Stress is a fact of life, and it is important to learn how to use stress constructively to improve performance. We now look at Gmelch's ideas for optimizing performance through stress.

The relationship between stress and performance can be divided into several sections. First is the perceived ability of an individual to accomplish a task. Next is the actual work to be accomplished. How difficult is the work, and how much effort is required? Then we need to look at the individual's actual capacity to perform the assigned work. For example, if your capacity is greater than your work, you will experience rustout. If your capacity equals your work, you will experience peak performance. And if your capacity is too low for the work you're trying to accomplish, then you will experience burnout.

How can you utilize the concept of stress to maintain high performance? Gmelch gives several suggestions. If you are experiencing rustout (work is less than capacity), then you need to take risks, try new techniques, meet new people, and stay alert. In other words, you need to do whatever is necessary to increase stress or arousal to its optimum level.

If you are at peak performance (work is equal to capacity), you need to continue to remain in control. You

FIGURE 12.9 Stress and Performance
Air traffic controllers are under constant stress because they cannot predict when a problem will develop. When too many demands are placed on people, they may not deliver peak performance.

should practice time-management skills, establish goals, and become aware of your stress points. In other words, you still have to work actively to keep performance at its peak level. If you don't, rustout or burnout will most likely result.

If you are experiencing burnout (work is greater than capacity), you need to reduce stress in order to optimize performance. You should learn the causes of your stress and take steps to reduce it. You need to learn to say no to additional requests and delegate responsibility to others. You should learn time-management skills and practice dividing up large projects into smaller ones. The more you become aware of the relationship between stress and performance, the more you can make stress work for you.

Personal Adjustment Problems

Stress causes us to adjust. Most of us are able to cope with stress much of the time but sometimes have more difficulty than usual in adjusting.

While most of us do not experience severe enough long-term stress to produce burnout, we usually experience some level of continuous stress. How much stress we experience at any one particular time depends upon a number of variables that include the stressors in our lives and our personality characteristics and coping abilities (Kessler & colleagues, 1985).

The number and severity of the stressors in our lives influence the degree of stress that we experience. In general, the more events that produce stress and the greater the severity of each one, the more stress we have. O'Brien (1981) pointed out that stress is diminished when we are able to predict it. For example, if you were aware that an examination was scheduled for tomorrow, you should feel less anxiety than if you were surprised when you arrived at class. People who believe they have control over the situation experience less stress than those who don't have this perceived control (Phares, 1991).

Individual Differences in Reactions to Stress
Our personality affects how well we are able to handle stress. Kobasa (1982) has identified the "hardy" personality style of handling stress well. Characteristics of *hardiness* include commitment, challenge, and control. *Commitment* is characterized by a sense of purpose in life and a belief in what we are doing. *Challenge* involves being flexible and having a positive attitude toward the demands that are made on us. *Control* is the belief that we are responsible for ourselves and can handle stressful

situations. Depue and Monroe (1986) argued that racial differences exist in perceiving the degree of stress. For instance, in one study they found that minorities indicated starting work or reducing work time is more stressful, whereas whites felt the birth of a child was very stressful.

Social support is also an important variable in how we react to stress. Cohen and Wills (1985) reported that people who have a social support system of family and friends are able to deal with stressful events better than those who don't. Our family and friends can provide financial or personal assistance, can help us make properly informed decisions, and can support us emotionally when we are in need of a buffer from our stress. Dakoff and Taylor (1990) found that social support is most useful when it is provided by people considered important in the stressed person's life. Holahan and Moos (1985) reported that men tended to be more independent and self-confident when dealing with stress, whereas women tended to utilize family members as a support system. Marriage apparently does not alleviate stress for students in academic settings. For example, Staats (1983) reported that marriage did not significantly alleviate the stress that college students tend to experience (such as worrying about not having enough money, doing poorly on tests, and earning low grades). Learning how to use the resources effectively that are available to us is important in handling stress in our lives.

Learned Helplessness   As we discussed in our opening story, Martin Seligman (1975) proposed a theory to explain why some people seem to give up and become helpless. He believed that when people are in a situation over which they have no control, they eventually learn that any response they make will not affect any particular outcome. Behaviorally, they will stop responding. Cognitively, they will believe that responding is useless. Emotionally, they will experience anxiety and depression. Seligman suggested that learned helplessness is a serious problem in our society because, if ignored, it can develop into depression.

Seligman's original theory was based largely on animal studies, and did not predict human depression as well as it might. So he reformulated it to take the complexity of people into account (Peterson & Seligman, 1985). The reformulated attributional theory of learned helplessness suggests that people have a need to believe that they have control over their lives. In particular, this theory focuses on how somebody answers the question "why?" when he or she encounters stressful events (that is, to what they attribute the stress). For example, assume that you failed a test. You could attribute the failure to yourself (internal explanation) or to the situation (external explanation). You could assume the cause is permanent (stable) or temporary (unstable). For example, a

stable cause might be low intelligence and an unstable cause might be the flu. And you could believe this situation is unique (specific) or part of a general pattern (global). Research suggests that people who are most likely to eventually become depressed tend to use internal, stable, and global explanations for a failure. Therefore, they feel that failure is their fault, is always their fault, and is the inevitable result of everything they attempt. Obviously, if a given event is truly uncontrollable, the person's behavior is not going to make a difference. But this one event may then be generalized to situations where the individual does have control, and this overgeneralization can contribute to a general feeling of helplessness.

Seligman suggests that parents sometimes encourage learned helplessness in children by not giving them more responsibility in making personal decisions. Teachers might encourage learned helplessness in students by not giving them more freedom in choosing assignments or learning from mistakes. As long as we tell others what to do, they learn that they have no control over the situation.

How can learned helplessness be prevented or treated? Seligman suggested that the basic problem in learned helplessness is that people expect that responding will not work. Therefore, they must be convinced that they do have some control over the situation. Parents can help children by giving them more responsibility. For example, let them choose to wear the red or the green jacket. Children will then feel they are important in making their own decisions. Teachers can let students experience mistakes. The most important factor is to convince people that they do make a difference. This concept is similar to Rotter's internal locus of control (see chapter 11, "Personality"). When we feel we can control our lives, we are much more capable of dealing with stress and anxiety.

Shyness   Shyness is a problem for many people and can involve a great deal of stress. Philip Zimbardo spent a number of years studying shyness and reported some interesting findings in his 1977 book on this topic. He stated that shyness is the awareness of our inability to act even when we want to and know how. Sometimes shyness is a fear of negative evaluation from ourselves as well as others. When we are shy, we feel uncomfortable with other people. Shyness can create problems in meeting new people, making friends, standing up for our rights, and enjoying ourselves.

Zimbardo surveyed nearly 5,000 people and found shyness to be much more prevalent than one might expect. More than 80 percent of those surveyed reported being shy at some point in their lives, and over 40 percent indicated that they were still shy. The majority of people surveyed agreed that shyness produced negative conse-

FIGURE 12.10 Shyness
Zimbardo (1977) reported that more than 80 percent of people experience shyness at some time in their lives. It can involve a great deal of personal stress. Realizing that others are also shy is one step toward dealing with this problem.

quences. Jones and Carpenter (1986) reported that shy people tend to experience loneliness and dissatisfaction with social relationships.

Shy people view shyness differently than do people who are not shy. They tend to see their shyness as a personality trait that is always with them. People who are not shy tend to view shyness as a reaction that might occur in specific situations, but not as something inherent in personality. Some researchers believe shyness might be inherited, whereas others prefer to emphasize the role of learning. For instance, people who become shy might have overreacted at one time to events in which they were embarrassed or where others made fun of them. In order to prevent it from happening again, they withdrew from social situations (Phillips, 1981). What we do know is that shyness often occurs at an early age and is sometimes encouraged by society.

Zimbardo (1986) has developed a clinic to help shy students; his ideas are appropriate for anyone with shyness. First, we should choose an atmosphere of non-evaluation where others will not be judging us and we feel confident. Second, we should realize that many other people are shy and that it is a perfectly normal experience. And third, we must try to develop assertiveness in interactions with others.

ADJUSTMENT TECHNIQUES

Everyone experiences stress in coping with the demands of daily living. People can give in to stress and become helpless, or they can adjust and learn techniques for confronting their problems head-on. Lazarus (1980) defined coping as the adjustment that people make to stress. Coping involves solving the problems that cause stress and managing the emotions that accompany stress. In this section, we review various techniques that we use to adjust to stress. Some of them are clearly more effective than others. One of the most common coping techniques is the use of defense mechanisms.

Defense Mechanisms

Defense mechanisms are psychological techniques (first described by Freud in 1894) with which we try to protect ourselves from anxiety and stress, to resolve conflicts within ourselves, and to preserve our self-esteem. Defense mechanisms have some useful functions. They help to protect us from very painful conflicts, which might otherwise cause so much stress that we would be overwhelmed. They allow us to maintain a positive self-evaluation, which can give us confidence. They allow us to deal effectively with short-term stress.

Defense mechanisms also have some negative aspects. They involve self-deception and ultimately prevent us from dealing with stress in an effective manner. They help us avoid the stress temporarily; but the stress is still there, and often manifests itself more intensely at a later time. We all use defense mechanisms, and as long as we don't use many of them very often, some of them are not too seriously harmful.

Repression In repression painful memories and unacceptable thoughts and motives are conveniently forgotten or *repressed* so that they will not have to be dealt with. The individual unconsciously expends a great deal of emotional energy to keep them in the unconscious. We mentioned repression when we discussed theories of memory. An example of repression is the way we conveniently forget we have a dental appointment because we are fearful of the visit.

Projection In projection a person attributes her unacceptable characteristics or motives to others instead of herself. For example, a messy person might complain about the slob she has for a roommate. Or someone who hates himself is convinced that others treat him badly because they hate him.

Fantasy In fantasy a person escapes from stress and anxiety by daydreaming that everything is perfect and all the problems are gone. Everyone daydreams once in a while, and it is a good relaxation technique. We have to worry only when we have trouble separating fantasy from reality.

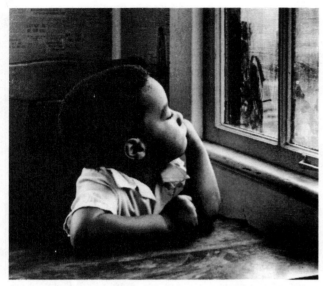

FIGURE 12.11   Defense Mechanism of Fantasy
Freud suggested that defense mechanisms are used to avoid anxiety and conflict. In fantasy, a person daydreams that all problems are solved and everything is ideal.

Regression   In regression a person retreats to an earlier, more immature form of behavior. If we were hammering a nail and hit our thumb instead, we might yell and hop around the floor the way a young child would. Or when we are having a tense argument, we might pout or scream. The result is that the stress is gone temporarily.

Compensation   In compensation a person deals with feelings of inadequacy by developing or focusing on a desirable characteristic. For example, if we are poor in mathematics, we might study extremely hard in English and do an outstanding job. Often, compensatory behaviors are not entirely effective, since they do not eliminate the basic weakness.

Rationalization   In rationalization a person makes up logical excuses to justify behavior rather than exposing the true motives. For instance, if we do poorly on a test, we might tell others that our notes were stolen, or we were sick, rather than admit to the truth that we didn't study. Of course if we really were sick, we would not be rationalizing.

Displacement   In displacement a person directs his or her aggression and hostility toward a person or object other than the one it should be directed toward. For example, if we have a difficult day at school, we might come home and yell at family members, who had nothing to do with our difficulties.

Sublimation   In sublimation a person redirects socially undesirable urges into socially acceptable behavior. A person who enjoys violence might become a police officer. A person who would like to beat up others might become a boxer. Or a person with strong sexual urges might become an artist who paints nude portraits.

Reaction Formation   In reaction formation a person masks an unconsciously distressing or unacceptable trait by assuming an opposite attitude behavior. For example, people who are basically shy or cowardly may act in forceful or even heroic ways to hide their fears—even from themselves. A person who hates kids might become an elementary school teacher. Or someone who hates animals might become the best-loved zookeeper of all time. How do you know if a person's behavior reflects true motives or is a reaction formation? It may be impossible to know for certain.

Some of the defense mechanisms appear to be useful, whereas others are so vague that they are useless. Still, the basic idea of the defense mechanism is that we can deal with stress by ignoring it or believing that it's not serious. Obviously, although they may postpone dealing with the stress temporarily, defense mechanisms are not very effective adjustment techniques in the long run. Task-oriented coping is often more effective in dealing with stress.

Coping Techniques

Coping techniques are ways of dealing with stress and anxiety. They are often done without thinking, and as such can be valuable ways of releasing tension. Morris (1990) described several important stress-reduction coping techniques as well as more direct task-oriented coping strategies. These stress-reduction techniques do not solve the problems that lead to stress, but rather serve to reduce the stress temporarily so that the individual can attempt more direct adjustment.

Crying is extremely useful in releasing tension from a stressful situation. Although adults (especially men) are taught not to cry in our society, we all sometimes cry when the pressure gets too high. This helps us to release tension, relax, and become reoriented.

An important way of dealing with stress is *talking* your problem over with someone else. A number of therapies (to be discussed in chapter 14, "Therapy") are based on the premise that if you share your problem with someone else, you will feel better. Crisis hotlines are springing up everywhere and help people with problems talk them out anonymously. Often we overlook this simple technique for dealing with excessive stress.

Humor is an excellent way of reducing stress. We've all heard the old saying, "laughter is the best medicine." If

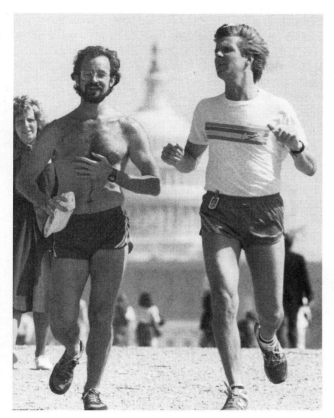

FIGURE 12.12 Coping With Stress
There are many ways of dealing with stress when it begins
to interfere with the ability to function in daily life. Meditation,
biofeedback, and exercise are some effective stress re-
ducers.

we can laugh about our mishaps, the stress is reduced
and we can then deal with the situation more effectively.
Through laughter we are able to accept hurt and disappointment and we can begin to solve our problems more
effectively.

It is often useful to use *reflection* when thinking
about our problems. I try to write my reflections down
and read them back to myself. Often we are so busy just
trying to get by that we forget to think seriously about
things that are important in our lives. If we take time to
think about a stressful situation, we will be able to
evaluate our responses to stress and develop more effective methods of dealing with it.

An additional coping technique is to *obtain help*
from others. Often we are not able to deal with problems
by ourselves most effectively. It's often hard to admit to
ourselves that we need outside help, but if we are to be
successful in dealing with our problems, we must get help
from other sources. Find information from the library.
Visit a counselor. Talk to an instructor. See a friend. We
ought to do whatever will make us clearly put the problem
into perspective. Then we can begin task-oriented adjustment.

Adjustment aimed at realistically solving the problems that cause the stress is often the most successful.
Task-oriented coping responses require that the person
evaluate the stressful situation objectively and then formulate a plan with which to solve the problem. Three
basic approaches to task-oriented coping include attack,
withdrawal, and compromise (Morris, 1990).

In *attack*, the person faces the problem head-on.
The first task is to survey the problem and determine a
course of action. It is important to remain flexible and
seek additional information and aid if the problem war-
rants it. For example, suppose you are doing poorly in
your biology class. You first survey the situation and
decide that you don't understand the material. Then you
visit the instructor and arrange for a tutor to help you
master the material. Because you attack the problem,
you will very likely be successful and your grade will
improve.

In chapter 8, "Language and Intelligence," we
discussed the problem-solving theory of Bourne and
colleagues (1986), which is effective in dealing with
stress-related problems. The steps include preparation
(understanding the problem and obtaining information),
production (considering solutions to the problem), and
evaluation (considering the appropriateness of the
solution).

Sometimes it is wise to reassess the situation and
decide to *withdraw*. If you have chosen an inappropriate
goal that is unattainable, it's wise to admit defeat, leave
the situation, and establish a new direction. For example,
let's suppose that your grades in biology do not improve.
You have your heart set on becoming a biologist, but you
cannot pass the introductory course. If you have given it
everything you have with no success, then it's time to
withdraw. You ought not to persist until learned helplessness occurs.

When you are unlikely to reach a particular goal, it's
time to sit back and think about your options. Perhaps
you could reach the goal through some other pathway.
Maybe you could accept a substitute goal. For example, if
you should find biology impossible, perhaps a degree in
animal psychology would satisfy you. *Compromise* techniques allow us to readjust our goals and the means of
obtaining these goals. Without them we would have
trouble solving many of the problems that cause us stress
and anxiety. Adjustment is often a matter of compromise.

There are many other techniques designed to reduce stress. In chapter 14, "Therapy," we discuss progressive relaxation, a technique for relieving stress by
relaxing in the presence of stressful stimuli. A particularly
effective approach to dealing with stress is stress inoculation. Donald Meichenbaum (1985) described three
phases of stress inoculation: education, rehearsal, and
implementation. In the *education phase*, specific information about what to expect is given to the individual. For

instance, someone going into the hospital for an operation is able to cope better if he or she knows exactly what to expect. In the *rehearsal phase*, the person practices the threatening event in safe surroundings. For example, if I need to give a talk to a group of people, I rehearse at home until I am confident of myself. In the *implementation phase* the person actually carries out the plan. Stress reduction techniques also include a change in diet (for example, ingesting less caffeine), building a social support system, practicing meditation, using biofeedback, exercising, and implementing time-management techniques.

Time Management

For most people, in school as well as out, time management is the most difficult aspect of adjustment. Most of us have problems managing our time. We tend to put things off—procrastinate—and wait until the last minute to do them (Keyes, 1991). We often miss deadlines and then have to hurry to get back on schedule. We spend much of our time on unimportant things. We don't have a schedule and we don't know what goals are most important. In this section, we discuss how to improve adjustment by learning how to manage time effectively.

An important point to remember is that we all have exactly the same amount of time. It does not matter whether we are rich or poor, we all own exactly the same number of minutes each day. So it is not a matter of getting more time. What counts is what you do with your time. If you use your time wisely, your adjustment will be easy and your stress level low.

Williams and Long (1991) discuss some techniques for effective time management. They suggest that before we even begin to implement time-management techniques, we must be motivated to manage our time. Commitment to solving our time problems and making time management a way of life is essential. Then we need to become fully aware of our use of time. One of the easiest methods of analyzing our use of time is to keep a time log for a week. Every half hour throughout the day, record what you are doing. Then analyze how much time you are spending on various activities. For instance, you might find that you are spending more time than you thought on traveling to and from your destinations each day, but less time on studying or socializing. You should be especially alert for potential time robbers, activities that take up a great deal of time but are not as important as some of your other activities.

In order to use the time we have effectively, you need to establish goals. Alan Lakein, in his 1973 book, *How to Get Control of Your Time and Your Life*, stated that successful people are more likely to write a list of daily goals. You should write a list that you can monitor to check your daily progress. As you accomplish each of

your goals, cross it off your list. By having an ongoing list, you will be able to allot your time for productive projects.

Once you have established your goals, you should examine the behaviors that will lead to these goals. For example, you should group similar tasks. If you go to the supermarket, you should stop at the bank on your way there, so you won't need to make a separate trip. Likewise, while you're in the library studying, you should look up the assignment for English class, so that you won't have to return later for that purpose. Make sure that your daily activities are organized to expend your time effectively. If you have spare time between projects, you should use it to study or read or relax, rather than to worry.

There are numerous reasons why people have difficulty with managing time. Often we are overcommitted and end up doing more than we should. One easy technique is to learn how to say "no" to requests that we cannot comply adequately with because of a lack of time. We can also learn to delegate responsibilities to others when appropriate.

Procrastination is one of the most common time-management problems. We have many reasons for procrastination, including fear of a large task, lack of motivation, interruptions, and general stress. Lakein proposed the "Swiss cheese technique" to help overcome procrastination. The basic idea is to poke holes in an overwhelming task to reduce it to bite-sized pieces. Divide a large task into small steps and begin with the easiest one. Then continue to complete small tasks until the large one is manageable. For example, perhaps your instructor

FIGURE 12.13 Effective Time Management

- Develop Commitment to Time Management
- Assess Values and Beliefs
- Analyze Current Use of Time
- Set Goals and Decide Priorities
- Be Flexible in Setting Goals
- Work on Highest Priorities First
- Take Time to Plan Each Day
- Subdivide Large Goals into Small Tasks
- Develop List of "To Do" Activities
- Accumulate Similar Tasks to Do Together
- Avoid Procrastination and Perfectionism
- Learn to Say No to Requests
- Learn to Delegate Tasks to Others
- Become Effective Rather Than Efficient
- Evaluate Progress Toward Goals
- Build in Time for Relaxation

Time-management techniques help us successfully adjust to stress in our environment.

assigned a term paper, but you have been procrastinating because it is such a huge assignment. Sit down and write an outline. Plan some time to go to the library to look up possible resources. Take a half hour to take a few notes from a resource or two. Now you have a good start on the term paper and should be able to continue to spend the required time to complete it.

The last step of a successful time-management program is to evaluate your program and make the necessary changes. For instance, perhaps you are spending too much time on low-priority tasks and need to modify the tasks you work on. You should be flexible in your time-management goals and ready to modify your goals as you progress. Remember that your main goal is effective time management. Efficiency is doing things right and effectiveness is doing the right things. In other words, don't spend a lot of time doing things that are not very important. You should give yourself lots of reinforcement when you progress toward your goals. And make sure that you leave time for relaxation. Time-management skills help us adjust to stress by finding efficient solutions to our time problems.

Adjustment and Well-Being

Everyone would prefer to be well-adjusted and happy, but too often people experience so much stress that they are not as happy as they would like to be. Well-being may be defined as a subjective, positive, emotional state with general life satisfaction (Diener, 1984). It involves the way the individual feels about himself or herself, and is due to achievement of goals in life. The successfully adjusted person is pleased with his or her life (Schwartz & Clore, 1983). In other words, the person is happy.

Staats (1983) reported that college students were generally happy if they were getting good grades, were making friends, achieving goals, had enough money, and were studying with good professors. Stassen and Staats (1988) found that American students were slightly happier and more satisfied than Canadian students. Both groups reported the greatest satisfaction with health and lowest satisfaction with financial security. These students generally reflected the level of satisfaction found in the general population (Diener, 1984).

The most common contributors to a sense of well-being include family life, standard of living, work, marriage, and financial security. Diener (1984) reported that happy people tend to have high self-esteem, a satisfying love relationship, a meaningful religious faith, and are socially active. Diener also reported that happiness does not appear to be related to age, race, sex, or education. Maslow (1970) identified the characteristics of the self-

actualized person in his humanistic approach (see chapter 11, "Personality"). Many of those characteristics are motives for the happy, well-adjusted individual.

Brodsky (1988) identified several characteristics of the person who is striving toward well-being. They include a strong positive affect, substantial satisfaction with life, and a reconciliation of values with realities of society. This person makes deliberate choices, practices self-control, and takes some risks to obtain goals. In addition, the well-adjusted person is a unique person and has a good self-image. In order to help more individuals reach this state of existence, more research will be done in the psychology of adjustment and health.

HEALTH PSYCHOLOGY

The field of health psychology is concerned with understanding the psychological influences on people's state of health, including how they stay healthy, why they become ill, and how their behavior relates to their state of health (Taylor, 1991). Health psychologists focus on a number of specific topics, including the promotion of health, the role of psychological factors in illness, the management of stress, and the improvement of health care and health-care policy. In this section, we discuss the role of psychological factors on physical disorders, Type A behavior pattern and health, and the promotion of health.

It has been estimated that up to 75 percent of all visits to physicians are because of stress-related problems (Charlesworth & Nathan, 1982). Health psychologists are studying the role of stress in various physical conditions, such as hypertension and coronary heart disease, disorders of the immune system (such as AIDS), and cancer (Brannon & Feist, 1992). Ultimately this information will allow us to modify stress-related behaviors through an approach called behavioral medicine.

Psychological Effects on Physical Conditions

The 1987 revision of the *Diagnostic and Statistical Manual of Mental Disorders (DSM-III-R)* uses the term *psychological factors affecting physical condition* to include those that contribute to the initiation or aggravation of a specific physical condition (we discuss DSM-III-R in chapter 13, "Psychological Disorders"). In the past, terms such as *psychosomatic illness* and *psychophysiological disorder* have been used. Although psychological and environmental stressors can affect physical conditions, they may also be due to strictly physiological causes.

DSM-III-R (1987) provides a listing of the physical conditions that are influenced by psychological factors. They include obesity, tension and migraine headache, painful menstruation, acne, asthma, ulcers, nausea, and colitis. Taylor (1991) described a number of the most extensively researched conditions, including ulcers, headaches, asthma, hypertension, and coronary heart disease.

Ulcers are holes in the lining of the stomach or duodenum. They are produced by excessive gastric-acid secretions from digestive processes that might be caused or aggravated by stress, hostility, anxiety, and uncontrollable events (Bachrach, 1982). The autonomic nervous system then causes a reduction of blood to the protective mucus layer of the stomach and an increase in the secretion of acid. Some research suggests that people susceptible to ulcers may not show the appropriate physiological responsiveness to stress (Weiss, 1984). Ulcers are generally treated through diet, medication, and relaxation techniques. The anti-ulcer drug *Zantac* is one of the most prescribed drugs in the United States today.

Migraine headache is the most common psychophysiological disorder, affecting up to 10 percent of the population of the United States. The migraine headache is caused by arteries under the scalp of the head that become dilated (enlarged) and press on the pain-sensitive nerves in the area. It has been theorized that migraine headache sufferers have scalp arteries that are extremely sensitive to autonomic nervous system activity. Migraine headaches are often treated with stress-reduction techniques, such as biofeedback and relaxation (Gannon & colleagues, 1987).

Asthma is a problem characterized by increased sensitivity of the respiratory tract, resulting in the narrowing of the airways and causing breathing difficulties. It is believed that bronchial asthma is caused largely by physiological factors, but that psychological and social stress are indirect contributors (Burg & Ingalls, 1985). However, psychological stress or emotional reactions such as fear, anger, or frustration can aggravate an asthmatic condition and increase its severity. Research indicates that the person with asthma can be helped by exercise and stress-management techniques (Parker, 1985).

Cardiovascular disorders include hypertension (high blood pressure) and coronary heart disease (CHD). Hypertension is an increase in blood pressure above acceptable levels (usually above systolic pressure of 160 and diastolic pressure of 120). The majority of cases of hypertension cannot be attributed to a specific organic cause; stress and anxiety appear to be important aggravating factors. Sympathetic nervous system activity leads to sharp increases in blood pressure during stress, and then the blood pressure declines to normal. Continued sympathetic arousal and constriction of the arteries may lead to hypertension. Hypertensives seem to show excessive blood pressure reaction to stressful events. Among blacks in the United States, high blood pressure ranks as one of the most serious health problems today.

Coronary heart disease (CHD) is the cause of nearly half of all deaths in the United States. CHD refers to any condition that causes a narrowing of the coronary arteries. A variety of risk factors are believed to contribute to CHD, including hypertension, obesity, diabetes, heredity, high-fat diet, high levels of cholesterol, smoking, inactivity, Type A behavior, and stress. In fact, stress is strongly implicated in about half of the cases of CHD (American Heart Association, 1989). We discuss the relationship of stress and the personality Type A behavior pattern to coronary heart disease in the next section.

Type A Behavior

Do you like to do everything quickly? Have you even found yourself completing someone's sentence in order to speed the conversation along? Do you hate to wait in lines? Are you always trying to do several things at the same time? Are you competitive? Are you impatient with others who cannot keep up with you? Are you hard-driving? If you answer these questions with a yes, you may be a Type A behavior person.

Physicians Meyer Friedman and Ray Rosenman have investigated the long-term effects of stress-producing behavior patterns on heart disease. For 20 years they have been studying a personality pattern of behavior that causes stress. In 1974 they published a popular book entitled *Type A Behavior and Your Heart*, in which they summarized many of their research findings.

Type A behavior describes a particular type of personality. According to Friedman and Rosenman, Type A people tend to be competitive, aggressive, hard-driving individuals who are constantly under excessive stress. Type A people are impatient with others who cannot keep up with them. They compete unendingly; when there's no one to compete with, they race against time. Type A people hate delays and often do several things at once (like reading the mail while driving to work). Type A individuals work extra hard to increase the level of their achievement. They are under stress *constantly*.

Type B behavior describes a different personality type. Sometimes Type B people are aggressive, competitive, impatient, and hardworking. But they also relax more. Type B people react to environmental demands and work hard when it is required. But they are not always in such a state of urgency that they experience constant stress.

Research on Type A and Type B people has shown that often Type A people are significantly more likely to develop coronary heart disease as they grow older. Type A and B individuals can be identified through a structured

FIGURE 12.14   Type A Behavior
Friedman and Rosenman (1974) describe the Type A person as being a competitive, hard-driving individual who is constantly under stress. The stock trader above, at the Chicago Board of Options Exchange, frantically tries to make himself heard on October 19, 1987, a day when the Dow Jones average dropped over 500 points.

interview procedure developed by Rosenman and his colleagues that focuses on competitiveness, deadlines, ambitiousness, impatience, aggressiveness, and hostility. There are also several questionnaires available, including the *Jenkins Activity Survey* and the *Framingham Type A Scale.* Unfortunately, there is disagreement among the measures of the Type A behavior pattern, which suggests a problem in accurate diagnosis (Matthews, 1988).

Research has shown that Type A people are especially affected by negative sources of stress over which they have no control (Carver & Humphries, 1982). They continue to respond to stress as if they had control, even if it is not possible for them to secure it. Matthews (1982) suggested that differences between Type A and Type B individuals become pronounced in situations that are competitive, require careful, slow performance, and are largely uncontrollable. Type A people can sometimes be more effective than Type B people when there are distracting conditions such as background noise, because they are better able to attend to both the work at hand and the distraction and still accomplish the task.

Mark Pittner and his colleagues reported (1983) that Type A individuals showed higher blood pressure rates when exposed to an aversive stimulus, even when the subjects had no control over such a stimulus. Kahn and colleagues (1980) suggested that Type A behavior might be the result of greater physiological reactions to stress, rather than a cause of the reactions. They found, for instance, that Type A people undergoing bypass surgery showed a greater increase in blood pressure than did Type B people, even though they were all unconscious.

Type A people show more sympathetic nervous system activity and more norepinephrine secretion than Type B people. Norepinephrine is a hormone that works with the sympathetic nervous system to prepare the body for emergency situations; high levels apparently contribute to CHD.

It has been discovered that not all characteristics of Type A behavior contribute to an increased risk of heart disease (Wright, 1988). One line of research argues that *hostility* (stemming from a belief that people are generally selfish and mean and therefore cannot be trusted) is the core characteristic of Type A behavior that leads to CHD (Williams, 1989). Dembroski and colleagues (1985) argued that an aggressive personality contributes to heart disease, but other Type A characteristics—such as doing things quickly, being ambitious, or working hard—do not. Spielberger and London (1982) found that people who react with anger to minor irritations are most likely to develop coronary heart disease, whereas Spielberger and colleagues (1985) found that people who suppress anger are more likely to have hypertension. They developed the *Anger-In Scale* to measure the tendency to suppress anger. This scale contains items such as "I keep things in" and "I am angrier than I am willing to admit."

Logan Wright (1988) reviewed the research on identifying the specific components of the Type A behavior pattern that significantly contribute to CHD. Originally he proposed a cluster of characteristics that included time urgency (concern with moment-to-moment time), chronic activation (always remaining active), and multiphasic activity (doing two or more things at the same time). After analyzing research data, Wright suggested that there are several independent factors that can contribute to heart disease, including heredity, self-imposed non-Type A risk (smoking, diet), anger-in (tendency to suppress anger), anger-out with time urgency and chronic activations, and the traditional Type A pattern first identified by Rosenman and Friedman. Wright concluded that anger-in was the best predictor of CHD, followed by a combination of anger-out (expressing anger and irritability readily) and time urgency/chronic activation. Other research also continues to implicate hostility, anger, cynicism, suspiciousness, and mistrust to CHD (Weidner & colleagues, 1989). Research will continue on identifying the specific characteristics and mechanisms that show a relationship between Type A behavior and coronary heart disease.

It is estimated that about 50 percent of the adult males in the United States are Type A. Fewer women exhibit Type A behavior, but as more women enter the competitive job market, it is likely that more of them will also become Type A. Research suggests that people can learn to modify their life-styles and perhaps change from Type A to Type B, but more research is needed on ways to help people modify their behavior to avoid coronary heart disease.

Health Enhancement Behavior

Earlier we mentioned a number of topics that health psychologists focus on, including the promotion of health, the role of psychological factors in illness, and the improvement of health care. One of the more successful current trends is the emphasis on behaviors and attitudes that contribute to good health. Here we discuss the health enhancement behaviors of exercise and proper nutrition.

Exercise   It is hard to find someone who is unaware of the current interest in aerobic exercise, such as the trend for people to engage in exercise. Aerobic exercise, such as walking, running, dancing, swimming, cycling, and cross-country skiing, involves increasing oxygen consumption over a period of time. This involves a number of body systems, especially the respiratory and coronary systems.

There are a variety of health benefits from a minimum of 15 minutes of exercise three times a week. These include weight control, cardiovascular fitness, regulation of cholesterol and glucose levels, stress management, and overall improvement of physical health (Taylor, 1991). Some research suggests that exercise may also benefit mental health, improve mood, and provide a sense of well-being and self-esteem (Rodin & Plante, 1989).   Rodin and Plante also noted that exercise programs in businesses and organizations can help improve worker morale, reduce absenteeism, and reduce health-care costs.

Although most people recognize the benefits of exercise, only 50 percent of those who begin some form of exercise program continue after 6 months (Dishman, 1982). Because of this low continuance, health psychologists have been working on increasing compliance to a schedule of exercise. Research indicates that those with a positive attitude toward exercise are more likely to continue to exercise. Dishman (1982) found that people are more likely to exercise when it is easy and convenient to do so. For instance, you would probably swim more regularly if you lived next to the YMCA. Belisle and colleagues (1987) reported that the probability of adhering to an exercise program increases if the participants are told the possible problems they will encounter and ways to deal with these problems. Exercise improves physical and mental health, and more people are learning to develop an exercise program. Have you had your walk today?

Nutrition   In a very real sense, we are what we eat. In chapter 9, "Motivation," we discussed obesity and weight control management. In addition to the quantity of food we consume, our health is also affected by the type of diet we maintain. Health psychologists are developing ways to help individuals improve health through diet and nutrition (Taylor, 1991).

There is little doubt that particular foods are related to illness. For instance, high salt intake is related to high blood pressure, and high-fat and high-cholesterol foods are related to various cancers and CHD. It is, however, difficult to convince people to eat properly (Hayes & Ross, 1987). Often individuals are not motivated to become more aware of nutrition and health, even when there is a medical problem. And those who do begin nutrition programs often do not adhere to the proper diet.

Taylor (1991) indicated that educational campaigns to improve a community's nutritional habits have had short-term success, but are ineffective over longer periods of time. More success has been obtained when an individual's family was involved in the diet (Carmody & colleagues, 1986). Additional research is needed to identify methods to obtain higher compliance rates to nutritional diets for improvement of health.

Health psychologists are making progress in informing at-risk individuals of the importance of life changes. In addition to exercise and nutrition, health psychologists are helping people to follow the advice of their physicians, adjust to life-style changes dictated by illness, and deal with illness. Health psychology is also helping many of us learn how to deal with stress more effectively. ■

Adjustment is an ongoing process. We can learn to be more successful in our adjustment, but there will always be new problems to solve. Stress is a fact of life. It's more important to learn to live with it than to try to eliminate it totally. As shown in the opening story on learned helplessness in dogs, learning may not always produce a positive outcome. But as we strive for successful adjustment and a state of well-being, we often learn how to cope with stressful demands made upon us.

"What do you mean '10 minutes'? I want my stress medicine *now*!"

CHAPTER REVIEW

What You've Learned About Adjustment and Health

1. Stress is anything that produces demands on us to adjust our behavior. It can result from physical dangers or psychological threats. How we react to the stress in our lives is called adjustment. Adjustment might be viewed as a continuum from maladjustment to adjustment to competence.

2. The *Social Readjustment Rating Scale* measures the amount of stress caused by specific changes in life. A second approach is to study the daily hassles (annoyances, aggravations, frustrations).

3. Pressure occurs when we strive to meet the demands imposed on us by ourselves (internal pressure) and others (external pressure). Conflict occurs when we experience incompatible demands and desires. Types of conflict include approach-approach conflict, avoidance-avoidance conflict, approach-avoidance conflict, and multiple approach-avoidance conflict. Frustration occurs when we are prevented from reaching our goals. There are many types of frustration, including time delays, daily hassles, lack of resources, losses, failure, and discrimination.

4. Anxiety is a vague unpleasant feeling of fear, worry, and apprehension and is often an emotional response to stress. It can be measured by examining self-reports, observing behavior, and recording physiological activity. Trait anxiety is viewed as a stable personality characteristic. Situation anxiety is associated with a particular event.

5. The general adaptation syndrome consists of three stages. The alarm reaction is the immediate response to stress, in which the body prepares for an emergency by activating the sympathetic nervous system. When stress is prolonged, we enter the stage of resistance. As the body continues to resist, it eventually depletes its energy, and we enter the stage of exhaustion.

6. Burnout is the depletion of our physical and mental resources. The helping professions are most likely to experience burnout. Symptoms include exhaustion, detachment, boredom, impatience, and a feeling of being unappreciated. Some of the remedies include setting realistic goals, taking breaks, learning to relax, and using support groups.

7. People who learn that their behavior is ineffective in reaching goals give up and experience learned helplessness. Seligman believes learned helplessness is related to depression. We can treat learned helplessness by helping people gain control over their environment. Shyness is an awareness of our inability to act when we want to and know how. Treatments include providing a nonevaluative environment, learning that shyness is common, and developing assertiveness techniques.

8. Defense mechanisms, a concept developed by Freud, are psychological techniques to help protect the individual from anxiety. In repression, painful memories are forgotten. In projection, unacceptable urges are attributed to other people. In fantasy, a person escapes from stress by daydreaming. In regression, a person reverts to earlier, more immature behavior. In compensation, a person makes up for a feeling of inadequacy by developing or focusing on a desirable characteristic. In rationalization, a person makes up logical excuses to justify behavior rather than exposing the true motives. In displacement, a person diverts aggression and hostility from their true objects to others. In sublimation, a person redirects socially undesirable urges into socially acceptable behavior. And in reaction formation, a person behaves in a way that is opposite to the true unconscious motives.

9. Task-oriented coping involves realistically solving the problem that leads to stress. We can attack the problem head-on, withdraw if it looks impossible, or compromise when necessary.

10. For most people, time management is the most difficult aspect of adjustment. It is important to know how we spend our time. Successful time management requires that we establish goals, analyze tasks, organize activities, and evaluate progress.

11. Well-being is a subjective positive emotional state with general life satisfaction. Contributors to a sense of well-being include family life, standard of living, work, marriage, and financial security.

12. The field of health psychology is concerned with understanding the psychological influences on people's state of health. Psychological stress can create or aggravate certain physical conditions; the most extensively studied include ulcers, migraine headaches, asthma, and coronary heart disease.

13. The Type A behavior pattern produces stress and leads to heart disease. Type A people are competitive, aggressive, hard-driving, and impatient. Type B people react more to environmental demands and are thus less subject to stress and heart disease. Specific aspects of the Type A behavior pattern, such as the tendency to suppress anger, may contribute to coronary heart disease.

14. Health psychologists focus on promoting good health. Two behaviors that people can show to improve their health are to exercise and eat properly.

CHAPTER 13

PSYCHOLOGICAL DISORDERS

When an individual is unable to adjust to daily life adequately, he or she has a psychological disorder. The milder types of abnormal behavior are called the anxiety disorders. The more severe psychological disorders include depression and schizophrenia. Psychologists are still trying to discover the causes of abnormal behaviors so they can treat them more effectively.

CRITICAL THINKING OBJECTIVES FOR CHAPTER 13

After reading chapter 13, you should be able to identify, apply, and evaluate what you have learned about the following questions:

What are the components in the definition of abnormal behavior?
What are the important models of abnormal behavior?
What is the role of anxiety in the anxiety disorders?
What are the theories of depression?
What are the clinical symptoms of schizophrenia?
What are the types of somatoform and dissociative disorders?

CHAPTER 14

THERAPY

Treating individuals who have psychological problems has long been a major activity of psychologists. Psychoanalysis was the first major systematic attempt to treat psychopathology. Today, psychologists utilize a variety of therapeutic approaches, including insight, behavior, and group therapies. Sometimes drug therapy is incorporated into the treatment program.

CRITICAL THINKING OBJECTIVES FOR CHAPTER 14

After reading chapter 14, you should be able to identify, apply, and evaluate what you have learned about the following questions:

What are the various types of psychological and biological therapy?
What is the history of therapy for mental disorders?
What are the distinctions between psychoanalysis and person-centered therapy?
What are the important types of reinforcement therapy?
What are the important types of group therapy?
What is the effectiveness of psychotherapy?
What are the major types of drugs used in therapy?

When there is a severe problem in personality, the area of psychology involved in its study is abnormal psychology. In this part of the textbook we cover abnormal disorders and the different types of therapies used to treat those disorders.

PART VI

Psychological Disorders and Therapy

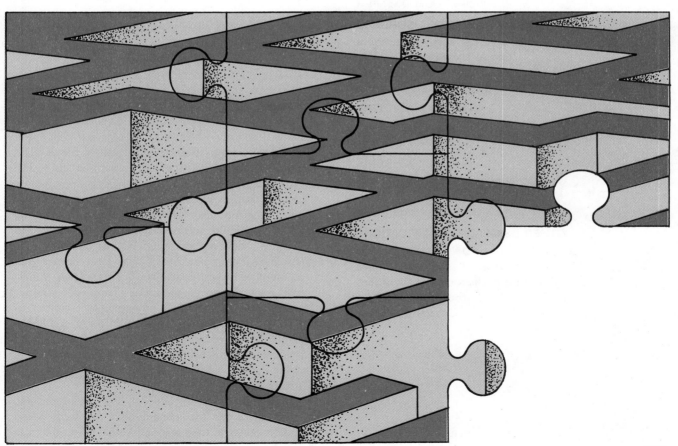

CHAPTER OBJECTIVES

What You'll Learn About Psychological Disorders

After studying this chapter, you should be able to:

1. Define abnormal behavior.
2. Identify the major models of abnormal behavior.
3. State the purpose of the DSM-III-R.
4. Describe the panic disorder and agoraphobia.
5. Describe the social and simple phobias.
6. Describe the obsessive compulsive disorder.
7. Describe the generalized anxiety disorder.
8. Describe the symptoms and theories of the mood disorder of depression.
9. Describe the bipolar disorder.
10. Identify the clinical symptoms of schizophrenia.
11. Describe the classification types of schizophrenia.
12. Identify the causes of schizophrenia.
13. Describe the delusional disorder.
14. Describe the organic mental disorders.
15. Describe the somatoform and dissociative disorders.
16. Describe the personality disorders and sexual disorders.

David Rosenhan's 1973 article, "On Being Sane in Insane Places," is a classic study in how we diagnose abnormal behavior. He noted it is often assumed that mental patients exhibit specific symptoms that can be categorized in order to distinguish them from normal people. In order to verify this assumption, Rosenhan had eight normal people admit themselves to mental hospitals for diagnosis and treatment.

Rosenhan's eight pseudopatients included a graduate student, three psychologists, a psychiatrist, a physician, an artist, and a homemaker. In the group were three women and five men. The eight pseudopatients were admitted to a total of twelve mental hospitals (four people were admitted to two hospitals each) located in both the eastern and western parts of the United States. The hospitals varied in size, age, research orientation, and staff-to-patient ratio.

When they arrived at the admitting offices of the hospitals, the pseudopatients complained of hearing voices. They said the voices were unclear, but seemed to say "empty," "hollow," and "thud." Other than complaining of these symptoms and giving false names and occupations, the pseudopatients were completely honest in their responses to all questions. They correctly described their relationships with other people, their frustrations as well as enjoyments. None of these conditions could be considered pathological. But as soon as they were admitted to the hospital, they stopped complaining of any symptoms, and behaved normally while trying to get released.

While in the mental hospital, the pseudopatients talked freely to the real patients and the staff. When asked how they felt, they responded that they no longer experienced any symptoms and they now felt fine. They

When an individual is unable to adjust to daily life adequately, he or she has a psychological disorder. The milder types of abnormal behavior are called the anxiety disorders. The more severe psychological disorders include depression and schizophrenia. Psychologists are still trying to discover the causes of abnormal behaviors so they can treat them more effectively.

13

Psychological Disorders

FIGURE 13.1 A State Mental Hospital
Rosenhan's pseudopatients admitted themselves to mental hospitals in order to see how long it would take to be released once they no longer showed abnormal symptoms.

cooperated fully with the staff (except they did not swallow any medication). The pseudopatients kept a record of observations in the hospital. At first these records were kept secretly, but it soon became apparent that no one cared what they did in the ward, so the pseudopatients openly wrote their observations.

Rosenhan told the pseudopatients that they had to work to get out of the mental hospital as quickly as possible. This motivated them to cooperate fully and behave as normally as possible. The staff reports later confirmed that these pseudopatients were friendly and cooperative and behaved normally at all times.

Not only were the pseudopatients not detected as fakes, but eleven out of twelve times they were diagnosed as having *schizophrenia* (a severe psychological disorder) when admitted, and they were all discharged with a diagnosis of "schizophrenia in remission." In remission means that although the patient no longer shows the symptoms of a psychological disorder, he or she might begin to show them in the future. Rosenhan pointed out that this diagnosis meant that the hospitals viewed the pseudopatients as continuing to have a psychiatric disorder, even though no abnormal symptoms were shown.

They had been kept in the mental hospitals for an average of 19 days (the range was 7 to 52 days), during which time staff personnel did not question their motives. Strangely enough, other patients did suspect that they were faking. During the first three admissions, 35 out of a total of 118 real patients voiced suspicions that the pseudopatients were normal. Some patients even accused the pseudopatients of being journalists or professors checking up on the hospital.

Because normal people were so readily diagnosed as abnormal, Rosenhan ran a second study to see if the reverse was also true. The staff of a mental hospital not used in the first study was informed that one or more pseudopatients would attempt to be admitted within the following 3 months. Each staff member was asked to rate the likelihood that a new patient was actually a pseudopatient. Of 193 patients admitted, 41 were suspected (with high confidence) of being pseudopatients by at least one staff member. Nineteen were suspected by a psychiatrist and another staff member. Actually, no pseudopatients were admitted during that time; this experiment again indicated the potential danger of labeling people and then treating them according to those labels.

Rosenhan's study demonstrates how easy it is in a mental hospital for normal people to be diagnosed as abnormal. He suggests further that the labels we use in diagnosing people are so general that they have little usefulness. And, as shown by the release diagnosis of "in remission," once one has been labeled as abnormal, it is extremely difficult to overcome that label. While some professionals question Rosenhan's research on methodological and ethical grounds, it does raise many questions about the diagnosis and treatment of the mentally disturbed.

WHAT IS ABNORMAL BEHAVIOR?

The distinction between the psychologically normal and the abnormal can be tricky. But it is a very important distinction, for how individuals are labeled in this respect determines how society treats them: whether they are allowed the same freedoms as everyone else, are hospitalized for treatment, or are treated even more severely (in times past, people with psychological disorders were even put to death so their evil spirits could not infect others).

Defining abnormal behavior is a difficult task. The criteria that have been proposed tend to emphasize a particular orientation—be it medical, psychological, biological, legal, statistical, or anthropological—while ignoring other perspectives (Sue & colleagues, 1990). Mental health can be approached from the point of view of society, the mental health profession, or the individual. How abnormal behavior is defined has implications for research as well as for therapy. For instance, if we define abnormal behavior as a disease (mental illness) or a biochemical imbalance, therapy would be very different than if it were defined as an inappropriate learned response. The type of therapy used also depends on the specific psychological disorder the person showing abnormal behavior is diagnosed as having.

While psychologists have not yet agreed on a single definition, there are some commonalities in abnormal behavior that can be incorporated into a working definition. Holmes (1991) suggested subjective distress of the individual, behavior that is psychologically or socially disabling, and behavior that deviates from social norms as criteria of abnormal behavior. Sue and colleagues (1990) proposed personal discomfort, inefficiency in coping with daily demands, and bizarre or unusual behavior in a specific culture as criteria. Carson and Butcher (1992) viewed abnormal behavior as being deviant from social norms and maladaptive for the individual. In this book, we define abnormal behavior as behavior that (a) contributes to *maladaptiveness* in an individual; (b) is considered *deviant* by the culture; or (c) leads to personal psychological *distress*.

Maladaptiveness may be defined as gross inadequacy in the handling of the events of daily life. If a person's state of mind becomes so confused that he or she is unable to accomplish even the ordinary tasks of day-to-day living efficiently, it is more than likely that he or she has a psychological disorder. Thus, the ability to adapt and function is a major criterion of sound psychological health.

A person may be judged abnormal if he or she behaves in a bizarre or highly deviant fashion. Such behavior can include *delusions* (the holding of obviously false beliefs), *hallucinations* (sensory experiences unrelated to the actual surroundings), and fears or odd rituals that serve no apparent purpose. Such behavior must, however, be seen against the background of the culture.

Perhaps the best indicator of psychological abnormality is the one that most closely resembles the criterion for determining physical illness: whether or not the person suffers acute distress. Depression, anxiety, and bodily complaints without corresponding physical ailments can all cause such subjective discomfort. The fact that an individual cannot eliminate such symptoms easily, and would welcome relief from them, is itself an indicator of psychological malfunctioning.

APPROACHES TO THE STUDY OF
ABNORMAL BEHAVIOR

Sometimes *abnormal psychology* is a controversial field, as we saw in our opening story. Some professionals have great confidence in the classification schemes used, while others question the value of labeling people. Most psychologists recognize the need for a systematic approach to the study of abnormal behavior and approve of some sort of classification scheme. This section reviews some of the major approaches used to study abnormal behavior and describes how psychological disorders are classified.

Models of Abnormal Behavior

There are many different approaches to the study of abnormal behavior. We examine some of the representative models of abnormality in this first section.

Psychoanalytic Model   An approach to abnormal psychology stemming from Sigmund Freud's theories of personality is the *psychoanalytic model*. This approach suggests that abnormal behavior is the result of a person's inner conflicts. In chapter 12, "Adjustment and Health," we discussed how we use defense mechanisms to deal with anxiety. When anxiety and conflict become too great for even the defense mechanisms to handle, abnormal behavior results. Thus, outward abnormal behavior is simply the symptom of some internal problem. The cure is to find the source of anxiety and solve the conflicts.

Biological Model   The idea that abnormal behavior is caused by biological factors is called the *biological model*. According to this approach, when the body's biochemical balance is upset, the person behaves abnormally. Historically, this approach was favored by psychiatrists, who are trained to treat disease. The cure is to alter the body biologically to restore balance. Thus, medical means, such as drugs or surgery, are used to treat abnormal behavior. Recently, much effort has focused on discovering the biological basis of behavior, including abnormal behavior.

Learning Model   Many psychologists find it more constructive to view mental abnormalities not as diseases, but as learned social maladjustments. According to the *learning model* of abnormality, the standards of normality are simply the social standards of society. Abnormal behavior is just the result of the individual's learning inappropriate role expectations. The cure, according to this view, is merely relearning the correct, socially acceptable behavior.

Cognitive Model   The *cognitive model* emphasizes inefficient thinking and problem solving as causes of abnormal behavior. The individual is not able to meet daily demands adequately because he or she cannot reason and understand the demands logically. The cognitive model is closely related to the psychoanalytic and learning models. The therapeutic cognitive approach would be to help the patient understand his or her problems and learn to solve them through thinking about the causes and consequences.

Legal Model   In the *legal model*, every society sets up its own laws and standards of behavior. If we break the law, our behavior might be considered insane, especially if we have no motive or cannot distinguish right from wrong. For example, walking naked down the street or harming oneself or others are examples of behavior that might be labeled legally insane. The legal definition of insanity is a topic of debate. Because he was declared insane, John Hinckley was sent to a mental institution instead of prison for shooting at President Ronald Reagan. The following Application explores the legal model in more depth.

APPLICATION

Insanity and the Law

In this chapter's opening story, we pointed out how difficult it is to define abnormal behavior. The issue becomes even more complicated when questions are raised in a court of law about a defendant's mental condition at the time he or she is alleged to have committed a crime. When the defendant pleads "not guilty by reason of insanity," the court must decide on his or her mental condition, based on legal precedent. The issue of insanity is decided by a judge or jury after listening to testimony of experts, who are usually psychologists or psychiatrists.

It is important to remember that in a court the concept of insanity is legal rather than psychological. The insanity plea is used in situations where the defendant is judged to be incapable of knowing right from wrong because of a mental disorder. Although psychologists may examine the individual and testify in court, the final decision is a legal one made by the courts.

As you are probably aware, even the experts are not in agreement over insanity as a legitimate defense. In some cases, insanity is used as a means to avoid prosecution. Normally, if one is judged insane, he or she is committed to a mental hospital until cured. If later judged sane, he or she is set free, sometimes after only a light sentence. One proposal to help solve the problem is to

FIGURE 13.2   Insanity and Law
Insanity is a legal term for an individual who is judged not capable of knowing right from wrong. John Hinkley (above) was sent to a mental institution rather than a prison after his attempted assassination of President Reagan, because he was declared insane.

replace the verdict of "not guilty by reason of insanity" with the verdict of "guilty but mentally ill." Individuals found "guilty but mentally ill" would be given the proper psychotherapy to treat their mental disorders, and when they were judged sane, they would be returned to prison to complete their sentences.

A related issue is the ability of the defendant to stand trial. In order to be brought to trial, an individual must understand the charge against him or her and be able to prepare a proper defense with a lawyer. Many times, instead of standing trial, the defendant is judged "incompetent to stand trial" and is committed to a mental institution for treatment. After being confined for a period of time, he or she is released if judged competent. Unfortunately, it is difficult to predict the future behavior of such a person. More research needs to be conducted on the application of psychological determinations to legal proceedings.

Statistical Model   Most abnormal behavior represents a magnification of some aspect of normal behavior. We have all experienced fear, daydreaming, fantasies, suspicions, or the desire to escape from people and their demands. These experiences are not only normal, they are sometimes necessary for adjustment. Abnormal behavior occurs when some of these processes are magnified out of proportion to reality and become predominant. The *statistical model* defines behavior as abnormal when its frequency or extent is vastly different from the normal population's.

It should be clear, then, that defining abnormal behavior is a difficult task. There are many approaches, and psychologists have not agreed totally on one particular theory to explain abnormality. Before we review the various psychological disorders themselves, we look at the classification scheme used by mental health professionals.

Classification and DSM-III-R

One of the most important tasks of clinical psychologists and other mental health experts is to diagnose and classify *psychological disorders* correctly. The American Psychiatric Association attempted to develop a standard set of diagnoses of abnormal behaviors by publishing the *Diagnostic and Statistical Manual of Mental Disorders (DSM)* in 1952. The DSM was revised in 1968, and again in 1980. The latest edition, DSM-III-R, was revised in 1987 and is used by psychologists and psychiatrists around the world to classify abnormal behavior patterns (Maser & colleagues, 1991). We refer to this revision throughout this book.

At press time, a task force was working on preparing DSM-IV, which is expected to be published in 1993 (Widiger & colleagues, 1991). Most of the classifications are expected to be similar to those now used. DSM-IV will be coordinated with the 10th edition of the *Manual of the International Statistical Classification of Diseases, Injuries, and Causes of Death (ICD-10)*, which will be published in 1993 by the World Health Organization (Kendell, 1991).

The purpose of DSM-III-R is to provide conformity and continuity among mental health professionals in the diagnosis of psychological disorders. The current edition emphasizes the patient's behavioral symptoms more than the assumptions of the underlying causes of the problem. Thus, it includes detailed criteria for classifying the various psychological disorders. It is also more complex than earlier editions.

DSM-III-R classifies the individual on five axes, or dimensions. First, there is the primary diagnosis, which concerns the major problem and symptoms (Axis I). The

FIGURE 13.3 DSM-III-R Major Classifications

AXIS I CLINICAL SYNDROMES

DISORDERS USUALLY FIRST EVIDENT IN INFANCY, CHILDHOOD, OR ADOLESCENCE
- Disruptive Behavior Disorders
  - Attention-deficit hyperactivity disorder
  - Conduct disorder
  - Oppositional defiant disorder
- Anxiety Disorders of Childhood or Adolescence
- Eating Disorders
  - Anorexia nervosa
  - Bulimia nervosa
- Gender Identity Disorders
- Tic Disorders
- Elimination Disorders
- Other Disorders of Infancy, Childhood, or Adolescence

ORGANIC MENTAL DISORDERS
- Dementias Arising in the Senium and Presenium
  - Primary degenerative demantia of the Alzheimer type
- Psychoactive Substance-Induced Organic Mental Disorders
- Organic Mental Disorders associated with Axis III physical disorders

PSYCHOACTIVE SUBSTANCE USE DISORDERS

SCHIZOPHRENIA
- Catatonic Schizophrenia
- Disorganized Schizophrenia
- Paranoid Schizophrenia
- Undifferentiated Schizophrenia
- Residual Schizophrenia

DELUSIONAL DISORDER

PSYCHOTIC DISORDERS NOT ELSEWHERE CLASSIFIED

MOOD DISORDERS
- Bipolar Disorders
  - Bipolar disorder
  - Cyclothymia
- Depressive Disorders
  - Major depression
  - Dysthymia

ANXIETY DISORDERS
- Panic Disorder With Agoraphobia
- Panic Disorder Without Agoraphobia
- Agoraphobia Without History of Panic Disorder
- Social Phobia
- Simple Phobia
- Obsessive Compulsive Disorder
- Post-traumatic Stress Disorder
- Generalized Anxiety Disorder

SOMATOFORM DISORDERS
- Body Dysmorphic Disorder
- Conversion Disorder
- Hypochondriasis
- Somatization Disorder
- Somatoform Pain Disorder
- Undifferentiated Somatoform Disorder

DISSOCIATIVE DISORDERS
- Multiple Personality Disorder
- Psychogenic Fugue
- Psychogenic Amnesia
- Depersonalization Disorder

SEXUAL DISORDERS
- Paraphilias
- Sexual Dysfunctions
- Other Sexual Disorders

SLEEP DISORDERS
- Dyssomnias
- Parasomnias

FACTITIOUS DISORDERS

IMPULSE CONTROL DISORDERS NOT ELSEWHERE CLASSIFIED

ADJUSTMENT DISORDER

PSYCHOLOGICAL FACTORS AFFECTING PHYSICAL CONDITION

AXIS II DEVELOPMENTAL DISORDERS

DISORDERS USUALLY FIRST EVIDENT IN INFANCY, CHILDHOOD, OR ADOLESCENCE
- Mental retardation
- Pervasive Developmental Disorders
- Autistic disorder
- Specific Developmental Disorders
  - Academic skills disorders
  - Language and speech disorders
  - Motor skills disorder
- Other Developmental Disorders

AXIS II PERSONALITY DISORDERS

PERSONALITY DISORDERS

individual's long-term personality characteristics or developmental problems are described (Axis II). Any physical problems that might be relevant to the disorder are also described (Axis III). The environment and sources of stress to which the individual is exposed are described (Axis IV). And finally, an evaluation is made on how well the individual has functioned in the past (Axis V). The extensive classification scheme is designed to help make more accurate diagnoses.

Not everyone is totally pleased with DSM-III-R. For instance, some psychologists argue that it is too specific in its classifications. For example, dependence on nicotine is included as a classification. Most people would probably not consider cigarette smoking a psychological disorder. And the five axes make DSM-III-R complex to understand and use.

DSM-III-R was designed not to perpetuate a particular viewpoint, although it has been criticized for emphasizing the medical model. Some psychologists feel that it includes too many disorder classifications (more than 230). Others worry about the tendency to think that the syndromes have been explained when they have only been described (McReynolds, 1989). There is concern over the reliability of the diagnoses made with DSM-III-R. And there is controversy over the reclassification of disorders. For instance, although homosexuality is no longer included as a psychiatric diagnosis, several other controversial disorders are included in an appendix for "proposed diagnostic categories needing further study." Among these are such disorders as the *late luteal phase dysphoric disorder*, which occurs in females who experience severe changes in physical and emotional functioning during menstrual cycles that cause marked impairment in social interactions. The *sadistic personality disorder* occurs when someone shows continual cruel, demeaning, and aggressive behavior toward other people. The *self-defeating personality disorder* occurs when a person shows a pattern of self-defeating behavior. There is continuing debate on the appropriateness of including these proposed diagnostic categories.

We review some of the major classifications of psychological disorders in DSM-III-R in this chapter. We cannot possibly cover every one of the 230 classifications, so we concentrate on the most relevant and representative examples of different types. Since anxiety and stress are often involved in behavior problems, we start with the anxiety disorders.

As we go through this chapter, you may recognize in your roommate, parents, friends, teachers, or even yourself some of the symptoms described. Chances are good that these people are normal. We all show little individual peculiarities or idiosyncrasies that make us unique. To be classified as abnormal, the conditions would have to be fairly serious. While we all experience some anxiety, for example, severe psychological disorders are fortunately relatively rare.

ANXIETY DISORDERS

Anxiety disorders are fairly long-lasting disruptions of the normal pattern of living, characterized by anxiety. Anxiety is usually defined as a vague feeling of fear and apprehension. As we discussed in chapter 12, "Adjustment and Health," anxiety might be thought of as a fear of the demands placed on the individual when the individual doesn't know exactly what the demands are. The person generally has no clear idea of the real cause of the anxiety; in fact, there is a tendency to avoid thinking about the fears, since that only seems to intensify them. The anxious person often develops specific ritualistic behaviors that serve to reduce anxiety temporarily, but that actually increase the problems because they don't solve them (Beck & Emery, 1985). Originally Freud used the term neurosis to describe abnormal behavior caused by anxiety. However, the term crept into popular usage and wasn't as specific as it might have been, and so in the DSM-III-R it is replaced with individual anxiety disorders.

We review four types of anxiety disorder: panic disorder and agoraphobia, social and simple phobias, obsessive compulsive disorder, and generalized anxiety disorder.

Panic Disorder and Agoraphobia

Panic disorder is identified by the occurrence of panic attacks, specific periods of intense anxiety characterized by shortness of breath, dizziness, faintness, trembling, sweating, nausea, numbness, chills or hot flashes, or a fear of dying. The person may feel apprehension and a sense of doom (DSM-III-R, 1987). Panic attacks may last from a few minutes up to an hour or more. They are unexpected and are not caused by anxiety-producing situations.

Usually panic disorders occur in young adults of both sexes. Panic attacks can occur several times a week, or, in some cases, daily. The disruption of an important social relationship can predispose an individual to panic disorder (Franklin, 1987). When panic disorder alone is experienced, there might be only a minimal impairment of social functioning; however, it is often accompanied by agoraphobia.

Agoraphobia occurs when the individual is afraid of places or situations that would be difficult or embarrassing to escape from, especially if incapacitating symptoms occur (Williams & colleagues, 1989). He or she may be afraid to be outside the home, in a crowd, or traveling; afraid of falling, becoming dizzy, or developing some embarrassing problem. Because of this intense fear, the person usually restricts travel. Sometimes he or she can travel with a companion and is willing to endure the anxiety situation in order to accomplish something. Typically, agoraphobia develops in young adults, with females being more likely to develop the disorder than males. The individual may or may not also experience full-blown panic attacks but may have any of the symptoms individually. Research suggests that agoraphobia and panic disorder are often experienced together, and may have a common genetic basis (Noyes & colleagues, 1986).

Social and Simple Phobias

Phobias are acute excessive fears of specific situations or objects, fears that have no convincing basis in reality. Persons with phobias usually recognize the irrationality of their fears, but cannot overcome them without outside help. People can develop phobias about an endless variety of things. Some of the more common phobias are fear of being closed in (claustrophobia), fear of heights (acrophobia), fear of crowds (ocholophobia), fear of animals (zoophobia), and fear of the dark (nyctophobia). There is a trend away from a long list of Greek words indicating specific phobias. DSM-III-R classifies phobias into three general categories, agoraphobia (which we've just discussed), social phobia, and simple phobia.

Social phobias are excessive irrational fears and embarrassment when interacting with other people. Social phobias include fear of assertive behavior, fear of criticism, fear of mistakes, and fear of public speaking. Social phobias often begin in adolescence and can be quite disruptive. The disorder is more common in males than in females. The individual with social phobia usually attempts to avoid the situations that cause the intense anxiety.

The individual with a simple phobia shows an excessive irrational fear toward a specific stimulus. The most common simple, or specific, phobias are directed toward dogs, snakes, insects, blood, closed-in spaces, darkness, and heights. Thus, one might have a simple phobia of snakes or a simple phobia of heights.

The simple phobias exclude fear of social situations (social phobias), fear of having a panic attack (panic disorder), or agoraphobia. Females more often experience simple phobias, and the problem can begin at any age from childhood on. The simple phobias are fairly common, and since they usually are not too disruptive, often people do not seek treatment for them.

Often fears toward specific objects are developed by simple classical conditioning. As we noted in chapter 6, "Learning," phobias do not develop at random, but rather appear to be learned from specific stimuli. A theory proposed by Martin Seligman (1972) states that we can learn phobias from stimuli that at some time in

FIGURE 13.4   Social Phobia
An individual who fears situations and objects inordinately when there is no reason to be afraid has a social phobia. An extreme fear of crowds, for example, can disrupt an individual's life and prevent him or her from enjoying many kinds of social events.

evolution were dangerous to people (such as snakes, darkness, or heights).

Fears become phobic when, without foundation, they interfere with daily living. For instance, they can prevent individuals from using public transportation, flying on an airplane, or going past the first floor of a building. When phobic persons encounter the objects of their phobias, typically they experience panic, nausea, and acute anxiety. On the other hand, phobias have the advantage of giving anxious persons reasons for anxiety and specific objects to avoid. Therefore, they can keep anxiety in check.

Obsessive Compulsive Disorder

One relatively common type of anxiety disorder is the obsessive compulsive disorder (OCD), which can take several forms. Anxious persons may have repetitive thoughts (obsessions) or constant urges to indulge in meaningless rituals (compulsions), which they find uncontrollable, irrational, and inconvenient. For example, they may imagine that someone is following them constantly or may check repeatedly to make sure a window is not open. The obsessions or compulsions cause significant distress, interfere with the individual's normal functioning, and are time-consuming (DSM-III-R, 1987).

Obsessive thoughts often involve fears of being unable to control impulses. The individual may continually fantasize about killing a relative, walking naked in public, or screaming obscenities. The chances of carrying out these actions are practically nonexistent, but the fantasies continually and involuntarily recur, until the person having them is afraid of losing control. Any attempt to stop these thoughts, however, results in acute anxiety.

Compulsive acts are equally disruptive to the individual. They range from minor routines, such as checking doors three times to assure that they are locked or stirring coffee exactly five times, to complex rituals, such as dressing and undressing seven times before going out or adding the numbers on all visible license plates before crossing a street. Again, any attempt to stop the behaviors results in acute anxiety.

Obsessions and compulsions are often combined in some way, such as when a person constantly worries about dirt and washes his or her hands every half hour. Or perhaps a person is afraid of being frozen, so he or she hoards blankets and sweaters. If the person has 1,000 sweaters, we can be pretty sure he or she is compulsive. We all have thoughts and mannerisms that we perform almost automatically. In the obsessive compulsive, however, these thoughts and acts become so dominant that they disrupt life.

To judge accurately whether a particular behavior is obsessive compulsive, the social context must be taken into consideration. For example, we would not consider an airline pilot disturbed for compulsively checking out the airplane's instruments before each takeoff. Likewise, a few years ago my wife had a beer can collection. She thought constantly about acquiring new cans and at times went out of her way to look at collections. If she had continued this hobby to the point of ignoring her family and becoming ill from not eating, then there would have been a serious problem. Obsessive compulsive individuals are relatively easy to treat, as this is usually considered a relatively mild form of maladjustment.

There are several theories of how obsessive compulsive disorders develop. The psychoanalytic model suggests that anxiety and guilt about some problem can overwhelm a person. The individual might find doing something else takes his or her mind off the problem. Thus a cycle begins: every time the anxiety is experienced, the ritualistic behavior is performed. The learning theory suggests that obsessive compulsive disorders develop in response to an anxiety-producing experience. When we are upset about something, we try various methods of reducing the anxiety. When we find something that works, we continue to do it. Dollard and Miller (1950) suggested that our compulsions may be behaviors that were rewarded in childhood. For example, washing our hands, getting dressed, or straightening our room

FIGURE 13.5 Obsessive Compulsive Disorders
An individual with an obsessive compulsive disorder may continually think about being contaminated or disorderly. These obsessive thoughts may lead to compulsive acts, such as constantly washing one's hands, cleaning the house, or constantly straightening the contents of drawers or closets even when they do not need it.

often earned us praise. As adults, we exaggerate these childhood behaviors. Since they are associated with reinforcement, they temporarily reduce our anxiety. Some research suggests that there is a biological basis for some forms of obsessive compulsive behavior. *Clomipramine*, an antidepressant drug that increases the level of serotonin, has been found to be effective in treating obsessive compulsive disorder (Zohar & colleagues, 1988).

Generalized Anxiety Disorder

Individuals with generalized anxiety disorder live in a state of constant tension. Anxious people usually do not know why they feel as if something dreadful is about to happen; their anxiety is generally free-floating, or unattached to any particular object or situation.

Individuals with generalized anxiety disorder feel inadequate and helpless in the face of life and its challenges. Of course, we all have had anxious experiences when faced with trying situations (for example, incompleted work assignments or difficult decisions to be made). But somehow we get through the situation without severe trauma. People with generalized anxiety disorder, however, cannot function when faced with problems that most of us handle without much difficulty. They are constantly apprehensive and find endless problems to worry about. Even when things are going well for them, they cannot relax because there are always tomorrow's problems to worry about.

DSM-III-R lists 18 symptoms, 6 of which are required for a diagnosis of generalized anxiety disorder. Muscle tension symptoms include trembling, muscle tension, restlessness, and fatigue. Autonomic hyperactivity symptoms include shortness of breath, rapid heart rate, sweating, dizziness, dry mouth, nausea, chills, difficulty swallowing, and frequent urination. Vigilance and scanning symptoms include feeling keyed up, an exaggerated startle response, insomnia, difficulty concentrating, and general irritability. The person must show these symptoms for at least 6 months to be diagnosed as having generalized anxiety disorder. Some evidence suggests that panic attacks can occur in individuals with generalized anxiety disorder (Barlow & colleagues, 1985).

Anxiety disorders represent the mild end of the continuum of maladjustment. While they are serious, as we see in chapter 14, "Therapy," they can often be treated successfully and the individual can then resume a productive life. Phobias are also often treated effectively with behavior therapy.

We turn next to the more severe categories of psychological disorders that are called psychotic disorders. The two major psychoses—the *mood disorders* and *schizophrenia*—are discussed here.

MOOD DISORDERS

When a person experiences a severe disruption in mood or emotional balance, we call the problem a mood disorder (formerly called an affective disorder). A mood disorder may involve one extreme of mood, *depression*, in which a person's emotions are at an all-time low and he or she loses interest in life. It may also involve the other extreme of mood, *mania*, which is a highly excitable, highly active, unrealistic, optimistic state. DSM-III-R includes two major mood disorders: *major depression* (or unipolar depression), which is characterized by a sad mood, coupled with feelings of guilt and worthlessness; and *bipolar disorder* (sometimes referred to as manic-depression), which is characterized by extreme mood swings from sad depression to joyful mania. Mania seldom occurs by itself.

Major Depression

Depression can vary widely in severity. It is normal for people to feel mildly depressed when they have failed to achieve something or when they lose someone important to them. One review by Winokur (1985) found that people become depressed when they have problems at

FIGURE 13.6   Depression
An individual who is depressed cannot adjust to the problems in life. He or she is usually sad and often has thoughts
of guilt and worthlessness. Scientists have several theories
that try to explain the basis for this mood disorder.

work, experience marital problems, or find they are
incompetent in something they want to do. Some research suggests that men become more depressed when
their spouses die then do women (Stroebe & Stroebe,
1983). We may become mildly depressed when we have
a fight with someone or receive a low grade on a test. As
mentioned in chapter 12, "Adjustment and Health,"
Seligman suggests depression is often an extension of
learned helplessness. Mild depression usually lasts briefly
and is followed by full recovery.

A more serious problem is dysthymia, in which the
person has a depressed mood much of the time for at
least 2 years. Symptoms of dysthymia include a major
change in eating and sleeping habits (loss of appetite or
overeating, insomnia or hypersomnia), fatigue, low self-
esteem, poor concentration, and feelings of hopelessness
(DSM-III-R, 1987). Dysthymia may be due to other
nonmood disorders, such as anorexia or drug use. The
individual with dysthymia usually experiences minor impairment in social interactions, and is rarely hospitalized
unless a suicide attempt occurs. The depression in dysthymia is moderate compared to major depression, which
is more severe and incapacitating.

Symptoms of Major Depression   Major depression occurs when an individual experiences one or
more *major depressive episodes*, the chief symptom of
which includes a depressed mood and loss of interest in
normal activities. Cognitive symptoms can include feelings of worthlessness or inappropriate guilt, an inability to
concentrate, and thoughts of death or suicide. Depressed
individuals typically have low self-esteem and a general
negative attitude toward life. Behavioral symptoms include sleep pattern changes, eating difficulty and weight
loss, reduction of sex drive, and a general disruption of
motor activities. In addition, depressed individuals have
little energy and complain of constantly feeling fatigued.
These symptoms occur most of the time for at least a
2-week period. People who are severely depressed describe themselves as sad and hopeless and may have no
motivation to continue living.

Major depression usually begins in early adulthood,
but a major depressive episode may occur at any age,
including infancy. A major episode usually lasts at least 6
months, and some of the symptoms can persist for a year
or more. Impairment of the depressed individual varies
from moderate disruption of normal relationships and
activities to complete inability to function as a person.
The largest problem in major depression is the possibility
of suicide.

APPLICATION

Suicide

Suicide is often a real possibility in cases of depression. Roughly 1 out of 10,000 Americans commit suicide
each year. Though more women attempt suicide, three
times more men actually die from suicide (probably
because men tend to use more violent methods). Whites
commit suicide twice as often as blacks. Although the
peak age for suicide attempts in America is about age 30,
studies indicate that the incidence of suicide is very
serious among teenagers and the elderly (Peck & colleagues, 1985). Recently, the greatest increase in suicide
rates has been in the 15- to 24-year-old range.

Why do people commit suicide? While there are
many different individual reasons, most have to do with
the fact that those who attempt suicide feel that life is not
worth living. As we indicated in this chapter, feelings of
hopelessness and guilt are prevalent in depression. If the
situation looks hopeless, it might induce the depressed
individual to commit suicide.

Some people believe that the act of suicide is a
desperate plea for help. Others argue that suicide gestures are ways of controlling other people. Holmes (1991)

FIGURE 13.7   Suicide
People who are severely depressed and feel hopeless may commit suicide. Scientists are trying to find ways to prevent this growing problem.

FIGURE 13.8   Symptoms of Major Depression

- Depressed mood most of the time
- Loss of interest in normal activities
- Inability to think or concentrate
- Feelings of worthlessness or guilt
- Low self-esteem
- General negative attitude toward life
- Thoughts of death/suicide attempts
- Constant feelings of fatigue
- Sleep pattern changes
- Eating difficulties and weight change
- Reduction of sex drive
- Disruption of normal motor activities

reported that nearly 80 percent of suicide victims provided some type of warning prior to the act itself. It appears that people who commit suicide are individuals who are unable to deal adequately with their stress and know of no other alternative.

There are some things that can be done to help prevent suicide, as discussed by Davison and Neale in their 1990 book, *Abnormal Psychology*. Getting potential suicide victims to promise not to commit suicide before seeing a counselor appears to be successful. Talking with them about how they feel might help reassure them until they can get professional help. If you are with a potential suicide victim, go with him or her to get help. A counseling center, hospital emergency room, or even a police station are places where professionals will know how to handle the situation. If indeed the person feels there is no reason to live, then the best treatment would seem to be one that provides the person with hope. Psychologists do not understand exactly why people commit suicide. They hope through continuing research to improve their understanding of the causes of suicide and learn how to prevent this tragic waste of human life.

Major depression can be diagnosed as having a seasonal pattern (also called *seasonal affective disorder*). DSM-III-R states that for a seasonal pattern there has to be a clear relationship between the onset of a major depressive episode and a particular time of the year, and a history of at least three episodes of depression in three separate years. Most often, patients with a seasonal pattern have depressive episodes in the winter months. One theory is that the depression is associated with the changes in the amount of daylight during winter months (Rosenthal & colleagues, 1985). A therapy that appears to be effective is exposing the patient to bright white light.

Theories of Depression   Depression is a common maladjustment problem, and there are a variety of theories that attempt to explain how it occurs. Psychoanalytic theory focuses on unconscious conflict and suggests that feelings of anger and hostility are displaced, or turned inward, with the result that the person becomes so miserable that life is no longer tolerable. Thus, he or she gives up and becomes depressed. Freud also compared depression to mourning. Beck's (1967, 1976) cognitive theory of depression emphasizes the negative and self-defeating thoughts of the person who is depressed. It suggests that when a person dwells on the negative for too long, low self-esteem and depression can result.

The learning theory (see chapter 12, "Adjustment and Health," for a discussion of helplessness) suggests that depression is the result of learning to be helpless. This popular theory proposed by Seligman (1975) assumes that when people discover that they do not have control over their lives, socially, economically, or psychologically, they tend to give up. They tend to attribute their problems to their own personalities and believe they cannot improve (Seligman & colleagues, 1988). This might help to explain why depression is so common among the poor and helpless.

Other learning theorists speculate that depression results from the reduction of social reinforcement and activity (Heiby, 1983). For example, after the loss of a wife, a husband no longer has much intimate reinforcement or enjoyment, and other people do not expect much from him. Soon he learns his new role, and continues to remain depressed. Help might consist of encouraging him to gain control over his life by taking up a hobby, becoming socially active, or going back to school.

Some research focuses on the role of interpersonal factors in depression. Hooley (1986) reported that problems in a relationship (such as hostility in marriage) often precede depression. Roy (1985) found that when a parent dies early, children are more likely to become depressed as adults. In general, any major life event that significantly decreases an individual's self-esteem or increases his or her stress level might contribute to maladjustment.

A number of biological theories have been proposed for depression. Seligman (1975) found that dogs that had learned to become helpless had very low levels of the neurotransmitter norepinephrine. In their classic theory of mood disorders, Schildkraut and Kety (1967) proposed that low levels of dopamine and especially norepinephrine were involved in depression. Drugs that increase levels of norepinephrine and serotonin have been successful in treating depression in humans (Cooper & colleagues, 1986). Some evidence exists that the loss of pleasurable reinforcement and enjoyment experienced by those who suffer from Parkinson's disease is due to lowered levels of dopamine (Fibiger, 1984). A theory of Janowsky and Risch (1984) suggests that depression and mania are caused by disturbances in the balance between the neurotransmitters norepinephrine and acetylcholine. Norepinephrine plays a role in the experience of pleasure in the brain when reinforcement occurs, thus linking the reinforcement-learning and biological theories. Researchers have found lower levels of the neurotransmitter GABA in individuals who are depressed than in those who are not (Petty & Sherman, 1984). Some research has focused on synaptic malfunctions and mood disorders (McNeal & Cimbolic, 1986). While the evidence is strong that a disturbance in the levels of neurotransmitters such as norepinephrine are involved in depression, at the present time the exact mechanism is not known. Some evidence also suggests that depression has a genetic component (Mendlewicz, 1985), and is affected by the endocrine system (Poland & colleagues, 1987).

Bipolar Disorder

The bipolar disorder, or *manic-depression*, is characterized by unpredictable extreme mood swings. Sometimes the manic-depressive's mood fluctuates wildly from great excitement to extreme melancholy. During the manic phase, the patient may become hyperexcited, talkative, boastful, uninhibited, and perhaps destructive. In this energy and excitement phase, he or she may talk about highly unrealistic projects. The person may have greatly increased self-confidence and is easily distracted. Suddenly, without warning, the patient with bipolar disorder becomes so gloomy and experiences such profound feelings of worthlessness that he or she will have difficulty sleeping and moving about and refuse to eat. There are not nearly as many people with bipolar disorder (about 1 percent of the population) as with unipolar depression (from 10 percent to 20 percent of the population in the United States). The bipolar disorder occurs with equal frequency in men and women.

People suffering from bipolar disorder differ in a number of ways from those experiencing major (unipolar) depression. Individuals who develop major depression tend to be older at the onset than those with bipolar disorder. When those with bipolar disorder experience a depression episode, they are lethargic, whereas people with major depression tend to be more agitated. Those who are suffering from a depressive episode of bipolar disorder are more likely than those with major depression to benefit from a prescription of lithium (a chemical salt that tends to level out extreme mood swings).

Some individuals experience a bipolar disorder called cyclothymia, which is a moderately severe problem with mood swings from hypomanic episodes to depression (but not as extreme as manic or major depressive episodes). A *hypomanic episode* is characterized by an elevated or irritable mood but is not severe enough to cause major disruption of normal functioning. It is also possible for an individual to have a seasonal pattern in a bipolar disorder, in which there is a relationship between an episode of bipolar disorder or depressive episode and the time of the year.

SCHIZOPHRENIA

I met Jerry at a local mental institution. A group of students and I were walking up to one of the wards when a young man approached and said he would help guide our tour. He proceeded to tell us about some of the patients and the therapies used at the institution. Then he warned us about the gunman and told us that he had to go ring the church bell. But he stopped and began to laugh, saying that he didn't know why we had strawberry jam in our pockets. Our tour guide, who had been with us the entire time, led Jerry back to his room. Later our guide explained that the best way to tell the patients from the workers was to ask for keys—only workers had keys.

Jerry had schizophrenia. Schizophrenia is the most common type of psychosis, and people with this psychological disorder tend to live in a world of their own imagining. Most people hospitalized with schizophrenia dress themselves, walk about, and indulge in such everyday activities as eating and smoking in much the same manner as everyone else. However, individuals with schizophrenia withdraw their interest in and concern for the events and people in the world around them. They are often preoccupied with fantasies, delusions, and hallucinations, which affect their speech and thoughts. Although there are several types of schizophrenia, most schizophrenics show some common symptoms.

Clinical Symptoms of Schizophrenia

As shown in our opening story, there is quite a bit of controversy over labeling a person as schizophrenic. Because it is the most common psychotic disorder, schizophrenia is sometimes used as a catchall for individuals who cannot be classified otherwise. Some psychologists, like David Rosenhan, argue that mental health professionals are too ready to diagnose someone as having schizophrenia. It was to illustrate this point that he designed the study that had normal people admit themselves into various psychiatric hospitals, complaining of hearing voices. As we discussed in our opening story, although it would be extremely difficult to diagnose a psychological disorder accurately from this symptom alone, in eleven out of twelve admissions, Rosenhan's

FIGURE 13.9   Clinical Symptoms of Schizophrenia

Content of thought:
delusions
Form of thought:
incoherence, unorganized thinking
Perception:
hallucinations (often voices)
Affect:
Flat or inappropriate emotions
Sense of self:
loss of sense of self
Volition:
inadequate interest or drive
impaired interpersonal functioning and relationship
to the external world
Psychomotor behavior:
disturbed actions, bizarre postures

pseudopatients were diagnosed as having schizophrenia. This study demonstrated the danger in labeling people with clinical diagnostic terms. The DSM-III-R helps to classify people when sufficient symptoms can be seen clearly. Following is a brief description of the major symptoms of schizophrenia. The DSM-III-R identifies several areas in which individuals with schizophrenia typically experience disturbances. They include thinking, perception, affect (emotion), sense of self, volition, relationship to the world, and behavior.

Disruption of Content and Form of Thought
Many individuals with schizophrenia have delusions, or beliefs not founded on reality. Some schizophrenics have delusions of persecution, and believe that someone is trying to kill or hurt them. They also have thoughts about agents controlling their thinking and behavior, as well as difficulty separating reality from fantasy. A common delusion in schizophrenia is thought broadcasting, in which people believe that their thoughts are broadcast so others can hear them. Thought insertion, in which people with schizophrenia believe thoughts from others are inserted into their heads, is another common delusion.

Individuals with schizophrenia often have problems with the form of their thoughts, called formal thought disorder. Often their thinking is unorganized and incoherent. They appear to have trouble associating current information with previous knowledge. In addition, they show confusion and lack of insight. Ideas shift from one topic to another, even though there is no relationship between topics of thought.

Disruption of Perception   Individuals with schizophrenia often report having hallucinations, or sensory experiences with no sensory stimuli present. Often they are auditory hallucinations, such as hearing voices that talk to the patient or just make sounds. Tactile hallucinations may also be experienced, and usually involve a tingling or burning feeling. Sometimes visual or olfactory hallucinations occur, such as seeing snakes crawling around the room.

Disruption of Affect   Many individuals with schizophrenia show abnormalities of emotional response. Sometimes they are emotionally flat and do not show any emotional arousal. They tend to stare straight ahead and appear apathetic. When they speak, their voices are monotone without any expression. Other individuals with schizophrenia show inappropriate emotional responses: for example, they laugh at sad news, or cry for no apparent reason; or they shift emotional moods quickly, and are not dependable in their reaction to a stimulus.

Disruption of Sense of Self and Volition   The sense of self is an important characteristic of the normal, healthy person. An individual with schizophrenia has difficulties in developing a personal identity, and may believe outside forces are directing his or her behavior.

A characteristic often observed in a person with schizophrenia is a disturbance in volition, or lack of goal-directed activation. The person does not show adequate motivation to follow through on an action. This, of course, causes the person to be unable to function properly in society.

Disruption of Relationships and Behavior   The individual with schizophrenia has great difficulty relating to other people. Often he or she will withdraw from social relationships. Because the person experiences delusions and hallucinations, he or she is unable to relate to the external world properly.

Especially in severe forms of schizophrenia, disturbances in behavior are observed. For instance, the person with schizophrenia may maintain a rigid posture or exhibit stereotypical spastic movements, or other bizarre mannerisms.

Types of Schizophrenia

Schizophrenia usually begins during childhood or early adolescence. Diagnosis of schizophrenia requires that the symptoms be present for at least 6 months. Usually a *prodromal phase* occurs first, in which there is a definite deterioration in functioning. In this phase, the individual often shows social withdrawal, neglect of personal hygiene, lack of motivation, and unusual perceptual experiences. During the *active phase*, psychotic symptoms (such as hallucinations and delusions) are exhibited. Finally, after the active phase is a *residual phase*, in which many of the prodromal phase characteristics are again evident.

DSM-III-R lists five major types of schizophrenia: *catatonic, disorganized, paranoid, undifferentiated,* and *residual.* They are often thought of as patterns of symptoms of the illness, rather than as distinct types of psychosis. They tend to overlap, and their use as diagnostic tools seems to be somewhat a matter of convenience.

Catatonic Schizophrenia   One fairly rare type of schizophrenia is catatonic schizophrenia, most often characterized by complete immobility and the apparent absence of the will to move and speak. The individual with catatonic schizophrenia is able, without shifting, to maintain the same—often quite uncomfortable—position for hours (called a catatonic stupor). Catatonics are sometimes suggestible, obeying the orders of others in a robot-like way. More often, they are negativistic, resisting

FIGURE 13.10   Catatonic Schizophrenia
An individual with catatonic schizophrenia sometimes maintains the same uncomfortable position for extended periods of time. This may be one way to avoid the anxiety of interacting with other people.

outside efforts to change their position or even to feed them. They may also show selective amnesia (forgetting) for some events along with an extraordinary memory at other times.

Disorganized Schizophrenia   The most severe personality disintegration occurs in disorganized schizophrenia. Previously, disorganized schizophrenia was called *hebephrenia* (from the Greek word "hebe" meaning childish or silly). Its onset most often occurs at an early age. It is characterized by flat or inappropriate emotions, including silliness and giggling, infantile reactions, bizarre behavior, incoherent speech and thought, hallucinations, and delusions.

Paranoid Schizophrenia   People with paranoid schizophrenia frequently have persecutory or grandiose delusions. With their elaborately and logically constructed persecutory delusions, individuals with paranoid schizophrenia often show great alertness, suspicion, and vigilance toward the "agents" who are "out to get them." They may also believe they are Christ or the object of a pursuit by the CIA, and may project feelings they think are "bad" onto others. This ability to transfer the "bad" part of themselves to others may result in feelings of omnipotence or all-powerfulness. Such grandiose delusions also provide paranoid schizophrenics with a rationale for why others are persecuting them.

One of the common symptoms of schizophrenia is sensory hallucination; individuals with paranoid schizophrenia may "hear voices" that confirm their supernatural powers. The individual with paranoid schizophrenia can be angry and at times violent. There is a chance the individual with paranoid schizophrenia can recover and function normally. The number of paranoid schizophrenics appears to be decreasing, whereas the number of individuals with undifferentiated schizophrenia is increasing.

Undifferentiated Schizophrenia The above three types of schizophrenia show specific psychotic symptoms. Sometimes the individual with schizophrenia does not fit into any particular category, or shows symptoms of more than one type. This patient is labeled as having undifferentiated schizophrenia. This type, sometimes called simple schizophrenia, is characterized by a gradual loss of interest in the world, in social relationships, and in personal hygiene, as well as increased withdrawal, apathy, and emotional indifference. This person displays delusions, hallucinations, incoherence, or disorganized behavior, but because such a person does not meet all of the diagnostic criteria he or she cannot be categorized as a catatonic, disorganized, or paranoid type.

Residual Schizophrenia Individuals with residual schizophrenia are without major psychotic symptoms but have had a schizophrenic episode in the past. They tend to exhibit symptoms such as social withdrawal, illogical thinking, and inappropriate emotions, although they can function fairly well. The individual who is classified as having residual schizophrenia is not quite "in remission" since the residual type still shows some signs of the disorder.

Causes of Schizophrenia

In the past 20 years or so, there has been considerable research into the possible biochemical and genetic causes of schizophrenia—specifically, research into the possibility that some genetically inherited substance in the brain might be responsible for schizophrenia. The disorder seems to run in families, and the incidence of schizophrenia among identical twins, even those reared in different homes, is high. But environmental forces seem to intensify the influence of suspected genetic factors. Let's first look at environmental influences on schizophrenia.

Environmental Influences Thorough investigation into the family background of individuals with schizo-

phrenia usually reveals a history of very great stress on the child, so great that he or she escapes from an intolerable reality into a fantasy world (Zubin & Ludwig, 1983). There are two family situations most commonly linked to schizophrenia (Roff & Knight, 1981). The first involves a mother who is indifferent to the family, resulting in disorganization and stress. The second involves one parent (usually the mother) who completely dominates the spouse and children, but is not nurturant. In both cases, conflict and stress result in increased vulnerability in the children. In another study (Doane & colleagues, 1981), it was found that communication patterns in the family were related to schizophrenic tendencies in children. Specifically, unclear and conflicting messages, criticism, and hostility are more often found in homes in which children develop schizophrenia.

Psychoanalytic theorists like Freud believed schizophrenia was the result of regression to primary narcissism, the oral phase before the ego has developed. The narcissistic individual is totally controlled by the id and seeks total self-gratification. Laing (1964) suggested that schizophrenia occurs when an individual decides no longer to accept the pressures and demands of society, and thus turns inward to a self-made fantasy world. Social learning theorists argue that schizophrenia is a learned behavior, produced through others' reinforcement of abnormal responses. If someone is ignored, then one way to gain attention is to show bizarre behavior.

A number of early studies showed that schizophrenia is more prevalent in the lower socioeconomic groups (Hollingshead & Redlich, 1958). People with schizophrenia in these economic groups show more physical and social symptoms of unhappiness, as well as more open friction with others. There are many possible but unproven reasons for these apparent class differences: less than adequate diagnostic procedures may be available to low-income people; the low-income disturbed person is less able to hold a well-paying job; the poor and the rich may raise their children in ways that predispose the children to react to stress differently; being poor may also give rise to feelings of hopelessness. Research into an explanation for apparent class differences in the incidence of schizophrenia is scanty; more research is needed. None of the environmental theories have fully explained schizophrenia, and there is, therefore, excitement in the research being done on the biological causes.

Biological Influences The chance of an individual having schizophrenia is very small: about 1 percent of the population in the United States has schizophrenia. Genetic research has shown that if one close genetic relative has schizophrenia, the chances are significantly higher that another will also have it. Twin studies have shown high *concordance* rates for schizophrenia (if one has it, the other does also), according to Zerbin-Rubin

(1972). As discussed in chapter 2, "Psychobiology," schizophrenia concordance is much higher for monozygotic (identical) twins than for dizygotic (nonidentical) twins. Gottesman and Shields (1972) reported a concordance rate of 42 percent for MZ twins but only 9 percent for DZ twins. Adoption studies also demonstrate that genetic influences are very important in schizophrenia (Kety, 1983). Typically, even if separated, twins who are adopted are likely to have high concordance rates.

A number of critiques have pointed out that, with the current methodology, it is extremely difficult to separate the environmental and genetic influences (Abrams & Taylor, 1983). The exact genetic mechanism responsible for schizophrenia has not yet been identified. However, recent evidence suggests that genes affect biochemical reactions that may lead to schizophrenic behavior. For example, Sherrington and colleagues (1988) reported a study in which many people with schizophrenia had a problem with a gene on chromosome number 5, which also influences dopamine activity.

Over the years a number of biochemical theories of schizophrenia have been proposed. Researchers have suggested vitamin deficiencies, blood-protein abnormalities, and urine chemical irregularities as causal factors. Often in the past researchers overlooked the fact that people institutionalized for schizophrenia are usually on drug therapy, which may account for these chemical differences. The most promising current biochemical theory is the *dopamine theory*.

Wise and Stein (1973) reported that persons with schizophrenia have significantly higher than normal levels of the neurotransmitter dopamine. Drugs called *phenothiazines*, which help treat the symptoms of schizophrenia by lowering dopamine levels, can, if not carefully monitored, produce symptoms of Parkinson's disease (which is normally caused by low levels of dopamine). Amphetamines tend to increase levels of dopamine and can lead to amphetamine psychosis, with schizophrenic symptoms (Angrist, 1983). Research by Wong and colleagues (1986) found that individuals with schizophrenia tend to have brains with significantly more dopamine receptors than usual. Unfortunately, the data are not as clear-cut as we would like. Antipsychotic drugs do not help all schizophrenics. And, while these drugs lower levels of dopamine, they also interfere with the functioning of norepinephrine, serotonin, and acetylcholine, and thus are not the complete solution to a complex situation. Researchers continue to try to find how neurochemicals are related to schizophrenia. There are some scientists who believe schizophrenia could be caused by a viral infection (Bower, 1985). Some viruses can affect the neurotransmitters, including dopamine.

Neuchterlein and Dawson (1984) proposed a vulnerability-stress model of schizophrenia that states that some people have a biological tendency (predisposition),

by inheriting particular genes, to develop schizophrenia if they are stressed enough by their environment. In particular, this theory suggests that certain people have difficulty processing information and maintaining attention. They overreact to social stressors and lack appropriate social competency and adjustment skills. Thus, when a supportive family is not present, the stress is severe enough to push the individual toward schizophrenia. Both biological and environmental factors are involved in the vulnerability-stress model.

We do not yet know exactly what causes schizophrenia. It seems to be produced and sustained by genetic, organic, biochemical, and environmental factors (Mirsky & Duncan, 1986). Like cancer, it probably isn't really one disorder, but rather a loose combination of physical and behavioral problems, only some of which we have identified. And like cancer, it is a disorder to which many people seem susceptible.

OTHER DSM-III-R CLASSIFICATIONS

As mentioned earlier in this chapter, there are over 230 clinical syndromes covered in DSM-III-R. In a book such as this, it is impossible to present each of these in detail. There are, however, some important disorders that students in general psychology courses should be familiar with. A brief review of other selected psychological disorders follows.

Delusional Disorder

The chief characteristic of the delusional disorder (formerly called paranoid disorder) is a persistent delusion not due to any other mental disorder (schizophrenia or a mood disorder), or to an organic factor. Other than the effects of the delusion on the individual's behavior, such as having great difficulties in interpersonal relationships, he or she is able to function fairly well. Research indicates that the delusional disorder is relatively rare and distinctly different from schizophrenia (Brennan & Hemsley, 1984).

DSM-III-R identifies five types of delusions that are common to individuals with this disorder. They include erotomanic, grandiose, jealous, persecutory, and somatic. The *erotomanic delusion* involves the belief that one is loved by another. In a *grandiose delusion*, the person believes that he or she is extremely important. The *jealous delusion* involves believing that one's spouse or lover is unfaithful. In the *persecutory delusion*, the person believes that others are out to get him or her, and will try to poison, harass, hurt, frustrate, or kill him or her. The *somatic delusion* involves the belief that insects are inside the person, or certain parts of the body are not functioning properly.

Organic Mental Disorders

The organic mental disorders involve a disruption of psychological functioning due to a dysfunction of the brain. *Primary degenerative dementia of the Alzheimer type* refers to the progressive and deteriorating disorder in which cognitive abilities such as memory, thinking, and personality functioning are severely disrupted. In the early stages, the individual experiences memory impairment and social withdrawal. Eventually, personality changes occur and the individual's cognitive functions deteriorate to the point that he or she is incapable of caring for himself or herself. This disorder is much more common in people older than 65 years (senile onset), but does occur in younger individuals (presenile onset). Approximately 3 percent of the population over 65 in the United States have primary degenerative dementia of the Alzheimer type.

Organic mental disorders can also be caused by disease or by an accident. For example, brain tumors, exposure to lead, mercury, or other toxic chemicals, certain nervous diseases, or advanced syphilis all can produce psychotic symptoms. The severity of the psychosis, however, is a function not just of the physical damage, but also of the person's individual personality traits and previous psychological disposition.

People also develop psychotic symptoms because they have taken certain drugs. Such *psychoactive substance-induced organic mental disorders* are a growing problem among the users of drugs such as LSD and "crack" cocaine, which interfere with the normal functioning of the nervous system (see chapter 5, "Sleep and Consciousness," for a review of psychoactive drugs). DSM-III-R identifies 11 classes of substances that can lead to organic mental disorders. They include alcohol, amphetamines, caffeine, cannabis, cocaine, hallucinogens, inhalants, nicotine, opioids, phencyclidine, and sedatives.

Somatoform and Dissociative Disorders

The somatoform and dissociative disorders are ways that individuals deal with extreme stress and anxiety. The somatoform disorders focus on physical symptoms and pain whereas the dissociative disorders focus on personality problems and memory loss.

Somatoform Disorders   Somatoform disorders are generally characterized by physical symptoms for which there are no obvious physical causes. About 2 percent of the population of the United States experience somatoform disorders at some point in their lives. DSM-III-R identifies five major types of somatoform disorders: body dysmorphic disorder, conversion disorder, hypochondriasis, somatization disorder, and somatoform pain disorder.

The chief symptom of body dysmorphic disorder is a preoccupation with an imaginary defect in the physical appearance of a physically healthy person. Common complaints include excessive facial hair, skin spots, shape of various facial features, or, rarely, of other body parts (hands, feet, breasts). The disorder often begins during adolescence or early adulthood, and often lasts for several years. Although social interactions are impaired, the individual is not usually incapacitated by this disorder.

In conversion disorder the person displays an obvious disturbance in physical functioning that suggests a physical disorder, though medical examination reveals no physical basis for the problem. The symptoms can be those of paralysis, loss of sensation, blindness, or insensitivity to pain. People with these symptoms are often surprisingly undisturbed by them and show resistance to having them cured. They are not pretending and the symptoms are not imaginary; but these people are under the control of psychological processes of which they may be unaware. The relatively rare conversion disorder usually occurs during adolescence or early adulthood, and typically does not last long.

In hypochondriasis the person is preoccupied with the fear of having a serious or deadly disease. Medical examinations do not reveal any physical problem that could account for the complaints. The person may be preoccupied with normal bodily processes such as heart rate or breathing, or may focus on insignificant sores or an occasional cough. Often the person believes he or she has a fatal disease such as cancer or AIDS. Hypochondriasis occurs most often during young adulthood, and is equally common in men and women.

Somatization disorder occurs when a person (most often a woman) has numerous medical complaints for which no physical cause is evident. She might have headaches, backaches, allergies, painful or irregular menstrual periods, gastrointestinal cramps, vomiting, diarrhea, or dizziness. Year after year, the patient develops new symptoms that must be treated. Somatization disorder is closely related to hypochondriasis, the distinction being mainly that in hypochondriasis the person is more concerned with fear of disease than in the symptoms of the disease itself, and the age of onset for somatization disorder is often adolescence rather than young adulthood.

The chief symptom of somatoform pain disorder

(formerly called psychogenic pain disorder) is the preoccupation with severe pain for which there is no known organic cause. In some cases, there is a relationship between a stressful event and the occurrence of the pain, but in other cases, there is no evidence of any environmental stress. Although the somatoform pain disorder can occur at any time, it most often occurs in early adulthood, and occurs twice as often in women. In many cases, the person becomes incapacitated and can no longer work or function normally.

The somatoform disorders appear to help a person avoid anxiety because the pain and other symptoms excuse him or her for failing to carry out responsibilities. Note that these are different from the psychological factors affecting a physical condition discussed in chapter 12, "Adjustment and Health." Those problems are real medical problems (such as ulcers, migraine headaches, high blood pressure) caused or aggravated by psychological stress.

Dissociative Disorders   The dissociative disorders involve a disturbance in memory, consciousness, or personality identity of an individual. Typically they are ways of escaping excessive anxiety through memory or identity loss. The DSM-III-R identifies four types of dissociative disorders. If the problem is primarily an identity loss, the individual must develop a new identity (multiple personality disorder) or alter his or her relationship to reality (depersonalization disorder). If it is primarily a memory loss, the individual cannot remember important personal events (psychogenic amnesia or psychogenic fugue).

Multiple personality is an extremely rare disorder in which several personalities are present in the same individual. One way to escape from overwhelming anxiety is to segment the personality into two or more alternatives that can more successfully deal with the situation. For example, one personality might be aggressive while another might be shy, and the two may or may not be aware of the existence of each other. Treatment of a woman called Sybil showed that she had 16 personalities. A recent celebrated case is that of William Milligan, an accused rapist of coeds at the Ohio State University campus in the late 1970s who exhibited at least 24 different personalities (Keyes, 1981).

Depersonalization disorder occurs when a person escapes from his or her own personality by believing he or she does not exist or that the environment is not real. The perception of the self is modified so that the individual can become detached from it. The person with depersonalization disorder often feels as if he or she is in a dream. The disorder often begins in adolescence or early adulthood, and may last for some time throughout the person's life.

Individuals with psychogenic amnesia lose their sense of identity, literally forgetting who they are, where they live, or what they do. It is a kind of selective amnesia, for they never forget their language or how to perform the tasks of daily life. It occurs most often in adolescents and young adults. Its onset is abrupt, and the disorder is usually temporary, with termination also abrupt and recovery complete.

Occasionally, the dissociated individual develops psychogenic fugue, and in addition to losing his or her memory, leaves the scene of his or her present life, going to a new geographic location and beginning life over as someone else, forgetting all of the unpleasant emotions connected with the old life. Often the fugue is less severe than this, and consists of a brief travel period, after which the individual recovers and returns home. This rare disorder occurs most often during a natural disaster or a war.

The dissociative disorders appear to be ways to deal with excessive anxiety or stress. *Disassociating* oneself from personal commitments is probably a means of escape from overwhelming anxiety. Often a traumatic event has occurred prior to the development of the disorder. The person loses his or her memory or identity, and hence he or she is no longer responsible for obligations.

Personality Disorders

Personality disorders are problems in the basic personality structure of the individual. Personality disorders are often seen in other disorders, and are long-term impairments in social and personal functioning. When the characteristics are maladaptive and cause distress or impairment in adjustment they are called personality disorders. Personality disorders often begin in adolescence and continue throughout a lifetime. Some researchers have argued that the diagnoses of personality disorders overlap significantly and thus the number of classifications should be reduced (Morey, 1988).

DSM-III-R groups the personality disorders into three clusters. For each cluster, we give a brief description of selected disorders. Cluster A includes paranoid, schizoid, and schizotypal personality disorders. The chief observation of individuals with these disorders is that they appear odd or strange in their daily functioning. Individuals with *paranoid personality disorder* have extreme suspiciousness and mistrust of others, even when there is no reason for suspicion. The chief symptom of individuals with *schizoid personality* is a total lack of interest in developing a social relationship. Those with *schizotypal personality disorder* tend to show odd behaviors, express bizarre thoughts, have unusual perceptual experiences, and express inappropriate emotions.

Cluster B includes borderline, histrionic, narcissistic, and antisocial personality disorders. People with these disorders are emotional and dramatic, and can be antisocial. Individuals with *borderline personality disorder* have persistent problems with self-image, mood, and social relationships, and tend to be impulsive and unpredictable. The *narcissistic personality disorder* is characterized by grandiose behavior, feelings of exaggerated importance, and lack of social skills.

One of the more serious adult personality disorders is the antisocial personality disorder, also known as *sociopathic personality* or *psychopathic personality*. DSM-III-R identifies the chief feature of this disorder as a pattern of irresponsible and antisocial behavior that begins in childhood or adolescence and continues into adulthood. In the United States, it is much more common in males (4.5 percent) than in females (less than 1 percent) according to a study by Robins and colleagues (1984). As a child, the individual with this personality disorder may lie, steal, fight, or run away from home. In adulthood, the irresponsibility and antisocial pattern continues, with the individual failing to honor obligations or conform to social norms, and impulsively exhibiting antisocial behaviors such as destroying property and harassing other people. He typically does not experience guilt over his activities and feels no shame. Often he repeats his antisocial behaviors and appears to be unable to learn not to do them. Some individuals with this disorder may become criminals, but many just have very serious problems adjusting in society.

Cluster C includes avoidant, dependent, obsessive compulsive, and passive aggressive personality disorders. These individuals are seen as anxious and fearful. Individuals with *avoidant personality disorder* are timid and fearful of negative evaluation from others. People who have *obsessive compulsive disorder* are characterized by perfectionism and inflexibility in everything they do.

Sexual Disorders

The last major group of disorders concerns sexual adjustment. Some are quite serious disorders, while others are more common problems of adjustment. DSM-III-R divides the sexual disorders into two groups: the sexual dysfunctions and the paraphilias. As we discussed in chapter 10, "Emotion," the more common sexual dysfunctions involve an inhibition of sexual desire or problems in the sexual response cycle. Here we discuss the paraphilias, which are sexual deviations characterized by the need for unusual behaviors for sexual arousal. This need interferes with normal sexual motives and activities. Paraphilia means deviant (para) attraction (philia).

The paraphilias are experienced almost exclusively by men. People who have a paraphilia tend to have repetitive sexual urges and fantasies that involve objects, humiliation, children, or nonconsenting people. DSM-III-R identifies eight specific paraphilias.

Exhibitionism is when one exposes the genitals to strangers in order to achieve sexual gratification. *Fetishism* is when a person becomes sexually excited primarily by objects (fetishes). *Frotteurism* involves the obtaining of sexual arousal from touching and rubbing against a nonconsenting person, often in a crowd in a public place. *Pedophilia* refers to sexual activities with young children. *Sexual sadism* involves inflicting suffering or humiliation on one's partner to achieve sexual arousal, and *sexual masochism* is when one achieves sexual arousal by receiving pain from one's partner. *Transvestic fetishism* involves obtaining sexual gratification from cross-dressing (usually a heterosexual man wearing women's clothing when alone). In *voyeurism* a person derives sexual satisfaction from looking at people who are either naked or engaging in sexual activities, without their knowledge or consent.

There are many explanations for the paraphilias, but some psychologists believe that learning is extremely important in these disorders. The behavioral model suggests that somehow the person learns to be reinforced by the inappropriate stimulus. As we discuss in the next chapter, treatment often includes relearning the appropriate behavior. ■

One of the potential dangers in the field of abnormal psychology is labeling a person as abnormal, as shown in the introductory story. Defining abnormal behavior is a very difficult task. The diagnostic categories in DSM have evolved as the identification of psychological disorders has become more sophisticated. There are many individual differences in personality, and what is thought to be abnormal in one society might be adaptive in another society. Psychologists try to understand abnormal behavior so they can treat it, as shown in the next chapter.

CHAPTER REVIEW

What You've Learned About Psychological Disorders

1. Behavior is abnormal when it contributes to maladaptiveness in an individual, is considered deviant by the culture, or leads to personal psychological distress.

2. There are a number of viewpoints on abnormal behavior, including the psychoanalytic model, the biological model, the learning model, the cognitive model, the legal model, and the statistical model.

3. The Diagnostic and Statistical Manual of Mental Disorders (DSM-III-R) was revised by the American Psychiatric Association in 1987. This is used as a basis for diagnosing and classifying psychological disorders.

4. The panic disorder is identified by the occurrence of panic attacks, specific periods of intense anxiety. Agoraphobia occurs when the individual is afraid of places or situations from which it would be difficult or embarrassing to escape. The individual with agoraphobia is especially afraid to be outside the home, in a crowd, or traveling.

5. Phobias are acute excessive fears of specific situations or objects when such fears have no convincing basis in reality. Social phobias are excessive fears and embarrassment when interacting with other people. Simple phobias are excessive, irrational fears of specific objects, such as dogs, snakes, or enclosed places.

6. In the obsessive compulsive disorder, the anxious person may have repetitive thoughts (obsessions) or have constant urges to indulge in meaningless rituals (compulsions). Any attempt to stop the behaviors results in increased anxiety.

7. An individual with a generalized anxiety disorder lives in a state of constant tension and feels inadequate and helpless most of the time. Symptoms include trembling, restlessness, fatigue, rapid heart rate, sweating, nausea, and dizziness.

8. Mood disorders involve disruption of the normal emotional responses of the individual. Major depression occurs when a person becomes unable to cope with daily activities. Depressed people are sad, have little interest in anything, have feelings of guilt, worthlessness, and inadequacy, and might have thoughts of suicide. Psychoanalytic theory suggests that feelings of anger and hostility are turned inward. Learning theory proposes that depression is the result of either learning to be helpless or a reduction in reinforcement from others. One physiological theory states that depression is the result of low levels of the neurotransmitter norepinephrine.

9. The bipolar disorder, or manic-depression, is characterized by unpredictable and extreme mood swings. In the manic state, the individual is hyperexcited, talkative, uninhibited, and perhaps destructive. Then, without warning, the patient becomes extremely depressed.

10. Individuals with schizophrenia show severe disturbances in the areas of thinking, perception, emotion, sense of self, volition, relationship to the world, and behavior. Often thinking is unorganized and incoherent. Many schizophrenics show delusions, or beliefs not founded on reality. They also have hallucinations, or sensory experiences with no sensory stimuli present. Many schizophrenics show inappropriate emotional responses.

11. An individual with catatonic schizophrenia is sometimes immobile and does not speak, but at other times is aggressive. Disorganized schizophrenia is characterized by inappropriate silliness and bizarre behavior. In paranoid schizophrenia, the person often has persecutory or grandiose delusions. Undifferentiated schizophrenia is characterized by a gradual loss of interest in the world. Residual schizophrenia is the label given to a person who is currently without major psychotic symptoms, but who has had at least one prior episode.

12. Research suggests that the family life of a schizophrenic is extremely stressful. Learning theorists suggest that abnormal behavior increases because it is reinforced by others. Psychoanalytic theorists believe schizophrenics become narcissistic and totally controlled by the id. A genetic component is likely to be involved in schizophrenia. A biochemical theory proposes that schizophrenia results from excessively high levels of the neurotransmitter dopamine.

13. The chief characteristic of the delusional disorder is a persistent delusion not due to any other mental disorder or to an organic factor. Common delusions include the erotomanic, grandiose, jealous, persecutory, and somatic.

14. Organic mental disorders involve problems in which there is a disruption of psychological functioning due to a dysfunction of the brain, whether caused by disease or accident.

15. Somatoform disorders are characterized by physical symptoms for which there are no obvious physical causes. They include body dysmorphic disorder, conversion disorder, hypochondriasis, somatization disorder, and somatoform pain disorder. Dissociative disorders involve a disturbance in memory, consciousness, or identity of an individual. They include multiple personality disorder, depersonalization disorder, psychogenic amnesia, and psychogenic fugue.

16. Personality disorders are problems in the basic personality structure of the individual. One of the most serious is the antisocial personality disorder. Sexual disorders include problems that people experience in their sexual adjustment. The paraphilias are sexual deviations such as exhibitionism, fetishism, frotteurism, pedophilia, sadism, masochism, transvestism, and voyeurism.

CHAPTER OBJECTIVES

What You'll Learn About Therapy

After studying this chapter, you should be able to:

1. Define therapy and identify its two major forms for psychological disorders.
2. Outline the history of the treatment of abnormal behavior.
3. Describe psychoanalysis.
4. Describe person-centered therapy.
5. Describe Gestalt therapy.
6. Describe reinforcement therapy.
7. Describe counterconditioning therapy.
8. Describe cognitive behavior therapy.
9. Describe encounter group therapy.
10. Describe family therapy.
11. Outline and evaluate the effectiveness of psychotherapy.
12. Describe drug therapy.
13. Describe psychosurgery.
14. Describe electroconvulsive therapy.

Behavior therapy, the application of reinforcement and punishment to modify behavior, became popular in the 1960s. One of the best-known early studies in the type of behavior therapy known as token economy was conducted at Anna State Hospital in Anna, Illinois, by Teodoro Ayllon and Nathon Azrin. Ayllon and Azrin described their study in their 1968 book *The Token Economy*.

The two psychologists worked in a ward in a mental hospital in which 44 female patients resided. The women, most of whom were diagnosed as psychotic (mainly schizophrenic), had been in the ward for an average of 16 years (the range was from 1 to 37 years). At the beginning of the study, many of the women did not cooperate and were difficult to manage. The women did not dress themselves, wash themselves, talk, eat properly, or keep their rooms neat. The hospital staff was frustrated and did not know how to control the patients except through the use of drugs.

Ayllon and Azrin set up a token economy program in which tokens (small plastic pieces) were awarded when subjects performed desired behaviors, such as making their beds, combing their hair, brushing their teeth, and eating properly, and withheld when the desired behaviors were not performed. The token economy was also used to decrease undesired behaviors, such as refusing to cooperate, being withdrawn, and acting bizarrely. Tokens are effective because they permit immediate reinforcement of an appropriate behavior, are not likely to cause the subject to become bored, are portable (subjects and experimenter can easily carry them around), and are durable (Ayllon & Azrin, 1968).

324

14

Therapy

Treating individuals who have psychological problems has long been a major activity of psychologists. Psychoanalysis was the first major systematic attempt to treat psychopathology. Today, psychologists utilize a variety of therapeutic approaches, including insight, behavior, and group therapies. Sometimes drug therapy is incorporated into the treatment program.

The patients collected these tokens and were allowed to cash them in for privileges. For example, for 10 tokens they could go for a walk on the hospital grounds, for 1 token they could listen to a radio or watch a movie, and for 100 tokens they could go for a trip into town. For specified numbers of tokens the patients could also select commissary items such as candy, cigarettes, toothpaste, lipstick, gloves, or newspapers.

In one part of this study the experimenters recorded the total number of hours the group performed the desired tasks. When reinforcement was contingent upon desired behaviors, the total for all of the patients was about 47 hours, which was maintained for 15 days. The next 15 days, no reinforcement was given, and performance fell quickly and drastically to about 10 hours per day, total time. The last 15 days of the study, reinforcement was again given and the performance swiftly returned to 45 hours, where it remained.

The results of this study were clear-cut. When the patients were being reinforced in the token economy system, desirable behaviors rose significantly, while undesirable behaviors greatly decreased. On the other hand, when the reinforcements were neither awarded for desired behaviors nor withheld for undesired behaviors, the undesirable behaviors increased dramatically.

Ayllon and Azrin had demonstrated the effectiveness of behavior therapy in successfully modifying the behavior of even severely disturbed mental patients. An important aspect of the token economy study is not that patients with schizophrenia could change the behaviors they exhibited (although this in itself is also important), but rather that the behavior of subjects could be quickly

FIGURE 14.1 Token Economy
In a token economy, the subject works to earn tokens (or points) that may then be cashed in for something desired. The token is a secondary reinforcer and the desired event is the primary reinforcer. Here, a resident of New Castle State Development Center in Indiana is purchasing items with tokens earned by successfully completing a bed-making program.

brought under the control of a reinforcement schedule. This valuable behavior modification technique has since been used with a wide variety of people, from retarded and disturbed individuals to very healthy, normal individuals in schools, homes, and at work.

325

WHAT IS THERAPY?

The opening story focuses on the application of behavior therapy in a mental ward. Although some forms of therapy are practiced with individuals who have severe psychological disorders, many of the same techniques are being used to treat the more common problems that affect relatively healthy people. A primary goal of research into the causes and nature of emotional distress is the development of effective methods for aiding people with a variety of problems. Better treatments are emerging from the research of medical experimenters, the clinical experience of psychotherapists, and refinement of psychological theories.

This chapter describes many of the measures being taken to treat individuals with psychological disorders, to enhance their ability to cope more successfully with stressful life situations. These measures make it possible for people with a wide variety of mild and severe psychological problems to gain greater control over their feelings, thoughts, and actions, and thus to decrease the incidence and severity of abnormal behavior. People seek therapy for a variety of reasons, from improved self-understanding to the elimination of incapacitating distress. Others are forced into treatment by relatives or the court.

There are many types of professionals who are involved with people who need help with psychological problems. For instance, clergy are often involved in counseling sessions to help people with marital problems or who are having emotional difficulties. Family physicians may spot a potential problem and refer a patient to a trained professional. There are three major classes of mental health professionals who provide therapy for psychological disorders. *Psychiatrists* are medical doctors who specialize in mental disorders. As an M.D., a psychiatrist can prescribe drugs or other medical treatment for patients. *Clinical psychologists* and *counseling psychologists* have graduate Ph.D. degrees in psychology, have typically worked in a mental hospital, and have had experience in counseling or psychotherapy. *Psychiatric social workers* have graduate training in social work and in counseling people and families.

There are two broad forms of therapy for psychological disorders—psychotherapy and biological (or biomedical) therapy—both of which we cover in this chapter. Psychotherapy is the treatment of behavioral and emotional problems using psychological techniques. Some psychologists reserve the term *psychotherapy* for the long-term intense process of helping severely disturbed individuals, and use the term *counseling* for the short-term process of helping normal individuals cope more effectively (Brammer & colleagues, 1989). In this book we use the term *psychotherapy* for treatment of

both mild and *severe* psychological disorders. Psychotherapy includes a variety of approaches, including insight, behavior, and group therapies. *Insight therapies* are largely based on the assumption that behavior is abnormal because people do not adequately understand the motivation causing their behavior. Thus, insight therapies attempt to help people gain insight into their behaviors, thoughts, and feelings. *Behavior therapies* are more concerned with modifying abnormal behavior than with gaining insight into motivation. They assume that when the behavior changes, the underlying motivation also changes. *Group therapies* attempt to help people with problems by letting them interact in a group setting; through interaction they may gain insight into their motivations as well as change their behavior.

Psychotherapy is a broad category that includes many different approaches. Carson and Butcher (1992) described some of the objectives of psychotherapy. According to them, it is used to reduce or eliminate maladaptive or abnormal behaviors, to increase self-understanding, or to improve interpersonal competency. Psychotherapy can help a person solve an immediate crisis as well as relieve personal distress over a longer period of time, help modify the environmental conditions contributing to the person's distress, and help the person modify misperceptions and inappropriate cognitions about the world. Although a particular psychotherapy focuses on specific objectives, many of these objectives overlap. It is important to point out that this chapter covers only a few of the many forms of psychotherapy available. In a sense, each psychotherapist uses an individualized, *eclectic* approach combining several types of therapy as may be appropriate for the patient.

Biological therapy is the treatment of behavior problems through biological techniques (Carson & Butcher, 1992). Biological therapy (or biomedical therapy) includes drug therapy, psychosurgery, and electroconvulsive therapy. The basic assumption of biological therapy is that a physiological disturbance causes the psychological disorder, and that if the person is treated biologically the behavior will change. Biological therapy is usually used by a psychiatrist, since he or she has the appropriate medical training. The use of a particular therapy often depends upon the therapist, patient, and nature of the problem being treated.

HISTORICAL OVERVIEW OF TREATMENT OF PSYCHOLOGICAL DISORDERS

For centuries, supposedly civilized societies looked upon psychologically disturbed humans as subhumans, to be tortured or locked away and forgotten. As a result, the history of the treatment of psychological disorders

FIGURE 14.2 Early Treatment of Mental Disorders
This drawing illustrates one of the torturous devices used in the treatment of mental disorders in the past.

FIGURE 14.3 Bicêtre Institution, 1793
This painting depicts Philippe Pinel ordering the release of the inmates who had been kept in chains at the Bicêtre mental hospital. Pinel, a French psychiatrist, campaigned for humane treatment of the insane at the end of the eighteenth century.

and insanity makes a grim story. For hundreds of years, because of its bizarreness, insanity was associated with the supernatural, and the disturbed were thought to be possessed by demons or the devil. One "cure" that dates back to the Stone Age involves cutting a hole in the

patient's skull to let out the evil spirits. In Europe during the seventeenth and eighteenth centuries hundreds of thousands of persons were tortured to "bring them to their senses." If that did not work, they were burned or hanged. Not only were the psychologically disturbed and insane miserable to begin with, but, because they frightened other people, often they received treatment that made them worse.

In 1793, during the French Revolution, Philippe Pinel brought about a startling new reform at the Bicêtre Asylum in Paris. He released the patients from their iron chains and called for "wiser and more moderate restraints." He reported that a number of previously violent patients, once freed of chains, became relaxed and talked quite agreeably with those in charge. Although he was not the first to do so, Pinel attempted to classify the different types of psychological disturbances and to suggest that different forms of insanity required different types of treatment. He showed the importance of keeping case histories and approaching each patient as worthy of individual treatment.

A major breakthrough for the mentally ill in the United States came in 1909 when Clifford W. Beers founded the National Committee for Mental Hygiene. Its purpose was to improve conditions in mental hospitals, encourage psychiatric research, enlarge the facilities for the care of the mentally ill, and make the public more aware of mental health.

Until recently, some modern treatments for psychological disorders included practices as brutal as many of those seen in asylums before Pinel. Psychosurgery, involving permanent destruction of portions of the brain, left thousands of patients with altered personalities, forced them to lead lives of limited potential, and deprived them of normal experiences. Great strides are now being made to provide better treatment of the psychologically disturbed. There has been a trend during the last couple of decades to get patients out of institutions and back into society. Here we look at some of the therapies used to treat psychological problems.

INSIGHT THERAPY

Insight therapy is designed to help people better understand who they are and why they have various behavior tendencies. The assumption is that when people understand themselves and the motivation behind their behavior, they will have greater control over their lives. We review several types of insight therapy, including psychoanalysis, person-centered therapy, and Gestalt therapy. We will start with one of the first insight therapies, Sigmund Freud's psychoanalysis.

Psychoanalysis

Therapists who have had psychoanalytic training and have personally undergone psychoanalysis are qualified to become psychoanalysts. Psychoanalysis is an intensive and prolonged exploration of a person's unconscious motivation. In psychoanalytic treatment, the patient is assumed to have repressed conflicts from childhood that are still unresolved and causing anxiety and psychological problems. The goal of psychoanalysis is to bring the repressed conflicts to consciousness, so that the patient can deal with them as an adult. Although few professionals use psychoanalysis in exactly the way Freud did, his method is important because many of the techniques he developed are employed in adaptations of the classical psychoanalytic approach. Psychoanalytic techniques include free association, dream analysis, and transference (Freud, 1949).

Free Association　In the classic psychoanalytic situation, the patient relaxes on a couch facing away from the analyst and is encouraged to use free association, a technique in which the patient is required to say everything that crosses his or her mind, without letting normal inhibitions stop him or her from saying anything obscene, hostile, foolish, or illogical. The psychoanalyst expresses no disapproval or emotional reaction to what the patient

FIGURE 14.4　Psychoanalysis
A therapeutic technique developed by Freud, psychoanalysis involves an intensive exploration of a patient's unconscious motivation. Here a patient expresses herself through free association.

talks about. As the therapist discerns patterns in the patient's associations, anxieties, slips of the tongue, and reports of dreams, the patient is encouraged to explore the areas of past life that seem to be significant. The assumption is that, with conscious control of thought reduced to a minimum, the patient may reveal unconscious motives and associations.

Usually, the patient will show resistance, unconsciously avoiding certain painful areas of discussion. The patient might suddenly change the topic or totally forget what was just said. If the therapist continues to prod, the patient interrupts the session by remaining silent, making jokes, or even becoming ill. In classical Freudian therapy, such resistance is usually thought to be connected with real or imagined sexual experiences in childhood. Hence psychoanalysis focuses on these past causes of current problems.

Dream Analysis　As we discussed in chapter 5, "Sleep and Consciousness," Freud (1900) believed that dream analysis can help the therapist break into the patient's unconscious mind, where true feelings can be expressed. Freud distinguished between the manifest dream content (what is remembered) and the latent dream content (the actual dream thoughts that occurred in the unconscious mind). The manifest dream content is a disguised representation of our unconscious wishes, and thus the therapist must focus on using free association to gain insight into the latent content of the dream. Freud believed that "dreams are the royal road to the unconscious mind," and provide a way for the therapist to understand the true nature of the patient's problems better. Often, patients are encouraged to use free association while recalling dreams in order to provide clues that the therapist can interpret.

Transference　Transference is an important means of bringing out the patient's emotional conflicts. The analyst, remaining in the background and saying very little, becomes a blank figure on which the patient *projects* the attributes of significant figures in his or her emotional life—the hated or loved mother, father, sister, or brother. Bringing these emotional reactions to light makes them recognizable for what they are and easier to deal with. Thus, the patient *transfers* feelings onto the therapist.

In the course of analysis, the analyst begins to get a picture of the unconscious problems that are the source of the patient's difficulties. The analyst can suggest this picture to the patient, who then gains some insight into the problem. According to psychoanalytic theory, the patient must become aware of unconscious motives and conflicts, as well as understand how they are operating, before the maladaptive behavior patterns can be changed.

The classic form of psychoanalysis requires three to five visits per week over a period of 5 years or more, and can cost thousands of dollars. Since it requires an ability to verbalize feelings in a sophisticated way, and also an ability to respond rationally, its use is restricted to people without significant mental disabilities or severe psychotic disorders.

The classic form of psychoanalysis is rarely used today, partly because of the time and cost factors. Neo-Freudians, or psychoanalysts who came after Freud, often stressed current behavior rather than historical conflict, and the ego as well as the id. However, psycho-analysis forms the basis for a variety of other therapies, many without specific names. Rather than free associa-tion, many analysts use a more direct probing technique. Psychoanalysis is important because it provided a frame-work within which other forms of psychotherapy could be developed. One major therapy that is very different from psychoanalysis is person-centered therapy.

Person-Centered Therapy

Person-centered therapy (formerly called *client-centered therapy*) was founded by the humanistic person-ality theorist Carl Rogers. Its main assumptions are that every individual has an innate capacity to be healthy psychologically and to become self-actualized. Psycho-logical maladjustment, according to this view, occurs when individuals deny important aspects of themselves, such as certain feelings and experiences, because they regard them as "unacceptable." To get back into contact with themselves, instead of clinging to the images im-posed upon them by others, they need an environment of acceptance that encourages free and open exploration of their personality. This will lead ultimately to self-understanding and mental health.

The function of the therapist is to provide a totally nonthreatening atmosphere of warmth and acceptance for the individual. To emphasize the active role he or she plays in the process, the person receiving therapy is called a client rather than a patient. In this *nondirective* approach the therapist does not instruct the client to change his or her life, nor give advice or offer interpreta-tions of what the client says. Rather, the therapist directs all efforts toward understanding the client totally and clarifying the feelings and reactions he or she is expres-sing. Rogers thought that the therapist should be sincere, sharing feelings with the client, while remaining a warm and sympathetic listener.

In his 1980 book, *A Way of Being*, Rogers described three core qualities—genuineness, unconditional positive regard, and empathy—that the therapist in person-cen-tered therapy should have. *Genuineness* means being authentic, open, and honest. The therapist can help the client by being genuine in the relationship and by disclos-

FIGURE 14.5   Person-Centered Therapy
Carl Rogers believed everyone has the capacity for devel-oping psychological health. The function of person-centered or nondirective therapy is to provide a warm and accepting environment that encourages an open exploration of per-sonality. Carl Rogers is pictured at the right leading a therapy session.

ing real thoughts and feelings when necessary. The therapist must view the client with *unconditional positive regard*, or total acceptance. The client must be treated always as a unique, important, and good human being. It is important to create an environment in which change can occur. The therapist must always have a positive, accepting attitude toward the client. The therapist must also show *empathy* for the client and try to understand the client's feelings and perceptions. In showing empathy, the therapist reflects the feelings and ideas of the client, so the client can see himself or herself more clearly. Active listening (devoting full attention to what is being said) on the part of the therapist is essential in gaining empathetic understanding of the other person. Thus, the therapist does not interpret or evaluate what the client says, but rather lets the client form his or her own conclusions as the therapy progresses.

In the person-centered therapy situation, the client begins to feel free to explore his or her personality and problems and to uncover experiences and feelings he or she had formerly suppressed. In the end, the client is expected to gain greater self-understanding and self-acceptance, which the person-centered therapist believes to be one and the same thing. The therapist believes also that the client's increased self-knowledge will facilitate discovery of more effective and rewarding ways of living and interacting with others.

BIOGRAPHICAL HIGHLIGHT

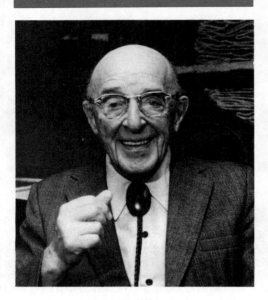

CARL R. ROGERS

Carl R. Rogers, the son of prosperous Illinois business people, was born in Oak Park, Illinois, in 1902. He was reared in a strict religious environment that placed great emphasis on the value of hard work and the sharing of responsibility. Rogers enrolled in the University of Wisconsin with the intention of studying agriculture. However, he soon decided to prepare for the ministry.

Leaving Wisconsin in 1924, he entered the Union Theological Seminary in New York. He became deeply involved in clinical work with disturbed children and his interests shifted to clinical psychology. He received his doctorate from Columbia University in 1931 and went to work at a guidance clinic in Rochester, New York. He taught at Ohio State University, the University of Chicago, and the University of Wisconsin, before settling at the Center for Studies of the Person in La Jolla, California.

Throughout his career, Rogers continued to work extensively with delinquent and underprivileged children, gathering the experience that led to his theory of nondirective, or person-centered therapy. He wrote many influential books, including *Client-Centered Therapy* (1951), *On Becoming a Person* (1961), and *A Way of Being* (1980). He was a leader of the humanistic psychology movement until his death in 1987.

Rogers believed that the person-centered approach applied to a wide variety of relationships, including therapist-client, parent-child, leader-group, teacher-student, or administrator-staff. Whenever the goal is to help the person develop, then the person-centered approach is appropriate. Some concerns, however, have been raised about Rogerian therapy. Evaluation focuses on the reports of the clients rather than on actual behavior changes, thus making it difficult to measure the effectiveness of the therapy. Also, since the client must actively participate in the therapeutic process, the person-centered therapy is appropriate only for mild problems.

Gestalt Therapy

Another humanistic therapy was described by Frederick ("Fritz") S. Perls in his 1969 book, *Gestalt Therapy Verbatim*. Perls had been trained as a psychoanalyst, but because he couldn't support many of Freud's ideas, he broke away and developed Gestalt therapy. Gestalt therapy is designed to help people become more aware of themselves and of their responsibility for their own behavior; it focuses on the whole individual and the person's perceptions of self and the surrounding world. Like

Rogers, Perls had an optimistic view of human nature and believed that people develop problems when their innate goodness is frustrated.

The therapist observes nonverbal cues, such as voice, hand gestures, and eye movements; and then helps people become aware of their own feelings expressed through the nonverbal cues. The clients are encouraged to talk in the present tense and first person. Much of the therapy session is devoted to acting out emotions. It may involve other people who are present, or imagined interactions with others. A goal of Gestalt therapy is to make people feel whole by helping them discover their feelings and reclaim the parts of personality that have been denied.

Like the other insight therapies, Gestalt therapy tries to improve the person's understanding of his or her own feelings. The emphasis of Gestalt therapy is on the present. The therapist takes a very active role in directing the person toward self-understanding. The therapist may question, goad, or use any other technique necessary to get the person to achieve self-awareness and take responsibility for his or her own life. Also, again like other insight therapies, Gestalt seems to suit people with minor problems who have good verbal skills and fairly high intelligence; behavior therapy, the next type of therapy discussed, is not restricted in these ways.

BEHAVIOR THERAPY

In behavior therapy, the "symptoms" are treated as constituting the disorder itself. This is much different from psychoanalysis, which treats emotional disturbances as symptoms of a disease whose roots extend far back into childhood. In behavior therapy, a disturbance in personality is considered a learned form of thinking, feeling, and behaving that can be modified through relearning. The aim of the relearning in behavior therapy is readaptation to present circumstances. Behavior therapy emphasizes learning new behavior to replace the old unwanted habits. It treats overt behavior by giving or withholding reinforcements, or by administering punishments (Thorpe & Olson, 1990). The therapeutic procedure is therefore more like training, using the principles of both classical and operant conditioning, than the gradual development of insight.

There are a great many types of behavior therapy that can be used singly or in combination, but most share a core of common characteristics (O'Leary & Wilson, 1987). Behavior therapists assume abnormal behavior is learned and can be modified through learning principles. The focus of therapy is to modify the current behavior in a wide range of settings rather than to try to determine its historical antecedents.

Reinforcement Therapy

Behavior therapy assumes that to correct maladjusted behavior the subject must relearn appropriate behavior. As you will recall from our discussion of operant conditioning, *reinforcement* is very important in learning and maintaining new behaviors. Reinforcement therapy simply applies the operant conditioning principles of reinforcement to increase the frequency of desired behavior (and decrease the frequency of undesired behaviors). Skinner's 1953 book *Science and Human Behavior* was influential in helping behavior therapy, or behavior modification, gain support among therapists. O'Leary (1984) reported that a survey of the 1983 issues of the *Archives of General Psychiatry* and *The Journal of Consulting and Clinical Psychology* showed that of the nondrug treatment studies, the majority involved a form of behavior therapy.

Shaping   A form of behavior modification that has been used successfully in therapy with individuals who are emotionally disturbed or mentally retarded is *shaping* (see chapter 6, "Learning"). Psychologist O. Ivar Lovaas (1977) used this conditioning technique to teach autistic children to speak. He did so by teaching them a series of new responses, each of which more closely approximated the ultimate desired response.

Lovaas gave each child a spoonful of food for every sound made. He also rewarded the child for looking at the teacher's mouth. When the child vocalized every 5 seconds or more often and spent at least half the time looking at the teacher's mouth, the next step began. For example, Lovaas said the word, "baby," every 10 seconds. If the child made any vocal response within 6 seconds of the adult's word, reinforcement was given. When the teacher's voice began to evoke a vocal response from the student fairly frequently, a further requirement for reinforcement was added: the pupil's reply actually had to match the teacher's.

Lovaas carefully chose the behavior to be reinforced. It had to be a syllable that the teacher was able to produce visibly. For example, the teacher said "ba" and

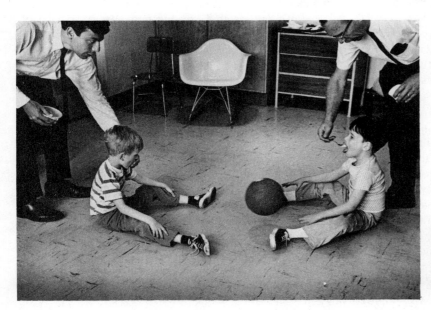

FIGURE 14.6 Reinforcement Therapy In this form of behavior therapy, a reward is used to increase the frequency of the desired behavior. Here, autistic children are immediately reinforced with food when they interact with each other.

held the child's lips closed with his finger, releasing them abruptly when the child exhaled; then the child was reinforced. On successive trials, the teacher moved his fingers away from the child's mouth, then to the cheek, finally touching the jaw.

In the next step, the teacher introduced a second sound, quite different from the first, and interspersed the two sounds randomly. Other sounds were added, and in this way, the child built up a large stock of imitative syllables and words. A noticeable increase in the words learned by the end of this period indicated that the child had learned not just certain vocal responses but the principle of imitation as well.

Other studies have shown that shaping is useful in solving a wide range of childhood problems, including thumb sucking, hyperactivity, poor school performance, and even shyness. Franks (1984) reported that the rate of improvement using behavior modification techniques was better than that obtained with other types of therapy. Parents can also use shaping to help children develop positive social skills and manners.

Extinction In *extinction* all reinforcements are withheld when the unwanted response occurs. When all delusional or psychotic remarks made by a mental patient are ignored, there will often be a marked drop in the frequency of these statements. At the same time, more realistically oriented statements can be reinforced. The parents of a baby who cries at bedtime might use extinction to eliminate the unwanted behavior.

Sometimes we inadvertently reinforce undesirable behavior rather than using extinction. For example, a teacher may ignore a student's classwork, but as soon as the student misbehaves, the teacher yells at him or her. If the student has been deprived of attention, he or she may interpret this yelling as attention (reinforcement) and actually increase the misbehavior because it was able to elicit the attention denied previously. What would you do to correct the situation? An effective therapy is to ignore the undesired behavior (unless it is too disruptive) and reinforce the desirable behavior to increase its frequency (Kazdin, 1989).

The Token Economy As discussed in our opening story, a token economy is a form of behavior modification in which desirable behaviors are immediately reinforced with tokens that can be exchanged at a later time for desired rewards such as food, television, or recreational activities (Kazdin, 1989). In some programs, tokens are taken away for undesirable behaviors.

As we saw in the Ayllon and Azrin study of a mental hospital ward, people's behavior quickly came under the control of the token reinforcements. When they briefly removed the tokens, the patients' undesirable behaviors again increased. As with other forms of behavior therapy,

the token economy can be used with severely disturbed individuals who do not have normal verbal capacities. Ayllon and Azrin (1968) found that a token economy could be administered easily by regular staff personnel. In recent years, token economies have not been used as frequently in mental institutions, partially because of the reduction in hospital staff as well as the trend toward hospitalization only for more severe psychological disorders (Carson & Butcher, 1992).

Token economies have also been used with the mentally retarded and with nondisabled people who want to change their behavior patterns in order to lose weight, manage their time better, stop biting their fingernails, or solve a host of other problems. In fact, your instructor may be using a form of token economy in your psychology class. How many tokens (points) do you need for an *A*?

Reinforcement therapy can be utilized by an individual wishing to modify unwanted habits, as shown in the following Application.

APPLICATION

Self-Directed Behavior Modification

It is possible to employ some of the principles of classical and operant conditioning in a program of self-directed behavior modification. You begin by choosing one problem to modify. Then you spend a week or so keeping a diary or journal of your normal behavior. The contents of this diary constitute the baseline data you will use to determine what aspects of your behavior need modifying and what actions and feelings that contribute to the problem may be susceptible to behavior modification.

Let's assume that you want to alter your habit of overeating or cut down on your smoking. In collecting your baseline data, you must include every instance of engaging in the target behavior, with entries indicating all the factors at work while you ate or smoked. You'll want to know how much you ate or smoked, whether you did so alone or with others, where you were, how you felt before, during, and after, and any other factors that might be related to your behavior.

Checking your completed baseline data, you may discover that certain people, situations, or feelings seem to be cues or stimuli for your target behavior. By using the behavior modification technique of stimulus control, you can begin to master the forces compelling you to engage in the habit. If, for instance, you find that you eat too much when you are out with others, control that stimulus by removing it—eat alone. Similarly, if you seem to smoke most while watching television or reading, confine your smoking to other occasions.

You can support your stimulus control efforts with a program of rewards or reinforcements for meeting certain behavioral goals. If you are in fact able to, say, restrict your eating only to mealtimes and only to the dining room, give yourself some predetermined reward, like the purchase of a book or an article of clothing. You can even set up your own token economy by awarding yourself points that add up to rewards you can collect later. You can keep track of the points by carrying toothpicks or similarly portable counters in one pocket or part of a purse and transferring them to another spot as you meet some behavioral goal you've established as worth a certain number of points.

You can also alter your actions behaviorally by changing the sequence of events, doing things in a novel order and thus disrupting the stimulus-response pattern that may be sustaining your target behavior. And you can employ incompatible behavior, whereby you do something else, rather than your target behavior. For example, if you always seem to bite your fingernails, in certain places at certain times, your can weaken the habit by becoming aware of the situations that reinforce it and arranging to have something in your hands on those occasions (thus acting incompatibly with the habit).

The success you achieve with self-directed behavior modification depends largely on your willingness to go slowly and stay with the program. You have to keep complete baseline records, consistently use the chosen technique—failure to do so every time, and as soon as your target behavior is manifested, can make your problem worse than before—and try to concentrate on one problem at a time. Make sure that you understand the basic principles of behavior modification before you begin your program, and always keep your goals obtainable, and you should have success in modifying your behavior.

Counterconditioning

The techniques of classical conditioning may be involved in behavior therapies. In counterconditioning, an unwanted response is replaced by conditioning a new response that is incompatible with the original one. An early study by Mary Cover Jones (1924) demonstrated counterconditioning. Jones was able to treat Peter, a young boy who was afraid of rabbits, by feeding him in the presence of a rabbit. Over a series of trials, the rabbit was brought closer and closer until Peter could pet the animal without fear. Put simply, the rabbit was presented prior to the food, and through classical conditioning, became associated with the food. A number of counterconditioning therapies have been developed.

Systematic Desensitization An important application of counterconditioning is systematic desensitization, a technique that in supervised therapy programs is very valuable in treating fears, phobias, shyness, and related problems. In systematic desensitization, individuals overcome anxieties by learning to relax in the presence of stimuli that had once made them unbearably nervous and afraid. First, patients are taught how to relax their muscles completely. Then, very gradually, anxiety-producing stimuli are introduced. As the patients learn to relax in the presence of these stimuli, stronger anxiety-arousing stimuli are added, until the patients are no longer made anxious by the original objects that caused them to seek help.

Systematic desensitization, a procedure developed by behaviorist Joseph Wolpe (1958) is based on the principle of reciprocal inhibition. This concept states that it is possible to break the bond between anxiety-provoking stimuli and responses manifesting anxiety by facing those stimuli in a calm, relaxed state. All this means is that there are actions or emotions that counter anxiety, and with them we can combat our tendency to feel anxious when encountering anxiety-provoking objects or situations. For example, eating seems to inhibit anxiety, which may be the reason so many people seem to choose

FIGURE 14.7 Progressive Relaxation

BODY AREA	RELAXATION TECHNIQUE
Feet	Point your feet straight out and curl your toes tightly. Then release and relax.
Lower Legs	Point your feet toward your face as high as they will go. Relax.
Upper Legs	Keeping your legs straight, lift your feet off the floor 10 inches. Relax.
Stomach	Take a deep breath and tighten the stomach muscles as you hold your breath. Relax.
Chest	Push your shoulders back and hold as you slowly exhale. Relax.
Upper Arms	Tighten the muscles in both of the upper arms. Relax.
Lower Arms	Tighten muscles as you move your hand toward your arm. Relax.
Hands	Make a tight fist and hold. Relax.
Neck	Smile and tighten throat muscles. Relax.
Forehead	Push your eyebrows up and tighten muscles. Relax.

In this program of self-relaxation, you tense and relax each area of the body in turn.

eating—and overeating—as a way of dealing with anxiety. They usually do so unconsciously and unsystematically, and therefore they often just gain weight and still continue to experience anxiety. Desensitization is a more carefully planned approach.

A basic component of desensitization is the ability to relax. We can actually teach ourselves how to relax. So many of our problems involve stress, tension, and anxiety that acquiring the ability to relax quickly and easily and in a variety of situations is an important first step toward gaining significant control over our feelings.

Progressive relaxation is a simple form of self-relaxation. This technique was developed in 1929 by a physician named Edmund Jacobson. All you have to do is assume a horizontal position and in turn alternately tense, then relax, the various muscle groups in the body. This permits you to identify the lingering tenseness in different parts of your body by learning the difference between what a tense and a relaxed muscle feels like. It takes only a half-hour or so to begin learning the method, and after a few daily or twice-daily sessions, you should begin to notice that you are able to relax yourself totally with less and less practice or effort.

By using such self-relaxation before bedtime, people can overcome some of their insomnia. Practiced before encounters expected to be stressful, it can precondition a person to experience less tension and anxiety than he or she would usually manifest in such encounters. By reducing residual muscle tension, many people discover they are less troubled by nervous habits that in the past may have caused tensions.

In systematic desensitization, after subjects have learned how to relax successfully, the therapist helps them draw up an anxiety hierarchy. The hierarchy starts with a mild anxiety-arousing situation and proceeds to terrifying events that are unlikely ever to occur. For example, let's suppose you have a snake phobia. The least anxiety-provoking stimuli might include seeing a picture of a snake or a worm at a distance; the most terrifying event might be actually handling or being bitten by a snake.

Now you are ready to proceed to relax in progressively more anxious situations. You might need a professional counselor for treatment, but in some cases, you can use systematic desensitization yourself. In a relaxed state, having freed yourself of muscle tensions, you produce the least anxiety-arousing stimulus in your desensitization hierarchy. You experience it, in all its details and threatening aspects, until you begin to feel tense or anxious. You stop; using self-relaxation you relax yourself again, and repeat the procedure until that part of the hierarchy doesn't produce any anxiety. You continue the method, moving up the anxiety hierarchy a few steps each session, until even the most frightening aspect of your problem causes you no anxiety when you confront it head-on.

Another form of desensitization, covert desensitization, is an effective technique for helping an individual overcome fears by learning to relax in the presence of *images* that arouse anxiety. Rather than actually presenting the feared stimulus, the therapist asks the subject to imagine the presence of it. Many students experience anxiety when taking examinations. If you could learn to relax during a test, you would be able to focus on the test questions, and ultimately improve your grade in the course. Let's take test anxiety as an example of covert desensitization.

FIGURE 14.8 Treatment of Snake Phobia
Using both desensitization therapy and modeling, subjects were able to reduce their fear of snakes significantly. In desensitization, subjects are taught how to relax in the presence of stimuli that cause increasing degrees of anxiety. In modeling, subjects observe how models interact with the stimuli, which helps lower their own fear levels.

After you have learned to relax, you need to construct an anxiety hierarchy. You should have about 10 items that can be placed in a sequence from most anxiety-producing to least anxiety-arousing. The most threatening situation might be taking a test, not knowing any of the answers, and panicking. Next might be taking a test and knowing only half the answers. A little less threatening is sitting in the classroom waiting for your instructor to hand you the test. Then might come walking down the hallway toward the classroom where the test will be taken. A little less threatening still might be awakening the morning of the test and thinking about it. Then might come studying for the test the night before. Finally might come scenes like reading the textbook or listening to a lecture a week before the test.

You need to find someplace quiet where you can relax. Once you've relaxed, imagine the least threatening item in your test anxiety hierarchy. As soon as you begin to feel anxious, stop imagining the item and practice relaxation again. Keep trying to imagine the stimulus until you can do so without feeling anxious. Then you're ready to try the next item on your hierarchy.

Continue until you have completed your anxiety hierarchy or until you have reached an item that you cannot relax with totally. The hierarchy should take several sessions to complete. If you experience much trouble, you need to divide the items up further. On the other hand, if you sail through the entire hierarchy, it is not threatening enough. Practice should help you decide on the procedure. When finished, you should be able to take tests without experiencing extreme anxiety.

Systematic desensitization is often successful (Spiegler, 1983). If the problem is fragmented into small enough parts, and if you proceed slowly and cautiously, even long-standing phobias and fears can usually be overcome.

Aversion Therapy   In aversion therapy unwanted responses are paired with unpleasant consequences (see also chapter 6, "Learning"). Alcoholics, for example, can be given a slight electric shock every time they take a drink. Or they may take a drug that makes them nauseated when they consume alcohol. The new habits learned by such methods are fairly fragile and can soon be replaced, as discussed by Wilson and O'Leary (1980). If, however, the alcoholic, or person with any such specific problem, genuinely wants to rid himself or herself of the problem, he or she may undergo aversion therapy to make it easier to break the unwanted habit.

Aversion therapy has been used to treat a variety of problems, including drinking, smoking, obesity, and sexual disorders. Usually the subject views, tastes, or imagines the problem stimulus while receiving an aversive stimulus. A person with a fetish for silk panties might view the panties while receiving an electric shock. Sometimes aversion can be accomplished by overindulgence. For

FIGURE 14.9   Aversion Therapy
When a subject undergoes aversion therapy, unwanted behaviors are associated with a negative stimulus. Here an alcoholic receives an electric shock to his hand each time he takes a drink.

example, you might form an aversion to chocolate ice cream if you ate three gallons of it at once.

Aversion therapy is controversial because of the ethical issues it raises. Some people question whether psychologists should ever be permitted to inflict pain on other people. Often, aversion therapy is used with other methods, or when other methods prove ineffective.

Cognitive Behavior Therapy

Behavior therapy implies that behavior alone is modified, and that identical techniques should work on animals and humans. Recently, some forms of behavior therapy have included thinking or *cognition* in the treatment program (see chapter 8, "Language and Intelligence"). Cognitive behavior therapy involves modifying a client's cognitions through behavioral techniques. A basic assumption of cognitive behavior therapy is that a person's thoughts and feelings affect his or her behavior. The goal is to change the person's thoughts, which will in turn have a positive effect on the person's adjustment. A number of different cognitive behavior therapies have been developed, most focusing on *cognitive restructuring*, the modification of the client's thoughts and perceptions that are contributing to his or her maladjustment. We discuss some of the most influential forms of cognitive behavior therapy here.

Rational-Emotive Therapy Albert Ellis (1962, 1984), the founder of rational-emotive therapy, argued that what we think has a significant influence on the way we feel and act. In particular, psychological maladjustment occurs when we hold certain self-defeating, irrational beliefs about our experiences in the world. The rational-emotive therapy (RET) model suggests that a significant activating event (A) is interpreted by a person's belief system (B) and leads to an emotional consequence (C). When the consequence is an undesirable one, such as anxiety or stress, it is due to the individual's irrational beliefs. RET attempts to dispute (D) the irrational belief system by challenging it rationally, with the result that the disturbed consequences eventually disappear (Ellis, 1984).

Ellis compiled a list of common irrational beliefs. For example, one should be loved by everyone; one must always be perfect in everything; one's self-worth is based on one's performance; a person has little control over emotions; and one should avoid life's problems. The aim of RET is to challenge beliefs such as these so the person can enjoy a happy, healthy life. For example, one of the irrational beliefs cited by Ellis is the belief that we must be competent in everything we do. Tom did not receive an *A* on his last test and now feels defeated and depressed. By understanding that everyone can't always come out on top, Tom can learn to accept himself, and in time even work harder to earn an *A* in that particular subject (or be satisfied with doing the best job possible).

Cognitive Therapy Aaron Beck (1976) argued that many disorders are caused by the negative thoughts and feelings people experience. He developed a cognitive therapy to restructure these negative, self-defeating thoughts and modify the way people view the world. Beck has largely applied his cognitive therapy to depression, although recently he extended it to the treatment of anxiety disorders (Beck, 1985).

Beck's cognitive therapy assumes that depression results because people hold illogical ideas that are maintained by self-defeating behaviors. For example, if Bill does poorly on a test, he may believe he is stupid and will never do well and thus should quit school. Thus, Bill might tend to perceive the world as harmful (teachers are out to get him), overgeneralize from his limited experiences (he will never do well in anything), and magnify the significance of an event (failing the test is the end of the world). In cognitive therapy, Bill would be encour-

aged to develop hypotheses from his beliefs and expectations and test these hypotheses to determine if they are true. Eventually, the client learns to restructure cognitive processes to obtain a more objective, unbiased view of the world. A number of studies have supported the effectiveness of cognitive therapy (Wilson & colleagues, 1983).

Modeling Albert Bandura (1986) argued that modeling and imitation are extremely important in learning everyday behaviors, and observing others can help an individual deal with problems. In addition to reinforcement, Bandura proposed that cognitive factors were important in therapy. For instance, a person with a simple phobia of snakes was helped by observing someone (a model) handle snakes without fear (Bandura & colleagues, 1969). Children can reduce their fear of surgery when exposed to a model of the surgical event before it is performed.

Bandura (1977) described several functions of modeling in therapeutic situations. It serves a *learning function* by providing observers examples of appropriate behaviors. It has an *eliciting function* by providing appropriate cues (for instance, causing the client to relax when the model relaxes in an anxiety-producing situation). Modeling serves a *disinhibiting function* when the observer is not afraid to engage in an activity after seeing someone else do it (for example, children might lose their inhibitions about petting a dog if they observe other children petting it). Modeling can also serve an *inhibiting function* (children can learn not to pet the dog when they observe it biting someone else). Modeling has been applied with great success to a variety of mild psychological disorders.

Bandura (1989) argued that the success of therapy is due to the improvement of a person's sense of mastery, or self-efficacy. This, according to Bandura, involves both cognitive and behavioral therapeutic techniques. Many psychologists believe that cognitive factors are important in learning behavior and play a major role in psychological disorders such as phobias and depression. Further research will explore how cognitive therapy can help people change attitudes and maladaptive behaviors.

Sometimes a brief crisis intervention can be provided by volunteers at a telephone crisis center, as discussed by the following Application.

APPLICATION

Telephone Crisis Centers

One problem with traditional forms of psychotherapy is that usually they take a long time and involve an intensive interaction between therapist and patient.

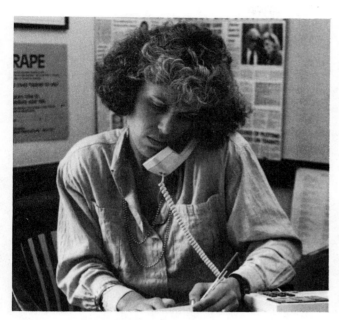

FIGURE 14.10   Telephone Crisis Hot Line
The telephone crisis hot line allows people with problems to talk to someone who will patiently listen. The benefits of this system consist of immediate attention from a volunteer paraprofessional and anonymity of the caller.

Unfortunately, we don't have enough professional therapists to have one always available when a crisis arises. During the past decade or so, many community mental health centers have established telephone crisis centers to help deal with this problem.

The telephone crisis hot line is usually staffed by paraprofessionals. These are people who volunteer their time and are intensively trained in the techniques of phone usage in emotional and mental emergencies. Because they can remain anonymous, people with serious personal problems will phone and talk with these workers. The problems range from suicide, rape, and incest to loneliness, anxiety, and indecision. The concept works because someone is willing to listen. If the caller wants professional help, he or she is referred to an appropriate agency; the call may even be switched to a professional who can be reached by phone.

Research in this area provides some suggestions for crisis hot line volunteers. First, the volunteer should be a good listener and try to develop empathy with the caller. Second, the volunteer must know where help can be obtained, including agencies, physicians, psychologists, or special centers for specific problems. Next, the volunteer should try to get the caller to promise to take some specific steps to solve the problem. And finally, it's important to reassure the caller that the crisis will end and life will not always seem so hopeless.

The popularity of telephone crisis centers has risen in recent years. However, evaluating their effectiveness is a difficult task. It has been shown that about 95 percent of the callers do not call again. And since callers are usually anonymous, it's usually impossible to do follow-up studies on them. Still, it seems likely that just having someone to talk to can make a critical difference to a person contemplating suicide. This type of service fills a gap that exists because there are insufficient professionals available at any given time.

GROUP THERAPY

Group therapy involves the treatment of several patients at the same time. In group therapy the therapist tries to remain in the background, while patients discuss and share their feelings and problems with one another. Feedback is encouraged from other members of the group, rather than only from the therapist.

This method originally emerged as an alternative to the high cost of individual therapy, but it is now believed by many psychotherapists to be of value in its own right and with definite advantages for some patients. Patients may be helped by getting to know that other people have difficulties similar to their own. In addition, an individual in group therapy can see how a variety of people actually respond to him or her, and can try out new ways of reacting and responding with a group of people whom he or she knows and trusts.

In many cases, the individual therapies already discussed can be adapted easily to group situations. A group of people with test anxiety or fear of snakes can go through systematic desensitization together rather than alone. Gestalt therapy is often conducted in groups rather than individually. As you might imagine, there is an unlimited variety of group therapies. Not all groups are successful, however, and for any type of therapy it is important to weigh carefully the advantages and disadvantages before joining a group (Kaul & Bedner, 1986).

Encounter Groups

In the past couple of decades, there has been a great deal of interest in encounter and sensitivity training groups. A group of people, usually no fewer than 7, and rarely more than 20, get together with the aim of shedding their ordinarily polite social masks and expressing their real feelings. The group usually emphasizes verbal interaction, games, and other activities that encourage open displays of approval, criticism, affection, dislike, and even anger and tears, rather than the tact and

FIGURE 14.11 Group Therapy
When several people are treated simultaneously, there is opportunity for interaction with supportive others who often share similar problems. Group therapy includes such types as encounter groups and family therapy.

it may meet as a *marathon group* for 24 continuous hours or more, with individuals dropping out for naps. It is thought that the intensity and prolonged time of the marathon group will break down social resistance faster, and accomplish as much as groups whose meetings are interspersed over longer periods of time. The goals of encounter groups include examining one's behavior and values, learning about people in general, becoming more successful in interpersonal relationships, and developing conflict resolution skills.

Related to encounter groups are groups that are designed especially for assertiveness training. These groups help individuals stand up for their rights without violating the rights of others. Typically, a group of about a dozen people are told the problems of not being assertive and how the group can help build confidence. Then members of the group role-play in various situations that require an assertive response. Feedback and encouragement are provided by the therapist, until individuals feel comfortable being assertive (Carson & Butcher, 1992).

Most people in encounter groups do not consider themselves involved in psychotherapy. Rather it is thought that anyone can benefit from the experience in encounters where there is complete candor—something very rare in our world. Some psychologists are concerned that these group experiences may trigger serious disturbances in some of the more troubled patients who participate in them. The success of these groups depends to a large degree on the skills of the leader and the personalities of the people involved. Be cautious and ascertain if the leader is properly trained and well respected before joining such a group.

Family Therapy

Family therapy assumes that ineffective communication and difficulty in interacting with members of the family unit are significantly involved in causing a problem (Gurman & colleagues, 1986). The task of the family therapist is to modify these social interactions and help improve communication patterns so family members can solve their own problems (Kutash & Wolf, 1986). In *conjoint family therapy*, the emphasis is on developing better relationships and self-esteem for all members of the family. *Structural family therapy* attempts to modify the organizational structure of the family so members can relate more positively and be supportive of one another. For instance, structural therapy might be used when a child appears to have more power than a parent.

Often the therapist sees only one member of the family at a time, while at other times the entire family is in the therapy session together. The goal of family therapy is to work with a whole family to help them change un-

inhibition of emotional expression that ordinarily govern our social behavior. The assumption in these groups is similar to that of person-centered therapy: the individual will grow in a positive way by resisting social restrictions and by interacting with others honestly and openly.

Sensitivity training groups originally tended to be less extreme than encounter groups, although the distinction between the two is thin, and the terms are often used interchangeably. The sensitivity training group (T-group) grew out of conferences on small-group dynamics held at the National Training Laboratory in Bethel, Maine, in 1947. Originally, T-groups were designed to help executives and managers become more sensitive or aware of the needs of their employees. The emphasis has shifted toward individual growth in healthy people. Carl Rogers is credited with starting some of the first T-groups when he trained counselors at the University of Chicago in the mid-1940s.

Encounter groups most often have a leader experienced at getting people to open up. The group may meet for several hours a week over some period of months, or successful patterns of behavior toward each other. A highly successful technique in family therapy involves making a videotape of the family members, in which they are interacting with one another. When people are able to view themselves "from the outside" in this way, they often find it easier to understand their unsuccessful behavior and to make progress toward improving it. While not everyone benefits from family therapy, for many it is a useful form of treatment.

When just husband and wife are treated together, it is called marital therapy. Sometimes this form is called *couple counseling* and includes nonmarried couples who are living together (Brammer & colleagues, 1989). It is essential that both partners be treated together, so that they can better understand their relationship and improve their adjustment. One of the difficult tasks of couple counseling is to help each partner overcome his or her intense emotions so that he or she can view the relationship objectively and appreciate the role each one plays in it. A study by Cookerly (1980) of the divorce rates of individuals undergoing marital therapy found that 56 percent of couples who underwent therapy together remained married for at least 5 years after the treatment. Of course, couples seeking therapy would be likely to be the most motivated to maintain the marriage in the first place. Hahlweg and Markman (1988) argued that more efforts need to be placed on prevention of marital distress early in the relationship.

EVALUATION OF THE EFFECTIVENESS OF PSYCHOTHERAPY

A true experimental test of the effectiveness of psychotherapeutic procedures would be complex, expensive, and probably impossible. It would require several groups of patients carefully matched for similarity of psychological disturbance, IQ, and family, educational, and economic background. One group would be treated with traditional psychoanalysis, one with person-centered therapy, one with behavior therapy, and another with group therapy. Also, we would need a control group whose members received no therapeutic help at all, since a study by Smith and Glass (1977) estimated that as many as one-fourth of all people with anxiety complaints get better without any professional help. Not only the extent of improvement would have to be measured, but also its duration.

Some investigations of psychotherapists suggest that there are common characteristics possessed by successful therapists (Lafferty & colleagues, 1989). The more successful the therapist, the more likely he or she is to have strong feelings of warmth and liking for his or her

FIGURE 14.12   Effectiveness of Psychotherapy

TYPE OF THERAPY	EFFECTIVENESS
Psychodynamic	72
Adlerian	76
Eclectic	68
Transactional Analysis	72
Rational-Emotive	78
Gestalt	60
Client-Centered	74
Systematic Desensitization	82
Implosive	74
Behavior Modification	78

(Effectiveness score = Client is better off than XX% of those untreated)

Smith and Glass (1977) reviewed the effectiveness of 10 types of therapy and found that the patient who is treated, regardless of method, is generally better off than about three-quarters of those not treated. Note that many of the therapies are similar in their effectiveness.

patients, to be readily able to imagine himself or herself in the situation of the patient, to be free of anxiety or other disturbances, to be open and honest, and to have had considerable experience in treating patients. The therapist should also be knowledgeable and objective in the therapy session.

Other researchers have focused on the characteristics of the patient in successful psychotherapy (Carson & Butcher, 1992). In general, the patient most likely to benefit from psychotherapy would have a moderate rather than a severe psychological disorder and a high degree of motivation to overcome the problem. The patient's confidence in the therapist appears to aid the effectiveness of the therapy. Other variables, such as the patient's age, sex, race, and education, also play a role in the success of therapy (Sue, 1988).

The task of evaluating specific types of psychotherapy is also extremely difficult because of the diversity of approaches used today. In a survey of 579 clinical psychologists who were members of the APA (American Psychological Association), Norcross and colleagues (1989) reported that 29 percent were eclectic (integrated aspects of various types to create a unique type) in their approach to therapy, 29 percent of psychologists used behavior or cognitive-behavior therapy, 33 percent used some form of insight therapy, and 9 percent indicated they used some other form of therapy. It seems likely therefore that over one-third (38 percent) of clinical psychologists do not readily fall into the categories of therapy we have discussed in this chapter.

Clearly, no certain measure of the effectiveness of the various forms of therapy has yet been devised. It is therefore largely up to the individual to decide which kind of therapy might best meet his or her needs. People who are otherwise normal but who may be troubled by anxiety, mild depression, difficulty in getting along with others, or related common emotional and behavioral complaints have a wide selection of therapeutic options. Of course, it is nearly impossible for most people (and especially those needing help) to have the expertise necessary to make this decision.

Depending on the particular problem involved, on the character and skill of the therapist, and on one's willingness to go along conscientiously with the therapeutic program he or she enters, one can confidently expect to see measurable results in a reasonable time. Howard and colleagues (1986) found that improvement was related to the number of therapy sessions participated in, with the greatest gains occurring within the first 6 months. Phillips (1988) argued that Howard's data base was limited, and that currently the most common length of psychotherapy (for all types and all problems combined) is six sessions. Psychoanalysis or some of the other insight therapies take years to see change and improvement, whereas behavior therapy can produce quite rapid results.

Although Smith, Glass, and Miller's (1980) analysis of psychotherapy outcome studies found that the patients were better off than 80 percent of untreated control subjects, there is no evidence to prove that one form of therapy is always better than another. Kazdin and Bass (1989) argued that until research is able to evaluate the effectiveness of different psychotherapies adequately, we must be extremely cautious in claiming that differences in effectiveness exist.

Further research will continue to examine the characteristics that make psychotherapy effective, and practitioners will continue to refine their techniques to provide quality service for their clients. It seems likely that the characteristics of the problem, the therapist, the patient, and the therapy itself will be more closely matched by mental health professionals in the future.

BIOLOGICAL THERAPY

Up to now we have discussed psychological therapies; this section deals with biological therapy, the treatment of behavior problems through biological techniques. The three major types of biological therapy, or biomedical therapy, are drug therapy, psychosurgery, and electroconvulsive therapy.

Drug Therapy

In the past 3 decades, remarkable discoveries of new psychoactive drugs have revolutionized treatment of psychological disorders. There are many types of drugs in use in drug therapy today. In chapter 5, "Sleep and Consciousness," we discussed the psychoactive drugs that are not usually used to treat psychological disorders. In this chapter, we concentrate on three major classes of drugs used in the treatment of psychological disorders: antianxiety drugs, antipsychotic drugs, and antidepressant drugs. Remember that only therapists with M.D. degrees can prescribe these drugs, and that psychologists must work with medical personnel when drugs are used to treat psychological disorders.

Antianxiety Drugs The antianxiety drugs, or antianxiety minor tranquilizers, are used to reduce anxiety. They are often given to patients who are under stress or experiencing pressure, tension, or insomnia. Sometimes antianxiety drugs are prescribed by general practitioners for people complaining of anxiety. Some people you know probably take Librium, Valium, Equanil, or Miltown.

In small doses for short periods of time, when a person is in a stressful situation, these drugs do reduce anxiety and allow the person to function effectively. Unfortunately, sometimes people take large doses over a long period of time and misuse this potentially valuable aid to effective coping. Ideally, antianxiety drugs are used to relieve overwhelming anxiety, so that other forms of psychotherapy can treat the real problem.

Antipsychotic Drugs Probably the greatest change in treating institutionalized schizophrenics occurred in 1955, when chlorpromazine was introduced in the United States. Antipsychotic drugs, also known as major tranquilizers, are effective in relieving the bizarre and antisocial symptoms of some schizophrenic patients. The antipsychotic drugs have made it possible for therapists to work with patients rather than just provide institutional custodial care. However, they have sometimes been abused. When given in large doses, these drugs can sedate patients to the point where they are incapable of responding to the environment.

As discussed in chapter 13, "Psychological Disorders," a current theory of schizophrenia is that it results from high levels of the neurotransmitter dopamine. Among its actions, chlorpromazine reduces the level of dopamine usage in the brain. At present we do not understand exactly how the antipsychotic drugs produce their dramatic effects.

Antipsychotic drugs are used extensively today, with the vast majority of institutionalized psychotic patients receiving regular medication. The trade name of chlor-

FIGURE 14.13 Drug Therapy

CLASS	GENERIC NAME	TRADE NAME
Antianxiety Drugs		
(minor tranquilizers)	alprazolam	Xanax
	chlordiazepoxide	Librium
	clorazepate	Tranxene
	diazepam	Valium
	flurazepam	Dalmane
	meprobamate	Miltown, Equanil
	oxazepam	Serax
Antipsychotic Drugs		
(major tranquilizers)		
phenothiazines	chlorpromazine	Thorazine
	fluphenazine	Prolixin
	perphenazine	Trilafon
	prochlorperazine	Compazine
	promazine	Sparine
	thioridazine	Mellaril
	trifluoperazine	Stelazine
butyrophenones	haloperidol	Haldol
thioxanthenes	chlorprothixene	Taractan
	thiothixine	Navane
Antidepressant Drugs		
tricyclics	amitriptyline	Elavil
	imipramine	Tofranil
	nortriptyline	Pamelor
	protriptyline	Vivactil
monoamine oxidase	isocarboxazid	Marplan
(MAO) inhibitors	phenelzine	Nardil
	tranylcpromine	Pamate
serotonin uptake inhibitor	fluoxetine	Prozac
lithium	lithium carbonate	Lithane

There are a variety of drugs used in therapy. Antianxiety drugs are used to relieve feelings of tension. Antipsychotic drugs are used to treat psychotic symptoms such as those found in schizophrenia. Antidepressant drugs are used to relieve depression.

promazine is Thorazine. Other often-used antipsychotic drugs include Mellaril, Stelazine, and Haldol. Sometimes antipsychotic drugs have been found to be more effective in modifying behavior than many forms of psychotherapy, but they produce maximum results when used with other forms of therapy.

Antidepressant Drugs The antidepressant drugs, like imipramine, help to relieve depression. The most common trade names include Tofranil, Elavil, and Nardil. As described in chapter 13, "Psychological Disorders," one current theory suggests that depression results from low levels of the neurotransmitter norepinephrine. These antidepressant drugs increase the levels of norepinephrine, and this probably contributes to their effectiveness. Prozac, an antidepressant drug introduced in 1987, works by

increasing levels of serotonin. Although Prozac appears to be extremely effective in relieving depression, some concerns have been raised about its possible side effects (Burton, 1991). Sometimes antidepressant drugs are useful in the treatment of other disorders, such as obsessive compulsive disorder, panic disorder, and eating disorders.

Recently, there has been an increased interest in the drug lithium carbonate as an effective treatment for bipolar disorder. This simple inorganic salt was discovered in Australia in 1949, but was not used in the United States for 20 years because it was considered dangerous and because physicians had serious doubts about its effectiveness. Lithium serves to calm the individual in the manic state of bipolar disorder and smooth out the extreme mood swings. Some research suggests that it might also help some forms of depression (Coppen &

colleagues, 1982). There is concern over its side effects, however, and blood levels must be carefully monitored in patients. Research is continuing on the effectiveness and safety of lithium carbonate as a drug.

Drug therapy is currently the most widely used biological therapy. It does, without a doubt, alter physiological reactions and, consequently, behavior. The major limitations of drug therapy include undesirable side effects and the potential of covering up the symptoms without helping the individual solve his or her problems. Another technique in biological therapy, popular before the introduction of drugs, is psychosurgery.

Psychosurgery

Psychosurgery was one of the earliest treatments for abnormal behavior. Some anthropologists suggest that the therapy practiced by cave dwellers consisted of cutting a hole in the skull to let the "evil spirits" out. Patients who survived very likely behaved differently and probably were much calmer than before.

Modern psychosurgery is credited to Portuguese neuropsychiatrist Antonio Caetano de Abreu Freire Egas Moniz, who in 1935 began performing prefrontal lobotomies on people. In a *prefrontal lobotomy*, the frontal lobes of the brain are disconnected from the rest of the brain. When this surgery is performed on violent patients, they become calm. During the 1950s thousands of patients received lobotomies, including those patients classified as having schizophrenia, depression, and even anxiety disorders.

Because of the frequent negative side effects, such as seizures, loss of emotionality, and problems in thinking, the number of lobotomies performed declined. Since the introduction of the antipsychotic drugs in the 1950s, extremely few psychosurgeries have been performed. Elliot Valenstein (1986) described the historical development of psychosurgery and argued that the reason for its initial success was psychiatry's need to gain respectability by having a surgical treatment for psychological disorders. Overall, psychosurgery is usually reserved for cases where other treatments have failed to produce any effects. When necessary, newer techniques allow neurosurgeons to isolate a very small area of the brain that is malfunctioning or has a tumor, and remove it.

Electroconvulsive Therapy

In the 1930s scientists began experimenting with convulsions as a therapy for schizophrenia and depression. One method was to inject insulin, which produced low blood-sugar level and coma. The other more popular method was electroconvulsive therapy (ECT), discovered by Italian physicians.

In electroconvulsive therapy (ECT), after a muscle relaxant has been administered, two electrodes are fastened to the patient's head and an electric current, about the same strength as household electricity, is passed between them for a very brief time. The patient goes through a brief period of extreme muscle contraction (a convulsion) and is temporarily unconscious. When the patient wakes up, he or she is drowsy and confused, but quickly recovers and shows less severe symptoms (sometimes ECT is incorrectly referred to as "shock" therapy). Side effects include temporary general disorientation and more serious memory impairments that can last for months (Palmer, 1981).

ECT is controversial and is not used as frequently as it was before the antidepressant drugs were introduced. It is generally reserved for the severely depressed. We do not know how it works, but it does produce some positive results in many severely depressed patients. It is, like psychosurgery, usually a last resort, because psychoactive drugs are generally much more effective in altering behavior. ∎

Many of the therapeutic techniques described in this chapter are extensions of everyday social interactions. Indeed, insight therapies such as psychoanalysis or person-centered therapy have as their chief goals improved perception and self-understanding. As we saw in the opening story, reinforcement behavior therapy involves the application of learning and reinforcement principles, and is effective in a variety of situations from mental institutions to classrooms. Unfortunately, no one type of therapy is totally effective for all problems or all people. Success of a therapy depends on many factors, including the the problem being treated and the personalities of the therapist and patient. In the next chapter we explore some of the influences that create individual differences in social behavior.

CHAPTER REVIEW

What You've Learned About Therapy

1. Professionals who provide therapy for psychological disorders include psychiatrists, clinical and counseling psychologists, and psychiatric social workers. Psychotherapy is the treatment of behavior problems, using psychological techniques such as insight, behavior, and group therapies. Biological therapy treats behavior problems with biological techniques that include drug therapy, psychosurgery, and electroconvulsive therapy.

2. Historically, people with behavior problems were treated inhumanely. There has been a trend during the past couple of decades to get patients out of institutions and back into society.

3. Insight therapy is largely based on the assumption that the patient behaves abnormally because he or she does not adequately understand the motivation underlying the behavior. Psychoanalysis is an insight therapy developed by Freud that is an intensive and prolonged exploration of the patient's unconscious motivation. The patient is assumed to have repressed conflicts from childhood that are unresolved and hence causing problems. The goal of psychoanalysis is to bring the repressed conflicts into consciousness so that the patient can deal with them. Techniques employed by psychoanalysts include free association, dream analysis, and transference.

4. Person-centered therapy is an insight therapy developed by Rogers that is based on the assumption that every individual has an innate capacity to be psychologically healthy and self-actualized. The therapist provides a nonthreatening atmosphere and lets the client choose the direction of the therapy. Therapists should show genuineness, unconditional positive regard, and empathy toward the client.

5. Gestalt therapy is an insight therapy designed to get people to become more aware of themselves and their responsibility for their own behavior. The therapist helps the person become aware of his or her own perceptions and act out his or her emotions.

6. Behavior therapy is concerned with modifying undesired behavior. Reinforcement therapy, one form of behavior therapy, is based on the assumption that abnormal behavior is learned, and therefore reinforcement can modify the behavior. The techniques of shaping and extinction are used in reinforcement therapy. In a token economy, desirable behaviors are immediately reinforced with tokens that can be exchanged at a later time for desired rewards.

7. In counterconditioning, an unwanted response is replaced by conditioning a response incompatible with it.

In systematic desensitization, individuals overcome fears and anxieties by learning to relax in the presence of stimuli that made them unbearably nervous. In aversion therapy, unwanted responses are paired with unpleasant consequences.

8. Cognitive behavior therapy involves modifying a client's cognitions through behavioral techniques. Cognitive restructuring involves the modification of the client's thoughts and perceptions that are contributing to his or her maladjustment. Rational-emotive therapy was developed by Ellis to get people to become aware of their irrational beliefs.

9. Group therapy attempts to treat problems by letting people interact in a group setting. Sensitivity training groups (or T-groups) grew out of efforts to help executives and managers become more aware of their employees' needs. There has been a shift toward self-awareness and self-growth in encounter groups. To be successful, an encounter group requires a leader experienced at getting people to open up and discuss their problems and feelings.

10. Family therapy and marital therapy are based on the assumption that poor communication and flawed social interactions within the family are causing the problem. The goal is to help family members change unsuccessful patterns of behavior.

11. No clear measure of the effectiveness of the various forms of therapy has been devised. Characteristics of the problem, therapist, patient, and therapy influence effectiveness. Research indicates that psychotherapy often accelerates adjustment.

12. Biological therapy includes drug therapy, psychosurgery, and electroconvulsive therapy. Drug therapy is the most widely used biological therapy and often alters behavior. Antianxiety drugs (minor tranquilizers) are used to reduce anxiety. Antipsychotic drugs (major tranquilizers) are used to relieve the symptoms of schizophrenia. Antidepressant drugs relieve depression, possibly by increasing the level of norepinephrine in the brain.

13. Psychosurgery, in the form of removing or destroying part of the brain, has never been very effective. Few such operations were performed after the 1950s, when antipsychotic drugs became available.

14. Electroconvulsive therapy (ECT) applies electricity to the brain to produce a convulsion. It sometimes relieves severely depressed patients, but is not as effective as antidepressant drugs.

CHAPTER 15

SOCIAL PSYCHOLOGY

Who influences what you think and do? It is likely that a number of people have a strong effect on you. Our behavior, thoughts, and feelings are often influenced by others. How people perceive others and form attitudes have long been major interests of social psychologists, who are also involved in research on social influence and group processes. An important goal of social psychology is to understand social interaction in all situations.

CRITICAL THINKING OBJECTIVES FOR CHAPTER 15

After reading chapter 15, you should be able to identify, apply, and evaluate what you have learned about the following questions:

What are the important theoretical approaches in social psychology?
What are the important theories of attribution?
What are the variables involved in attitude change?
What are the types of compliance?
What are the variables that influence group effectiveness?
What are the important theories of aggression?

CHAPTER 16

APPLIED PSYCHOLOGY

Psychologists are interested in applying their skills and research findings to practical problems. Psychologists can apply their skills to everyday problems in industry, education, the effects of a person's surroundings (environment) on his or her behavior, in police departments, prisons, and even in sports, as well as in other interesting areas.

CRITICAL THINKING OBJECTIVES FOR CHAPTER 16

After reading chapter 16, you should be able to identify, apply, and evaluate what you have learned about the following questions:

What are the major areas of applied psychology?
What are the variables that influence jury behavior?
What are the variables that influence motivation in organizations?
What are the topics in environmental psychology?
What are the topics in educational psychology?

344

Part VII explores some of the influences others have on the individual. The areas of social psychology and psychology applied to industry, legal systems, and the environment are reviewed.

Social Processes

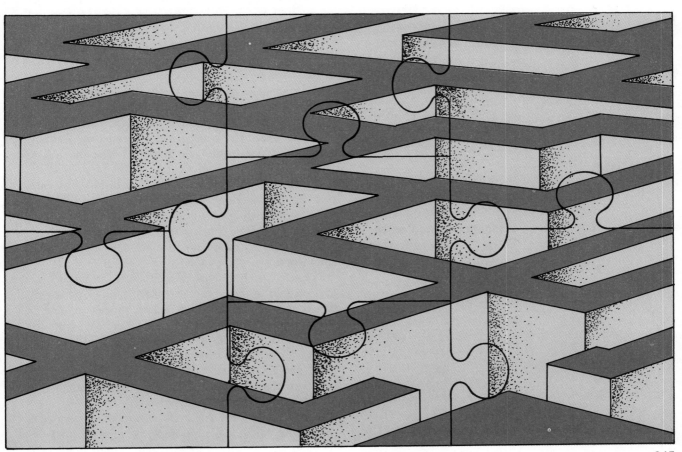

CHAPTER OBJECTIVES

What You'll Learn About Social Psychology

After studying this chapter, you should be able to:

1. Define social psychology.
2. Describe the process of person perception.
3. Describe the process of attribution.
4. Define attitude and outline how attitudes are formed and measured.
5. Describe how attitudes can be changed.
6. Outline the theory of cognitive dissonance.
7. Define the concept of prejudice.
8. Identify two theories of conformity.
9. Describe four techniques of compliance.
10. Outline Milgram's research on obedience.
11. Describe the processes that influence group effectiveness.
12. Describe Zajonc's theory of social facilitation.
13. Outline the research on cooperation, competition, and conflict.
14. Outline the research on leadership.
15. Define aggression and outline three theories of aggression.
16. Outline the steps that lead to helping behavior.

WHAT IS SOCIAL PSYCHOLOGY?

SOCIAL COGNITION
Person Perception
Attribution

ATTITUDES
Attitude Formation
Attitude Measurement
Attitude Change
Cognitive Dissonance
Prejudice

SOCIAL INFLUENCE
Conformity
Compliance
Obedience

GROUP PROCESSES
Group Effectiveness
Social Facilitation
Cooperation, Competition, and Conflict
Leadership

AGGRESSION AND HELPING BEHAVIOR
Aggression
Helping Behavior

Yale psychologist Stanley Milgram's 1963 experiment on obedience produced frightening results. He describes it in his book, *Obedience to Authority* (1974). Milgram wanted a general cross section of people, so he placed an advertisement in a New Haven, Connecticut, newspaper, offering $4 for anyone between the ages of 20 and 50 willing to participate in a 1-hour study of memory and learning. Subjects who responded included teachers, post office workers, engineers, and factory workers. Their education ranged from high school to professional degrees. Originally only men were accepted, but women participated in some of the later studies.

The subjects were told that they were participating in a test to gauge the effects of punishment on learning. Each individual subject was asked to take the role of "teacher" and to deliver electric shocks to a "learner," who was actually a secret accomplice of Milgram. Supposedly, the "learner" was attempting to memorize 40 word pairs, such as *blue-box* and *wild-duck*, and was to be given an electric shock when he failed to remember a pair, the shocks becoming stronger if he continued to miss words.

Each "teacher" was provided with an impressive-looking (but actually harmless) electric shock generator, which, he was told, could deliver shocks ranging in intensity from 15 to 450 volts to the "learner," who was strapped to a chair in a separate room. The "teacher" was to decide on the strength of the shock to be administered and then actually pull the switch. As part of the scenario, the "learner" deliberately made mistakes in recalling 30 out of the 40 word pairs.

The purpose of the study was to investigate obedience. As the shocks supposedly became stronger (remember, no shocks were actually administered), the

Who influences what you think and do? It is likely that a number of people have a strong effect on you. Our behavior, thoughts, and feelings are often influenced by others. How people perceive others and form attitudes have long been major interests of social psychologists, who are also involved in research on social influence and group processes. An important goal of social psychology is to understand social interaction in all situations.

15
Social Psychology

FIGURE 15.1 Obedience Experiment
These photographs were taken at Yale University during the course of Milgram's experiments in obedience. **(A)** The "shock generator." **(B)** A "teacher" (subject) helps the experimenter strap the "learner" (confederate) into the chair and connect him to the shock apparatus. **(C)** A teacher receives a sample shock from the generator. **(D)** The teacher refuses to administer any more shocks to the learner and gets up from his chair in protest.

"learner" began to moan and cry out. At still higher levels, the "learner" demanded to be let out of the experiment, claiming to have a weak heart. At about 300 volts, he screamed in agony, then lapsed into silence.

Despite these apparent signs of the "learner's" distress, the experimenter urged the "teacher" to continue. If a "teacher" hesitated or resisted, the experimenter said, "You must go on."

Although many of the subjects showed signs of great conflict, 65 percent of them continued to administer what they thought were real shocks until the end of the study. Right up through the three highest possible voltages, they pulled switches that delivered these shocks even to a screaming, protesting human being who they were led to

believe had a weak heart. Not one subject refused to participate in so seemingly cruel an exercise. They showed obedience to the authority represented by the "expert."

Milgram ran 18 different experiments in his study of obedience. The variables studied included proximity, personnel, institutional context, authority figure, and group decisions. Generally, as the physical proximity of the victim to the subject increased, the subjects' level of obedience fell significantly (although there was considerable variability). Although some criticize Milgram's study of obedience on ethical grounds (Miller, 1986), it demonstrates how social psychology is often involved in understanding everyday behavior.

WHAT IS SOCIAL PSYCHOLOGY?

It is hard to imagine a day in which our lives are not influenced by other people, directly or indirectly. We form impressions of other people every day. We make decisions about the motives of our friends and acquaintances, and decide whether we like new people that we meet. When we attribute motives to others (attribution) we rely on perceptual cues that we have learned through social interactions. Through our experiences and interactions with other people, we form and modify our attitudes. How we form these social perceptions is an important area of study in social psychology.

Another area of social psychology examines social influence on behavior. When you attend class, you may sit politely and listen to the instructor. You may also comply with requests, such as helping to hand out class papers. And, as shown in our opening story, you obey the orders of people in authority. These are social influences.

Social psychology also covers the influences that groups have on their members. In class discussions, a few people become leaders and guide the group's other members into the paths these discussions will take. Aggression and helping behavior are the final topics of social psychology that we will discuss in this chapter.

Although there are a number of variations, most psychologists accept Gordon Allport's (1985) definition of social psychology. Allport stated that social psychology is an attempt to understand how the thoughts, feelings, and behavior of individuals are influenced by the actual, imagined, or implied presence of others. In this text we define social psychology as the study of how an individual's behavior, thoughts, and feelings are influenced by others. When someone asks you a question, you respond with an answer. Someone else's personality and physical characteristics can either attract or repel you. For instance, you are more inclined to notice an attractive person than you are to notice someone unattractive. You are also influenced indirectly by others: through books, movies, television, and newspapers people you have never met help shape your opinions and tastes.

Social psychology is a behavioral and social science, and as such its emphasis is on the individual. However, it focuses primarily on interpersonal interactions, and the influences that other people have on the individual. Many basic topics that we have already discussed are relevant in this social approach to behavior. For instance, perception, learning, cognition, motivation, and personality all contribute to our understanding of social interactions. Other topics, such as social influences, behavior in groups, aggression, and helping behavior, are uniquely social phenomena. As we go through this chapter, try to recall the previous topics and apply them in this new context.

Sears and colleagues (1991) described six major theories that dominate social psychology: learning, cognitive, motivational, decision-making, social exchange, and social role theories. The social learning theory proposes that social behavior is learned and maintained through the processes of observation, imitation, and reinforcement, and that learned behavior is particularly relevant in aggression. The cognitive theory focuses on thinking and language, and is important when discussing their effect on social perception and attitudes. The motivational theory emphasizes needs and desires, and is involved in determining social influence on behavior. Decision-making theories assume that people logically select most appropriate actions. The social exchange theory focuses on the evaluation of the costs and benefits of interpersonal interactions. The social role theory emphasizes the norms or expectations that influence a person's behavior in a social situation. As you can see, social psychology is a complex area that covers a variety of topics from a number of different approaches. We begin this chapter with a look at how people develop impressions of others.

SOCIAL COGNITION

Social cognition is the process of understanding other people and ourselves (Fiske & Taylor, 1991). This area of social psychology explores how we make sense out of ourselves and other people by forming and utilizing information about the social world. Social cognition includes the study of person perception and attribution. It stresses the cognitive functioning of the individual in everyday social situations. In this section, we will first discuss person perception, the process of forming impressions of other people, and then we will discuss attribution, the process of making inferences about the motives of ourselves and others.

Person Perception

Most people have an amazing ability to recognize and respond to the important aspects of another's personality. When we first meet people, we quickly determine whether or not we like them through the process of impression formation. Even hearing a bit of information about someone or observing a person allows us to make judgments about him or her. Solomon Asch (1946) argued that we perceive people as wholes. Thus, when given only partial information, we tend to fill the gaps in our impressions with traits of people similar to those we perceive, however inaccurately. The process of person

FIGURE 15.2   Person Perception
The first impression we form of someone tends to be the overriding factor in interpreting later impressions of them. Physical attractiveness and manner of dress contribute to first impressions.

perception involves using the information we gather in forming impressions of other people to evaluate them.

First Impressions   Much research has centered around which is more important in forming enduring impressions of people: first impression (*primacy effect*) or last impression (*recency effect*). In an early study, Asch (1946) reported that subjects who heard a personality profile of someone who was described as "intelligent, industrious, impulsive, critical, stubborn, and envious" rated the person as significantly more happy and sociable than other subjects who heard the exact same personality traits read in the reverse order. It appears the first words we hear, favorable or otherwise, are the ones that remain with us and influence our perceptions and behaviors. After we form an impression, we tend to ignore later information.

In a classic experiment by Harold Kelley (1950), one group of students was told a new lecturer was "a rather warm person, industrious, critical, practical, and determined." If this person came to give a talk to your class, how would you react? Would you be likely to interact with the person or remain silent? Kelley found 56 percent of his students entered into class discussion with the lecturer, and the vast majority of students rated him as informed, considerate, sociable, popular, generous, and humorous. Another group of students were told that the guest was "a rather cold person, industrious, critical,

practical, and determined." Now how would you react? Kelley found that only 32 percent of the subjects entered into class discussion with this person, and most rated him as self-centered, formal, unsociable, irritable, and humorless. Of course, the only difference was the substitution of the word "cold" instead of "warm" in the description. Our first impressions do influence our behaviors.

Consistency and Positivity Bias   Research has shown that once we have formed a general impression of someone, we tend to interpret additional information about this person in a manner consistent with our general impression. The tendency to be consistent in evaluation impressions is called the halo effect. Nisbett and Wilson (1977) had college students view a videotape of a professor. In one version, the professor was warm and friendly, whereas in the other version, he acted cold and uncaring. Not surprisingly, in an example of the halo effect, students who saw the warm version liked the professor better and rated all other characteristics in a much more positive fashion than did those subjects who saw the cold version.

Other research has shown that we tend to provide positive evaluations when we evaluate other people (Sears, 1983). The tendency to evaluate others positively is called positivity bias. In one study, Sears reported that college students rated 97 percent of the college professors they were taking classes from above average (in reality, only 50 percent could be above average, since 50 percent are below average). We empathize with people and thus evaluate them more highly if they are individuals rather than groups. Sears also reported that 74 percent of the time instructors were rated higher than the courses they taught, emphasizing the human element in the evaluation phenomenon.

Physical Attractiveness   An important dimension in forming an impression of someone is what that person looks like. If he or she dresses sloppily, is clumsy, and is physically unattractive, we are inclined to dislike him or her, or in general think negatively about him or her, while to many people an attractive person can do no wrong. This is due partially to the halo effect.

Karen Dion (1972) reported that physical attractiveness does indeed influence other people's impressions. She had women read reports of severe classroom disruptions by elementary schoolchildren. In some cases the report was accompanied by a photograph of a very attractive child, while in other cases the photo was of an unattractive boy or girl. The subjects tended to blame the disruptive behavior on the ugly children, saying that it was easy to see that they were "brats." On the other hand, when the photo was of a beautiful child the women tended to excuse him or her.

Do adults make judgments on the basis of attractiveness? They certainly do, according to a study by Dion and her colleagues, Ellen Berscheid and Elaine Walster (1972). They showed college students photographs of attractive students, average students, and unattractive students, and asked them to rate the people in the photos on 27 personality traits. As expected, the attractive people received the most positive ratings.

Cunningham (1986) had male college students rate photographs of beauty contest finalists and ordinary-looking college women, and then analyzed the differences in facial features between the two groups. One way that they differed was that the beauty contest women tended to have "widely spaced eyes, small noses, small chins, wide pupils, high eyebrows, and a big smile." These features were associated with positive personality ratings, such as intelligent, sociable, and assertive. Thus, overall, research supports the claim that beautiful people are perceived as having excellent personalities.

Attribution

Are we able to observe a person's behavior and somehow decide what that person is really like? How do we attribute a person's personality to his or her behaviors? Attribution is the social cognitive process of determining the causes of behavior of other people and understanding their motives and personality (Jones, 1990). Essentially, we are interested in attributing the motivation for a behavior to either situational or dispositional factors. *Situational factors* involve the external environment, whereas *dispositional factors* involve the individual's internal personality. Common sense tells us that there are many times that we want to know whether a person's behavior is due to external or internal causes. For example, if someone does poorly on an exam, is it because the test is very difficult (external) or the individual does not know the material well (internal)? Through attribution, we are able to predict what a person is likely to do in a given situation, and we gain a better understanding of the person's motivation for engaging in certain behaviors.

Correspondent Inference Theory   Often we are interested in knowing more about an individual's personality. We usually observe the individual's behavior and then make inferences about his or her motivation and personality based on what we observe. Jones and Davis (1965), in their theory of correspondent inference, suggested that attribution is often successful because we focus on certain types of behaviors. People have many traits in common, but we tend to focus on the ways in which a person is unique or different from others. For example, try to describe the personality of someone who drives a car to work every day. It's a very difficult task, since many people drive cars to work. Now, try to describe the personality of someone who rides a lion to work every day.

Jones and Davis also suggested that we tend to focus on behaviors that could have only one motive. For example, Mary just accepted a new position. Let's assume that the new position is in a very attractive part of the country, consists of interesting work, and pays an extremely high salary. Why did she accept the new job? She might have any of several reasons. But let's assume that the new position is in an unattractive part of the country, consists of boring work, and pays an extremely high salary. We now most likely assume that Mary is interested in money.

Covariation Theory   Often the main task in attribution is to determine whether a person's behavior was caused by internal or external motives. Harold Kelley (1973) proposed a covariation theory to account for *causal attribution*. Kelley suggested we consider three factors (consensus, consistency, and distinctiveness) in determining whether a behavior was internally or externally motivated. Often these factors will covary (occur together), helping us to predict causation. Consensus is the extent to which other people react in the same way the subject does in a particular situation. Consistency is the extent to which the subject always behaves the same way in a particular situation. And distinctiveness is the extent to which the subject reacts the same way in other situations.

FIGURE 15.3   Causal Attribution

	Internal	External
Consensus	Low Others do not act this way in this situation	High Most others act this way in this situation
Consistency	High Person always acts same way in this situation	High Person always acts same way in this situation
Distinctiveness	Low Person acts same way in other situations	High Person does not act same way in other situations

Kelley stated that the factors of consensus, consistency, and distinctiveness must be considered in determining whether a behavior is internally or externally motivated.

If we conclude that we have conditions of low consensus, high consistency, and low distinctiveness, we attribute the subject's behavior to internal causes. If we have high consensus, high consistency, and high distinctiveness, then we attribute the person's behavior to external causes. For example, the mail carrier takes one look at your big dog and runs off down the street. If no one else avoids your dog (low consensus), the mail carrier always avoids your dog (high consistency), and he or she avoids all dogs (low distinctiveness), we conclude that he or she is afraid of dogs. If however, everyone avoids your dog, the mail carrier avoids your dog, and he or she doesn't avoid other dogs, we would conclude that the mail carrier is afraid of your dog because your dog is a vicious animal who bites people. Apparently, the process of attribution is so ingrained in us that we often don't realize that we use it. Some research, however, suggests that we often jump to conclusions rather than analyze all of the potential influences on behavior (Lupfer & colleagues, 1990).

Attribution Bias   In general, when trying to explain the behavior of others we often overestimate the role of disposition (personality, inner motivation) and underestimate the role of situation (external environment). This bias is called the fundamental attribution error (Ross, 1977). For instance, what if you asked a librarian a question and were met with a sharp, sarcastic reply? Chances are that you would explain this behavior as due to his unpleasant personality (disposition) rather than the possibility that he had a rough day or the job is very demanding (situation).

An interesting finding is that the fundamental attribution error holds true when we observe others, but not when we perceive our own behavior. If the person sitting next to you in class did poorly on an exam, you would probably conclude that he or she was not very bright. But what if you did poorly on an exam? Perhaps you might think the test was tricky, the instructor misled you, or there was not enough time to finish it. We tend to attribute the behavior of other people to internal causes, while we often attribute our own behavior to external causes. This tendency is sometimes called actor-observer bias (Jones & Nisbett, 1972). If we are aware of this attribution bias tendency, we can make more accurate attributions.

Attribution, Success, and Failure   Bernard Weiner (1974, 1986) described a model of attribution that focuses on the causes of success and failure. In addition to the internal-external dimension (disposition-situation), he added a stable-unstable dimension to the model, as well as a controllability component. Essentially, we can attribute a behavior to effort (internal-unstable), luck (external-unstable), ability (internal-stable) or task difficulty (external-stable). In addition, each outcome could be due to controllable or uncontrollable factors. For

FIGURE 15.4   Weiner's Theory of Attribution

According to Weiner, success or failure can be attributed to an internal or external locus of control as well as to a stable or unstable personality. He also added a controllability factor, generally stating that success is due to internal controllable factors and failure to external uncontrollable factors.

instance, to what would we attribute the success of the school's football team's perfect record? We might agree it was due to effort (internal-unstable-controllable cause) or ability (internal-stable-uncontrollable cause). What if the team had not won any games? Perhaps we would suggest it was due to bad luck (external-unstable-uncontrollable cause) or having to play away games (external-unstable-uncontrollable cause). Weiner's theory has been supported by research studies in many countries (Schuster & colleagues, 1989).

Research indicates that we tend to attribute success to internal causes and failure to external causes. This tendency is called the self-serving bias. For instance, if you receive a high grade on a term paper, you are likely to attribute your success to your own ability and effort, but if you receive a low grade, you probably will blame the instructor.

We don't like to experience failure, especially if it is due to our own lack of ability. Sometimes people prepare for failure by using the self-handicapping strategy (Baumeister & Scher, 1988). They behave in ways that produce obstacles to success so that when they eventually do fail, they can place blame on the obstacle and not their own lack of ability. For example, a student who stays up all night studying can blame his poor test performance on fatigue rather than lack of knowledge. A cross-country runner who goes to a party the night before a big meet can blame a poor running time on lack of sleep rather than her lack of ability. And should the person perform well, his or her success is even more impressive, since he or she had to overcome the obstacle to achieve it.

ATTITUDES

We may like carrots but dislike broccoli, and we may approve of a president's personality but disapprove of his or her politics. Our feelings, thoughts, and behavioral tendencies toward other people, objects, or ideas constitute our <u>attitudes</u>. Attitudes are learned dispositions that actively guide us toward specific behaviors (Shavitt, 1990). They help us to interpret our world and to make appropriate decisions about it. Petty and Cacioppo (1985) suggested that attitudes consist of long-lasting, general evaluations of people, objects, or issues.

The *ABC model* of attitudes divides the concept of attitude into three distinct components: affect, behavior, and cognition (Breckler, 1984). The affective component refers to our emotional reactions. The behavioral component refers to our actions that carry out our evaluations. The cognitive component refers to the thinking aspect of forming an attitude. Affect, behavior, and cognition are present in almost every attitude we have. Consider your attitude toward marijuana. All three components will be present: you will have affective responses to marijuana (you will either view it as pleasant or unpleasant); you will have behavioral responses (you will either use it yourself or refrain from using it); and you will have cognitions about marijuana (you will believe either that it is harmful or that it is harmless).

FIGURE 15.5 ABC Model of an Attitude

Attitudes are learned dispositions that involve affect, behavior, and cognition. The three components can be found in all attitudes, and interrelate with each other.

Social psychologists have generally assumed that attitudes automatically predict behavior (Greenwald, 1989). For instance, people vote for the candidate they believe is most qualified, and marry people with whom they fall in love. Sometimes, however, the link between attitude and behavior appears weak. For example, many people who smoke cigarettes believe that smoking is bad for their health. Ajzen and Fishbein (1977) pointed out that the more specific the attitude, the more likely it is that it will accurately predict a specific behavior. For example, if you like mushrooms on pizza (a specific attitude), you are likely to ask for mushrooms when you order a pizza, but if you enjoy music (a general attitude), it would be difficult to predict which new CD you might purchase.

Attitude Formation

Obviously, no one is born with a clear set of attitudes. Psychologists suspect that early childhood experiences are related to the development of attitudes, although later experiences can modify and sometimes change them radically. Both classical and operant conditioning are involved in attitude formation (Baron & Byrne, 1991).

Some attitudes are formed as a result of direct contact: a person severely frightened by a dog in childhood may continue to fear dogs throughout life. However, most attitudes are learned indirectly from other people. Parents teach certain attitudes deliberately—controlling television viewing, selecting playmates, or sending children to special schools. McGuire (1985) pointed out the close similarity of the political attitudes of parents and children. But parents can also contribute to attitude development in quite inadvertent ways. The mother who encourages her daughter to play with dolls and wear frilly "feminine" clothes is laying the groundwork for a particular sex-role attitude, although she may be totally unconscious of doing so. The father whose behavior encourages his son to avoid doing the dishes or housecleaning because they are "woman's chores" is also fostering sex-role attitudes.

Schools and peer groups play an important part in attitude development, for children learn a great deal about life by observing and interacting with their teachers and with other children. The social learning theory proposes that the mass media have a powerful influence in shaping attitudes (Roberts & Maccoby, 1985). In 98 percent of all American homes, the occupants view a television set an average of 6 hours a day. Some psychologists think we learn attitudes toward violence from television. For example, between the ages of 5 and 14 the average child witnesses the annihilation of thousands of human beings on the television screen. This must have some effect on the child.

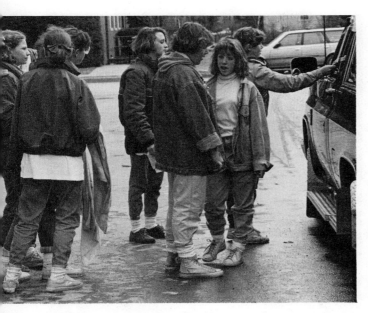

FIGURE 15.6   Attitude Formation
Parents, families, schools, peer groups, and the mass media all contribute to the formation of attitudes in an individual.

Another way we form attitudes is through inadvertent learning. We adopt attitudes toward people or events because we associate them with pleasant or unpleasant experiences. For instance, we may adopt a negative attitude toward the Republican party because we didn't like the food at a fund-raising dinner, or we may form a favorable view of a city we have visited simply because the weather was great and we met people we liked.

Attitude Measurement

Since attitudes involve cognitions and emotions, they cannot be studied easily. Psychologists have devised several techniques for measuring attitudes. One approach is simply to ask people what their attitudes are, either by interview or by questionnaire. Interviews are particularly useful for in-depth studies of small numbers of people; questionnaires are quicker to complete and more useful for larger samples. If the questionnaire is given to a representative number of people, the findings can serve as a useful indicator of the attitudes of the general population. As we discussed in chapter 1, "The Study of Psychology," one problem with interviews and questionnaires is that we cannot always be sure that people are telling the truth.

To reduce the risk of inaccuracy in their findings, psychologists sometimes use *projective techniques* in studying attitudes. The idea here is to get people to project their attitudes in a way that they may not recognize, but that the trained psychologist will. For example, the subjects might be given a set of incomplete sentences to finish; their answers sometimes reveal truer attitudes than when they are questioned directly.

Social psychologists also use *behavioral measures*, which involve observing a person's actual behavior. For example, they might measure people's willingness to sign petitions or attend a rally for a particular cause. Or they might observe where a person ate and conclude that he or she had a positive attitude about the chosen restaurant. Fast-food chains and soft-drink companies use behavioral measures when they ask people to engage in taste tests and use the results to indicate attitude preferences.

Social psychologists often use *attitude scales*, which consist of a series of statements expressing attitudes toward a particular issue. On a *Likert Scale* the subjects are asked to indicate their degree of agreement or disagreement with each of the statements, often using a five-point scale ranging from "strongly agree" to "strongly disagree." The responses are then computed, and the subjects can be ranked as having favorable or unfavorable attitudes toward the issue in question.

Attitude Change

People are bombarded from all directions by advertisements and persuasive communications designed to change their attitudes (and ultimately their behavior). As we watch television or listen to the radio, we are exposed to countless advertisements that try to convince us to use specific products or vote for particular candidates. Psychologists are involved actively in these campaigns to change attitudes and behaviors. What is the most effective way to alter someone's attitude? The research into attitude change is divided usually into three areas: the source of the communication (the communicator), the communication itself (the message), and the receiver of the communication (the audience).

The Communicator   What are the characteristics of the successful communicator? Research suggests that successful communicators are credible, trustworthy, attractive, and similar to their audience (Petty & Cacioppo, 1981). The higher the communicator's social status and expertise, the more credible his or her message becomes. This is why advertisers use testimonials from professionals, as well as from popular athletes and entertainers.

We are more influenced also by someone we trust. Hence, as Wood and Eagly (1981) report, we look for what the communicator has to gain if we are persuaded; we are influenced more readily by someone who does not have a great deal to gain. For example, we would probably be more influenced to purchase a new Ford if the president of General Motors, rather than the president of Ford, urged us to do so. Obviously, the president of General Motors has nothing to gain (and in fact much to lose) if we purchase a car from Ford.

We are persuaded more easily by attractive people, as demonstrated by Chaiken (1979), who asked college students to persuade other students to sign a petition. She found that those students who were most attractive were significantly more successful at persuading others to sign a petition than those who were unattractive. We like attractive people and perceive them as being friendly, trustworthy, and more like ourselves; thus we can identify with them more easily, and therefore trust the message.

The Message   When trying to change attitudes, what is said is as important as who says it. Research on the message has focused on how different it is from the audience's previous views, whether opposition evidence should be included, and how emotional it should be. Rajecki (1989) argued that attitudes are changed much more easily by mild persuasion (soft sell) than by a barrage of extreme propaganda (hard sell). Some religious and political groups overlook this fact and run the risk of being dismissed as fanatics.

Should we use two-sided arguments, or only present our own case? Often this choice depends on the audience. If our audience already favors our views, then a one-sided argument is more effective. If the audience is unfavorably disposed toward them, however, it is best to use the two-sided approach, as this gives us more credibility and helps build an immunity to the claims of the opposing side.

If we need to present both sides of an argument (or if someone else is presenting the other side), which side should be presented first for maximum impact? Petty and Cacioppo (1981) pointed out that if the attitude measurement is to take place several days after the talks, the primacy effect prevails and the side presented first is remembered best. However, if there is a length of time between the first and second talk, and the attitude measurement takes place immediately after the second talk, it has more impact due to the recency effect.

Under some conditions, the use of fear and other emotional appeals might change attitudes. Fear alone is likely to cause people to avoid the message completely. However, if the fear is coupled with instructions of what to do about it, it may be effective. For example, Leventhal, Singer, and Jones (1965) reported that college students were more likely to obtain a tetanus shot when presented with a warning, or fear, message about the danger of lockjaw caused by an infected cut, coupled with instructions about how to get the shot, than when they were presented with the fear message only or the instruc-

FIGURE 15.7   Attitude Change
Research on attitude change focuses on the communicator, the message, and the audience. Many variables interact to determine whether or not the audience will change its mind. President George Bush's approval rating underwent a dramatic reverse in 1991: according to *Washington Post–ABC News* polls, Bush had a reelection approval rating of 68 percent at the end of the Persian Gulf War (in February); by late October this rating had fallen to 47 percent.

tion to report for shots only. But emotional appeals do not always work, and more research is needed before we can draw definite conclusions.

The Audience   It appears that some people are persuaded more easily than others. It is easier to convince people who have a need for a product. For example, if you are in the market for a new car, you will be motivated to listen to car advertisements. Other research has shown that people with a high need for social approval will often be persuaded because they want others to like them. And, in general, more intelligent people will be more resistant to persuasion than less intelligent people. However, there are many individual differences, and at the present time the conclusions in this area are still somewhat tentative. For instance, Baumeister and Covington (1985) found that people with high self-esteem were as easily persuaded as people with low self-esteem, but the people with high self-esteem did not want to admit it. And Eagly and Carli (1981) reported that men were no more or less likely to change their attitudes than women were.

Cognitive Dissonance

What is the underlying basis of attitude change? Leon Festinger theorized about attitude changes in his book, *A Theory of Cognitive Dissonance* (1957). According to Festinger, the essence of persuasion consists of introducing into a person's mind material that, though inconsistent with existing attitudes, is difficult to dismiss. Some people are able to ignore inconsistencies, at least to some extent, but most people find that when they have two psychologically inconsistent ideas they will experience cognitive dissonance, an uncomfortable psychological state characterized by tension and conflict.

Cognitive Dissonance Theory   Naturally, individuals in such an unpleasant state will try to remove the source of their dissonance. They may do this either by changing one or the other of their dissonant (conflicting) attitudes or by adopting additional attitudes that will help reconcile the conflicting elements. As an example, Festinger cites the case of a cigarette smoker who is presented with evidence that smoking causes cancer. This

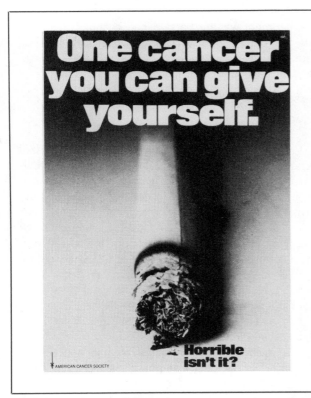

FIGURE 15.8 Cognitive Dissonance
Festinger's theory of cognitive dissonance predicts that when people hold two inconsistent beliefs, they experience tension that drives them to reconcile their thoughts. Anti-smoking campaigns produce dissonance for smokers who enjoy smoking but know it is harmful.

arouses cognitive dissonance, as the person does not wish to believe that the habit may be deadly. The smoker has several options. He or she can stop smoking, disbelieve the cancer report, or reason that the pleasures of smoking make the risk of cancer worthwhile.

Another example of how cognitive dissonance can be aroused is when a person acts in ways that conflict with stated attitudes. In this case, the theory predicts that the person will change attitudes so that they will be consistent with existing behavior. The more willingly the person engages in behavior that is contrary to his or her attitudes, the more cognitive dissonance will be experienced, and the more he or she will be motivated to change attitudes.

Festinger and Carlsmith (1959) illustrated this principle in their classic study, in which they paid subjects who had engaged in an extremely boring, senseless experiment to tell other subjects that the experiment had been exciting and fun. The subjects were paid either $20 or $1. Cognitive-dissonance theory predicted that if a subject was paid $20, the money would justify that person telling a lie and hence no dissonance would be experienced: the subject told a lie and was paid $20 for it. On the other hand, if the subject were paid $1, that would not justify the lie, and dissonance would be produced.

Later, the subjects were interviewed and asked their true feelings about the experiment. As predicted, the high-dissonance group reported that the experiment had been interesting and worthwhile, while the low-dissonance group, as well as a control group who were not asked to lie, felt the experiment was boring. The high-dissonance group had apparently adjusted their attitudes about the task, making them consistent with their actions.

Cooper and Fazio (1984) reported that the experience of dissonance is dependent upon two conditions. First, the behavior must lead to an aversive consequence (in Festinger's study, lying to someone would be aversive). Second, the person must assume personal responsibility in choosing the behavior (in Festinger and Carlsmith's study, the subjects could say no). Scher and Cooper (1989) stated that when a person chooses an action that turns out poorly, he or she feels responsible, and dissonance occurs. For example, let's assume that a store sells two new music CDs that you want and you purchase one of them. If when you get home and listen to it you are disappointed with it, you will probably be sorry that you didn't select the other CD, and you will likely experience dissonance.

Application of Cognitive Dissonance   Festinger's theory of cognitive dissonance spurred many other psychologists to research the applications of this theory. For instance, Axsom and Cooper (1985) had some patients in a weight-loss program exert a great effort on a task at an initial meeting while others did not.

BIOGRAPHICAL HIGHLIGHT

Leon Festinger was born in New York City in 1919. Being interested in psychology, he started college at the City College of New York, and after getting his bachelor's degree, went to the State University of Iowa, where he obtained his Ph.D. in 1942. He taught at a number of universities before going to Stanford University in 1955. In 1968 he went to the New School for Social Research in New York City, where he remained until his death in 1990.

Although Festinger contributed a large number of concepts and theories to the field of social psychology, probably none has had greater impact that his ideas from his 1957 book, *Theory of Cognitive Dissonance*. Festinger viewed people as thinking individuals who need to have balance in their thoughts as well as their actions. This idea of balance is key to his theory of cognitive dissonance. Much research is still being conducted today in social psychology to answer some of the questions that cognitive dissonance has raised.

LEON FESTINGER

Six months later, those who engaged in the difficult task were more committed to the weight-loss program and had lost significantly more weight than those who did not have to do the task. Apparently the successful weight-loss subjects experienced cognitive dissonance because of their extra effort, and this led them to continue to work on losing weight.

Elliott Aronson described some excellent examples of cognitive dissonance applied to an educational setting in his 1991 book, *The Social Animal*. Aronson described the typical classroom procedure: If teachers want students to learn, they often give them large amounts of external rewards. For example, when students perform well on a test, teachers give them As, gold stars, or praise. But perhaps students learn their lessons only to obtain the high grades. Aronson suggests that if teachers provide inadequate rewards, the students will still learn, but for internal justification, not external rewards. In other words, if students can be convinced to learn without receiving high grades for the assignment, dissonance is produced that can be eliminated when the students feel they actually enjoy the work. Inadequate rewards may influence many attitudes and behaviors in our society.

Self-Perception Theory Cognitive dissonance theory provided an explanation of attitude change, and has been widely accepted. Daryl Bem (1967) proposed an alternative explanation in his self-perception theory. He suggested that the formation and change in our attitudes are often based on our perceptions of our own behavior. For example, if we move into a new home and grow roses in our garden, we assume we must like roses and thus have a positive attitude toward them. In his reanalysis of Festinger and Carlsmith's original study,

Bem argued that subjects who received the larger sum of money ($20) perceived themselves as being motivated mainly by money, whereas those receiving the smaller amount of money ($1) perceived that they really believed the experiment was fun, and hence changed their attitudes. Self-perception theory is most applicable in cases where we don't already have strong attitudes toward something (Tybout & Scott, 1983).

Prejudice

Prejudice is an attitude of special interest to social psychologists. Prejudice is an unjustified attitude involving a fixed, usually negative, way of thinking about a person or object. Prejudices do not easily adjust to new information or experience; instead, new facts are either readjusted to fit into the existing pattern of prejudice or simply ignored. For example, if racially prejudiced persons encounter a pleasant member of a disliked group, they will more than likely view him or her as "an exception to the rule" rather than change their attitude toward the group as a whole.

Like all attitudes, prejudice has affective, behavioral, and cognitive components. The affective component of prejudice includes negative feelings, such as anger, hate, or disgust. The cognitive component of prejudice is the stereotype, an exaggerated and rigid mental image of a particular group of persons or objects. The stereotype is applied indiscriminantly to all members of the category and is often used to justify the negative feelings and behavior toward the group (Devine, 1989). Discrimination refers to the unfair behaviors toward members of the group. Common forms of prejudice include racism, sexism, and ageism. People with disabilities, people with AIDS, gay men and lesbians, and people with uncommon religious faiths are sometimes victims of prejudice.

Causes of Prejudice Prejudice appears to have many causes; even individuals with the same prejudice can have different reasons for it. For example, usually people like people who resemble themselves or those they think resemble themselves. This generalization extends not only to similarities in skin color or other physical attributes, but also to tastes, interests, beliefs, attitudes, and values. Research has shown that we assume that individuals of our race share our attitudes and that those of a different race share different attitudes (Brewer, 1986). Another source of prejudice is the mutuality of attitudes in the community or subculture in which the individual is raised. Psychologists have discovered regional, cultural, and group differences in prejudiced attitudes. Individuals who move to different areas or become identified with different groups tend to alter their prejudiced attitudes to conform to the norms, or standards, of their new social environment.

Much of this culturally based prejudice is transmitted to a child at an early age by parents, neighbors, peers, schools, the media, and other influences. The transmission does not need to involve direct teaching. Instead, children receive approval and disapproval for associating with particular playmates. They overhear conversations of adults, imitate their behavior, and take on their attitudes and thoughts.

Overcoming Prejudice The government has enlisted the help of psychologists in dealing with racial prejudice, a real problem for a multiracial country devoted to the ideal of the individual's equal rights and opportunities. Psychologists have studied prejudiced people and tried to learn what causes prejudice and what functions it serves. They have discovered, for example, that prejudiced people lump other people into easily identifiable or stereotyped groups and treat them all alike, rather than as individuals. A racially prejudiced employer, for example, may simplify decisions about hiring by simply rejecting all applicants of a different race.

What can be done to decrease intergroup prejudice? Allport (1954) proposed the *contact theory*, which included three conditions necessary for the reduction of intergroup hostility. First, there must be close contact on a regular basis (such as in school, at work, and in living situations). Second, there must be cooperative interdependence, in which the groups need each other to accomplish goals. And third, the contact must take place in a situation where both groups have equal status. A number of recent research programs have confirmed this theory. For instance, Cook (1984) studied students in a school system and found that the contact over a period of

time decreased racial prejudice. Brewer and Miller (1984) pointed out that the requirement of equal status can be very difficult to achieve when the different groups impose artificial barriers between themselves and others. For instance, in a school system, students might have certain dress codes for their particular group and might ignore those who do not wear appropriate clothes (because of cultural or economic reasons).

Social psychologists have worked hard to reduce racial prejudice. Kenneth Clark, emeritus professor of psychology of the City College of New York, has established a firm to help promote successful race relations. Clark has also written a number of books that explain the dangers of prejudice, in the hope of educating people and reducing the incidence of prejudice. Still, research shows that prejudice continues to be a problem in America (Hochschild & Herk, 1989).

Sex Roles and Stereotypes People sometimes hold beliefs about what men and women should be like. Often these sex stereotypes are learned as children but continue to influence the behavior of adults. For example, some people believe that women are overly emotional, and men are interested only in money. Often the sex stereotype characteristics of women are more negative than those of men (Heilman & colleagues, 1988).

Sandra Bem (1974) developed the *Bem Sex-Role Inventory (BSRI)*, a 60-adjective sex-role questionnaire to measure feminine and masculine traits in people. She found that specific traits were stereotypically associated with each sex. Feminine traits include being gentle, sensitive, warm, and soft-spoken, and loving children. Masculine traits include being ambitious, dominant, competitive, aggressive, and having leadership qualities. Bem found that while many people score high on either the feminine or masculine scale, some people score high on both stereotype scales, a personality characteristic called androgyny. Bem suggested that masculine individuals tend to do better in assertive situations, feminine people tend to do well in nurturing situations, and androgynous individuals do well in both types of situations. People who are androgynous are less likely to be influenced by sex stereotypes (Bem, 1975).

Research has shown that, like racism, sexism continues to be a problem in our society. Zinkhan and Stoiadin (1984) found that if a man and woman are waiting for service in a department store, the man is significantly more likely to be served first. Many studies have documented the bias that exists against hiring women for all types of employment. Kluegel and Smith (1986) argued that beliefs and stereotypes about women are often part of historical traditions, but are not readily acknowledged by most people. Presumably, continuing research and education will play a major role in helping to reduce prejudice of all kinds.

FIGURE 15.9   Gender Identity
Gender identity, or sex role, is an important part of our personality. The sex roles of men and women are not as divergent as was once believed. Researchers such as Sandra Bem show people can have traits of both sexes. Men in today's society no longer feel their identity threatened by performing tasks once believed to be strictly feminine.

SOCIAL INFLUENCE

A great deal of human social encounters consist of influencing and being influenced by other people. We try to persuade our friends to go to the movies with us. We often ask favors of our friends. We are likely to obey people in authority, such as police, teachers, and parents. Attempts at changing the attitudes or behavior of others can be thought of as social influence (Cialdini, 1988). The areas of social influence that have been most thoroughly studied include conformity, compliance, and obedience.

Conformity

Conformity has been studied extensively by social psychologists. Conformity is defined as the changing of one's behavior in order to fit social norms or expectations more closely. It is a major type of social influence. We know that we conform to social expectations a good deal of the time.

Social psychologist Solomon Asch conducted a classic experiment on conformity in 1955. He assembled several groups, each composed of seven college students. Each group was presented with a series of 18 cards on which four lines were drawn. One of the lines on each card was the "standard" and the other three were comparison lines. One of the comparison lines was the same length as the standard line, and each student had to declare aloud which comparison line matched the standard line in each case. But six of the seven subjects in each group were actually Asch's accomplices and had been coached beforehand to give incorrect answers on 12 of the 18 trials. For the first two cards, there was unanimous agreement. But then the accomplices started agreeing on wrong answers on most of the remaining cards.

The subjects who were not accomplices yielded to the majority and gave a wrong answer on 36.8 percent or more of the trials. (Subjects in a control group, by contrast, made mistakes less than 1 percent of the time.) There were considerable personal differences: some subjects yielded to the majority all the time, some yielded only part of the time, and about 25 percent maintained their independence as a minority of one.

Why did some subjects seem to disbelieve the evidence of their senses? When Asch interviewed them, they gave three types of reasons for bowing to group pressure. Some believed the majority was wrong, but did not want to be "different" by giving the right answer. A second group, which included most of the subjects, did not trust their own judgment when the majority disagreed. They thought they knew the right answer but were not sufficiently sure of themselves. A third group suffered from an actual distortion of perception and claimed to perceive the lines the way the majority seemed to.

We often conform for two basic reasons: to be liked by others (normative influence) and to show appropriate behavior (informational influence). With normative influence, we learn that it is rewarding to be accepted and punishing to be rejected. If we deviate, we are subjected immediately to group pressure to conform. Thus, we alter our behavior to meet social expectations. With informational influence, whenever we are unsure of ourselves in a new situation, we look to others to see how things are done. We internalize the appropriate norms and adopt the expected role. We alter our behavior to match what others are doing.

Leon Festinger accounts for this latter type of conformity in his social comparison theory. We all have a need to evaluate the correctness of our opinions and the worth of our abilities. If some standard exists by which we can make these evaluations—a score on an examination, for

FIGURE 15.10   Asch's Conformity Study

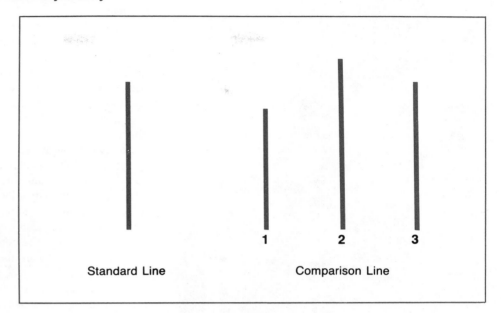

Solomon Asch (1955) found that subjects yielded to a majority over one-third of the time and give wrong answers in a line comparison task. Which of the lines on the right is equal in length to the line on the left?

Standard Line   Comparison Line

example—we will use it. But how do we assess the correctness or adequacy of our views about politics, religion, athletic ability, or our social skills? We look to the other people around us. We ask their opinions, examine their performance, and compare our own behavior with theirs. Since everyone does this, our attitudes and behavior tend to converge, and we remain pretty much like one another. Festinger's theory also suggests why cultural norms retain their cohesion: we all validate them constantly to ensure that they will guide us through an ambiguous world.

Compliance

When an insurance salesperson visits my home, first he tells me how nice it is; then he compliments me on my three beautiful children. Just before he gets down to work, usually he asks for a small favor—a glass of water or to use the bathroom. These actions are designed for my compliance and to get me ready to comply by signing on the dotted line. Compliance is a type of social influence in which an individual changes his or her behavior because of a direct request from someone else. There are a number of techniques that can be used to obtain compliance, including ingratiation, multiple requests, and low-balling. Most of the techniques work much of the time with most people.

Ingratiation   The salesperson described above seeks to obtain compliance through ingratiation. He attempts to get me to like him by complimenting me on my

home and children. Ingratiation is any technique that increases the attractiveness of a person trying to seek compliance from us. Ingratiation might include giving compliments, doing favors, agreeing with someone, or just being nice.

Multiple Requests   Often *multiple requests* are made in order to obtain compliance. The salesperson asked for a small favor (a drink of water) before he made the big request (buying insurance). This compliance technique of first making a small request and then making a large request is called the foot-in-the-door technique. A study by Freedman and Fraser (1966) demonstrates the effectiveness of this method. They called homemakers on the phone and asked them to answer several simple questions about the soap products that they used in their home. This was the small request. A few days later, they called back and asked if a 5-person crew could come into the person's home and take a complete inventory of all the products in the house. What would you say to such an enormous request? Almost 53 percent of the subjects agreed to this second request, compared to only 22 percent of a control group who had not been asked for a small request earlier.

In getting customers to buy more, salespersons frequently make a small request followed by a large request. For example, they might encourage you to purchase a relatively inexpensive model of their product, and then, when you agree, begin to talk about the advantages of the higher-priced model, or about all the accessories that you will certainly need. This technique is very effective when the salespersons have the time to

FIGURE 15.11 Compliance
Research indicates that one way to obtain compliance is to first make a small request and follow it with a large request. This is called the foot-in-the-door technique.

implement it. But can it also work when they don't have time to talk someone into it?

Psychologists Robert Cialdini and David Schroeder (1976) tested this idea in an experiment with solicitors for contributions to the American Cancer Society. They reasoned that if they could get people to contribute anything, they might get them to contribute more. Thus, they had two teams of solicitors (each team consisting of a male and female college student) use a standard request ("I'm collecting money for the American Cancer Society. Would you be willing to help by giving a donation?"). Another two teams used the same approach, but added the phrase "Even a penny will help" at the end. Forty-two people were canvassed with each approach.

Which approach was more effective? With the standard approach, 12 out of 42 people donated, while with the "Even a penny will help" approach, the teams received 21 contributions (out of 42 tries). Clearly, the small-favor approach worked to increase contributions. But if the contributions were smaller (since even pennies were acceptable), then it still might not be as effective as the regular pitch. The standard approach earned a total of $18.55, while the penny approach earned a total of $30.34. Cialdini and Schroeder suggested that saying "Even a penny would help" was the equivalent of asking for a small favor, and once a person made the decision to help, he or she would actually contribute a larger amount because he or she didn't want to appear cheap.

Some research suggests that the foot-in-the-door effect is due to a change in self-perception, in which people view themselves as more helpful after they respond to an initial small request (Eisenberg & colleagues, 1987). Then they are motivated to be consistent, and hence also help with a later large request. The foot-in-the-door technique is not always effective, however. Some research suggests that if the first request results in a bad experience for the person solicited, he or she is less likely to comply with the second request (Crano & Sivacek, 1982).

Surprisingly, the opposite technique is also successful. The compliance technique of first making a large request and then making a small request is called the door-in-the-face technique, or the rejection-then-retreat technique (Cialdini, 1988). Suppose someone comes to the door and asks you to subscribe to an expensive magazine for 3 years. After you refuse, he or she then asks if you will buy the current issue. Chances are good that you will comply with this second small request. Cialdini and his colleagues demonstrated the effectiveness of this technique in a 1975 study. When they approached college students and asked them if they would volunteer to serve as counselors for several hours a week for the next 2 years, none of them agreed. Then they asked the students if they would take a group of delinquents to the zoo. About 50 percent agreed to this smaller request, compared to only about 17 percent of a control group who had not received the larger request first.

Cialdini (1988) described a number of situations in which the door-in-the-face technique is often used. Labor negotiators might make extreme demands at first and then settle for more realistic requests later. Cialdini also described television scriptwriters who deliberately put extreme statements in their scripts, knowing the censors would delete them, so they then could keep the statements they really wanted in the first place.

The Low-ball Procedure A technique called the low-ball procedure is also used to obtain compliance. When shopping for insurance, I found that three salespersons quoted me a very low price. When I told them to write the policy, they suddenly "discovered" an error, and the premium was actually significantly higher. Often, people will continue to make the purchase even if it is more expensive. Cialdini (1988) described a couple of low-balling techniques used by some automobile salespersons. Sometimes the customer is offered a great deal and is encouraged to like the car, then an error is "discovered" and the price is several hundred dollars higher than originally stated. Or an overgenerous trade-in allowance is offered, and when the new car is picked up, a "reevaluation" reduces the allowance by several hundred dollars. Since the customer really wants the new car, chances are good he or she will go ahead with the higher-priced deal anyway.

Cialdini and his colleagues (1978) tested the effectiveness of the low-balling technique on college students enrolled in a psychology course. They called the subjects on the phone and asked them to participate in an experiment for which they would get credit for the course. After the subjects agreed, they were told the study would start at 7 A.M. Over 55 percent of the subjects showed up for their appointments, compared to only about 24 percent of control subjects who were told about the 7 A.M. time *before* agreeing to participate.

The That's-Not-All Technique   Have you ever seen something in a store you were considering purchasing, but, before you decided, the sales clerk added a bonus to sweeten the deal? If so, you have experienced the "that's-not-all" compliance technique. In the that's-not-all procedure, a deal is presented, and then, while the person is considering it, the phrase "that's not all" is added to the pitch. Jerry Burger (1986) tested this technique with a study in which college students held a psychology bake sale on campus. In a control condition, people who asked the price of cupcakes were told that a prepackaged set of one cupcake and two cookies were being sold for 75 cents. In the that's-not-all experimental condition, students were told that a cupcake cost 75 cents. Then, before the students could respond, they were told that they could get a cupcake and two cookies for 75 cents. In the control condition, 40 percent of the students bought cupcakes, whereas in the that's-not-all condition, 73 percent bought cupcakes.

By understanding the techniques used to obtain compliance, we can be more free to make our own decisions. Sometimes we are not asked for a favor, but are told what to do. The study of obedience has important implications for social psychology.

Obedience

When Adolf Eichmann was on trial for his role in the mass murder of Jews in Nazi Germany during World War II, he justified his action by stating that he was "just following orders." At the My Lai massacre during the Vietnam War, American troops led by Lieutenant William

FIGURE 15.12   Proximity Effect on Obedience

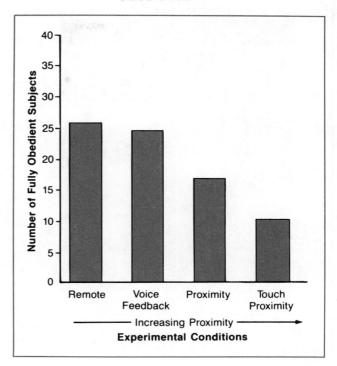

Milgram conducted four studies that examined the effect of proximity of the victim on the subject's level of obedience. The number of subjects out of 40 in each study who gave the maximum shock levels are presented here. In Experiment 1 (Remote Feedback), the victim-learner could not be seen or heard but pounded on the wall at 300 volts. In Experiment 2 (Voice Feedback), the learner's yells could be heard through the wall. In Experiment 3 (Proximity), the victim was in the same room as the subject. And in Experiment 4 (Touch Proximity), the subject had to hold the learner's hand on a plate for the shock to be delivered.

L. Calley opened fire on unarmed women and children, although there were no enemy forces in the vicinity. When Calley was charged with the crime, his defense was that he believed he was "acting under orders." During the Watergate investigation, some of the defendants claimed that they were following orders, or carrying out the demands of their superiors. Is this kind of behavior the result of a psychopathic personality? Or might a great many of us behave in a similar way in a similar situation?

In this chapter's opening story, we described Stanley Milgram's classic experiment on obedience. In this study, subjects were led to believe that they were participating in an experiment to test the effects of punishment on learning. The subjects served as "teachers," and had to deliver increasingly larger shocks when the "learners" made mistakes on a memory task. Actually, no shocks

BIOGRAPHICAL HIGHLIGHT

STANLEY MILGRAM

Stanley Milgram was born in New York City in 1933. His high school interests centered around science, as evidenced by his earning the school's gold medal in biology. Following graduation from high school he enrolled at Queens College of the City University of New York, where he majored in political science.

Eventually he decided to major in social psychology at Harvard University, where he studied with Solomon Asch and earned a doctorate in 1960. Milgram taught at Yale University and Harvard University before finally settling at the Graduate Center of the City University of New York in 1967.

Milgram conducted a large number of studies in social psychology. Perhaps the best known is his controversial obedience study described in his 1974 book, *Obedience to Authority*. Milgram's research was often creative and original. For example, he dropped letters from a helicopter to measure prejudice, asked people to hand a package to someone they knew to study communication channels, and took photographs of people to study social interactions.

Milgram received numerous awards for his creative contributions to psychology. He produced an award-winning film on his work on urban life and overload. Stanley Milgram died in December 1984 at the age of 51.

were given, and the real purpose of the study was to investigate obedience in the subjects who were the "teachers." As we indicated in our opening story, 65 percent of the subjects continued to deliver shocks at the 450-volt level, even when the "learner" complained of a weak heart and screamed to be released. The study demonstrated obedience to authority.

Milgram had conducted his study at Yale University, and it occurred to him that the subjects might be obeying him because of the prestige of the university and the belief that the experimenters must know what they are doing. To test this idea, he set up his experiment elsewhere—in a run-down office in downtown Bridgeport, Connecticut. This time he claimed to represent a research firm rather than a university. Interestingly, the new subjects proved to be about as obedient as those in his Yale laboratory.

In the light of these findings, the attitude of the American public to the Calley trial should come as no surprise. Just before the trial, a national sample of Americans was asked about a hypothetical situation in which "soldiers in Vietnam are ordered to shoot all inhabitants of a village suspected of assisting the enemy, including old men, women, and children." The subjects were asked what they thought most people would do in that situation. Some 65 percent thought that most Americans would follow orders and shoot; and 51 percent

thought they themselves would shoot women and children under those circumstances. To them, following orders was an obligation that outweighed all other considerations.

In a variation on his original experiment, Milgram (1965) introduced a second "teacher," also an accomplice, who flatly refused to continue to administer shocks when the "learner" protested. When Milgram instructed his real subjects to proceed with the shocks in these new circumstances, 36 out of 40 sided with the other "teacher" and refused to obey orders. This experiment demonstrated that when the subjects administered the electric shocks they were doing so not out of any basic cruelty, but out of simple obedience to authority. They apparently would have preferred not to cause pain, yet they were unable to defy Milgram's orders until there was sufficient social support to justify their actions.

Why do people obey and how can we learn to resist when obedience is destructive? People with authority assume responsibility for decisions and actions, thus allowing others to obey more readily. Milgram argued that we learn to obey people in authority because this often results in positive reinforcement, a connection that most people learn as children. As an experiment, Bushman (1984) had someone stop pedestrians and order them to give a dime to a person who appeared to need it for a parking meter. Significantly more people obeyed when the person giving orders was dressed in a firefighter uniform (nearly 80 percent) than when dressed in a business suit or old clothes (40 percent). The firefighter seemingly had authority and hence was obeyed. Milgram found several factors that might reduce the level of destructive obedience (Sears & colleagues, 1991). Obedience is reduced if the victim's suffering is immediate, if people are made to feel responsible for their own actions, and if people are taught to consider the motives of people in authority. If someone else resists an order for destructive obedience, others are likely to resist also. Some research suggests that personality variables are important when predicting obedience (Blass, 1991). Although there are times when we should obey people in authority, we need to evaluate the situation to decide the most appropriate action.

GROUP PROCESSES

We are highly social animals, and we spend a great deal of our lives in groups—family, friends, classes, clubs, organizations, companies. Not every collection of people is a group, however; a number of people standing in line for a bus is simply an aggregate of individuals. The difference between a group and an aggregate of people lies in the fact that group members perceive themselves as group members who have common goals, and interact with one another (Paulus, 1989).

Every group functions according to norms—the explicit or implicit rules and standards that regulate the behavior of members in the group situation. The norms may vary from group to group and depend on the values and objectives that members consider important and relevant. A weekend pleasure group may stress such norms as instant gratification and the enjoyment of leisure; a business group may stress such norms as deferred gratification for future profit and the value of a decent day's work; a baseball team may stress winning and teamwork.

The degree to which group norms influence an individual's behavior depends to some extent on whether or not the group is a reference group for that person. We all belong to a number of groups—some formal, some informal—but among these groups certain ones are more influential than others. These influential groups, which psychologists call reference groups, are those from which a person derives his or her values, attitudes, and identity. Reference groups may be large—such as a person's race, religion, native country, or political affiliation; or they may be small—such as a club or a team or a group of friends. But regardless of their size or formal status, the reference groups we belong to have a profound influence on our individual behavior.

FIGURE 15.13 Groups
We spend a large amount of time interacting with members of groups. Each group functions according to its own rules (called *norms*).

Group Effectiveness

Most institutions in our society operate on the assumption that "two heads are better than one." Colleges, corporations, and governments are run by committees, in the belief that group decisions are wiser and more efficient than decisions made by an individual working alone. But is this assumption always justified? The answer depends on several factors: the task, the size and composition of the group, the nature of the leadership, and the way the members relate to one another.

Group Tasks Steiner (1972) described several types of tasks that groups might perform, and compared the productivity of groups to that of individuals. In *additive tasks* the contributions of each member are combined into the final group product. For example, pushing an automobile that is stuck in the mud involves the efforts of everyone, and the group is more effective than an individual. In *disjunctive tasks*, there is a single problem for the group to solve. The most competent person in the group usually finds the solution. A group of people working collectively will be more likely to hit on the right answer than one person working alone. For example, a group of people is more likely to solve a difficult crossword puzzle than is a single individual; a group of scientists working on a cure for cancer is more likely to succeed than is a scientist working alone. A *conjunctive task* requires all group members to work toward the goal, and productivity is limited to the least competent member. For example, if a group is tied together when climbing a mountain, every member is essential, and if even one does not keep up, the group is ineffective. Here, often individual performance is better than a group's. Hill (1982) noted that research has confirmed Steiner's divisions, and that in most cases the performance of a group is better than the performance of the average individual (but often worse than that of the best individual).

Brainstorming   Alex Osborn (1957) developed the technique of brainstorming as a means to create innovative ideas in business advertising. Basically, a problem is presented to the group and the members are to come up with as many different solutions as possible in a brief time. Osborn listed several rules, including not allowing criticism during the session and encouraging combinations of previous ideas. Brainstorming has been used in a wide variety of situations and is used in education, business, and social groups. Brainstorming can also be done by individuals, and some research shows that individuals working alone can produce more solutions than can groups (Diehl & Stroebe, 1987).

Groupthink   Psychologist Irving Janis (1982) has pointed out that some group decisions, which he terms groupthink, can be dangerous. Groupthink occurs when the members of a group are so committed to and optimistic about the group that they feel it is invulnerable, and the members are so concerned with maintaining consensus that criticism is muted. McCauley (1989) suggested that groupthink is due to conformity to group expectations and coming to accept the group norms as your own.

According to Janis, an example of groupthink occurred in April 1980 when President Jimmy Carter and his advisers decided to use military force to rescue the U.S. hostages in Iran. The plan was ill-conceived and contained major errors; even though there was some opposition to the plan, the majority of the president's advisers agreed to it and it was put into effect. The plan failed completely. Nearly 20 years earlier, in 1961, one of the worst military and diplomatic blunders in U.S. history was the result of groupthink. President John F. Kennedy, on the advice of a group of brilliant statesmen and advisers, launched the ill-fated invasion of Cuba at the Bay of Pigs. Several members of the group had very strong private

objections to the plan, but the pressures toward unanimity were so great that the dissenters kept silent.

Janis (1982) suggested several precautions to prevent groupthink in group decisions. The leader should encourage members to voice objections and doubts about decisions. The leader should be impartial in discussions, rather than state his or her preference at the outset. If possible, several groups should work independently on the same problem, so different proposals can be evaluated. And, after a decision has been made, a "second chance" meeting should be held to air doubts or alternatives. Janis suggested that groupthink is most dangerous when it occurs in groups setting national policies; therefore these precautions might be unwarranted for simple everyday problem-solving sessions.

Group Polarization   Group discussion can often stimulate ideas that would not have been thought of otherwise, and groups can evaluate critically ideas that an individual might accept too readily. But, on the other hand, a solution may be evaluated according to the status in the group of the person who offers it, rather than according to its merits. It has also been found that groups are more likely to take an extreme position than would an individual by himself or herself.

The tendency for groups to make riskier decisions than an individual would make is called the risky-shift phenomenon (Stoner, 1961). Davis and his colleagues (1976) discussed several possible reasons why risky-shift might occur. In a group situation, people feel less personal responsibility: if something goes wrong, no particular person will be blamed. People in a group generally tend to conform, and individuals do not want to be seen as deviating from the established norm. And it's possible that the group members who are the ones most likely to take risks are the same persons who can influence others to go along with them. Groups can therefore make risky decisions.

Originally, it was believed that groups always tended to move only in more risky directions. More recent research has shown that, although groups are likely to move to the extreme, it can be either the *risky* extreme or the *conservative* extreme (Isenberg, 1986). The tendency for a group to move toward an extreme position is called group polarization. The *persuasive argument* explanation for group polarization suggests that people gain information as the discussion develops, and thus the more persuasive an argument is that is proposed for a particular position, the more likely it will be adopted. The *social comparison* explanation emphasizes the tendency for members to compare their views with others in the group. As they discover that some other members have even more extreme views than they do, they align their opinions with the extreme view to appear as competent as those in the group.

Social Loafing If a single person puts enough energy into a cheer to make a loud noise, theoretically a group of eight people should make a noise eight times as loud. This is not what happens, however. Bibb Latané reported in 1981 that in a group of people each person actually does less than he or she would do alone. This effect is called social loafing. Latané explains social loafing by his theory of social impact, which says that because each member of the group shares the responsibility equally, each individual performs at a somewhat lessened rate.

Cognitive factors also appear to contribute to social loafing. Jackson and Harkins (1985) argued that if people think others are not working as hard as they are, they are likely to also do less. It is likely that when people believe others cannot recognize their contribution they do not feel a responsibility to try hard. Jackson and Williams (1985) reported that social loafing decreased when people believed they contributed something important to the group effort, when individual contributions were identifiable, or when the task was very difficult. It appears that leaders can lessen the effects of social loafing by helping each member of the group feel a sense of importance and responsibility. Harkins and Szymanski (1989) reported that social loafing decreased when members of a group were able to compare their group's performance to that of other groups.

FIGURE 15.14   Social Loafing
When we are part of a group, we tend to contribute less than we would if we were alone, because we feel less responsibility for the outcome of a situation.

APPLICATION

Theory of Social Impact

Bibb Latané has been involved actively in trying to understand the influence of others on social behavior. His early work with John Darley demonstrated that people are less likely to help someone in an emergency if there are other people around. The concept of *diffusion of responsibility* explains the bystander effect by saying that responsibility for helping is equally distributed among all of the people present. Hence, if you are alone, the responsibility of helping or not helping is totally yours, but if you are only one of four people, only 25 percent of it is yours.

Latané has also investigated the phenomenon of *social loafing*, which states that in a group of people each one contributes less than he or she would contribute alone. He found that when eight people clapped their hands, the sound was not eight times as loud as the sound of each one individually, and that in a game of tug-of-war the force was not multiplied by the number of people pulling on the rope.

Latané combined much of his research into a new theory called the *theory of social impact*. There are several principles included in this theory. First, the more people present, the more influence they will have on each individual. Additionally, the more important the people are to the individual, the more influence they will have on him or her. This explains why someone is more nervous when delivering a presentation to a large group of important people than when he or she is delivering it to a small group of friends.

Second, the theory of social impact states that while the impact of others on the individual increases as the number of people increases, the rate of increase in impact grows less as each new individual is added. For example, if you are giving a presentation to three people and a fourth one joins the group, this is more significant than if you were giving a presentation to 31 people and one more joined.

Third, each individual can influence others, but the more people present, the less influence any one individual will have. Thus, we are more likely to listen attentively to a speaker if we are in a small group than if we were in a large group.

Latané has tested his theory of social impact in a variety of situations. In his 1981 paper, he reports that people tip more if they have separate bills than if they share in a group bill. In parties of six, if each person is given an individual bill, the tipping is about 19 percent, while in groups of six with a group bill each individual contributes only about 13 percent.

In another study, Latané tested the hypothesis that Billy Graham would be more effective in front of small audiences. He researched the numbers of people who responded to Graham's appeal for converts in various-sized audiences. He found that when the audiences were small, people were more willing to sign cards allowing local ministers to contact them than when the audiences were large.

Social psychologists are just beginning to research the theory of social impact (Jackson, 1987). Already it has made many predictions that could be useful in understanding human behavior. Further research will test the validity of these predictions.

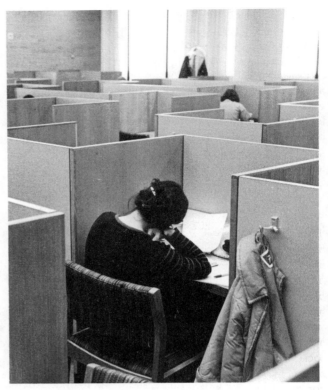

FIGURE 15.15   Social Facilitation
Zajonc proposed a theory of social facilitation that states that the presence of others enhances the possibility of an individual's expected response. One application of this theory is that you should study alone when learning new material, but with others after you know the material fairly well.

Social Facilitation

Our behavior is sometimes different in front of a group than when we are alone. Social psychologists have known this basic fact for many years. The problem is that sometimes our performance improves when we have an audience, while at other times it deteriorates. For a long time no one could explain this audience effect.

In 1965 social psychologist Robert Zajonc (whose last name rhymes with science) proposed a motivational drive theory of social facilitation. His theory states that the presence of others enhances the emission of the individual's dominant response. Effectively, the presence of others causes an increase in arousal, which contributes to an increase in the dominant (most likely) response (see chapter 9, "Motivation").

If the dominant response is a well-learned behavior, such as eating, doing math problems, or running, then the presence of others (either as an audience or as coactors) will usually lead to improved performance. If, on the other hand, the response is a new behavior, not yet well-learned, then the dominant response will most likely be an impaired performance. In this case, if you add an audience, the arousal increases and leads to a decrease in behavior. Learning new nonsense syllables or learning a complicated maze are examples of behaviors in which the subject is likely to make many mistakes in the beginning.

The social facilitation prediction was tested in a study by Michaels and colleagues (1982) in a college student union. The researchers observed pairs of students while the students were playing pool. Then a group of four confederates approached the students and closely watched them continue to play. Zajonc's theory predicts that the good players should improve while the poor

players should show decreased scores. This hypothesis was confirmed: the good players increased their accuracy from 71 percent to 80 percent, whereas the poor players decreased their accuracy from 36 percent to 25 percent when they were observed.

Several other explanations for the social facilitation drive have been proposed. Baron (1986) suggested the *distraction-conflict theory*, which states that others cause arousal because they distract the individual from the task. Sanna and Shotland (1990) argued for an *evaluation apprehension* explanation. They found that subjects who performed in front of a group only did better than those who performed alone when they anticipated a positive evaluation from the audience. When they expected a negative evaluation, their performance was actually worse.

The past 2 decades have seen a great deal of research devoted to social facilitation (Guerin, 1986) and although all the particulars have not yet been settled, it is clear that social facilitation is an important phenomenon that can be used in everyday life. For example, when you are learning something new (such as the material in this chapter), you should study alone until you begin to master the material. Then, once you have learned it fairly well, study in a group so that social facilitation can improve your performance and prepare you for your test.

Cooperation, Competition, and Conflict

When individuals or groups interact, they might engage in cooperation, competition, or conflict. Here we explore some factors that determine how they might interact.

Cooperation and Competition In some situations, cooperation is dominant, whereas in others, competition is. Factors such as personalities of the individuals, amount of communication, size of the group, and reciprocity of actions determine whether individuals compete or cooperate in a social situation. These factors have been the focus of research conducted in laboratory game simulations of everyday situations. In the game theory approach there are two kinds of games of interest to social psychologists: zero-sum and non-zero-sum. In zero-sum games, the total gains and losses equal zero. For example, in chess or tennis there is a winner and a loser. In non-zero-sum games the sum of the payoffs is not zero. There is value in cooperation in non-zero-sum games, since if both players cooperate both can gain and no one has to lose. Two non-zero-sum games are described below.

The trucking game was developed by Deutsch and Krauss (1960) to explore the bargaining behavior of individuals in a social situation. Each player owns a trucking company and tries to make a shipment as quickly as possible. Each has a long route to the destination as well as a short route that converges into a one-lane road. In order to use the short-cut (and make "money") the players have to cooperate and take turns using the road. However, each person also had control of a gate to prevent the other trucking company from using the road. The best strategy is to cooperate, and yet the researchers found that when the players had a weapon (the gate), the majority of the time was spent competing and threatening the other.

In the prisoner's dilemma, two prisoners are isolated and each is accused of a crime. If neither prisoner confesses, each receives a light sentence of 1 year of imprisonment, and if both confess, each receives a heavy sentence of 10 years. If one confesses but the other does not, the one who confesses is given a very light sentence of 3 months and the other receives a very heavy sentence of 20 years. There is an advantage for both prisoners in cooperating and remaining silent, thereby guaranteeing both a relatively light sentence, but, over a series of trials, personal gain favors competition: by

confessing and hoping the other person does not, one of the two might obtain the lightest possible sentence. Typically, subjects show competition in this game also.

These games illustrate the factors that determine whether an individual competes or cooperates. Some research suggests that Americans are especially competitive, and that this characteristic is learned during childhood (Werner, 1979). There are personality differences, with some people always competing, some always cooperating, and some dependent upon the other person (they begin by cooperating, but will compete if the other person does). Communication is also a very important factor. Wichman (1970) found that when there was no communication between individuals in the prisoner's dilemma, about 40 percent of the responses were cooperative, but if verbal communication were allowed, the cooperation level increased to around 70 percent. The size of the group also makes a difference. When the prisoner's dilemma was modified so groups could play, it was found that as the size of group increased, cooperation decreased (Komorita & Lapworth, 1982). Reciprocity also plays a role, and many people will go along with whatever strategy the other begins. Cooperation and competition are important forces in today's world, and social psychologists are attempting to understand how groups and even nations can learn to increase cooperation.

Conflict Sometimes cooperation does not occur and competition escalates into conflict. Thomas (1990) stated that conflict occurs when one individual or group perceives that another individual or group has caused or will cause harm. The types of conflict vary, and for instance can include individuals or groups in an athletic contest, or nations in a war.

Conflict can be caused by a variety of factors. One of the most common causes of conflict is competition for limited resources. For people who live or work together, space is often a source of conflict (Who gets the larger office or room? How is furniture arranged?). How income is spent can be the source of marital conflict. Indeed, wars between nations are also often due to territorial conflict or competition for limited resources. Poor communication is often a source of conflict in social and international situations. Marital conflict, group unrest, employee discontent, and even international hostilities are often due to poor communication. In fact, Baron and colleagues (1990) have reported that ineffective communication is the greatest contributor to conflict in work situations.

Social psychologists and those working in the field of peace psychology are interested in reducing destructive conflict. A number of *conflict management* techniques have been identified by researchers (Barash, 1991). Because poor communication is often the cause of a conflict, improving communication between sides can help resolve differences, as shown above in the prisoner's dilemma game. Sometimes a third-party mediator, such as a marriage counselor, a courtroom judge, or the United Nations, is needed to help negotiations (Lim & Carneval, 1990). Labor negotiations may involve an outside arbitrator. Conflict is sometimes reduced when the opposing sides work together on some common goal (called a superordinate goal). For instance, nations that were previously at war can become allies when confronted by a common enemy (Barash, 1991).

The most common method of effectively resolving conflict is bargaining. Although circumstances vary widely, *bargaining* involves both sides making a series of offers and counteroffers so that an acceptable agreement can be reached. The effective bargaining strategy called GRIT (graduated and reciprocated initiatives in tension reduction) was proposed by Charles Osgood (1962). In the GRIT procedure, one side announces that it wants to reduce tension and then shows a small conciliatory act. Then it is up to the other side to show compromise also. GRIT has been very effective in increasing cooperation and trust in laboratory simulations, and peace psychologists are investigating its use in international conflicts (Milburn & Christie, 1989). Obviously, the ideal outcome is when both sides can cooperate and enjoy mutual success.

Leadership

One element—leadership—is always present in groups, even in those informal groups that try to avoid it. A leader is someone who is able to exert influence over the other members of a group. He or she need not necessarily occupy a formal position of power. There may be a "power behind the throne," some person who actually exercises more influence than the leader who has been designated officially or informally (Ridgeway, 1983). Usually group members agree on who the leader is. Leadership involves a number of qualities, such as the capacity to direct others effectively, speak convincingly, represent the group to the outside world, initiate and organize programs of action, mediate between disputing members, raise morale, and obtain consensus from the group members.

Social psychologists have been anxious to discern any consistent attributes shared by leaders in general. Initially, these psychologists focused on personality and attempted to establish recurrent character traits in leaders. But this research proved inconclusive. Leaders often are quite unlike one another, and the only commonly occurring characteristics seem to be that leaders are more intelligent and verbally fluent than nonleaders.

A subsequent situational approach focused on the position of leadership rather than on the person who

FIGURE 15.16   Leadership
There are many traits that leaders might possess. Authoritarian leaders **(A)** are most effective in situations where speed and efficiency are needed to carry out tasks. Democratic groups **(B)** require leaders who are effective at social interaction and group maintenance.

held it. The assumption was that any person can be a leader as long as he or she can satisfy the current objectives of the group. Since the demands of the role will change over time, different persons will emerge to satisfy these elements (Fiedler, 1981). If a political group decides to initiate a fund-raising campaign, for example, leadership may pass from one who excels at politics to one who is good at raising money.

A more recent approach is based on "process," which attempts to take into account the broader relationships among leaders, members, and the group situation. The concept of a leader as a person who just gives orders is far too simplistic. The way he or she leads depends on the expectations and needs of the followers as well as on the varying demands of the situation.

Extensive research on leadership has demonstrated that one cannot label a leader "good" or "bad" without understanding the conditions under which he or she operates. There is a wide range of leadership styles, from democratic (consulting and persuading others) to authoritarian (making decisions alone and issuing orders). No one leader is effective in all situations, and a person who is quite inefficient in one environment might be a superb leader in different circumstances. For instance, authoritarian leaders are most effective in emergency situations where speed and efficiency outweigh any other considerations. Armies thus have a very authoritarian power structure. On the other hand, democratic leaders are far more effective in situations where group members are concerned about individual rights and where there is some disagreement about goals. Discussion groups usually adopt a democratic structure for this reason.

Halpin (1966) described two dimensions often present in leadership: task orientation and group-maintenance orientation. The task leader is the one who gets the job done. He or she can direct others to carry out task goals efficiently. The social leader is the one who tries to keep the people in the group happy with one another. He or she is the group-maintenance leader, and is more concerned with social interaction than with the accomplishment of the task at hand. Often a group will have separate leaders for the task and social functions. Permanent groups usually need both types of leaders to carry out their long-term goals effectively.

Besides the group dynamics described above, there are additional ways in which other people can influence individual behavior. We end this chapter by reviewing the areas of aggression and helping behavior.

AGGRESSION AND HELPING BEHAVIOR

None of us lives in this world alone. Our actions and reactions have either a positive or negative effect on those around us. Social psychologists are interested in discovering what influences people to hurt others or help others in social interactions. In this last section, we review what is known about aggression and helping behavior.

Aggression

Every time we pick up a newspaper or watch a television newscast, we are bombarded by stories of aggression and violence. Armed struggles in Central America, belligerence in the Middle East, viciousness in Northern Ireland, and crime in the United States all remind us that human beings can be very aggressive creatures.

What is aggression? What causes it? How does it develop? How can it be controlled? Do human beings have to be aggressive, or do they learn to be? How can we reduce destructive aggression? Social psychologists seek answers to these questions.

Definition of Aggression   Aggression is a difficult concept to define and is widely used and misused (Scott, 1975). To you or me, it could be the behavior of a child hitting another youngster or a thief robbing a bank; but it could also be an act of war by a nation. People continue to debate the scope of aggression. For example, how loudly do we yell or tense up inside if we see somebody kill an insect, an animal, or another person? Aggression may include two animals fighting with claws and teeth, or it may be expanded to people fighting with guns or knives. In order to understand aggression in the context of human behavior, psychologists often limit the scope of their research. Here we focus our discussion on destructive human aggression.

Social psychologist Robert Baron (1983) defined aggression as behavior intended to harm another member of the same species. This definition eliminates cross-

FIGURE 15.17   Frustration and Aggression
When we are frustrated, it can lead to aggression. Here two children both want the same puzzle. Since only one can have it, frustration will probably result in aggresson.

FIGURE 15.18 Imitation of Aggression
Bandura and his colleagues found that after children observed a film of adult aggression, they would imitate the aggressive behavior. This research supports the social learning theory of aggression.

species aggression (hunting), accidental aggression, and aggression toward objects in the environment. For social psychologists studying humans, aggression is behavior directed toward harming another person.

Aggressive behavior can take many forms. It may be physical behavior, such as attacking with fists or weapons, or it may be verbal behavior, such as threats. Or it may be an indirect action, such as destroying another person's property or harming his or her loved ones.

Aggression is a behavior, but it is accompanied by emotion (anger) and influenced by motivation. Roger Johnson (1972) pointed out that aggression is a multidimensional concept with many influences. Psychologists have studied the relationships between aggression and such factors as heredity, sex, territory, dominance, ecology, physiology, development, learning, and social organization.

Theories of Aggression Aggression has been studied from three approaches: instinct theory, frustration-drive theory, and social learning theory.

The oldest theory of aggression holds that people are naturally aggressive. Probably the most famous proponent of the instinct theory was Sigmund Freud (1930) who argued that aggression is the result of a death instinct (Thanatos) inherent in all human beings. Freud proposed that destructive energy builds up and has to be released through aggressive behavior.

A more modern instinct theory of aggression has been proposed by the European ethologist Konrad Lorenz. Lorenz (1966) argued that people evolved ag-

gressive behavior to survive. Other more powerful animals have inhibitions against harming one another. Because a human without weapons is fairly powerless against other people, Lorenz argues, humans didn't develop the same inhibitions against fighting that most other species have. The instinct to be aggressive, combined with the development of weapons, has made the human the most dangerous animal in nature. The instinct theory takes a fairly pessimistic view of human aggression.

The frustration-drive theory provides a little more hope for us. The frustration-drive theory of aggression was proposed by social psychologists Dollard, Doob, Miller, Mowrer, and Sears (1939). The theory hypothesizes that frustration leads to the arousal of an aggressive drive to hurt the source of the frustration. For example, if you wanted to have a party but your best friend objected, your frustration might lead to aggression toward your friend. This theory suggests that all aggression is the result of frustration, and the way to control aggression is to eliminate potential frustrations in the environment. In other words, if everyone had everything he or she needed or wanted, which unfortunately seems highly unlikely, there would be no frustration and hence no aggression.

Social learning theory proposes that aggression is a form of learned social behavior. Albert Bandura (1973) and Robert Baron (1977) represent the current view that aggression is learned through observation and imitation of other people and is maintained through positive reinforcement.

A classic experiment conducted by Bandura and his colleagues (1963) demonstrated the social learning concept of aggression. The researchers had children watch a film of an adult attacking a large inflatable "Bobo" doll that stands upright. The adult model used some unusual aggressive behaviors with the doll. Later, when the children were allowed to play with the doll, most of them imitated the aggressive behaviors shown by the adult in the film. They learned to be aggressive by observing someone else.

Children watch aggression on television and observe it in other children and adults. They then imitate the aggressive behaviors and are reinforced when they get what they want. The social learning theory suggests that the way to control aggression is to reduce the number of aggressive models available to children and to eliminate reinforcement when aggression occurs (Eron, 1982).

APPLICATION

Television and Aggression

In 1982 the National Institute of Mental Health published a 10-year study of the effects of watching television. Its conclusion was that watching violence on television can contribute to aggressive behavior. The response from the television networks was that the research was incomplete. The question of television and aggression is complex and has not yet been fully answered.

We do know that the average household spends about 6 hours a day watching television. And we know that the level of violence on television is higher than it was 10 years ago. Does watching crime and violence on television influence children? The evidence suggests that it probably does (Hearold, 1986).

Bandura's (1963) early research on young children's imitation of aggressive acts seen in a film suggests that we might learn aggression by watching television. Leonard Berkowitz (1984) has shown that in watching violence on television we learn to associate a variety of cues with aggression. He studied television-watching habits of a group of boys when they were 9 years old and then returned to examine them again 10 years later. He found that those boys who watched the most violence on TV were the most aggressive when they were 19. Phillips (1983) reported that the number of homicides in the United States significantly increased after championship boxing matches were aired on television.

Opponents argue that perhaps the most aggressive children like to watch violence on television the most. Although it seems logical that we can learn to be aggressive through watching television, some research suggests that television violence reduces the tendency to become anxious when experiencing real aggression (Thomas, 1982). And some experts believe that we can take out

FIGURE 15.19   Television and Aggression
A great deal of research has been done on the relationship between watching television violence and behaving aggressively. No conclusive results have been reached, but the findings so far suggest a positive correlation.

our aggressive impulses through watching violence on TV. Thus, while it seems that television can teach us to be aggressive, the issue is not completely settled (Freedman, 1988).

An alarming statistic is the high rate of aggressive behavior in close relationships, such as families and dating couples (Laner, 1983). Straus and colleagues (1980) reported that nearly 75 percent of parents used some form of physical aggression on children (20 percent striking their children with an object). The causes of violence in families are varied, and include having grown up in a violent family with a great deal of stress and frustration. Overall, it appears that males are slightly more aggressive than females (Eagly & Steffen, 1986). Men tend to use more physical aggression than do women, and both men and women direct aggression more often toward other men.

Aggression is a very serious problem for humankind. We need to increase research into the causes of aggression and work to reduce aggression in our society. Baron and Byrne (1991) suggested several techniques to control human aggression, including punishment, exposure to nonaggressive models, and training in basic social skills. J. P. Scott (1975) emphasized the importance of scientific research in trying to make the world a safer place to live in, and argued that the consequences of not reducing aggression are too painful to consider.

Helping Behavior

It is early evening. You are at home, relaxing. Suddenly you hear screams coming from your neighbor's home next door. It sounds like a fight, with crashes and bangs. What should you do? Should you help? What if they consider the fight to be their personal business? What if it's only the television? What if they begin to attack you instead? The decision to help is sometimes complex and difficult to make. The problem of increasing helping has received the attention of social psychologists during the past couple of decades.

We help others for a number of reasons. Sometimes we expect to be rewarded. Sometimes it's our job. Sometimes we do it just to be nice. Helping behavior is often called *prosocial behavior*, and when we help others without any expectation of reward for ourselves, it is called *altruistic behavior*.

FIGURE 15.20 Altruistic Behavior
When we help others without expectation of a reward, we are engaging in altruistic behavior. This photograph shows Lennie Skutnik saving a victim of an airplane crash in the icy water of the Potomac River in January 1982.

Steps in Helping Behavior In their 1970 book *The Unresponsive Bystander: Why Doesn't He Help?* Bibb Latané and John Darley proposed a series of steps that we must go through before actually helping in an emergency situation. The first step is to notice that something is happening. If we don't pay attention to the problem, we will not be able to do anything. Next, we must interpret the situation correctly. We have to make sure that it is an emergency. We then must assume responsibility for taking action. If we believe someone else will take care of it, or that it is none of our business, then we will not help. After we decide that we must help, we must decide what to do. Should we call the police, rush in ourselves, get reinforcements, or announce politely that we are here to help? Finally, after we decide to help, we must engage in the helping behavior itself. Latané and Darley explain that unless all of the above steps are taken, helping behavior will not occur.

The Bystander Effect Sometimes we see an emergency situation but we do not help. Social psychologists have discovered that we are actually less likely to help when other people are present. The fact that a single person by himself or herself is much more likely to help in an emergency than when he or she is in a group of people is called the bystander effect. Latané and Darley tested the bystander effect in numerous experiments. In a 1968 study they had students fill out questionnaires, some in a room by themselves and others in a room with two other people. While they were working, smoke began to pour into the rooms. The lone subjects reported the smoke immediately, while the subjects in groups tended to ignore the smoke completely, even though it got so thick they couldn't breathe properly.

Latané and Darley explain the bystander effect by saying that when we are in a group a diffusion of responsibility occurs, so that each individual feels less responsibility to take action. Also, in a group you can preserve anonymity: no one recognizes you as an individual expected to help. Furthermore, we hesitate to become involved because of the possibility that there may not be an emergency after all and we would be embarrassed if we made the mistake of acting as if there is one when there really is not.

How can we increase the incidence of helping? Research has shown that people are more likely to help when they feel good (O'Malley & Andrews, 1983) and when they feel responsible. In this situation the presence of other people can actually increase the likelihood of helping (Yinon & colleagues, 1982). Some research has suggested that personality characteristics influence the probability of helping behavior (Amato, 1985). For example, people who have a strong need for approval or who have high moral standards are more likely to help. A

FIGURE 15.21   Diffusion of Responsibility

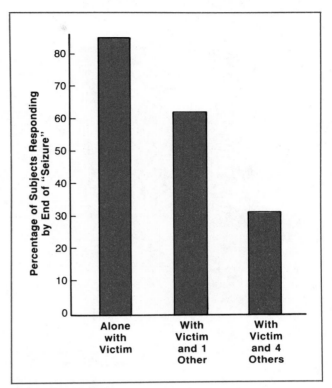

When other people are present, each person feels less responsible to take action. In one experiment on helping, Latané and Darley (1970) found that the percentage of subjects reporting a victim's seizure decreased dramatically as the number of people in the group increased.

person who has made a prior commitment to help others is much more likely to carry through on that commitment. Eagly and Crowley (1986) reported that men are more likely to help than women, especially when helping is defined as a heroic act for a distressed stranger, but not necessarily when everyday friendship and family assistance are taken into account. Latané and Darley's research suggests that we need to help people recognize emergencies. Helping behavior is very important to a society, and social psychologists will continue to work to increase its incidence in emergency situations. ■

Social behavior is a major part of being human. We continually influence other people and they in turn influence us. As shown in our opening story on obedience, sometimes the social influence can have drastic consequences, while at other times we are not even aware of the influence. Many of the topics we discussed earlier are relevant when exploring social psychology. To become truly effective social citizens, we must understand the many ways that social interaction pervades our daily life.

© 1983 The Register and Tribune Syndicate, Inc.

CHAPTER REVIEW

What You've Learned About Social Psychology

1. Social psychology is the study of how an individual's behavior, thoughts, and feelings are influenced by others. Important areas in social psychology include social cognition, attitudes, social influence, group processes, aggression, and helping behavior.

2. Social cognition is the process of understanding other people and ourselves. Person perception is the process of developing an impression of another person. Once we form a general impression of someone, we tend to interpret additional information about that person in a manner consistent with our general impression (the halo effect). Physical attractiveness and first impressions are important variables in impression formation.

3. Attribution is the process of determining the causes of behavior in a given individual. Situational factors involve the external environment, whereas dispositional factors involve the individual's internal personality. Actor-observer attribution bias is the tendency to attribute the behavior of others to internal causes while attributing our own behavior to external causes.

4. Attitudes are learned dispositions that actively guide us toward specific behaviors. Attitudes include affective, behavioral, and cognitive components. Attitudes are formed through conditioning. We develop attitudes from our experiences with our parents, schools, peers, and mass media. We can measure attitudes through interviews, questionnaires, projective techniques, and behavioral testing.

5. Research on attitude change has concentrated on the communicator, message, and audience. The effective communicator is credible, trusted, attractive, and similar to the audience. Two-sided arguments should be used when the audience is unfavorable, but single-sided arguments work best when the audience is favorable. Emotional appeals work only under certain conditions.

6. Festinger's cognitive dissonance theory states that when a person has two attitudes that are in disagreement, tension is produced. The person tries to reduce this tension by changing attitudes. An extension of cognitive dissonance is the concept of inadequate rewards, in which a person develops an internal reward when the external rewards are inadequate.

7. Prejudice is an unjustified attitude involving a fixed, usually negative, way of thinking about a person or object. A stereotype is an exaggerated and rigid mental image of a particular class of persons or objects. Racial prejudice can be reduced when the prejudiced person interacts with members of the disliked group. Sex stereotypes are often learned when we are children. People who score high on both feminine and masculine scales are androgynous.

8. A good deal of human social encounters consist of influencing and being influenced by other people. Conformity is the changing of behavior in order to fit social norms or expectations more closely. We conform to be

liked by others or to show appropriate behavior. The social comparison theory states that we use other people to judge our own perceptions and conform to others.

9. Compliance is a type of social influence in which an individual changes his or her behavior because of a direct request from someone else. Ingratiation increases the attractiveness of the person making the request. The foot-in-the-door technique is making a small request followed by a large one. The door-in-the-face technique is making a very large request and following it up with a smaller one. Low-balling is making an attractive offer and then changing it once it has been accepted.

10. Stanley Milgram extensively studied obedience, in which one person makes a demand of another. He showed that when conditions are right, a large number of people tend to obey authority. In one classic study, Milgram found 65 percent of the subjects continued to deliver 450-volt "shocks" to a learner who complained of a weak heart.

11. We spend a great deal of time interacting in groups that function according to norms—rules and standards that regulate the behavior of group members. Groupthink occurs when the group makes decisions that individuals would not. Groups tend to make extreme decisions, a phenomenon called group polarization. People in groups tend to exert less energy than they would by themselves, a finding called social loafing. Latané's theory of social impact proposes that (a) the more people present, the more influence they have on each individual, (b) the rate of influence grows less as each new individual is added, and (c) the more people present, the less influence any one will have.

12. Zajonc's theory of social facilitation proposes that when in the presence of others, we tend to exhibit our dominant responses. Thus, when we are learning something new, we should practice it alone, but once it is well-learned, it's better to perform in front of an audience.

13. Social psychologists use the game theory approach to study competition and cooperation. Factors that influence competition or cooperation include personality, communication, reciprocity, and group size. Conflict occurs when one individual or group perceives that another individual or group has or will cause harm.

14. Groups have leaders, people who are able to exert influence over other group members. Research has not been able to totally define what makes a great leader. Two dimensions of leadership include task orientation and social orientation.

15. Aggression is behavior intended to harm another member of the same species. Aggressive behavior can be physical, verbal, or indirect. The instinct theory states that people are aggressive because of genetic tendencies. The frustration-drive theory proposes that frustration leads to the arousal of an aggressive drive to hurt the source of the frustration. The social learning theory views aggression as a behavior that is learned through observation and maintained through reinforcement.

16. Latané and Darley suggest that in order to help in an emergency, we must notice something is happening, interpret it as an emergency, assume responsibility, decide what to do, and take action. The bystander effect describes the fact that a single person is more likely to help in an emergency than a group of people. Diffusion of responsibility means that each member of the group has only partial responsibility, with the result that none help.

CHAPTER OBJECTIVES

What You'll Learn About Applied Psychology

After studying this chapter, you should be able to:

1. Identify the areas of applied psychology.
2. Describe the role of psychologists in assisting police departments.
3. Describe how psychologists are involved in the courtroom.
4. Describe how psychologists are involved in prisons.
5. Identify three tasks performed by psychologists in personnel psychology.
6. Identify the major theories of motivation in organizational psychology.
7. Describe the field of engineering psychology.
8. Identify the areas of research in consumer psychology.
9. Outline how personal space influences behavior.
10. Outline the effects of crowding on behavior.
11. Describe the effects of noise on behavior.
12. Describe how psychology is applied to sports.
13. Describe how psychology is applied to education.

Between 1924 and 1932 the Hawthorne Works telephone equipment plant of the Western Electric Company, near Chicago, was the site of an important research program. There the management was interested in how different types of working conditions influenced productivity. A number of scientists, including Elton Mayo and Fritz Roethlisberger, were involved.

One series of experiments focused on levels of illumination (Roethlisberger, 1941) in order to study if the productivity of employees increased or decreased, depending on the amount of lighting. A control group of women worked, in one study, under constant illumination (10 footcandles), whereas a test group of women worked under different illumination intensities (24, 46, and 70 footcandles). A footcandle is the illumination produced on a 1-foot-square surface located 1 foot from a candle. Surprisingly, the results showed that the productivity level in both groups increased, and at about the same rate.

In the next experiment, the illumination level in the experimental test group's room was decreased to 3 footcandles. Again the results were puzzling: productivity increased in both the experimental and control groups. This seemed to suggest that there was no systematic

Psychologists are interested in applying their skills and research findings to practical problems. Psychologists can apply their skills to everyday problems in industry, education, the effects of a person's surroundings (environment) on his or her behavior, in police departments, prisons, and even in sports, as well as in other interesting areas.

16

Applied Psychology

relationship between level of illumination and work output.

The third experiment on illumination involved making the workers believe that the lighting levels were being changed, when in fact they stayed constant. The workers thanked the researchers for the "improved" lighting conditions when the illumination levels were "increased" and complained when the lighting was "decreased." But there was no significant change in productivity.

In a final experiment, the illumination level was decreased to only .06 footcandle (the amount of light given off by the moon). When this low level of lighting was reached, worker productivity decreased.

Roethlisberger described the situation as "screwy," and spent considerable time trying to figure out what went wrong. The results were definitely negative in the sense that the researchers could not draw any conclusions about the effects of illumination levels on employee productivity, which was the original purpose of the experiments. Eventually, after a number of other experiments and employee interviews, the researchers concluded that they had been trying to deal with a human situation in nonhuman terms.

Rather than view the workers from a psychological perspective, the Hawthorne experiments only focused on physical conditions. They changed light bulbs and counted output, but forgot that the workers were human beings with social and psychological needs. Eventually, Mayo and his colleagues realized that work settings are complex social systems. In order to understand the research results, it was necessary to understand worker attitudes, patterns of communication, social norms, and worker motivation.

They concluded that in the illumination experiments, productivity levels increased because the workers knew they were being observed and enjoyed the special attention they were receiving. The changes in the level of illumination were incidental and did not actually affect performance significantly. Thus, social factors were responsible for the results of the research.

The research conducted at the Hawthorne Works was flawed. Groups of subjects were not matched, testing rooms were not identical, and appropriate dependent variables were not identified. However, the finding that behavior can be influenced just by participation in a research study was a valuable lesson, and is generally referred to as the *Hawthorne effect*. Researchers are now much more sensitive to the Hawthorne effect when designing experiments.

WHAT IS APPLIED PSYCHOLOGY?

Although most people are aware of the contributions psychologists make to solving individual behavioral problems, they sometimes forget that the findings of psychological research are also of great value in dealing with a wide range of applied social problems that affect us all. Some of the information psychologists have gathered has already benefited society. For example, the basic principles of learning have been employed effectively in improving teaching techniques in the classroom and in reducing behavior problems in schools, homes, and institutions. Psychologists have investigated the effects of television violence, created educational programs such as the popular *Sesame Street*, helped people find satisfying careers, helped people improve their physical health, and studied the causes of crime.

Applied psychology is concerned with helping to solve practical problems. Two large segments of applied psychology are clinical and counseling psychology, areas we have already discussed in chapters 12, "Adjustment and Health," 13, "Psychological Disorders," and 14, "Therapy." Historically, the other major segment of applied psychology has been industrial psychology, which includes personnel selection, training, job satisfaction, and consumer behavior.

In addition to clinical and industrial applications, psychologists are involved in investigating crime, the legal system, and prisons; and improving mental health care in the community. Some other applied psychology specialties include sport psychology, medical psychology, peace psychology, traffic and transportation, pet psychology, and leisure psychology. Applied social psychology includes such areas as the environment, health, and organization (Rodin, 1985). These areas are an extension of the principles of social psychology. You will notice the application of some of the research from the social psychology chapter (chapter 15) in the topics discussed here.

Goldstein and Krasner (1987) stressed that basic and applied research are interrelated, and that applied psychology refers more to where the information is being used than to what information is being used. They argued that areas of modern applied psychology include clinical, industrial, health, legal, educational, and sports applications. The *Journal of Applied Psychology*, established in 1917, continues to have a heavy emphasis on industrial psychology applications. It also covers applications in settings such as police and corrections, urban affairs, government, health, and education. Until 1946 the scientific and applied (mainly clinical and industrial) areas had two separate organizations, the American Association for Applied Psychology for practitioners and the American Psychological Association for scientists. These two organizations merged into the APA in 1946, with the goal of advancing psychology as a science and a profession.

Although the applications of psychology to our social activities are wide and varied, the interests of psychologists discussed here will serve to illustrate how they are applying research findings to everyday behaviors. We begin this chapter with a look at the field of legal psychology.

LEGAL PSYCHOLOGY

After a rash of airplane skyjackings, the federal government called in psychologists to develop a profile of the typical skyjacker. Interviews with the skyjackers who had been caught and a study of their motives, life history, and methods of operation provided psychologists with data for a composite profile of the typical skyjacker, so that people concerned with the security of flights could recognize someone likely to try to take over an airplane. Developing profiles of potential criminals is but one of many roles psychologists play in law enforcement. Forensic psychologists work in police departments, courts, and prisons to detect and prevent crime and to assess and rehabilitate those convicted of criminal behavior (Hans, 1989).

Police Departments

To reduce the crime rate we need an effective police department. They must deal with the public carefully, uphold the laws, ensure that people accused of a crime are treated fairly, and, when off duty, be able to function socially. Psychologists are involved in selecting, training, and counseling police officers, as well as in helping to detect and prevent crime (Goldstein & Krasner, 1987).

Psychologists have skills in assessing personality, motivation, attitudes, perception, abilities, and adjustment. The methods of testing, observation, and interviewing that have already been described in this book can be helpful in selecting capable police officers (see chapter 11, "Personality"). These methods should predict characteristics such as skills in human relations, communication, decision-making, emotional maturity, and adjustment, which are necessary in police departments because they need officers who can tolerate stress, behave objectively, act compassionately, and yet be firm and obedient.

Once the proper persons have been selected, they must receive instruction on how to carry out their duties.

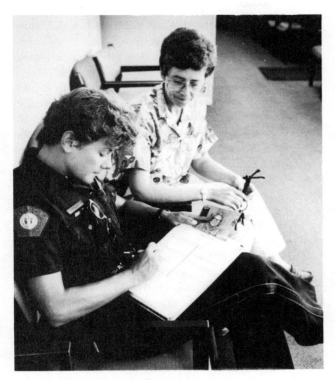

FIGURE 16.1   Police Officers
Psychologists are involved in the training and counseling of police officers. They help police deal with their high level of stress and may help develop and interpret methods of solving crimes.

Psychologists can help teach police officers about motivation, personality, social interactions, prejudice, aggression, abnormal behavior, and various kinds of treatment. The psychologist is able to provide information about how to deal with problems such as drug abuse, aggression, youth delinquency, and race relations. This information is of immense value to the police officer who has to deal with these problems daily.

Police officers experience a high level of stress from exposure to danger, dealing with people, making crucial decisions, and scheduling their lives around the department's demands. Bartol (1983) reported the most significant sources of stress for police officers include lack of supervisory support, shiftwork, physical danger, and negative public image. Psychologists can help them deal with this stress. Maslach (1982) has reported that stress management workshops are routinely conducted by police departments.

Psychologists also assist police in the detection and prevention of crime. They compile criminal profiles. They advise on the techniques for interviewing suspects, on ways to deal with the public, and on methods of handling dangerous situations. Once a suspect has been arrested, psychologists often participate in the legal process as expert witnesses.

Courts

"But I saw it with my own eyes!" is a statement many of us have heard. But whether a person really saw something or merely thought he or she did may be debatable, because perception is sometimes confused with sensation. However, as the Gestalt psychologists point out, perception and sensation are often quite different; and in a courtroom where legal decisions are made, this distinction can make a critical difference.

Expert Testimony   To understand crime and the people involved in it, most court systems need the assistance of psychologists and other specialists. Psychologists may be called as expert witnesses to give a clinical evaluation of a defendant or to evaluate scientifically the testimony and evidence. For example, psychologists might be asked to share their expertise in areas such as identification techniques, interpretation of memory, and identification of perception or motivation. They might also interpret a score on a personality or intelligence test.

Eyewitness Testimony   Imagine you are a juror watching a videotape of an automobile accident. If the prosecutor asks "How fast were the cars going when they hit each other?" what might you respond? What if the prosecutor asked "How fast were the cars going when they collided?" How about "bumped," "contacted," or "smashed"? A single word in a question can elicit quite different responses, even when the actual perception is the same. We discussed this study by Elizabeth Loftus (1979) in chapter 1, "The Study of Psychology." You should recall that the highest speed was reported by a witness when the word used by the prosecutor was "smashed," and the lowest speed was reported when the word "contacted" was used. The analysis and application of courtroom eyewitness testimony is an important concern of applied psychology.

Psychologists are aware that perception and memory distortions can lead to inaccurate descriptions of events. For instance, when Buckhout (1980) had subjects watch a film of a staged crime and then attempt to identify the "criminal" in a line-up, only 14 percent of the subjects were able to identify the correct person. Other research suggests that there is no relationship between the confidence of the eyewitness and the accuracy of the testimony (Wells & Murray, 1983).

One research finding relevant to eyewitness testimony is the *other-race face perception effect*. This other-race effect (or own-race bias) refers to the finding that recognition memory tends to be better for faces of one's own race than for faces of people of other races. Lindsay and colleagues (1991) examined black and white college students and found that the white subjects did better at correctly identifying photographs of white students. Black students, however, were equally adept at identifying photographs of white and black individuals. If you were ever called to serve on a jury it would be important to be aware of the limitations of perceptual identification in listening to evidence.

Does eyewitness testimony influence jurors? Yes, according to Leippe (1985), who had subjects participate in a mock robbery trial with all variables held constant except the testimony of the "eyewitnesses." In one situation, two witnesses (the victim and a bystander) both identified the defendant as the guilty person, whereas in another situation, one of the witnesses decided the defendant was not guilty. When the witnesses agreed, 70 percent of the jurors felt the defendant was guilty, compared to only 13 percent when the witnesses disagreed. Thus, eyewitness testimony does have a significant impact on jurors in a trial.

Jury Behavior   Research on the behavior of juries is probably the earliest interest of legal psychology. Early studies focused on how small groups make decisions. Research in social psychology on topics such as leadership, groupthink, and risk-taking (which are discussed in chapter 15, "Social Psychology") is directly relevant to the functioning of juries.

to help understand the prevalent attitudes on the issues that will be raised during the trial. It is also designed to match up some of these attitudes with specific demographic variables (age, sex, religion, occupation).

Next, information is obtained on each of the potential individual jurors, especially background information pertinent to the issues likely to be raised during the trial.

In the preliminary sessions, the behavior of the potential individual juror is observed in the courtroom. Then the psychologist collates all the information collected together and develops his or her predictions about the juror's behavior, as well as his or her possible interactions with the other jurors. Social psychological principles of small group behavior are helpful in making these predictions.

Finally, after the trial, the psychologist interviews the jury, as well as those prospective jurors eliminated in the jury selection sessions. Through these interviews, the psychologist can measure the effectiveness of his predictions.

While this area is still relatively young, there is some evidence that the predictions have been somewhat effective (Hans & Vidmar, 1986). However, questions concerning the ethics of the involvement of psychologists in the process of jury selection have been raised. In the future, we will need to decide what limits should be placed on the applications of psychology in our judicial processes.

APPLICATION

Jury Selection

Sometimes psychologists help attorneys predict the behavior of individual jurors, and thereby enable the attorneys to select jurors they believe are sympathetic to their case. Richard Christie (1976) described the procedures used by psychologists to help select jurors.

The first step is to conduct a survey in the community in which the trial will be held. This survey is designed

FIGURE 16.2   Jury Selection
The process in which a jury is selected is complex and includes a wide variety of people. Psychologists are involved in conducting surveys and interviews, and making observations to help predict jury behavior.

More recent research on jury behavior has concentrated on interviewing jurors directly after a trial, or monitoring simulated trials with volunteer subjects (often college students) as mock jurors. Jury research has studied variables such as the personal background of jurors, the order of presentation of evidence in the courtroom, and the effects of the instructions given by the judge (Pennington & Hastie, 1990). Personality findings include the fact that younger jurors and those with more education are more likely to vote for acquittal than older ones or those with less education. Monahan and Loftus (1982) reported that the more similar in age and education the juror is to the defendant the more likely that he or she will vote for a verdict that ensures a less severe sentence.

Research has shown that the verdict reached by the jury depends to a large degree on the severity and number of the possible alternatives available to it. For instance, if the only possible verdicts allowable are first-degree murder and not guilty, more jurors will vote not guilty than when the possible verdicts are manslaughter and not guilty. Even fewer would vote for not guilty when more alternatives, such as negligent homicide or second-degree murder, are added to first-degree murder and manslaughter as choices.

The order of presentation of evidence in a trial appears to have an influence on the decision of the jurors. Consistent with other research in social psychology, it has been found that a *recency effect* occurs. That is, information presented at the end of a trial is more persuasive than that presented at the beginning of the trial. A classic study was done by Weld and Roff (1938), who divided prosecution and defense evidence into distinct units. In one condition, subjects (mock jurors) were presented with all of the prosecution evidence first, followed by all of the defense evidence. In the other condition, part of the prosecution evidence was presented, followed by the defense evidence, with the rest of the prosecution evidence presented last. Subjects in the latter group were more likely to believe the defendant was guilty. While research such as this gives some insight into how jurors may function, it is important to remember that the research was not conducted under ideal conditions, and that it is impossible to predict human behavior infallibly in such settings.

Prisons

Once convicted, a person may be sentenced to a term in prison. Prison psychologists may evaluate new prisoners, counsel inmates, and train prison personnel.

Usually prison psychologists have clinical or counseling backgrounds. One of their important duties is to evaluate newly admitted prisoners. The new prisoner is given a battery of tests, including intelligence, interest, personality, and social tests (see chapter 11, "Personality") to determine how he or she is likely to respond to the pressures of confinement, whether he or she will become violent in prison, and how the prison system might best help rehabilitate him or her. Most prisons have educational opportunities (including college courses) and some type of vocational training program.

While the inmates are incarcerated, they may require some sort of counseling, either as part of an ongoing assessment of rehabilitation procedures or to help them cope with the demands of prison life. In some cases, prisoners just need the opportunity to talk to someone who is interested in them as individuals. The outcome of counseling sessions can be an important factor in parole decisions, and so most inmates take them very seriously.

Like the police officer, the prison staff member is under a great deal of stress. Prison guards are especially vulnerable to the strains of the prison environment and need psychological counseling and training.

Among other psychologists concerned with the

FIGURE 16.3   Prison Environment
Psychologists evaluate and counsel prisoners and train prison personnel. They may assist in the design of the prison environment so that the need for personal space and privacy can be met. Ultimately, psychologists may positively influence the prison system itself.

prison system are environmental psychologists, who assist in designing new facilities or help the staff understand the prisoner's need for personal space and privacy (Paulus, 1988). Also involved in prisons are correctional psychologists, who make recommendations to parole boards; and educational psychologists, who set up and run educational programs for the inmates. (When I teach General Psychology at the local correctional institution, I am greatly impressed with the ability and motivation of my inmate students to learn the course material. In a small research study, I found my inmate students to be similar to my regular college students in both class performance and the need for social approval.)

Unquestionably, crime is one of the major social problems in the United States, more so than in most other countries. Some people feel that the only solution to the crime problem is to catch criminals and put them in prison so that they may recognize the evil of their ways, acquire useful skills, and emerge rehabilitated and prepared to lead productive, law-abiding lives. But, as shown in a simulated prison study by Philip Zimbardo, our present-day penal system tends to bring out the worst in both prisoners and guards. According to Zimbardo's results, the flaw seems to lie more in the system than in the personalities of the individuals.

Zimbardo's Simulated Prison Study   Researchers, led by Philip Zimbardo, created a mock prison in 1973 in a laboratory basement, using as subjects 21 healthy male undergraduate volunteers. Each person was to receive 15 dollars a day for 2 weeks. Nine of the students were randomly selected to be "prisoners" while the rest were divided into three shifts of "guards," who worked around the clock.

Within a brief time, the "guards" and "prisoners" became totally absorbed in their respective roles. As the guards grew more aggressive, the prisoners became passive and apathetic. No sense of solidarity developed among them. They spent only a tenth of their conversation talking about subjects unrelated to imprisonment. The rest of the time they talked about escape, the quality of the food, and the causes of their discontent.

At first, it was an exciting game, but it quickly became an unpleasant way of living. An hour after the prisoners went to sleep, the guards abruptly woke them

FIGURE 16.4   Simulated Prison Study
In a study that simulated a prison environment, college students played the roles of guards or prisoners. Zimbardo found that both guards and prisoners soon took their roles too seriously. The study had to be ended early because of the possible negative consequences.

and made them line up and repeat their ID numbers. The guards made the prisoners do push-ups until they were exhausted. When the prisoners revolted, they were placed in solitary confinement and even made to clean toilets with their bare hands. The guards then began using psychological tactics, isolating and recombining prisoners until the prisoners no longer trusted one another.

Finally, after only 6 days, the experiment had to be halted. Even with his significant training in social psychology, Zimbardo was unprepared for the psychological influences that totally took control of the social environment. He quickly became convinced that behavior does not exist in a vacuum, but is due to a complex variety of variables that psychologists have only begun to understand.

This striking example of psychological research shows how the behavior of the individual can be shaped by the demands of the environment. The fact that prisoners are convicted criminals or that guards may be strict may have little to do with the brutalizing effect of prisons on both prisoners and guards. It also demonstrates how the study of psychology can shed light not only on questions about individual behavior, but also on questions of practical concern to society.

INDUSTRIAL AND ORGANIZATIONAL PSYCHOLOGY

Industrial psychology, or industrial-organizational (I-O) psychology, is an area of applied psychology that will have a great impact on your life (Landy, 1989). Someday you will take a job. After you are hired, you will need additional training in the precise skills and procedures of that job. Your performance will be evaluated regularly for promotion and raises. You will be motivated to work hard and be happy when you achieve job satisfaction. While working, the environment will influence your performance. And when you get paid, you will become a consumer and purchase the goods you need or desire. Industrial-organizational (I-O) psychology includes personnel psychology, organizational psychology, engineering psychology, and consumer psychology.

Personnel Psychology

Personnel psychology involves employee selection, training, and evaluation. In the process of selection, the employer decides what type of employee is needed, solicits and receives applications, and conducts interviews. Training prepares new employees for their jobs and helps older employees learn more effective tech-

FIGURE 16.5   Personnel Selection
The selection of new employees often involves personnel psychologists who may aid in the selection procedure. This usually includes evaluation of an application blank, letters of recommendation, tests, and a personal interview with the applicant.

niques for doing their jobs. Finally, employees are periodically evaluated for promotions and pay raises. The personnel psychologist participates in all phases of an employee's career (Landy, 1989).

Selection   The basic idea of selection is to obtain the best applicant for the job. There are several steps involved in a successful selection process. First, a *job analysis* is undertaken to determine exactly what the new employee will be doing. It usually consists of a job description and personnel specifications. The job description is a detailed description of what the worker does and the conditions under which he or she works. It is obtained by examining published analyses of similar jobs, interviewing people already doing the job, or observing people as they work on the job. Personnel specifications describe the characteristics of the person required for the position and might include such things as personality, physical ability, mental ability, experience, and motivation).

There are numerous indicators involved in the process of employee selection, but the most common include application blanks, references, tests, and interviews (Landy, 1989). The *application blank* is virtually universal and is

usually the initial step in the selection process. Customarily, the application requests routine biographical information, work experience, qualifications, and sometimes personal information (from finances to hobbies). Care is taken to meet guidelines of fair employment legislation.

A common selection technique is to require that the applicant submit the names of several *references* who can testify to the applicant's abilities, or provide several *letters of recommendation*. The major limitation of letters of recommendation is that they tend to be rather positive regardless of the qualities of the applicant, since the applicant often can choose who will write the letters.

Often the selection process includes tests of mental ability, aptitude, motor ability, and personality. These tests help the employer match the applicant with a particular job. The last method almost always included in the selection process is the personal *interview*. As we discussed in chapter 11, "Personality," an interview can be structured or unstructured, and depends for its success mostly on the ability of the interviewer (Hakel, 1982). In many cases, the structured interview is the more effective.

Training   Training is the process of learning something new. After someone has been hired, he or she is trained to perform the job efficiently. Along with developing job knowledge and skills, sometimes training programs serve to inform the employee about the organization and to modify employee attitudes and develop employee loyalty.

There are several steps in designing and conducting training programs. They are usually specific to the particular organization, so the first step is to decide the function of the training (to orient new employees, teach employees how to use machines, or help them improve their attitudes). Then the actual training is conducted to meet the objectives that have been developed. Finally, the effectiveness of the training program is evaluated by observing the behavior and performance of the employees.

There are many different types of training programs. Orientation training is designed to develop job skills and provide knowledge of the organization. Usually on-the-job training is handled by a supervisor who teaches an apprentice how to improve job performance. Off-the-job training is a professional type of instruction and may consist of lectures, programmed instruction, or simulations (practice in a simulated environment). Training programs for managers concentrate on social and psychological skills, and include techniques such as role-playing, sensitivity training, and business games (Saal & Knight, 1988).

Evaluation   Evaluation of performance is routine in most organizations. Functions of evaluation include gaining feedback on effectiveness of selection procedures, recognizing areas that require additional training, provid-

BIOGRAPHICAL HIGHLIGHT

ANNE ANASTASI

Anne Anastasi was born in New York City in 1908. As a child, she excelled in school, skipping several grades. She was admitted to Barnard College at the age of 15 and received her Ph.D. degree from Columbia University at age 21.

From childhood, Anastasi was fascinated with mathematics. In college, she began combining mathematics and psychology—an interest that led to her eventual contributions to psychological testing and differential psychology. She researched how trait development is influenced by genetic and environmental influences and how the measurement of traits is influenced by experiences and training. Her work has helped psychologists better understand testing and measurement.

Anastasi taught at Barnard College and Queens College of the City University of New York before she settled at Fordham University in 1947. She remained at Fordham University conducting research and teaching courses in psychological testing, applied psychology, and intelligence.

Among Anastasi's popular textbooks are *Fields of Applied Psychology* (1979) and *Psychological Testing* (1988). Anastasi has also been active in psychological societies, including the presidency of APA in 1971. In 1981 she received the APA Distinguished Scientific Award for the Applications of Psychology and in 1984 was awarded the American Psychological Foundation Gold Medal.

ing feedback for employee improvement, and determining promotions and salaries.

In evaluating job performance, employers try to appraise for merit or to determine areas where the employee can be coached to improve performance. Anastasi (1988) stated that when appraising for merit, we often use rating scales, which are standardized forms for recording personal evaluation. There are several types of rating scales, including ranking employees from best to worst, forced-choice comparisons of statements about the worker, and behavior checklists. Anastasi (1988) pointed out that there are problems with many rating scales, including ambiguity, the halo effect, the *error of central tendency* (tendency to evaluate everyone in the middle range and avoid extreme ratings) and the *error of leniency* (tendency not to evaluate anyone negatively). Ambiguity can be decreased by having clear adjectives that *everyone* understands. One way to reduce the halo effect, for example, is to define the traits being measured in terms of specific behaviors (such as "is slower than average," "is late at least once a week," or "is always dressed neatly"). One way to reduce error of central tendency and error of leniency is to force *rankings* of individuals within the organization.

When appraising progress, the management by objectives (MBO) approach is often used. In this technique, originally developed by Peter Drucker to improve man-

agement-employee relations, the worker and supervisor jointly agree on objectives for the worker to accomplish, and then both evaluate progress toward these measurable goals. This can lead to increased performance and increased job satisfaction, both goals of organizational psychology. MBO is an extremely popular technique, and is often very successful for both the employee and management (Steers, 1991).

Organizational Psychology

Organization theory is frequently described as an interdisciplinary study that examines the structure and functioning of organizations and the behavior of the people within organizations (Mitchell & Larson, 1987). Usually the term organizational psychology refers to the area of industrial psychology derived from social and personality psychology. Baron and Greenberg (1990) stated that organizational psychology is the field that focuses on understanding and predicting human behavior in organizational settings. Steers (1991) defined organizational psychology as the area concerned with management functions and their implications for an organization. Employee motivation is one of the key areas of organizational psychology.

The Hawthorne Study   As indicated in our opening story, one of the most influential studies in organizational psychology was the Hawthorne study, in which the researchers realized that the workers were not responding just to the level of illumination in the plant. Rather, they were motivated to work harder just because the management cared enough about them to try to find ideal working conditions. Although the original study had some flaws, the term Hawthorne effect now refers to the fact that behavior can be influenced just by participation in a research study. Motivation can be extremely important in a work setting.

McGregor's Theory X and Theory Y   Douglas McGregor (1960) summarized two possible views of management in worker motivation. Theory X is the traditional view of direction and control. It states that the worker dislikes work and tries to avoid it. The function of management, therefore, is to force the employee to work, through coercion and threats of punishment. The worker prefers in most cases to be directed and wants to avoid responsibility. The main motivator for the worker, therefore, is money.

Theory Y is the humanistic/self-actualization approach to human motivation. Sometimes called the human resources model, it states that work is natural and can be a source of satisfaction, and when it is, the worker can be highly committed and motivated. Workers often seek responsibility and need to be more fully involved with management to become motivated. Theory Y is most likely to be used when management utilizes worker participation in organizational decisions. In their book, *In Search of Excellence*, Peters and Waterman (1982) stated that one of the chief differences between American and Japanese management is that American managers tend to use Theory X and Japanese managers tend to use Theory Y. This difference may be lessening, as evidenced by the practices of the management of the General Motors' Saturn plants.

In his book, *Theory Z*, William Ouchi (1981) described the characteristics of the Japanese companies that produce high employee commitment, motivation, and productivity. Many Japanese employees are guaranteed a position for life, increasing their loyalty to the company. Careful evaluation occurs over a period of time, and the responsibility for success or failure is shared among employees and management. Most employees do not specialize in one skill area, but work several different tasks, learning more about the company as they develop. And Japanese companies are often concerned about all aspects of their employees' lives, on and off the job. According to Ouchi, type Z organizations tend to have stable employment, high productivity, and high employee morale and satisfaction. Many of these outcomes are similar to Theory Y, and research will continue

to evaluate the feasibility of implementing some of them in American companies (Landy, 1989).

Herzberg's Motivator-Hygiene Theory   Frederick Herzberg (1966) proposed the motivator-hygiene theory to account for worker motivation. Herzberg believes that there are two motivation systems for the worker: the need for personal growth (job satisfaction) and the need to avoid unpleasantness (job dissatisfaction). He calls the factors that lead to job satisfaction motivator needs. They include responsibility, the nature of the work, possibility for advancement, the chance for achievement, and recognition for a good job. Hygiene needs, or maintenance needs, include company policy, supervision, salary, interpersonal relations, and working conditions. If hygiene needs are met, they do not necessarily produce job satisfaction, but if they are not met, they do produce dissatisfaction. In many ways, the hygiene needs are similar to Maslow's basic needs, whereas the motivator needs are similar to Maslow's higher needs (see chapter 9, "Motivation"). In order for job satisfaction to occur, the worker must be able to experience personal growth and development on the job.

Unfortunately, research has not strongly supported Herzberg's theory, largely due to Herzberg's use of the *critical incident* approach, which confuses the job and the people involved (Thayer, 1983). The critical incident

FIGURE 16.6 Employee Motivation
Research has demonstrated that people are motivated by a wide variety of needs. While basic maintenance needs such as salary and working conditions must be met, the greatest worker satisfaction is obtained only by meeting such needs as responsibility, achievement, and personal recognition.

approach used by Herzberg involved asking employees to list specific events that they thought produced work satisfaction or dissatisfaction. Unfortunately, he found that different people answered in contradictory ways. Thus, it is difficult to identify a few universal variables that always lead to satisfaction or dissatisfaction with work for everyone. Psychologists now recognize that work motivation is influenced by many variables. Each individual has a unique personality, interests, abilities, and experiences. The work environment, including the physical and social structures, management, location, and task difficulty helps determine the compatibility between worker and job. Research is being continued in this important area.

Organizational psychologists have become interested in developing strategies to help workers develop *quality of work life (QWL)*. Lawler (1982) suggested several strategies for improving job satisfaction and QWL, including improving work conditions and security, increasing worker responsibility, and providing financial stability. Other strategies include enhancing the worker's sense of self-worth and providing opportunities for social relationships to develop within the organization. Job satisfaction is an area of organizational psychology that will continue to be important in the future.

Engineering Psychology

Engineering psychology, or human factors psychology, is concerned with how work is performed, the design of equipment, and the work environment. The ideal objective of engineering psychology is to design a job so that anybody could perform it.

As early as the 1880s, Frederick Taylor went into plants with a stopwatch and timed how long it took to perform particular tasks. Then he set time standards by which workers were compared. In the early part of this century, Frank Gilbreth brought a camera into factories and took pictures of people working. Then he figured out ways to simplify the jobs. Essentially, time and motion studies helped people work more efficiently to increase productivity. Workers and labor unions have argued, however, that these studies only benefit the company and not the employees, who often feel they must continually strive to work harder to be more productive.

Engineering psychology is concerned with designing the work space for efficient utilization by the worker. Not surprisingly, research has discovered that materials and tools should be placed in the order in which they are needed. Incidentally, this principle also holds for study areas. When you study, do you have all of your materials where you need them?

We often need to obtain information about the machines we use. Engineering psychology is concerned

with producing information displays that are efficient and cost-effective. There are three categories of visual display: quantitative (information in numerical form, such as a thermometer); qualitative (information in three or more categories, such as cold, warm, hot); and dichotomist (information in two categories, such as on-off). Sleight (1948) examined the effectiveness of different types of quantitative displays. It was found that the semicircular display was more efficient than the horizontal, which was more efficient than the vertical.

Engineering psychologists are involved in technological projects such as nuclear power plants. After the Soviet Chernobyl nuclear power plant accident, psychologists have played an even more prominent role in designing equipment to prevent "human error." They are also working closely with NASA on the space shuttle program to help design efficient control panels for the astronauts.

Engineering psychology also evaluates the physical and social conditions of the workplace (Prince, 1980). Research has examined factors such as noise, light, and color. Color can have an effect on our moods and perceptions. For example, a dark room seems smaller than a lighter-colored room. And in some situations, the colors of blue and green appear cool, while the colors of red and orange appear warm. It has been found that fish in an aquarium tend to relax and soothe the people around them. However, caution must be used in this area, since many studies have not been replicated, and often the effects are smaller than what would have been expected.

Finally, engineering psychology is concerned with the temporal conditions of work. Research has been conducted on the hours of work, the 4-day workweek (compressed workweek), flexible working hours (flextime), job sharing, telecommuting, and rest periods during the workday (Steers, 1991). Overall, shorter hours decrease boredom and fatigue and increase productivity. Companies that have converted to a 4-day week have generally experienced increases in productivity, a reduction in absenteeism, and increased employee satisfaction. Flexible working hours, or flextime, in which employees can help determine which time they will work (for example, 9am-5pm, 7am-3pm, or 8am-4pm, has also proven very satisfactory, both to employees and their companies. In general, productivity slightly increases, tardiness is significantly reduced, and employee morale is improved (Friedman, 1990).

Consumer Psychology

Consumer psychology deals with the behavior of the consumer when he or she goes out to purchase a product. It includes advertising, research on consumers, packaging, and psychological factors such as memory and perception (Mowen, 1989).

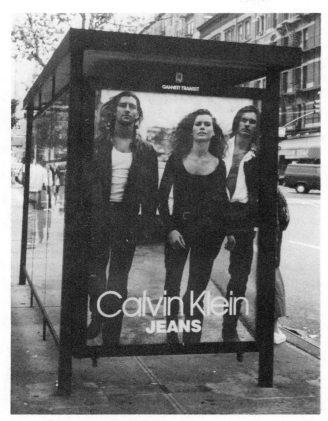

FIGURE 16.7 Advertising
It is assumed that sexually attractive models will sell any product; however, research in this area is not conclusive. When you see an advertisement like this one, do you remember the product or the models?

Consumer psychologists often use an approach called psychographics to identify the attitudes of buyers and their preferences for particular products. Once consumers who like a product are studied, a profile is developed to help market the product. Decisions about advertising, pricing, and distributing the product can then be made effectively (Mowen, 1989). For example, Perri (1990) reported that psychographic profiles revealed that consumers who valued being respected and being accepted by others were significantly more likely to purchase health and beauty products.

Advertising Do you pay attention to advertisements? Probably, because as Schrank (1977) explained, advertising is a reflection of people's needs. Advertising makes promises to us, and we listen because we want to hear those messages. For instance, we might drink diet Coca-Cola "just for the taste of it," or Pepsi because we want to share "the choice of a new generation."

But advertising can be deceptive, according to Schrank. When an aspirin manufacturer tells us "no other aspirin is better," we assume that brand of aspirin to

be the best, unless we know that all aspirin is alike. As another example, I once bought a can of chocolate-flavored syrup only to find out that it contained no chocolate; it contained only chemicals to make it taste like chocolate.

Childers and Houston (1984) compared the importance of pictures to words in advertising. When the experimenters asked the subjects to pay attention to the visual content of the advertisement, they remembered the name of the product better than when they were told to pay attention to the words. Color and repetition are also effective in getting people to remember a product, but are not always used (Lee & Barnes, 1990). On the other hand, sometimes advertisers put too much information into an advertisement and consumers have difficulty remembering it, a phenomenon called information overload (Jacoby, 1984).

Advertisers sometimes use very attractive, seductive, and sexually appealing models. Sex appeal is used to sell everything from automobiles to after-shave lotion and soft drinks. Most consumers (as well as advertisers) assume automatically that the use of sexually attractive models will guarantee the success of a product. Actually, relatively few conclusive research results have been found in this area of advertising.

Sexually attractive models do get the attention of both men and women. People tend to look at advertisements using sexually attractive models more often than they look at other ads. But research shows that often the wrong audience is reached with the ad. For instance, both men and women look at advertisements containing pictures of sexually attractive women, but the actual advertising message is read more often by women. Thus, using an attractive female to get men to read an advertisement often doesn't work. Likewise, advertisements using attractive males are actually read more often by men. While more research is needed in this area, it appears that sex in advertising is not always effective (Caballero & colleagues, 1989).

Consumer Purchase Process   There are many reasons why we buy something. In order to understand consumer behavior we must first examine individual, social, and cultural variables. For example, we may buy something because it makes us feel good, impresses other people, or is part of our ethnic heritage. Or we may buy something simply because it is on sale. To understand the consumer purchase process, we need to take these cognitive, emotional, and motivational variables into account.

Lavidge and Steiner (1961) identified six stages the consumer goes through to reach the purchase stage:

1. *Awareness.* Learns that a product exists.
2. *Knowledge.* Learns what the product offers.

3. *Liking.* Develops favorable attitudes toward the product.

4. *Preference.* Begins to prefer the product.

5. *Conviction.* Believes that purchase of the product would be wise.

6. *Purchase.* Buys the product.

To illustrate this process, I bought a personal computer in order to help me write this book. I first became aware that the company made a computer. Then I began to study the characteristics of a number of different computers. I decided one was better than the others and developed a preference for it. I did this by reading computer magazines and actually looking over various makes of computers. I developed a conviction that the computer would be useful to me, and eventually bought it (when it was on sale).

FIGURE 16.8 Consumer Psychology
The consumer is affected by such variables as advertising, cost, and availability. Because the consumer's perception of these variables as well as his or her own needs can be influenced rather easily, advertisers and marketing specialists seek to understand the psychology of consumer behavior.

Consumer Behavior Research What has research in consumer psychology found out about consumer behavior? Brettman (1986) described a number of findings. Consumer perception is important in pricing. For example, would you be more inclined to buy a product selling for $4.95 or $5.00? If you're like most people, $4.95 sounds much less expensive than $5.00. Gotlieb and Dubinsky (1991) reported that advertisements that provide comparative price information influence consumer attitudes and behaviors positively.

Perception is also important in developing a brand image, or recognition of a particular brand of a product. A large number of studies demonstrate that people feel secure in buying a name brand (even if it is identical to an unknown brand). For example, Makens (1965) gave two identical samples of turkey meat to customers in a grocery store. One was labeled with a national brand, and the other one was an unknown brand (both samples were actually identical and were the national brand). Shoppers chose the sample marked with the national brand as being more tender and tasty. Other shoppers were given a choice between two unmarked samples of turkey, one tough and the other tender. Shoppers all thought the tender sample was the national brand.

When something happens to disrupt people's confidence in a product, a brand image can have serious problems, as shown when Tylenol capsules laced with cyanide resulted in the death of seven Chicago residents. However, because of its strong brand image and an aggressive advertising strategy to get customers back, McNeil Laboratory was able to win back the public's confidence.

How do people decide where to shop? A survey of over 500 people found that nearly 50 percent depended upon advertisements for information (Hirschman & Mills, 1980). Those people who relied on advertisements were more concerned with price and better informed about the product than those who didn't. Newspapers were the most widely used sources of information (35 percent), followed by mail brochures (7 percent), and television commercials (6 percent). What influenced the rest of the shoppers? Over 50 percent decided on where to shop at any particular time strictly by habit. Consumer behavior can be difficult to predict.

Psychology of Packaging An important part of advertising is the package a product comes in. Several companies manufacture antihistamine tablets for allergies or colds. One brand's tablet is twice the size of another, even though they both contain exactly the same amount of drug. Which one sells more? More consumers believe the bigger tablet must be better (even though they are identical in strength). So size is important.

Dichter suggested (1975) that a package must satisfy the following six criteria to be effective: *convenience* (the package is a good size for how you use it), *adaptability* (the package must fit in the space you have for it), *security* (the package may come in tamper-proof containers), *status* (the package gives you a sense of importance), *dependability,* (the package holds up to handling), and *aesthetic satisfaction* (the package is pleasing to look at). The next time you buy a product, note whether you were influenced by the package.

Psychology is used to sell many products. The shopper who understands how advertisers use psychology can become a wiser consumer.

ENVIRONMENTAL PSYCHOLOGY

Environmental psychologists are interested in discovering how the environment influences human behavior. Holahan (1986) described these variables as pollution, noise, crowding, and weather. Some psychologists consider environmental psychology a subarea of social psychology, whereas others view it as a unique and separate field of study. In the next section we cover the variables of personal space, crowding, and noise.

Personal Space

People surround themselves with a "bubble" of personal space that they claim as their own, and they tend to become stressed when other people invade their "bubble." Our personal space protects us from too much arousal and helps us feel comfortable when we communicate with other people.

Interpersonal Distance   Hall (1966) called the study of interpersonal distance proxemics. From observing Americans, Hall concluded that four interpersonal distances were important in our social interaction: intimate, personal, social, and public.

Intimate distance is from 0 to 1.5 feet. What can be done at this close range? Vision is minimal, and we rely on our senses of smell and touch. Making love or comforting someone are intimate activities, usually restricted to private encounters, that can be performed comfortably at intimate distances. We tend not to get this close to people we are not intimate with and try to escape if we do.

Personal distance is from about 1.5 feet to around 4 feet. At this distance, touch is minimal (except perhaps when shaking hands), and vision and hearing become

FIGURE 16.9   Interpersonal Distance
Hall proposed that Americans have four distinct interpersonal distances that they use in social interactions: intimate, personal, social, and public. Social distance is appropriate for activities where the participants know each other, but aren't necessarily friends.

important. This is the distance we use to interact with friends. Within this range, normal conversations can take place easily. We might allow strangers into the outer limits, but reserve the inner limits strictly for friends.

Social distance extends from approximately 4 to 12 feet, and includes the space required for more formal social interactions. Hearing and vision are the primary senses involved. The social distance is often utilized in business, for example, in interviewing new applicants for employment or negotiating for a raise.

Public distance includes distances greater than 12 feet. Hall suggested that after 25 feet, interpersonal interaction is not possible. At this distance, there is little detail involved in communication. A public speaker (actor, politician) communicates only one way with an audience.

Research suggests that we feel uncomfortable when we are too close or too distant from another person (Scott, 1984). How do we learn appropriate social distances? Baxter (1970) suggested that we imitate others in our culture. He reported cultural differences in interpersonal spacing, with Mexicans being closest, white Americans next, and black Americans being farthest apart.

Sex differences have been reported in personal spacing as well, with women usually being closer than men (Ashton & colleagues, 1980). Still other research suggests that interpersonal distance is influenced by social relationships. Women prefer more distance between themselves and an opposite-sex stranger than do men. Ashton and colleagues found that when they asked pairs of friends and strangers to stand at various distances from each other, both men and women felt more comfortable when an opposite-sex friend stood close (about 1 1/2 feet) than when a stranger of either sex stood at that distance. In general, women tend to stand closer when talking with friends than do men. Understanding these sex differences can help us behave appropriately in social situations with both men and women.

Invasion of Personal Space When sitting with a same-sex friend, do you tend to sit next to or across from the person? Research has shown that there are sex differences in seating preference that extend the interpersonal distance concept one step farther. Byrne, Baskett, and Hodges (1971) found that males prefer to sit across from someone they like, while females prefer to sit next to a friend.

Fisher and Byrne (1975) extended this finding by showing that males are most disturbed by an invasion from the front, while females dislike an intrusion on the side of their personal space. They had students invade the personal space of other students who were working alone at tables in the library. The invasion came either across from or next to the subject. When interviewed later, males were most disturbed by invasions from across

FIGURE 16.10 Invasion of Personal Space
Environmental psychologists Fisher and Byrne have found that there are sex differences in the reactions we have to invasion of our personal space. Males are most disturbed by an invasion from the front, whereas females are more upset with an invasion from the side.

the table, whereas females were most disturbed by invasions from the same side of the table. Fisher and Byrne further found that males tend to "defend" the space on the library table in front of them by placing books on it, while females place their books to the side to block the area from which they fear incursions.

Understanding personal space can have practical applications. For example, if we understand the "acceptable" or "appropriate" distance from someone in a given situation, we can communicate more effectively with that person. When we first meet someone we should be careful not to get too close (intimate distance), but should also not stay too far away (public distance), and we should try to avoid sitting across from males or next to females. It's also important to keep in mind the cultural variations that exist. Sometimes we do not have a choice in regulating personal space. When too many people occupy too little space, we experience crowding.

Crowding

Environmental psychologists distinguish between the physical measurement of density and the psychological feeling of crowding. Density is defined as the physical area available to the given number of individuals present, while crowding is the psychological feeling of not having enough space available. Paulus (1980) concluded that while high density (a large number of individuals per area space) is usually necessary for crowding, it does not always produce the negative feeling of crowding. For example, at an enjoyable party or an exciting football game, we might have high density but not really think of it as being crowded. On the other hand, if we are on a deserted beach and someone else comes within view, we might feel crowded, even though the density is not high. Crowding is a psychological phenomenon.

There have been a number of animal studies on crowding; one of the most notable is John Calhoun's 1962 experiment using Norway rats. Calhoun placed a small population of rats in large enclosures with an abundance of food and water. The rats multiplied quickly and soon reached a high density. As the density reached maximum, the rats started behaving very strangely. The males became sexually motivated by females not ready to mate, young females, and even other males. Many became aggressive and violent. The females often ignored their young. Calhoun concluded that the crowded conditions caused normal social behavior to break down. This is not always the case, however. In a 1980 study I was involved with, it was found that a litter of dogs could tolerate severe restrictions of space for short periods of time without any disruptions in the social hierarchy.

Crowding research with humans also has produced conflicting results.

Most people think of crowding as definitely bad. It is usually assumed (but often unproven) that crowding automatically leads to aggression, violence, and crime. A number of studies have reported positive correlations between high density and negative social conditions, such as crime. For example, Schmitt (1966) found that as the density of the population in Honolulu increased, the crime rate, death rate, and mental-disorder rate also increased. But Freedman (1975) argued that when social factors such as economic level, educational level, and ethnicity are taken into account, the relationship between crowding and crime disappears. Thus, it seems that the issue of crowding is more complex than we first believed it to be.

In research studies, usually it is found that performance decreases as density increases. But we feel less crowded with friends than with strangers. It is likely that someone with a large personal space need would feel crowded sooner than someone with a small personal space need. Sex differences have been reported by Freedman and his colleagues, with males usually experiencing more stress in high-density situations.

The importance of cognitive factors in crowding was demonstrated in a 1984 experiment by Worchel and Brown. The experimenters showed either an arousing film (which was humorous, aggressive, or sexual in

FIGURE 16.11 Crowding
The psychological feeling of not having enough space is defined as crowding. People living in large cities are more likely to experience this psychological phenomenon.

content) or a nonarousing film to college students who were seated inappropriately close to one another. Subjects who were watching an arousing film attributed their arousal feelings to the film and thus did not experience crowding. However, subjects who were watching the nonarousing film could not attribute their arousal (actually caused by the inappropriately close seating arrangement) to the film, and so felt crowded. Crowding, therefore, was dependent upon the perception of the source of the arousal.

In his 1975 book, *Crowding and Behavior*, Jonathan Freedman argued that crowding is neither good nor bad. Instead, in his density-intensity theory of crowding he suggests that as density increases, the intensity of our moods and behavior increases. Thus, if we expect to have a good time at a party and the party is crowded, we'll really enjoy ourselves. But if we expect to have a bad time, crowding makes us feel miserable. Baum and colleagues (1981) argued that when people are aware of the density level beforehand they will feel less crowded than those who do not know what to expect. In an urban setting, if crime is a dominant behavior, crowding will increase the crime level. But if positive social behaviors predominate, crowding will produce beneficial effects. Freedman argues that therefore it is important to make sure that positive social environments exist in high-density areas.

Noise and Behavior

We measure noise with the decibel (dB) scale. The threshold for hearing is 0 dB. Normal conversation is about 40 dB, while the noise around a busy street is about 70 dB, and a rock band might be 120 dB. Long exposure to 90 dB can damage the eardrums. Sometimes noise is defined as any sound of a high enough intensity to inflict physical harm, but usually the definition includes the idea that noise is disturbing, either psychologically or physically. Thus, lower levels of sound can also be considered noise, especially when sounds are unpleasant and uncontrollable.

A study reported by Cohen and his colleagues (1986) found that children living on the lower floors of a high-rise apartment building had poorer hearing abilities and more problems with reading than did children on the upper floors. The apartment building was built near a noisy freeway and the noise levels were blamed for the deficiencies of the children living on the lower floors. Smith and Stansfeld (1986) reported that noise also affects adults in daily life. For instance, people living in a noisy neighborhood tended to make more mistakes in simple tasks, forgot common things, and even dropped things more often.

Noise can be objectionable, but does it actually affect our social behavior? Yes, according to a number of

FIGURE 16.12 Noise and Behavior
The perception of noise as a stressful condition is a psychological phenomenon, but constant exposure to stressful noise, such as a busy street or a nearby airport, can adversely affect behavior.

research studies. For instance, Mathews and Canon (1975) found that people were less likely to help someone pick up dropped books when a noise of 85 dB was present. The same results were obtained whether the research took place in a laboratory situation or on a street where a lawn mower provided the noise. Other studies have shown that people living in noisy neighborhoods have fewer social interactions, are more aggressive, and tend to dislike their neighbors more.

Some research suggests that stressful noise can have an influence on our behavior even after we stop hearing it. In 1972 David Glass and Jerome Singer placed people in a noisy environment and either told them that they could control the noise (with a switch) or that they had no control over the noise. The group with control did not often use it, but when both groups were tested on a task afterward, the performance of the group who had control was significantly better. Glass and Singer proposed that noise is a source of stress and that uncontrollable stress leads to a feeling of helplessness. Thus, those in the group with control could relieve helplessness because of their belief that they could control its cause. This suggests that the psychological interpretation of environmental stressors such as noise, crowding, or heat plays an important role in determining our reactions to them.

OTHER APPLICATIONS OF PSYCHOLOGY

Psychology can be applied to a wide variety of areas, as we've seen thus far in this chapter. In this last section, we discuss two additional applications. Sport psychology is one of the newest applied areas, and educational psychology is one of the oldest.

Sport Psychology

Although the principles of psychology have been applied to sports for many years, it has only been in the past couple of decades that a formal discipline has developed. Sport psychology is the application of the principles of psychology to sport activities (Browne & Mahoney, 1984). Many of the topics discussed throughout this book are clearly relevant to the athlete and sports coach, such as motivation to play well, personality differences among athletes or coaches, social influences when playing, and attitudes toward sports and aggression.

Sport psychology has three main areas of focus. It studies performance factors that concentrate on identifying and explaining the behaviors of athletes as compared to nonathletes. Second, sport psychologists are interested

in social variables that influence performance, such as teamwork, cohesion, or goal setting by a team. And, third, sport psychologists have recently become interested in nonperformance factors related to sports, such as violence at games, the morality of athletes, their career development, and retirement. In this section we discuss personality and motivational influences on athletic performance.

Personality of Athletes   There have been many studies of the personality differences between athletes and nonathletes, in an attempt to identify the qualities that contribute to successful athletic performance. Overall, this has been an extremely difficult task, and has not resulted in many significant findings (Browne & Mahoney, 1984). In general, as might be supposed, successful athletes tend to be assertive, internally motivated, dominant, self-confident, and have a high need for achievement.

Goldstein and Krasner (1987) argued that the lack of clear-cut personality profiles of successful athletes is likely due to the fact that there is such a wide variety of sports, and success depends on numerous variables other than just personality. In other words, the successful athlete is a person who possesses the ability to do well in sports, and has had appropriate motivation and successful experiences. They suggest that future research should focus on the interaction of a sportsperson's personality with others and his or her actions rather than on personality alone.

Motivation of Athletic Performance   The successful coach is one who can motivate athletes to exhibit their best performance. Alderman (1980) suggested several incentives that motivate athletes to perform well, including meeting the needs of independence, power, success, aggression, stress (excitement), affiliation, and excellence. Alderman found affiliation and excellence to be the most important motivators for athletes. Landers (1982) investigated the role that arousal plays in athletic performance and concluded that a medium arousal level is often more effective than being too "psyched up" for an activity. A relatively new technique for coaches is to help athletes learn how to monitor their arousal levels through biofeedback and control the excess arousal or anxiety (Paterson, 1984).

What is the optimum coaching strategy for motivating athletes? Duquin (1980) suggested that the successful athlete should be intrinsically motivated and not dependent upon the coach for reinforcement. For instance, my son's cross country running coach encourages the runners to compete against themselves, trying to beat their best time rather than competing against other people. The runners gain self-confidence and self-reward when they can set a new personal record. The coach needs to

FIGURE 16.13 Motivation of Athletic Performance
A successful coach is able to motivate athletes to perform their best. He or she understands the athlete's need for attaining success and excellence, as well as the need to control and utilize stress and arousal levels. Being too "psyched up" may result in a less than effective game or performance.

motivate players, encourage team spirit, and promote social cohesiveness (LeUnes & Nation, 1989). Emphasis should be on the success of the individual as a person and not only on the victory. These strategies are often successful in producing a winning team. It is important to remember that sport psychology involves the coach, the team members, the particular sport, and the ability of the athletes, as well as personality and motivational factors.

Educational Psychology

We have all benefited greatly from the applications of psychology to education. Throughout our school years, our learning, thinking, and memory abilities have been guided and evaluated through procedures that educational psychologists designed. *School psychologists* give psychological tests to students, consult with students, teachers and parents, and try to help students adjust to academic requirements. You have probably had contact with school psychologists at various stages of your academic career. You are much less likely to have had contact with educational psychologists, who often work behind the scenes conducting research or consulting with school officials to help maximize the effectiveness of the educational system. The field of *educational psychology* focuses on how students learn and how instructors teach (Thornburg, 1984).

Learning Applications Much of what we discussed in chapter 6, "Learning," is relevant to educational psychology. The theories and techniques of learning, reinforcement, and punishment have been applied in the classroom for many years. For example, when students do well they are reinforced with praise, high grades, or leisure activities, and when they do poorly, they are punished with detentions, low grades, or threats. Edward Thorndike wrote *Educational Psychology* in 1903, in which he emphasized the role of reinforcement in learning, and encouraged teachers to evaluate students' progress. John Dewey also contributed to the techniques used in education with his emphasis on "learning by doing." Since learning is at the core of education, anything that enhances learning contributes to the success of education.

Instructional Process In order to help students learn effectively, instructors have a number of tasks to perform. Gage and Berliner (1988) outlined several tasks involved in the instructional process. Instructors should develop a set of learning objectives that students are expected to achieve. Instructors ought to understand the personalities, problems, interests, and abilities of their students as well as how their students can best learn. To achieve these goals, instructors ought to have an understanding of learning theories and psychological principles that influence the learning process. With this understanding, instructors must then decide which teaching methods to use—lecture, discussion, demonstration, programmed instruction, computer-assisted instruction, or hands-on experience. Instructors must also evaluate the achievements of their students. Ultimately, education is a joint venture between instructors and students.

In addition to deciding which teaching methods to use in the classroom, instructors must also understand and facilitate student motivation. Jere Brophy (1983) suggested several techniques instructors might use to facilitate classroom motivation. Classroom performance is unique because it is largely cognitive, usually compulsory, and often publicly evaluated. From an examination of these three characteristics, Brophy draws several implications. Students are most likely to be motivated when they can achieve success through gradual steps rather than abrupt leaps (for example, small reports rather than a large paper). Likewise, students are likely to learn most readily when motivation is moderate rather than intense and stressful. Brophy suggested that the instructor must reduce obstacles to successful motivation, such as anxiety and fear of failure. The instructor should make sure the reinforcement value is appropriate for the effort of the student. And, the instructor can motivate students by helping them apply what they learn in a variety of situations.

Learning Styles   Today's students are diverse and require a variety of teaching approaches to maximize learning. Understanding <u>learning styles</u> is one way to improve the educational process.

There are a number of theories of learning styles. Claxton and Murrell (1987) described four levels of learning style models. Differences in *personality* form the core of learning styles in one model. A second model examines how personality affects the style of *information processing* used by the student. The *social interaction* model focuses on how the student behaves in the classroom, whereas the *instructional preference* the student has determines whether the teaching style is appropriate for effective learning.

The field dependent—field independent dimension is one theory of learning style (Witkin, 1976). Those students who are *field dependent* (influenced strongly by the environment) prefer interpersonal interactions that might be found in areas such as social science and humanities. *Field independent* (not influenced strongly by the environment) students prefer areas that involve analytic skills, such as mathematics and science. These different types of students would learn best in environments in which their learning styles were matched with appropriate instructional formats. The *Myers-Briggs Type Indicator* is one test that has been used to identify different learning styles (Myers & Myers, 1980).

Anthony Grasha and Sheryl Riechmann proposed six student learning styles. *Competitive students* are motivated to do better than other students and want to win at learning. *Collaborative students* prefer working with others as they learn and view the classroom as a social environment. *Avoidant students* are not interested in learning and would prefer to be elsewhere. *Participant students* enjoy class and take responsibility for learning what is required. *Dependent students* view the teacher as an authority and learn only what is required. *Independent students* prefer to think for themselves and are confident of their ability to learn. Hruska and Grasha (1982) reported that students become more independent and participate more as they get older. Women tend to be more collaborative in school than do men, but otherwise sex differences in learning styles are not usually significant.

Perhaps Gregorc's (1986) model of learning style best illustrates how style of teaching and learning can be matched, even in today's educational system. Gregorc proposed that students tend to vary on two dimensions, concrete-abstract and sequential-random. Students with a *concrete-sequential* style of learning tend to be organized, task-oriented individuals who focus on factual

FIGURE 16.14   Learning Styles
Educational psychologists have discovered that students have different learning styles. The challenge is to meet those diverse needs in one classroom. One effective way is to vary the presentation of material and the physical setting; by researching such methods, educational psychologists help both teachers and students improve the educational process.

details. They need an instructional program that is structured and provides practical, hands-on experiences. Students with a *concrete-random* learning style tend to be independent risk-takers who focus on experiential components of learning. They need an instructional program that provides open-ended activities for them to explore and experiment with different options. Students who have an *abstract-sequential* learning style tend to be analytical and focus on theoretical aspects of learning. They prefer an instructional program that provides information and allows them to develop concepts and theories. Students with an *abstract-random* style of learning tend to be imaginative, flexible, and global. They need a program of instruction that involves interpretation of concepts and examples of applications.

Instructors can learn to help students with different styles of learning by presenting information in a variety of ways. For example, college instructors might provide an outline of the material for concrete-sequential students, give concrete-random students problems to solve, give abstract-sequential students theoretical background information, and use audio-visual materials for abstract-random students. Most can become better students if they understand their style of learning and attend to those activities that help them learn the course material.

Contributions of Psychology to Everyday Life

This chapter has touched on only a few of the many applications of psychology in our everyday lives. In the various fields of psychology, there are many more. By developing new methods of education and ways to increase the intellectual potential of individuals; by finding better ways to determine the effects of drugs; by treating people with emotional disturbances, alcoholism, drug addiction, and sexual problems; by training people with mental retardation; by rehabilitating prisoners; by increasing cooperation and establishing effective communication between individuals and nations; by learning how policy decisions can be made more effectively; by finding ways to reduce conflict between groups; and by increasing job satisfaction, psychologists help resolve our social problems.

In recent years the contributions of psychology have been enriched and broadened. Research and clinical work in such areas as the biochemical foundations of behavior have revealed how and why people think and act as they do, and have suggested new means for treating emotional ailments long thought beyond the reach of therapy. Ethological studies examining basic animal behavior are demonstrating the limits and potentials of human learning. And advances in behavior therapy are opening new avenues to greater self-awareness and meaningful self-control.

Applied psychology is intertwined with our daily lives. New methods of training pets are being developed by animal behaviorists. The space program is going to need social psychologists to help establish societies on space stations. The health profession continues to depend more and more on public awareness for its effectiveness in treating disorders and encouraging health. As our society changes, career counseling psychologists will play a major role in helping people adjust to new careers and life-styles. More time will be spent in leisure pursuits, and personality and motivation psychologists will help people relax and enjoy life as they engage in leisure activities. In our homes, schools, organizations, and recreational places, we will continue to enjoy the benefits of applied psychology.

In chapter 1, "The Study of Psychology," we learned that psychology is a relatively young science. Although it has already probed many of the mysteries of human behavior, there is still a great deal to be done. Research at all levels, basic as well as applied, needs to be encouraged by everyone, in the many areas of and approaches to psychology that have been described in this book. Such a multidisciplinary approach can guide us toward our common goal—better understanding of ourselves and our environment. ▪

I hope you have really enjoyed this book and will continue to apply what you have learned in psychology throughout your life. Good luck!

CHAPTER REVIEW

What You've Learned About Applied Psychology

1. Applied psychology is the area that is concerned with helping people solve practical problems. Along with clinical and counseling psychology, applied psychology includes legal psychology, industrial psychology, environmental psychology, and educational psychology.

2. Forensic psychologists work in police departments and prisons to detect and prevent crime and to assess and rehabilitate those accused of criminal behavior. In police departments, psychologists are involved in selecting, training, and counseling police officers and assisting in crime fighting.

3. In court systems, psychologists serve as expert witnesses and conduct research on eyewitness testimony and on the behavior of juries. Psychologists may be called upon as expert witnesses to give a clinical evaluation of the defendant or to evaluate scientifically the testimony and evidence. Research on jury behavior has shown that the verdict depends in part upon the number of possible verdicts and severity of various possible penalties.

4. Some psychologists work in a prison setting. Their chief duties include evaluating new prisoners, counseling the inmates, and training the prison staff. Zimbardo's study of a simulated prison demonstrated the effects of a prison environment on the behavior of inmates and guards.

5. Industrial psychology is the area concerned with behavior in organizations and businesses. It includes personnel psychology, organizational psychology, engineering psychology, and consumer psychology. Personnel psychology includes selection, training, and evaluation of new applicants and current employees. Selection involves developing a job analysis, receiving applications and references, giving tests, and conducting interviews. Training programs help the employee develop job skills. Evaluation helps provide feedback on performance for promotions and improvement.

6. Organizational psychology involves the study of the social variables found in a work setting. The Hawthorne study demonstrated the influence of interest on performance levels. McGregor's Theory X and Theory Y illustrate the extremes of motivation expectations of managers. And Herzberg's motivator-hygiene theory attempts to explain the variables involved in job satisfaction.

7. Engineering psychology is concerned with how work is performed, the design of equipment, and the actual work environment. Areas in engineering psychology have focused on how to simplify work behaviors, how to design an efficient work space, how to display information efficiently, how to produce a pleasant work area, and how to maximize productivity by varying work time.

8. Consumer psychology is concerned with purchasing behavior. Consumer psychologists study the steps a consumer goes through before buying a product, how perception influences pricing and brand image, and how to package and advertise a product effectively.

9. Environmental psychologists are interested in discovering how the environment influences human behavior. When other people invade our personal space, we tend to become stressed. People usually maintain appropriate interpersonal distances. Four distances are: intimate (for lovers), personal (for friends), social (for acquaintances), and public (for audiences). Sex differences are found in seating preferences, with males tending to sit across from people they like and females tending to sit next to favored others. Since these seating preferences are favored for friends, they also produce the greatest disturbances when invaded by strangers.

10. Environmental psychologists distinguish between density (the physical area available to a given number of individuals) and crowding (the psychological feeling of not having enough space available). When in crowded conditions, we often show poor performance. Freedman's density-intensity theory of crowding proposes that crowding intensifies the already prevalent feelings and behaviors. Often performances decrease as density increases.

11. Noise is any sound loud enough to inflict psychological or physical harm or discomfort. Noise can result in hearing damage, reading deficits, and a decrease in helping behavior.

12. Sport psychology is the application of the principles of psychology to sport activities. Successful athletes are people who possess the ability to do well in sports and have had the appropriate motivation and experiences.

13. The field of educational psychology focuses on how students learn and how instructors teach. Educational psychologists study learning, the instructional process, and learning styles.

Glossary

A

abnormal behavior Behavior that contributes to maladaptiveness; is considered deviant by the culture; or behavior that leads to personal psychological distress. 306

absolute threshold The minimum amount of physical energy required to produce a sensation. 80

accommodation Process in cognitive development; involves altering or reorganizing the mental picture to make room for a new experience or idea. 61

acetylcholine A neurotransmitter involved in memory. 31

achievement style The way people behave in achievement situations; achievement styles include the direct, instrumental style, and relational style. 228

achievement test Test designed to measure what a person can currently accomplish. 193

acquisition In conditioning, forming associations in first learning a task. 132

action potential An electrical charge in a neuron (neural impulse) that travels down the length of the neuron. 30

activation synthesis theory Theory of dreaming that states that during REM sleep the brain activates itself and then synthesizes the information generated into dreams. 113

actor-observer bias Tendency to attribute the behavior of other people to internal causes and our own behavior to external causes. 351

acupuncture Oriental practice involving the insertion of needles into the body to control pain. 100

adjustment How we react to stress; some change that we make in response to the demands placed upon us. 282

adolescence Period of human development between puberty and adulthood. 64

adoption studies Technique in human behavior genetics in which comparisons can be made between children and their adoptive parents as well as between children and their biological parents. 46

adrenal glands Endocrine glands involved in stress and energy regulation. 40

adrenaline A hormone produced by the adrenal glands that is involved in physiological arousal; adrenaline is also called epinephrine. 40

adulthood Period of human development after adolescence. One becomes an adult when one leaves home or gets married. 66

aerial perspective Monocular depth cue in which we use brightness, color, and detail to determine distance; closer objects tend to look brighter. 91

aerobic exercise Any activity that involves increasing oxygen consumption, such as walking, running, swimming, or cycling. 300

afterimages Images that last in the nervous system for a brief time after being received; visual persistence. 92

aggression Behavior intended to harm another member of the same species. 369

aggressive personality In Horney's personality theory, the personality type that is characterized by a need to act aggressively in a world seen as hostile. 265

agoraphobia Anxiety disorder in which an individual is excessively afraid of places or situations from which it would be difficult or embarrassing to escape. 310

agreeableness The dimension in the five-factor personality theory that includes traits such as warmth, generosity, pleasantness, cooperativeness, and cheerfulness; also called friendliness. 268

AIDS Acquired immune deficiency syndrome; a sexually transmitted fatal disease of the immune system. 253

alarm reaction The first stage in Selye's general adaptation syndrome. The alarm reaction is the immediate response to stress; adrenaline is released and digestion slows. The alarm reaction prepares the body for an emergency. 288

algorithm (random search strategy) Strategy in problem solving in which every solution is tried. 187

all-or-none law The principle that states that a neuron only fires when a stimulus is above a certain minimum strength (threshold), and when it fires, it does so at full strength. 30

alpha Brain-wave activity that indicates that a person is relaxed and resting quietly; 8-12 Hz. 107

altered state of consciousness (ASC) A state of consciousness in which there is a redirection of attention, a change in the aspects of the world that occupy a person's thoughts, and a change in the stimuli to which a person responds; a mental state qualitatively different from a person's normal, waking consciousness. 106

Alzheimer's disease A degenerative disorder of the brain that results in irreversible memory loss, confusion, and intellectual deterioration. 71, 174

amacrine cells With the horizontal cells, they interconnect the neurons in the retina. 84

ambivalent attachment Type of infant-parent attachment in which the infant seeks contact but resists once the contact is made. 57

Ames room Experimental room constructed so that it looks normal even though the walls and windows are trapezoidal and one corner is much farther away from the observer than the other; a visual illusion. 87

amniocentesis Procedure of testing for genetic abnormalities during prenatal development. 52

amphetamine A strong stimulant; increases arousal of the central nervous system. 117

amplitude Intensity of sound waves; amplitude determines loudness of sound. 95

analytical psychology The personality theory of Carl Jung. 263

androgen Male sex hormone produced by the testes; androgen produces male characteristics such as facial hair and low-pitched voice. 41

androgyny Personality in which a person shows both masculine and feminine traits. 250, 357

animism Process of attributing living characteristics to inanimate objects; for example, in young children, believing the sun is sleeping for the night. 61

anorexia nervosa Eating disorder in which an individual becomes severely underweight because of self-imposed restrictions in eating. 221

antianxiety drug A minor tranquilizer that reduces anxiety; used in treatment of anxiety disorders. 340

antianxiety minor tranquilizers Drugs prescribed for treating anxiety, pressure, and insomnia. 116

antidepressant drug A drug that relieves depression. 341

antidiuretic hormone (ADH) Hormone secreted by the pituitary gland to cause the kidneys to slow down their production of urine; this restores body fluids. 40

antipsychotic drug Major tranquilizer used to treat severe disruptions of psychological functioning; relieves psychotic and schizophrenic symptoms. 120, 340

antisocial personality disorder Personality disorder in which the individual who engages in antisocial behavior experiences no guilt or anxiety about his or her actions; sometimes called sociopathy or psychopathy. 322

anxiety A vague feeling of fear and apprehension; a fear of the demands placed upon an individual that he or she is unable to identify clearly. 286, 310

anxiety disorder Fairly long-lasting disruption of the person's ability to deal with stress; often accompanied by feelings of fear and apprehension. 310

anxiety hierarchy Method of systematic desensitization that starts with a mild anxiety-producing situation and progresses to the most anxiety-producing. 334

aphagia Disorder in which the person does not eat. 220

aphasia Disorder in which a person loses the ability to understand speech. 97

apnea Sleep disorder in which the person stops breathing and wakes up after falling asleep. 114

apparent motion Perceived movement of an object when in fact there is none; a visual illusion. 92

applied psychology The area of psychology that is most immediately concerned with helping to solve practical problems; includes clinical and counseling psychology, industrial, environmental, and legal psychology. 378

applied research Research conducted to help solve a practical or pressing question or problem. 15

approach-approach conflict When we are attracted to two equally desirable goals that are incompatible. 284

approach-avoidance conflict When we are faced with a single goal that has positive and negative aspects. 285

aptitude test Any test designed to predict what a person with the proper training can accomplish in the future. 192

archetypes In Jung's personality theory, unconscious universal ideas shared by all humans. 263

arousal theory Theory that focuses on the energy (arousal) aspect of motivation; it states that we are motivated to initiate behaviors that help to regulate overall arousal level. 214

artificial intelligence (AI)   The area of cognitive science that simulates human thinking; the ability of computers to perform in ways that normally require intelligence. 186

asocial phase   Phase in attachment development in which the neonate doesn't distinguish people from objects. 56

aspartate   Amino acid excitatory neurotransmitter found chiefly in thalamus and spinal cord. 31

assertiveness training   Training that helps individuals stand up for their rights while not denying rights of other people. 338

assimilation   Process in cognitive development; occurs when something new is taken into the child's mental picture. 60

association areas   Areas of the cortex of the brain that help integrate information. 35

asthma   Psychophysiological disorder characterized by increased responsiveness of the respiratory tract that results in the narrowing of the airways, thus causing breathing difficulties. 298

attachment   Process in which the individual shows behaviors that promote proximity with a specific object or person. 56

attention   Process of focusing on particular stimuli in the environment. 159

attitude   Learned disposition that actively guides us toward specific behaviors; attitudes consist of feelings, beliefs, and behavioral tendencies. 352

attribution   The cognitive process of determining the motives of someone's behavior, and whether they are internal or external. 218, 350

auditory canal   Canal leading from the outer ear into the middle ear. 95

auditory nerve   Nerve that carries auditory information from the ear to the brain. 96

autokinetic effect   Perception of movement of a stationary spot of light in a darkened room. 92

autonomic nervous system   The part of the peripheral nervous system that carries messages from the central nervous system to the endocrine glands, the smooth muscles controlling the heart, and the primarily involuntary muscles controlling internal processes; includes the sympathetic and parasympathetic nervous systems. 39

autosomes   Chromosomes that carry genes that regulate various bodily processes and characteristics, such as eye color or intelligence. 43

aversion therapy   A counterconditioning therapy in which unwanted responses are paired with unpleasant consequences. 335

avoidance conditioning   Learning situation in which a subject avoids a stimulus by learning to respond appropriately before the stimulus begins. 145

avoidance-avoidance conflict   Conflict that occurs when we must choose between two equally undesirable demands. 285

avoidant attachment   Type of infant-parent attachment in which the infant avoids the parent. 57

axon   The tail end of a neuron along which messages (neural impulses) are conducted; contains terminal buttons that release neurotransmitters into the synapse. 29

axon hillock   The place at which the axon of a neuron meets the cell body. 29

B

Babinski reflex   Reflex that occurs when you stroke the bottom of the baby's feet; the baby first spreads the toes out and then curls them in. 53

backward conditioning   A procedure in classical conditioning in which the US is presented and terminated before the termination of the CS; very ineffective procedure. 133

bait shyness   A form of conditioned taste aversion in which an animal learns to avoid eating a particular poison. 136

barbiturates   Depressant drugs that can be used as tranquilizers to relieve anxiety or as sleep inducers. 116

basal metabolism   The rate at which a body converts food to energy. 220

basic research   Research conducted to obtain information for its own sake. 15

basilar membrane   Partition in the cochlea of the ear; involved in sound sensation. 95

bed-wetting (enuresis)   NREM sleep disorder in which the person wets the bed at night; occurs mainly in children. 114

behavior   Anything you do or think, including various bodily reactions. Behavior includes physical and mental responses.6

behavior genetics   How genes influence behavior. 43

behavior modification   Another term for behavior therapy; the modification of behavior through psychological techniques; often the application of conditioning principles to alter behavior. 146, 331

behavior potential   In Rotter's personality theory, the probability that a particular behavior occurs in a specific situation. 272

behavior therapy   Any therapy in which the symptoms are treated as constituting the disorder itself; sometimes called behavior modification. 331

behaviorism   The school of thought founded by John Watson; it studied only observable behavior. 10

belongingness and love needs   Third level of motives in Maslow's hierarchy; includes love and affection, friends, and social contact. 217

beta   Brain-wave activity that indicates that a person is alert, 13-30 Hz. 107

between-subject experiment   An experimental design in which different subjects are included in the experimental and control groups. 19

binaural   Condition in which sound is delivered to both ears simultaneously. 97

binocular depth cues   Visual cues that depend on both eyes; used to detect distance. 91

biological motives   Motives that have a definite physiological basis and are biologically necessary for survival of the individual or species. 218

biological response systems   Systems of the body that are important in behavioral responding; include the senses, endocrines, muscles, and nervous system. 28

biological therapy   Treatment of behavior problems through biological techniques; major biological therapies include drug therapy, psychosurgery, and electroconvulsive therapy. 340

bipolar cells   Cells in the retina of the eye; light causes the rods and cones to send electrical energy to the bipolar cells, then pass on neural impulses to ganglion cells. 84

bipolar disorder   Mood disorder characterized by extreme mood swings from sad depression to joyful mania; sometimes called manic-depression. 315

blind spot   Place in the retina where the optic nerve begins; a person cannot see at this location. 84

blinding technique   In an experiment, a control for bias in which the assignment of a subject to the experimental or control group is unknown to the subject or experimenter or both (a double-blind experiment). 20

body dysmorphic disorder   Somatoform disorder characterized by a preoccupation with an imaginary defect in the physical appearance of a physically healthy person. 320

body language   Communication through position and movement of the body. 248

bottom-up processing   The psychoanalytic process of understanding communication by listening to words, then interpreting phrases, and finally understanding ideas. 180

brain   Part of the central nervous system that is housed in the skull. 33

brainstorming   Technique in which a group attempts to come up with numerous creative solutions to a problem without evaluating or criticizing the ideas being presented. 364

brand image   In consumer psychology, the consumer's recognition of a particular brand of product. 388

brightness   Intensity of light; determined by wave amplitude. 82

brightness constancy   Tendency to see objects as continuing to have the same brightness even though light or shadow may change their immediate sensory properties. 86

bulimia nervosa   Eating disorder in which an individual eats large amounts of calorie-rich food in a short time and then purges the food by vomiting or using laxatives. 221

burnout   The depletion of our physical and mental resources due to stress; burnout occurs when we have more energy going out than coming in. 289

bystander effect   Phenomenon in an emergency situation in which a person is more likely to help when alone than when in a group of people. 373

C

caffeine   Stimulant drug that causes central nervous system arousal; often contained in coffee, tea, chocolate, and cola drinks. Causes alertness in people. 117

California Psychological Inventory (CPI)   An objective personality test used to study normal populations. 276

cannabis sativa   The plant from which marijuana is derived. 118

Cannon-Bard theory of emotion   Theory of emotion which states that the emotional feeling and the physiological arousal occur at the same time. 239

cardinal traits   In Allport's personality theory, the traits of an individual that are so dominant that they are expressed in everything the person does; few people possess cardinal traits. 265

cardiovascular disorders   Psychophysiological disorders that involve the heart and circulatory system; include hypertension and coronary heart disease. 298

case study   Research method in which the events of a person's life are reconstructed to gain insight into a current problem; a scientific biography. 18

CAT scan (computerized axial tomography)   Method of studying the brain that uses a series of X rays. 37

catatonic schizophrenia   A type of schizophrenia that is characterized by periods of complete immobility and the apparent absence of will to move or speak. 317

catatonic stupor   Immobility and absence of will to move by someone with catatonic schizophrenia. 317

CCK (cholecystokinin)   Hormone involved in regulation of eating behavior. 219

cell body (soma) The central portion of a body cell; includes the nucleus and genes. 29

central nervous system The part of the human nervous system that interprets and stores messages from the sense organs, decides what behavior to exhibit, and sends appropriate messages to the muscles and glands; includes the brain and spinal cord. 32

central tendency In statistics, measures of central tendency give a number that represents the entire group or sample. 22

central traits In Allport's personality theory, the traits of an individual that form the core of the personality; they are developed through experience. 265

cerebellum The part of the hindbrain that is involved in balance and muscle coordination. 33

cerebral cortex The outermost layer of the cerebrum of the brain where higher mental functions occur. The cerebral cortex is divided into sections, or lobes, that control various activities. 34

cerebrum (cerebral hemisphere) Largest part of the forebrain involved in cognitive functions; the cerebrum consists of two hemispheres connected by the corpus callosum. 34

chemical senses The sense of smell and taste; sensory stimulation of the chemical sense receptors involves contact with chemical substances. 97

childhood The period of human development roughly between 2 and 11 years. 58

chorionic villi sampling Prenatal test in which a sample of embryonic tissue is examined for genetic defects. 52

chromosomes Bodies in the cell nucleus that contain the genes. 43

chunking Process of combining stimuli in order to increase memory capacity. 160

classical conditioning The form of learning in which a stimulus is associated with another stimulus that causes a particular response. Sometimes called Pavlovian conditioning or respondent conditioning. 131

clinical psychology Subfield in which psychologists assess psychological problems and treat people with behavior problems using psychological techniques (called psychotherapy). 13

closure Perceptual principle of organization of filling in the gaps in a figure to perceive a complete form. 89

cocaine A stimulant derived from the leaves of the South American coca plant. 117

cochlea A spiraled organ in the inner ear that is involved in sound sensation. 95

code of ethics Code of conduct that ensures that research will be conducted properly and that subjects will not be harmed, mentally or physically. 16

cognition Mental processes, such as perception, attention, memory, language, thinking, and problem solving; cognition involves the acquisition, storage, retrieval, and utilization of knowledge. 6, 178

cognitive behavior therapy A form of behavior therapy that identifies self-defeating attitudes and thoughts in a subject, and then helps the subject to replace these with positive, supportive thoughts. 335

cognitive development Changes over time in mental processes such as thinking, memory, language, and problem solving. 60

cognitive dissonance Festinger's theory of attitude change that states that when people hold two psychologically inconsistent ideas they experience tension that forces them to reconcile the conflicting ideas. 355

cognitive expectancy The condition in which an individual learns that certain behaviors lead to particular goals; cognitive expectancy motivates the individual to exhibit goal-directed behaviors. 218

cognitive learning Type of learning that theorizes that the learner utilizes cognitive structures in memory to make decisions about behaviors. 148

cognitive map A mental representation of an area; concept used by Tolman in cognitive learning. 149

cognitive psychology The area of psychology that includes the study of mental activities involved in perception, memory, language, thought, and problem solving. 13, 15, 178

cognitive therapy Therapy developed by Beck in which an individual's negative, self-defeating thoughts are restructured in a positive way. 336

cognitive-motivational-relational theory of emotion A theory of emotion proposed by Lazarus that includes cognitive appraisal, motivational goals, and relationships between an individual and the environment. 240

collective unconscious Jung's representation of the thoughts shared by all humans. 263

color blindness Visual condition in which the person cannot discriminate all possible color variations. 85

color constancy Tendency to see familiar objects as the same color regardless of the illumination. 86

common fate Gestalt perceptual principle in which groups of stimuli, or objects moving together, are seen as a unit. 90

companionate love An emotion characterized by deep attachment, trust, respect, affection, loyalty, and familiarity; called conjugal love by married partners. 244

comparative psychology Subfield in which experimental psychologists study and compare the behavior of different species of animals. 15

compensation   Defense mechanism by which the individual deals with feelings of inadequacy by focusing on a desirable characteristic. 294

competence   Theory of motivation that states that people are motivated to interact successfully with the environment; condition that occurs when a person goes beyond just meeting challenges to improving his or her life and achieving his or her goals. 226, 282

compliance   Type of social influence in which an individual changes his or her behavior because of a direct request from someone else. 359

compliant personality   In Horney's personality theory, the personality type that is characterized by a strong need to be loved and needed by others. 265

composite standard age score   The overall score on the Stanford-Binet Intelligence Scale; average score is 100 with standard deviation of 16. 194

compulsive acts   Rituals performed by the compulsive-obsessive to reduce anxiety. 311

computer assisted instruction (CAI)   The technique of using the computer to present learning material and help students learn; CAI has become popular with the advent of microcomputers. 147

computer simulation   Process in which a computer is programmed to approximate some event or activity. 186

concept   A set of features that share one or more common properties. 183

concept formation (concept learning)   The development of the ability to respond to common features of categories of objects or events. 183

concrete operations period   Stage in cognitive development; from 7 to 11 years, the time in which the child's ability to solve problems with reasoning greatly increases. 62

conditioned response (CR)   The response or behavior that occurs when the conditioned stimulus is presented (after the CS has been associated with the US). 132

conditioned stimulus (CS)   An originally neutral stimulus that is associated with an unconditioned stimulus and takes on the latter's capability of eliciting a particular reaction. 132

conditioned taste aversion (CTA)   An aversion to particular tastes associated with stomach distress; usually considered a unique form of classical conditioning because of the extremely long interstimulus intervals involved. 136

conditioning   A term applied to two types of learning (classical and operant). Conditioning refers to the scientific aspect of the type of learning. 131

conduction   The ability of a neuron to carry a message (a neural impulse) along its length. 29

conduction deafness   Type of deafness resulting from structures in the outer or middle ear not functioning properly. 96

cones   One type of vision receptor; cones respond to color variations in bright light. 83

confirmation bias   When solving problems, the tendency to seek information that confirms a hypothesis. 189

conflict   Situation that occurs when we experience incompatible demands or desires; or, the outcome when one individual or group perceives that another individual or group has caused or will cause harm. 284, 367

conformity   Type of social influence in which an individual changes his or her behavior to fit social norms or expectations. 358

congruence   In Rogers's personality theory, the state in which the different aspects of the personality—the real self, perceived self, and ideal self—are essentially the same. 269

conscientiousness   The dimension in the five-factor personality theory that includes traits such as practical, cautious, serious, reliable, careful, and ambitious; also called dependability. 268

conscious   Being aware of experiencing sensations, thoughts, and feelings at any given point in time. 9

conscious mind   In Freud's psychoanalytic theory of personality, the part of personality that we are aware of in everyday life. 106

consciousness   The processing of information at various levels of awareness; state in which a person is aware of sensations, thoughts, and feelings. 106

consensus   In causal attribution, the extent to which other people react as the subject does in a particular situation. 350

conservation   The ability to recognize that something stays the same even if it takes on a different form; Piaget tested conservation of mass, number, length, and volume. 62

consistency   In causal attribution, the extent to which the subject always behaves in the same way in a situation. 350

consolidation   The biological neural process of making memories permanent; possibly short-term memory is electrically coded and long-term memory is chemically coded. 174

consumer psychology   Area of psychology that is concerned with the behavior of the consumer when he or she goes out to purchase a product. 386

contact comfort   In attachment, comfort felt by infants in physical contact, especially when it is soft or warm. 57

continuity   The Gestalt rule of perceiving a straight line as continuing to be straight. 89

continuous reinforcement   Situation in which every correct response is followed by reinforcement. 142

continuum of preparedness   Seligman's proposal that animals are biologically prepared to learn certain responses more readily than they are prepared to learn others. 151

control   A goal of psychology; modifying behavior through manipulation of the environment. 7

control group   Subjects in an experiment who do not receive the independent variable; the control group determines the effectiveness of the independent variable. 19

conventional morality   Level II in Kohlberg's theory, in which moral reasoning is based on conformity and social standards. 63

convergence   Binocular depth cue in which we detect distance by interpreting the kinesthetic sensations produced by the muscles of the eyeballs. 91

conversion disorder   Somatoform disorder in which a person displays obvious disturbance in the nervous system without a physical basis for the problem. 320

coping   The adjustment people make to stress; coping involves solving the problems that cause stress and managing the emotions that accompany it. 293

cornea   Outer membrane that covers the eyeball. 83

coronary heart disease (CHD)   Any condition that causes a narrowing of the coronary arteries. 298

corpus callosum   The nerve bundle that connects the two hemispheres of the cerebrum. 34

correlation   Statistical technique to determine the degree of relationship that exists between two variables. 21

correlation coefficient   A statistical measure of the degree to which two factors are related; perfect positive correlation is +1.0, while no correlation is 0.0 and perfect negative correlation is −1.0. The stronger the relationship, the closer the correlation score is to 1.0. 21

correspondent inference theory   This attribution theory states that people observe an individual and then make inferences about his or her behavior. 350

counseling psychology   Subfield in which psychologists help people with emotional or personal problems. 14

counterbalancing   Experimental design in which subjects receive all treatments, but in different orders. 20

counterconditioning   A behavior therapy in which an unwanted response is replaced by conditioning a new response that is incompatible with it. 333

courtship   The behavioral process whereby sexually mature animals of a species become mating pairs. 222

covariation theory   This attribution theory states that certain factors (consensus, consistency, and distinctiveness) occur together, helping an individual predict causation. 350

covert desensitization   A technique for helping an individual overcome fears by learning to relax in the presence of images of anxiety-arousing thoughts. 334

crack   A potent form of cocaine made by mixing baking soda and water with the crystalline form of cocaine and heating it. 118

cranial nerves   Set of 12 peripheral nerves that enter the central nervous system in the brain. The cranial nerves include sensory and motor nerves from the somatic nervous system. 33

creativity   A process of coming up with new or unusual responses to familiar circumstances. 189

critical period   Period of time during development in which particular learning or experiences normally occur; if learning doesn't occur, the individual has a difficult time learning it later. 54, 151

crowding   The psychological feeling of not having enough space available. 391

crystallized intelligence   Verbal reasoning and comprehension of cultural concepts. 71

culture-bound   The idea that a test's usefulness is limited to the culture in which it was written and utilized. 191

culture-fair   Ideally, a test which is completely independent of cultural influences. 199

cumulative response curve   Graphed curve that results when responses for a subject are added to one another over time; if subjects respond once every 5 minutes, they will have a cumulative response curve value of 12 after an hour. 143

curiosity motive   Motive that causes the individual to seek out a certain amount of novelty. 225

cyclothymia   A bipolar disorder that is a moderately severe problem with mood swings from hypomanic episodes to depression. 315

D

dark adaptation   Process in which the retina's rods and cones adjust to changes in dim light. 83

daydreaming   An altered state of consciousness that occurs without effort and involves a brief escape from reality into fantasy. 113

death instinct   (also called thanatos) Freud's term for an instinct that is destructive to the individual or species; aggression is a major expression of death instinct. 213, 262

debriefing   Procedure of explaining the true purpose of an experiment in which deception was used. 17

decay Theory of forgetting in which sensory impressions leave memory traces that fade away with time. 168

decenter The ability to realize that your way of looking at the world is only one perspective. 62

decibel Unit for measuring loudness. 95

deep structure The actual meaning of a sentence. 180

defense mechanisms Psychological techniques to help protect ourselves from stress and anxiety, to resolve conflicts, and to preserve our self-esteem. 293

delayed conditioning A procedure in classical conditioning in which the presentation of the CS precedes the onset of the US and the termination of the CS is delayed until the US is presented; most effective procedure. 133

delusion The holding of obviously false beliefs; for example, imagining someone is trying to kill you. 316

delusional disorder Psychological disorder in which the individual shows a persistent delusion not attributable to any other mental disorder; formerly called paranoid disorder. 319

demand characteristics In an experiment, the situation in which subjects feel they are required to act in a certain way; demand characteristics can bias the outcome of the study. 20

dendrites Projections that extend from the neuron and receive messages (neural impulses) from adjacent neurons. 29

density The physical area available to the given number of individuals present. 390

density-intensity theory Freedman's crowding theory; as density increases, the intensity of our moods and behavior also increases. 392

deoxyribonucleic acid (DNA) Organic molecules that genes are composed of; DNA has a double helix pattern that allows the gene to transcribe its message and direct the formation of biochemicals that can be utilized to ultimately produce the characteristics of the individual. 43

dependent variable In psychology, the behavior or response that is measured; it is dependent on the independent variable. 19

depersonalization disorder Dissociative disorder in which the individual escapes from his or her own personality by believing that he or she doesn't exist or that his or her environment is not real. 321

depolarization Any change in which the internal electrical charge becomes more positive. 30

depressants Drugs that have a sedative effect. 115

depth of processing In memory encoding, how relevantly or meaningfully the material is encoded; meaningful material is processed more deeply. 162

depth perception Ability to judge distance to object. 90

description A goal of psychology; recording accurate observations of behavior. 7

descriptive statistics Techniques that help summarize large amounts of data information. 22

detached personality In Horney's personality theory, the personality type that is characterized by a need to maintain distance from others. 265

development Changes in the physical, cognitive, and personality-social characteristics of the individual over time. 50

developmental psychology Study of physical and mental growth and behavioral changes in individuals from conception to death. 15, 50

developmentally handicapped (DH) Individuals who are not able to learn as rapidly as classmates in school. Except for special needs, DH children are often mainstreamed in regular classrooms. 203

dichromat A person who is partially color blind; a person who lacks one of the three types of cones. 85

difference threshold The minimum amount of energy change required to produce a difference in sensation. 80

diffusion of responsibility Finding that groups tend to inhibit helping behavior; responsibility is shared equally by members of the group so that no one individual feels a strong commitment. 373

digit-span memory test Test of short-term memory in which the subject is asked to recall a string of numbers. 160

discrimination The behaviors toward members of a group that are unfair when compared to behavior toward others. 356

disorganized schizophrenia A type of schizophrenia that is characterized by a severe personality disintegration; the individual often displays bizarre behavior. 317

displacement Defense mechanism by which the individual directs his or her aggression or hostility toward a person or object other than the one it should be directed toward; in Freud's dream theory, the process of reassigning emotional feelings from one object to another one. 111, 294

dissociative disorder Psychological disorder that involves a disturbance in the memory, consciousness, or identity of an individual; types include multiple personality disorder, depersonalization disorder, psychogenic amnesia, and psychogenic fugue. 321

distinctiveness In causal attribution, the extent to which the subject reacts the same way in other situations. 350

distress Stress that is harmful or unpleasant; anxiety and fear are examples of distress. 282

distributed practice Learning material over an extended period of time, with breaks between sessions. 171

dizygotic twins Nonidentical twins produced when two separate eggs are fertilized by two separate sperm at the same time. 45

dominant Form of a gene that is always reflected in the phenotype. 43

door-in-the-face technique The technique to obtain compliance from a person by first making a large · request and then making a small request. 360

dopamine A neurotransmitter involved in moods. 31

Down syndrome Form of mental retardation caused by having three number 21 chromosomes (trisomy 21). 203

dream analysis Psychoanalytic technique in which a patient's dreams are reviewed and analyzed to discover true feelings. 328

drive Motivational concept used to describe the internal forces that push an organism toward a goal; sometimes identified as psychological arousal arising from a physiological need. 213

drug therapy A biological therapy in which drugs are given to modify abnormal behaviors. 340

DSM-III-R Diagnostic and Statistic Manual of Mental Disorders; latest edition at press time was published in 1987 by the American Psychiatric Association. 308

duodenum The initial segment of the small intestine. 219

dyssomnia Sleep disorder in which the chief symptom is a disturbance in the amount and quality of sleep; they include insomnia and hypersomnia. 113

dysthymia Mood disorder in which the person suffers moderate depression much of the time for at least two years. 313

E

eardrum Thin membrane stretched across the inner end of the auditory canal. 95

echoic memory Auditory information that is encoded into the sensory memory store. 159

educational psychology Subfield in which psychologists help improve the effectiveness of textbooks, classroom organization, teaching methods, and test design. 14

EEG imaging A brain research technique in which electrodes are placed on the scalp and the wires are connected to a computer to record brain activity. 37

ego Freud's term for individual's sense of reality. 262

egocentrism Seeing the world only from your perspective. 61

eidetic imagery Photographic memory; ability to recall great detail accurately after briefly viewing something. 160

elaborative rehearsal Thinking about the meaning of information and trying to form associations with information already in memory. 162

Electra complex The Freudian idea that the young girl feels inferior to boys because she lacks a penis. 263

electrical stimulation of the brain (ESB) Procedure in which a tiny electric current is sent into a precise location in the brain to alter behavior. 34

electroconvulsive therapy (ECT) A type of biological therapy in which electricity is applied to the brain in order to relieve severe depression. 342

electroencephalogram (EEG) Record of measuring brain-wave activity. 107

electroencephalography (EEG) Technique of measuring brain-wave activity; the record is an electroencephalogram. 37

electrophysiological Bodily measures that can be recorded electrically. 107

embryonic stage Stage in prenatal development; from about two to eight weeks, during which three layers of cells form. 50

emotion A response to a stimulus that involves physiological arousal, subjective feeling, cognitive interpretation, and overt behavior. 234

emotional stability The dimension in the five-factor personality theory that includes traits such as relaxation, calmness, unemotionalism, security, and patience; negative pole is neuroticism. 268

encoding The process of putting information into the memory system. 157

encounter group As in a sensitivity training group, this is a therapy where people become aware of themselves in meeting others. 338

endocrine glands Ductless glands that secrete chemicals called hormones into the bloodstream. 40

endorphins Several neuropeptides that function as neurotransmitters. The opiate-like endorphins are involved in pain, reinforcement, and memory. 31, 100

engineering psychology Area of psychology that is concerned with how work is performed, design of equipment, and work environment; also called human factors psychology. 386

engram The physical memory trace or neural circuit that holds memory; also called memory trace. 173

environmental psychology Area of psychology that is concerned with discovering how the physical environment influences human behavior. 389

episodic memory Highest memory system; includes information about personal experiences. 164

equity theory   Theory of interpersonal relationships that states that people are motivated to maintain a fair balance in relationships. 242

Eros   Freud's term for an instinct that helps the individual or species survive; also called life instinct. 213, 262

escape conditioning   Learning situation in which a subject is presented with an aversive stimulus from which he or she must escape. 145

esteem needs   Fourth level of motives in Maslow's hierarchy; includes high evaluation of oneself, self-respect, self-esteem, and respect of others. 217

estrogen   Female sex hormone secreted by the ovaries; produces female characteristics such as breasts and wide hips and makes the female sexually receptive. 41, 222

estrus   Period of sexual receptivity in a female animal. 222

ethogram   A detailed description of all the behaviors shown by a species; this is the first step for the ethologist when studying animal behavior. 211

ethology   The science of the behavior of animals in their natural environment. 211

eustress   Stress that results from pleasant and satisfying experiences; earning a high grade or achieving success produce eustress. 282

excitement phase   First phase in the human sexual response cycle; the beginning of sexual arousal. 250

expectancy   In experimental research, a type of experimenter bias in which the experimenter subtly influences the outcome of an experiment; sometimes called the self-fulfilling prophecy. In Rotter's personality theory, the individual's belief that if he or she exhibits a certain behavior in a specific situation, it will result in reinforcement. 20, 272

expectancy-value   Theory of motivation that proposes that behavior is the result of expectations of achieving goals and the value placed on those goals. 218

experiment   Research method in which environmental conditions can be controlled in order to discover the cause-effect relationship between two conditions. 19

experimental group   Subjects in an experiment who receive the independent variable. 19

experimental psychology   Subfield in which psychologists research the fundamental causes of behavior. Many experimental psychologists conduct experiments in basic research. 15

experimenter bias   Source of potential error in an experiment from the action or expectancy of the experimenter; might influence the experimental results in ways that mask the true outcome. 20

expert witness   In a courtroom, a person who is judged to be highly competent in the area under investigation and who can evaluate the evidence presented. 379

explanation   A goal of psychology; understanding the influences on behavior. 7

exploration   Sensory inspection of the environment. 225

external locus of control   In Rotter's personality theory, the perception that reinforcement is independent of a person's behavior. 273

external pressure   Pressure that results from the demands made on us by other people. 284

extinction   The elimination of behavior by, in classical conditioning, the withholding of the US, and in operant conditioning, the withholding of the reinforcement. 135

extraneous variables   In an experiment, the conditions or influences that are not of interest to the researcher. 19

extraversion   The dimension in the five-factor personality theory that includes traits such as sociability, talkativeness, boldness, fun-lovingness, adventurousness, and assertiveness; also called surgency. The personality concept of Jung in which the personal energy of the individual is directed externally. 263, 268

extrinsic motivation   Motivation outside of the individual; reinforcement comes from the environment. 226

eyewitness testimony   In a courtroom, an account of an incident given by someone who saw it firsthand. 165, 379

F

facial expressions   Communication of emotion through movement and position of facial muscles. 246

facial feedback hypothesis   Theory proposed by Tomkins that brain networks underlie each emotion and a specific facial expression is associated with each emotion. 247

factor analysis   A statistical procedure used to determine the relationship among variables. 267

family therapy   Group therapy that treats the social interactions of the family unit. 338

fantasy   Defense mechanism in which a person escapes from stress and anxiety by daydreaming that everything is perfect and that all the problems are gone. 293

fear of failure   Motivation in which an individual does not want to fail in a task; individuals who score low on need for achievement tend to have a high fear of failure. 227

fear of success Motivation in which an individual does not want to succeed on a task. 227

fetal alcohol syndrome (FAS) Condition in which defects in the newborn child are caused by the mother's excessive alcohol intake. 50, 116

fetal stage Stage in prenatal development, from eight weeks until birth. 52

figure-ground relationship Perceptual organization rule that explains our tendency to separate a scene into a main figure and a background. 88

five-factor model of personality tracts A trait theory of personality that includes the factors of extraversion, agreeableness, conscientiousness, emotional stability, and openness. 267

fixed action pattern (FAP) Unlearned, inherited, stereotyped behaviors that are shown by all members of a species; term used in ethology. 211

fixed interval (FI) schedule Schedule of reinforcement where the subject receives reinforcement for a correct response given after a specified time interval. 143

fixed ratio (FR) schedule Schedule of reinforcement in which the subject is reinforced after a certain number of responses. 143

flashbulb memory Memory of an event that is so important that significant details are vividly remembered for life. 164

flavor Property of food that is due to smell, appearance, texture, and temperature. 98

flextime Flexible working hours; type of temporal working condition in which employees help determine the hours they work. 386

flow chart Diagram showing the possible choices at each step in solving problems. 186

fluid intelligence The ability to solve novel problems. 71

foot-in-the-door technique The technique to obtain compliance from a person by first making a small request and then making a large request. 359

forebrain The largest and most complex part of the brain; located in the front, it controls higher level functions. 34

foreclosure In Marcia's adolescent identity theory, the status of individuals who make a commitment to values and roles without struggling with personal problems. 65

forensic psychology Area of psychology that includes work in police departments, courts, and prisons to detect and prevent crime and assess and rehabilitate those accused of criminal behavior. 378

forgetting In memory, not being able to retrieve the original learning. The part of the original learning that cannot be retrieved is said to be forgotten. 166

formal concept Type of concept that has a clear and unambiguous rule that specifies exactly which attributes define the category. 184

formal operations period Period in cognitive development; at 11 years, the adolescent begins abstract thinking and reasoning. This period continues throughout the rest of life. 62

fovea The middle area of the retina in which the cones are clustered. 83

free association Psychoanalytic technique in which the patient says everything that comes to mind. 328

free recall A verbal learning procedure in which the order of presentation of the stimuli is varied and the subject can learn the items in any order. 167

frequency Number of peaks of sound pressure per second; determines the pitch of sound. 94

frequency distribution Tabulation of data that shows the number of times each score occurs. 22

frequency theory of hearing Theory of hearing that states that the frequency of vibrations at the basilar membrane determines the frequency of firing of neurons carrying impulses to the brain. 96

frontal lobes The part of the cerebral cortex that is involved in higher mental activities such as thinking. 34

frustration A cause of stress that results from the blocking of a person's goal-oriented behavior. 285

frustration-drive theory Theory of aggression that states that it is caused by frustration. 370

functional fixedness A special case of a set that interferes with problem solving; the longer we use an object the less likely we are to find new uses for it. 188

functionalism School of thought that studied the functional value of consciousness and behavior. 10

fundamental attribution error Attribution bias in which people overestimate the role of internal disposition and underestimate the role of external situation. 351

G

GABA Gama-aminobutyric acid; amino acid inhibitory neurotransmitter found throughout the central nervous system. 31

ganglion cells Cells in the retina of the eye; the ganglion cells receive messages from the bipolar cells. Axons of the ganglions form the optic nerve. 84

gate-control theory of pain Theory of pain that proposes that there is a gate that allows pain impulses to travel from the spinal cord to the brain. 99

gay male A male homosexual; a man who has a same gender sexual orientation. 252

gender identity   A person's sense of maleness or femaleness; the learned psychological identification with a particular sex. 56, 249

gender-identity disorder   Incongruence between assigned sex and gender identity. 253

gender-identity/role   Term that incorporates gender identity (the private perception of one's sex) and gender role (the public expression of one's gender identity). 250

gene   The basic unit of heredity; the gene is composed of deoxyribonucleic acid (DNA). 42

general adaptation syndrome (GAS)   Selye's theory of how the body responds to stress over time. GAS includes alarm reaction, resistance, and exhaustion. 287

generalized anxiety disorder   Anxiety disorder in which the individual lives in a state of constant severe tension, continuous fear and apprehension. 312

genetics   The study of heredity; genetics is the science of discovering how traits are passed along generations. 42

genotype   The complete set of genes inherited by an individual from his or her parents. 42

gerontology   The study of late adulthood and aging. 67

Gestalt psychology   A school of thought that studied whole or complete perceptions. 11

Gestalt therapy   Insight therapy designed to help people become more aware of themselves in the here and now and to take responsibility for their own actions. 330

glucostatic theory   Theory that states that hunger is due to low glucose metabolism in individual cells. 219

glutamate   Amino acid neurotransmitter; principal excitatory transmitter in brain's cortex. 31

glycine   Amino acid inhibitory neurotransmitter found chiefly in the spinal cord and hindbrain. 31

gonads   The reproductive glands; ovaries in the female, testes in the male. 41

grammar   The set of rules that structures a language. 178

grandiose delusion   Distortion of reality; one's belief that he or she is extremely important or powerful. 317

GRIT   Graduated and reciprocated initiatives in tension reduction. This procedure, proposed by Osgood, occurs when one side announces that it wants to reduce tension and then shows a conciliatory act. 368

group   A collection of people who have a common goal and work toward that goal. 363

group polarization   Tendency for a group to move toward an extreme position—either more risky or more conservative. 364

group therapy   Treatment of several patients at the same time. 337

groupthink   When group members are so committed to, and optimistic about, the group that they feel it is invulnerable; they become so concerned with maintaining consensus that criticism is muted. 364

growth hormone   Hormone secreted by the pituitary gland that helps regulate growth. 40

GSR (galvanic skin response)   A measure of autonomic nervous system activity. In the GSR measurement technique a slight electric current is passed over the skin; the more nervous a subject is, the easier the current will flow. 236

gustation   The taste sensation. 98

H

hallucination   A sensory impression reported when no external stimulus exists to justify the report; often hallucinations are a symptom of mental illness. 316

hallucinogens   Psychedelic drugs that result in hallucinations at high doses, and other effects on behavior and perception in mild doses. 118

halo effect   The finding that once we form a general impression of someone, we tend to interpret additional information about the person in a consistent manner. 349

haptic sense   Sense of touch. 99

Hawthorne effect   The finding that behavior can be influenced just by participation in a research study. 385

health psychology   Field of psychology that studies psychological influences on people's health, including how they stay healthy, why they become ill, and how their behavior relates to their state of health. 282, 297

helping   The act of providing aid or assistance to someone; sometimes called prosocial behavior. 372

heredity   The natural capability of an individual to develop the characteristics possessed by his or her ancestors. 41

heuristic   Problem-solving strategy; a person tests solutions most likely to be correct. 187

hierarchy of needs   Maslow's list of motives in humans, arranged from the biological to the uniquely human. 216

higher order conditioning   Learning to make associations with stimuli that have been learned previously. 136

hindbrain   The back part of the brain that controls basic life-support of the body. 33

hippocampus   Brain structure in the limbic system that is important in learning and memory. 34

homeostasis   The state of equilibrium that maintains a balance in the internal body environment. 40, 313

homosexual   Sexual preference and activities directed toward other people of the same sex. 252

horizontal cells   The cells that interconnect the neurons in the retina. 84

hormones   Chemicals produced by the endocrine glands that regulate activity of certain bodily processes. 40

hospice   Program of supportive services that provide physical, psychological, social, and spiritual aid for the dying. 72

hue   The color we perceive; hue is determined by the wavelength of light. 82

humanistic   Psychological school of thought that believes that people are unique beings. 216

humanistic psychologist   Psychologist who concentrates on developing theories based on the uniqueness of the human personality. 269

humanistic psychology   Psychological school of thought that believes that people are unique beings who cannot be broken down into parts. 13

hygiene needs   In Herzberg's theory, the factors that can produce job dissatisfaction if not met. They include company policy, supervision, salary, interpersonal relations, and working conditions. 385

hyperopia (farsightedness)   Visual disorder in which the eyeball is unusually short and the image is focused beyond the retina. 84

hyperphagia   Disorder in which the individual continues to eat until he or she is obese; can be caused by damage to ventromedial hypothalamus. 220

hypersomnia   Sleep disorder in which an individual falls asleep at inappropriate times; narcolepsy is a form of hypersomnia. 114

hypertension   An increase in blood pressure above acceptable levels. 298

hypnagogic hallucination   Symptom of narcolepsy in which very vivid dreams occur as the narcoleptic begins a sleep attack. 114

hypnosis   Altered state of consciousness characterized by heightened suggestibility. 120

hypochondriasis   Somatoform disorder in which the individual is obsessed with fears of having a serious medical disease. 320

hypothalamus   Part of the brain's limbic system; involved in motivational behaviors, including eating, drinking, and sex. 34

hypothesis   In the scientific method, an educated guess or prediction about future observable events. 16

hypothyroidism   Condition resulting from an underactive thyroid; symptoms are sluggishness, sleepiness, and weight gain. 40

I

iconic memory   Visual information that is encoded into the sensory memory store. 158

id   Freud's representation of the basic instinctual drives; the id always seeks pleasure. 262

identification   The process in which children adopt the attitudes, values, and behaviors of their parents. 58

identity achievement   In Marcia's adolescent identity theory, the status of individuals, who have struggled with values and beliefs and have made a personal commitment. 65

identity diffusion   In Marcia's adolescent identity theory, the status of individuals who have failed to make a commitment to values and roles. 65

illusion   An incorrect perception that occurs when sensation is distorted. 92

immediate memory span   Sperling's measure of sensory memory capacity; subjects were asked to recall information immediately after it was presented to them. 158

impossible figure   A figure that logically cannot exist; a visual illusion. 93

impression formation   Developing an evaluation of another person from your perceptions; first, or initial, impressions are often very important. 348

imprinting   A form of early learning in which birds follow a moving stimulus (often the mother); may be similar to attachment in mammals. 151

inbred strain   Genetically identical individuals produced by artificial selection. 44

incentive   An external stimulus that pulls the individual toward some goal. 214

independent variable   The condition in an experiment that is controlled and manipulated by the experimenter; it is a stimulus that will cause a response. 19

indiscriminate attachment phase   Stage of attachment in which babies prefer humans to nonhumans, but do not discriminate among individual people. 56

individual psychology   The personality theory of Alfred Adler; this theory focuses on the uniqueness of each individual person. 264

individuation   Jung's concept of the process leading to the unification of all parts of the personality. 263

induced motion   Situation in which we attribute motion to an object that is not really moving; when we incorrectly attribute motion to figure rather than background. 92

industrial/organizational psychology   Subfield of psychology in which psychologists work in businesses and organizations to increase communication, improve employee satisfaction, and help design training programs; includes personnel psychology, organizational psychology, engineering psychology, and consumer psychology. 15, 382

infancy Period of the first two years of life during which the neonate becomes a small, achieving child. 52

inferential statistics Techniques that help researchers make generalizations about a finding based on a limited number of subjects. 24

inferiority complex Adler's personality concept that states that because children are dependent on adults and cannot meet the standards set for themselves they feel inferior.264

information-processing theory Memory theory that relies on computer models to describe the flow of information through the memory system. 157

ingratiation Any technique that increases the attractiveness of a person trying to seek compliance from us; examples include giving compliments, doing favors, or just being nice. 359

insight A sudden grasping of the means necessary to achieve a goal; important in the Gestalt approach to problem solving. 148

insight therapy Therapy based on the assumption that behavior is abnormal because people do not adequately understand the motivation causing their behavior. 327

insomnia The inability to sleep. 114

instinct Highly stereotyped behavior common to all members of a species that often appears in virtually complete form in the absence of any obvious opportunities to learn them. 151, 210

instinct theory Any theory that attempts to explain behavior as being determined by instincts. 210

instinct theory Theory proposed by Freud that aggression is the result of a death instinct inherent in all human beings. 370

instinctive drift The process of learned behavior moving over time toward more innate responses. 151

instrumental conditioning Operant conditioning. 138

intellectually gifted Upper extreme of intelligence, usually when an individual has an IQ score of 130 or higher; intellectually gifted individuals tend to be successful in life. 204

intelligence Capacity to learn and behave adaptively. 191

intelligence quotient (IQ) An index of a person's performance on an intelligence test relative to others in the culture; ratio of a person's mental age to chronological age. 194

intelligence test A test designed to measure a broad range of mental abilities; intelligence tests are often used to predict future academic success. 193

interference Theory of forgetting in which information that was learned before (proactive interference) or after (retroactive interference) causes the learner to be unable to remember the material of interest. 168

internal locus of control In Rotter's personality theory, the perception that reinforcement is contingent upon behavior. 272

internal pressure Pressure that results when we attempt to maintain self-esteem by forcing ourselves to achieve higher standards. 284

interneuron (also called association neuron) A neuron connected with other neurons. 29

internship A period of time (usually one year) in which a person works under the supervision of others before being on his or her own, usually part of a clinical or counseling psychology program. 14

interpersonal attraction Our behavior and attitudes toward other people; can be positive or negative. 241

interposition Monocular depth cue in which one object partially blocks another; we assume the overlap is due to the first one being closer. 90

interstimulus interval Time interval between two stimuli; in classical conditioning, it is the elapsed time between the CS and the US. 133

interview Research method in which in-depth information is obtained through verbal interaction with a subject. 18

intimate distance Hall's closest interpersonal distance category, 0 to 1.5 feet. 389

intrinsic motivation Motivation inside the individual; we do something because we receive satisfaction from it. 226

introspection Method in which a subject gives a self-report of his or her immediate experience. 9

introversion The personality concept of Jung in which the personal energy of the individual is directed inward; characterized by introspection, seriousness, inhibition, and restraint. 263

irritability The characteristic of a neuron to change in response to stimulation. 29

J

James-Lange theory of emotion Theory of emotion which states that the physiological arousal and behavior come before the subjective experience of an emotion. 238

just noticeable difference (JND) Difference threshold: minimum amount of energy required to produce a difference in sensation. 80

K

kinesthesis   The sense of bodily movement. 101

L

language   Communication utilizing manipulation of symbols to convey meaning to others or one's self. 178

language acquisition device (LAD)   Hypothesized biological structure that accounts for the relative ease of acquiring language, according to Chomsky. 181

latent dream content   In Freud's dream theory, the true thoughts in the unconsciousness; the true meaning of the dream. 111

latent learning   Learning that occurs when an individual acquires knowledge of something but does not show it until motivated to do so. 149

lateral hypothalamus (LH)   Part of the hypothalamus involved in initiating eating behavior. 219

lateral preoptic area   Area of the hypothalamus in which osmoreceptor cells are sensitive to blood and cellular dehydration due to the amount of salt. 221

law of effect   Thorndike's law that if a response produces satisfaction it will be repeated; reinforcement. 138

leader   Someone who is able to exert influence over the other members of a group. 368

learned helplessness   Condition in which a person learns that his or her behavior has no effect on his or her environment; when an individual gives up and stops trying. 292

learned social motives   Social motives that are learned; include achievement and affiliation. 226

learning   The relatively permanent change in behavior or behavioral ability of an individual that occurs as a result of experience. 130

learning styles   The preferences students have for learning; theories of learning styles include personality differences, styles of information processing, and instructional preferences. 395

learning to learn   Principle in which the skill learned in one situation is transferred to a new situation. 188

lens   Part of the eye that focuses on stimuli. 83

lesbian   A female homosexual; a woman who has a same gender sexual orientation. 252

libido   Freud's term for psychic energy that builds up in the id and powers motivation. 213, 262

life instinct   (also called Eros) Freud's term for an instinct that helps the individual or species survive; sex is the major expression of life instinct. 213, 262

life structure   In Levinson's theory of adult personality development, the underlying pattern of an individual's life at any particular time; seasonal cycles include preadulthood, early adulthood, middle adulthood, and late adulthood. 68

light waves   A type of electromagnetic energy; light waves stimulate the eyes to produce vision. 82

limbic system   The structures of the forebrain that control motivation and emotion. 34

linear perspective   Monocular depth cue in which lines converging depict distance; example is railroad tracks receding in the distance. 91

linguistic relativity hypothesis   Proposal that the perception of reality differs according to the language of the observer. 183

lipostatic theory   Theory of eating behavior motivation that proposes that body weight regulation is due to storage of body fat; when fat is decreased in diet, subjects eat more. 219

lobe   One of the four parts of the cerebral cortex of the brain; the cerebral cortex is divided into the frontal lobe, temporal lobe, parietal lobe, and occipital lobe. Each lobe has certain distinct functions in interpreting information received by the brain. 34

locus coeruleus   Area in the pons area of the brain stem that appears to be involved in REM sleep; this area inhibits muscle tone during REM sleep, paralyzing the person from acting out dreams. 110

locus of control   Rotter's theory in which a person's beliefs about reinforcement are classified as internal or external. 272

long-term memory   The permanent memory where rehearsed information is stored. 162

love   An emotion characterized by knowing, liking, and becoming intimate with someone. 242

low-ball procedure   The compliance technique of presenting an attractive proposal to someone and then switching it to a more unattractive proposal. 360

lucid dream   A dream in which the sleeper appears to be aware of the dream. 113

M

magic number 7   The finding that most people can remember about seven items of information for a short time (in short-term memory). 160

magnetic resonance imaging (MRI)   A method of studying brain activity using magnetic field imaging. 38

maintenance rehearsal   Repeating information over and over without thinking about it. 161

major depression   Severe mood disorder in which a person experiences one or more major depressive episodes; sometimes referred to simply as depression. 313

maladjustment   Condition that occurs when a person utilizes inappropriate abilities to respond to demands placed upon him or her. 282

management by objectives (MBO)   Procedure in industry where the worker and supervisor jointly agree on work objectives and evaluate the progress. 384

manifest dream content   In Freud's dream theory, what is remembered about a dream upon waking; a disguised representation of the unconscious wishes. 111

marijuana   A psychoactive drug derived from the leaves and flowers of the cannabis plant. 118

marital therapy   Family therapy where just the husband and wife are treated. 339

massed practice   Learning as much material as possible in long continuous stretches. 170

masturbation   Erotic self-stimulation. 252

maturation   The genetically controlled process of growth that results in orderly changes in behavior. 42, 50

mean   The arithmetic average, in which the sum of scores is divided by the number of scores. 23

meaningfulness   The informational value of material to be learned; high meaningful material is better encoded. 159

medial forebrain bundle   A tract of neurons that runs through the limbic system in the brain. 34

median   The middle score in a group of scores that are arranged from lowest to highest. 23

meditation   The practice of some form of relaxed concentration while ignoring other sensory stimuli. 122

medulla   The part of the hindbrain that helps regulate blood pressure and breathing. 33

meiosis   The process in which chromosomes in the sex cells divide to half of their number. Unlike the other body cells which have 46 chromosomes, each sex cell (sperm or egg) has only 23 chromosomes. 43

memory   The process of storing information so that it can be retrieved and used later. 156

memory attributes   The critical features of an event that are used when the experience is encoded or retrieved. 169

memory trace   A hypothetical circuit that occurs because of learned information and fades due to disuse. 168

menarche   Onset of menstruation in females. 64

menopause   End of menstruation in women. 67

mental age   The age level on which a person is capable of performing; used in determining intelligence. 194

mental retardation   Lower extreme of intelligence range, when a person scores less than 70 on an IQ test and has problems adjusting. 202

mental set   Condition in which a person's thinking becomes so standardized that he or she approaches new problems in fixed ways. 188

metamemory   The knowledge of one's own memory ability. 166

method of loci   Mnemonic technique that associates places with words to be remembered. 171

midbrain   Region connecting hindbrain and forebrain. 34

migraine headache   Headache caused by arteries under the scalp of the head that become dilated and press on pain-sensitive nerves in the area; psychophysiological disorder. 298

mild retardation   Largest segment of the mentally retarded; includes individuals with IQs of 52 to 68. 202

Minnesota Multiphasic Personality Inventory (MMPI-2)   An objective personality test that was originally devised to identify personality disorders. 275

miscarriage   Spontaneous abortion during pregnancy, when the unborn life is terminated naturally. 52

mnemonic technique   Method of improving memory by combining and relating chunks of information. 171

mode   The most frequently occurring score. 23

modeling   A process of learning by imitation in a therapeutic situation. 336

moderate retardation   Level of mental retardation in which individuals have IQs of 36 to 51. 202

monaural   Condition in which sound is delivered only to one ear. 97

monochromat   A person who can see only light and dark; a person who is totally color-blind. 85

monocular depth cues   Visual cues that depend on only one eye; used to detect distance. 90

monozygotic twins   Identical twins produced when one egg fertilized by one sperm divides into two. 45

mood disorder   Psychological disorder in which a person experiences a severe disruption in mood or emotional balance. 312

moon illusion   Illusion in which the moon looks larger on the horizon than when high in the sky. 94

moral development   Development of individuals as they adopt their society's standards of right and wrong; development of awareness of ethical behavior. 63

moratorium   In Marcia's adolescent identity theory, the status of individuals who are struggling with identity issued but have not make a commitment. 65

Moro reflex   Reflex that occurs when something in the environment changes quickly and the baby quickly extends both arms and brings the feet close to the body (startle reflex). 53

morpheme   Smallest meaningful unit of language. 179

motion parallax   Monocular depth cue where objects close by seem to move faster than objects farther away. 91

motivated forgetting (repression)   Theory which suggests that people want to forget unpleasant events. 170

motivation   The forces that initiate and direct behavior, and the variables that determine the intensity and persistence of the behavior. 210

motivator needs   In Herzberg's theory, the factors that lead to job satisfaction; they include responsibility, the nature of the work, advancement, and recognition. 385

motivator-hygiene theory   Theory of Herzberg to account for motivation and job satisfaction. 385

motive   Anything that arouses the individual and directs his or her behavior toward some goal. Three categories include biological, stimulus, and social motives. 210

motor division   A part of the somatic nervous system that carries neural information to the skeletal muscles directing their voluntary movements. 39

motor neuron   (also called efferent neuron) A neuron that carries messages from the central nervous system to the muscles and glands. 29

Müller-Lyer illusion   A well-known illusion, in which two horizontal lines have end lines either going in or out; the line with the end lines going in appears longer. 93

multiple approach-avoidance conflict   Conflict that occurs when an individual has two or more goals, both of which have positive and negative aspects. 285

multiple attachment phase   Later attachment stage in which the baby begins to form attachments to people other than the primary caretaker. 57

multiple personality   Dissociative disorder in which several personalities are present in the same individual. 321

myelin sheath   A fatty substance that provides insulation for the axon; neural impulses travel faster in myelinated axons. 29

Myers-Briggs Type Indicator (MBTI)   Objective personality test based on Jung's type theory. 278

myopia (nearsightedness)   Visual disorder in which the eyeball is unusually long and the image is focused in front of the retina; nearsighted people cannot see long-range stimuli. 84

N

nanometer (nm)   One billionth of a meter. 82

narcolepsy   Sleep disorder characterized by inappropriate daytime attacks of sleep. 114

narcotic analgesics   Drugs that have an effect on the body similar to morphine; these relieve pain and suppress coughing. 116

natural concept   Type of concept that is intuitively used in everyday life. 184

naturalistic observation   Research method in which behavior of people or animals in their normal environment is accurately recorded. 17

Necker cube   A visual illusion. The Necker cube is a drawing of a cube designed so that it is difficult to determine which side is toward you. 93

need   A physiological deprivation that results in a drive to restore balance. 213

need for achievement   The desire to perform at some high standard of excellence. 227

need for affiliation   The desire to be with others. 228

need for power   The desire to control or exert influence over other people. 228

negative afterimage   Visual image that is the opposite colors of the original; occurs when you stare at an image and then look at a white surface. 85

negative reinforcement   Removing something unpleasant from a subject to increase the probability that the preceding behavior will be repeated. 144

NEO Personality Inventory (NEO-PI)   An objective personality test developed by Costa & McCrae to measure the five major factors in personality; consists of 181 questions. 277

neonate   Newborn infant; the individual immediately after birth. 52

nerve deafness   Type of deafness resulting from damage to the auditory nerve. 96

nervous system   All of the neurons in the body; the human nervous system carries messages from sense organs to the brain, stores information, and carries decisions to the muscles for action. 28

neural impulse   The electrical message that is conducted down the length of a neuron. 29

neuron   A specialized cell that functions to conduct messages throughout the body. 29

neuropeptides   Short chains of amino acids that can sometimes serve as neurotransmitters. 31

neurosis   A Freudian term that was used to describe abnormal behavior caused by anxiety; it has been largely eliminated from DSM-III. 310

neurotic needs   In Horney's personality theory, needs that are irrational in dealing with basic anxiety. 264

neurotransmitter Chemical that carries messages across the synapse. 30

neutral stimulus A stimulus that does not cause the response of interest; the individual may show some response to the stimulus but not the associated behavior. 131

nicotine A stimulant contained in the tobacco of cigarettes; it is absorbed by the lungs and distributed by the bloodstream. 117

nodes of Ranvier Gaps along the myelin sheath of an axon. The nodes of Ranvier help the neural impulse travel quickly along the axon. 29

noise Any sound of a high enough intensity to disturb an individual. 392

norepinephrine A neurotransmitter involved in moods. 31

norm A sample of scores representative of a population. 193

normal curve When scores of a large number of random cases are plotted on a graph, they often fall into a bell-shaped curve; as many cases on the curve are above the mean as below it. 22

norms Explicit or implicit rules and standards that regulate the behavior of members in the group. 363

NREM (non REM) Nonrapid eye-movement sleep; type of sleep in which the eyes are very slowly moving back and forth; a restful sleep time. 107

O

obedience Type of social influence in which an individual gives the behavior required by a command. 361

obesity Condition of significant overweight. 220

object permanence The ability to realize that objects continue to exist even if we can no longer see them. 61

objective personality tests Measures of personality administered and scored according to standardized instructions. 275

observation Research method that involves watching an individual's behavior in everyday situations over a period of time; also called naturalistic observation. 274

observational learning In social learning theory, learning by observing someone else behave; people observe and imitate in learning socialization. 150

obsessive compulsive disorder Anxiety disorder in which the individual has repetitive thoughts (obsessions) that lead to constant urges (compulsions) to engage in meaningless rituals. 311

obsessive thoughts Repetitive thoughts in the obsessive compulsive disorder; often involves fears of being unable to control impulses. 311

occipital lobe Part of the cerebral cortex of the brain that is involved in interpreting visual sensations. 34, 84

Oedipus complex The Freudian idea that the young boy has sexual feelings for his mother and is jealous of his father and must identify with his father to resolve the conflict. 263

off-the-job training Training often done by a professional away from the actual job site. 383

olfaction The smell sense. 97

olfactory bulbs Part of brain involved in smell. 97

olfactory epithelium Sense receptor for smell that reacts chemically with odors to produce neural impulses. 97

on-the-job training Training of the current employee designed to increase job performance effectiveness; usually taught by the supervisor. 383

openness The dimension in the five-factor personality theory that includes traits such as imagination, creativity, perception, knowledge, artistic ability, curiosity, and analytical ability; also called culture or intellect. 268

operant conditioning Form of learning in which behavior followed by reinforcement (satisfaction) increases in frequency. 139

opiates Narcotic analgesics; drugs whose effect on the body is similar to morphine, the analgesic ingredient derived from the opium poppy plant. 116

opponent-process theory Theory that when one emotion is experienced, the other is suppressed. 241

opponent-process theory of color vision Theory of color vision that postulated the existence of receptors sensitive to opposing pairs of colors. 85

optic chiasma Junction in the optic nerve that connects the nerve tracts from each eye carrying information from the same side of the visual field. 84

optic nerve Nerve that travels from the retina of the eye to the brain. 84

optimum level of arousal Motivation theory that states that the individual will seek a level of arousal that is comfortable. 214

organ of Corti Sensory receptor for sound. 96

organic mental disorders Psychological disorders that involve physical damage to the nervous system; can be caused by disease or by an accident. 320

organizational psychology Area of industrial psychology that focuses on worker attitudes and motivation; derived primarily from personality and social psychology. 384

orgasm The climax of intense sexual excitement; release from building sexual tension, usually accompanied by ejaculation in men. 251

orientation training Training in an organization which is designed to develop job skills and give knowledge of the organization to the new employee. 383

osmoreceptors Cells in the anterior hypothalamus sensitive to the relative amount of water in the blood. 221

ovaries Female reproductive glands. 41

overlearning Continuing to rehearse information after the initial learning is accomplished. 171

P

pain Skin sense that detects strong pressure. 99

paired-associate learning A verbal learning procedure in which the subject is presented with a series of pairs of items to be remembered. 167

panic attack A specific period of intense anxiety, characterized by shortness of breath, dizziness, faintness, trembling, and nausea. 310

panic disorder Anxiety disorder characterized by the occurrence of specific periods of intense fear. 310

papillae Small bumps on the surface of the tongue that contain the taste buds. 98

paradoxical cold A phenomenon in which a person sometimes senses warm stimuli of 45° C (112° F) as cold. 101

paranoid schizophrenia A type of schizophrenia in which the individual often has delusions of grandeur and persecution, thinking that someone is out to get him or her. 317

paraphilia Sexual deviation characterized by the need for unusual behaviors for sexual arousal that interfere with normal sexual activities. 322

parasomnia Sleep disorder in which the chief symptom is an unusual event that disturbs sleep; they include sleep terror disorder, bed-wetting, and sleepwalking. 113

parasympathetic nervous system The branch of the autonomic nervous system that is more active under normal circumstances; it decreases breathing and heart rate. 39

parietal lobes The section of the cerebral cortex of the brain in which sensations such as touch are interpreted. 35

partial reinforcement Any schedule of reinforcement in which reinforcement follows only some of the correct responses. 142

partial reinforcement extinction effect The finding that partial reinforcement produces a response that takes longer to extinguish than continuous reinforcement. 142

passionate love An intense emotional experience that includes sexual desire, elation, anxiety, ecstasy, and tenderness; also called romantic love. 243

pattern recognition Memory process in which information attended to is compared with information already permanently stored in memory. 159

peace psychology Subfield of psychology in which members are interested in reducing destructive conflict; new division of APA. 367

pegword A mnemonic technique that starts with a rhyme or series in which the key words serve as anchors to associate with other items to be remembered. 171

perception The active process in which the sensory information that is carried through the nervous system to the brain is organized and interpreted; the interpretation of sensation. 78

perceptual constancy The tendency to perceive objects in a consistent manner despite the changing sensations received by sense organs; constancy plays an important role in helping us to adapt to the environment successfully. 85

periaqueductal gray (PAG) In a theory of pain, the area of the brainstem that produces endorphins that then inhibit the neurons in the spinal cord from transmitting pain. 100

peripheral nervous system The part of the human nervous system that receives messages from the sense organs and carries them to the muscles and glands; everything outside of the brain and spinal cord. 32

persecutory delusion A delusion in which the individual has a distortion of reality; the belief that other people are out to get one. 317

person perception The process of using the information we gather in forming impressions of people to make evaluations of others. 349

personal distance One of Hall's interpersonal distance categories, 1.5 to 4 feet. 389

personal space Space around a person that he or she claims as his or her own. 389

personal unconscious Jung's representation of the individual's repressed thoughts and memories. 263

personality The distinctive and enduring patterns of behavior and cognition that characterize a person's adaptation to life. 260

personality disorder Psychological disorder in which there are problems in the basic personality structure of the individual. 321

person-centered approach Rogers's personality theory in which the emphasis is on the individual. 269

person-centered therapy Founded by Carl Rogers. The therapist provides a nonthreatening atmosphere of warmth and acceptance; also called client-centered therapy. 329

personnel psychology   Area of industrial psychology that includes selection, training, and evaluation of new applicants and current employees. 382

perspective   Changes in the appearance of objects or surfaces as the distance from the perceiving increases; monocular depth cues help us perceive distance correctly. 90

PET scan (Positron Emission Tomography)   Examining brain-cell activity by recording utilization of radioactive glucose. 37

petting   Sexual contact with the opposite sex excluding intercourse. 252

phantom-limb pain   Phenomenon in which people who have lost an arm or leg feel pain in the missing limb. 100

phencyclidine hydrochloride (PCP)   Animal anesthetic that functions as a hallucinogen. 118

phenomenal field   In Rogers's personality theory, the sum total of an individual's experiences. 269

phenotype   The complete set of observable characteristics of an individual. 42

phenylketonuria (PKU)   Form of mental retardation caused by a single gene; the body cannot metabolize the substance phenylalanine. 44

pheromones   Chemical signals used by some animals to communicate by olfaction. 98, 222

phi phenomenon   Perception of movement between two lights that are alternately going on and off; *see* stroboscopic motion. 92

phobias   Acute excessive fears of specific situations or objects that have no convincing basis in reality. 310

phoneme   Basic speech sound in a language. 179

phrenology   Method developed by Franz Gall to describe behavioral characteristics by measuring bumps on the head. 36

physical dependence   A condition in which the habitual user's body becomes biochemically dependent upon the drugs; addiction. 115

physiological   Refers to biological responses that occur inside the body. 6

physiological needs   First level of motives in Maslow's hierarchy; includes the biological needs of hunger, thirst, sex, exercise, and rest. 216

physiological psychology   Subfield in which psychobiologists study the physiological processes involved in animal behavior. 15

pinna   Large flap of outer ear. 95

pituitary gland   Endocrine gland that is called the master gland; it secretes hormones that cause other endocrine glands to function. 40

PKU (phenylketonuria)   Form of mental retardation caused by a single gene; the body cannot metabolize the substance phenylalanine. 203

place theory of hearing   Emphasizes the place on the basilar membrane that produces pitch differences. 96

placebo   An inert or inactive substance given to control subjects to test for bias effects. 20

placenta   The connection between the fetus and mother, through which blood and nutrients pass. 50

plateau phase   Second phase in the human sexual response cycle, during which the physiological arousal becomes more intense. 251

pleasure principle   In Freudian theory, the idea that the instinctual drives of the id unconsciously and impulsively seek immediate pleasure. 262

Poggendorff illusion   Illusion in which a straight line looks distorted. 94

polarization   Normal electrical charge of a passive neuron in which there are more negative ions (such as chloride) inside the neuron and more positive ions (such as sodium and potassium) outside. 30

polygraph   Instrument that records a variety of physiological responses, such as heart rate, respiration rate, blood pressure, and GSR. 236

pons   The part of the hindbrain that is involved in breathing, feeding, and facial movement. 33

Ponzo illusion   An illusion in linear perspective where a line that looks larger is actually closer. 94

population   Includes all of the individuals from the large group that the subjects were selected from. 24

positive reinforcement   Presenting a subject something pleasant to increase the probability that the preceding behavior will be repeated. 144

positivity bias   In forming impressions, the tendency to evaluate others positively. 349

postconventional morality   Level III in Kohlberg's theory, in which moral reasoning is based on personal standards and beliefs; highest level of moral thinking. 63

post-traumatic stress disorder   Condition that can occur when a person experiences a severely distressing event; characterized by constant memories of the event, avoidance of anything associated with it, and general arousal. 286

Prägnanz (law of)   Gestalt psychologist law that states that people have a tendency to group stimuli according to rules, and that people do this whenever possible. 89

preconscious mind   In Freud's psychoanalytic theory of personality, the part of personality that contains information that we have learned but that we are not thinking about at the present time. 106

preconventional morality   Level I of Kohlberg's theory, in which moral reasoning is largely due to the expectation of rewards and punishments. 63

prediction   A goal of psychology; making educated guesses about future behavior. 7

prefrontal lobotomy Severing frontal lobes of brain. 36

prejudice An unjustified fixed, usually negative, way of thinking about a person or object. 356

Premack Principle Principle that states that, of any two responses, the one that is more likely to occur can be used to reinforce the response that is less likely to occur. 147

premenstrual syndrome (PMS) The distinct changes that many women experience in their physical and psychological functioning just prior to menstruation. 41

prenatal development The growth of an individual from conception until birth. 50

preoperational thought period Period in cognitive development; from two to seven years, the period during which the child learns to represent the environment with objects and symbols. 61

pressure In sensation, the skin sense that detects contact on the skin. In psychology, what we experience when we strive to meet the social and psychological demands placed upon us; internal pressure results from self-demands, while external pressure results from demands from others. 99, 284

primacy effect Phenomenon where items are remembered because they come at the beginning of a list. 167

primary appraisal Activity of determining whether a new stimulus event is positive, neutral, or negative; first step in appraisal of stress. 288

primary narcissism A Freudian term that refers to the oral phase before the ego has developed; the individual constantly seeks pleasure. 318

primary reinforcement Reinforcement that is effective without having been associated with other reinforcers; sometimes called unconditioned reinforcement. 143

prisoner's dilemma Social simulation developed to measure competition and cooperation in a social situation (confessing to a crime to avoid heavy punishment). 367

proactive interference Interference caused by information learned before the material of interest. 169

probability (p) In inferential statistics, the likelihood that the difference between the experimental and control groups is due to the independent variable. 24

procedural memory The most basic type of long-term memory; involves the formation of associations between stimuli and responses. 163

profound retardation Lowest level of mental retardation; it includes individuals with IQs below 20. 203

programmed learning Form of instruction in which the student is guided by reinforcement and feedback through a series of small steps toward some goal; similar to personalized system of instruction (PSI). 147

progressive relaxation Technique in which the individual learns to alternately tense and relax various parts of the body. 334

projection Defense mechanism in which a person attributes his or her unacceptable characteristics or motives to others rather than himself or herself. 293

projective personality test A personality test that presents ambiguous stimuli to which subjects are expected to respond with projections of their own personality. 277

proprioceptive senses The body sense of kinesthesis (bodily movement) and the vestibular sense (body balance). 99

proxemics The study of the interpersonal distance between people. 389

proximity Closeness in time and space. In perception, it is the Gestalt perceptual principle in which stimuli next to one another are included together. 90

psyche According to Jung, the thoughts and feelings (conscious and unconscious) of an individual. 263

psychedelic drugs Drugs that produce changes in emotional feelings and perceptions of the external world; also called hallucinogens. 118

psychiatrist A physician who specializes in treatment of abnormal behavior. 13

psychoactive drug A drug that produces changes in behavior and cognition through modification of conscious awareness. 114

psychoanalysis The school of thought founded by Sigmund Freud that stressed unconscious motivation. In therapy, a patient's unconscious motivation is intensively explored in order to bring repressed conflicts up to consciousness; psychoanalysis usually takes a long time to accomplish. 12, 328

psychobiology (also called biological psychology or physiological psychology) The subfield of experimental psychology concerned with the influence of heredity and the biological response systems on behavior. 15, 28

psychogenic amnesia A dissociative disorder in which an individual loses his or her sense of identity. 321

psychogenic fugue A dissociative disorder in which an individual loses his or her sense of identity and goes to a new geographic location, forgetting all of the unpleasant emotions connected with the old life. 321

psychographics A technique used in consumer psychology to identify the attitudes of buyers and their preferences for particular products. 387

psycholinguistics The psychological study of how people convert the sounds of a language into meaningful symbols that can be used to communicate with others. 178

psychological dependence   Situation in which a person craves a drug even though it is not biologically needed by the body. 115

psychological disorder   A diagnosis of abnormal behavior; syndrome of abnormal adjustment, classified in DSM-III-R. 307

psychological types   Jung's term for different personality profiles; Jung combined two attitudes and four functions to produce eight psychological types. 264

psychology   Science of behavior and cognition. 6

psychopharmacology   Study of effects of psychoactive drugs on behavior. 115

psychophysics   An area of psychology in which researchers compare the physical energy of a stimulus with the sensation reported. 80

psychosexual stages   Freud's theoretical stages in personality development. 59

psychosurgery   Surgery on the brain for treatment of psychological problems. 342

psychotherapy   Treatment of behavioral disorders through psychological techniques; major psychotherapies include insight therapy, behavior therapy, and group therapy. 326

psychotic disorders   The more severe categories of abnormal behavior. 312

puberty   Sexual maturation; the time at which the individual is able to perform sexually and reproduce. 64

public distance   Hall's widest interpersonal distance category, more than 12 feet. 390

punishment   Any event that decreases the likelihood that the behavior preceding it will be repeated. 145

pupil   Part of the eye that adjusts to light intensities; when the pupil constricts, less light is permitted into the eye. 83

R

range   In statistics, a measure of variability; the highest score minus the lowest score. 23

raphe nucleus   Area in the back of the brain; this area appears to be involved in NREM sleep. 110

rating scales   Standardized forms for recording personal evaluations of a subject. 274, 384

rational-emotive therapy   A cognitive behavior modification technique in which a person is taught to identify irrational, self-defeating beliefs and then to overcome them. 336

rationalization   Defense mechanism in which a person makes up logical excuses to justify his or her behavior rather than exposing the true motives. 294

reaction formation   Defense mechanism in which a person masks an unconsciously distressing or unacceptable trait by assuming an opposite attitude or behavior pattern. 294

readiness to learn   Children cannot learn until they are mature enough to be able to use their muscles properly. 54

real motion   In perception, a situation in which we correctly perceive an object as moving. 92

realistic love   Knox's theory that this type of love is characterized by a practical, calm, solid emotion. 243

reality principle   In Freudian theory, the idea that the drives of the ego try to find socially acceptable ways to gratify the id. 262

recall (reconstruction)   In memory, a measure of retention in which the subject is required to retrieve learned information from memory. 167

recency effect   A phenomenon in which items are remembered because they come at the end of a list. 167

recessive   Form of a gene that is only reflected in the phenotype when both genes at a particular location are identical. 43

reciprocal determinism   The concept proposed by Bandura that the behavior, the individual, and the situation interact and influence each other. 272

reciprocal inhibition   Concept of Wolpe that states that it is possible to break the bond between anxiety-provoking stimuli and responses manifesting anxiety by facing those stimuli in a state antagonistic to anxiety. 333

recognition   A measure of retention in which the subject identifies items which were previously learned. 167

reconstructive memory   Procedure in which an individual combines actual details of an event with other available information to fill in the gaps. 165

reference groups   Group from which a person derives his or her values, attitudes, and identity. 363

reflex   An automatic movement that occurs in direct response to a stimulus. 32

refractory period   In physiological psychology, a brief period of time after a neuron has fired during which it cannot fire again. 30

regression   Defense mechanism in which a person retreats to an earlier, more immature form of behavior. 294

reinforcement   Any event that increases the probability that the behavior that precedes it will be repeated; also called a reinforcer; similar to a reward. 142

reinforcement therapy   A behavior therapy in which reinforcement is used to modify behavior. Techniques in reinforcement therapy include shaping, extinction, and token economy. 331

reinforcement value   In Rotter's personality theory, the importance or values a person attaches to a particular reinforcement. 272

releaser (sign stimulus)   Specific environmental cues that stimulate a stereotyped behavior to occur; releasers cause fixed action patterns. 211

reliability   The degree of consistency in the results of measurements taken at various times. 22, 193

REM (rapid eye movement)   Type of sleep in which the eyes are rapidly moving around; dreaming occurs in REM sleep. 107

renin   Hormone secreted by the kidneys that causes water retention and thirst. 221

repression   Defense mechanism in which painful memories and unacceptable thoughts and motives are conveniently forgotten so that they will not have to be dealt with. 293

reproductive glands   Endocrine glands involved in sexual motivation and secondary sexual characteristics; testes and ovaries. 41

residual schizophrenia   Type of schizophrenia in which the individual currently does not have symptoms but has had a schizophrenic episode in the past. 318

resistance   Psychoanalytic term used when a patient avoids a painful area of conflict. 328

resolution phase   The last phase in the human sexual response cycle; the time after orgasm that the body gradually returns to the unaroused state. 251

response   Specific actions taken by an individual in reaction to something in the environment. 130

resting potential   The normal electrical charge of a passive (resting) neuron. 30

Restricted Environmental Stimulation Technique (REST)   Research technique in which environmental stimuli available to an individual are reduced drastically; formerly called sensory deprivation. 124

reticular formation   Network of neurons extending from the medulla to the forebrain centers of incoming information; sometimes the reticular formation is referred to as the reticular activating system (RAS). 33

retina   A patch of tissue in which lie the rods and cones of the eye; the "film" of the eye. 83

retinal disparity   Binocular cue in which each eye receives slightly different sensory information that must be combined for normal vision. 91

retrieval   The process of pulling information out of the memory system. 157

retroactive interference   Interference caused by information learned after the material of interest. 169

retrograde amnesia   Forgetting information recently learned because of disruptive stimulus such as electric shock. 174

reversal   The ability to work a problem backwards. 62

reversible figure   In perception, a situation in which the figure and ground seem to reverse themselves; an illusion in which objects alternate as the main figure. 88

rhodopsin   Photosensitive pigment that breaks down into chemicals that stimulate neurons sending visual messages to the brain. 83

risky-shift   The tendency for groups to make riskier decisions than individuals. 364

rods   One type of vision receptor; rods respond to differences in brightness but not to color variations. 83

romantic love   Knox's theory that this type of love is characterized by excitement, arousal, and urgency. 243

rooting reflex   Reflex that occurs when you touch a baby's cheek and he or she turns his or her head toward the source. 53

Rorschach Inkblot Test   A projective personality test in which subjects are asked to discuss what they see in cards containing blots of ink. 277

S

safety needs   Second level of motives in Maslow's hierarchy; includes security, stability, dependency, protection, freedom from fear and anxiety and the need for structure and order. 216

sample   Actual subjects that are used in a study. 24

savings (relearning)   Measure of retention in which the subject first learns a task and then is required to relearn it; if it takes less time to relearn, savings has occurred. 168

Schachter-Singer theory of emotion   Theory of emotion that states that we interpret our arousal according to our environment and label our emotions accordingly. 240

scheme   A unit of knowledge that the person possess; used in Piaget's cognitive development theory. 60

schizophrenia   Severe psychotic disorder that is characterized by disruptions in thinking, perception, and emotion. 316

school of thought   An approach to a discipline containing certain beliefs and methods. 8

school psychology   Subfield in which psychologists are responsible for administering and interpreting tests for students, and consulting with teachers about student academic needs. 14

scientific method   An attitude and procedure that scientists use to conduct research. The steps include:

stating the problem, forming the hypothesis, collecting the information, evaluating the information, and drawing conclusions. 16

secondary appraisal In appraisal of stress, this is the evaluation that an individual's abilities and resources are sufficient to meet the demands of a stressful event. 289

secondary reinforcement Reinforcement that is effective only after it has been associated with a primary reinforcer; also called conditioned reinforcement. 144

secondary traits In Allport's personality theory, the less important situation-specific traits that help round out personality; include attitudes, skills, and behavior patterns. 266

secure attachment Type of infant-parent attachment in which the infant actively seeks contact with the parent. 57

selective attention The perception process of screening out irrelevant information while focusing on significant stimuli in the environment. 78, 159

selective breeding Procedure used in genetics in which similar animals are mated for many generations. 45

self In Rogers's humanistic personality theory, the individual's perception of "I" or "me" in relation to others. 269

self-actualization A humanistic term describing the state in which all of an individual's capacities are developed fully. Fifth and highest level of motives in Maslow's hierarchy; this level, the realization of one's potential, is rarely reached. 217, 269

self-concept An individual's knowledge of who he or she is. 59

self-efficacy An individual's sense of self-worth and success in adjusting to the world. 272

self-handicapping A strategy that people use to prepare for failure; people behave in ways that produce obstacles to success so that when they do fail they can place the blame on the obstacle. 351

self-perception theory Attitude theory that states that attitudes are based on an individual's perceptions of his or her own behavior. 356

self-serving bias An attribution bias in which an individual attributes success to his or her own behavior but failure to external environmental causes. 351

semantic memory Type of long-term memory that can use cognitive activities, such as everyday knowledge. 163

semantics The meaning of language. 179

semicircular canals Canals in the inner ear that are receptors for the vestibular sense. 102

sensation The passive process in which stimuli are received by sense receptors and transformed into neural impulses that can be carried through the ner-

vous system; first stage in becoming aware of environment. 78

sensation seeking Theory that states that people will seek stimulation until they reach their optimum, after which they will avoid it. 216

sense receptors Structures at the end of neurons directly affected by environmental stimuli. 78

sensitivity training group (T-group) Therapy group that has the goal of making participants more aware of themselves and their ideas. 338

sensorimotor period Period in cognitive development; first two years, during which the infant learns to coordinate sensory experiences with motor activities. 61

sensory adaptation Tendency of the sense organs to adjust to continuous stimulation by reducing their functioning; a stimulus that once caused sensation and no longer does. 81

sensory deprivation Situation in which normal environmental sensory stimuli available to an individual are reduced drastically; also called REST. 123

sensory division A part of the somatic nervous system that carries messages from the sense organs to the central nervous system. 38

sensory memory The memory store that sensory information first enters in the memory system. 158

sensory neuron (also called afferent neuron) A neuron that carries messages from the sense organs toward the central nervous system. 29

serial learning A verbal learning procedure in which the stimuli are always presented in the same order, and the subject has to learn them in the order in which they are presented. 166

serial position effect Finding of Ebbinghaus that people remember words at the beginning and end of a list better than those in the middle. 167

serotonin Neurotransmitter involved in sleep, motivation, and perception. 31

set-point theory Theory of obesity that suggests that obese people have a hypothalamus that maintains their weight at a point higher than normal. 220

severe retardation Level of retardation that includes individuals with IQs of between 20 and 35. 203

sex chromosomes Chromosomes that carry genes that determine the genetic sex of the individual. 43

sex roles The set of behaviors and attitudes that are determined to be appropriate for one sex or the other in a society. 55, 249

sex stereotypes A prejudiced rigid mental image of what males and females are like. 357

sexual dysfunctions Problems in normal sexual behavior, usually characterized by inhibitions in sexual arousal or problems in the sexual response cycle. 253

shape constancy The tendency to perceive familiar objects as having a permanent shape, even if we look at the objects from different angles. 86

shaping In operant conditioning, the gradual process of reinforcing behaviors that get closer to some final desired behavior. Shaping is also called successive approximation. 139

short-term memory The memory store, with a capacity of about 7 items and enduring for up to 30 seconds, which handles current information. 159

shyness An uncomfortable feeling in the presence of other people; when we are shy, we lack confidence in our ability to act appropriately in social situations. 292

signal detection theory Research approach in which the subject's behavior in detecting threshold is treated as a form of decision-making. 81

similarity Gestalt principle in which similar stimuli are perceived as a unit. 90

simple phobia Excessive irrational fear that does not fall into other specific categories such as fear of dogs, insects, snakes, or closed-in places. 310

simultaneous conditioning A procedure in classical conditioning in which the CS and US are presented at exactly the same time. 133

situation anxiety Anxiety associated with a particular event. 287

Sixteen Personality Factor Questionnaire (16PF) Cattell's personality test to measure source traits. 276

size constancy Tendency to perceive objects as the same size even though the retinal size changes. 87

size perspective Monocular depth cue in which we normally interpret distance by the relative size of an object; the smaller an object, the farther away it seems. 90

skin senses Senses with receptors in or under the body's skin; include pressure, pain, cold, and warmth. 99

Skinner box B. F. Skinner's animal cage with a lever that triggers reinforcement for a subject. 140

sleep terror disorder (pavor nocturnus) NREM sleep disorder in which the person (usually a child) wakes up screaming and terrified, but cannot recall why. 114

sleepwalking (somnambulism) NREM sleep disorder in which the person walks in his or her sleep. 114

social cognition The process of understanding other people and ourselves by forming and utilizing information about the social world. 348

social cognitive theory Bandura's approach to personality that proposes that individuals use observation, imitation, and cognition to develop personality. 272

social comparison Theory proposed by Festinger that we tend to compare our behavior to others to ensure that we are conforming. 358

social distance One of Hall's interpersonal distance categories—4 to 12 feet. 390

social exchange theory Theory of interpersonal relationships that states that people evaluate the costs and rewards of their relationships and act accordingly. 242

social facilitation Phenomenon in which the presence of others increases dominant behavior patterns in an individual; Zajonc's theory states that the presence of others enhances the emission of the dominant response of the individual. 366

social influence Influence designed to change the attitudes or behavior of other people; include conformity, compliance, and obedience. 358

social leader The one who tries to keep the people in a group happy with one another; the group maintenance leader. 369

social learning theory An approach to social psychology that emphasizes observation and modeling. Social learning theory states that reinforcement is involved in motivation rather than in learning, and proposes that aggression is a form of learned behavior. 272, 370

social loafing Each individual in a group puts in less effort than if he or she were acting alone. 365

social phobia Excessive irrational fear and embarrassment when interacting with other people. Social phobias may include fear of assertive behavior, fear of making mistakes, or fear of public speaking. 310

social psychology The study of how an individual's behavior, thoughts, and feelings are influenced by other people. 14, 348

sociobiology Study of the genetic basis of social behavior. 212

somatic nervous system The part of the peripheral nervous system that carries messages from the sense organs and relays information that directs the voluntary movements of the skeletal muscles. 38

somatization disorder Somatoform disorder in which a person has medical complaints without physical cause. 320

somatoform disorders Psychological disorders characterized by physical symptoms for which there are no obvious physical causes. 320

somatoform pain disorder Somatoform disorder in which the individual complains of severe, long-lasting pain for which there is no organic cause. 320

sound waves Rapid changes in air pressure caused by vibrating object in contact with the air. 94

source traits In Cattell's personality theory, the traits basic to the core of an individual's personality. 267

specific attachment phase Stage at about six months, in which the baby becomes attached to a specific person. 57

spinal cord   Bundles of nerves that form a communication link between the brain and the peripheral nervous system; housed in the spinal backbone. 32

spinal nerves   The peripheral nerves that connect with the central nervous system through the spinal cord. 32

split-brain research   Popular name for Sperry's research on the syndrome of hemisphere deconnection; research on individuals with the corpus callosum severed. Normal functioning breaks down in split-brain subjects when different information is presented to each hemisphere. 35

spontaneous recovery   In conditioning, reappearance of behavior that had disappeared during extinction. 135

sport psychology   The field in which principles of psychology are applied to sports activities. 393

SQ5R   A technique to improve learning and memory. Components include survey, question, read, record, recite, review, and reflect. 173

Stage 1   NREM sleep stage during which a person makes transition from relaxation to sleep; EEG characterized by theta activity with a frequency of 4-7 Hz. 107

Stage 2   NREM sleep stage characterized by EEG theta activity and sleep spindles—brief bursts of 12-14 Hz waves; people spend 50 percent of sleep time in Stage 2. 107

Stage 3   NREM sleep stage, characterized by sleep spindles and delta activity of 1-3 Hz. 107

Stage 4   Deepest NREM sleep stage, characterized by over 50 percent delta activity of 1-3 Hz. 107

stage of exhaustion   Third stage in Selye's general adaptation syndrome. As the body continues to resist stress, it depletes its energy resources and the person becomes exhausted. 288

stage of resistance   Second stage in Selye's general adaptation syndrome. When stress is prolonged, the body builds some resistance to the effects of stress. 288

standard deviation   Measure of variability that describes how scores are distributed around the mean. 23

standardization   The process of obtaining a representative sample of scores in the population so that a particular score can be interpreted correctly. 193

Stanford-Binet Intelligence Scale   An intelligence test first revised by Lewis Terman at Stanford University in 1916; still a popular test used today. 194

state-dependent learning   Situation in which what is learned in one state can only be remembered when the person is in that state of mind. 172

statistically significant   In inferential statistics, a finding that the independent variable did influence greatly the outcome of the experimental and control group. 24

stereochemical theory   Theory of olfactory coding that states that the odor receptors have holes the same shape as the odor molecules. 98

stereotype   An exaggerated and rigid mental image of a particular class of persons or objects. 356

stimulants   Drugs that have an arousing effect on the central nervous system and the body. 116

stimulus   A unit of the environment that causes a response in an individual; a physical or chemical agent acting on an appropriate sense receptor. 130

stimulus discrimination   Responding to relevant stimuli. 136

stimulus generalization   Responding to stimuli similar to the stimulus that had caused the response. 135

stimulus motives   Motivating factors that are internal and unlearned, but do not appear to have a physiological basis; stimulus motives cause an individual to seek out sensory stimulation through interaction with the environment. 225

stimulus trace   The perceptual persistence of a stimulus after it is no longer present. 158

storage   The process that keeps information in the memory system. 157

strange situation procedure   A measure of attachment developed by Ainsworth that consists of eight phases during which the infant is increasingly stressed. 57

strategies   Plans for attacking problems. 187

stress   Anything that produces demands on us to adjust and threatens our well-being. 282

stress innoculation   Technique for dealing with stress through education, rehearsal, and implementation. 295

stroboscopic motion   Perception of movement when a series of still pictures are seen rapidly; each successive one is slightly different from the earlier one; the basis of movies. 92

Strong Interest Inventory   An objective personality test that compares people's personalities to groups that achieve success in certain occupations. 275

structuralism   First school of thought in psychology; studied conscious experience to discover the structure of the mind. 9

structured interview   An interview in which a standard set of questions is asked. 274

subject bias   Source of potential error in an experiment from the action or expectancy of a subject; a subject might influence the experimental results in ways that masks the true outcome. 20

subjective organization   Long-term memory procedures in which the individual provides a personal method of organizing information to be memorized. 165

sublimation Defense mechanism; a person redirects his or her socially undesirable urges into socially acceptable behavior. 294

substantia gelatinosa Area of the spinal cord that acts as a gate for pain. 99

successive approximation Shaping; in operant conditioning, the gradual process of reinforcing behaviors that get closer to some final desired behavior. 139

sucking reflex Reflex that occurs when something touches the baby's lips and he or she attempts sucking. 53

sudden infant death syndrome (SIDS) Situation in which a seemingly healthy infant dies suddenly in its sleep; also called crib death. 114

superego Freud's representation of conscience. 262

surface structure The sequence of morphemes we hear or see in a sentence. 179

surface traits In Cattell's personality theory, the observable characteristics of a person's behavior and personality. 267

survey Research method in which questions are given to people for their responses. 18

symbolization In Freud's dream theory, the process of converting the latent content of a dream into manifest symbols. 111

sympathetic nervous system The branch of the autonomic nervous system that is more active in emergencies; it causes a general arousal and increased breathing, heart rate, and blood pressure. 39

synapse The space between the axon of one neuron and the dendrites of the next. 30

syntax A subset of rules of grammar that governs the order of words in sentences. 179

systematic desensitization Application of counterconditioning, in which the individual overcomes anxiety by learning to relax in the presence of stimuli that had once made him or her unbearably nervous. 333

T

task leader Leadership orientation in which the leader tries to get the work accomplished by directing members to carry out their tasks efficiently. 369

task-oriented coping Adjustment responses in which the person evaluates a stressful situation objectively, and then formulates a plan with which to solve the problem. 295

taste buds Receptors for sense of taste; taste buds are located on top and sides of the tongue. 98

telegraphic speech Speech of children in which they use two-word sentences. 180

temperament Emotional part of personality; ways of responding to the environment that begin in infancy. 54

temporal lobes The section of the cerebral cortex of the brain in which auditory sensations are interpreted. 35

terminal buttons The end branches at the end of an axon; the terminal buttons contain the neurotransmitters that are released into the synapse. 29

test of significance An inferential statistical technique used to determine whether the difference in scores between the experimental and control groups is really due to the effects of the independent variable or to random chance. If the probability of an outcome is extremely low, we say that outcome is significant. 24

testes Male reproductive glands. 41

testing method Method of assessing a person's interests, personality, abilities, or intelligence in a standard form. 19

texture gradient Monocular depth cue in which small objects close to us show more detail than objects farther away. 91

thalamus The part of the forebrain involved in relay of sensory information. 34

Thanatos Freud's term for a destructive instinct such as aggression; also called death instinct. 213, 262

that's-not-all procedure A compliance technique in which a deal is presented and then while the person is considering it, the phrase "that's not all" is added to the pitch. 361

Thematic Apperception Test (TAT) Projective personality test in which subjects are shown pictures of people in everyday settings; subjects must make up a story about the people portrayed. 227, 278

theory of social impact Latané's theory of social behavior; it states that each member of a group shares the responsibility equally. 365

Theory X McGregor's theory that states that the worker dislikes work and must be forced to do it. 385

Theory Y McGregor's theory that states that work is natural and can be a source of satisfaction, and, when it is, the worker can be highly committed and motivated. 385

therapy In psychology, the treatment of behavior problems; two major types of therapy include psychotherapy and biological therapy. 326

thinking Mental activity manipulating symbols. 183

threshold The minimum strength of a stimulus required for a neuron to fire. 30

thyroid gland Gland that secretes thyroxin, a hormone that helps determine rate of metabolism in the body. 40

thyroxin A hormone secreted by the thyroid gland that influences the rate of metabolism. 40

timbre   Complexity of the mixture of sound waves. 95

time and motion studies   In engineering psychology, studies that analyze the time it takes to perform an action and the movements that go into the action. 386

tip-of-the-tongue phenomenon   A phenomenon in which the closer a person comes to recalling something, the more accurately he or she can remember details, such as the number of syllables or letters. 165

token economy   A behavior therapy in which desired behaviors are reinforced immediately with tokens that can be exchanged at a later time for desired rewards, such as food or recreational privileges. 147, 332

tolerance   When greater doses of drugs are necessary to produce the same effects. 115

top-down processing   The psycholinguistic process of communicating by beginning with a meaningful thought, selecting phrases to express the idea, and producing speech sounds that make up the words and phrases of our sentences. 180

trace conditioning   A procedure in classical conditioning in which the CS is a discrete event that is presented and terminated before the US is presented. 133

trait   A distinctive and stable attribute in people. 265

trait anxiety   Anxiety that is long-lasting; a relatively stable personality characteristic. 287

transduction   The process of changing the stimulus energy from the environment into neural impulses that travel through the nervous system. 79

transference   Psychoanalytic term used when a patient projects his feelings onto the therapist. 328

transformational grammar rules   The rules that allow us to take ideas (deep structures) and convert them into meaningful sentences (surface structures). 180

transsexualism   A condition in which a person feels trapped in the body of the wrong sex. 253

trial and error learning   Trying various behaviors in a situation until the solution is found. 138

triangular theory of love   Sternberg's theory that states that love consists of intimacy, passion, and decision/commitment. 244

triarchic theory of intelligence   Robert Sternberg's theory of intelligence that states that it consists of three parts: componential, experiential, and contextual subtheories. 192

trichromat   A person with normal color vision. 85

trichromatic theory   Young-Helmholtz idea of color vision. 85

trucking game   Social simulation developed to measure bargaining of individuals in a social situation (delivering goods by truck). 367

Type A behavior   Behavior shown by a particular type of individual; a personality pattern of behavior that can lead to stress and heart disease. 298

Type B behavior   Behavior shown by an individual who is able to relax. 298

U

ulcer   A hole in the lining of the stomach or duodenum; can be caused or aggravated by stress. 298

ultrasound   Testing procedure in which extremely high-pitched sound waves are bounced off the embryo or fetus to produce a picture. 52

unconditional positive regard   Part of Rogers's personality theory; occurs when we accept someone regardless of what he or she does or says. 269

unconditioned response (UR)   An automatic reaction elicited by a stimulus. 132

unconditioned stimulus (US)   Any stimulus that elicits an automatic or reflexive reaction in an individual; it does not have to be learned in the present situation. 132

unconscious mind   In Freud's psychoanalytic theory of personality, the part of personality that is unavailable to us; Freud suggests that instincts and unpleasant memories are stored in the unconscious mind. 106

undifferentiated schizophrenia   Type of schizophrenia that does not fit into any particular category, or fits into more than one category. 318

unstructured interview   An interview in which there is no specific list of questions that must be followed. 273

V

validity   The degree to which you actually measure what you intend to measure. 22, 193

variability   In statistics, variability measures the range of the scores. 23

variable interval (VI) schedule   Schedule of reinforcement in which the subject is reinforced for the first response given after a certain time interval, with the interval being different for each trial. 143

variable ratio (VR) schedule   Schedule of reinforcement in which the subject is given reinforcement after a varying number of responses; the number of responses required for reinforcement is different for every trial. 143

vascular theory of emotion   Theory of emotion proposed by Zajonc that changes in facial expressions influence the blood vessels that regulate brain temperature; increases are associated with negative emotions and decreases with positive ones. 248

ventromedial hypothalamus (VMH)   Part of the hypothalamus involved in stopping eating behavior. 219

verbal learning   Learning that involves responses to words or symbols. 166

vestibular sense   Sense that helps keep our balance. 101

visual acuity   Ability of a person to discriminate fine details when looking at something. 84

visual capture   The tendency for vision to dominate the other senses. 82

visual cliff   Apparatus used to test depth perception. 91

vulnerability-stress model   Theory of schizophrenia that states that some people have a biological tendency to develop schizophrenia if they are stressed enough by their environment. 319

W

waking consciousness   The awareness of sensations and thoughts while the person is awake and alert; also called conscious awareness. 106

wave amplitude   The height of a light wave (amplitude) determines the experience of brightness. 82

wavelength   The wavelength of light waves is the distance between any point on a wave and the corresponding point of the wave in the next cycle; wavelength determines experience of hue. 82

Weber's Law   Law that states that the difference threshold depends on the ratio of the intensity of one stimulus to another rather than on an absolute difference. 81

Wechsler Adult Intelligence Scale (WAIS)   An intelligence test for adults, first published by David Wechsler in 1955; it contains verbal and performance subscales. 195

well-being   A subjective positive emotional state characterized by general satisfaction of one's life. 297

Wernicke's area   Area of the brain important in speech perception. 97

withdrawal   Unpleasant physical reactions that a drug-dependent user experiences when he or she stops taking the drug. 115

within-subject experiment   An experimental design in which each subject is given all treatments, including the control condition; subjects serve in both experimental and control groups. 20

Y

Yerkes-Dodson Law   Popular idea that performance is best when arousal is at a medium level. 216

Z

zygote   A fertilized egg; at conception a sperm fertilizes an egg to produce the zygote. 43

zygote stage   First stage in prenatal development; first two weeks after conception; the zygote divides and travels down the fallopian tube to become attached to the wall of the uterus. 50

References

A

Abel, E. (1984). Opiates and sex. *Journal of Psychoactive Drugs, 16,* 205-216.

Abrams, S.R., & Taylor, M. (1983). The genetics of schizophrenia: A reassessment using modern criteria. *American Journal of Psychiatry, 140,* 171-175.

Abramson, L., Seligman, M.E.P., & Teasdale, J. (1978). Learned helplessness in humans: Critique and reformulation. *Journal of Abnormal Psychology, 87,* 49-74.

Adams, D., Gold, A., & Burt, A. (1978). Rise in female-initiated sexual activity at ovulation and its suppression by oral contraceptives. *New England Journal of Medicine, 299,* 1145-1150.

Adler, A. (1939). *Social interest.* New York: Putnam.

Agnew, J.W., Jr., Webb, W. B., & Williams, R. L. (1964). The effects of stage four sleep deprivation. *Electroencephalography and Clinical Neurophysiology, 17,* 68-70.

Ainsworth, M.D.S. (1979). Infant-mother attachment. *American Psychologist, 34,* 932-937.

Ainsworth, M.D.S. (1989). Attachments beyond infancy. *American Psychologist, 44,* 709-716.

Ainsworth, M.D.S., Blechar, M., Waters, E., & Wall, S. (1978). *Patterns of attachment: A psychological study of the strange situation.* Hillsdale, NJ: Erlbaum.

Ajzen, I., & Fishbein, M. (1977). Attitude-behavior relations: A theoretical analysis and review of empirical research. *Psychological Bulletin, 84,* 888-918.

Alberts, P., & Alberts, M. (1990). Unvalidated treatment of premenstrual syndrome. *International Journal of Mental Health, 19,* 69-80.

Alcock, J. (1989). *Animal behavior: An evolutionary approach* (4th ed.). Sunderland, MA: Sinauer.

Alderman, R.B. (1980). Strategies for motivating young athletes. In W. Straub (Ed.), *Sports psychology: An analysis of athletes' behavior.* Ithaca, NY: Mouvement.

Aldrich, M.S. (1990). Narcolepsy. *New England Journal of Medicine, 323,* 389-394.

Alkon, D. (1989). Memory storage and neural systems. *Scientific American, 258,* 42-50.

Allen, G. (1987). Cognitive influences on the acquisition of route knowledge in children and adults. In P. Ellen & C. Thinus-Blanc (Eds.), *Cognitive processes and spatial orientation in animal and man* (Vol. 2). Boston: Martinus Nijhoff.

Allison, J. (1989). The nature of reinforcement. In S.B. Klein & R.R. Mowrer (Eds.), *Contemporary learning theories: Instrumental conditioning theory and the impact of biological constraints in learning.* Hillsdale, NJ: Erlbaum.

Allport, G.W. (1954). *The nature of prejudice.* Garden City, NY: Doubleday.

Allport, G.W. (1961). *Patterns and growth in personality.* New York: Holt, Rinehart & Winston.

Allport, G.W. (1985). The historical background of social psychology. In G. Lindzey & E. Aronson (Eds.), *Handbook of social psychology* (Vol. 1) (3rd ed.). New York: Random House.

Amabile, T.M. (1983). *The social psychology of creativity.* New York: Springer-Verlag.

Amabile, T.M. (1987). The motivation to be creative. In S. Isaksen (Ed.), *Frontiers in creativity: Beyond the basics.* Buffalo, NY: Bearly Limited Publishers.

Amato, P. (1985). An investigation of planned helping behavior. *Journal of Research in Personality, 19,* 232-252.

Amelang, M., & Borkenau, P. (1982). On the factor structure and external validity of some questionnaire scales measuring dimensions of extraversion and neuroticism. *Zeitschrift fur Differentielle und Diagnostische Psychologie, 3,* 119-146.

American Heart Association. (1989). *1989 Heart facts.* Dallas, TX: American Heart Association.

American Psychiatric Association. (1987). *Diagnostic and statistical manual of mental disorders* (3rd ed., rev.). Washington, DC: American Psychiatric Association.

American Psychological Association. (1986). *Careers in psychology.* Washington, DC: Author.

American Psychological Association. (1990). Ethical principles of psychologists. *American Psychologist, 45,* 390-395.

Amoore, J.E. (1970). *Molecular basis of odor.* Springfield, IL: Thomas.

Amoore, J.E., Johnston, J.W., Jr., & Rubin, M. (1964). The stereochemical theory of odor. *Scientific American, 210,* 42-49.

Anastasi, A. (1988). *Psychological testing* (6th ed.). New York: Macmillan.

Anderson, J.R. (1990). *Cognitive psychology and its implications* (3rd ed.). New York: Freeman.

Anderson, N.B. (1989). Racial differences in stress-induced cardiovascular reactivity and hypertension: Current status and substantive issues. *Psychological Bulletin, 105,* 89-105.

Angoff, W. (1988). The nature-nurture debate, aptitudes, and group differences. *American Psychologist, 43,* 713-720.

Angrist, B. (1983). Psychoses induced by central nervous system stimulants and related drugs. In I. Creese (Ed.), *Stimulants: Neurochemical, behavioral and clinical perspectives.* New York: Raven.

Arnett, J. (1990a). Drunk driving, sensation seeking, and egocentrism among adolescents. *Personality and Individual Differences, 11,* 541-546.

Arnett, J. (1990b). Contraceptive use, sensation seeking, and adolescent egocentrism. *Journal of Youth and Adolescence, 19,* 171-180.

Aronson, E. (1992). *The social animal* (6th ed.). New York: Freeman.

Asch, S. (1946). Forming impressions of personality. *Journal of Abnormal and Social Psychology, 41,* 258-290.

Asch, S. (1955). Opinions and social pressure. *Scientific American, 193*(5), 31-35.

Aserinsky, E., & Kleitman, N. (1953). Regularly occurring periods of eye motility and concomitant phenomena during sleep. *Science, 118,* 273-274.

Ashton, N., Shaw, M., & Worsham, A. (1980). Affective reactions to interpersonal distances by friends and strangers. *Bulletin of the Psychonomic Society, 15,* 306-308.

Astin, G., & Barber, H. (1982). *The rise and fall of national test scores.* New York: Academic Press.

Atchley, R.C. (1985). *Social forces and aging: An introduction to social gerontology.* Belmont, CA: Wadsworth.

Atkinson, J.W. (1981). Studying personality in the context of an advanced motivational psychology. *American Psychologist, 36,* 117-128.

Atkinson, J.W., & Birch, D. (1978). *Introduction to motivation* (2nd ed.). New York: Van Nostrand.

Atkinson, J.W., & Litwin, G. (1960). Achievement motive and test anxiety conceived as motive to approach success and motive to avoid failure. *Journal of Abnormal and Social Psychology, 60,* 52-63.

Atkinson, R.C., & Shiffrin, R.M. (1971). The control of short-term memory. *Scientific American, 225,* 82-90.

Averill, J.R. (1969). Autonomic response patterns during sadness and mirth. *Psychophysiology, 5,* 399-414.

Averill, J.R. (1983). Studies on anger and aggression: Implications for theories of emotion. *American Psychologist, 38,* 1145-1160.

Ax, A.F. (1953). The physiological differentiation between fear and anger in humans. *Psychosomatic Medicine, 15,* 433-442.

Axsom, D., & Cooper, J. (1985). Cognitive dissonance and psychotherapy: The role of effort justification in inducing weight loss. *Journal of Experimental Social Psychology, 21,* 149-160.

Ayllon, T., & Azrin, N.H. (1968). *The token economy: A motivational system for therapy and rehabilitation.* East Norwalk, CT: Appleton-Century-Crofts.

Azarin, N. (1959). Some notes on punishment and avoidance. *Journal of the Experimental Analysis of Behavior, 2,* 260.

B

Bachrach, W.H. (1982). Psychological elements of gastrointestinal disorders. In W. Fann, I. Karacan, A. Pokorny, & R. Williams (Eds.), *Phenomenology and treatment of psychophysiological disorders.* New York: Spectrum.

Baddeley, A. (1986). *Working memory.* New York: Oxford University Press.

Badia, P., Wesensten, N., Lammers, W., & Culpepper, J. (1990). Responsiveness to olfactory stimuli presented in sleep. *Physiology and Behavior, 48,* 87-90.

Bahrick, H.P., Bahrick, P.O., & Wittlinger, R.P. (1975). Fifty years of memory for names and faces: A cross-sectional approach. *Journal of Experimental Psychology: General, 104,* 54-75.

Baldwin, J., & Bell, Y. (1985). The African self-consciousness scale: An African personality questionnaire. *Western Journal of Black Studies, 9,* 61-68.

Bandura, A. (1973). *Aggression: A social learning analysis.* Englewood Cliffs, NJ: Prentice-Hall.

Bandura, A. (1977). *Social learning theory.* Englewood Cliffs, NJ: Prentice-Hall.

Bandura, A. (1978). The self system in reciprocal determinism. *American Psychologist, 33,* 344-458.

Bandura, A. (1982). Self-efficacy mechanism in human agency. *American Psychologist, 37* 122-147.

Bandura, A. (1986). *Social foundations of thought and action: A social cognitive theory.* Englewood Cliffs, NJ: Prentice-Hall.

Bandura, A. (1989). Human agency in social cognitive theory. *American Psychologist, 44,* 1175-1182.

Bandura, A., Ross, D., & Ross, S.A. (1961). Transmission of aggression through imitation of aggressive models. *Journal of Abnormal and Social Psychology, 63,* 575-582.

Bandura, A., Ross, D., & Ross, S.A. (1963). Imitation of film-mediated aggressive models. *Journal of Abnormal and Social Psychology, 66,* 3-11.

Banks, M., & Salapatek, P. (1983). Infant visual perception. In M. Haith & J. Campos (Eds.), *Handbook of child psychology* (Vol. 2). New York: Wiley.

Barabasz, A., & Barabasz, M. (1989). Effects of restricted environmental stimulation: Enhancement of hypnotizability for experimental and chronic pain control. *International Journal of Clinical and Experimental Hypnosis, 36,* 217-231.

Barash, D.P. (1982). *Sociobiology and behavior* (2nd ed.). New York: Elsevier.

Barash, D.P. (1991). *Introduction to peace studies.* Belmont, CA: Wadsworth.

Barber, T.X. (1969). *Hypnosis: A scientific approach.* Princeton, NJ: Van Nostrand.

Bard, P. (1928). A diencephalic mechanism for the expression of rage with special reference to the sympathetic nervous system. *American Journal of Physiology, 84,* 490-515.

Barkley, R.A. (1987). The assessment of attention deficit-hyperactivity disorder. *Behavioral Assessment, 9,* 207-233.

Barlow, D.H., Vermilyea, J., Blanchard, E., Vermilyea, B., & DiNardo, P. (1985). The phenomenon of panic. *Journal of Abnormal Psychology, 94,* 320-328.

Baron, R.A. (1981). Olfaction and human behavior: Effects of a pleasant scent on attraction and social perception. *Personality and Social Psychology Bulletin, 7,* 611-616.

Baron, R.A. (1983). *Human aggression.* New York: Plenum.

Baron, R.A., & Byrne, D. (1991). *Social psychology: Understanding human interaction* (6th ed.). Newton, MA: Allyn & Bacon.

Baron, R.A., & Greenberg, F. (1990). *Behavior in organizations* (3rd ed.). Newton, MA: Allyn-Bacon.

Baron, R.A., Fortin, S.P., Frei, R.L., Hauver, L.A., & Shack, M.L. (1990). Reducing organizational conflict: The role of socially-induced positive affect. *International Journal of Conflict Management, 1,* 133-152.

Baron, R.S. (1986). Distraction-conflict theory: Progress and problems. In L. Berkowitz (Ed.), *Advances in experimental social psychology* (Vol. 20). New York: Academic Press.

Bartol, C. (1983). *Psychology and American law.* Belmont, CA: Wadsworth.

Bartus, R., Dean, R. III, Beer, B., & Lippa, A. (1982). The cholinergic hypothesis of geriatric memory dysfunction. *Science, 217,* 408-417.

Baum, A., Fisher, J., & Solomon, S. (1981). Type of information, familiarity, and the reduction of crowding stress. *Journal of Personality and Social Psychology, 40,* 11-23.

Baumeister, R.F., & Covington, M.V. (1985). Self-esteem persuasion and retrospective distortion of initial attitudes. *Electronic Social Psychology, 1,* 1-22.

Baumeister, R.F., & Scher, S.J. (1988). Self-defeating behavior patterns among normal individuals: Review and analysis of common self-destructive tendencies. *Psychological Bulletin, 104,* 3-22.

Baxter, J.C. (1970). Interpersonal spacing in natural setting. *Sociometry, 33,* 444-456.

Beatty, W., Butters, N., & Janowsky, D. (1986). Patterns of memory failure after scopolamine treatment: Implications for cholinergic hypothesis of dementia. *Behavioral and Neural Biology, 45,* 196-211.

Beck, A.T. (1967). *Depression: Clinical, experimental, and theoretical aspects.* New York: Harper & Row.

Beck, A.T. (1976). *Cognitive therapy and emotional disorders.* New York: International Universities Press.

Beck, A.T. (1985). Theoretical perspectives on clinical anxiety. In A. Tuma & J. Maser (Eds.), *Anxiety and the anxiety disorders.* Hillsdale, NJ: Erlbaum.

Beck, A.T., & Emery, G. (1985). *Anxiety disorders and phobias: A cognitive perspective.* New York: Basic Books.

Beck, R.C. (1990). *Motivation: Theories and Principles* (3rd ed.). Englewood Cliffs, NJ: Prentice Hall.

Bee, H.L. (1989). *The developing child* (5th ed.). New York: Harper & Row.

Belisle, M., Roskies, E., & Levesque, J. (1987). Improving adherence to physical activity. *Health Psychology, 6,* 159-172.

Bell, A., & Weinberg, M. (1978). *Homosexuality: A study of diversity among men and women.* New York: Simon & Schuster.

Bell, A., Weinberg, M., & Hammersmith, S. (1981). *Sexual preference: A study of human diversity.* New York: Simon & Schuster.

Bellezza, F.S. (1981). Mnemonic devices: Classification, characteristics and criteria. *Review of Educational Research, 51,* 247-275.

Bem, D.J. (1967). Self-perception: An alternative interpretation of cognitive dissonance phenomena. *Psychological Review, 74,* 183-200.

Bem, S.L. (1974). The measurement of psychological androgyny. *Journal of Consulting and Clinical Psychology, 42,* 155-162.

Bem, S.L. (1975). Sex-role adaptability: One consequence of psychological androgyny. *Journal of Personality and Social Psychology, 31,* 634-643.

Bem, S.L. (1987). Masculinity and femininity exist only in the mind of the perceiver. In J. Reinisch, L. Rosenblum, & S. Sanders (Eds.), *Masculinity/femininity: Basic perspectives.* New York: Oxford University Press.

Benjamin, L.T., Jr. (1988). *A history of psychology.* New York: McGraw-Hill.

Benson, A. (1982). The vestibular sensory system. In H. Barlow & J. Mollon (Eds.), *The senses.* London: Cambridge University Press.

Berko, J. (1958). The child's learning of English morphology. *Word, 14,* 150-177.

Berkowitz, L. (1984). Some effects of thoughts on anti- and pro-social influences of media events: A cognitive neo-association analysis. *Psychological Bulletin, 95,* 410-427.

Berlyne, D.E. (1960). *Conflict, arousal, and curiosity.* New York: McGraw-Hill.

Berlyne, D.E. (1966). Curiosity and exploration. *Science, 153,* 25-33.

Bernstein, I.L. (1985). Learned food aversions in the progression of cancer and its treatment. In N. Braverman & P. Bernstein (Eds.), Experimental assessments and clinical application of conditioned food aversions. *Annals of the New York Academy of Sciences* (Vol. 443).

Berscheid, E. (1983). Emotion. In H. Kelley, E. Berscheid, A. Christensen, J. Harvey, T. Huston, G. Levinger, E. McClintock, L. Peplau, & D. Peterson (Eds.), *Close relationships.* New York: Freeman.

Berscheid, E., Dion, K., Walster, E., & Walster, G.W. (1971). Physical attractiveness and dating choice: A test of the matching hypothesis. *Journal of Experimental Social Psychology, 7,* 173-189.

Blasi, A. (1980). Bridging moral cognition and moral action: A critical review of the literature. *Psychological Bulletin, 88,* 1-45.

Blass, T. (1991). Understanding behavior in the Milgram obedience experiment: The role of personality, situations, and their interactions. *Journal of Personality and Social Psychology, 60,* 398-413.

Block, J. (1983). Differential premises arising from differential socialization of the sexes: Some conjecture. *Child Development, 54,* 1335-1354.

Bloom, F.E. (1983). The endorphins: A growing family of pharmacologically pertinent peptides. *Annual Review of Pharmacology and Toxicology, 23,* 151-170.

Bolles, R., & Faneslow, M. (1982). Endorphins and behavior. *Annual Review of Psychology, 33,* 87-101.

Bouchard, T.J. (1984). Twins reared apart: What they tell us about human diversity. In S. Fox (Ed.), *Individuality and determinism: Clinical and biological basis.* New York: Plenum Press.

Bouchard, T.J., & McGue, M. (1981). Familial studies of intelligence: A review. *Science, 212,* 1055-1059.

Bourne, L., Dominowski, R., Loftus, E., & Healy, A. (1986). *Cognitive processes.* Englewood Cliffs, NJ: Prentice-Hall.

Bower, B. (1985). The infection connection: The controversial role of viruses in schizophrenia is being examined from new angles. *Science News, 128,* 346-347.

Bower, G.H. (1981). Mood and memory. *American Psychologist, 36,* 129-148.

Bowlby, J. (1982). *Attachment and loss: Vol. 1. Attachment* (2nd ed.). New York: Basic Books.

Bradley, R., & Caldwell, B. (1984). The relation of infants' home environments to achievement test performance in first grade: A follow-up study. *Child Development, 55,* 803-809.

Brammer, L.M., Shostrom, E., & Abrego, P. (1989). *Therapeutic psychology: Fundamentals of counseling and psychotherapy* (5th ed.). Englewood Cliffs, NJ: Prentice Hall.

Brannon, L., & Feist, J. (1992). *Health psychology: An introduction to behavior and health.* Belmont, CA: Wadsworth.

Bransford, J.D., & Stein, B.S. (1984). *The IDEAL problem solver: A guide for improving thinking, learning, and creativity.* New York: Freeman.

Braveman, N.S., & Bronstein, P. (Eds.). (1985). Experimental assessments and clinical applications of conditioned food aversions. *Annals of the New York Academy of Sciences* (Vol. 443).

Breckler, S.J. (1984). Empirical validation of affect, behavior, and cognition as distinct components of attitude. *Journal of Personality and Social Psychology, 47,* 1191-1205.

Bregman, E. (1934). An attempt to modify the emotional attitudes of infants by the conditioned response technique. *Journal of Genetic Psychology, 45,* 169-198.

Brehm, S.S. (1992). *Intimate relationships* (2nd ed.). New York: McGraw-Hill.

Breier, A., & Paul, S.M. (1990). The GABA-A/benzodiazepine receptor: Implications for the molecular basis of anxiety. *Journal of Psychiatric Research, 24,* 91-104.

Breland, K., & Breland, M. (1961). The misbehavior of organisms. *American Psychologist, 16,* 681-684.

Brennan, J.H., & Hemsley, D.R. (1984). Illusory correlations in paranoid and nonparanoid schizophrenia. *British Journal of Clinical Psychology, 23,* 225-226.

Brent, D. (1989). Suicide and suicidal behavior in children and adolescents. *Pediatrics in Review, 10,* 269-275.

Brewer, M. (1986). The role of ethnocentrism in intergroup conflict. In S. Worchel & W. Austin (Eds.), *Psychology of intergroup relations* (2nd ed.). Chicago: Nelson-Hall.

Brewer, M., & Miller, N. (1984). Beyond the contact hypothesis: Theoretical perspectives on desegregation. In N. Miller & M. Brewer (Eds.), *Groups in contact: The psychology of desegregation.* New York: Academic Press.

Brewer, W., & Pani, J. (1983). The structure of human memory. In G.H. Bower (Ed.), *The psychology of learning and motivation: Advances in research and theory* (Vol. 17). New York: Academic Press.

Bridges, K.M.B. (1932). Emotional development in early infancy. *Child Development, 3,* 324-341.

Bridges, L.J., Connell, J.P., & Belsky, J. (1988). Similarities and differences in infant-mother and infant-father interaction in the strange situation: A component process analysis. *Developmental Psychology, 24,* 92-100.

Brodsky, S.L. (1988). *The psychology of adjustment and well-being.* New York: Holt, Rinehart & Winston.

Brooks-Gunn, J., & Peterson, A.C. (1983). *Girls at puberty: Biological and psychosocial perspectives.* New York: Plenum Press.

Brophy, J.E. (1983). Conceptualizing student motivation. *Educational Psychologist, 18,* 200-215.

Brown, J. (1958). Some tests of the decay theory of immediate memory. *Quarterly Journal of Experimental Psychology, 10,* 12-21.

Brown, R., & Kulik, J. (1977). Flashbulb memories. *Cognition, 5,* 73-79.

Brown, R.W., & McNeill, D. (1966). The "tip-of-the-tongue" phenomenon. *Journal of Verbal Learning and Verbal Behavior, 5,* 325-337.

Browne, M., & Mahoney, M. (1984). Sport psychology. *Annual Review of Psychology, 35,* 605-626.

Bruck, M., Cavanagh, P., & Ceci, S. (1991). Fortysomething: Recognizing faces at one's 25th reunion. *Memory and Cognition, 19,* 271-228.

Bruner, J., Goodnow, J., & Austin, G. (1956). *A study of thinking.* New York: Wiley.

Buchoff, R. (1990). Attention deficit disorder: Help for the classroom teacher. *Childhood Education, 67,* 86-90.

Buckhout, R. (1980). Nearly 2,000 witnesses can be wrong. *Bulletin of the Psychonomic Society, 16,* 307-310.

Burg, I., & Ingalls, C. (1985). The immune system. In L. Hayman & E. Sporing (Eds.), *Handbook of pediatric nursing.* New York: Wiley.

Burger, J.M. (1986). Increasing compliance by improving the deal: The that's-not-all technique. *Journal of Personality and Social Psychology, 51,* 277-283.

Burgess, A. (1963). *A clockwork orange.* New York: Norton.

Burt, C. (1966). The genetic determination of differences in intelligence: A study of monozygotic twins reared together and apart. *British Journal of Psychology, 57,* 137-153.

Burton, J. (1991). Scientologists fail to persuade FDA on Prozac. *The Wall Street Journal,* August 2, 1991, 8.

Busemeyer, J., & Myung, E.J. (1988). A new method for investigating prototype learning. *Journal of Experimental Psychology: Learning, Memory and Cognition, 14,* 3-11.

Bushman, B.J. (1984). Perceived symbols of authority and their influence on compliance. *Journal of Applied Social Psychology, 14,* 501-508.

Buss, D.M. (1989). Sex differences in human mate preferences: Evolutionary hypotheses tested in 37 cultures. *Behavioral and Brain Sciences, 12,* 1-14.

Butler, R.A., & Harlow, H.F. (1954). Persistence of visual exploration in monkeys. *Journal of Comparative and Physiological Psychology, 47,* 258-263.

Byrne, D., Baskett, G., & Hodges, L. (1971). Behavioral indicators of interpersonal attraction. *Journal of Applied Social Psychology, 1,* 137-149.

Békésy, G. von (1960). *Experiments in hearing.* New York: McGraw-Hill.

C

Caballero, M., Lumpkin, J., & Madden, C. (1989). Using physical attractiveness as an advertising tool: An empirical test of the attraction phenomenon. *Journal of Advertising Research, 29,* 16-22.

Cacioppo, J.T., Martzke, J., Petty, R., & Tassinary, L. (1988). Specific forms of facial EMG response index emotions during an interview: From Darwin to the continuous flow hypothesis of affect-laden information processing. *Journal of Personality and Social Psychology, 54,* 592-604.

Cacioppo, J.T., Petty, R.E., Losch, M., & Kim, H.S. (1986). Electromyographic activity over facial muscle regions can differentiate the valence and intensity of affective reactions. *Journal of Personality and Social Psychology, 50,* 260-268.

Calhoun, J.B. (1962). Population density and social pathology. *Scientific American, 206,* 139-148.

Cameron, P., Frank, R., Lifter, M., & Morrissey, P. (1968). Cognitive functionings of college students in a general psychology class. Paper presented at the American Psychological Association, San Francisco.

Cannon, W.B. (1927). The James-Lange theory of emotions: A critical examination and an alternative theory. *American Journal of Psychology, 39,* 106-124.

Cannon, W.B. (1939). *The wisdom of the body.* New York: Norton.

Cannon, W.B., & Washburn, A.L. (1912). An explanation of hunger. *American Journal of Physiology, 29,* 441-454.

Cappella, J., & Palmer, M. (1990). Attitude similarity, relational history, and attraction: The mediating effects of kinesic and vocal behaviors. *Communication Monographs,* 57, 161–183.

Capute, A. (1984). Primitive reflex profile: A quantitation of primitive reflexes in infancy. *Developmental Medicine and Child Neurology, 26,* 375–383.

Carmody, J., Istvan, J., Matarazzo, J., Conner, S., & Conner, W. (1986). Applications of social learning theory in the promotion of heart-healthy diets: The Family Heart Study dietary intervention model. *Health Education Research, 1,* 13–27.

Carson, R.C., & Butcher, J.N. (1992). *Abnormal psychology and modern life* (9th ed.). New York: HarperCollins.

Carter, R. (1978). Sleep and dreams, part II. *Annual Review of Psychology, 29,* 223–252.

Caspi, A., Elder, G., & Bem, D.J. (1988). Moving away from the world: Life-course patterns of shy children. *Developmental Psychology, 24,* 824–831.

Cattell, R.B. (1965). *The scientific analysis of personality.* Baltimore: Penguin.

Cavanagh, P., & LeClerc, Y. (1989). Shape from shadows. *Journal of Experimental Psychology: Human Perception and Performance, 15,* 3–27.

Cermak, L. (1975). *Improving your memory.* New York: Norton.

Cernoch, J., & Porter, R. (1985). Recognition of maternal axillary odors by infants. *Child Development, 56,* 1593–1598.

Charlesworth, E., & Nathan, R. (1982). *Stress management: A comprehensive guide to wellness.* Houston: Biobehavioral Press.

Chase, M. (1986). Overview of sleep research, circa 1985. *Sleep, 9,* 452–457.

Chase, M., & Morales, F. (1983). Subthreshold excitatory activity and motor neuron discharge during REM periods of active sleep. *Science, 221,* 1195–1198.

Chesney, M.A., Eagleston, J.R., & Rosenman, R.H. (1981). Type A behavior: Assessment and intervention. In C. Prokop & L. Bradley (Eds.), *Medical psychology: Contributions to behavioral medicine.* New York: Academic Press.

Childers, T., & Houston, M. (1984). Conditions for a picture superiority effect on consumer memory. *Journal of Consumer Research, 11,* 643–654.

Chojnacki, T.J., & Walsh, W.B. (1990). Reliability and concurrent validity of the Sternberg Triangular Love Scale. *Psychological Reports, 67,* 219–224.

Chomsky, N. (1965). *Aspects of the theory of syntax.* Cambridge, MA: MIT Press.

Chomsky, N. (1968). *Language and mind.* New York: Harcourt Brace Jovanovich.

Chorover, S., & Schiller, P. (1965). Short-term retrograde amnesia in rats. *Journal of Comparative and Physiological Psychology, 59,* 73–78.

Christensen, L.B. (1991). *Experimental methodology* (5th ed.). Boston: Allyn & Bacon.

Christie, R. (1976). Probability vs. precedence: The social psychology of jury selection. In G. Bermant, C. Nemeth, & N. Vidmar (Eds.), *Psychology and the law: Research frontiers.* Lexington, MA: Lexington Books.

Cialdini, R. (1988). *Influence: Science and practice* (2nd ed.). Glenview, IL: Scott, Foresman.

Cialdini, R., & Schroeder, D. (1976). Compliance by legitimizing paltry contributions: When even a penny helps. *Journal of Personality and Social Psychology, 34,* 599–604.

Cialdini, R., Cacioppo, J., Bassett, R., & Miller, J. (1978). Low-ball procedure for producing compliance: Commit-

ment then cost. *Journal of Personality and Social Psychology, 36,* 463–476.

Cialdini, R., Vincent, J., Lewis, S., Catalan, J., Wheeler, D., & Darby, B. (1975). Reciprocal concessions procedure for inducing compliance: The door-in-the-face technique. *Journal of Personality and Social Psychology, 31,* 206–215.

Clark, K.B., & Clark, M.K. (1939). The development of consciousness of self and the emergence of racial identification in Negro pre-school children. *Journal of Social Psychology, 10,* 591–599.

Clark, K.B., & Clark, M.K. (1947). Racial identification and preference in Negro children. In T. Newcomb & E. Hartley (Eds.), *Readings in Social Psychology.* New York: Holt.

Clark, K.J., & Horch, K.W. (1986). Kinesthesia. In K. Boff, L. Kaufman, & J.P. Thomas (Eds.), *Handbook of perception and human performance* (Vol. 1). New York: Wiley.

Claxton, C., & Murrell, P. (1987). *Learning styles: Implications for improving educational practices.* ASHE-ERIC Higher Education Report No. 4. Washington, DC: Association for the Study of Higher Education.

Cohen, L.H. (1988). *Life events and psychological functioning: Theoretical and methodological issues.* Newbury Park, CA: Sage.

Cohen, S., & Hoberman, H. (1983). Positive events and social supports as buffers of life change stress. *Journal of Applied Social Psychology, 13,* 99–125.

Cohen, S., Evans, G., Stokols, D., & Krantz, D. (1986). *Behavior, health and environmental stress.* New York: Plenum.

Cohen, S., Glass, D.C., & Singer, J.E. (1986). Apartment noise, auditory discrimination, and reading ability in children. *Journal of Experimental Social Psychology, 9,* 407–422.

Cohen, S., & Wills, T. (1985). Stress, social support, and the buffering hypothesis. *Psychological Bulletin, 98,* 310–357.

Colangelo, N., Kelly, K., & Schrepfer, R. (1987). A comparison of gifted, general, and special learning needs students on academic and social self-concept. *Journal of Counseling and Development, 66,* 73–77.

Coles, C., Smith, I., Lancaster, J., & Falek, A. (1987). Persistence over the first month of neurobehavioral differences in infants exposed to alcohol prenatally. *Infant Behavior and Development, 10,* 23–37.

Conger, J., & Peterson, A. (1984). *Adolescence and youth* (3rd ed.). New York: Harper & Row.

Cook, S. (1984). Cooperative interaction in multiethnic contexts. In N. Miller & M. Brewer (Eds.), *Groups in conflict: The psychology of desegregation.* New York: Academic Press.

Cookerly, J.R. (1980). Does marital therapy do any lasting good? *Journal of Marital and Family Therapy, 6,* 393–397.

Cooper, J., & Fazio, R. (1984). A new look at dissonance theory. *Advances in Experimental Social Psychology, 17,* 229–266.

Cooper, J., Bloom, F., & Roth, R. (1986). *The biochemical basis of neuropharmacology* (5th ed.). New York: Oxford University Press.

Cooper, R., & Zubek, J. (1958). Effects of enriched and restricted early environments on the learning ability of bright and dull rats. *Canadian Journal of Psychology, 12,* 159–164.

Coppen, A., Metcalfe, M., & Wood, K. (1982). Lithium. In E. Pakel (Ed.), *Handbook of affective disorders.* New York: Guilford.

Coren, S., & Porac, C. (1987). Individual differences in visual-geometric illusions: Predictions from measures of spatial cognitive abilities. *Perception and Psychophysics, 41,* 211-219.

Coren, S., & Ward, L.M. (1989). *Sensation and perception* (3rd ed.). San Diego: Harcourt Brace Jovanovich.

Costa, P.T., Jr., & McCrae, R.R. (1980). Still stable after all these years: Personality as a key to some issues in adulthood and old age. In P. Baltes & O. Brim (Eds.), *Life span development and behavior* (Vol. 3). New York: Academic Press.

Costa, P.T., Jr., & McCrae, R.R. (1985). *The NEO personality inventory: Manual, form S and form R.* Odessa, FL: Psychological Assessment Resources.

Costa, P.T., Jr., Zonderman, A.B., McCrae, R.R., & Williams, R.B., Jr. (1985). Content and comprehensiveness in the MMPI: An item factor analysis in a normal adult sample. *Journal of Personality and Social Psychology, 48,* 925-933.

Couch, J.V. (1987). *Fundamentals of statistics for the behavioral sciences* (2nd. ed.). St. Paul, MN: West.

Cowan, N. (1988). Evolving conceptions of memory storage, selective attention, and their mutual constraints within the human information-processing system. *Psychological Bulletin, 104,* 163-191.

Cowart, B.J. (1981). Development of taste perception in humans: Sensitivity and preference throughout the life span. *Psychological Bulletin, 90,* 43-73.

Cowart, B.J. (1989). Relationships between taste and smell across the adult life span. *Annals of the New York Academy of Sciences, 561,* 39-55.

Cox, H. (1984). *Later life: The realities of aging.* Englewood Cliffs, NJ: Prentice-Hall.

Craik, F., & Lockhart, R. (1972). Levels of processing: A framework for memory research. *Journal of Verbal Learning and Verbal Behavior, 11,* 671-684.

Craik, F., & Watkins, M. (1973). The role of rehearsal in short-term memory. *Journal of Verbal Learning and Verbal Behavior, 12,* 599-607.

Crick, F., & Mitchison, G. (1983). The function of dream sleep. *Nature, 304,* 111-114.

Crowder, R.G. (1982). Decay of auditory memory in vowel discrimination. *Journal of Experimental Psychology: Learning, Memory, and Cognition, 8,* 153-162.

Crowe, R.R. (1990). Panic disorder: Genetic considerations. *Journal of Psychiatric Research, 24,* 129-134.

Crusco, A.H., & Wetzel, C.G. (1984). The Midas touch: The effects of interpersonal touch on restaurant tipping. *Personality and Social Psychology Bulletin, 10,* 512-517.

Cunningham, M.R. (1986). Measuring the physical in physical attractiveness: Quasi-experiments on the sociobiology of female facial beauty. *Journal of Personality and Social Psychology, 50,* 925-935.

Curry, S., Wagner, E., & Grothaus, L. (1990). Evaluation of intrinsic and extrinsic motivation interventions with a self-help smoking cessation program. *Journal of Consulting and Clinical Psychology, 59,* 318-324.

Cutler, W.B., Preti, G., Krieger, A., Huggins, G.R., Garcia, C., & Lawley, H.J. (1986). Human axillary secretions influence women's menstrual cycles: The role of donor extract from men. *Hormones and Behavior, 20,* 463-473.

Cutting, J. (1987). Rigidity in cinema seen from the front row, side aisle. *Journal of Experimental Psychology: Human Perception and Performance, 13,* 323-334.

D

Dakoff, G.A. & Taylor, S.E. (1990). Victims' perceptions of social support: What is helpful to whom? *Journal of Personality and Social Psychology, 58,* 80-89.

Darwin, C. (1859). *The origin of species by means of natural selection.* London: Murray.

Darwin, C. (1965). *The expression of the emotions in man and animals.* Chicago: University of Chicago Press. (Original work published London: Murray, 1872).

Darwin, C.J., Turvey, M.T., & Crowder, R.G. (1972). An auditory analog of the Sperling partial report procedure: Evidence for brief auditory storage. *Cognitive Psychology, 3,* 255-267.

Davies, P. (1985). A critical review of the role of the cholinergic system in human memory and cognition. *Annals of the New York Academy of Sciences, 444,* 212-217.

Davis, J., & Smith, T. (1984). *General social surveys, 1972-1984: Cumulative data.* New Haven, CT: Roper Center for Public Opinion Research.

Davis, J., Laughlin, P., & Lomorita, S. (1976). The social psychology of small groups: Cooperative and mixed-motive interaction. *Annual Review of Psychology, 27,* 502-516.

Davis, R., Freeman, R., & Garner, D. (1988). A naturalistic investigation of eating behavior in bulimia nervosa. *Journal of Consulting and Clinical Psychology, 56,* 273-279.

Davison, G.C., & Neale, J.M. (1990). *Abnormal psychology: An experimental clinical approach* (5th ed.). New York: Wiley.

Dawkins, R. (1976). *The selfish gene.* New York: Oxford University Press.

DeCarvalho, R.J. (1990). A history of the "third force" in psychology. *Journal of Humanistic Psychology, 30,* 22-44.

DeCasper, A., & Fifer, W. (1980). Of human bonding: Newborns prefer their mothers' voices. *Science, 208,* 1174-1176.

DeLuce, J., & Wilder, H.T. (Eds.). (1983). *Language in primates: Perspectives and implications.* New York: Springer-Verlag.

Deci, E.L. (1975). *Intrinsic motivation.* New York: Plenum.

Deci, E.L. (1980). *The psychology of self-determination.* Lexington, MA: Lexington Books.

Deci, E.L., & Ryan, R.M. (1985). *Intrinsic motivation and self-determination in human behavior.* New York: Plenum Press.

Delack, J.B. (1976). Aspects of infant speech development in the first year of life. *Canadian Journal of Linguistics, 21,* 17-37.

Delgado, J.M.R. (1969). *Physical control of the mind: Toward a psychocivilized society.* New York: Harper & Row.

Dembroski, T.M., MacDougall, J., Williams, B., & Haney, T. (1985). Components of Type A, hostility, and anger-in: Relationship to angiographic findings. *Psychosomatic Medicine, 47,* 219-233.

Dement, W.C. & Kleitman, N. (1957). Cyclic variations in EEG during sleep and their relation to eye movement, body motility, and dreaming. *Electroencephalography and Clinical Neurophysiology, 9,* 673-690.

Dement, W.C. (1960). The effect of dream deprivation. *Science, 131,* 1705-1707.

Dement, W.C. (1976). *Some must watch while some must sleep.* New York: Norton.

Denes, P.B., & Pinson, E.N. (1963). *The speech chain*. Murray Hill, NJ: Bell Laboratories.

Dennis, W., & Dennis, M.G. (1940). The effect of cradling practices upon the onset of walking in Hopi children. *Journal of Genetic Psychology, 56*, 77-86.

Depue, R., & Monroe, S. (1986). Conceptualization and measurement of human disorder in life stress research: The problem of chronic disturbances. *Psychological Bulletin, 99*, 36-51.

Deutsch, J.A. (1983). Dietary control and the stomach. *Progress in Neurobiology, 20*, 313-332.

Devine, P. (1989). Stereotypes and prejudice: Their automatic and controlled components. *Journal of Personality and Social Psychology, 56*, 5-18.

Diamond, G., Gurdin, P., Wiznia, A., & Belman, A. (1990). Effects of congenital HIV infection on neurodevelopmental status of babies in foster care. *Developmental Medicine and Child Neurology, 32*, 999-1004.

Dichter, E. (1975). *Packaging: The sixth sense*. Boston: Cahners.

Diehl, M., & Stroebe, W. (1987). Productivity loss in brainstorming groups: Toward a solution of a riddle. *Journal of Personality and Social Psychology, 53*, 497-509.

Diener, E. (1984). Subjective well-being. *Psychological Bulletin, 95*, 542-575.

Digman, J.M. (1988). Personality structure: Emergence of the five-factor model. *Annual Review of Psychology, 41*, 417-440.

Digman, J.M. (1990). Personality structure: Emergence of the five-factor model. In M. Rosenzweig & L. Porter (Eds.), *Annual Review of Psychology, 41*, 417-440. Palo Alto, CA: Annual Reviews.

Digman, J.M., & Takemoto-Chock, N.K. (1981). Factors in the natural language of personality: Re-analysis, comparison, and interpretation of six major studies. *Mutlivariate Behavioral Research, 16*, 149-170.

Dion, K.K. (1972). Physical attractiveness and evaluations of children's transgressions. *Journal of Personality and Social Psychology, 24*, 207-213.

Dion, K.K. (1980). Physical attractiveness, sex roles, and heterosexual attraction. In M. Cook (Ed.), *The bases of sexual attraction*. New York: Academic Press.

Dion, K.K., Berscheid, E., & Walster, E. (1972). What is beautiful is good. *Journal of Personality and Social Psychology, 24*, 285-290.

Dion, K.L., & Dion, K.K. (1987). Belief in a just world and physical attractiveness stereotyping. *Journal of Personality and Social Psychology, 52*, 775-780.

Dishman, R.K. (1982). Compliance/adherence in health-related exercise. *Health Psychology, 1*, 237-267.

Doane, J., West, M., Goldstein, M., & Rodnick, E. (1981). Parental communication deviance and affective style: Predictions of subsequent schizophrenia spectrum disorders in vulnerable adolescents. *Archives of General Psychiatry, 38*, 679-685.

Dodge, K.A. (1983). Behavioral antecedents of peer social status. *Child Development, 54*, 1386-1399.

Doherty, W.J., & Baldwin, C. (1985). Shifts and stability in locus of control during the 1970s: Divergence of the sexes. *Journal of Personality and Social Psychology, 48*, 1048-1053.

Dolan, B. (1991). Cross-cultural aspects of anorexia nervosa and bulimia: A review. *International Journal of Eating Disorders, 10*, 67-79.

Dollard, J., & Miller, N.E. (1950). *Personality and psychotherapy*. New York: McGraw-Hill.

Dollard, J., Doob, L.W., Miller, N.E., Mowrer, O.H., & Sears, R.R. (1939). *Frustration and aggression*. New Haven: Yale University Press.

Doty, R.L., Green, P.A., Ram, C., & Uankell, S.L. (1982). Communication of gender from human breath odors: Relationship to perceived intensity and pleasantness. *Hormones and Behavior, 16*, 13-22.

Duncker, K. (1945). On problem solving. *Psychological Monographs, 58*, No. 270.

Dunn, J., Plomin, R., & Daniels, D. (1986). Consistency and change in mothers' behavior toward young siblings. *Child Development, 57*, 348-356.

Duquin, M. (1980). The dynamics of athletic persistence. In W. Straub (Ed.), *Sports psychology: An analysis of athletes' behavior*. Ithaca, NY: Mouvement.

Dutton, D., & Aron, A. (1974). Some evidence for heightened sexual attraction under conditions of high anxiety. *Journal of Personality and Social Psychology, 30*, 510-517.

E

Eagly, A.H., & Carli, L.L. (1981). Sex of researchers and sex-typed communications as determinants of sex differences in influenceability: A meta-analysis of social influence studies. *Psychological Bulletin, 90*, 1-20.

Eagly, A.H., & Crowley, M. (1986). Gender and helping behavior: A meta-analysis of the social psychological literature. *Psychological Bulletin, 100*, 283-308.

Eagly, A.H., & Himmelfarb, S. (1978). Attitudes and opinions. *Annual Review of Psychology, 29*, 517-554.

Eagly, A.H., & Steffen, V.J. (1986). Gender and aggressive behavior: A meta-analysis of the social psychological literature. *Psychological Bulletin, 100*, 309-330.

Ebbinghaus, H. (1913). *Memory*. (H.A. Ruger and C.E. Bussenius, Trans.). New York: Columbia University Press. (Original work published 1885).

Eibl-Eibesfeldt, I. (1972). *Love and hate: The natural history of behavior patterns*. New York: Holt, Rinehart & Winston.

Eisenberg, N., Cialdini, R.B., McCreath, H., & Shell, R. (1987). Consistency-based compliance: When and why do children become vulnerable? *Journal of Personality and Social Psychology, 52*, 1174-1181.

Eisenberg, N., Shell, R., Pasternack, J., Lennon, R., Beller, R., & Mathy, R. (1987). Prosocial development in middle childhood: A longitudinal study. *Developmental Psychology, 23*, 712-718.

Ekman, P. (1982). *Emotion and the human face* (2nd ed.). New York: Cambridge University Press.

Ekman, P. (1985). *Telling lies: Clues to deceit in the marketplace, politics, and marriage*. New York: Norton.

Ekman, P., & Friesen, W.V. (1981). Measuring facial movement with the facial action coding system. In P. Ekman (Ed.), *Emotion in the human face* (2nd ed.). Cambridge: Cambridge University Press.

Ekman, P., & Friesen, W.V. (1986). A new pan-cultural facial expression of emotion. *Motivation and Emotion, 10*, 159-168.

Ekman, P., Friesen, W., O'Sullivan, M., Chan, H., Diacoyanni-Tarlatzis, I., Heider, K., Krause, R., LeCompte, W., Pitcairn, T., Ricci-Bitti, P., Scherer, K., Tomita, M., & Tzauaras, A. (1987). Universals and cultural differences in the judgments of facial expressions of emotion. *Journal of Personality and Social Psychology, 53*, 712-717.

Ekman, P., Levenson, R.W., & Friesen, W.V. (1983). Autonomic nervous system activity distinguishes among emotions. *Science*, 1208-1210.

Ellis, A. (1962). *Reason and emotion in psychotherapy*. New York: Stuart Press.

Ellis, A. (1984). Rational-emotive therapy. In R.J. Corsini (Ed.), *Current psychotherapies* (3rd ed.). Itasca, IL: Peacock.

Ellis, H. (1987). Recent developments in human memory. In V.P. Makowsky (Ed.), *The G. Stanley Hall Lecture Series* (Vol. 7). Washington, DC: American Psychological Association.

Epstein, A. (1982). The physiology of thirst. In D. Pfaff (Ed.), *The physiological mechanisms of motivation*. New York: Springer-Verlag.

Epstein, R., Kirshnit, C., Lanza, R., & Rubin, L. (1984). "Insight" in the pigeon: Antecedents and determinants of an intelligent performance. *Nature, 308*, 61-62.

Erikson, E.H. (1963). *Childhood and society* (2nd ed.). New York: Norton.

Erikson, R.P. (1985). Definitions: A matter of taste. In D. W. Pfaff (Ed.), *Taste, olfaction, and the central nervous system*. New York: Rockefeller University Press.

Erlich, S.S., & Itabashi, H.H. (1986). Narcolepsy: A neuropathologic study. *Sleep, 9*, 126-132.

Eron, L.D. (1982). Parent-child interaction, television violence, and aggression of children. *American Psychologist, 37*, 197-211.

Eysenck, H.J. (1952). *The scientific study of personality*. London: Routledge & Kegan Paul.

Eysenck, H.J. (1967). *The biological basis of personality*. Springfield, IL: Thomas.

Eysenck, H.J. (1975). *The structure of human personality*. London: Methuen.

Eysenck, H.J. (1982). *Personality, genetics, and behavior*. New York: Springer-Verlag.

F

Fabbro, F., Brusaferro, A., & Bava, A. (1990). Opposite musical-manual interference in young vs. expert musicians. *Neurophychologia, 28*, 871-877.

Fagot, B. (1985). Changes in thinking about early sex role development. *Developmental Review, 5*, 83-98.

Falbo, T. (1982). Only children in America. In M.E. Lamb & B. Sutton-Smith (Eds.). *Sibling relationships: Their nature and significance across the lifespan*. Hillsdale, NJ: Erlbaum.

Fantz, R.L. (1961). The origin of form perception. *Scientific American, 204*, 66-72.

Farrell, J., Pavel, M., & Sperling, G. (1990). The visible persistence of stimuli in stroboscopic motion. *Vision Research, 30*, 921-936.

Fechner, G.T. (1966). *Elements of psychophysics*, edited by D.H. Howes & E.G. Boring, (H.E. Adler Trans.). New York: Holt, Rinehart & Winston, (Original work published 1860).

Feldman, S., Nash, S., & Aschenbrenner, B. (1983). Antecedents of fathering. *Child Development, 54*, 1628-1636.

Ferster, C., & Skinner, B.F. (1957). *Schedules of reinforcement*. East Norwalk, CT: Appleton-Century-Crofts.

Feshbach, S., & Weiner, B. (1986). *Personality* (2nd ed.). Lexington, MA: Heath.

Festinger, L. (1954). A theory of social comparison processes. *Human Relations, 7*, 117-140.

Festinger, L. (1957). *A theory of cognitive dissonance*. Stanford, CA: Stanford University Press.

Festinger, L., & Carlsmith, J.M. (1959). Cognitive consequences of forced compliance. *Journal of Abnormal and Social Psychology, 58*, 203-210.

Festinger, L., Schachter, S., & Back, K. (1950). *Social pressures in informal groups: A study of human factors in housing*. New York: Harper & Row.

Feuerstein, R. (1980). *Instrumental enrichment: An intervention program for cognitive modifiability*. Baltimore: University Park Press.

Fibiger, H.C. (1984). The neurobiological substrates of depression in Parkinson's disease. *Canadian Journal of Neurological Sciences, 11*, 105-107.

Fiedler, F. (1981). Leadership effectiveness. *American Behavioral Scientist, 24*, 619-632.

Field, T. (1987). Interaction and attachment in normal and atypical infants. *Journal of Consulting and Clinical Psychology, 55*, 853-859.

Fisher, J.D., & Byrne, D. (1975). Too close for comfort: Sex differences in response to invasions of personal space. *Journal of Personality and Social Psychology, 32*, 15-20.

Fisher, J.D., Rytting, M., & Heslin, R. (1976). Hands touching hands: Affective and evaluative effects of an interpersonal touch. *Sociometry, 39*, 416-421.

Fishman, J. (1985, September). Mapping the mind. *Psychology Today*, 18-19.

Fiske, S.T., & Taylor, S.E. (1991). *Social cognition* (2nd ed.). New York: McGraw Hill.

Fitzpatrick, V., Pasnak, R., & Tyer, Z. (1982). The effect of familiar size at familiar distances. *Perception, 11*, 89-91.

Flaherty, C.F. (1985). *Animal learning and cognition*. New York: Knopf.

Flavell, J.H. (1982). Structures, stages, and sequences in cognitive development. In W. Collins (Ed.). *The concept of development: The Minnesota symposia on child psychology* (Vol. 15). Hillsdale, NJ: Erlbaum.

Flavell, J.H. (1985). *Cognitive development* (2nd ed.). Englewood Cliffs, NJ: Prentice-Hall.

Flavell, J.H. (1986). The development of children's knowledge about the appearance-reality distinction. *American Psychologist, 41* 418-425.

Fleming, J. (1983). *The impact of college environments on black students*. San Francisco: Jossey-Bass.

Foa, E., Steketee, G., & Young, M. (1984). Agoraphobia: Phenomenological aspects, associated characteristics, and theoretical considerations. *Clinical Psychology Review, 4*, 431-457.

Fodor, E. (1984). The power motive and reactivity to power stress. *Journal of Personality and Social Psychology, 47*, 853-859.

Fordham, S. & Ogbu, J. (1986). Black students' school success: Coping with the "burden of acting white." *Urban Review, 18*, 176-206.

Fosson, A., Knibbs, J., Bryant-Waugh, R., & Lask, B. (1987). Early onset anorexia nervosa. *Archives of Disease in Children, 62*, 114-118.

Fouts, R.S., & Bodamer, M. (1987). Preliminary report to the National Geographic Society on "Chimpanzee intrapersonal signing." *Friends of Washoe, 7*, 4-12.

Fouts, R.S., Fouts, D.H., & Schoenfeld, D.J. (1984). Sign language conversational interaction between chimpanzees. *Sign Language Studies, 42*, 1-12.

Francoeur, R. (1991). *Becoming a sexual person* (2nd ed.). New York: Macmillan.

Frankenburg, W.K., & Dodds, J.B. (1967). The Denver developmental screening test. *Journal of Pediatrics, 71*, 181-191.

Franklin, J. (1987). The changing nature of agoraphobic fears. *British Journal of Clinical Psychology, 26*, 127-133.

Franks, C.M. (1984). Behavior therapy with children and adolescents. In G.T. Wilson, C.M. Franks, K.D. Brownell, & P.C. Kendall (Eds.), *Annual review of behavior therapy: Theory and practice.* New York: Guilford Press.

Frederickson, R.C., & Geary, L.E. (1982). Endogenous opiod peptides: Review of physiological pharmacological and clinical aspects. *Progress in Neurobiology, 19*, 19-69.

Freedman, J.L. (1975). *Crowding and behavior.* San Francisco: Freeman.

Freedman, J.L. (1988). Television violence and aggression: What the evidence shows. In S. Oskamp (Ed.), *Television as a social issue.* Newbury Park, CA: Sage.

Freedman, J.L., & Fraser, S.C. (1966). Compliance without pressure: The foot-in-the-door technique. *Journal of Personality and Social Psychology, 4*, 195-202.

Freud, S. (1915). The unconscious. In S. Freud, *Collected papers*, Vol. IV. London: Hogarth Press, 1949.

Freud, S. (1930). *Civilization and its discontent.* London: Hogarth.

Freud, S. (1933). *New introductory lectures on psychoanalysis.* New York: Norton.

Freud, S. (1940). *An outline of psycho-analysis.* Translated by J. Strachey in 1949. New York: Norton.

Freud, S. (1950). The interpretation of dreams. In J. Strachey (Ed. and Trans.), *The standard edition of the complete psychological works.* London: Hogarth. (Original work published 1900).

Freudenberger, H.J. (1980). *Burnout: How to beat the high cost of success.* New York: Bantam.

Friedlund, A.J., Ekman, P., & Oster, H. (1987). Facial expressions of emotion. In A. Siegman & S. Feldstern (Eds.), *Nonverbal communication and behavior* (2nd ed.). Hillsdale, NJ: Erlbaum.

Friedlund, A.J., Fowler, S.C., & Pritchard, D.A. (1980). Striate muscle tension patterning in frontalis EMG biofeedback. *Psychophysiology, 17*, 47-55.

Friedman, D.E. (1990). Corporate responses to family needs. *Marriage and Family Review, 15*, 77-98.

Friedman, L., Bliwise, D., Yesavage, J., & Salom, S. (1991). A preliminary study comparing sleep restriction and relaxation treatments for insomnia in older adults. *Journal of Gerontology, 46*, 1-8.

Friedman, M., & Rosenman, R. (1974). *Type A behavior and your heart.* New York: Knopf.

Frijda, N.H. (1988). The laws of emotion. *American Psychologist, 43*, 349-358.

Fromm, E. (1956). *The art of loving.* New York: Harper & Row.

G

Gackenbach, J., & Bosveld, J. (1989). *Control your dreams.* New York: Harper & Row.

Gage, N.L., & Berliner, D.C. (1988). *Educational Psychology* (4th ed.). Boston: Houghton Mifflin.

Galanter, E. (1962). Contemporary psychophysics. In R. Brown, E. Galanter, E. Hess, & G. Mandler (Eds.), *New directions in psychology* (Vol. 1). New York: Holt, Rinehart & Winston.

Galicki, S., & McEwen, M. (1989). The relationship of residence at a predominantly white university. *Journal of College Student Development, 30*, 389-394.

Galinsky, E. (1981). *Between generations: The six stages of parenthood.* New York: Berkley.

Ganchrow, J., Steiner, J., & Daher, M. (1983). Neonatal facial expressions in response to different qualities and intensities of gustatory stimuli. *Infant Behavior and Development, 6*, 189-200.

Gannon, L.R., Haynes, S.N., Cuevas, J., & Chavez, R. (1987). Psychophysiological correlates of induced headaches. *Journal of Behavioral Medicine, 10*, 411-423.

Garcia, J. (1989). Food for Tolman: Cognitions and catharis in concert. In T. Archer & L. Nilsson (Eds.), *Aversion, avoidance and anxiety: Perspectives on aversively motivated behavior.* Hillsdale, NJ: Erlbaum.

Garcia, J., & Koelling, R. (1966). Relation of cue to consequence in avoidance learning. *Psychonomic Science, 4*, 123-124.

Garcia, J., Kimeldorf, D., & Koelling, R. (1955). Conditioned aversion to saccharin resulting from exposure to gamma radiation. *Science, 122*, 157-158.

Gardner, H. (1983). *Frames of mind.* New York: Basic Books.

Gardner, H. (1983). Prodigies' progress. *Psychology Today*, May, 75-79.

Gardner, R.A., & Gardner, B.T. (1969). Teaching sign language to a chimpanzee. *Science, 165*, 664-672.

Gazzaniga, M.S. (1983). Right hemisphere language following brain bisection: A 20 year perspective. *American Psychologist, 38*, 525-537.

Gazzaniga, M.S. (1987). Perceptual and attentional processes following callosal section in humans. *Neuropsychologia, 25*, 119-133.

Gazzaniga, M.S. (1989). Organization of the human brain. *Science, 245*, 947-952.

Gelfand, D.M., & Hartmann, D.P. (1980). The development of prosocial behavior and moral judgement. In R.L. Ault (Ed.), *Developmental perspectives.* Santa Monica, CA: Goodyear.

Gelman, R., & Gallistel, C.R. (1978). *The young child's understanding of number: A window on early cognitive development.* Cambridge, MA: Harvard University Press.

Gennaro, S., Tulman, L., & Fawcett, J. (1990). Temperament in pre-term and full-term infants at three and six months of age. *Merrill-Palmer Quarterly, 36*, 201-215.

George, V. (1986). Talented adolescent women and the motive to avoid success. *Journal of Multicultural counseling and Development, 14*, 132-139.

Giannini, A., Martin, D., & Turner, C. (1990). Beta-endorphin decline in late luteal phase dysphoric disorder. *International Journal of Psychiatry in Medicine, 20*, 279-284.

Gibson, E.J., & Walk, R.D. (1960). The visual cliff. *Scientific American, 202*, 64-71.

Glass, D.C., & Singer, J.E. (1972). Behavioral aftereffects of unpredictable and uncontrollable aversive events. *American Scientist, 60*, 457-465.

Glick, P. (1989). The family life cycle and social change. *Family Relations, 38*, 123-129.

Gmelch, W. (1982). *Beyond stress to effective management.* New York: Wiley.

Goebel, B.L., & Brown, D.R. (1981). Age differences in motivation related to Maslow's need hierarchy. *Developmental Psychology, 17*, 809-815.

Gold, S., & Henderson, B. (1990). Daydreaming and curiosity: Stability and change in gifted children and adolescents. *Adolescence, 25*, 701-708.

Goldberg, L. (1990). An alternative "description of personality": The big-five factor structure. *Journal of Personality and Social Psychology, 59,* 1216-1229.

Goldstein, A.P., & Krasner, L. (1987). *Modern applied psychology.* New York: Pergamon.

Goleman, D.J. (1977). *The varieties of meditative experience.* New York: Dutton.

Goleman, D.J. (1980). 1,528 little geniuses and how they grew. *Psychology Today, 14,* 28-53.

Gotlieb, J.B., & Dubinsky, A.J. (1991). Influence of price on aspects of consumers' cognitive process. *Journal of Applied Psychology, 76,* 541-549.

Gotmark, F. (1987). White underparts in gulls function as hunting camouflage. *Animal Behavior, 35,* 1786-1792.

Gottesman, I.I., & Shields, J. (1972). *Schizophrenia and genetics: A twin study vantage point.* New York: Academic Press.

Gottlieb, A. (1988). *Blood magic.* Berkeley: University of California Press.

Gough, H.G. (1969). *Manual for the California psychological inventory* (rev. ed.). Palo Alto, CA: Consulting Psychologists Press.

Gouras, P. (1985). Color vision. In E. Kandel & J. Schwartz (Eds.), *Principles of neural science.* New York: Elsevier.

Graham, W., & Balloun, J. (1973). An empirical test of Maslow's need hierarchy theory. *Journal of Humanistic Psychology, 13,* 97-108.

Granud, C. (1986). Binocular vision and spatial perception in 4 and 5 month old infants. *Journal of Experimental Psychology: Human Perception and Performance, 12,* 36-49.

Grasha, A.F. (1987). *Practical applications of psychology* (3rd ed.). Boston: Little, Brown.

Grasha, A.F., & Kirschenbaum, D.S. (1986). *Adjustment and competence: Concepts and applications.* St. Paul, MN: West.

Gravetter, F.J., & Wallnau, L.B. (1992). *Statistics for the behavioral sciences* (3rd ed.). St. Paul, MN: West.

Green, B.F. (1981). A primer of testing. *American Psychologist, 36,* 1001-1011.

Green, D.M., & Swets, J.A. (1966). *Signal detection theory and psychophysics.* New York: Wiley.

Greenbaum, P., & Rosenfeld, H. (1978). Patterns of avoidance in response to interpersonal staring and proximity: Effects of bystanders on drivers at a traffic intersection. *Journal of Personality and Social Psychology, 36,* 575-587.

Greene, R.L. (1987). Effects of maintenance rehearsal on human memory. *Psychological Bulletin, 102,* 403-413.

Greeno, J. (1989). A perspective on thinking. *American Psychologist, 44,* 134-141.

Greenwald, A.G. (1989). Why are attitudes important? In A. Partkanis, S. Breckler, & A. Greenwald (Eds.), *Attitude structure and function.* Hillsdale, NJ: Erlbaum.

Gregorc, A.F. (1986). *An adult's guide to style.* New York, NY: Gabriel Systems.

Greiser, C., Greenberg, R., & Harrison, R.H. (1972). The adaptive function of sleep: The differential effects of sleep and dreaming on recall. *Journal of Abnormal Psychology, 80,* 280-286.

Grief, E., & Ulman, K. (1982). The psychological impact of menarche on early adolescent females: A review of the literature. *Child Development, 53,* 1413-1430.

Griffith, R.M., Miyagi, O., & Tago, A. (1958). The universality of typical dreams: Japanese vs. Americans. *American Anthropologist, 60,* 1173-1179.

Grinker, J. (1982). Physiological and behavioral basis of human obesity. In D. Pfaff (Ed.), *The physiological mechanisms of motivation.* New York: Springer-Verlag.

Guilford, J.P. (1967). *The nature of human intelligence.* New York: McGraw-Hill.

Guilford, J.P. (1982). Cognitive psychology's ambiguities: Some suggested remedies. *Psychological Review, 89,* 48-59.

Gurman, A., Kniskern, D. & Pinsof, W. (1986). Research on marital and family therapies. In S.L. Garfield & A. Bergin (Eds.), *Handbook of psychotherapy and behavior change.* New York: Wiley.

Gustavson, C.R., & Gustavson, J.C. (1985). Predation control using conditioned food aversion methodology: Theory, practice, and implications. In N. Braverman & P. Bernstein (Eds.), Experimental assessments and clinical application of conditioned food aversions. *Annals of the New York Academy of Sciences,* Vol. 443.

H

Haber, R.N. (1980). Eidetic images are not just imaginary. *Psychology Today, 14,* 72-82.

Hager, J., & Ekman, P. (1979). Long-distance transmission of facial affect signals. *Ethology and Sociobiology, 1,* 77-82.

Hakel, N.D. (1982). Employment interviewing. In K. Rowland & C. Ferris (Eds.), *Personal management.* Boston: Allyn & Bacon.

Hales, P. (1986). *The complete book of sleep.* Reading, MA: Addison-Wesley.

Hall, C.S. (1966). *The meaning of dreams.* New York: McGraw-Hill.

Hall, C.S. (1984). An "ubiquitous sex difference in dreams" revisited. *Journal of Personality and Social Psychology, 46,* 1109-1117.

Hall, C.S., & Lindzey, G. (1985). *Introduction to theories of personality.* New York: Wiley.

Hall, E.T. (1966). *The hidden dimension.* New York: Doubleday.

Hall, G.S. (1916). *Adolescence.* New York: Appleton.

Hall, J. (1986). The cardiopulmonary failure of sleep disordered breathing. *Journal of the American Medical Association, 255,* 930-933.

Hallahan, D., Kauffman, J., & Lloyd, J. (1985). *Introduction to learning disabilities* (2nd ed.). Englewood Cliffs, NJ: Prentice-Hall.

Halpin, A.W. (1966). *Theory and research in administration.* New York: Macmillan.

Hancock, P.A. (1986). The effect of skill on performance under an environment stressor. *Aviation, space, and environmental medicine. 57,* 59-64.

Haney, C., Banks, C., & Zimbardo, P.G. (1973). Interpersonal dynamics in a simulated prison. *International Journal of Crime and Penology, 1,* 69-97.

Hans, V. (1989). Psychology and the law. In W.L. Gregory and W.J. Burroughs (Eds.), *Introduction to applied psychology.* Glenview, IL: Scott-Foresman.

Hans, V., & Vidmar, N. (1986). *Judging the jury.* New York: Plenum.

Hansen, J.C., & Campbell, D.P. (1985). *Manual for the SVIB-SCII* (4th ed.). Stanford, CA: Stanford University Press.

Harkins, S., & Szymanski, K. (1989). Social loafing and group evaluation. *Journal of Personality and Social Psychology, 56,* 934-941.

Harlow, H.F. (1949). The formation of learning sets. *Psychological Review, 56*, 51-65.

Harlow, H.F. (1958). The nature of love. *American Psychologist, 13*, 673-685.

Hartmann, E.L. (1973). *The functions of sleep.* New Haven: Yale University Press.

Hatfield, E. (1988). Passionate and companionate love. In R.J. Sternberg & M.L. Barnes (Eds.), *The psychology of love.* New Haven, CT: Yale University Press.

Hayes, D., & Ross, C. (1987). Concern with appearance, health beliefs, and eating habits. *Journal of Health and Social Behavior, 28*, 120-130.

Hayflick, L. (1980). The cell biology of human aging. *Scientific American, 242*(1), 58-65.

Hays, R.B. (1985). A longitudinal study of friendship development. *Journal of Personality and Social Psychology, 48*, 909-924.

He, L. (1987). Involvement of endogenous opiod peptides in acupuncture. *Pain, 31*, 99-122.

Hearold, S. (1986). A synthesis of 1043 effects of television on social behavior. In G. Comstock (Ed.), *Public Communication and behavior.* New York: Academic Press.

Hebb, D.O. (1949). *The organization of behavior.* New York: Wiley.

Hebb, D.O. (1955). Drives and the C.N.S. (conceptual nervous system). *Psychological Review, 62*, 243-253.

Hecht, S., & Shlaer, S. (1938). An adaptometer for measuring human dark adaptation. *Journal of the Optical Society of America, 28*, 269-275.

Heffeth, S., & Hayes, C. (Eds.). (1987). *Risking the future: Adolescent sexuality, pregnancy, and childbearing: Vol 2. Working papers and statistical reports.* Washington, DC: National Academy Press.

Heibeck, T., & Markman, E. (1987). Word learning in children: An examination of fast mapping. *Child Development, 58*, 1021-1034.

Heiby, E.M. (1983). Depression as a function of the interaction of self- and environmentally-controlled reinforcement. *Behavior Therapy, 14*, 430-433.

Heider, F. (1958). *The psychology of interpersonal relations.* New York: Wiley.

Heilman, M., Martell, R., & Simon, M. (1988). The vagaries of sex bias: Conditions regulating the underevaluation, equivaluation, and overevaluation of female job applicants. *Organizational Behavior and Human Decision Processes, 41*, 98-110.

Helmholtz, H.L.F. von (1863). *Die lehre von den tonemp findug en als physiologische Grundlage fur die theorie der Musik.* Braunschweig: Viewig V. Sohn.

Hendrick, C., & Hendrick, S. (1989). Research on love: Does it measure up? *Journal of Personality and Social Psychology. 56*, 784-794.

Hensel, H. (1982). *Thermal sensations and thermoreceptors in man.* Springfield, IL: Thomas.

Heron, W. (1957). The pathology of boredom. *Scientific American, 196*, 52-56.

Hertzog, C. (1989). Influences of cognitive slowing on age differences in intelligence. *Developmental Psychology, 25*, 636-651.

Hertzog, C., Dixon, R., & Hultsch, D. (1990). Relationships between metamemory, memory predictions, and memory task performance in adults. *Psychology and Aging, 5*, 215-227.

Herzberg, F. (1966). *Work and the nature of man.* New York: Crowell.

Hess, E.H. (1959). Imprinting. *Science, 130*, 133-141.

Hilgard, E.R. (1979). Divided consciousness in hypnosis: The implications of the hidden observer. In E. Froom & R. Shor (Eds.), *Hypnosis: Developments in research and new perspectives.* New York: Aldine.

Hilgard, E.R. (1987). Research advances in hypnosis: Issues and methods. *International Journal of Clinical and Experimental Hypnosis, 35*, 248-264.

Hilgard, E.R., & Hilgard, J.R. (1983). *Hypnosis in the relief of pain.* Los Altos, CA: Kaufmann.

Hill, G.W. (1982). Group versus individual performance: Are N + 1 heads better than one? *Psychological Bulletin, 91*, 517-539.

Hinz, L., & Williamson, D. (1987). Bulimia and depression: A review of the affective variant hypothesis. *Psychological Bulletin, 102*, 150-158.

Hirschman, E., & Mills, M. (1980). Sources shoppers use to pick stores. *Journal of Advertising Research, 20*, 47-51.

Hobfoll, S.E. (1989). Conservation of resources: A new attempt at conceptualizing stress. *American Psychologist, 44*, 513-524.

Hobson, J.A. (1989). *Sleep.* New York: Freeman.

Hobson, J.A., & McCarley, R.W. (1977). The brain as a dream state generator: An activation-synthesis hypothesis of the dream process. *The American Journal of Psychiatry, 134*, 1335-1348.

Hochschild, J., & Herk, M. (1989). Yes but . . . : Principals and caveasts in American racial attitudes. In J. Chapman (Ed.), *NOMOS: Majorities and minorities: Political and philosophical perspectives.* New York: New York University Press.

Holahan, C.J. (1986). Environmental psychology. *Annual Review of Psychology, 37*, 381-407.

Holahan, C.J., & Moos, R.H. (1985). Life stress and health: Personality, coping, and family support in stress resistance. *Journal of Personality and Social Psychology, 49*, 739-747.

Holden, C. (1980). The hospice movement and its implications. In R. Fox (Ed.), *The social meaning of death: Annals of the American academy of political and social psychology.*

Hollingshead, A.B., & Redlich, F.C. (1958). *Social class and mental illness: A community study.* New York: Wiley.

Holmes, D.S. (1984). Meditation and somatic arousal reduction: A review of the experimental evidence. *American Psychologist, 39*, 1-10.

Holmes, D.S. (1991). *Abnormal psychology.* New York: HarperCollins.

Holmes, J., & Boon, S. (1990). Developments in the field of close relationships: Creating foundations for intervention strategies. *Personality and Social Psychology Bulletin, 16*, 23-41.

Holmes, T.H., & Rahe, R.H. (1967). The social readjustment rating scale. *Journal of Psychosomatic Research, 11*, 213-218.

Homans, G.C. (1961). *Social behavior: Its elementary forms.* New York: Harcourt Brace Jovanovich.

Hooley, J.M. (1986). Expressed emotion and depression: Interactions between patients and high-versus-low-expressed emotion spouses. *Journal of Abnormal Psychology, 95*, 237-246.

Horn, J.L., Donaldson, G., & Engstrom, R. (1981). Apprehension, memory, and fluid intelligence decline in adulthood. *Research on Aging, 3*, 33-84.

Horn, J.M. (1983). The Texas adoption project. Adopted children and their intellectual resemblance to biological and adoptive parents. *Child Development, 54*, 268-275.

Horner, M.S. (1972). Toward an understanding of achievement-related conflicts in women. *Journal of Social Issues, 28*, 157-175.

Horney, K. (1939). *New ways in psychoanalysis*. New York: Norton.

Horowitz, F.D., & O'Brien, M. (1986). Gifted and talented children: State of knowledge and directions for research. *American Psychologist, 41*, 1147-1152.

Hothersall, D. (1990). *History of psychology* (2nd ed.). New York: McGraw Hill.

Houston, J.P. (1991). *Fundamentals of learning and memory* (4th ed.). New York: Harcourt Brace Jovanovich.

Houston, L.N. (1990). *Psychological principles and the Black experience*. Lanham, MD: University Press of America.

Howard, K., Kopta, S., Krause, M., & Orlinski, D. (1986). The dose-effect relationship in psychotherapy. *American Psychologist, 41*, 159-164.

Hruska, S., & Grasha, A. (1982). The Grasha-Riechmann student learning style scales. In *Student styles and brain behavior*. Reston, VA: National Association of Secondary School Principals.

Hull, C.L. (1920). Quantitative aspects of the evolution of concepts. *Psychological Monographs*, Whole No. 123.

Hull, C.L. (1943). *Principles of behavior*. East Norwalk, CT: Appleton-Century-Crofts.

Hull, C.L. (1952). *A behavior system: An introduction to behavior theory concerning the individual organism*. New Haven, CT: Yale University Press.

Hunt, M. (1974). *Sexual behavior in the 1970s*. Chicago: Playboy Press.

Hunziker, V. & Barr, R. (1986). Increased carrying reduces infant crying: A randomized control trial. *Pediatrics, 77*, 641-648.

Huston, A. (1983). Sex-typing. In P. Mussen (Ed.), *Handbook of child psychology* (Vol. 4) (4th ed.). New York: Wiley.

Hyde, J.S. (1990). *Understanding human sexuality* (4th ed.). New York: McGraw-Hill.

Hyde, T., & Jenkins, J. (1969). Differential effects of incidental tasks on the organization of recall of a list of highly associated words. *Journal of Experimental Psychology, 82*, 472-481.

I

Intons-Peterson, M.J., & Fournier, J. (1986). External and internal memory aids: When and how often do we use them? *Journal of Experimental Psychology: General, 115*, 267-280.

Isenberg, D.J. (1986). Group polarization: A critical review and meta-analysis. *Journal of Personality and Social Psychology, 50*, 1141-1151.

Iversen, L.L. (1987). Neurotransmitters. In G. Adelman (Ed.), *Encyclopedia of neuroscience*. Boston: Birkhauser.

Izard, C.E. (1972). *Patterns of emotions: A new analysis of anxiety and depression*. New York: Academic Press.

Izard, C.E. (1977). *Human emotions*. New York: Plenum.

Izard, C.E. (1979). Emotions as motivations: An evolutionary-developmental perspective. In R.A. Dienstbier (Ed.), *1978 Nebraska Symposium on Motivation*. Lincoln, NE: University of Nebraska Press.

Izard, C.E. (1980). The psychology of emotion comes of age on the coattails of Darwin. *Contemporary Psychology, 27*, 426-429.

Izard, C.E. (1990). Facial expressions and the regulation of emotions. *Journal of Personality and Social Psychology, 58*, 487-498.

Izard, C.E., Huebner, R., Risser, D., McGinnes, G., & Dougherty, L. (1980). The young infant's ability to produce discrete emotional expressions. *Developmental Psychology, 16*, 132-140.

J

Jackson, J.M. (1987). Social impact theory: A social forces model of influence. In B. Mullen and G.R. Goethals (Eds.), *Theories of group behavior*. New York: Springer-Verlag.

Jackson, J.M., & Harkins, S.G. (1985). Equity in effort: An explanation of the social loafing effect. *Journal of Personality and Social Psychology, 49*, 1199-1206.

Jackson, J.M., & Williams, K.D. (1985). Social loafing on difficult tasks: Working collectively can improve performance. *Journal of Personality and Social Psychology, 49*, 937-942.

Jacobs, B.L. (1987). How hallucinogenic drugs work. *American Scientist, 75*, 386-392.

Jacobson, E. (1929). *Progressive relaxation*. Chicago: University of Chicago Press.

James, W. (1884). What is an emotion? *Mind, 9*, 188-205.

James, W. (1890). *Principles of psychology*. New York: Holt.

James, W. (1904). Does consciousness exist? *Journal of Philosophy, Psychology, and Scientific Methods, 1*, 447-491.

Janis, I.L. (1982). *Groupthink: Psychological studies of policy decision and fiascoes* (2nd ed.). Boston: Houghton Mifflin.

Janowsky, D., & Risch, S. (1984). Adrenergic and cholinergic balance and affective disorders. *The Psychiatric Hospital, 15*, 163-171.

Jensen, A.R. (1969). How much can we boost IQ and scholastic achievement? *Harvard Educational Review, 39*, 1-123.

John, R., Hollander, B., & Perry, C. (1983). Hypnotizability and phobic behavior: Further supporting data. *Journal of Abnormal Psychology, 92*, 390-392.

Johnson, B., Williams, T., Sanabria, H., & Del, Kojo. (1989). Social impact of crack dealing in the inner city. *National Institute on Drug Abuse: Research Monograph Series, 95*, 326-327.

Johnson, C., & Conners, M. (1987). *The etiology and treatment of bulimia nervosa*. New York: Basic Books.

Johnson, C., & Larson, R. (1982). Bulimia: An analysis of moods and behavior. *Psychosomatic Medicine, 44*, 341-351.

Johnson, D. (1990). Animal rights & human lives: Time for scientists to right the balance. *Psychological Science, 1*, 213-214.

Jones, B.E., Harper, S.T., & Halaris, A.E. (1977). Effects of coeruleus lesions upon cerebral meonamine content, sleep wakefulness states and the response to amphetamine in the cat. *Brain Research, 124*, 473-496.

Jones, E.E. (1990). *Interpersonal perception*. New York: Freeman.

Jones, E.E., & Davis, K. (1965). From acts to dispositions: The attribution process in person perception. In L. Berkowitz (Ed.), *Advances in experimental social psychology* (Vol. 2). New York: Academic Press.

Jones, E.E., & Nisbett, R.E. (1972). The actor and the observer: Divergent perceptions of the causes of behavior.

Jones, M. (1965). Psychological correlates of somatic development. *Child Development, 36*, 899-911.

Jones, M.C. (1924). A laboratory study of fear: The case of Peter. *Pedagogical Seminary, 31*, 308-315.

Jones, N., Kearins, J., & Watson, J. (1987). The human tongue show and observers' willingness to interact: Replication and extensions. *Psychological Reports, 60,* 759-764.

Jouvet, M. (1967). Neurophysiology of the states of sleep. *Physiological Reviews, 47,* 117-177.

Julien, R.M. (1992). *A primer of drug action* (6th ed.). New York: Freeman.

Jung, C.G. (1923). *Psychological types.* London: Rutledge and Kagan Paul.

Jung, C.G. (1939). *The integration of the personality.* New York: Farrar & Rinehart.

K

Kagan, J. (1982). Canalization of early psychological development. *Pediatrics, 70*(3), 474-483.

Kahn, J.P., Kornfield, P., Frank, L., Heller, S., & Hoar, P. (1980). Type A behavior and blood pressure during coronary artery bypass surgery. *Psychosomatic Medicine, 42,* 407-414.

Kaitz, M., Good, A., Rokem, A., & Eidelman, A. (1987). Mothers' recognition of their newborns by olfactory cues. *Developmental Psychology, 206,* 587-591.

Kaitz, M., Meschulach-Sarfaty, O., & Averbach, J. (1988). A re-examination of newborns' ability to imitate facial expressions. *Developmental Psychology, 24,* 3-7.

Kaplan, E., & Kaplan, G. (1971). The prelinguistic child. In J. Elliot (Ed.), *Human development and cognitive processes.* New York: Holt, Rinehart & Winston.

Karabenick, S. (1977). Fear of success, achievement and affiliation dispositions, and the performance of men and women under individual competitive conditions. *Journal of Personality, 45,* 117-149.

Kaufman, L., & Rock, I. (1962). The moon illusion, I. *Science, 136,* 953-961.

Kaul, T., & Bednar, R. (1986). Experiential group research: Results, questions, and suggestions. In S. Garfield and A. Bergin (Eds.), *Handbook of Psychotherapy and behavior change: An evaluative analysis.* New York: Wiley.

Kazdin, A.E., & Bass, D. (1989). Power to detect differences between alternative treatments in comparative psychotherapy outcome research. *Journal of Consulting and Clinical Psychology, 57,* 138-147.

Kazkin, A.E. (1989). *Behavior modification in applied settings* (4th ed.). Pacific Grove, CA: Wadsworth.

Kelley, H.H. (1950). The warm-cold variable in first impressions. *Journal of Personality, 18,* 431-439.

Kelley, H.H. (1973). The processes of causal attribution. *American Psychologist, 28,* 107-128.

Kellman, P.J., Gleitman, H., & Spelke, E.S. (1987). Object and observer motion in the perception of objects by infants. *Journal of Experimental Psychology: Human Perception and Performance. 13,* 586-593.

Kelly, D.D. (1981). Disorders of sleep and consciousness. In E.R. Kandel & J.H. Schwartz (Eds.), *Principles of neural science.* New York: Elsevier.

Kelly, G.F. (1992). *Sexuality today: The human perspective* (3rd ed.). Guilford, CT: Dushkin.

Kendell, R.E. (1991). Relationship between the DSM-IV and the ICD-10. *Journal of Abnormal Psychology, 100,* 297-301.

Kessler, R., Price, P., & Worthman, C. (1985). Social factors in psychopathology: Stress, social support, and coping processes. *Annual Review of Psychology, 36,* 531-572.

Kety, S. (1983). Mental illness in the biological and adoptive relatives of schizophrenic adoptees: Findings relevant to genetic and environmental factors in etiology. *American Journal of Psychiatry, 140* 720-727.

Keyes, R. (1991). *Timelock.* New York: HarperCollins.

Kiester, E., Jr. (1980). Images of the night. *Science 80, 1,* 36-43.

Kihlstrom, J.F. (1987). The cognitive unconscious. *Science, 237,* 1445-1452.

Kimble, G.A. (1961). *Hilgard and Marquis' conditioning and learning.* East Norwalk, CT: Appleton-Century-Crofts.

Kinsey, A.C., Pomeroy, W.B., & Martin, C.E. (1948). *Sexual behavior in the human male.* Philadelphia: Saunders.

Kinsey, A.C., Pomeroy, W.B., Martin, C.E., & Gebhard, P.H. (1953). *Sexual behavior in the human female.* Philadelphia: Saunders.

Kirk, S.A., & Gallagher, J.J. (1986). *Education's exceptional children* (5th ed.). Boston: Houghton Mifflin.

Klatzky, R.L. (1984). *Memory and awareness: An information processing perspective.* New York: Freeman.

Klein, S.B. (1991). *Learning* (2nd ed.). New York: McGraw-Hill.

Kleinke, C.L. (1986). Gaze and eye contact: A research review. *Psychological Bulletin, 100,* 78-100.

Kleinke, C.L., Meeker, F., & LaFong, C. (1974). Effects of gaze, touch and use of name on evaluation of "engaged" couples. *Journal of Research in Personality, 7,* 368-373.

Klineberg, O. (1938). Emotional expression in Chinese literature. *Journal of Abnormal and Social Psychology, 33,* 517-520.

Klinger, E. (1987). The power of daydreams. *Psychology Today, 21,* 36-44.

Klinnert, M., Emde, R., Butterfield, P., & Campos, J. (1986). Social referencing: The infant's use of emotional signals from a friendly adult with mother present. *Developmental Psychology, 22,* 427-432.

Kluegel, J., & Smith, E. (1986). *Beliefs about inequality.* New York: Aldine.

Knox, D.H., Jr. (1970). Conceptions of love at three developmental levels. *The Family Coordinator, 19,* 151-157.

Knox, D.H., Jr. (1985). *Choices in relationships.* St. Paul: West.

Kobasa, S.C. (1982). The hardy personality: Toward a social psychology of stress and health. In G. Snaders & J. Suls (Eds.), *Social psychology of health and illness.* Hillsdale, NJ: Erlbaum.

Kohlberg, L. (1966). A cognitive-developmental model analysis of children's sex-role concepts and attitudes. In E. Maccoby (Ed.), *The development of sex differences.* Stanford: Stanford University Press.

Kohlberg, L. (1969). *Stages in the development of moral thought and action.* New York: Holt, Rinehart & Winston.

Kohlberg, L. (1985). *Essays on moral development. Volume 1: The philosophy of moral development.* New York: Harper & Row.

Köhler, W. (1927). *The mentality of apes.* E. Winter (Trans.). 1st Eng ed., 1925. 2nd Eng. ed. New York: Harcourt, Brace.

Kokoszka, A. (1988). An integrated model of the main states of consciousness. *Imagination, Cognition, and Personality, 7*, 285–294.

Kolata, G. (1983). First trimester prenatal diagnosis. *Science, 22*, 1031–1032.

Kolb, B., & Whishaw, I. (1985). *Human neuropsychology*. New York: Freeman.

Kraly, F. (1984). Physiology of drinking elicited by eating. *Psychological Review, 91*, 478–490.

Kübler-Ross, E. (1969). *On death and dying*. New York: Macmillan.

Kübler-Ross, E. (1981). *Living with death and dying*. New York: Macmillan.

Kulik, J.A., Kulik, C.C., & Gangert-Drowns, R.L. (1985). Effectiveness of computer-based education in elementary schools. *Computers in Human Behavior, 1*, 59–74.

Kuo, Z.Y. (1921). Giving up instincts in psychology. *Journal of Philosophy, 17*, 645–664.

Kutash, I., & Wolf, A. (Eds.). (1986). *Psychotherapists' casebook*. San Francisco: Jossey-Bass.

L

LaBerge, S. (1986). *Lucid dreaming*. New York: Ballantine Books.

Lafferty, P., Beutler, L., & Crago, M. (1989). Differences between more and less effective psychotherapists: A study of select therapist variables. *Journal of Consulting and Clinical Psychology, 57*, 76–80.

Lahey, B. & Carlson, C. (1991). Validity of the diagnostic category of attention deficit disorder without hyperactivity: A review of the literature. *Journal of Learning Disabilities, 24*, 110–120.

Laing, R.D. (1964). Is schizophrenia a disease? *International Journal of Social Psychiatry, 10*, 184–193.

Lakein, A. (1973). *How to get control of your time and your life*. New York: Signet.

Landers, D. (1982). Arousal, attention, and skilled performance: Further considerations. *Quest, 33*, 271–283.

Landers, S. (1988). Skinner joins aversive debate. *APA Monitor, 19*, 22–23.

Landy, F.J. (1989). *Psychology of work behavior* (4th ed.). Pacific Grove, CA: Brooks-Cole.

Laner, M. (1983). Courtship abuse and aggression: Contextual aspects. *Sociological Spectrum, 3*, 69–83.

Lange, C.G. (1885). *The emotions*. Baltimore: Williams & Wilkins.

Langlois, J., Ritter, J., Roggman, L., & Vaughn, L. (1991). Facial diversity and infant preferences for attractive faces. *Developmental Psychology, 27*, 79–84.

Lanyon, R.I. (1984). Personality assessment. *Annual Review of Psychology, 35*, 667–701.

Lashley, K. (1950). In search of the engram. *Symposia of the Society of Experimental Biology, 4*, 454–482.

Latané, B. (1981). The psychology of social impact. *American Psychologist, 36*, 343–356.

Latané, B., & Darley, J.M. (1968). Group inhibition of bystander intervention in emergencies. *Journal of Personality and Social Psychology, 10*, 215–221.

Latané, B., & Darley, J.M. (1970). *The unresponsive bystander: Why doesn't he help?* New York: Appleton-Century-Crofts.

Lavidge, R., & Steiner, G. (1961). A model for predictive measurements of advertising effectiveness. *Journal of Marketing, 25*, 59–62.

Lawler, E.E. (1982). Strategies for improving the quality of work life. *American Psychologist, 37*, 486–493.

Lazar, I., & Darlington, R. (1982). Lasting effects of early education: A report from the Consortium of Longitudinal Studies. *Monographs of the Society for Research in Child Development, 47*, Whole Number 195.

Lazarus, R.S. (1980). The stress and coping paradigm. In L. Bond & J. Rosen (Eds.), *Competence and coping during adulthood*. Hanover, NH: University Press of New England.

Lazarus, R.S. (1981). Little hassles can be hazardous to health. *Psychology Today, 15*, 58–62.

Lazarus, R.S. (1981). The stress and coping paradigm. In C. Eisdorfer, D. Cohen, A. Kleinman, & P. Maxim (Eds.), *Models for clinical psychopathology*. New York: Spectrum.

Lazarus, R.S. (1984). On the primacy of cognition. *American Psychologist, 39*, 124–129.

Lazarus, R.S. (1991a). Cognition and motivation in emotion. *American Psychologist, 46*, 352–367.

Lazarus, R.S. (1991b). Progress on a cognitive-motivational-relational theory of emotion. *American Psychologist, 46*, 819–834.

Lazarus, R.S., & Folkman, S. (1984). *Stress, appraisal, and coping*. New York: Springer.

Lazarus, R.S., DeLongis, A., Folkman, S., & Gruen, R. (1985). Stress and adaptational outcomes. *American Psychologist, 40*, 770–779.

LeUnes, A.D. & Nation, J.R. (1989). *Sport psychology: An introduction*. Chicago: Nelson-Hall.

Leal, L. (1987). Investigation of the relation between metamemory and university students' examination performance. *Journal of Educational Psychology, 79*, 35–40.

Lebow, M., Goldberg, P., & Collins, A. (1977). Eating behavior of overweight and nonoverweight persons in the natural environment. *Journal of Consulting and Clinical Psychology, 45*, 1204–1205.

Lederman, S., & Klatzky, R. (1990). Haptic classification of common objects: Knowledge-driven exploration. *Cognitive Psychology, 22*, 421–459.

Lee, C., & Lindsey, C. (1985). Black consciousness development: A group counseling model for Black elementary school students. *Elementary School Guidance and Counseling, 19*, 228–236.

Lee, S., & Barnes, J. (1990). Using color preferences in magazine advertising. *Journal of Advertising Research, 29*, 25–30.

Leeming, F., & Little, G. (1977). Escape learning in houseflies. *Journal of Comparative and Physiological Psychology, 91*, 260–269.

Lepper, M.R., Greene, D., & Nisbett, R.E. (1973). Undermining children's intrinsic interest with extrinsic rewards: A test of the "overjustification" hypothesis. *Journal of Personality and Social Psychology, 28*, 129–137.

Leventhal, H., & Tomarken, A. (1986). Emotion: Today's problems. *Annual Review of Psychology, 37*, 565–610.

Leventhal, H., Singer, R., & Jones, S. (1965). The effects of fear and specificity of recommendation upon attitudes and behavior. *Journal of Personality and Social Psychology, 2*, 20–29.

Levinson, D.J. (1978). *The seasons of a man's life*. New York: Ballantine.

Levinson, D.J. (1986). A conception of adult development. *American Psychologist, 41*, 3-13.

Levinson, D.J. (1987). *The seasons of a woman's life*. New York: Knopf.

Levinthal, C.F. (1990). *Introduction to physiological psychology* (3rd ed.). Englewood Cliffs, NJ: Prentice Hall.

Lewin, K. (1935). *A dynamic theory of personality*. New York: McGraw-Hill.

Liebert, R.M., & Speigler, M.D. (1990). *Personality: Strategies and issues* (6th ed.). Pacific Grove, CA: Brooks-Cole.

Lim, R., & Carnevale, J. (1990). Contingencies in the mediation of disputes. *Journal of Personality and Social Psychology, 58*, 259-272.

Linberg, K.A., & Fisher, S.K. (1986). An ultrastructural study of interplexiform cell synapses in the human retina. *The Journal of Comparative Neurology, 243*, 561-576.

Lindsay, D.S., Jack, P.C., Jr., & Christian, M. (1991). Other-race face perception. *Journal of Applied Psychology, 76*, 587-589.

Lipman-Blumen, J., Handley-Isaksen, A., & Leavitt, H. (1983). Achieving styles in men and women: A model, an instrument, and some findings. In J.T. Spence (Ed.), *Achievement and achievement motives: Psychological and sociological approaches*. San Francisco: Freeman.

Loehlin, J.C., & Nichols, R.C. (1976). *Heredity, environment, and personality*. Austin: University of Texas Press.

Loftus, E.F. & Loftus, G.R. (1980). On the permanence of stored information in the human brain. *American Psychologist, 35*, 409-420.

Loftus, E.F. (1979). *Eyewitness testimony*. Cambridge, MA: Harvard University Press.

Loftus, E.F. (1980). *Memory*. Reading, MA: Addison-Wesley.

Loftus, E.F. (1983). Misfortunes of memory. *Philosophical transactions of the Royal Society, London, 302*, 413-421.

Loftus, E.F. (1984). Eyewitness: Essential but unreliable. *Psychology Today*, February, 22-27.

Logue, A.W. (1991). *The psychology of eating and drinking: An introduction* (2nd ed.). New York: Freeman.

Lorenz, K. (1937). The companion in the bird's world. *Auk, 54*, 245-273.

Lorenz, K. (1965). *Evolution and modification of behavior*. Chicago: University of Chicago Press.

Lorenz, K. (1966). *On aggression*. New York: Harcourt Brace & World.

Lovaas, O.I. (1977). *The autistic child: Language development through behavior modification*. New York: Irvington.

Lubin, B., Larsen, R., Matarazzo, J., & Seever, M. (1985). Psychological test usage patterns in five professional settings. *American Psychologist, 40*, 857-861.

Lucero, M.A. (1970). Lengthening of REM sleep duration consecutive to learning in the rat. *Brain Research, 20*, 319-322.

Luchins, A.S. (1942). Mechanization in problem solving: The effect of Einstellung. *Psychological Monographs, 54* (Whole No. 248).

Luh, C. (1922). The conditions of retention. *Psychological Monographs*. No. 142.

Lupfer, M., Clark, L., & Hutcherson, H. (1990). Impact of context on spontaneous trait and situational attributions. *Journal of Personality and Social Psychology, 58*, 239-249.

Luria, Z., Friedman, S., & Rose, M. (1987). *Human sexuality*. New York: Wiley.

M

MacFarlane, J.A. (1977). *The psychology of childbirth*. Cambridge, MA: Harvard University Press.

MacLean, P.D. (1949). Psychosomatic disease and the "visceral brain": Recent developments bearing on the Papez theory of emotion. *Psychosomatic Medicine, 11*, 338-353.

MacLean, P.D. (1968). The hypothalamus and emotional behavior. In W. Haymaker (Ed.), *The hypothalamus*. Springfield, IL: Thomas.

MacNichol, E.F., Jr. (1964). Three-pigment color vision. *Scientific American, 211*, 48-56.

MacNichol, E.F., Jr. (1986). A unifying presentation of photopigment spectra. *Vision Research, 29*, 543-546.

Maccoby, E. (1980). *Social development: Psychological growth and the parent-child relationship*. New York: Harcourt Brace Jovanovich.

Mahowald, M. & Rosen, G. (1990). Parasomnias in children. *Pediatrician, 17*, 21-31.

Makens, J. (1965). Effect of brand preference upon consumer's perceived taste of turkey meat. *Journal of Applied Psychology, 49*, 261-263.

Marcel, A.J. (1983). Conscious and unconscious perception: An approach to the relation between phenomenal experience and perceptual processes. *Cognitive Psychology, 15*, 238-300.

Marcia, J.E. (1980). Identity in adolescence. In J. Adelson (Ed.), *Handbook of adolescent psychology*. New York: Wiley.

Marfo, F., & Ryan, R. (1990). A comparison of average and poor readers in their recall performance, strategy use, and metamemory. *Alberta Journal of Educational Research, 36*, 241-255.

Marsh, J., Schubarth, G., Brown, W., & Riege, W. (1990). PET and P300 relationships in early Alzheimer's disease. *Neurobiology of Aging, 11*, 471-476.

Martin, L., & Pullum, G. (1991). *The great Eskimo vocabulary hoax*. Chicago: University of Chicago Press.

Martin, P. (1987). Psychology and the immune system. *New Scientist*, April 9, 46-50.

Maser, J., Kaelber, C., & Weise, R. (1991). International use and attitudes toward DSM-III and DSM-III-R: Growing consensus in psychiatric classification. *Journal of Abnormal Psychology, 100*, 271-279.

Maslach, C. (1979). Negative emotional biasing of unexplained arousal. *Journal of Personality and Social Psychology, 37*, 953-969.

Maslach, C. (1982). *Burnout: The cost of caring*. Englewood Cliffs, NJ: Prentice-Hall.

Masland, R. (1986). The functional architecture of the retina. *Scientific American, 255*, 102-111.

Maslow, A.H. (1968). *Toward a psychology of being* (2nd ed.). New York: Van Nostrand.

Maslow, A.H. (1970). *Motivation and personality* (2nd ed.). New York: Harper & Row.

Maslow, A.H. (1987). *Motivation and personality* (3rd Ed.). New York: Harper & Row. (Revised by R. Frager, J. Fadiman, C. McReynolds, & R. Cox)

Masters, W.H., & Johnson, V.E. (1966). *Human sexual response*. Boston: Little, Brown.

Masters, W.H., Johnson, V.E., & Kolodny, R.C. (1992). *Human sexuality* (4th ed.). New York: HarperCollins.

Matheny, A.P. Jr., Riese, M.L., & Wilson, R.S. (1985). Rudiments of infant temperament: Newborn to 9 months. *Developmental Psychology, 21,* 486-494.

Mathews, K.E., & Canon, L.K. (1975). Environmental noise level as a determinant of helping behavior. *Journal of Personality and Social Psychology, 32,* 571-577.

Matlin, M.W. (1987). *The psychology of women.* New York: Holt, Rinehart & Winston.

Matlin, M.W. (1989). *Cognition* (2nd ed.). New York: Holt, Rinehart & Winston.

Matlin, M.W., & Foley, H.J. (1992). *Sensation and perception* (3rd ed.). Boston: Allyn-Bacon.

Matsumota, D. (1987). The role of facial response in the experience of emotion: More methodological problems and a meta-analysis. *Journal of Personality and Social Psychology, 52,* 769-774.

Matthews, K.A. (1982). Psychological perspectives on the Type A behavior pattern. *Psychological Bulletin, 91,* 293-323.

Matthews, K.A. (1988). Coronary heart disease and Type A behaviors: Update on an alternative to the Booth-Kewley and Friedman (1987) quantitative review. *Psychological Bulletin, 104,* 373-380.

Mayer, J. (1953). Glucostatic mechanism of regulation of food intake. *New England Journal of Medicine, 249,* 13-16.

McAlpine, C., Singh, N., & Kendall, K. (1991). Development and validation of videotaped role plays of the six basic facial expressions of emotion. *Bulletin of the Psychonomic Society, 29,* 117-120.

McAuley, E., Wraith, S., & Duncan, T. (1991). Self-efficacy, perceptions of success, and intrinsic motivation for exercise. *Journal of Applied Social Psychology, 21,* 139-155.

McCanne, T.R., & Anderson, J.A. (1987). Emotional responding following experimental manipulation of facial electromyographic activity. *Journal of Personality and Social Psychology, 52,* 759-768.

McCarley, R.W., & Hoffman, E. (1981). REM sleep dreams and the activation-synthesis hypothesis. *American Journal of Psychiatry, 138,* 904-912.

McCauley, C. (1989). The nature of social influence in groupthink: Compliance and internalization. *Journal of personality and Social Psychology, 57,* 250-260.

McClelland, D.C. (1958). Methods of measuring human motivation. In J.W. Atkinson (Ed.), *Motives in fantasy, action and society.* Princeton, NJ: Van Nostrand.

McClelland, D.C. (1978). Managing motivation to expand human freedom. *American Psychologist, 33,* 201-210.

McClelland, D.C. (1985a). *Human motivation.* Glenview, IL: Scott, Foresman.

McClelland, D.C. (1985b). How motives, skills, and values determine what people do. *American Psychologist, 40,* 812-825.

McClelland, D.C., Atkinson, J.W., Clark, R.A., & Lowell, E.L. (1953). *The achievement motive.* East Norwalk, CT: Appleton-Century-Crofts.

McCloskey, M., Wible, C., & Cohen, N. (1988). Is there a special flashbulb memory mechanism? *Journal of Experimental Psychology: General, 117,* 171-181.

McConkey, K., & Kinoshita, S. (1988). The influence of hypnosis on memory after one day and one week. *Journal of Abnormal Psychology, 97,* 48-53.

McConnell, J.V. (1990). Negative reinforcement and positive punishment. *Teaching of Psychology, 17,* 247-249.

McCrae, R.R., & Costa, P.T., Jr. (1985). Updating Norman's "Adequate Taxonomy": Intelligence and personality dimensions in natural language and in questionnaires. *Journal of Personality and Social Psychology, 49,* 710-721.

McCrae, R.R., & Costa, P.T., Jr. (1986). Clinical assessment can benefit from recent advances in personality psychology. *American Psychologist, 41,* 1001-1003.

McCrae, R.R., & Costa, P.T., Jr. (1987). Validation of the five-factor model of personality across instruments and observers. *Journal of Personality and Social Psychology, 52,* 81-90.

McCrae, R.R., & Costa, P.T., Jr. (1989a). More reasons to adopt the five factor model. *American Psychologist, 44,* 451-452.

McCrae, R.R., & Costa, P.T., Jr. (1989b). Reinterpreting the Myers-Briggs Type Indicator from the perspective of the five-factor model of personality. *Journal of Personality, 57,* 17-40.

McCrae, R.R., & Costa, P.T., Jr. (1990). *Personality in adulthood.* New York: Guilford.

McDougall, W. (1908). *Social psychology.* New York: G.P. Putnam's Sons.

McDougall, W. (1921). *An introduction to social psychology.* Boston: Luce.

McGaugh, J.L. (1983). Preserving the presence of the past: Hormonal influences on memory storage. *American Psychologist, 38,* 161-174.

McGeer, P., & McGeer, E. (1980). Chemistry of mood and emotion. *Annual Review of Psychology, 31,* 273-307.

McGregor, D. (1960). *The human side of enterprise.* New York: McGraw-Hill.

McGuigan, F. (1984). Progressive relaxation: Origins, principles, and clinical applications. In R. Woolfolk & P. Lehrer (Eds.), *Principles and practice of stress management.* New York: Guilford.

McGuire, W.J. (1985). Attitudes and attitude change. In G. Lindzey & E. Aronson (Eds.), *Handbook of social psychology* (Vol. 2) (3rd ed.). New York: Random House.

McHugh, P.R., & Moran, T.H. (1985). The stomach: A conception of its dynamic role in satiety. *Progress in Psychobiology and Psychology, 11,* 197-232.

McMaster, N.L. (1990). The courts and hypnotically refreshed memory: A review of the literature. *Australian Journal of Clinical Hypnotherapy and Hypnosis, 11,* 1-9.

McMinn, M. (1984). Mechanisms of energy balance in obesity. *Behavioral Neuroscience, 98,* 375-393.

McNeal, E.T. & Cimbolic, P. (1986). Antidepressants and biochemical theories of depression. *Psychological Bulletin, 99,* 361-374.

McReynolds, P. (1989). Diagnosis and clinical assessment: Current status and major issues. *Annual Review of Psychology, 40* 83-108.

Meichenbaum, D. (1985). *Stress in oculation training.* New York: Pergamon.

Mellor, S. (1990). How do only children differ from other children? *Journal of Genetic Psychology, 151,* 221-230.

Melzack, R., & Wall, P.D. (1965). Pain mechanisms: A new theory. *Science, 150,* 971-979.

Mendlewicz, J. (1985). Genetic research in depressive disorders. In E. Beckham & W. Leber (Eds.), *Handbook of depression: Treatment, assessment, and research.* Homewood, IL: Dorsey.

Messing, R., & Sparber, S. (1985). Greater taste difficulty amplifies the facilitatory effect of des-glycinamide arginine vasopressin on appetitively motivated learning. *Behavioral Neuroscience, 99,* 1114-1119.

Milburn, T.W., & Christie, D.J. (1989). Rewarding in international politics. *Political Psychology, 10* 625-645.

Milgram, S. (1963). Behavioral study of obedience. *Journal of Abnormal and Social Psychology*, 67, 371-378.

Milgram, S. (1965). Some conditions of obedience and disobedience to authority. *Human Relations*, 18, 57-76.

Milgram, S. (1974). *Obedience to authority*. New York: Harper & Row.

Miller, A.G. (1986). *The obedience experiments: A case study of controversy in social science*. New York: Praeger.

Miller, G.A. (1956). The magical number seven, plus or minus two: Some limits on our capacity for processing information. *Psychological Review*, 63, 81-97.

Miller, L., & Branconnier, R. (1983). Cannabis: Effects on memory and the cholinergic limbic system. *Psychological Bulletin*, 93, 441-456.

Miller, N., & Gold, M. (1988). The human sexual response and alcohol and drugs. *Journal of Substance Abuse Treatment*, 5, 171-177.

Miller, N.E. (1973). *Biofeedback and self-control*. Chicago: Aldine.

Miller, N.E. (1978). Biofeedback and visceral learning. *Annual Review of Psychology*, 29, 421-452.

Miller, N.E. (1985). The value of behavioral research on animals. *American Psychologist*, 40, 423-440.

Miller, N.E., & Banuazizi, A. (1968). Instrumental learning by curarized rats of a specific visceral response, intestinal or cardiac. *Journal of Comparative and Physiological Psychology*, 65, 1-17.

Miner, J.B. (1984). The validity and usefulness of theories in an emerging organizational science. *Academy of Management Review*, 9, 296-306.

Mirsky, A.F., & Duncan, C.C. (1986). Etiology and expression of schizophrenia: Neurobiological and psychosocial factors. *Annual Review of Psychology*, 37, 291-319.

Mischel, W. (1986). *Introduction to personality* (4th ed.). New York: Holt, Rinehart & Winston.

Mishkin, M. & Appenzeller, T. (1987). The anatomy of memory. *Scientific American*, 256, 80-89.

Mitchell, T.R., & Larson, J.R., Jr. (1987). *People in organizations: An introduction to organizational behavior*. New York: McGraw-Hill.

Mittelman, W. (1991). Maslow's study of self-actualization: A reinterpretation. *Journal of Humanistic Psychology*, 31, 114-135.

Moen, P. (1982). The two-provider family: Problems and potentials. In M. Lamb (Ed.). *Nontraditional families: Parenting and child development*. Hillsdale, NJ: Erlbaum.

Moldofsky, H., & Scarisbrick, P. (1976). Induction of neurasthenic musculoskeletal pain syndrome by selective sleep stage deprivation. *Psychosomatic Medicine*, 38, 35-44.

Monahan, J., & Loftus, E.F. (1982). The psychology of law. *Annual Review of Psychology*, 33, 441-475.

Money, J. (1987). Propaedeutics of diecious G-I/R: Theoretical foundations for understanding dimorphic gender-identity/role. In J. Reinisch, L. Rosenblum, & S. Sanders (Eds.), *Masculinity/femininity: Basic perspectives*. New York: Oxford University Press.

Money, J., & Ehrhardt, A. (1972). *Man and woman, boy and girl*. Baltimore: Johns Hopkins University Press.

Monroe, S.M. (1982). Life events and disorder: Event-symptom associations and the course of disorder. *Journal of Abnormal Psychology*, 91, 14-24.

Moreland, R., & Zajonc, R. (1982). Exposure effects in person perception: Familiarity, similarity, and attraction. *Journal of Experimental and Social Psychology*, 18, 395-415.

Morey, L.C. (1988). Personality disorders in DSM-III and DSM-III-R: Convergence, coverage, and internal consistency. *American Journal of Psychiatry*, 145, 573-577.

Morley, J., Bartness, T., Gosnell, B., & Levine, A. (1985). Peptidergic regulation of feeding. *International Review of Neurobiology*, 27, 207-298.

Morris, C.G. (1990). *Contemporary psychology and effective behavior* (7th ed.). Glenview, IL: Scott-Foresman.

Morris, N., & Udry, J. (1978). Pheromonal influences on human sexual behavior: An experimental search. *Journal of Biosocial Science*, 10, 147-157.

Mowen, J.C. (1989). Consumer psychology. In W.L. Gregory & W.J. Burroughs, (Eds.), *Introduction to Applied Psychology*, Glenview, IL: Scott-Foresman.

Mowrer, O.H., & Mowrer, W.M. (1938). Enuresis—a method for its study and treatment. *American Journal of Orthopsychiatry*, 8, 436-459.

Mudd, E., & Taubin, S. (1982). Success in family living: Does it last? A twenty-year follow-up. *Journal of Family Therapy*, 10, 59-67.

Murray, H.A. (1938). *Explorations in personality*. New York: Oxford University Press.

Mussgay, L., & Hertwig, R. (1990). Signal detection indices in schizophrenia on a visual, auditory, and bimodal continuous performance test. *Schizophrenia Research*, 3, 303-310.

Musto, D.F. (1991). Opium, cocaine and marijuana in American history. *Scientific American*, 265, 40-47.

Muuss, R. (1985). Adolescent eating disorder: Anorexia nervosa. *Adolescence*, 79, 525-536.

Myers, I.B. (1962). *Manual: The Myers-Briggs Type Indicator*. Princeton: Educational Testing Service.

Myers, I.B. (1987). *Introduction to type*. Palo Alto, CA: Consulting Psychologists Press.

N

Neiss, R. (1988). Reconceptualizing arousal: Psychological states in motor performance. *Psychological Bulletin*, 103, 345-366.

Neuchterlein, K., & Dawson, M.E. (1984). A heuristic vulnerability/stress model of schizophrenic episodes. *Schizophrenic Bulletin*, 10, 300-311.

Nichols, D., & Thorn, B. (1990). Stimulation-produced analgesia and its cross-tolerance between dorsal and ventral PAG loci. *Pain*, 41, 347-352.

Nickerson, R.S., & Adams, M.J. (1979). Long-term memory for a common object. *Cognition Psychology*, 11, 287-307.

Nisbett, R.E. (1972). Hunger, obesity, and the ventromedial hypothalamus. *Psychological Review*, 79, 433-453.

Nisbett, R.E., & Wilson, T. (1977). The halo effect: Evidence for the unconscious alteration of judgments. *Journal of Personality and Social Psychology*, 35, 450-456.

Norcross, J., Prochaska, J., & Gallagher, K. (1989). Clinical psychologists in the 1980s: II. Theory, research, and practice. *Clinical Psychologist*, 42, 45-52.

Norman, W.T. (1963). Toward an adequate taxonomy of personality attributes: Replicated factor structure in peer nomination personality ratings. *Journal of Abnormal and Social Psychology*, 66, 574-583.

Noyes, R., Jr., Crowe, R., Harris, E., Hamra, B., & McChesney, C. (1986). Relationship between panic disorder and agoraphobia: A family study. *Archives of General Psychiatry*, 43, 227-232.

O

O'Leary, K.D. (1984). The image of behavior therapy: It is time to take a stand. *Behavior Therapy*, *15*, 219-233.

O'Leary, K.D., & Wilson, G.T. (1987). *Behavior therapy: Application and outcome* (2nd ed.). Englewood Cliffs, NJ: Prentice-Hall.

Olds, J., & Milner, P. (1954). Positive reinforcement produced by electrical stimulation of septal area and other regions of rat brain. *Journal of Comparative and Physiological Psychology*, *47*, 419-427.

Onyehalu, A. (1981). Identity crisis in adolescence. *Adolescence*, *16*, 629-632.

Orme-Johnson, D.W. (1987). Medical care utilization and the Transcendental Meditation program. *Psychosomatic Medicine*, *49*, 493-507.

Ornstein, R.E. (1986). *The psychology of consciousness* (rev. ed.). New York: Penguin Books.

Osgood, C.E. (1962). *An alternative to war or surrender*. Urbana, IL: University of Illinois Press.

Ouchi, W.G. (1981). *Theory Z: How American business can meet the Japanese challenge*. Reading, MA: Addison-Wesley.

Overholser, J. (1990). Fetal alcohol syndrome: A review of the disorder. *Journal of Contemporary Psychotherapy*, *20*, 163-176.

Ozanne, A., Krimmer, H., & Murdoch, B. (1990). Speech and language skills in children with early treated phenylketonuria. *American Journal on Mental Retardation*, *94*, 625-632.

P

Palmer, R. (1981). (Ed.). *Electroconvulsive therapy: An appraisal*. New York: Oxford University Press.

Palumbo, S.R. (1978). *Dreaming and memory: A new information-processing model*. New York: Basic Books.

Pam, A., Plutchik, R., & Conte, H. (1975). Love: A psychometric approach. *Psychological Reports*, *37*, 83-88.

Panksepp, J. (1986). The neurochemistry of behavior. *Annual Review of Psychology*, *37*, 77-107.

Papez, J.W. (1937). A proposed mechanism of emotion. *Archives of Neurology and Psychiatry*, *38*, 725-743.

Park, D., Smith, A., & Cavanaugh, J. (1990). Metamemories of memory researchers. *Memory and Cognition*, *18*, 321-327.

Parke, R.D., & Sawin, D.B. (1980). The family in early infancy: Social interactional and attitudinal analyses. In F. Pedersen (Ed.), *The father-infant relationship: Observational studies in the family setting*. New York: Praeger.

Parker, J.G. & Asher, S.R. (1987). Peer relations and later personal adjustment: Are low-accepted children at risk? *Psychological Bulletin*, *102*, 357-389.

Parker, S.R. (1985). Future directions in behavioral research related to lung disease. *Annals of Behavioral Medicine*, *7*, 21-25.

Parlee, M. (1983). Menstrual rhythms in sensory processes: A review of fluctuations in vision, olfaction, audition, taste, and touch. *Psychological Bulletin*, *93*, 539-548.

Paterson, C.E. (1984). The effects of a program of muscle relaxation, cue control relaxation, and image training program on the batting and pitching performance of college baseball players. Unpublished master's thesis, The Ohio State University.

Paterson, C.E., & Pettijohn, T.F. (1982). Age and human mate selection. *Psychological Reports*, *51*, 70.

Patterson, F.G. (1978). The gestures of a gorilla: Language acquisition in another pongid. *Brain and Language*, *5*, 72-97.

Pattison, E.M. (1977). The experience of dying. In E.M. Pattison (Ed.), *The experience of dying*. Englewood Cliffs, NJ: Prentice-Hall.

Pauk, W. (1984). *How to Study in College* (3rd ed). Boston: Houghton Mifflin.

Paulus, P.B. (1980). Crowding: In P. Paulus (Ed.), *Psychology of group influence*. Hillsdale, NJ: Erlbaum.

Paulus, P.B. (1988). *Prison crowding: A psychological perspective*. New York: Springer-Verlag.

Paulus, P.B. (1989). *Psychology of group influence* (2nd ed.). Hillsdale, NJ: Erlbaum.

Pavlov, I. (1927). *Conditioned reflexes*. London: Clarendon Press.

Peabody, D. (1984). Personality dimensions through trait inferences. *Journal of Personality and Social Psychology*, *46*, 384-403.

Peabody, D., & Goldberg, L. (1989). Some determinants of factor structures from personality trait descriptors. *Journal of Personality and Social Psychology*, *57*, 552-567.

Peck, J., & Novin, D. (1971). Evidence that osmoreceptors mediating drinking in rabbits are in the lateral preoptic area. *Journal of Comparative and Physiological Psychology*, *74*, 134-147.

Peck, M., Farberow, N., & Litman, R. (Eds.). (1985). *Youth suicide*. New York: Springer.

Pedersen, W. (1991). Mental health, sensation seeking and drug use patterns: A longitudinal study. *British Journal of Addiction*, *86*, 195-204.

Pekala, R., & Forbes, E. (1990). Subjective effects of several stress management strategies with reference to attention. *Behavioral Medicine*, *16*, 39-43.

Penfield, W. (1975). *The mystery of the mind*. Princeton, NJ: Princeton University Press.

Pennington, N., & Hastie, R. (1990). Practical implications of psychological research on juror and jury decision making. *Personality and Social Psychology Bulletin*, *16*, 90-105.

Perkins, D. (1982). The assessment of stress using life events scales. In L. Goldberger & S. Breznitz (Eds.), *Handbook of stress: Theoretical and clinical aspects*. New York: Free Press.

Perls, F.S. (1969). *Gestalt therapy verbatim*. Moab, UT: Real People Press.

Perri, M. (1990). Application of the List of Values alternative psychographic assessment scale. *Psychological Reports*, *66*, 403-406.

Perris, C. (1982). The distinction between bipolar and unipolar affective disorders. In E. Paykel (Ed.), *Handbook of affective disorders*. New York: Guilford Press.

Peters, T., & Waterman, R., Jr. (1982). *In search of excellence: Lessons from America's best-run companies*. New York: Harper & Row.

Peterson, C., & Seligman, M.E.P. (1985). The learned helplessness model of depression: Current status of theory and research. In E. Beckham & W. Leber (Eds.), *Handbook of depression*. Homewood, IL: Dorsey.

Peterson, L., & Peterson, M. (1959). Short-term retention of individual items. *Journal of Experimental Psychology*, *58*, 193-198.

Petri, H.L. (1991). *Motivation: Theory and research* (3rd ed.). Belmont, CA: Wadsworth.

Pettijohn, T.F. (1979). Effects of alcohol on agonistic behavior in the Telomian dog. *Psychopharmacology, 60,* 295-301.

Pettijohn, T.F. (1981). Conditioned social aversion in the male Mongolian gerbil. *Journal of Comparative and Physiological Psychology, 95,* 228-239.

Pettijohn, T.F. (1985). Development of a computer tutoring and testing program for the general psychology course. *Teaching of Psychology, 12*(2), 103-104.

Pettijohn, T.F. (1988) Content of dreams in college students. Unpublished manuscript.

Pettijohn, T.F., Davis, K., & Scott, J.P. (1980). Influence of living space on agonistic interaction in Telomian dogs. *Behavioral and Neural Biology, 28,* 343-349.

Petty, F., & Sherman, A. (1984). Plasma GABA levels of psychiatric illness. *Journal of Affective Disorders, 6,* 131-138.

Petty, R.E., & Cacioppo, J.T. (1981). *Attitudes and persuasion: Classic and contemporary approaches.* Dubuque, IA: W.C. Brown.

Petty, R.E., & Cacioppo, J.T. (1985). The elaboration likelihood model of persuasion. In L. Berkowitz (Eds.), *Advances in experimental social psychology* (Vol. 19). New York: Academic Press.

Phares, E.J. (1991). *Introduction to personality* (3rd ed.). New York: HarperCollins.

Phillips, D.P. (1983). The impact of mass media violence on U.S. homicides. *American Sociological Review, 48,* 560-568.

Phillips, E.L. (1988). Length of psychotherapy and outcome: Observations stimulated by Howard, Kopta, Krause, and Orlinsky. *American Psychologist, 43,* 669-670.

Phillips, G.M. (1981). *Help for shy people.* Englewood Cliffs, NJ: Prentice-Hall.

Phillips, J.L. (1981). *Piaget's theory: A primer.* San Francisco: Freeman.

Piaget, J. (1960). *The child's conception of the world.* London: Routledge.

Piaget, J. (1967). *Six psychological studies.* New York: Vintage Books.

Piaget, J., & Szeminska, A. (1952). *The child's conception of number.* (C. Gattegno & F. Hodgson, translators). New York: Humanities Press.

Pinel, J.P.J. (1990). *Biopsychology.* Boston: Allyn-Bacon.

Pines, A., & Aronson, E. (1988). *Career burnouts: Causes and cures.* New York: Freeman.

Pion, G.M., Bramblett, J.P., Jr., & Wicherski, M. (1987). Preliminary report: 1985 doctoral employment survey. Washington, DC: American Psychological Association.

Pittenger, D.J., & Pavlik, W.B. (1988). Analysis of the partial reinforcement extinction effect in humans using absolute and relative comparisons of schedules. *American Journal of Psychology, 101,* 1-14.

Pittner, M., Houston, B., & Spiridigliozzi, G. (1983). Control over stress, type A behavior pattern, and response to stress. *Journal of Personality and Social Psychology, 44,* 627-637.

Plomin, R. (1989). Environment and genes: Determinants of behavior. *American Psychologist, 44,* 105-111.

Plomin, R., & DeFries, J.C. (1980). Genetics and intelligence: Recent data. *Intelligence, 4,* 15-24.

Plomin, R., DeFries, J.C., & McClearn, G. (1990). *Behavioral genetics: A primer* (2nd ed.). New York: Freeman.

Plutchik, R. (1962). *The emotions: Facts, theories, and a new model.* New York: Random House.

Plutchik, R. (1980). *Emotion: A psychoevolutionary synthesis.* New York: Harper & Row.

Plutchik, R. (1983). *Foundations of experimental psychology* (3rd ed.). New York: Harper & Row.

Poland, R., Rubin, R., Lesser, I., Lane, L., & Hart, P. (1987). Neuroendocrine aspects of primary endogenous depression. *Archives of General Psychology, 44,* 790-796.

Pomeroy, W. (1972). *Dr. Kinsey and the Institute for Sex Research.* New York: Harper & Row.

Potgieter, J., & Bischoff, F. (1990). Sensation seeking among medium-and low-risk sports participants. *Perceptual and Motor Skills, 71,* 1203-1206.

Premack, D. (1965). Reinforcement theory. *Nebraska Symposium on motivation.* Lincoln: University of Nebraska Press.

Premack, D. (1971). Language in chimpanzees? *Science, 172,* 808-822.

Pressey, A., & Martin, N. (1990). The effects of varying fins in Müller-Lyer and Holding illusions. *Psychological Research, 52,* 46-53.

Q

Quintanar, L., Crowell, C., & Pryor, J. (1982). Human-computer interaction: A preliminary social psychological analysis. *Behavior Research Methods and Instrumentation, 14*(2), 210-220.

R

Rahe, T., Romo, M., Bennett, L., & Siltanen, P. (1974). Recent life changes, myocardial infarction, and abrupt coronary death: Studies in Helsinki. *Archives of Internal Medicine, 133,* 221-228.

Raichle, M. (1983). Positron emission tomography. *Annual Review of Neuroscience, 6,* 249-267.

Rajecki, D.W. (1989). *Attitudes* (2nd ed.). Sunderland, MA: Sinaver.

Randall, C., Ekblad, V., & Anton, R. (1990). Perspectives on the pathophysiology of fetal alcohol syndrome. *Alcoholism: Clinical and Experimental Research, 14,* 807-812.

Ray, W.J., & Ravizza, R. (1988). *Methods: Toward a science of behavior and experience.* Belmont, CA: Wadsworth.

Raymond, C. (1986). Popular, yes, but jury still out on apnea surgery. *Journal of the American Medical Association, 256,* 439-441.

Rediehs, M., Reis, J., & Creason, N. (1990). Sleep in old age: Focus on gender differences. *Sleep, 13,* 410-424.

Reisberg, B. (Ed.). (1983). *Alzheimer's disease: The standard reference.* New York: Free Press.

Reisenzein, R. (1983). The Schachter theory of emotion: Two decades later. *Psychological Bulletin, 94,* 239-264.

Reiser, R.A. (1984). Reducing student procrastination in a personalized system of instruction course. *Educational Communication and Technology: A Journal of Theory, Research, and Development, 32,* 41-49.

Reynolds, C., Chastain, R., Kaufman, A., & McLean, J. (1987). Demographic characteristics and IQ among adults: Analysis of the WAIS-R standardization sample as a function of the stratification variables. *Journal of School Psychology, 25,* 323-342.

Reynolds, R.I., & Takooshian, H. (1988). Where were you on August 8, 1985? *Bulletin of the Psychonomic Society, 26,* 23-25.

Rice, P.L. (1987). *Stress and health: Principles and practice for coping and wellness.* Monterrey, CA: Brooks/Cole.

Richardson, J. (1983). Mental imagery in thinking and problem solving. In J. Evans (Ed.), *Thinking and reasoning: Psychological approaches.* London: Routledge & Kegan Paul.

Ridgeway, C. (1983). *The dynamics of small groups.* New York: St. Martin's Press.

Rivest, J., Ono, H., & Saida, S. (1989). The roles of convergence and apparent distance in depth constancy with motion parallax. *Perception and Psychophysics, 46,* 401-408.

Roberts, A.H. (1985). Biofeedback: Research, training, and clinical roles. *American Psychologist, 40,* 938-941.

Roberts, D., & Maccoby, N. (1985). Effects of mass communication. In G. Lindzey & E. Aronson (Eds.), *Handbook of social psychology* (Vol. 2) (3rd ed.). New York: Random House.

Roberts, E. (1986). GABA: The road to neurotransmitter status. In *Benzodiazepine/GABA receptors and chloride channels: Structural and functional properties.* New York: Alan Liss.

Robins, L., & Helzer, J. (1986). Diagnosis and clinical assessment: The current state of psychiatric diagnosis. *Annual Review of Psychology, 37,* 409-432.

Robins, L., Helzer, J., Weissman, M., Oruaschel, H., Gruenberg, E., Burke, J., & Regier, D. (1984). Lifetime prevalence of specific psychiatric disorders in three sites. *Archives of General Psychiatry, 41,* 949-958.

Rodin, J. (1981). Current status of the internal-external hypothesis for obesity. *American Psychologist, 36,* 361-371.

Rodin, J. (1985). The application of social psychology. In G. Lindzey & E. Aronson (Eds.), *Handbook of Social Psychology* (Vol. 2) (3rd ed.). New York: Random House.

Rodin, J., & Plante, T. (1989). The psychological effects of exercise. In R. Williams and A. Wellece (Eds.), *Biological effects of physical activity.* Champaign, IL: Human Kinetics.

Roethlisberger, F.J. (1941). *Management and morale.* Cambridge, MA: Harvard University Press.

Roff, J.D., & Knight, R. (1981). Family characteristics, childhood symptoms, and adult outcome in schizophrenia. *Journal of Abnormal Psychology, 90,* 510-520.

Roffwarg, H.P., Muzio, J.N., & Dement, W.C. (1966). Ontogenetic development of the human sleep-dream cycle. *Science, 152,* 604-619.

Rogers, C.R. (1951). *Client-centered therapy.* Boston: Houghton Mifflin.

Rogers, C.R. (1961). *On becoming a person.* Boston: Houghton Mifflin.

Rogers, C.R. (1970). *Carl Rogers on encounter groups.* New York: Harper & Row.

Rogers, C.R. (1971). A theory of personality. In S. Maddi (Ed.), *Perspectives on personality.* Boston: Little, Brown.

Rogers, C.R. (1980). *A way of being.* Boston: Houghton Mifflin.

Rogers, D. (1980). *The adult years: An introduction to aging.* Englewood Cliffs, NJ: Prentice-Hall.

Root, M. (1990). Disordered eating in women of color. *Sex Roles, 22,* 525-536.

Rorschach, H. (1921). *Psychodiagnostics.* Berne: Hans Huber.

Rosch, E. (1978). Principles of categorization. In E. Rosch & B. Lloyd (Eds.), *Cognition and categorization.* Hillsdale, NJ: Erlbaum.

Rosenhan, D.L. (1973). On being sane in insane places. *Science, 179,* 250-258.

Rosenstein, D., & Oster, H. (1988). Differential facial response to four basic tastes in newborns. *Child Development, 59,* 1555-1568.

Rosenthal, N., Sack, D., Carpenter, C., Parry, B., Mendelson, W., & Wehr, T. (1985). Antidepressant effects of light in seasonal affective disorder. *American Journal of Psychology, 142,* 163-170.

Rosenthal, R., & Jacobson, L. (1968). *Pygmalion in the classroom.* New York: Holt, Rinehart & Winston.

Ross, L. (1977). The intuitive psychologist and his shortcomings: Distortions in the attribution process. In L. Berkowitz (Ed.), *Advances in experimental social psychology* (Vol. 10). New York: Academic Press.

Rotter, J.B. (1954). *Social learning and clinical psychology.* Englewood Cliffs, NJ: Prentice-Hall.

Rotter, J.B. (1966). Generalized expectancies for internal versus external control of reinforcement. *Psychological Monographs, 80,* (Whole No. 609), 1-28.

Rotter, J.B. (1971). External control and internal control. *Psychology Today, 5*(1), 37-42, 58-59.

Roy, A. (1985). Early parental separation and adult depression. *Archives of General Psychiatry, 42,* 987-991.

Rubenstein, C. (1983). The modern art of courtly love. *Psychology Today,* June, 39-49.

Rubin, Z. (1970). Measurement of romantic love. *Journal of Personality and Social Psychology, 16,* 265-273.

Rubin, Z. (1973). *Liking and loving.* New York: Holt, Rinehart & Winston.

Ruch, L.O., & Holmes, T.H. (1971). Scaling of life change: Comparison of direct and indirect methods. *Journal of Psychosomatic Research, 15,* 221-227.

Rumbaugh, D.M. (Ed.). (1977). *Language learning by a chimpanzee: The Lana project.* New York: Academic Press.

Russek, M. Lora-Vilchis, M., & Islas-Chaires, M. (1980). Food intake inhibition elicited by intraportal glucose and adrenaline in dogs on a 22-hour fasting 2-hour feeding schedule. *Physiology and Behavior, 24,* 157-161.

Russell, J.A. (1980). A circumplex model of affect. *Journal of Personality and Social Psychology, 39,* 1161-1178.

Russell, J.A. (1990). The preschooler's understanding of the causes and consequences of emotion. *Child Development, 61,* 1872-1881.

Russell, J.A., & Bullock, M. (1985). Multidimensional scaling of emotional facial features: Similarity from preschoolers to adults. *Journal of Personality and Social Psychology, 48,* 1290-1298.

Russell, J.A., & Bullock, M. (1986). Fuzzy concepts and the perception of emotion in facial expressions. *Social Cognition, 4,* 309-341.

Russell, J.A., & Fehr, B. (1987). Relativity in the perception of emotion in facial expressions. *Journal of Experimental Psychology: General, 116,* 223-237.

Russell, J.A., Lewicka, M., & Niit, T. (1989). A cross-cultural study of a circumplex model of affect. *Journal of Personality and Social Psychology, 57,* 848-856.

Russell, M.J., Switz, G.M., & Thompson, K. (1980). Olfactory influences on the human menstrual cycle. *Pharmacology, Biochemistry, and Behavior, 13,* 737-738.

Rutherford, W.A. (1886). A new theory of hearing. *Journal of Anatomy and Physiology, 21,* 166-168.

S

Saal, F.E., & Knight, P.A. (1988). *Industrial/organizational psychology: Science and practice*. Pacific Grove, CA: Brooks-Cole.

Sanduik, E., Diener, E., & Larsen, R. (1985). The opponent process theory and affective reactions. *Motivation and Emotion, 9*, 407-418.

Sanna, L.J., & Shotland, R.L. (1990). Valence of anticipated evaluation and social facilitation. *Journal of Experimental Social Psychology, 26*, 82-92.

Sarason, I.G., & Sarason, B.R. (1989). *Abnormal psychology: The problem of maladaptive behavior* (6th ed.). Englewood Cliffs, NJ: Prentice-Hall.

Sarbin, T., & Coe, W. (1979). Hypnosis and psychopathology: Replacing old myths with fresh metaphors. *Journal of Abnormal Psychology, 88*, 506-526.

Sassin, J.F., Parker, D.C., Mace, J.W., Gotlin, R.W., Johnson, L.C., & Rossman, L.G. (1969). Human growth hormone release: Relation to slow-wave sleep and sleep-walking cycles. *Science, 165*, 513-515.

Savage-Rumbaugh, E.S. (1987). Communication, symbolic communication, and language: Reply to Seidenberg and Petitto. *Journal of Experimental Psychology: General, 116*, 288-292.

Savage-Rumbaugh, E.S., Rumbaugh, D.M., & Boysen, S. (1980). Do apes use language? *American Scientist, 68*, 49-61.

Savage-Rumbaugh, E.S., Sevcik, R.A., Rumbaugh, D.M., & Rubert, E. (1985). The capacity of animals to acquire language: Do species differences have anything to say to us? *Philosophical Transactions, Royal Society of London, B308*, 177-185.

Saxe, L., Doughterty, D., & Cross, T. (1985). The validity of polygraph testing: Scientific analysis and public controversy. *American Psychologist, 40*, 355-366.

Scarr, S., & Weinberg, R.A. (1983). The Minnesota adoption studies: Genetic differences and malleability. *Child Development, 54*, 260-267.

Schachter, S. (1959). *The psychology of affiliation: Experimental studies of the sources of gregariousness*. Stanford, CA: Stanford University Press.

Schachter, S. (1971a). *Emotion, obesity and crime*. New York: Academic Press.

Schachter, S., & Gross, L. (1968). Manipulated time and eating behavior. *Journal of Personality and Social Psychology, 10*, 98-106.

Schachter, S., & Singer, J. (1962). Cognitive, social, and physiological determinants of emotional state. *Psychological Review, 69*, 379-399.

Schaffer, H.R., & Emerson, P.E. (1964). The development of social attachments in infancy. *Monographs of the Society for Research in Child Development, 29*, (Whole No. 94).

Scheerer, M. (1963). Problem-solving. *Scientific American, 208*(4), 118-128.

Scher, S., & Cooper, J. (1989). Motivational basis of dissonance: The singular role of behavioral consequences. *Journal of personality and Social Psychology, 56*, 899-906.

Schiffman, S.S., Reynolds, M.L., & Young, F.L. (1981). *Introduction to multidimensional scaling*. New York: Academic Press.

Schildkraut, J.J., & Kety, S.S. (1967). Biogenic amines and emotion. *Science, 156*, 21-30.

Schmitt, R.C. (1966). Density, health and social disorganization. *Journal of the American Institute of Planners, 32*, 38-40.

Schneider, W., & Sodian, B. (1991). A longitudinal study of young children's memory behavior and performance in a sort-recall task. *Journal of Experimental Child Psychology, 51*, 14-29.

Schuster, B., Forsterling, F., & Weiner, B. (1989). Perceiving the causes of success and failure: A cross-cultural examination of attributional concepts. *Journal of Cross-Cultural Psychology, 20*, 191-213.

Schwartz, B. (1984). *Psychology of learning and behavior*. New York: Norton.

Scott, J.A. (1984). Comfort and seating distance in living rooms: The relationship of interactants and topic of conversation. *Environment and Behavior, 16*, 35-54.

Scott, J.P. (1968). *Early experience and the organization of behavior*. Belmont, CA: Brooks-Cole.

Scott, J.P. (1971). Attachment and separation in dog and man. In H.R. Schaffer (Ed.). *The origin of human social relations*. New York: Academic Press.

Scott, J.P. (1975). *Aggression* (2nd ed.). Chicago: University of Chicago Press.

Scott, J.P., & Fuller, J. (1965). *Genetics and the social behavior of the dog*. Chicago: University of Chicago Press.

Sears, D.O. (1983). The person-positivity bias. *Journal of Personality and Social Psychology, 44*, 233-250.

Sears, D.O., Peplau, L.A., & Taylor, S.E. (1991). *Social psychology* (7th ed.). Englewood Cliffs, NJ: Prentice Hall.

Sedney, M. (1987). Development of androgyny: Parental influences. *Psychology of Women Quarterly, 11*, 311-326.

Seligman, M.E.P. (1970). On the generality of the laws of learning. *Psychological Review, 77*, 406-418.

Seligman, M.E.P. (1971). Phobias and preparedness. *Behavior Therapy, 2*, 307-320.

Seligman, M.E.P. (1972). Phobias and preparedness. In M.E.P. Seligman & J.L. Hagen (Eds.), *Biological boundaries of learning*. Englewood Cliffs, NJ: Prentice-Hall.

Seligman, M.E.P. (1974). Depression and learned helplessness. In R.J. Friedman & M.M. Katz (Eds.), *The psychology of depression: Contemporary theory and research*. Washington, DC: Winston-Wiley.

Seligman, M.E.P. (1975). *Helplessness: On depression, development and death*. San Francisco: Freeman.

Seligman, M.E.P., & Maier, S.F. (1967). Failure to escape traumatic shock. *Journal of Experimental Psychology, 74*, 1-9.

Selye, H. (1976). *The stress of life* (rev. ed.). New York: McGraw-Hill.

Selye, H. (1980). The stress concept today. In E. Kutash & L. Schlesinger (Eds.), *Handbook on stress and anxiety*. San Francisco: Jossey-Bass.

Shapiro, C., Bortz, R., Mitchell, D., Bartel, P., & Jooste, P. (1981). Slow-wave sleep: A recovery period after exercise. *Science, 214*, 1253-1254.

Shapiro, D. (1985). Clinical use of meditation as a self-regulation strategy. Comments on Holmes' conclusions and implications. *American Psychologist, 40*, 719-722.

Shavitt, S. (1990). The role of attitude objects in attitude functions. *Journal of Experimental Social Psychology, 26*, 124-148.

Sherif, M. (1936). *The psychology of social norms*. New York: Harper & Row.

Sherman, J.E. (1978). U.S. inflation with trace and simultaneous fear conditioning. *Animal Learning and Behavior, 6*, 463-468.

Sherrick, C., & Cholewiak, R. (1986). Cutaneous sensitivity. In K. Boff, L. Kaufman, & J.P. Thomas (Eds.), *Handbook of perception and human performance* (Vol. 1). New York: Wiley.

Sherrington, R., Bynjolfsson, J., Petursson, H., Potter, M., Dudleston, K., Barraclough, B., Wasmuth, J., Dobbs, M., & Gurling, H. (1988). Localization of a susceptibility locus for schizophrenia on chromosomes 5. *Nature, 336,* 164-167.

Shinn, M., Rosario, M., Morch, H., & Chestnut, D. (1984). Coping with job stress and burn-out in the human services. *Journal of Personality and Social Psychology, 46,* 854-876.

Shostrom, E. (1964). An inventory for measurement of self-actualization. *Educational and Psychological Measurement, 24,* 207-218.

Siegel, S., Hinson, R., Krank, M., & McCully, J. (1982). Heroin overdose death: Contribution of drug associated environmental cues. *Science, 216,* 436-437.

Simpson, J.B., & Routtenberg, A. (1973). Subfornical organ: Site of drinking elicitation by angiotensin II. *Science, 181,* 1172-1174.

Singer, J.L. (1975). Navigating the stream of consciousness: Research in daydreaming and related inner experience. *American Psychologist, 30,* 727-738.

Skalka, P. (1984). *The American Medical Association guide to health and well-being after fifty.* New York: Random House.

Skeels, H.M. (1966). Adult status of children with contrasting early life experiences. *Monographs of the Society for Research in Child Development,* (Whole No. 31), 1-65.

Skinner, B.F. (1938). *The behavior of organisms: An experimental analysis.* East Norwalk, CT: Appleton-Century-Crofts.

Skinner, B.F. (1948). *Walden two.* New York: Macmillan.

Skinner, B.F. (1953). *Science and human behavior.* New York: Free Press.

Skinner, B.F. (1957). *Verbal behavior.* Englewood Cliffs, NJ: Prentice-Hall.

Skinner, B.F. (1958). Teaching machines. *Science, 128,* 969-977.

Skinner, B.F. (1961). Teaching machines. *Scientific American, 205,* 90-102.

Skinner, B.F. (1962). Two "synthetic social relations." *Journal of the Experimental Analysis of Behavior, 5,* 531-533.

Skinner, B.F. (1971). *Beyond freedom and dignity.* New York: Knopf.

Skinner, B.F. (1987). *Upon further reflection.* Englewood Cliffs, NJ: Prentice-Hall.

Skinner, B.F. (1987). What ever happened to psychology as the science of behavior? *American Psychologist, 42,* 780-786.

Skinner, B.F. (1988). *Personal communication.*

Slater, A., Mattock, A., & Brown, E. (1990). Size constancy at birth: Newborn infants' responses to retinal and real size. *Journal of Experimental Child Psychology, 49,* 314-322.

Smith, A., & Stansfeld, S. (1986). Aircraft noise exposure, noise sensitivity, and everyday errors. *Environment and Behavior, 18,* 214-226.

Smith, D. (1982). Trends in counseling and psychotherapy. *American Psychologist, 37,* 802-809.

Smith, G., & Gibbs, J. (1976). Cholecystokinin and satiety: Theoretic and therapeutic implications. In D. Novin, W. Wihyrwicka, and G. Bray (Eds.), *Hunger: Basic mechanisms and clinical implications.* New York: Raven.

Smith, M.E. (1926). An investigation of the development of the sentence and the extent of vocabulary in young children. *University of Iowa Studies in Child Welfare, 3*(5), 1-92.

Smith, M.L., & Glass, G.V. (1977). Meta-analysis of psychotherapy outcome studies. *American Psychologist, 32,* 752-760.

Smith, M.L., Glass, G.V., & Miller, T.I. (1980). *The benefits of psychotherapy.* Baltimore: Johns Hopkins University Press.

Solomon, R.L. (1980). The opponent-process theory of acquired motivation: The costs of pleasure and the benefits of pain. *American Psychologist, 35,* 691-712.

Solomon, R.L., & Corbit, J.D. (1974). An opponent-process theory of motivation. I. Temporal dynamics of affect. *Psychological Review, 81,* 119-145.

Solomon, R.L., & Wynne, L.C. (1953). Traumatic avoidance learning: Acquisition in normal dogs. *Psychological Monographs, 67* (Whole No. 354).

Solomon, Z., Mikulincer, M., & Avitzur, E. (1988). Coping locus of control, social support, and combat-related post traumatic stress disorder: A prospective study. *Journal of Personality and Social Psychology, 55,* 279-285.

Solso, R.L. (1988). *Cognitive psychology* (2nd ed.). Boston: Allyn Bacon.

Sommer, B., & Sommer, R. (1991). *A practical guide to behavioral research: Tools and techniques* (3rd ed.). New York: Oxford University Press.

Sorce, J.F., Emde, R.N., Campos, J., & Klinnert, M.D. (1985). Maternal emotional signaling: Its effect on the visual cliff behavior of 1-year-olds. *Developmental Psychology, 21,* 195-200.

Spearman, C. (1904). General intelligence objectively determined and measured. *American Journal of Psychology, 15,* 201-293.

Speilberger, C.D., & London, P. (1982). Rage boomerangs. *American Health, 1,* 52-56.

Sperling, G. (1960). The information available in brief visual presentations. *Psychological Monographs, 74,* (Whole No. 498), 1-29.

Sperry, R. (1968). Hemisphere deconnection and unity in conscious awareness. *American Psychologist, 23,* 723-733.

Spielberger, C.D., Johnson, E., Russell, S., Crane, R., Jacobs, G., & Worden, T. (1985). The experience and expression of anger. In M. Chesney, S. Goldston, & R. Rosenman (Eds.), *Anger and hostility in cardiovascular and behavioral disorders.* New York: Hemisphere.

Spurlock, J. (1986). Development of self-concept in Afro-American children. *Hospital and Community Psychiatry, 37,* 66-70.

Squire, L.R. (1987). *Memory and the brain.* New York: Oxford University Press.

Squire, L.R., Ojemann, J.G., Miezin, F.M., Petersen, S.E., Videen, T.O., & Raichle, M.E. (in press). Activation of the hippocampus in normal humans: A functional anatomical study of memory. *Proceedings of the National Academy of Science.*

Staats, S. (1983). Perceived sources of stress and happiness in married and single college students. *Psychological Reports, 52,* 179-184.

Stapp, J., Tucker, A., & VanderBos, G. (1985). Census of psychological personnel: 1983. *American Psychologist, 40,* 1317-1351.

Stassen, M., & Staats, S. (1988). Hope and happiness: A comparison of some discrepancies. *Social Indicators Research*, *20*, 45-58.

Stechler, G., & Halton, A. (1982). Prenatal influences on human development. In B. Wolman (Ed.), *Handbook of developmental psychology*. Englewood Cliffs, NJ: Prentice-Hall.

Steers, R.M. (1991). *Introduction to organizational behavior*. New York: HarperCollins.

Steinberg, L. (1988). Reciprocal relation between parent-child distance and pubertal maturation. *Developmental Psychology*, *24*, 122-128.

Steiner, I.D. (1972). *Group processes and productivity*. New York: Academic Press.

Sterling, P. (1983). Retinal microcircuitry. *Annual Review of Neuroscience*, 149-185.

Sternberg, R.J. (1982). Who's intelligent? *Psychology Today*, *16*, 30-39.

Sternberg, R.J. (1984). Toward a triarchic theory of human intelligence. *The Behavioral and Brain Science*, *7*, 269-315.

Sternberg, R.J. (1985). *Beyond IQ: A triarchic theory of human intelligence*. New York: Cambridge University Press.

Sternberg, R.J. (1986a). *Intelligence applied: Understanding and increasing your intellectual skills*. San Diego: Harcourt Brace Jovanovich.

Sternberg, R.J. (1986b). A triangular theory of love. *Psychological Review*, *93*, 119-135.

Sternberg, R.J. (1987). Liking versus loving: A comparative evaluation of theories. *Psychological Bulletin*, *102*, 331-345.

Sternberg, R.J. (1988). *The triangle of love: Intimacy, passion, commitment*. New York: Basic Books.

Sternberg, R.J., & Davidson, J. (1982). The mind of the puzzler. *Psychology Today*, *16*, 37-44.

Sternberg, R.J., & Davidson, J.E. (1985). Cognitive development in the gifted and talented. In F.D. Horowitz & M. O'Brien (Eds.), *The gifted and talented: Developmental perspectives*. Washington, DC: American Psychological Association.

Sternberg, S. (1966). High-speed scanning in human memory. *Science*, *153*, 652-654.

Sternberg, S. (1969). Memory-scanning: Mental processes revealed by reaction-time experiments. *American Scientist*, *57*, 421-457.

Stevens, D., & Truss, C. (1985). Stability and change in adult personality over 12 and 20 years. *Developmental Psychology*, *21*, 568-584.

Stevens, J.C. (1979). Variation of cold sensitivity over the body surface. *Sensory Processes*, *3*, 317-326.

Stier, D.S., & Hall, J.A. (1984). Gender differences in touch: An empirical and theoretical review. *Journal of Personality and Social Psychology*, *47*, 440-459.

Stinnett, N., Walters, J., & Kaye, E. (1984). *Relationships in marriage and the family*. New York: Macmillan.

Stock, M.B., & Smythe, P.M. (1963). Does undernutrition during infancy inhibit brain growth and subsequent intellectual development? *Archives of Disorders in Childhood*, *38*, 546-552.

Stoner, J. (1961). A comparison of individual and group decisions involving risk. Unpublished master's thesis. Massachusetts Institute of Technology, School of Industrial Management.

Stout, A. (1986). Premenstrual symptoms in Black and White community samples. *American Journal of Psychiatry*, *143*, 1436-1439.

Straus, M., Gelles, R., & Steinmetz, S. (1980). *Behind closed doors: Violence in the American family*. Garden City, NJ: Anchor Books.

Striegel-Moore, R., Silberstein, L., & Rodin, J. (1986). Toward an understanding of risk factors for bulimia. *American Psychologist*, *41*, 246-263.

Stroebe, M.S., & Stroebe, W. (1983). Who suffers more? Sex differences in health risks of the widowed. *Psychological Bulletin*, *93*, 279-301.

Sue, D., Sue, D., & Sue, S. (1990). *Understanding abnormal behavior* (3rd ed.). Boston: Houghton Mifflin.

Sue, S. (1988). Psychotherapeutic services for ethnic minorities. *American Psychologist*, *43*, 301-308.

Suedfeld, P. (1980). *Restricted environmental stimulation: Research and clinical applications*. New York: Wiley.

Suedfeld, P., & Baker-Brown, G. (1986). Restricted environmental stimulation therapy and aversive conditioning in smoking cessation. *Behavior Research and Therapy*, *24*, 421-428.

Suedfeld, P., & Coren, S. (1989). Perceptual isolation, sensory deprivation, and REST: Moving introductory psychology texts out of the 1950s. *Journal of Canadian Psychology*, *30*, 17-29.

Suedfeld, P., & Kristeller, J. (1982). Stimulus reduction as a technique in health psychology. *Health Psychology*, *1*, 337-357.

Sweep, C., & Wiegant, V. (1989). Release of B-endorphin-immunoreactivity from rat pituitary and hypothalamus in vitro: Effects of isoproterenol, dopamine, corticotropin-releasing factor and arginine-vasopressin. *Biochemical and Biophysical Research Communications*, *161*, 221-228.

T

Tanner, J.M. (1981). Growth and maturation during adolescence. *Nutrition Review*, *39*, 43-55.

Tart, C. (1975). *States of consciousness*. New York: Dutton.

Tavris, C., & Wade, C. (1984). *The longest war: Sex differences in perspective* (2nd ed.). San Diego: Harcourt Brace Jovanovich.

Taylor, J.A. (1953). A personality scale of manifest anxiety. *Journal of Abnormal and Social Psychology*, *48*, 285-290.

Taylor, S.E. (1991). *Health psychology* (2nd ed.). New York: McGraw-Hill.

Terman, L.M. (1916). *The measurement of intelligence*. Boston: Houghton Mifflin.

Terman, L.M. (1925). *Genetic studies of genius*. Stanford, CA: Stanford University Press.

Termine, N.T., & Izard, C.E. (1988). Infants' responses to their mothers' expressions of joy and sadness. *Developmental Psychology*, *24(2)*, 223-229.

Terrace, H.S. (1979). *Nim: A chimpanzee who learned sign language*. New York: Knopf.

Terrace, H.S. (1985). In the beginning was the "name." *American Psychologist*, *40*, 1011-1028.

Thayer, P.W. (1983). Industrial/organizational psychology: Science and application. In C.J. Scheirer & A.M. Rogers (Eds.), *The G. Stanley Hall lecture series* (Vol. 3). Washington, DC: American Psychological Association.

Thoits, P.A. (1983). Dimensions of life events as influences upon the genesis of psychological distress and associated conditions: An evaluation and synthesis of the literature. In H.B. Kaplan (Ed.), *Psychosocial stress: Trends in theory and research*. New York: Academic Press.

Thomas, A., & Chess, S. (1986). The New York Longitudinal Study: From infancy to early adult life. In R. Plomin & J. Dunn (Eds.), *The study of temperament: Changes, continuities, and challenges*. Hillsdale, NJ: Erlbaum.

Thomas, K.W. (1990). Conflict and negotiation processes. In M.D. Dunnette (Ed.), *Handbook of industrial and organizational psychology* (2nd ed.). Chicago: Rand McNally.

Thomas, M.H. (1982). Physiological arousal, exposure to a relatively lengthy aggressive film, and aggressive behavior. *Journal of Research in Personality, 16,* 72-81.

Thompson, R. (1985). *The brain*. San Francisco: Freeman.

Thompson, R. (1986). The neurobiology of learning and memory. *Science, 233,* 941-947.

Thornburg, H. (1984). *Introduction to educational psychology*. St. Paul, MN: West.

Thorndike, E.L. (1898). Animal intelligence. *Psychological Review, 2,* Whole No. 8.

Thorndike, E.L. (1932). *The fundamentals of learning*. New York: Teachers College Press.

Thorpe, G.L., & Olson, S.L. (1990). *Behavior therapy: Concepts, procedures, and applications*. Boston: Allyn Bacon.

Thurstone, L.L. (1938). Primary mental abilities. *Psychometric Monographs, 1.* Chicago: University of Chicago Press.

Tiedeman, D.V., & O'Hara, R.P. (1963). *Career development: Choice and adjustment*. New York: College Entrance Examination Board.

Tinbergen, N. (1952). The curious behavior of the stickleback. *Scientific American, 182,* 22-26.

Tolman, E.C. (1923). The nature of instinct. *Psychological Bulletin, 20,* 200-218.

Tolman, E.C. (1932). *Purposive behavior in animals and men*. New York: Appleton-Century-Crofts.

Tolman, E.C. (1948). Cognitive maps in rats and men. *Psychological Review, 55,* 189-208.

Tolman, E.C., & Honzik, C.H. (1930). Introduction and removal of reward, and maze performance in rats. *University of California Publications in Psychology, 4,* 257-275.

Tomkins, S.S. (1962). *Affect imagery consciousness. Vol. 1, The positive affects*. New York: Springer.

Tomkins, S.S. (1981). The quest for primary motives: Biography and autobiography of an idea. *Journal of Personality and Social Psychology, 41,* 306-329.

Tomkins, S.S., & McCarter, R. (1964). What and where are the primary affects? Some evidence for a theory. *Perceptual and Motor Skills, 18,* 119-158.

Tracy, R., & Ainsworth, M.D.S. (1981). Maternal affectionate behavior and infant-mother attachment patterns. *Child Development, 52,* 1341-1343.

Trapnell, P., & Wiggins, J. (1990). Extension of the interpersonal adjective scales to include the big five dimensions of personality. *Journal of Personality and Social Psychology, 59,* 781-790.

Tryon, R.C. (1940). Genetic differences in maze-learning ability in rats. *Yearbook of the National Society for the Study of Education, 1,* 111-119.

Tulving, E. (1962). Subjective organization in free recall of unrelated words. *Psychological Review, 69,* 344-354.

Tulving, E. (1972). Episodic and semantic memory. In E. Tulving & W. Donaldson (Eds.), *Organization and memory*. New York: Academic Press.

Tulving, E. (1983). *Elements of episodic memory*. New York: Oxford University Press.

Tulving, E. (1985). How many memory systems are there? *American Psychologist, 40,* 385-398.

Tupes, E.C., & Christal, R.E. (1961). Recurrent personality factors based on trait ratings. *USAF ASD Technical Report* (No. 61-97).

Turing, A.M. (1950). Computing machinery and intelligence. *Mind, 59,* 433-460.

Tybout, A., & Scott, C. (1983). Availability of well-defined internal knowledge and the attitude formation process: Information aggregation versus self-perception. *Journal of Personality and Social Psychology, 44,* 474-491.

U

U.S. Bureau of the Census. (1982). Current population reports, Series P-20, No. 371. Washington, DC: U.S. Government Printing Office.

Underwood, B.J. (1983). *Attributes of memory*. Glenview, IL: Scott, Foresman.

V

Valenstein, E.S. (1986). *Great and desperate cures*. New York: Basic Books.

Van Lawick-Goodall, J. (1971). *In the shadow of man*. New York: Dell.

Veninga, R.L., & Spradley, J.P. (1981). *The work stress connection*. Boston: Little, Brown.

Vernon, P.E. (1979). *Intelligence: Heredity and environment*. San Francisco: Freeman.

Veroff, J. (1982). Assertive motivations: Achievement versus power. In D. Winter & A.J. Stewart (Eds.). *Motivation and Society*. San Francisco: Jossey-Bass.

Vertes, R.P. (1983). Brainstem control of the events of REM sleep. *Progress in Neurobiology, 22,* 241-288.

Vogel, S., & Adelman, P. (1990). Extrinsic and intrinsic factors in graduation and academic failure among LD college students. *Annals of Dyslexia, 40,* 119-137.

Von Frisch, K. (1967). *The dance language and orientation of bees* (L. Chadwick, Trans.). Cambridge, MA: Harvard University Press.

W

Wachtel, S. (1983). *H-Y antigen and the biology of sex determination*. New York: Grune & Stratton.

Wadsworth, T. (1984). *Piaget's theory of cognitive and affective development*. New York: Longman.

Wagner, H.L., MacDonald, C.J., & Manstead, A.S.R. (1986). Communication of individual emotions by spontaneous facial expressions. *Journal of Personality and Social Psychology, 50,* 737-743.

Wallace, B., & Fisher, L.E. (1991). *Consciousness and behavior*, (3rd ed.). Boston: Allyn & Bacon.

Wallace, R.K., & Benson, H. (1972). The physiology of meditation. *Scientific American, 226,* 84-90.

Wallbott, H. (1991). The robustness of communication of emotion via facial expression: Emotion recognition from photographs with deteriorated pictorial quality. *European Journal of Social Psychology, 21,* 89-98.

Walsh, W.B., & Betz, N. (1990). *Tests and assessment* (4th ed). Englewood Cliffs, NJ: Prentice Hall.

Walster, E., & Walster, G.W. (1978). *A new look at love.* Reading, MA: Addison-Wesley.

Walster, E., Walster, G.W., & Berscheid, E. (1978). *Equity theory and research.* Boston: Allyn & Bacon.

Warner, C. (1988). Understanding your learning disability. Unpublished manuscript. The Ohio State University.

Wason, P. (1968). On the failure to eliminate hypotheses—a second look. In P. Wason & P. Johnson-Laird (Eds.), *Thinking and reasoning.* Baltimore: Penguin.

Watson, J.B. (1924). *Behaviorism.* New York: Norton.

Watson, J.B., & Rayner, R. (1920). Conditioned emotional reactions. *Journal of Experimental Psychology, 3,* 1-14.

Watson, J.D., & Crick, F. (1953). Genetical implications of the structure of deoxyribonucleic acid. *Nature, 171,* 964-967.

Webb, W.B. (1974). Sleep as an adaptive response. *Perceptual and Motor Skills, 38,* 1023-1027.

Webb, W.B. (1975). *Sleep: The gentle tyrant.* Englewood Cliffs, NJ: Prentice-Hall.

Webb, W.B. (1981). The return of consciousness. In L.T. Benjamin, Jr. (Ed.), *The G. Stanley Hall lecture series* (Vol. 1). Washington, DC: American Psychological Association.

Webb, W.B., & Campbell, S. (1983). Relationships in sleep characteristics of identical and fraternal twins. *Archives of General Psychiatry, 40,* 1093-1095.

Wechsler, D. (1975). Intelligence defined and undefined. *American Psychologist, 30,* 135-139.

Weidner, G., Friend, R., Ficarroto, T., & Mendell, N. (1989). Hostility and cardiovascular reactivity to stress in women and men. *Psychosomatic Medicine, 51,* 36-45.

Weil, A.T. (1973). *The natural mind.* Boston: Houghton Mifflin.

Weiner, B. (1974). *Achievement motivation and attribution theory.* Morristown, NJ: General Learning Press.

Weiner, B. (1986). *An attributional theory of motivation and emotion.* New York: Springer-Verlag.

Weinstein, S. (1968). Intensive and extensive aspects of tactile sensitivity as a function of body part, sex, and laterality. In D. Kenshato (Ed.), *The skin senses.* Springfield, IL: Thomas.

Weisberg, R. (1986). *Creativity: Genius and other myths.* New York: Freeman.

Weiss, J.M. (1984). Behavioral and psychological influences on gastrointestinal pathology: Experimental techniques and findings. In W. Gentry (Ed.), *Handbook of behavioral medicine.* New York: Guilford.

Weiss, R. (1987). How dare we? *Science News, 132,* 57-59.

Weld, H., & Roff, M. (1938). A study of the formation of opinion based upon legal evidence. *American Journal of Psychology, 51* 609-628.

Wells, G.L., & Murray, D.M. (1983). What can psychology say about the Neil vs. Biggers criteria for judging eyewitness accuracy? *Journal of Applied Psychology, 68,* 347-362.

Werner, E. (1979). *Cross-cultural child development.* Monterey, CA: Brooks-Cole.

Wetzel, C., & Insko, C. (1982). The similarity-attraction relationship: Is there an ideal one? *Journal of Experimental Social Psychology, 18,* 253-276.

Wever, E.G. (1949). *Theory of hearing.* New York: Wiley.

Wever, E.G., & Bray, C. (1937). The perception of low tones and the resonance-volley theory. *Journal of Physiology, 3,* 101-114.

White, R.W. (1959). Motivation reconsidered: The concept of competence. *Psychological Review, 66,* 297-333.

Whitten, W.B., & Leonard, J. (1981). Directed search through autobiographical memory. *Memory and Cognition, 9,* 566-579.

Whorf, B.L. (1956). Language, thought and reality. In J.B. Carroll (Ed.), *Selected writings of Benjamin Lee Whorf.* New York: Wiley.

Wichman, H. (1970). Effects of isolation and communication on cooperation in a two-person game. *Journal of Personality and Social Psychology, 16,* 114-120.

Widiger, T., Frances, A., Pincus, H., Davis, W., & First, M. (1991). Toward an empirical classification for the DSM-IV. *Journal of Abnormal Psychology, 100,* 280-288.

Wilks, J. (1986). The relative importance of parents and friends in adolescent decision making. *Journal of Youth and Adolescence, 15,* 325-334.

Williams, R.B., Jr. (1989). *The trusting heart: Great news about Type A behavior.* New York: Random House.

Williams, R.B., Jr., Barefoot, J., & Shekelle, R. (1984). The health consequences of hostility. In M. Chesney, S. Goldston, & R. Rosenman (Eds.), *Anger: Hostility in behavior medicine.* Washington, DC: Hemisphere.

Williams, R.L., & Long, J.D. (1991). *Toward a self-managed life style* (4th ed.). Boston: Houghton Mifflin.

Williams, S., Kinney, P., & Falbo, J. (1989). Generalization of therapeutic changes in agoraphobia. The role of perceiving self-efficacy. *Journal of Consulting and Clinical Psychology, 57,* 436-442.

Wilson, E.O. (1975). *Sociobiology: The new synthesis.* Cambridge, MA: Harvard University Press.

Wilson, G.T., & O'Leary, K.D. (1980). *Principles of behavior therapy.* Englewood Cliffs, NJ: Prentice-Hall.

Wilson, R.S. (1983). The Louisville twin study: Developmental synchronies in behavior. *Child Development, 54,* 298-316.

Wilson, T.D., Goldin, J.C., & Charbonneau-Powis, M. (1983). Comparative efficacy of behavioral and cognitive treatments of depression. *Cognitive Therapy and Research, 7,* 111-124.

Winokur, G. (1985). The validity of neurotic-reactive depression: New data and reappraisal. *Archives of General Psychiatry, 42,* 1116-1122.

Winter, D.G. (1973). *The power motive.* New York: Free Press.

Winter, D.G. (1982). *The power motive in women.* Unpublished manuscript.

Wise, C.D., & Stein, L. (1973). Dopamine-beta-hydroxylase deficits in the brain of schizophrenic patients. *Science, 181,* 344-347.

Wise, R., & Bozarth, M. (1984). Brain reward circuitry: Four circuit elements "wired" in apparent series. *Brain Research Bulletin, 12,* 203-208.

Witkin, H.A. (1976). Cognitive style in academic performance and in teacher-student relations. In S. Messick (Ed.), *Individuality in learning.* San Francisco: Jossey-Bass.

Wolpe, J. (1958). *Psychotherapy by reciprocal inhibition.* Stanford, CA: Stanford University Press.

Wong, D., Wagner, H., Tune, L., Dannals, R., Pearlson, G., Links, J., Tamminga, C., Broussolle, E., Ravert, H., Wilson, A., Toung, J., Malat, J., Williams, J., O'Tuma, L., Snyder, S., Kunar, M., & Gjedde, A. (1986). Position emission tomography reveals elevated D2 dopamine receptors in drug-naive schizophrenics. *Science, 234,* 1558-1563.

Wood, W., & Eagly, W. H. (1981). Stages in the analysis of persuasive messages: The role of causal attributions and message comprehension. *Journal of Personality and Social Psychology, 40,* 246-259.

Woodworth, R.S. (1918). *Dynamic psychology.* New York: Columbia University Press.

Wright, L. (1988). The Type A behavior pattern and coronary artery disease: Quest for the active ingredients and the elusive mechanism. *American Psychologist, 43,* 2-14.

Wurtman, R.J. (1987). Ways that food can affect the brain. *Nutrition Reviews, 4,* 2-5.

Y

Yinon, Y., Sharon, I., Gonen, Y., & Adam, R. (1982). Escape from responsibility and help in emergencies among persons alone or within groups. *European Journal of Social Psychology, 12,* 301-305.

Yonas, A. (1984). Reaching as a measure of infant spatial perception. In G. Gottlieb & N. Krasnegor (Eds.), *Measurement of audition and vision in the first year of postnatal life: A methodological review.* Norwood, NJ: Ablex.

Z

Zajonc, R.B. (1965). Social facilitation. *Science, 149,* 269-274.

Zajonc, R.B. (1984). On the primacy of affect. *American Psychologist, 39,* 117-123.

Zajonc, R.B. (1986). The decline and rise of scholastic aptitude scores: A prediction derived from the confluence model. *American Psychologist, 41,* 862-867.

Zajonc, R.B., & Markus, G.B. (1975). Birth order and intellectual development. *Psychological Review, 82,* 74-88.

Zajonc, R.B., Murphy, S., & Inglehart, M. (1989). Feeling and facial efference: Implications of the vascular theory of emotion. *Psychological Review, 96,* 395-416.

Zerbin-Rubin, E. (1972). Genetic research and the theory of schizophrenia. *International Journal of Mental Health, 1,* 42-62.

Zhang, G., & Simon, H.A. (1985). STM capacity for Chinese words and idioms: Chunking and acoustical loop hypotheses. *Memory and Cognition, 13,* 193-201.

Zigler, E., & Berman, W. (1983). Discerning the future of early childhood intervention. *American Psychologist, 38,* 894-906.

Zimbardo, P.G. (1977). *Shyness: What it is and what to do about it.* Reading, MA: Addison-Wesley.

Zimbardo, P.G. (1986). The Stanford Shyness Project. In W. Jones, J. Cheek, & S. Briggs (Eds.), *Shyness: Perspectives on research and treatment.* New York: Plenum.

Zimbardo, P.G., Andersen, S., & Kabat, L. (1981). Induced hearing deficit generates experimental paranoia. *Science, 212,* 1529-1531.

Zinkhan, G.M., & Stoiadin, L.F. (1984). Impact of sex role stereotypes on service priority in department stores. *Journal of Applied Psychology, 69,* 691-693.

Zohar, J., & Insel, T. (1987). Obsessive compulsive disorder: Psychological approaches to diagnosis, treatment, and pathophysiology. *Biological Psychiatry, 22,* 667-687.

Zohar, J., Insel, T., Zohar-Kadouch, R., Hill, J., & Murphy, D. (1988). Serotenergic responsitivitiy in obsessive compulsive disorder. *Archives of General Psychiatry, 45,* 167-175.

Zorumski, C., & Isenberg, K. (1991). Insights into the structure and function of GABA-benzodiazepine receptors: Ion channels and psychiatry. *American Journal of Psychiatry, 148,* 162-173.

Zubenko, G., Sullivan, P., Nelson, J., & Belle, S. (1990). Brain imaging abnormalities in mental disorders in late life. *Archives of Neurology, 47,* 1107-1111.

Zubin, J., & Ludwig, A. (1983). What is schizophrenia? *Schizophrenic Bulletin, 9,* 331-334.

Zuckerman, M. (1979). *Sensation seeking: Beyond the optimal level of arousal.* Hillsdale, NJ: Erlbaum.

Zuckerman, M. (1980). Sensation seeking. In H. London and J. Exner (Eds.), *Dimensions of personality.* New York: Wiley.

Zuckerman, M. (1984). Experience and desire: A new format for sensation seeking scales. *Journal of Behavioral Assessment, 6,* 101-114.

Zuckerman, M., & Como, P. (1983). Sensation seeking and arousal systems. *Personality and Individual Differences, 4,* 381-386.

Zuckerman, M., & Wheeler, L. (1975). To dispel fantasies about the fantasy-based measure of fear of success. *Psychological Bulletin, 82,* 932-946.

Index

Page references in **bold** indicate glossary terms.

A

ABC model of attitudes, 352
Abnormal behavior: **306**-307; approaches to study of, 307-308; classification, 308-310; disorders, 310-322
Absolute threshold, **80**
Abstract-random learning style, 395
Abstract-sequential learning style, 395
Acceptance, psychological stage of dying and, 72
Accommodation, cognitive development and, **61**
Acetylcholine, **31**
Achievement motive, 227-228
Achievement style, **228**
Achievement test, **193**
Acquired immunodeficiency syndrome (AIDS), effect of, on sexual behavior, **253**-254
Acquisition: in classical conditioning, **132**-133, 134; in operant conditioning, 140
ACTH, 40
Action potential, **30**
Activation synthesis theory, of dreams, **113**
Active phase, of schizophrenia, 317
Actor-observer bias, **357**
Acupuncture, **101**
Acute phase, of psychological stages of dying, 72
Adaption, sensory, 79-80
Addiction, drug, 115
Additive tasks, groups and, 363
Adjustment, **282**
Adler, Alfred, theory of individual psychology of, 264
Adolescence: **64;** personality development in, 64-65; physical development, 64; problems in, 65; sex in, 65; social development in, 65
Adoption studies, genetic versus environmental influences on: behavior in, **46;** intelligence in, 198, 200-201; schizophrenia in, 319
Adrenal glands, **40**-41

Adrenal medulla, 40-41
Adrenaline, **40**
Adulthood: parenthood in, 68-69; personality development in, 67-68; physical development in, **66**-67; social development in, 68-69
Advertising, consume psychology and, 387
Aerial perspective, as depth cue, **91**
Aerobic exercise, health in, **300**
Affective disorders, see Mood disorders
Afferent neurons, 29
Affiliation, need for, 228-230
Affirmation rule, 184
African Americans, see Blacks; Black psychologists
Afterimage: **92;** negative, 85
Aggression: **369,** 372; definition of, 369-370; television and, 371-372; theories of, 370-371
Aggressive personality, **265**
Agoraphobia, **310**
Agreeableness, in five-factor personality model, **268**
AIDS (acquired immunodeficiency syndrome), sexual behavior and, **253**-254
Ainsworth, Mary, 57
Alarm reaction, general adaptation syndrome and, **288**
Alcohol: 115-116, 119; adolescents and, 65; fetal alcohol syndrome and, 50, 116
Algorithm, **187**
All-or-none law, of neurons, **30**
Allport, Gordon W., trait theory of, 265-266
Alpha, activity, **107**
Alpha state biofeedback, 123
Altered states of consciousness, **106**-107
Altruistic behavior, 372-373
Alzheimer's disease: **71, 174;** acetylcholine and, 31, 71; aging 71; memory and, 174
Amacrine cells, **84**
Ambivalent attachment, **57**
American Association for Applied Psychology, 378

American Psychological Association (APA): 378; divisions of, 14; ethics in research and, 16-17; formation of, by G. Stanley Hall, 9; psychological organizations and, 13; publication of psychological research and, 16; see also, DSM-III-R
American Psychological Society (APS), 13
American Sign Language, primate language studies and, 182
Ames room, **87**
Amino acids, as neurotransmitters, 31
Amnesia: psychogenic, 321; selective, in catatonic schizophrenia, 317
Amniocentesis, **52**
Amphetamine, **117,** 119
Amphetamine psychosis, 117
Amplitude, of sound waves, **95**
Amygdala, 34
Anal stage, of psychosexual development, 59
Analysis of variance, 24
Analytical psychology, personality theory of Carl Jung and, **263**-264
Anastasi, Anne, 384
Androgen, 40, **41**
Androgyny, **250, 357**
Angel dust, see PCP; phencyclidine hydrochloride
Angell, James, 10
Anger, psychological stages of dying and, 71, 72
Animal behavioralists, see Comparative psychologists
Animal courtship, 222-224
Animals: courtship of, 222-224; studies of, and genetics, 44-45; treatment of, in psychological research, 17
Animism, in cognitive development, **61**
Anorexia nervosa, 65, **221**
Antianxiety drug(s), 115, 116, 119, **340,** 341
Antianxiety minor tranquilizers, 115, **116,** 119, 340, 341
Antidepressant drug(s), 118, 119, **341**-342
Antidiuretic hormone (ADH), **40,** 221

455

F

Credits & Acknowledgments

continued from page iv

Diego; 215 United Nations photo by Gasten Guarda; 217 courtesy Bertha Maslow; 218 © Arlene Collins—Monkmeyer Press Photo Service; 219 courtesy Dr. Neal E. Miller; 220 Figure 9.12 copyright 1971 by the American Psychological Association, adapted by permission; 223 Francisco Enze—Bruce Coleman; 224 © Kit Hedman—Jeroboam, Inc.; 225 University of Wisconsin Primate Lab; 229 Mimi Forsyth—Monkmeyer Press Photo Service; Figure 9.18 adapted with permission from "The Psychology of Affiliation: Experimental Studies of the Sources of Gregariousness" by S. Schachter, 1959, Stanford University Press; 234 Elaine Ward; 235 Robert Reynolds; 236 courtesy Los Angeles Police Department; 237 United Nations photo by John Isaac; 238 Figure 10.5 from *Emotion: The Psychoevolutionary Synthesis* by Robert Plutchik, copyright © 1980 by Robert Plutchik, reprinted by permission of HarperCollins Publishers; Daniel Brody, Stock • Boston; 239 The Bettmann Archive, Inc.; 241 Figure 10.8 copyright 1974 by the American Psychological Association, reprinted by permission; 243 Figure 10.9 from "Measurement of Romantic Love" by Z. Rubin, 1970, *Journal of Personality and Social Psychology*, Vol. 16, No. 2, pp. 265-273; 244 © Chuck Fishman—Woodfin Camp & Associates; 245 © David Hathcox; 247 Ekman & Friesen Human Interaction Laboratory; Figure 10.12 reprinted with permission of Psychology Today Magazine, copyright © 1975 Sussex Publishers, Inc.; 248 Spencer Grant—Monkmeyer Press Photo Service; 250 courtesy Sean Connelly; 251 Figure 10.15 reprinted by permission of Masters and Johnson Institute; 253 © Bodhan Hrynewych—Stock • Boston; 254 Rhoda Sidney—Stock • Boston; 259 Figure 11.1 from "External Control and Internal Control" by J. Rotter, 1971, *Psychology Today* Vol. 5, no. 1, pp. 37-42; 261 The Bettmann Archive, Inc.; 263 The Bettmann Archive, Inc.; 265 UPI/Bettmann Newsphotos; 266 Institute for Personality and Ability Testing; 270 Figure 11.7 from *Motivation and Personality* by A. Maslow, 1970, New York: Harper & Row; 271 United Nations photo; Southern Christian Leadership Conference; The Bettmann Archive, Inc.; courtesy Apple Computers; 274 Mimi Forsyth—Monkmeyer Press Photo Service; 276 MMP1-2 Profiles from S. R. Hathaway and J. C. McKinley, *The Minnesota Multiphasic Personality Inventory*, copyright © the University of Minnesota, 1942, 1943 (renewed 1970), this form 1948, 1976, 1982, reprinted by permission of the University of Minnesota Press; 278 Card 12F Thematic Apperception Test Manual reprinted by permission of the publishers from Henry A. Murray, **Thematic Apperception Test,** Cambridge, MA: Harvard University Press, copyright © 1943 by the President and Fellows of Harvard College, © 1971 by Henry A. Murray; 281 United Nations photo by P. S. Sudhakaran; 283 "Social Readjustment Rating Scale" by T. H. Holmes and R. H. Ruch, 1971, *The Journal of Psychosomatic Research*, 15, 221-227; 284 © Melanie Carr—Zephyr Pictures; 286 M. Marcuss Oslander; 287 Edith G. Haun—Stock • Boston; 286 Figure 12.7 from *The Stress of Life* by H. Selye, 1976, New York: McGraw-Hill; 289 The Bettmann Archive, Inc.; 290 Cheryl Nicholas Greenleaf; 291 courtesy FAA; 293 Arthur Tress—Photo Researchers, Inc.; 294 Augil Berill, Magnolia, TX—courtesy Scholastic Photography Awards; 295 UPI/Bettmann; 299 UPI/Bettmann; 305 Zalesky/Clemmer—Black Star; 308 UPI/Bettmann Newsphotos; 309 DSM-111-R major classifications reprinted by permission from the American Psychiatric Association, *Diagnostic and Statistical Manual of Mental Disorders, Third Edition, Revised,* Washington, DC: American Psychiatric Association, 1987; 311 United Nations photo by Paulo Fridman; 312 Cheryl Nicholas Greenleaf; 313 W. Marc Beinsau—The Image Works; 314 © Miro Vintoniv—Stock • Boston; 317 Grunnitus—Monkmeyer Press Photo Service; 325 New Castle State Developmental Center; 327 Culver Pictures; 328 Judith D. Sedwick—The Picture Cube; 329 Michael Rougler—*Life* magazine, © Time Inc.; 330 Tim Koors—NYT Pictures; 331 photo by Allan Grant, courtesy Dr. Ivar Lovers; 334 Albert Bandura—Stanford University; 335 Curt Gunther; 337 © Rhoda Sidney—The Image Works; 338 Bohdan Hrynewych—Stock • Boston; 347 © 1965 by Stanley Milgram, film *Obedience,* courtesy Alexandra Milgram; 349 Robert Kalman—The Image Works; 353 Robert Kalman—The Image Works; 354 UPI/Bettmann; 355 courtesy American Cancer Society; 356 photo by Karen Zebulon, courtesy Leon Festinger; 358 Spencer Grant—The Picture Cube; 360 Cheryl Nicholas Greenleaf; 362 photo by Erik Kroll, courtesy Alexandra Milgram; 363 United Nations photo by Bedrich Grunzweig; 365 WHO photo by L. Almsay/E. Mandelmann; 366 Daniel S. Brody—Stock • Boston; 368 Robert V. Eckert, Jr.—EKM Nepenthe; © Bodhan Hrynewych—Stock • Boston; 369 Peter Vandermark—Stock • Boston; 370 Albert Bandura, Stanford University; 371 Peter Menzei—Stock • Boston; 372 © ABC-TV News, 1982/AP/Wide World; 373 Figure 15.21 from *The Unresponsive Bystander: Why Doesn't He Help?* by Bibb Latané and John M. Darley, © 1970, adapted by permission of Prentice-Hall, Inc., Englewood Cliffs, NJ; 379 © Bob Daemrich—The Image Works; 381 UPI/Bettmann Newsphotos; 382 courtesy Philip Zimbardo; 383 Jim Pickerell—Tony Stone Worldwide; 384 courtesy Anne Anastasi; 385 Steve Goldberg—Monkmeyer Press Photo Service; 387 Rebecca Holland; 388 Pamela Carley Petersen; 389 Spencer Grant—Monkmeyer Press Photo Service; 390 Pamela Carley Petersen; 391 © Dion Ogust—The Image Works; 392 Robert V. Eckert, Jr.—Stock • Boston; 394 M. Marcuss Oslander; 395 © Spencer Grant—Photo Researchers, Inc. **Color Insert Page 1:** © Donald Fawcett—Science Source/Photo Researchers, Inc.; © Lennart Nilsson *A Child Is Born*; © Lennart Nilssen *A Child Is Born* **Page 2:** Ralph Eagle—Science Source/Photo Researchers: © Karl Maslowski—Photo Researchers, Inc.; Richmond Products **Page 4:** I. V. Bergman & Associates, Inc.; courtesy Drs. Michael Phelps & John Mazziota, UCLA School of Medicine; © Howard Sochurek 1983—Woodfin Camp & Associates; © Howard Sochurek 1986—Woodfin Camp & Associates.

Staff

Editor John S. L. Holland
Copy Editor Robert Mill
Production Manager Brenda S. Filley
Designers Harry Rinehart and Charles Vitelli
Photo Editor Pamela Carley Petersen
Editorial Assistant Diane Barker
Typesetting Supervisor Libra Ann Cusack
Typesetter Juliana Arbo
Production Assistant Steve Shumaker
Systems Coordinator Richard Tietjen

Anatomical figures were drawn by Mel Erikson.

The text was printed in narrow web offset lithography and bound by the Banta Company, Inc., at Harrisonburg, VA. The text paper is 50 lb. Butte des Morts.

The cover material is 10 pt. Carolina coated one-side (softbound) and an impregnated Latex Type II (Alcolite S11), non-woven stock manufactured by Appleton Papers, Inc., Appleton, WI (casebound).